On This Day
BY RANDY WALKER
IN TENNIS HISTORY

T0164220

On This Day

BY RANDY WALKER

IN TENNIS HISTORY

A Day-by-Day Anthology of Anecdotes and Historical Happenings

New Chapter Press

On This Day In Tennis History is published by New Chapter Press (www.newchapterpressmedia.com) and is distributed by the Independent Publishers Group (www.ipggroup.com).

ISBN—978-0942257427

Cover photos of Andre Agassi, John McEnroe, Venus and Serena Williams, Jimmy Connors and Suzanne Lenglen are courtesy of Getty Images.

Design by Visible Logic

Printed in Canada

Visit www.tennisgrandstand.com to sign up and receive a daily electronic email version of *On This Day In Tennis History* with content not found in the book!

From the Author

Tennis is my first love, but golf is a close second. I distinctly remember years ago Jack Whitaker of ABC Sports talk about the grand history of golf during the U.S. Open golf championships saying that "a sport that respects its history is destined to prosper and flourish." That sentiment has always stayed with me. Sports and sporting events that have well-documented histories and traditions—Wimbledon, the Masters and U.S. Open golf and tennis, Major League Baseball—stand out. Why are the major tennis tournaments—the Australian Open, the French Open, Wimbledon and the U.S. Open—the biggest and most prestigious events? It's because of their well-documented histories and traditions.

I took Whitaker's words with me when I started my position at the United States Tennis Association's Marketing and Communications Division in 1993. It was during another major golf tournament—The Masters—where I first heard CBS announcers informally discussing on air about events that happened on this day in Masters history. I thought that this was a terrific concept and great way to incorporate the history of an event into the current context of the sport. It didn't take long for me to give birth to a compilation "On This Day In U.S Open History" as part of the media information I authored at the USTA. Soon, the history of U.S. Open came to life on air on CBS television in the United States and in approximately 200 countries around the world.

When I became the press officer for the U.S. Davis Cup team in 1997, "On This Day In U.S. Davis Cup History" soon came into being. I recall one particularly poignant moment came in 2000 when in Zimbabwe with the U.S. Davis Cup Team and Captain John McEnroe. The U.S. clinched a come-from-behind 3-2 win over the tiny African nation seven years to the day after Arthur Ashe, the greatest African-American tennis player and the former U.S. Davis Cup player and captain, died from complications due to AIDS. Said McEnroe of Ashe in a TV interview following the win, "Arthur died seven years ago today and he was with us today."

After my departure from the USTA in 2005, as a hobby more of less, I started to compile a grander list of events and happenings in the sport. My research and compilation soon became "On This Day In Tennis History."

I have always been an avid tennis player and fan with a keen interest in history and documenting events. My enthusiasm for tennis history stems from all of the musings, anecdotes and stories from Bud Collins during his "Breakfast at Wimbledon" broadcasts with NBC through the years. He was—and continues to be—a great role model and I am proud that I have been able to work with Bud through the years at the U.S. Open, Davis Cup, as well as through New Chapter Press publishing *The Bud Collins History of Tennis*. Dan Magill, the legendary men's tennis coach at the University of Georgia, was another major influence on me. As a freshman at Georgia in the fall of 1987, Magill included me as part of the Bulldog tennis program, eventually resulting in my earning "walk-on" status on the team. Magill is also an avid chronicler of the game, founding and serving as curator of the Collegiate Tennis Hall of Fame. Not only do I remember admiring how Coach Magill documented all the extraordinary happenings and victories of all the top collegiate players in the museum, but also his accounting of the NCAA tennis championships held at the University of Georgia complex (now named for Magill) via newspaper articles laminated onto posters underneath the stadium's bleachers.

There are a lot of other people who have helped me along my way around what my friend Bill Mountford calls "the tennis carousel." My mother and father—Gisela and Ewing Walker—obviously started me in the game, but I was also helped by many others along the way, in playing and non-playing capacities, including Larry Wolf, Bill Jenkins, Dan Borgman, Manuel Diaz, Joe Lynch, Bruce Levy, Artie Campbell, Page Crosland, Rick Ferman, Joe Favorito, David Newman, Chris Widmaier, Arlen Kantarian, Marshall Happer, Pierce O'Neil, Tom Gullikson, Ron Woods, Lynne Rolley, Jeff Ryan, David Brewer, Patrick McEnroe, Jim Courier and Jon Venison among others. Others I want to thank for help and support with this book include Ben Sturner, Manfred Wenas, Joel Drucker, Kat Anderson, Greg Sharko, Janey Marks, Emily Brackett, DeAnne McCaslin and "The Mountfords" (Bill, Cat and Jack).

I hope you enjoy this compilation and take something away from the great history of tennis.

—Randy Walker
New York, N.Y., 2008

January 1

1921 Bill Tilden and Bill Johnston complete a 5-0 American sweep of Australasia in the 1920 Davis Cup Challenge Round, played in the 1921 calendar year at the Domain Cricket Ground in Auckland, New Zealand. Tilden defeats Gerald Patterson 5-7, 6-2, 6-3, 6-3, while Johnston defeats Norman Brookes 5-7, 7-5, 6-3, 6-3. The United States team, which is officially handed the Davis Cup trophy in a banquet ceremony on January 3, does not relinquish possession of the Cup until August of 1927.

1973 Fighting off on-court temperatures of 115 degrees and a pulled stomach muscle, Margaret Court defeats Evonne Goolagong 6-4, 7-5 to win the Australian Open women's singles title for an incredible 11th time. No player in tennis history wins as many singles titles at a major tournament than Court at the Australian Open. The title is her 22th of a record 24 major singles titles. Aussie John Newcombe defeats Onny Parun of New Zealand 6-3, 6-7, 7-5, 6-1 to win his first Australian Open singles title. Parun is the first Kiwi in a major final since Harry Parker loses the 1913 Australian men's singles final.

1974 Engaged couple Jimmy Connors and Chris Evert both compete in the men's and women's singles finals, respectively, at the Australian Open. Connors becomes only the fourth American since 1946 to win the title, defeating Australia's Phil Dent 7-6, 6-4, 4-6, 6-3. Evert, however, falls to Evonne Goolagong 7-6, 4-6, 6-0. Says Connors after the match, "I know it is the first Grand Slam, but I am not going to make any predictions because then it becomes a psychological battle to win the next three." Connors goes on to win Wimbledon and the U.S. Open in 1974, but is not allowed to play in the French Open due the French Tennis Federation's ban on players competing in World Team Tennis.

1975 Playing in her first major singles final, 18-year-old Martina Navratilova is defeated by Evonne Goolagong 6-3, 6-2 in the women's singles final of the Australian Open. John Newcombe upsets Jimmy Connors 7-5, 3-6, 6-4, 7-6 (9-7) to win the Australian Open men's singles title. Connors, who won the 1974 Australian Open in his first visit to the tournament, never again plays in Australia's national championship.

January 2

1912 Australasia clinches victory over the United States in the 1911 Davis Cup championship matches played in the 1912 calendar year. Norman Brookes and Alfred Dunlop defeat the U.S. doubles team of Beals Wright and Maurice McLoughlin 6-4, 5-7, 7-5, 6-4 to give the Australasia an insurmountable 3-0 lead over the United States at Hagley Park in Christchurch, New Zealand. The matches are staged in New Zealand to honor Kiwi tennis ace Tony Wilding, the reigning Wimbledon champion. Wilding, however, does not make himself available to play in the matches, choosing to stay home at his new residence in England with full confidence that Brookes will be able to lead the team to victory over the Americans.

1979 Arthur Ashe lets two match points slip away and is defeated in the semifinals of the Australian Open by unheralded, No. 188-ranked John Marks of Australia, by a 6-4, 6-2, 2-6, 1-6, 9-7 margin. Marks leads 4-1 in the fifth set, before Ashe wins four games in a row and holds two match points in the 10th game of the final set. The match ultimately becomes Ashe's final match at the Australian Open, the tournament where he hoists the winner's trophy in 1970, as Ashe retires from the sport after suffering a heart attack later in the year. No. 1 seed Guillermo Vilas also advances to the final, defeating American Hank Pfister 6-2, 6-0, 6-3.

1980 Guillermo Vilas wins his second straight Australian Open men's singles title, defeating feisty and tempermental American John Sadri 7-6, 6-3, 6-2 in the final. Sadri, best known for losing a five-set NCAA singles final in 1978 to John McEnroe, causes controversy during the tournament with what the Associated Press describes as "offensive finger gestures" as well as foul language and the smashing of an on-court ice bucket during his semifinal match with Colin Dibley the previous day. The only incident during the final with Vilas, according to the Associated Press, is when Sadri "gestured to an open court" where as "Vilas returned the sign." Says Vilas of Sadri following the match, "There are persons who are born stupid. If he does those things, he may be funny, but he will have to try a little better to make me laugh." Earlier in the day, American Barbara Jordan, ranked No. 68 in the world, becomes the unlikely winner. of the Australian women's singles title, defeating unheralded fellow American Sharon Walsh 6-3, 6-3 in the final.

January 3

1939 New York's Madison Square Garden is the scene of the professional debut of Don Budge. Fresh off winning the first "Grand Slam" of tennis in 1938, Budge defeats Ellsworth Vines 6-3, 6-4, 6-2 in 1 hour, 2 minutes. Writes Allison Danzig of the *New York Times,* "The invincibility associated with the name of Donald Budge as the world's foremost amateur tennis player for the past two years was reaffirmed last night with the first appearance in the role of a professional at Madison Square Garden. In the presence of a capacity gathering of 16,725 spectators who paid $47,120, the red-headed giant from Oakland, Calif., the only player in history to make a grand slam of the world's four major tennis titles, administered a crushing defeat to Ellsworth Vines of Pasadena, Calif., the recognized professional champion."

1972 Nineteen years after first winning the Australian Open, 37-year-old Ken Rosewall wins his nation's title for a fourth time, defeating 36-year-old Mal Anderson 7-6, 6-3, 7-5. Rosewall's 1972 Australian Open title is his eighth and final major singles title. The battle of "thirty-something" Australians is almost the all-time oldest men's singles final in a major. The combined age of 73 of the two finalists is second to the combined age of the 1908 Wimbledon finalists—40-year-old Arthur Gore over 37-year-old Herbert Roper Barrett. A record crowd of over 13,000 at Melbourne's Kooyong Tennis Club also watches Virginia Wade of Great Britain defeat Evonne Goolagong of Australia 6-4, 6-4 to win the women's singles title.

1979 Guillermo Vilas wins the Australian Open for the first time in his career, defeating unlikely finalist, No. 188-ranked John Marks of Australia 6-4, 6-4, 3-6, 6-3 in the men's singles final. Says Vilas after the match, "I decided in July that I wanted to play in Australia and win one big tournament on grass." In the women's final, Chris O'Neill of Australia, ranked No. 111 in the world, wins the women's title, defeating Betsy Naglesen of the United States 6-3, 7-6 in the women's final.

2006 Yugoslav-born Jelena Dokic, playing in her first WTA tournament in eight months, serves an incredible 28 double faults, losing to Germany's Julia Schruff 5-7, 7-6(3), 6-1 in the first round of the ASB Classic in Auckland, New Zealand.

January 4

1976 Twenty-one-year-old Mark Edmondson, three months removed from working as a janitor to supplement his tennis income, becomes the lowest-ranked player to win a major singles title when, ranked No. 212, he registers one of the biggest upsets in major tournament tennis in defeating fellow Australian and defending champion John Newcombe 6-7, 6-3, 7-6, 6-1 in the final of the Australian Open. Says Edmonson after the final, "I'm suffering from shock and exhilaration or something. It is just too good to believe. I think I might have a couple of bottles of bubbly tonight." The two-and-half-hour final is delayed for 30 minutes due to a severe weather conditions in which, according to the Associated Press, features 45 mile-per-hour wind gusts and a temperature drop "from 104 degrees to 79 in five minutes." Earlier in the day, Australia's Evonne Goolagong defeats Czech Renata Tomanova 6-2, 6-2 to win the Australian women's singles title.

1981 Brian Teacher of the United States defeats Aussie Kim Warwick 7-5, 7-6, 6-3 to win his first and only major title at the Australian Open. With the victory, Teacher wins the biggest paycheck of his career—$50,000—as well as tennis immortality. Says Teacher after the match, "Until today, I didn't think I would ever win a Grand Slam tournament." The day is a long one for Warwick, who outlasts No. 1 seed Guillermo Vilas 6-7, 6-4, 6-2, 2-6, 6-4 earlier in the day in his suspended semifinal match and then, following the singles final, he pairs with countryman Mark Edmondson to defeat fellow Aussies Peter McNamara and Paul McNamee 7-5, 6-4 in the men's doubles final.

2006 Forty-year-old former Wimbledon champion Pat Cash has a short-lived, novelty comeback on the ATP Tour, pairing with local Indian Karan Rastogi in the doubles competition at the Chennai Open in Chennai, India, losing in the first round to Germans Rainer Schuettler and Alexander Waske 6-2, 6-2.

January 5

1973 Virginia Wade is heckled by Australian tennis fans and defeated by Evonne Goolagong 7-5, 4-6, 6-4 in the semifinals of the New South Wales Open in Sydney. After flurry of disputed calls that go against her, Wade screams to the crowd, "Where are all the umpires?" only to be met with heckles and jeers.

1978 A crowd of 18,590—the biggest crowd to ever watch a sanctioned tournament match at the time in the United States—watch a rematch of the U.S. Open men's singles final from four months earlier as Guillermo Vilas again defeats Jimmy Connors 6-4, 3-6, 7-5 in round robin play at the Masters Championships at Madison Square Garden in New York City. Vilas also beat Connors in four sets in the final of the U.S. Open at the West Side Tennis Club in Forest Hills, Queens, N.Y. the previous September. Connors roars back from a 2-5 final-set deficit to nearly defeat the Argentine lefty. Neil Amdur of the *New York Times* describes the confrontation as a "three-hour tennis classic that will rank among the sport's more inspiring moments." Vilas clinches the 84th match victory of his last 85 matches in the early morning of January 6, as Connors drills a final forehand into the net at 12:42 am.

1994 World No. 1 Pete Sampras loses to world No. 204 Karim Alami of Morocco 3-6, 6-2, 6-4 in the first round of the Qatar Open in Doha, in one of the biggest upsets by ranking in the history of men's tennis. Says Alami after the match, "I had already made a flight reservation to leave Doha tonight when I found out I was due to play Sampras."

2008 Lindsay Davenport wins her 54th career WTA Tour singles title— moving her past Monica Seles into eighth place all-time—defeating Aravane Rezai of France 6-2, 6-2 to win the ASB Classic in Auckland, New Zealand. The title is Davenport's third in four events since she gives birth of her son, Jagger Leach, the previous spring. Davenport launched her comeback four months earlier in August and won singles titles in Bali, Indonesia and Quebec City, Canada. Says Davenport after her win Auckland, "I came here to win the tournament—mission accomplished. I played five matches in six days and only lost one set so I'm happy with the way I played."

January 6

1992 Twenty-year-old Stefano Pescosolido of Italy is defaulted from his final round qualifying match at the New South Wales Open in Sydney, Australia, when, after being aced by his opponent, Johan Anderson of Australia, he slams his racquet to the ground in disgust and drop kicks the racquet into the stands, striking a 22-year-old woman in the face. The woman is taken to the hospital where she receives stitches over her right eye. Pescosolido is also fined $1,500.

2007 Ivan Ljubicic of Croatia wins "the golden falcon"—the championship trophy of the Doha Open in Qatar—when he defeats Andy Murray of Scotland 6-4, 6-4 in the men's singles final for his seventh career ATP tournament title. Says Ljubicic, "This trophy is one of the most beautiful we have in tennis—the golden falcon. I wanted it so bad. Andy was a very good opponent. He fought hard and didn't miss many balls, but I was patient. I knew I had to be aggressive but not too aggressive. Against someone like Andy you need to find the perfect balance, because if you go to the net too much, he will pass you. And if you stay at the baseline, he's too solid. So the combination was the key today."

2008 World No. 2 Rafael Nadal has nothing left in the tank in a 57-minute, 6-0, 6-1 loss to Russia's Mikhail Youzhny in the final of the Chennai Open in India. The previous night, Nadal defeats fellow Spaniard Carlos Moya 6-7 (3), 7-6 (8), 7-6 (1) in 3 hours, 54 minutes—saving four match points in the second-set tie-break—in the longest three-set match on the ATP Tour in 15 years."Rafa was not Rafa," says Youzhny of Nadal winning only one game against him in the final. "I did not win today, it was Rafa who lost. I did not expect it to be so easy. I was lucky as he just couldn't move and couldn't play." Says a classy Nadal, "Maybe I was a bit tired after the long semifinal, but I lost the final because Mikhail played very well."

2007 Dinara Safina of Russia, the younger sister of U.S. and Australian Open champion Marat Safin, wins her fifth career WTA title, defeating Martina Hingis 6-3, 3-6, 7-5 in the final of the Australian women's hard court championships on the Gold Coast. Says Hingis of Safina, "Today she was just too good and everyone should watch her because she's gonna be maybe even better than her brother. Marat is such a genius. He can play unbelievable tennis. She (Safina) definitely doesn't have as much touch but she has more will and desire."

January 7

1979 Sixteen-year-old Tracy Austin wins her third title in as many tournaments since turning professional, defeating Martina Navratilova 6-3, 6-2 in the women's singles final at the Avon Championships of Washington, D.C.

2006 Roger Federer defeats Gael Monfils of France 6-3, 7-6 (5) to win the Exxon Mobil Open in Doha, Qatar for second straight year. The title is his 34th career singles title and his fifth straight title in the Middle East. Says Federer of his success in the Middle East, "It's almost like Wimbledon. I play and I win."

1980 Using what Barry Lorge of the *Washington Post* describes as a "relentless serve and-volley attack with quickness and remarkable touch," Martina Navratilova overwhelms Tracy Austin, 6-2, 6-1 to win the $250,000 Colgate Series Championship in Washington, D.C.

2008 Fabrice Santoro of France ends James Blake's bid to become the first player since Australian legend John Bromwich in 1940 to win a three straight titles at the Sydney International, defeating the two-time defending champion 7-6 (4), 6-2 in the first round. Says Blake of the match, "Maybe it was him, maybe it was the court, but it seemed so slow. It was tough for me to put balls away. I think I got a bit ahead of myself." At the U.S. Open the previous summer, Blake and Santoro play a memorable five-setter, Blake winning 6-4, 3-6, 6-2, 4-6, 6-4 after Santoro suffers cramps in the fifth set. The win was Blake's first five-set victory after nine defeats.

2007 Xavier Malisse of Belgium wins singles and doubles titles at the Chennai Open in India, becoming only the second ATP tour player to turn the double in the last 12 months. The Belgian wins his second career singles title, defeating Stefan Koubek of Austria 6-1, 6-3 in the singles final, then teams with countryman Dick Norman to defeat Rafael Nadal and Bartolome Salva-Vidal of Spain 7-6 (4), 7-6 (4) in the doubles final. Jose Acasuso of Argentina is the only player in the previous 12 months to win singles and doubles titles at the same event when he won both titles in Vina del Mar, Chile 10 months earlier.

January 8

1947 The Davis Cup lands on U.S. soil for the first time since 1939 as the triumphant U.S. Davis Cup team and the trophy touch down in Oakland, Calif., after the U.S. team of Jack Kramer, Frank Parker, Ted Schroeder and Gardnar Mulloy defeat Australia 5-0 in Melbourne, Australia. The landing concludes the first-ever plane flight for the Davis Cup trophy.

1978 Jimmy Connors defeats Bjorn Borg 6-4, 1-6, 6-4 to win the Masters Championships at Madison Square Garden in New York City and the first-ever $100,000 paycheck in the history of the year-end championships. Says Connors to the crowd following the victory, "I don't think you'll see any better tennis from me. It's certainly the best I can play. I had to play that way to beat Borg today. Every time I come to New York, you bring out the best in me. I'm getting to like it here." The victory for Connors muddles the argument on who the true No. 1 player in the world in men's tennis is for the 1977 season, between Borg, the Wimbledon champion, Guillermo Vilas, the French and U.S. Open champion, and Connors, the U.S. and Wimbledon runner-up. Connors receives the official year-end ATP No. 1 ranking, but observers, players and media argue over the label of world No. 1. Says Borg to the media after the match, "Who's No. 1? You decide." Says Connors to the media, "Let's play it all over. Borg beat me at Wimbledon. Vilas won Forest Hills. I won here....Just don't rank all three of us No. 1. That would be a cop out."

1978 Martina Navratilova defeats Betty Stove 7-5, 6-4 to capture her third Virginia Slims of Washington title. Navratilova is offered a choice of a $20,000 winners' check and a Russian sable mink coat, but chooses the money. Says Navratilova, "I want the coat, but my manager wants the cash."

2005 World No. 1 Roger Federer begins his 2005 season defeating Ivan Ljubicic of Croatia 6-3, 6-1 in the final of the Qatar Open in Doha for his 21st straight match win. The Swiss star wins his 14th tournament final in a row (dating to October of 2003) wins every service game he plays during the week and loses only 23 games in five matches during the event. "At the moment I think Federer is playing better than Sampras did," says Ljubicic after the match. "It's just that Pete went on for seven years. We will have to see through the years how Roger copes."

January 9

1977 Hard-serving lefty Roscoe Tanner out of Lookout Mountain, Tenn., and Stanford University, wins his only major singles title, defeating Guillermo Vilas 6-3, 6-3, 6-3 in 85 minutes in the final of the Australian Open. In his 2005-published book *Double Fault*, Tanner admits that he receives coaching from his doubles partner Arthur Ashe during the match. Ashe sits in the courtside photographer's pit during the final, taking pictures for a proposed coffee table book. Writes Tanner, "During changeovers, he would maneuver himself so that he was behind my chair. With my back turned to him, I heard Arthur whisper advice such as 'Serve to his forehand' or 'Chip and charge on the next break point.'" Earlier in the day, Kerry Reid defeats fellow Aussie Dianne Fromholtz 7-5, 6-2 in the women's singles final to also win her first and only major singles title.

1977 Martina Navratilova defeats Chris Evert 6-2, 6-3 in the final of the Virginia Slims of Washington tennis tournament. The $20,000 singles first prize is presented in fresh-one dollar bills. Quips Navratilova, "That's for 20 years of tipping, I guess."

2003 Two-time U.S. Open champion and two-time Wimbledon finalist Patrick Rafter of Australia announces his retirement in an open letter to the media. "I will have regrets that the Wimbledon and Davis Cup trophies are not in my cupboard, but that's sport. You win some and you lose some," writes Rafter. "However, I feel I can leave the game, satisfied with my achievements, knowing that I gave it my all." Rafter makes his announcement after a 12-month sabbatical from the sport, last competing in the 2001 Davis Cup Final in Melbourne.

2005 Carlos Moya of Spain defeats Paradorn Srichaphan 3-6, 6-4, 7-6 (5) in the men's singles final of the ATP Chennai Open in India and then donates the $68,439 first-prize pay check to victims of the tragic tsunami that struck India, Indonesia and other Asian nations. Says Moya, "I want the money I have earned here to help the survivors of one of the worst tragedies of our times. It is a small contribution which I hope will help the affected families. They deserve all the help they can get." The title is Moya's 18th career ATP singles title.

January 10

1934 With fans literally standing in the aisles, a crowd of 14,637—the largest crowd to ever assemble to watch a tennis match at the time—packs New York's Madison Square Garden as Ellsworth Vines makes his professional debut against Bill Tilden. The 41-year-old Tilden emerges victorious in the debut match of a 73-match barnstorming tour, beating the 23-year-old Vines 8-6, 6-3, 6-2. The match grosses $30,125 with courtside tickets being sold for $5. Vines wins the overall tour 47 matches to 26 with the overall tour grossing $243,000—the most ever for a pro tour.

1980 In what *Washington Post* tennis writer Barry Lorge calls "a tennis match for all seasons" Bjorn Borg defeats Jimmy Connors 3-6, 6-3, 7-6 (7-4) in 2 hours, 38 minutes in the second day of round-robin play at the Grand Prix Masters at Madison Square Garden in New York City. In front of an electric atmosphere featuring 16,753 fans, Connors trails Borg 2-5 in the 74-minute final-set, before furiously fighting back to force the third set tiebreak. Writes Lorge, "This was tennis and drama of the highest order, its fierce intensity and shifting fortunes more than making up for a few patches of ragged play. In the end, it was marked by the quality that has set the best Borg-Connors confrontations above all others of the modern era in tennis. The combativeness was palpable, the sustained pace and boldness of the shotmaking extraordinary. Each man made spectacular shots in turn, and ultimately every point became a war."

1982 In a match in which Jimmy Connors and John McEnroe nearly come to blows, Connors edges John McEnroe, 6-7, 7-5, 6-7, 7-5, 6-4, in the final of the Michelob Light Challenge in Rosemount, Ill.—an eight-player exhibition event used as warm-up to the Masters tournament. The match is highlighted by several point penalties and verbal exchanges between the two rivals, including a fifth-set confrontation that nearly gets physical. Writes Neil Amdur of the *New York Times*, "Connors stepped across the net and confronted McEnroe for what Connors considered abusive language and delay tactics; the two players were "about a whisker apart," in Connors's words, before being restrained by officials." One day later, in a pre-Masters press event in New York, Connors is asked what McEnroe said to him to irk him so much. Says Connors, "I hope I misunderstood what he said." Continues Connors of his relationship with McEnroe, "I think we both have the same attitudes. He's aggressive, I'm aggressive. We both stick up for our rights. But I stick up for my rights in a different way. If I feel like I'm in the right, I'll step up. I want some respect, not sloughing off. But there are certain limits."

2007 Serena Williams, playing in her first tournament in four months, loses to unheralded No. 53-ranked Sybille Bammer of Austria, 3-6, 7-5, 6-3 in the quarterfinals of Hobart, Australia. Says Williams, "I think she played the match of her life. I've never heard of her quite frankly. You just wish these players would play like this all the time instead of just against me." Williams, ranked No. 94 in the world after suffering through an injury-plagued 2006 season, uses the loss to Bammer as a motivational springboard as she goes on to win the Australian Open in surprising style three weeks later.

January 11

1988 Play begins at the Australian Open at the new $60 million Australian National Tennis Center at Flinders Park in Melbourne with American qualifier Wendy Wood winning the first match played in the new stadium court, later to be known as Rod Laver Arena, beating No. 14 seed Dianne Balestrat of Australia. Wood, 23, from Lexington, Mass., defeats the top-ranked Australian woman 6-2, 4-6, 8-6, registering her first professional match victory after playing only two previous WTA Tour-level events. "I'm very nervous now. I'm not used to these kind of situations," says Wood, whose father Wilbur Wood was a standout pitcher for the Chicago White Sox in the 1960s. "I knew I was going to be nervous, but I figured she had more reason to be nervous than me." Balestrat, 31, and an Australian Open finalist in 1977, says she has some difficulty adapting to the court—the synthetic Rebound Ace hard court surface—used for the for the first time at the Australian Open after a switch from grass courts. Pat Cash, the No. 4 seeded Australian and reigning Wimbledon champion, plays the second stadium court match and is greeted with boos and shouts from a group of anti-apartheid protestors who, in protest of Cash playing in South Africa the previous year, also throw black tennis balls on the court before being escorted from the stadium. Cash is fined $500 for swearing at a linesman in the final game of his 7-5, 6-1, 6-4 win over 20-year-old Thomas Muster of Austria. Also on the day, Yannick Noah of France, the No. 5 seed, staves off two match points before overcoming Roger Smith of the Bahamas 6-7, 5-7, 6-4, 6-2, 16-14 in 4 hours, 51 minutes, the longest-recorded match at the time at the Australian Open. Says Noah, who saves the match points in the 16th game of the final set, "After I saved the match points, I felt much stronger."

1998 Lleyton Hewitt wins his first ATP singles title as a 16-year-old wild card ranked No. 550 in the world, defeating fellow Australian Jason Stoltenberg 3-6, 6-3, 7-6 (4) at the Australian Men's Hard Court Championships in his hometown of Adelaide. At the age of 16 years, 11 months, Hewitt becomes the youngest player to win an ATP singles title since Michael Chang, at the age of 16 years, eight months, wins the title in San Francisco in 1988. Says Stoltenberg after the match, "He just played like a 16-year-old. You do what comes naturally rather than thinking what you should do."

2008 Justine Henin comes back from 0-3 down in the third set and defeats Svetlana Kuznetsova 4-6, 6-2, 6-4 to win the women's singles title at Sydney International. The win is Henin's 28th match victory in a row.

January 12

1980 Declaring in his post-match press conference, "Nobody beats Vitas Gerulaitis 17 times in a row," Gerulaitis ends a 16-match losing streak to Jimmy Connors with a 7-5, 6-2 victory in the semifinals of the Masters Championships at Madison Square Garden.

2007 Kim Clijsters wins her 34th—and final—WTA Tour singles title, defeating Serbia's Jelena Jankovic 4-6, 7-6 (7-1), 6-4 in the final of the Sydney International. Clijsters, who announced that 2007 is her final season, saves a match point with Jankovic serving for the match at 5-4 in the second set. Says Clijsters, who cuts short her final tennis season four months later, "I was down match point, so it's easy to think it's over but you should never think like that. You should always try to find a way to make the next point better. Even if you make a mistake, don't think about it any more, just refocus and forget about it and just start all over."

2008 In a rare match that doesn't feature a single break point opportunity, Russian Dmitry Tursunov defeats hard-serving Australian left-hander Chris Guccione 7-6 (3), 7-6 (4) to win the Sydney International. Says Tursunov, "I'm not really surprised that there were no breaks, because that's kind of his game. He goes for a lot of risky shots on the returns, and he knows that he's not going to get broken too often. That's pretty much the scenario. That was very expected." Tursunov becomes the first Russian to win the title since Alex Metreveli in 1972, although Metreveli was representing the Soviet Union.

2008 Philipp Kohlschreiber becomes the first German in the Open era to win the men's singles title at the Heineken Open in Auckland, New Zealand, defeating former world No. 1 Juan Carlos Ferrero 7-6 (4), 7-5 in the final. Kohlschreiber continues his fine form the following week at the Australian Open by upsetting another former world No. 1, Andy Roddick, in an epic five-set third-round match.

1981 Eighteen-year-old Tracy Austin defeats fifteen-year-old Andrea Jaeger 6-2, 6-2 in the final of the Colgate Series Championship in Landover, Md.— marking the two youngest players to compete in a women's championship match at the time.

January 13

1980 Bjorn Borg finally wins in New York as the two-time U.S. Open runner-up wins the Masters Championships at Madison Square Garden, defeating Vitas Gerulaitis 6-2, 6-2 in the championship match. "I wanted to win a tournament here for a long time," says Borg, who would play—and lose—two more U.S. Open finals in his career.

1985 John McEnroe wins his third—and final—Masters singles championship, defeating Ivan Lendl 7-5, 6-0, 6-4 in the final at New York's Madison Square Garden. Says Lendl of McEnroe in the post-match press conference, "I would say that he played very well. Unfortunately, I've seen him play very well many times." The only hiccup in the match comes with McEnroe serving for the first set at 6-5 and, while bouncing balls off his racquet, waiting for photographers to settle down in their courtside positions, he bounces one of the balls higher than anticipated that hits his eye and requires McEnroe to engage in a three-minute injury time-out. Says McEnroe of the freak injury, "I couldn't see for a couple of minutes. I've hit myself before never when it hurt that way."

1997 Unheralded Spaniard Carlos Moya upsets defending champion Boris Becker 5-7, 7-6 (4), 3-6, 6-1, 6-4 in the first round of the Australian Open in oppressive 95-degree temperatures, with on-court readings registering as high as 135 degrees. "The weather was maybe the key to the match," Moya says after contesting only his third five-set match. "I was also tired, but I think he was more tired than me. I am a young man, he is 29...I played a good match. Nobody can beat Boris when he's playing 100 per cent. I was sure at least to fight (out) the match and put pressure on him." Moya, a future French Open champion and world No. 1, goes on to reach the final of the tournament, where he loses to Pete Sampras.

2003 Two-time defending champion Jennifer Capriati becomes the first defending women's singles champion to lose in the first round of the Australian Open, losing to German Marlene Weingartner 2-6, 7-6 (6), 6-4. Capriati partially blames the loss on recent eye surgery in late 2002.

2007 In a rare, ironic twist, James Blake wins the Sydney International with a 6-3, 5-7, 6-1 win over Carlos Moya, the same player he is scheduled to play in the first round of the following week's Australian Open. Three days later, Blake again beats Moya, registering a 7-6 (8), 6-2, 6-4 first round win. Blake joins four-time champion Lleyton Hewitt and two-time titlist Pete Sampras as the only players to win back-to-back titles in Sydney in the Open era.

1974 Six weeks after losing the 1973 Davis Cup final to lose its five-year hold on the Davis Cup trophy, the United States is dealt its earliest loss ever in Davis Cup play as Jairo Velasco defeats Erik van Dillen 6-0, 7-5, 4-6, 6-3 to clinch Colombia's 4-1 first round win over the United States in Bogota, Colombia. A 45-minute rain delay at the end of the third set snuffs out any momentum that van Dillen can muster as the American double-faults 10 times in the fourth set to go down in defeat. After clinching the historic victory, Velasco is carried around the court by enthusiastic fans.

1998 Martina Hingis becomes the first No. 1 ranked woman ever to lose her opening match of a calendar year, losing 3-6, 6-4, 7-5 to fellow 17-year-old Venus Williams in the first round of the Sydney International.

January 14

1979 Nineteen-year-old John McEnroe saves two match points and defeats 35-year-old Arthur Ashe 6-7 (5), 6-3, 7-5 in 2 hours, 34 minutes to win the first of his three year-end Masters Championships at New York's Madison Square Garden. Ashe leads 4-1 in the final set and holds double match point with McEnroe serving at 4-5, 15-40, but is unable to hold on. Ashe praises McEnroe following the match stating, "The situation calls for a certain kind of challenge and he met it. What he had to do was compose himself and find out why he was winning and change his game if he was losing. That may be difficult for a 19-year-old who's had coaching all of his life."

2008 Austria's Tamara Paszek serves for the match five times in the final set, but is unable to punch through and upset world No. 3 Jelena Jankovic in the first round of the Australian Open, losing 6-2, 2-6, 12-10. The final set of the match is highlighted by an incredible and unlikely unprecedented 15 service breaks. Jankovic saves three match points in the 3-hour, 9-minute match and goes on to reach the semifinals of the event, losing to eventual champion Maria Sharapova. Says Jankovic, "I was just trying to stay positive somehow and I found a way to win. It was unbelievable when I was down those match points and I was really in some tough points and I was maybe lucky a few times."

2006 Jarkko Nieminen becomes the first player from Finland to win an ATP singles title, defeating Mario Ancic from Croatia 6-2, 6-2 to win the Heineken Open in Auckland, New Zealand.

1996 Playing in her first tournament in Australia following her post-stabbing hiatus from professional tennis, Monica Seles saves a match point and defeats Lindsay Davenport, 4-6, 7-6 (9-7), 6-3 to win the Sydney International tennis championships. Seles goes on to return to the winner's circle at the Australian Open in Melbourne two weeks later, beating Anke Huber in the title match for her fourth Aussie championship.

2005 Chinese women sweep the singles and doubles titles at the Moorilla International Championships in Hobart, Tasmania, Australia for the first time ever in the history of the WTA Tour. Jie Zheng defeats Gisela Dulko of Argentina 6-2, 6-0 in the singles final and then teams with Zi Yan to defeat Dinara Safina of Russia and Anabel Medina Garrigues of Spain 6-4, 7-5 in the final. Says Dulko of how Zheng plays in the singles final, "I felt like I was playing against the Great Wall of China because she didn't miss one ball."

1981 Gene Mayer shocks John McEnroe 3-6, 7-6 (5), 6-2 in round-robin play at the Masters Championships at Madison Square Garden in New York City. Says Mayer, "It's one thing believing you can beat the best players. It's another thing doing it on the court." McEnroe, however, is hampered in the match by an upset stomach and a turned ankle, and limps through the last few games of the match.

2002 Stefan Koubek of Austria pulls off a stunning comeback on the first day of the Australian Open, fighting back from a 0-6, 1-6, 1-4 (15-40) deficit to defeat Cyril Saulnier of France 0-6, 1-6, 7-6 (6), 6-4, 8-6, staving off a match point in the third set. Koubek comes back from a two-sets-to-love deficit to beat James Blake of the United States in the second round and goes on to defeat Kristian Pless in the third round and Fernando Gonzalez in the fourth round en route to the quarterfinals of the event. There, he loses to Jiri Novak of the Czech Republic.

January 15

1962 Rod Laver, the reigning Wimbledon champion, defeats Roy Emerson, the reigning U.S. champion, 8-6, 0-6, 6-4, 6-4 to win the Australian Championships in sweltering conditions at White City, Sydney, Australia. The title is the first leg of Laver's eventual 1962 "Grand Slam" campaign, where he sweeps the four major singles titles.

1964 President Lyndon Johnson hosts the victorious 1963 U.S. Davis Cup team at the White House. Johnson spends 45 minutes with team members Dennis Ralston, Chuck McKinley and Marty Riessen as well as U.S. captain Bob Kelleher and U.S. Lawn Tennis Association President Ed Turville. As Johnson introduces the team to his press secretary Pierre Salinger he says, "There's my tennis player. If I can teach Salinger to ride a horse, maybe he can teach me to play tennis."

1981 Bjorn Borg, the calm, cool and collected "ice man" of tennis, puts John McEnroe—and a stunned crowd of 19,103—in shock by losing his temper and is assessed two penalty points that virtually gives McEnroe the second set of his 6-4, 6-7, 7-6 round-robin win at the Masters at Madison Square Garden in New York. With the score knotted at 3-3 in the second-set tie-break, Borg hits a forehand that the linesman calls good, but chair umpire Mike Lugg overrules the call, giving McEnroe the 4-3 lead. Says Borg after his victory, "It should have been 4-3 for me, a very important point." Borg walks to the chair and argues the call. After 30 seconds, Lugg announces a warning against Borg, then, after another 30 seconds, he gives Borg a point penalty. After continued arguments, Borg is assessed another point penalty, giving McEnroe a 6-3 lead in the tie-break, that he claims when he wins the next point. Writes Bud Collins of the *Boston Globe* of Borg's lost temper, "It seemed as likely as the statue of the same name in Columbus Circle leaping and screaming that the world was flat after all." Says McEnroe of Borg's behavior, "Unbelievable. I was in shock watching Bjorn do that. He gave me the second set when he kept arguing and got those penalties. Borg hasn't played a tournament in about six weeks, and I guess he got a little nervous, but I really can't explain it. He just never does that."

1994 In his 144th and final appearance in a professional singles final, Ivan Lendl loses to Pete Sampras 7-6 (5), 6-4 in the final of the Sydney International. Sampras does not lose serve in the match, which is delayed by several hours due to rain and for 19 minutes with Sampras leading 6-5 in the first set.

1986 John McEnroe loses what ultimately becomes a career-altering match to Brad Gilbert in the first round of the year-end Masters Championships in New York. McEnroe, ranked No. 2 and struggling to find motivation, loses to the No. 15-ranked Gilbert 5-7, 6-4, 6-1 in front of 9,798 fans at Madison Square Garden. "I'm very ashamed of the way I played tonight," McEnroe says after the match. "I'm not moving well. I'm making too many mistakes. I'm out of condition—that's the bottom line. If I continue to play like this, I'll stop playing tournament tennis. I have no business being on the court." The match is also highlighted by verbal sparring between McEnroe and Gilbert as well as the New York crowd turning against McEnroe, their native grown champion. Gilbert does not repeat to reporters the words that McEnroe says to him during their exchange, Gilbert claiming them not fit for print. He does, however, say: "One of the things he said was that I didn't belong on the same court as him. The last time I played him (in Los Angeles) he got on me as well. I seem to bring out the worst in him." Writes Julie Cart in the *Los Angeles Times*, "McEnroe fought with the line judges, he fought with Gilbert and he fought with himself." Following the loss, McEnroe takes a sabbatical from tennis, where he marries his first wife, Tatum O'Neal. He returns to tournament tennis at the Volvo International at Stratton Mountain, Vermont in August, but never again reaches a major singles final.

1984 Hana Mandlikova ends Martina Navratilova's streak of victories at 54 with a 7-6, 3-6, 6-4 victory in the final of the Virginia Slims of California at the Oakland Coliseum Arena. Navratilova, the world's No. 1 player, enters the match needing two victories to equal the Open era record of 56 straight held by Chris Evert Lloyd. Navratilova, however, goes on to win 74 straight matches following the loss, setting a new Open era record.

1990 Eighteen-year-old Pete Sampras defeats Tim Mayotte 7-6, 6-7, 4-6, 7-5, 12-10 in 4 hours, 59 minutes in the first round of the Australian Open in what at the time was the longest match in the history of the tournament. Sampras and Mayotte's match is upstaged one year later when Boris Becker defeats Omar Camporese in 5:11 in the 1991 third round. Mayotte loses the match by double-faulting the last two points of the match. Says Mayotte of Sampras, a future 14-time major singles titlist who wins his first major eight months later at the U.S. Open, "Pete, talent-wise, is right up there among the best players. He's got the weapons, but it is whether he's got the commitment. He doesn't have the talent of Agassi or the commitment of Chang. But he has the talent of Chang, so if he's willing to put it together, he can be in the top 10."

2002 Top-seed Lleyton Hewitt crashes out in the first round of the Australian Open, losing to Spain's Alberto Martin 1-6, 6-1, 6-4, 7-6 (4) to become the first No. 1 seeded man in the history of the tournament to lose in the first round. With the first-round loss the previous day of No. 2 seed Gustavo Kuerten and the withdrawal of No. 3 seed Andre Agassi, the 2002 Australian Open becomes the first major event to start the second round without any of the top three seeded men's players.

2008 Frenchman Fabrice Santoro sets a longevity record in professional tennis as the 35-year-old Tahitian-born double-fisted player competes in his 62nd career major championship in beating American John Isner 6-2, 6-2, 6-4 in the first round of the Australian Open. Santoro, playing in his 38th straight major tournament, breaks the record he previously shares with Andre Agassi. Says Santoro of his achievement, "The thing is when you look at the history of game and see all these champion, like Sampras, Agassi, before like Connors, who had a huge and long career, all these past champion, (this is) the only point I'm a little bit in front of them. Because I have a huge respect for them, this record means a lot to me. I mean, I can't match against them about many things, except this one." Santoro, nick-named "The Magician" because of his abilities to hit a wide variety of slices, spins and seeming "magic" shots, plays his first major tournament at the 1989 French Open as a 16-year-old. His best singles showing at a major comes in reaching the quarterfinals of the 2006 Australian Open. His secret to his longevity? "I love the game more than many players, or more than normally. I always try to improve my game, to understand what's going on on the court, to listen to my body, stay healthy, just try to be the best every day."

2008 Andrea Petkovic's first-ever match in a major championship lasts only six points as the 20-year-old German ruptures her anterior cruciate ligament in the first game of her first-round match against No. 6 seed Anna Chakvetadze of Russia at the Australian Open. Says Petkovic, "I was running into the forehand and I tried to catch up the run, and as I stepped on my right foot, my knee just went like this (showing a twisting motion). The doctor said I should retire immediately."

January 16

2006 Eighteen-year-old Tszvetana Pironkova of Bulgaria, ranked No. 94 in the world and playing in her first major tournament, defeats three-time Wimbledon champion Venus Williams 2-6, 6-0, 9-7 on the opening day of the Australian Open. Says Williams of her upset loss, "I couldn't get it right today, but in general, I am playing really well. It's just like, `Wow, it was the wrong time to hit wrong.'"

2007 Top-seed Maria Sharapova blows a 5-0 third-set lead, but holds on and wins an excruciating first-round match with No. 62-ranked Camille Pin of France 6-3, 4-6, 9-7 at the Australian Open. The match is played on a 102-degree day in Melbourne causing for additional discomfort and challenges for both players. Says Sharapova of the heat, "It was hard to think about what you were going to do on court."

2003 In what eventually becomes her final match at the Australian Open, 29-year-old Monica Seles sprains her ankle and is eliminated in the second round, losing to Czech qualifier Klara Koukalova 6-7 (6), 7-5, 6-3. Seles injures her ankle in the third game of the match and braves through the three-set match with her left foot wrapped. Says Seles, "It was just bad luck, what can you do? It was a struggle from the moment I sprained it. I knew I was in trouble and I tried to fight it but she was just too good."

2002 Yevgeny Kafelnikov, the No. 4 seed and the 1999 Australian Open champion, is straight-setted by American qualifier and No. 234-ranked Alex Kim 6-3, 7-5, 6-3 in the second round the Australian Open.

1900 James Dwight, the president of the United States Lawn Tennis Association (USLTA), writes a letter to G.R. Mewburn, the honorary secretary of the Lawn Tennis Association, enclosing conditions for a competition between the United States and Britain that would evolve into the Davis Cup.

January 17

1981 After defeating Gene Mayer 6-3, 6-4 to reach the singles final of the Grand Prix Masters, Ivan Lendl denies charges from Jimmy Connors that he tanked his final round-robin match to ensure a better semifinal match-up in the year-end championships. In a match that concludes 18 minutes after midnight earlier in the day, Connors calls Lendl "a chicken" for allegedly not trying in the second set of his 7-6, 6-1 victory. With both players having already qualified for the semifinals with 2-0 round robin records, the semifinal pairings hinge on the winner and loser of the Connors-Lendl match. The loser of the match would face Gene Mayer, while the winner would draw Wimbledon and French Open champion Bjorn Borg. Writes Barry Lorge of the *Washington Post*, "Given those circumstances, the result of an unfortunate flaw in the hybrid round-robin-knockout Masters format, there was every temptation for a player to deliberately lose, and play Mayer rather than Borg. Since the loser would be due back on court in less than 13 hours, there was also incentive for the man who lost the first set to lose the second quickly." Lendl loses the second set to Connors in 18 minutes, winning only 10 points and, according to Lorge, rushing the net "suicidally." Says Connors, "I think he's a chicken. No matter what happens, you're supposed to try your hardest on every point." Asked his reaction to Connors calling him "a chicken," Lendl says, "That can be his opinion. If he thinks I didn't try, it is better that he says that, and doesn't say he thinks I tried. It is his opinion. Everybody is entitled to his opinion...I understand how somebody can say I did, but I say I didn't." Connors goes on to lose to Borg in a highly-intense semifinal by a 6-4, 6-7, 6-3 margin, while Lendl loses to Borg 6-4, 6-2, 6-2 in the championship match.

1982 Trailing two-sets-to-love and down match point in the third set tie-break, Ivan Lendl stages one of the great comebacks in the history of the Masters Championships, defeating Vitas Gerulaitis 6-7 (5), 2-6, 7-6 (6), 6-2, 6-4 in the 3-hour, 52-minute final at Madison Square Garden in New York. Lendl saves his match point at 5-6 in the third-set tie-break and also fights off two break points, trailing 0-2, 15-40 in the third-set that would have put him down a double-service break. Says Lendl of his two-set deficit, "I just wanted to come back. All you can do is keep fighting and fighting and fighting." Says Gerulaitis, "'You just know Lendl's not going to give up.'" The win was Lendl's 35th straight match victory, dating back to his round of 16 loss to Gerulaitis at the U.S. Open the previous summer.

2003 Todd Woodbridge wins his record 79th career doubles title when he teams with Jonas Bjorkman to beat Bob and Mike Bryan 7-6(3), 7-5 in the doubles final of the Adidas International in Sydney, Australia. Woodbridge previously shares the record of 78 doubles titles with Dutchman Tom Okker. Says Woodbridge following his record-breaking win, "There's still plenty to achieve in tennis and in life, isn't there? But I've got to tell you, I'm a little happier and fulfilled than I thought I would be about today. The crowd was fantastic. I didn't know what I expected. But it was a full house who knew what they were watching today—the verge of breaking a record and seeing a part of, I guess tennis history written. To be able to say that I won more than anybody in the history of doubles tennis is something I never began in my career to go after; but I got there, and I'm pretty happy with that."

2006 Playing on a court where she won three of her five major singles titles, Martina Hingis plays in her first major tournament in three years and defeats No. 30 seed Vera Zvonareva of Russia 6-1, 6-2 in the first round of the Australian Open. "I just came out here the other day. I could already feel the atmosphere coming from the previous years," the 25-year-old Hingis says after the match. "You don't know how good it feels. This surface, this stadium has been so good for me."

2004 Seventeen-year-old Rafael Nadal, appearing in his first ATP Tour singles final, loses to Dominik Hrbaty of Slovakia 4-6, 6-2, 7-5 in the final of the Heineken Open in Auckland, New Zealand. Says Nadal following the loss, "This was my first final. I was a bit nervous and a lot tired."

2007 Bobby Reynolds of the United States and Andreas Seppi of Italy finish their first round Australian Open match at 3:34 am as Seppi defeats Reynolds 6-1, 6-7 (4), 6-7 (5), 7-6 (3), 6-3. The match begins at 11:45 pm as Australian Open officials attempt to finish as many matches as possible due to play being suspended earlier in the day due to heat. "It felt like one of those late-nighters you have in college when you've got a paper to write and you need to drink a couple Cokes and get it done," Reynolds, a former Vanderbilt University standout, tells Chris Clarey of the *New York Times*.

January 18

1991 Boris Becker of West Germany and Omar Camporese of Italy play the longest match in the history of the Australian Open, as Becker prevails 7-6 (4), 7-6 (5), 0-6, 4-6, 14-12 in the third-round match in 5 hours, 11 minutes. "I had no idea how to finish it," says the 23-year-old Becker. "At the end, I guess I made one more shot than him. It was a great match from both players. For me, it was one of the top five matches I've played in. You can't get any closer." Becker goes on to win the tournament, beating Ivan Lendl in the final.

2000 Future world No. 1 Roger Federer plays and wins his first main draw match at the Australian Open, defeating Michael Chang 6-4, 6-4, 7-6 (5) in the first round in Melbourne. Federer goes on to reach the third round, losing to Arnaud Clement 6-1, 6-4, 6-3.

1996 Defending champion and No. 4 seed Mary Pierce loses in the second round of the Australian Open, falling to Russian Elena Likhovtseva 6-4, 6-4. Says Pierce, "I can just say basically that I had a really bad day."

1996 Boris Becker rallies from a two-sets-to-love deficit to defeat Thomas Johansson of Sweden 4-6, 3-6, 6-2, 6-1, 6-4 in the second round of the Australian Open. Becker goes on to win the tournament—his sixth and final major singles title—defeating Michael Chang in the final. Six years later, Johansson also hoists the Norman Brookes Challenge Trophy as the unlikely winner at the 2002 Australian Open as the No. 16 seed.

2008 Unheralded Australian left-hander Casey Dellacqua stuns Amelie Mauresmo to become the darling of her nation's major championship as she defeats 2006 Australian Open champion and No. 18 seeded Mauresmo 3-6, 6-4, 6-4 in the third round. Ranked No. 78, Dellacqua benefits from two double faults from the oft-nervous Frenchwoman in the final game of the match to advance. Says Dellacqua, "I knew that (Mauresmo) was struggling (with the pressure), I thought she was struggling a little bit. I know the last match and the match before that, when it comes to the crunch, I've had a lot of confidence ... I think maybe that's what helped me through....I could feel the whole crowd. I could feel Rod Laver (Arena) almost vibrating because the crowd was so loud. It was just awesome."

1993 No. 4 seed Boris Becker is stunned by an aging qualifier Anders Jarryd 3-6, 7-5, 3-6, 6-3, 6-2 in the first round of the Australian Open. "It was the first time in a long time that I can ever remember having to qualify," says the 31-year-old Jarryd. "I wanted to play a lot of tennis and get ready for the doubles. But when I saw Boris in the draw, I figured it would be too tough for me." Becker is slowed by a pulled muscle in his right thigh suffered two weeks earlier in Qatar. "I had treatment all day yesterday," says Becker. "I thought about withdrawing, but I figured that I had come all this way, so that I should give it a try. I was hoping for a short match."

1994 American MaliVai Washington upsets No. 2 seed Michael Stich of Germany 7-6 (4), 6-3, 3-6, 6-2 in the first round of the Australian Open. The confrontation is a re-match of a first round encounter from the 1991 Australian Open, where Washington squanders a two-sets-to-love lead in falling to the German. Says the 26th-ranked Washington of the memory of his blown match from 1991, "It actually kind of inspired me, because I wasn't going to let the two-set-to-love lead get away like it did back in '91. It didn't get me nervous or play a negative role."

1981 Bjorn Borg wins the Masters for second time, defeating Ivan Lendl 6-4, 6-2, 6-2 in the championship match at Madison Square Garden in New York in front of 18,297 fans. The match ultimately becomes the Swede's Masters swan song as he never again plays the event. Says Lendl, "I think Bjorn played very, very, very well."

January 19

1989 Suffering from motivation problems after achieving the apex of his tennis career, world No. 1 Mats Wilander is defeated by India's Ramesh Krishnan 6-3, 6-2, 7-6 in the second round of the Australian Open. Just three months after winning the U.S. Open to clinch the No. 1 ranking and finish off an incredible 1988 season winning three of the four major tournaments, Wilander admits in the post-match press conference that he was not in the match mentally. "It has been difficult for me to motivate myself since the U.S. Open," Wilander says. "That was such a big thing for me. Maybe being number one has got to me, because from there, you can only go down."

1997 Amanda Coetzer of South Africa ends Steffi Graf's 45-match winning streak in major tournaments, defeating the world No. 1 6-2, 7-5 in the fourth round of the Australian Open. Graf, the winner of the last six major tournaments that she entered, fails to reach the quarterfinals of a major championship for only the second time in a decade. Her last loss at a major comes in the 1994 U.S. Open final to Arantxa Sanchez Vicario. The match with Coetzer is played in heat in excess of 100 degrees—temperatures on-court reaching 140 degrees—with Graf being treated many times in the match with ice packs. The No. 3, No. 5 and No. 7 women's seeds also fall by the wayside during the day—No. 3 Conchita Martinez losing to Sabine Appelmans of Belgium 2-6, 7-5, 6-1, Mary Pierce defeating No. 5 Anke Huber and Kimberly Po upsetting No. 7 Lindsay Davenport 7-6 (13), 6-4—the latter match featuring a 28-point tie-break that is third-longest in the history of women's tennis.

1993 Thirty-two-year-old Ivan Lendl is beaten in the first round of the Australian Open by Swede Christian Bergstrom 6-4, 6-4, 2-6, 6-4—Lendl's first opening round loss at a major tournament since Wimbledon twelve years earlier. The No. 8 seed Lendl plays his first match in two months after suffering from strained groin muscles at the end of the 1992 season. Lendl's last first-round loss in a major came at the hands of Australian Charlie Fancutt at Wimbledon in 1981.

2007 Serena Williams wins her first match against a top 10 ranked player in two years, defeating No. 5 seed Nadia Petrova of Russia 1-6, 7-5, 6-3 in the third round of the Australian Open. When presented with this stat in her post-match press conference, Williams laughs and says, "Has it been that long? That's a terrible stat!" Her last previous win over a top 10 player comes at the 2005 Australian Open when she defeats Lindsay Davenport in the final.

2008 Philipp Kohlschreiber of Germany finishes off Andy Roddick 6-4, 3-6, 7-6 (9), 6-7 (3), 8-6 in an epic third-round match at the Australian Open that ends just after 2 am local time in Melbourne. In the losing effort, Roddick fires 42 aces and hits 79 winners. Kohlschreiber hits an incredible 104 winners during the nearly four-hour match. "I took his best stuff for five sets and I thought I was going to get him to break or to fold," says Roddick. "I thought if I kept it on him long enough that that would happen. Tonight he played like a great, great player. His backhand was extremely impressive." Says the No. 29-ranked Kohlschreiber, "That was just amazing. It's the best that happened to me in tennis. I enjoyed every second. It was just high-class tennis from both players." Later in the day, as the sun rises, world No. 1 Roger Federer plays an epic match of survival, fending off the upset challenge of No. 49-ranked Janko Tipsarevic of Serbia 6-7 (5), 7-6 (1), 5-7, 6-1, 10-8 in the third round. Federer serves a personal record 39 aces to win the match in 4 hours, 27 minutes. Says Federer, "I don't often get to play five-setters unless they're against Nadal at Wimbledon. It was good to be part of something like this."

1992 John McEnroe advances into the quarterfinals of the Australian Open with a thrilling 7-5, 7-6 (4), 4-6, 2-6, 8-6 win over Emilio Sanchez of Spain, saving three match points in a 4-hour, 41-minute epic played in temperatures near 120 degrees. The match, which ultimately becomes McEnroe's final match victory at the Australian Open, comes two days after the 32-year-old McEnroe straight-sets defending champion Boris Becker 6-4, 6-3, 7-5. McEnroe fights off his three-match points with Sanchez serving for the match at 6-5 in the fifth—Sanchez double-faulting and missing a forehand at 40-15 and missing a backhand add ad-in. Writes Sandy Harwitt in the *New York Times* of the match's conclusion, "When it was over, they hugged. McEnroe first raised his hand in the air to acknowledge the thunderous applause, but then just dropped to the ground, lying on his back, in disbelief and relief." McEnroe goes on to lose in the quarterfinals to Wayne Ferreira of South Africa.

January 20

1996 Pete Sampras is stunned in the third round of the Australian Open by 19-year-old Mark "Scud" Philippoussis, as the Australian native son fires 29 aces in a 6-4, 7-6 (9), 7-6 (3) victory that costs Sampras the No. 1 world ranking. "I didn't have a sniff at getting a serve back," says Sampras, who beat Philippoussis in four sets at the U.S. Open the previous September. "When he's serving that big, there's nothing you can do." Philippoussis agrees with Sampras in his post match comments, saying, "I felt like I could just toss it up and ace how I wanted to. It was an unbelievable feeling I did feel like I was in the zone."

2008 At 4:33 am local time in Melbourne, local favorite Lleyton Hewitt and Marcos Baghdatis of Cyprus complete the latest concluded match in the history of major championships and one of the Australian Open's most extraordinary matches, Hewitt prevailing 3-6, 7-5, 7-5, 6-7 (4), 6-3 in 4 hours, 45 minutes to advance into the fourth round. Hewitt, who calls the victory "one of my best wins mentally," leads 5-1 in the fourth set and holds a match point at 5-2, before Baghdatis rallies to extend the match deeper into the early morning hours. Due to a back-log of matches, including top-seed Roger Federer's 10-8 in the fifth-set third-set survival against Janko Tipsarevic, the match does not start until 11:47 pm the previous day. The previous latest finish of a match was at the 2007 Australian Open, when Italy's Andreas Seppi defeated American Bobby Reynolds 6-1, 6-7 (4), 6-7 (5), 7-6 (3), 6-3 at 3:34 am (play delayed during the day due to excessive heat, causing for the match to start at 11:45 pm local time).

1987 No. 71-ranked Wally Masur of Australia posts one of the biggest wins of his career—and one of the biggest upsets at the Australian Open—defeating two-time reigning Wimbledon champion Boris Becker 4-6, 7-6, 6-4, 6-7, 6-2 in the fourth round. Becker is fined $2,000 for a series of unsportsmanlike episodes—$500 for receiving illegal coaching from the sidelines by Gunther Bosch, another $500 for smashing his racquet in the second-set tie-break and another $1,000 for other offensive behavior, including throwing balls at the umpire, spitting water in the direction of the umpire and hitting three balls out of the Kooyong Tennis Stadium. Says Becker, "I couldn't serve or return and suddenly I started to lose my cool. Then I got bad calls. It made me completely crazy."

1997 Pete Sampras performs a great escape in the fourth round of the Australian Open, coming back from a 2-4 fifth-set deficit to defeat 19-year-old Dominik Hrbaty of Slovakia, 6-7 (4), 6-3, 6-4, 3-6, 6-4. With on-court temperatures soaring close to 140 degrees, Hrbaty folds in the final set, losing the final four games and double-faulting three times in his final two service games. Says Sampras of the fifth set and the result, "It's really not about tennis at that point. It's about luck. He played well enough to beat me. I got a little bit lucky, and sometimes that's what it takes."

1990 Rebound Ace, the controversial court surface of the Australian Open since 1988, is thrown under the microscope and criticized as two players, Gabriela Sabatini and Mark Woodforde, suffer ankle injuries that force them to leave the court in wheelchairs in third-round matches. Sabatini, ranked No. 3 in the world, leads Claudia Porwik of West Germany 6-2, 1-0 when, rushing to retrieve a drop shot, turns her ankle, forcing her to default. Says Porwik, who eventually reaches the women's semifinals, "It doesn't feel like a victory at all…I saw her foot stick on the surface. It happens on hard courts like this when you can't slide. Within a minute, it (Sabatini's ankle) was like an egg and it must have been very painful." Woodforde, trailing David Wheaton 3-6, 5-4, also turns his ankle forcing him to default. Says Boris Becker, a routine winner on the day over Olivier Delaitre of France, of the court surface, "The court is very sticky and when you're a little tired and just hanging in there, that's when your ankle can go."

January 21

1990 Saying "I don't really have anyone to blame but myself," John McEnroe becomes the first player in 27 years to be tossed out of a major tennis tournament for misconduct. Leading Sweden's Mikael Pernfors 6-1, 4-6, 7-5, 2-4 in the round of 16 a the Australian Open, McEnroe is disqualified by chair umpire Gerry Armstrong after breaking a racquet and uttering a flurry of four-letter words. "This is like a long story that culminates in me getting defaulted in a big tournament," McEnroe says in the post-match press conference. "I mean, I guess it was bound to happen. It's too bad. I don't feel good about it, but I can't say that I'm totally surprised." McEnroe is fined $6,500 for behavior in the match—$5,000 for racquet abuse, $500 for verbal abuse and $1,000 for the default. The previous disqualification came in 1963 when Colombian-born Spaniard Willie Alvarez is defaulted out of the French Championships.

1998 In their first-ever professional meeting, 17-year old Venus Williams defeats 16-year-old younger sister Serena 7-6 (4), 6-1 in the second round of the Australian Open. The two sisters go on to dominate tennis, winning multiple major titles in singles and doubles and, during a stretch between 2001 and 2003, play five major finals against each other. Says Venus of the second-round match, "I kept seeing Serena across the net. It was a little bit odd, but it is to be expected. In the future it will be the same...I feel good that I won. Even though it was Serena, I'm still a competitor. After the match I told her, 'Serena, I'm sorry I took you out. I didn't want to, but I had to do it.'" Says Serena, "It felt OK, I just tried to keep thinking of her as someone else. I tried to treat it as a normal match. I think in the end it was a normal match. I think we handled this very well. In the future we will be able to handle it even easier. If I had to lose in the second round, no better than to Venus."

1988 Chris Evert defeats rival Martina Navratilova 6-2, 7-5 to advance into the women's singles final at the Australian Open, in what ultimately becomes her last appearance in a major singles final. Says Evert, "I was under no pressure at all; Martina had all the pressure on her. I'm always relaxed when I play Martina. She was No. 1 for so long. It is no crime to lose to her." Top-seeded Steffi Graf loses the first two games at love but rallies to beat eighth-seeded Claudia Kohde-Kilsch 6-2, 6-3, in 45 minutes in the other women's semifinal.

1999 One round after hitting 23 double faults in the first round of the Australian Open, Anna Kournikova serves 31 double faults—the most recorded in a professional match—in a 1-6, 6-4, 10-8 second round win over Japan's Miho Saeki. Says Kournikova of her serving troubles, "I'm really frustrated about it, just like everybody who's watching. In practice, I feel fine. I serve normal and there's no sign of doubles faults, but when I come to the line when I play, there is something happening. I'm just going to have to get over it and try to fight through, just like I did today."

2007 Defending champion Amelie Mauresmo is ousted in the fourth round of the Australian Open by unseeded Lucie Safarova of the Czech Republic 6-4, 6-3. The 19-year-old Safarova enters the match having won just one match in six previous major tournaments. "It's amazing. I still can't believe it," says Safarova, ranked No. 70. "I'm so happy. It's incredible." Svetlana Kuznetsova, the 2004 U.S. Open champion and the No. 3 seed, is also dismissed from the tournament, losing 6-4, 6-2 to Shahar Peer of Israel.

2002 Pete Sampras plays what ultimately becomes his final match at the Australian Open, losing in the fourth round to Marat Safin 6-2, 6-4, 6-7 (5), 7-6 (10-8). Sampras trails 2-4 in the third set, but rallies to nearly take the match to a fourth set. Says Safin, "It would not be very nice to go five sets with Pete, because you never know."

2008 Daniela Hantuchova of Slovakia and Agnieszka Radwanska of Poland advance into the quarterfinals of the Australian Open with remarkable comeback victories. Hantuchova fights back from a 6-1, 4-1 deficit—winning at one point 17 straight points—to defeat Russian Maria Kirilenko 1-6, 6-4, 6-4, while Radwanksa comes back from a 6-1, 3-0 hole to beat Nadia Petrova of Russia 1-6, 7-5, 6-0. Radwanska, who becomes the first Polish woman to reach the quarterfinals of a major championship, benefits from Petrova straining her groin, which severely hampers her play. "I was losing 6-1, 3-0 and I was thinking, 'What am I doing wrong?"says Radwanska, who upset No. 2 seed Svetlana Kuznetsova in the third round. "It was so quick and she was using the wind very well, and I wasn't. I think that was the most important point in this match. Then I started to play, try to do something else. It was very long games and I won the second set. It was so close. In the third set, I don't know what she was doing, but it's not a question for me."

January 22

2003 Andy Roddick and Younes El Aynaoui compete in one of the greatest matches ever at the Australian Open, locking horns for 4 hours, 49 minutes before Roddick emerges victorious in the quarterfinal confrontation 4-6, 7-6 (5), 4-6, 6-4, 21-19. The fifth-set is the longest fifth set in a major tournament in the Open era in games (40) and in time (2 hours, 23 minutes), while the 83-game match is the longest match at the Australian Open since the introduction of the tie-break. The win advances Roddick into a major semifinal for the first time in his career, where, worn out, he falls meekly to Rainer Schuettler of Germany. Against El Aynaoui, Roddick saves a match point in the 10th game of the fifth set and serves for the match at 11-10, but is broken to extend the match. "My respect level for him just grew and grew throughout the match," says Roddick following the epic victory. "I'm sure it's vice-versa. I don't even remember ever talking to Younes before this match. But down the line, I mean, we could see each other 10 years down the line and know that we did share something special."

2008 Maria Sharapova ends world No. 1 Justine Henin's 32-match winning streak with a 6-4, 6-0 win in the quarterfinals of the Australian Open. Sharapova's father, Yuri, performs a "throat slash" gesture to his daughter at the end of the match, which is met with much disdain by Henin, the WTA Tour and the tennis industry. Earlier in the day, defending champion Serena Williams is eliminated, losing to No. 3 seed Jelena Jankovic of Serbia 6-3, 6-4 also in the quarterfinals.

1988 Australian Pat Cash and Swede Mats Wilander both register five-set semifinal victories at the Australian Open. Cash defeats No. 1 seed Ivan Lendl 6-4, 2-6, 6-4, 4-6, 6-2, winning the final four games losing only four points. Wilander defeats No. 2 seed and two-time defending champion Stefan Edberg 6-0, 6-7, 6-3, 3-6, 6-1 to end Edberg's bid to become the first man since Australia's Roy Emerson 20 years earlier to win the Australian Open three years in a row.

2006 No. 2 seed Andy Roddick is upset by unheralded and unseeded Marcos Baghdatis of Cyprus, 4-6, 6-1, 3-6, 4-6 in the fourth round of the Australian Open to set up a quarterfinal match with Croatia's Ivan Ljubicic. Asked in his post-match press conference whether he would watch any tapes of his Croatian opponent, Baghdatis says, "I think my coach will watch and I'll be sleeping with my girlfriend."

January 23

1991 Saying to the assembled media in the post-match press conference "It's just like you all expected-Edberg, Lendl, McEnroe and Becker," Patrick McEnroe, the younger brother of former world No. 1 John McEnroe, joins the illustrious list of tennis greats in the semifinals of the Australian Open with a 7-6 (7-2), 6-3, 4-6, 4-6, 6-2 victory over Italy's Cristiano Caratti. McEnroe, ranked No. 114 world, moves into the semifinals of the event with No. 1 ranked Stefan Edberg, No. 2 ranked Boris Becker and No. 3 ranked Ivan Lendl, all rivals for major championships with his brother John over the last six to 10 years. The younger McEnroe's run comes to an end in the semifinals, losing to eventual champion Becker.

1988 Steffi Graf downs Chris Evert 6-1, 7-6 to win the women's singles title at the Australian Open in Evert's last appearance in a major final. The match also marks the first time a major final is played indoors as the retractable roof at the facility is closed due to rain. Graf leads Evert 2-1 in the first set when rain begins to fall and after a 90-minute delay, Australian Open officials decide to close the roof for the duration of the match. "Steffi is a much better indoor player than I am," Evert says. "It took time to get used to the conditions. It's a lot different to outdoors. She just handled it better."

2005 Andre Agassi endures a record 51 aces from Joachim Johansson in defeating the six-foot-six Swede 6-7 (4), 7-6 (5), 7-6 (3), 6-4 in the round of 16 at the Australian Open. Johansson breaks the previous record for most aces in a match set by Richard Krajicek, who slams 49 aces in his quarterfinal loss to Yevgeny Kafelnikov at the 1999 US Open.

1983 Ivan Lendl routs John McEnroe 6-4, 6-4, 6-2 to win the Grand Prix Masters at Madison Square Garden for the second straight year. After defeating McEnroe for a seventh straight time, Lendl collects $100,000, raising his earnings for the 1982 season to $2,028,850, a men's record at the time. Lendl completes the 1982 season—with the Masters as the season-ending event—with a record of 107-9. While raised on clay in Czechoslovakia, Lendl's win ensures that he remains undefeated in his last 59 indoor matches, dating back to April of 1981. When asked what surface he felt would be his best against Lendl, McEnroe says grass, but then jokes, with his current bad form, "At this point, maybe mud."

1996 In a marathon major women's singles match, 19-year-old Chanda Rubin outlasts Arantxa Sanchez Vicario 6-4, 2-6, 16-14 in 3 hours, 33 minutes to reach the semifinals of the Australian Open in the longest women's match in the history of the Australian Championships. The third set alone lasts 2 hours, 22 minutes.

2003 Serena Williams fights off two match points and a 1-5 third-set deficit to beat Kim Clijsters 4-6, 6-3, 7-5 to dramatically advance into the final of the Australian Open. Williams advances into the final to meet sister Venus Williams, whom she defeats to clinch her "Serena Slam" run of four consecutive major tournament titles. "It was just an unbelievable battle out there," says Serena of the comeback win. "I thought, 'I don't want to lose, 6-1.' Then I said, 'I don't want to lose, 6-2.' So I just kept fighting. Next thing I know, I came back."

1983 The Swedish newspaper *Kvallposten* in Malmo, Sweden runs a story quoting Bjorn Borg that he will not play a Grand Prix schedule or any major tournaments in 1983, virtually ending his professional career. "I cannot give 100 percent," the paper quotes Borg as saying, "and if I cannot do that, it would not be fair to myself to go on. Tennis has to be fun if you are to get to the top, and I don't feel that way anymore. That's why I quit."

2007 Unseeded Serena Williams edges No. 16 seed Shahar Peer of Israel 3-6, 6-2, 8-6 in the quarterfinals of the Australian Open. Says Williams following the match, "I am the ultimate competitor...I'm definitely ready to create some more carnage. I feel absolutely no pressure. I don't think anyone thought I would get this far, except for me and my mom." Williams fights off 10 of 13 break points against her serve and comes back from a 1-4 deficit in the final set.

January 24

1988 Mats Wilander of Sweden wins the Australian Open for a third time, defeating hometown hero Pat Cash 6-3, 6-7, 3-6, 6-1, 8-6 in a dramatic 4-hour, 28-minute final—the first Australian men's final played on hard courts at the new Flinder's Park National Tennis Center facility. The 23-year-old Swede, who won the 1983 and 1984 Australian titles on grass courts, claims a major singles title on his third difference surface to go with his 1982 and 1985 French titles, joining Jimmy Connors as the only man to achieve the rare feat. Cash was attempting to become the first Australian since Mark Edmondson in 1976 to win his homeland's men's singles title.

1995 In a match lasting 3 hours, 58 minutes, concluding at 1:09 in the morning, world No. 1 Pete Sampras edges Jim Courier 6-7(4), 6-7(3), 6-3, 6-4, 6-3 in the quarterfinals of the Australian Open. The match is highlighted by tearful exhibitions from Sampras in the fifth set after a fan yells to Sampras to "win it for your coach" referring to Tim Gullikson, Sampras's coach who flies home earlier in the day back to the United States after being plagued by seizures caused by an eventual diagnosis of brain tumors. "I realized early, going into the second set, something special was happening out there," says Courier, ranked No. 11, in the post-match press conference. "We were both not missing much and all the points were being fought for." Says Sampras, "Win or lose, I thought it was one of the better matches I've ever taken part in. I just didn't quit and tried to do everything I could to try to win. You know, we both showed a lot of heart out there."

1996 In an epic day of play at the Australian Open, defending champion Andre Agassi comes back from two-sets-to-love down for the first time in his career to beat Jim Courier 6-7 (9-7), 2-6, 6-3, 6-4, 6-2 and take over the No. 1 ranking. The match, halted by rain in the 10th game the previous night, doesn't resume until 17 hours later with the total playing time of the match being 3 hours, 16 minutes. Earlier in the day, South African Amanda Coetzer ends the run of 15-year-old Martina Hingis of Switzerland, the youngest quarterfinalist ever in the Australian Open, 7-5, 4-6, 6-1 in 2 hours, 15 minutes. After the roof is closed due to rain, Anke Huber of Germany defeats Conchita Martinez 4-6, 6-2, 6-1. Following the conclusion of the Agassi-Courier epic, Boris Becker defeats Yevgeny Kafelnikov 6-4, 7-6 (9), 6-1, and Mark Woodforde defeats Thomas Enqvist 6-4, 6-4, 6-4.

1970 Dennis Ralston concludes his 93-game 19-17, 20-18, 4-6, 6-3 victory over John Newcombe in the second round of the Australian Open—the longest match in games in the history of the Australian Open. The playing time for the match is 4 hours, 41 minutes.

1987 Hana Mandlikova wins the Australian Open women's singles final, defeating Martina Navratilova 7-5, 7-6 (1) snapping Navratilova's 58-match winning streak. Mandlikova wins her second Australian Open title, to go with her 1980 title, while Navratilova fails in her attempt to win her fourth singles title Down Under. Says Mandlikova, "It is always nice to beat Martina. I respect her as a player and a person, and I've learned a lot from her."

2004 Lisa Raymond, known mainly for her astute doubles play, wins the singles match of her career, upsetting Venus Williams 6-4, 7-6 (5) in the third round of the Australian Open. Says Williams following the match, "I'm pretty much in shock. I definitely had some high hopes to win here."

2008 Ana Ivanovic loses the first eight games of the match, but rallies in dramatic fashion to defeat Daniela Hantuchova 0-6, 6-3, 6-4 to advance into the women's final of the Australian Open. Ivanovic does not win a game until the 46th minute of the match. Says Ivanovic, "I didn't find my rhythm and I knew I had to go for the shots before her, because she likes to dominate. I tried to hang in there. But I just tried to tell myself that she can't keep up that level throughout the whole match. I knew I would get a chance at some point, and that helped me a lot." In the other women's semifinal, Maria Sharapova defeats Jelena Jankovic 6-3, 6-1.

2008 Unseeded Jo-Wilfried Tsonga of France shocks the tennis world by steam-rolling world No. 2 Rafael Nadal 6-2, 6-3, 6-2 in the semifinals of the Australian Open, becoming only the third Frenchman to reach the men's singles final at the Australian Championships. Nadal commits only 12 unforced errors against the No. 38-ranked Tsonga, but the Frenchman responds with 49 winners and 17 aces. Says Tsonga, "For me it's a big dream. It's just amazing—I played unbelievable. Everything went in. My backhand worked a lot and my serve also. My forehand, my volley, my drop shot, everything. I was moving on the court like never I move, so everything was perfect." Tsonga joins 2001 finalist Arnaud Clement and 1928 champion Jean Borotra as the only men from France to reach the final round in Australia.

January 25

1997 At the age of 16 years, three months, 26 days, Martina Hingis of Switzerland becomes the youngest player to win a major singles title, defeating Mary Pierce of France 6-2, 6-2 in the women's singles final at the Australian Open. Hingis commits only 11 unforced errors in her first major final.

2003 Serena Williams clinches "The Serena Slam" beating older sister Venus Williams 7-6 (7-4), 3-6, 6-4 to win the Australian Open and complete her sweep of four consecutive major championships. Venus, ironically, is the final-round victim of Serena's in all four of the major tournaments. Serena joins Maureen Connolly, Margaret Court, Martina Navratilova and Steffi Graf as the only women to hold all four major tournament titles at the same time. "I never get choked up, but I'm really emotional right now," says Serena in the post-match ceremony. "I'm really, really, really happy. I'd like to thank my mom and my dad for helping me." The win for Serena places her ahead in her head-to-head series with Venus by a 5-4 margin. Says Venus of her younger sister, "I wish I could have been the winner, but of course you have a great champion in Serena and she has won all four Grand Slams, which is something I'd love to do one day."

1987 Stefan Edberg of Sweden wins his second straight Australian Open fighting off Aussie Pat Cash 6-3, 6-4, 3-6, 5-7, 6-3 in the last Australian Open played on grass courts at Kooyong Stadium in Melbourne.

2008 Roger Federer's streak of consecutive major singles finals is snapped at 10 as Novak Djokovic of Serbia upsets the world No. 1 7-5, 6-3, 7-6 (5) in the semifinals of the Australian Open. Federer, the two-time defending champion and the owner of 12 major singles titles, fails to reach the singles final at a major event for the first time since the 2005 French Open. Says Federer, "I've created a monster that I need to win every tournament." Says the 20-year-old No. 3-seeded Djokovic, "I am just very amazed I coped with the pressure today. In the most important moments, I played my best tennis. It's just amazing, indescribable, to beat the No. 1 player of the world, one of the best players this sport has ever had, in straight sets."

1992 Eighteen-year-old Monica Seles wins her second Australian Open title and her fifth major singles title, defeating Mary Joe Fernandez 6-2, 6-3 in the women's singles final. Aussies Mark Woodforde and Todd Woodbridge, the legendary Australian doubles pairing, win their first major doubles title as a pair, beating Americans Kelly Jones and Rick Leach 6-4, 6-3, 6-4.

1996 Monica Seles ends the major tournament title dream of Chanda Rubin, defeating the 19-year-old from Lafayette, La., 6-7, 6-1, 7-5 in the semifinals of the Australian Open. Rubin leads 5-2 in the third set and is two points away from reaching her first major final, but wins only two of the last 16 points of the match. Anke Huber of Germany advances into a major singles final for the first time in her career, defeating Amanda Coetzer 4-6, 6-4, 6-2.

2007 Roger Federer crushes Andy Roddick 6-4, 6-0, 6-2 in the semifinals of the Australian Open in one of the most devastating displays of top-level tennis ever seen. After Roddick leads 4-3 in the first set, Federer reels off 15 of the next 17 games with incredible shot-making that leaves Roddick mesmerized. Says Federer, "I had one of those days where everything worked and I was unbeatable. It's just unreal. I'm shocked myself. I've played good matches here, but never really almost destroyed somebody. That's a highlight of my career."

1989 Ivan Lendl dominates John McEnroe 7-6, 6-2, 7-6 in the quarterfinals of the Australian Open—their 10th and final meeting in a major tournament. Lendl wins the all-time head-to-head with McEnroe in majors 7-3. Lendl's quarterfinal win places their head-to-head at 15-14 and, after seven more career meetings, he wins the all-time head-to-head with his arch-rival 21-15.

January 26

2002 In one of the greatest major singles final ever, Jennifer Capriati endures on-court temperatures of 130 degrees, fights back from a 6-4, 4-0 deficit and saves four match points to defeat Martina Hingis 4-6, 7-6 (7), 6-2 to successfully defend her Australian Open singles title. Before Capriati, no woman had ever saved four match points to win a major singles final. Says Capriati, "I don't know which one was better for me, winning last year or winning this year. I was down match points and it was such a struggle for me and I didn't know if I was really going to pull that out or if I was going to win, and I just kept going, point by point, and things turned around. I had a lot on my shoulders, being the defending champion, trying to keep the No.1 status, and dealing with the conditions. I didn't feel like I was playing my best tennis in the beginning, but I really fought hard out there, so it means a lot to me." Says Hingis after the match, "I felt like my head was all over the place, but after I lost the second set, she had the momentum."

1992 Twenty-one-year-old Jim Courier defeats Stefan Edberg 6-3, 3-6, 6-4, 6-2 to win his first Australian Open singles title, putting him in position to become the first American man to rank No. 1 since John McEnroe in 1985. Courier becomes the first American man to win the Australian Open in 10 years and celebrates his win by running out of the stadium and jumping into the nearby Yarra River, one of the most polluted rivers in the world. Courier assumes the No. 1 ranking on Feb. 10.

1997 World No. 1 Pete Sampras wins his second Australian Open singles title and ninth career major singles title, needing only 87 minutes to defeat unseeded Carlos Moya 6-2, 6-3, 6-3 in the final. "He's No. 1 and he showed it today," says Moya, the first Spanish man to reach the Australian final since Andres Gimeno lost to Rod Laver in the 1969 final. "For him, it was his 11th Grand Slam final. For me, it was my first. I'm 20 and he's 25. He has more experience. But I learned many things today, more than in the last two weeks of the tournament."

2008 No. 5 seed Maria Sharapova wins her third major singles title, defeating Ana Ivanovic 7-5, 6-3 to win the Australian Open. Sharapova's victory comes one year after she is embarrassed by Serena Williams 6-1, 6-2 in the Australian final in one of the most one-sided major women's finals ever. The 20-year-old Sharapova claims the title without losing a set in seven matches and adds the Australian title to her major tournament trophy case that also includes the 2004 Wimbledon title and the 2006 U.S. Open title. The "Siberian Siren" tells the crowd in the post-match trophy ceremony of the text message she receives from tennis great Billie Jean King before the match that says "Champions take chances and pressure is a privilege." Says Sharapova, "I took mine."

1970 Arthur Ashe advances into the men's singles final of the Australian Open in Sydney when Dennis Ralston is forced to retire from the semifinal match with a strained back, trailing 3-6, 10-8, 3-6, 1-2. Dick Crealy of Australia also advances into the men's singles final, upsetting Roger Taylor of Great Britain 6-3, 9-11, 8-6, 3-6, 8-6.

1990 Ivan Lendl and Stefan Edberg rout their semifinal opponents in straight sets to set up a meeting in the Australian Open final. Defending champion Lendl defeats Yannick Noah 6-4, 6-1, 6-2, while Edberg hands Mats Wilander his worst defeat in his previous 155 major tournament matches by a 6-1, 6-1, 6-2 margin. "I had one of those days where I almost played perfect tennis," says Edberg.

2006 Marcos Baghdatis, ranked No. 54 in the world, becomes an unlikely finalist at the Australian Open with a dramatic 3-6, 5-7, 6-3, 6-4, 6-4 win over No. 4 seed David Nalbandian in the semifinals. With Baghdatis just three points from the upset, serving at 5-4, 15-15 in the fifth set, rain forces a temporary suspension of play and resumes when the roof of the Rod Laver Arena is closed. The 20-year-old Baghdatis returns after the delay and needs four points to close out the victory. Baghdatis, the junior champions in Melbourne in 2003, becomes only the fourth unseeded man to reach the Aussie Open final, by virtue of his 3-hour, 27-minute semifinal win.

2007 Fernando Gonzalez becomes the second Chilean to advance to a major final when he crushes No. 12 seed Tommy Haas of Germany 6-1, 6-3, 6-1 in just 91 minutes in the most lopsided Australian Open semifinal since 1990. Marcelo Rios was the first Chilean to reach a major final at the Australian Open in 1998, losing to Petr Korda. Gonzalez slams an incredible 42 winners against only three unforced errors in dominating the German. "It was a really good day for me," says Gonzalez. "I have been playing great tennis. I am enjoying it a lot." Says Haas, "I played actually pretty good tennis. Every time I tried to do something differently, he came up with the answer. That's quite frustrating after a period of time. I just have to hand it to him, tip the hat, say that's too good tonight. Nothing I could have done."

January 27

1969 Rod Laver defeats Andres Gimeno of Spain 6-3, 6-4, 7-5 to win the men's singles title at the Australian Open in Brisbane—the first leg of his eventual 1969 Grand Slam. Laver's toughest test of the championship comes in the semifinals against Tony Roche, who beat him earlier in the month of the New South Wales Open in Sydney. Roche and Laver battle for more than four hours in 105-degree heat before Laver prevails 7-5, 22-20, 9-11, 1-6, 6-3. Writes Bud Collins in *The Bud Collins History of Tennis* of the Laver-Roche semifinal match, "Both players got groggy in the brutal sun, even though they employed an old Aussie trick of putting wet cabbage leaves in their hats to help stay cool. It was so close that it could easily have gone either way, and a controversial line call helped Laver grasp the final set." Before Laver's win over Gimeno, Margaret Court beats Billie Jean King 6-4, 6-1 to win the women's singles title for an eighth time.

1970 Playing in a drizzle and swirling wind on the grass courts of White City in Sydney, Arthur Ashe wins the Australian Open men's singles title, defeating Australian Dick Crealy 6-4, 9-7, 6-2. The singles title is Ashe's second at a major tournament—to go with his 1968 triumph at the U.S. Open. Margaret Court needs only 40 minutes to win the Australian Open women's title for a ninth time, defeating Kerry Melville 6-3, 6-1 in the women's singles final.

1990 Twenty-year-old Steffi Graf wins her third straight Australian Open women's singles title, defeating 18-year-old first-time major singles finalist Mary Joe Fernandez 6-3, 6-4 in the women's singles final. The win also marks Graf's third consecutive major title and her 48th straight singles match victory. "I didn't play my best but I won it," Graf says. "Mary Joe played as I expected her to. When you're in a Grand Slam final, you tend to play your best."

2001 Anointed for greatness before she hit first ball as a professional at age 13, Jennifer Capriati breaks through and finally wins her major tournament title, defeating Martina Hingis 6-4, 6-3 to win the Australian Open women's singles title. The 24-year-old Capriati, the No. 12 seed playing in her first major tournament final, becomes the lowest seed to win a women's major in the Open era at the time. Seven years after dropping off the women's tennis circuit due to personal problems, Capriati's victory becomes the feel-good story in tennis for the year. Says Capriati after the match, "I'm no longer going to doubt myself in anything. If I can come home with a Grand Slam, now I know anything is possible."

1991 Boris Becker wins the Australian Open for the first time in his career, defeating Ivan Lendl 1-6, 6-4, 6-4, 6-4 in the men's singles final to clinch the world No. 1 ranking for the first time in his career. "This is an unbelievable moment for me. I can't say much, I'm sorry," says the 23-year-old Becker in the on-court trophy ceremony.

2002 Thomas Johansson of Sweden, ranked No. 18 and seeded No. 16, is the unlikely winner of the men's singles title at the Australian Open, defeating world No. 11 and former world No. 1 Marat Safin of Russia 3-6, 6-4, 6-4, 7-6 (4) in the singles final, spoiling Safin's 22nd birthday. "These two weeks have been the best two weeks in my life and today was just a dream come true," says the 26-year-old Johansson. "It was unbelievable, and I don't have words to say how happy I am." The No. 9 seeded Safin is the highest-ranked player Johansson beats in the tournament, which is ravaged by the first-round upsets of No. 1 seed Lleyton Hewitt and No. 2 seed Gustavo Kuerten, the withdrawal of No. 3 seed Andre Agassi, and the second-round losses of No. 4 seed Yevgeny Kafelnikov and No. 5 seed Sebastien Grosjean.

1996 Monica Seles wins her first major singles title since returning to tennis after tragically being stabbed on court in Germany in 1993, defeating Anke Huber 6-4, 6-1 to win the Australian Open. The win is the fourth for Seles at the Australian Open in as many visits and her ninth career major singles championship. Says Seles, "Standing up and holding that trophy I held in '93, I thought I was going to hold in '94, not being able to do that in '95 and now in '96, again holding it, it's very special."

2005 Roger Federer lets a match point slip away in his titanic 5-7, 6-4, 5-7, 7-6 (6), 9-7 loss to Marat Safin in the semifinals of the Australian Open. Federer fails in his attempt to become the first man since Pete Sampras in 1994 to capture three consecutive major titles. The four-and-a-half-hour defeat—in which Federer holds a match point in the fourth-set tie-break—is Federer's first loss in 30 matches since the previous year's Athens Olympics and first loss against a top 10 rival in 24 matches stretching back to October 2003. It is also the first time the runaway world No.1 drops a set—let alone the match—in five major semifinals, and only the third occasion from 62 matches that the brilliant Swiss loses after winning the first set in a major match. Says Federer, "It's a real pity. I mean, I had my chances but he didn't allow me to take them. It's really unfortunate. I thought I played, under the circumstances, really well."

2007 Twenty-five-year-old Serena Williams overwhelms Maria Sharapova 6-1, 6-2 in the women's singles final of the Australian Open to win her eighth and most unlikely major women's singles title. Williams, ranked No. 81 and having played only four tournaments in the last year due to a bad knee, becomes only the second unseeded woman to win the Australian title in the Open era, joining Chris O'Neill, who was ranked No. 111 when she won the 1978 Australian Open. "It was an awesome win, because I had so many critics. So many people ... saying negative things," says Williams. "Saying I wasn't fit, when I felt that I was really fit, and I could last three sets....It's always like, tell me no and I'll show you that I can do it. I get the greatest satisfaction just holding up the Grand Slam trophy and proving everyone wrong." Says Sharapova, "She came out today and she really played flawless tennis."

2005 Serena Williams saves three match points in defeating Maria Sharapova 2-6, 7-5, 8-6 in an epic women's semifinal at the Australian Open. Says Williams, "I'm still the top fighter out there. Those are always the best wins when you're down match point." Williams, seeded No. 7, fights off the three match points with Sharapova serving for the match at 5-4 in the third. At 6-6 in the third, Sharapova has three break point chances with Williams serving. After holding her serve for a 7-6 lead, Williams converts on her first match point to advance into the women's singles final. Of the match points Williams says, "I though. 'OK, Serena, you're down match point, but that's OK, you've been down match point before'. It's a little closer this time so I thought, 'OK, I could do this.' When the third match point came around I was like 'OK, haven't been in this position before. It's a new experience for me but I can keep fighting.'" Says Sharapova, "I didn't take my chances when I could—and that's what this game is about. If you don't take your chances you lose. Of course I'm sad but I've got a long way ahead of me. I'm 17-years-old and I got to the semifinals of the Australian Open. Nothing's negative...I think she (Williams) is one of the best competitors out there."

2008 Novak Djokovic outlasts unseeded Frenchman Jo-Wilfried Tsonga 4-6, 6-4, 6-3, 7-6 (2) to win the men's singles title at the Australian Open— his first major singles title. Seeded No. 3, the 20-year-old Djokovic becomes the first man from Serbia to a major singles title. Djokovic snaps a streak of

11 straight major championships won by either world No. 1 Roger Federer or No. 2 Rafael Nadal. Tsonga, ranked No. 38, was attempting to become the first Frenchman in 80 years (Jean Borotra in 1928) to win the Australian men's singles championship.

2006 The No. 12 seeded doubles team of Zi Yan and Jie Zheng of China save two match points and upset No. 1 seeds Lisa Raymond and Samantha Stosur to give China its first ever major tennis title with a 2-6, 7-6 (7), 6-3 win in the women's doubles final at the Australian Open. Says Yan of the significance of the title, "It will be good for Chinese tennis. In the near future, I think we could be better, make a progress, improve a lot, and it can stimulate (the sport) a little bit."

1998 Twenty-three-year-old Karol Kucera of Slovakia upsets No. 1 seed Pete Sampras 6-4, 6-2, 6-7 (5), 6-3 in the quarterfinals of the Australian Open. Sampras, gunning for his 11th major singles title, commits 46 unforced errors (28 off the forehand side) against the 20th-ranked opponent and is out-aced 18-7. Says Sampras, "You're hoping something will crack, but nothing did. He played tough as nails. He returned my serve as well as anyone ever does; he played the match of his life and I just didn't come up with the goods. It's pretty disappointing, but I just ran into a hot player who had nothing to lose, and I had a bad day. I was just missing." Says Kucera, "I didn't try something special; I was just running for every ball. I was pretty cool, and it could be that he was a little nervous. This is my biggest victory of my career."

2004 Andy Roddick loses to Marat Safin in the quarterfinals of the Australian Open to lose his world No. 1 ranking. Safin's 2-6, 6-3, 7-5, 6-7 (0-7), 6-4 win over Roddick, which comes on the Russian's 24th birthday, opens the door for Roger Federer or Juan Carlos Ferrero to ascend to the world No. 1 ranking (which Federer achieves by beating Ferrero in the men's semifinals.) Safin, ranked No. 86 after missing most of the previous season due to injury, is serenaded with "Happy Birthday" by the Aussie crowd at the match's conclusion. Roddick, seeded No. 1 at a major tournament for the first time in his career, smashes his racquet in disgust before leaving the court. Says Safin, "I can't ask for anything else. It's probably the best birthday I ever had."

January 28

2006 Amelie Mauresmo breaks through and finally wins her first major singles title at the Australian Open, but in an unusual and somewhat anti-climatic fashion. Leading Justine Henin-Hardenne 6-1, 2-0 in the final, Henin-Hardenne quits the match, claiming an upset stomach, giving Mauresmo the somewhat hallow victory. It marks the first time in the Open era that a major women's singles final ends in a retirement and rivals Helen Wills Moody's retirement against Helen Jacobs in the 1933 U.S. final when trailing 3-0 in the third set. Asked about the professional—or non-professional nature—of the withdrawal, Mauresmo responds in the post-match press-conference, "What can I say? Am I going to make controversy about that? No. That's not the day for this for me." Henin-Hardenne is restrained in giving praise to Mauresmo in her post-match press conference saying, "I think she had a lot of time because I was very far from my baseline, no energy, nothing in my ball. So she had a lot of time. When you have this kind of time, it's pretty hard to do mistakes.

1946 John Bromwich wins the men's singles title at the Australian Championships—the first major championships held in the post World War II era, defeating 19-year-old fellow Australian Dinny Pails 5-7, 6-3, 7-5, 3-6, 6-2 in the final.

1996 Thirty-year-old Stefan Edberg leaves the Australian Open in style, pairing with Petr Korda of the Czech Republic to beat Canadian Sebastien Lareau and American Alex O'Brien 7-5, 7-5, 4-6, 6-1 in the men's doubles final in Edberg's final Australian Open appearance.

1989 Steffi Graf wins her second Australian Open singles title, defeating Helena Sukova 6-4, 6-4 in the women's singles final. The 19-year-old Graf shrugs off talk of a second-consecutive Grand Slam after claiming her fifth straight major singles title, saying "I had an incredible year last year and I've started awfully well this year, but I'm not going to get myself in trouble and say it's going to happen again."

1990 Ivan Lendl repeats as men's champion at the Australian Open when Stefan Edberg is forced to retire in the men's singles final with a torn stomach muscle, marking the first time in the Australian Open's 85-year history that a men's finalist quit in the middle of a match. Lendl leads 4-6, 7-6 (7-3), 5-2 when Edberg is unable to continue. Edberg admits that he hurt himself in the last service game of his semifinal win over fellow Swede Mats Wilander two days earlier. "It kept getting worse and worse," he says after the match. The only other finalist to retire in mid-match in a men's major final comes at Wimbledon 1911 when H. Roper Barrett quits after four sets against Anthony Wilding.

1994 Todd Martin wins three tie-breakers to defeat No. 4 seed Stefan Edberg 3-6, 7-6 (7), 7-6 (7), 7-6 (4) in 3 hours, 50 minutes to advance into his first major singles final at the Australian Open. Pete Sampras ends Jim Courier's two-year-reign at the Australian Open, defeating the two-time defending champion 6-3, 6-4, 6-4 to advance into his first Australian Open final. Says Sampras, "That's one of the better matches I've played so far in my career. Everything really clicked today. I couldn't play any better." Courier, seeded No. 3, falls short of trying to become the first man to win three straight Australian Open titles since Roy Emerson wins five straight from 1963-67.

1995 Canadian-born Franco-American Mary Pierce wins her first major singles title, defeating Arantxa Sanchez-Vicario 6-3, 6-2 in the women's singles final at the Australian Open. The win avenges Pierce's loss to Sanchez-Vicario in the final of the previous year's French Open women's singles final. Pierce, 20, becomes the first French woman to win a major singles title since Francoise Durr wins the 1967 French women's singles title.

1996 At the age of 28, Boris Becker wins his sixth and what eventually becomes his final major singles title, defeating Michael Chang 6-2, 6-4, 2-6, 6-2 in the men's singles final at the Australian Open.

2001 Sixth-seeded Andre Agassi successfully defends his men's singles title at the Australian Open, defeating Frenchman Arnaud Clement, the No. 15 seed, 6-4, 6-2, 6-2, in the final. The title is Agassi's third at the Australian Open and his seventh overall in a major tournament, which puts him in a tie for 10th on the all-time major tournament singles titles list. Agassi is the first man to successfully defend his Australian Open title since Jim Courier in 1993.

2007 Roger Federer wins his 10th major singles title, defeating Fernando Gonzalez of Chile 7-5, 6-4, 6-4 in the final of the Australian Open. Federer becomes only the fourth man in the Open era to win a major title without the loss of a set—the last being Bjorn Borg at Roland Garros in 1980.

January 29

1938 Don Budge defeats Australian John Bromwich 6-4, 6-2, 6-1 to win the Australian Championships at Memorial Drive in Adelaide, Australia. The title marks the first leg of Budge's eventual "Grand Slam" sweep of all four major championships.

1955 Ken Rosewall hands Tony Trabert what turns out to be his only singles loss in a major championship for the 1955 calendar year, defeating the American 8-6, 6-3, 6-3 in the semifinals of the Australian Championships in Adelaide, Australia. Trabert goes on to win the French Championships, Wimbledon and the U.S. Championships to complete one of the most successful seasons in the history of tennis. Rosewall wins the title two days later on January 31, defeating fellow Australian Lew Hoad 9-7, 6-4, 6-4

1968 Billie Jean King of the United States and Bill Bowrey of Australia win the final "amateur" major championships at the Australian Championships—King beating Margaret Smith Court of Australia 6-1, 6-2 and Bowrey beating Juan Gisbert of Spain 5-7, 2-6, 9-7, 6-4 in the singles finals. The 1968 Australian Championships are the last major tournament to be played before the legislatures of tennis "open" the game to professionals in addition to the amateurs. King, who breaks Court's service six times on the day in the windy conditions at the Kooyong Tennis Club in Melbourne, says after the match that she is planning to retire from the sport in the next 18 months to two years. "I do not want to go on playing much longer. I want to settle down," says King, who never "settled down" playing up through 1983 and remaining active in tennis and women's sports for decades.

1989 Ivan Lendl wins his first Australian Open singles title and his seventh career major singles title defeating fellow Czech Miloslav Mecir 6-2, 6-2, 6-2 in the men's singles final. The win guarantees that Lendl will take back the world No. 1 ranking from Mats Wilander, the man who took it from him by winning the U.S. Open the previous September.

1994 Steffi Graf easily defeats Aranxta Sanchez Vicario 6-0, 6-2 in 57 minutes in the women's singles final at the Australian Open. The title is Graf's fourth—and final—singles title at the Australian after winning in 1988, 1989 and 1990.

1995 Andre Agassi wins his first Australian Open title, defeating and dethroning top-ranked Pete Sampras 4-6, 6-1, 7-6 (6), 6-4 in the men's singles final. The win is the second straight major singles title for Agassi after his U.S. Open triumph in 1994. "I came here believing in myself, believing that I could win," Agassi says after the final. "It was the first time I ever came into a Grand Slam believing like that. And now, I'm not worried about winning all of them, I worry about winning each one." Says Sampras of Agassi, "I don't know how much room there is for improvement. If he stays fit, he's a threat to win every single major title of the year."

2003 Former world No. 1 Marat Safin of Russia ends Andre Agassi's five-year winning streak at the Australian Open with a 7-6 (6), 7-6 (6), 5-7, 1-6, 6-3 win the men's semifinals. "I don't have the words to describe what I'm feeling right now," Safin says after the match. "To be on the same court as Andre Agassi and to win in five sets after he came back from 2-0 down, it's great. I came here to try and win it and I'm almost there. I have one match left to go. Everything is going my way." In the women's semifinals, Justine Henin-Hardenne of Belgium defeats No. 32 seed Fabiola Zuluaga of Colombia 6-2, 6-2, while fellow Belgian Kim Clijsters, beats Patty Schnyder of Switzerland 6-2, 7-6 (2).

2005 Serena Williams wins her seventh major singles title, defeating Lindsay Davenport 2-6, 6-3, 6-0 in the women's singles final at the Australian Open. Williams' win is her first major since she won Wimbledon in 2003. Says Williams after the match of the suggestion that her career was in decline, "It is a very fashionable way to decline....It's that much sweeter because people are always wondering about what's happening to us. It's been a long way coming back. But I'm almost to my goal, and it feels great."

2006 Roger Federer gets emotional, cries and hugs all-time great Rod Laver during the post-match ceremony following his 5-7, 7-5, 6-0, 6-2 win over upstart Cypriot Marcos Baghdatis in the final of the Australian Open. Federer has difficulty putting to words the emotions he feels during the post-match ceremony and sobs after receiving the trophy from Laver. "I hope you know how much this means to me," he says as he wipes away tears. Federer becomes the first player to win three consecutive major tournaments since Pete Sampras wins at the 1994 Australian Open. The title is his seventh career major title, tying him with John McEnroe, John Newcombe and Mats Wilander.

January 30

1967 Roy Emerson wins the Australian men's singles title for a fifth straight year, beating Arthur Ashe 6-4, 6-1, 6-4 in the title match played in Adelaide, Australia. Emerson needs only 75 minutes to beat Ashe in front of a crowd of 6,000 for his 11th major singles title. The turning point of the match comes with the score knotted at 4-4 in the first set and Ashe serves three straight double faults to lose his serve, allowing Emerson to serve out the set and roll to the straight-sets win. Unknowingly at the time, as statisticians and media representatives were yet to keep track of stats and records, but Emerson's title makes him the all-time men's singles major championship winner, moving him past Bill Tilden, who won 10 major singles titles from 1920 to 1930. In the women's singles final, Nancy Richey beats Lesley Turner 6-1, 6-4 to win her first major title.

1961 Roy Emerson wins his first of 12 major singles titles, defeating fellow Aussie Rod Laver 1-6, 6-3, 7-5, 6-4 to win the Australian men's singles title in Melbourne. Eighteen-year-old Margaret Smith wins the women's singles title, defeating Jan Lehane 6-1, 6-4.

1980 Saying, "I don't enjoy winning, and I don't enjoy losing. I just don't enjoy playing any more," 25-year-old Chris Evert announces her retirement from professional tennis. However, Evert's retirement doesn't last as she returns to professional tennis after only three months on the sidelines. Evert goes on to win nine more major titles and officially retires for a final time in 1989.

1993 Nineteen-year-old Monica Seles edges Steffi Graf 4-6, 6-3, 6-2 to win the women's singles title at the Australian Open, her eighth major singles victory. "I knew I had to run down every ball and never give up," Seles says after the match. "It was a close match all the way. We both hit the ball so hard you have to concentrate all the time. I never thought I'd be doing so well in Grand Slams. It's incredible." Says Graf, "She really deserved to win today. She just has incredible willpower and confidence. Once she gets in the groove, she just plays every point as hard as she can. That is very difficult because you do not get any easy points or easy games. That is definitely her strength."

1994 Pete Sampras wins his third consecutive major singles title, slamming 13 aces with speeds as fast as 126 mph in defeating first-time major finalist

Todd Martin 7-6(4), 6-4, 6-4 at the Australian Open. "He's just too good and he really deserves what he's succeeding at, because he's really working his butt off," Martin says of Sampras.

1951 Dick Savitt becomes the third American to win the men's singles title at the Australian Championships, defeating Australia's Ken McGregor 6-3, 2-6, 6-3, 6-1 in the final played in Sydney. Savitt, from Orange, N.J. and a graduate of Cornell University, joins 1905 champion Fred Alexander and 1938 champion Don Budge as "Yanks" to win Down Under. He defeats defending champion Frank Sedgman in the semifinals.

2005 Five years after winning his first major title at the U.S. Open, Marat Safin wins his elusive second major title, defeating native son Lleyton Hewitt 1-6, 6-3, 6-4, 6-4 in the final of the Australian Open. Safin is able to break through and win "Down Under" after having lost in the Australian Open final two times in the last three years. Hewitt falls short of attempting to become the first Australian to win his country's national championship since Mark Edmondson in 1976. "Today it was a relief for me," Safin says following the final. "Two Grand Slams, it's already something. One Grand Slam, you can win by mistake, like I did in 2000 U.S. Open, but this one, I've worked really hard for that."

1966 Margaret Smith is awarded her seventh straight Australian women's singles title—setting a new record—when Nancy Richey is unable to play due to an injured knee following her 6-2, 8-6 win over Kerry Melville in the semifinals. Smith's seventh straight title moves her past Nancye Wynne's record of six straight titles from 1937 to 1951.

2000 The U.S. Davis Cup team arrives in Zimbabwe for its first-ever tie on the African continent. First-year Davis Cup captain John McEnroe spends his first full-day on the ground as U.S. captain by visiting Zimbabwe's No. 1 tourist attraction, Victoria Falls, for publicity photos.

January 31

1927 Gerald Patterson of Australia hits 29 aces—against 29 double faults—in beating Jack Hawkes 3-6, 6-4, 3-6, 18-16, 6-3 to win the men's singles title at the Australian Championships in Melbourne.

1993 For the second consecutive year, Jim Courier defeats Stefan Edberg in the men's singles final at the Australian Open. Courier wins his fourth—and ultimately his last—major singles title, with a 6-2, 6-1, 2-6, 7-5 victory. Says Courier, "It's always very special to win Grand Slams, and to come back and defend makes it twice as special." The final is played in blistering heat, with on-court temperatures measuring 150 degrees. Says Edberg of the blistering conditions, "At one stage, you feel like death."

1998 Seventeen-year-old Martina Hingis wins her fourth major championship, defeating Conchita Martinez 6-3, 6-3 in the women's singles final at the Australian Open. Hingis becomes the youngest player in 100 years to defend a major singles titles. "To defend the title is much harder than coming here for the first time (when) nobody expected me to win," Hingis says after the final. "There was so much pressure....This is the hardest Grand Slam I've won. There were so many different expectations on me, especially the pressure I put on myself. Everybody told me this year is going to be very hard. I'm proud of myself for what I did the last two weeks." No player, male or female, had defended a Grand Slam title at a younger age since 16-year-old Charlotte "Lottie" Dod won her second straight Wimbledon in 1888. In the 30-year Open era, Monica Seles was two months older than Hingis when she won her second straight French Open championship in 1991.

2004 Justine Henin-Hardenne wins her third major title—and her first Australian Open title—defeating fellow Belgian Kim Clijsters 6-3, 4-6, 6-3 in a hard-fought women's singles final. Says Henin-Hardenne, "It was really emotional, both of us were really nervous. I have three Grand Slam titles now, it's wonderful."

February 1

1960 Rod Laver and Margaret Smith win their first career major singles titles at the Australian Championships in Brisbane. Laver stages an incredible two-sets-to-love comeback to defeat reigning U.S. champion Neale Fraser 5-7, 3-6, 6-3, 8-6, 8-6 in 3 hours, 15 minutes. Laver, who goes on to win 11 major singles titles—including two Grand Slam sweeps in 1962 and 1969—saves a match point at 4-5 in the fourth set. Following the match, Fraser collapses in the dressing room in cramps and fatigue. Margaret Smith—later Margaret Court—wins the first of her eventual 11 Australian singles titles at the age of 17, defeating fellow Australian teenager—18-year-old Jan Lehane—by a 7-5, 6-2 margin. Court goes on to win a record 24 major singles titles.

1998 At the age of 30, Petr Korda wins his first—and only—major singles championship, defeating 22-year-old Marcelo Rios of Chile 6-2, 6-2, 6-2 in 85 minutes in the men's singles final of the Australian Open. Korda knocks 32 winners passed Rios in becoming the oldest man to win a major title since Andres Gomez, a few months older, wins the 1990 French Open. "The Korda Kick" becomes a fad in tennis after the match as Korda celebrates his victories and winning shots in the tournament with scissor-kick type leaps. "I was waiting for this a long, long time," Korda tells the crowd after the final. "It's been such a long ride. It's fantastic. I got to the last stop. I feel I'm on top of the world at the moment…I just put all the pieces together for this tournament. It was really a very enjoyable ride for me."

2004 Roger Federer wins his first Australian Open crown, his second career major singles title and puts an exclaimation point on taking over the world's No. 1 ranking with a 7-6 (3), 6-4, 6-2 win over Marat Safin in the men's singles final at the Australian Open. "What a great start to the year for me, to win the Australian Open and become No. 1 in the world," Federer says. "To fulfill my dreams, it really means very much to me."

2005 The comeback attempt by former world No. 1 Martina Hingis stalls in Pattaya, Thailand as the Swiss standout is defeated by Germany's Marlene Weingartner 1-6, 6-2, 6-2 in the first round of the Volvo Women's Open. Hingis, a five-time major singles titlist, appears in her first WTA Tour event since October of 2002.

February 2

1945 American Davis Cupper and 1943 U.S. Champion Joseph Hunt dies as his Navy fighter plane crashes in the ocean off Florida. Hunt, 26, the highest-regarded American player to die in the war, was expected to major force in the game at the conclusion of the war.

1982 Still distraught over the shooting death of friend and fellow tennis player Andrea Buchanan, tennis legend Billie Jean King walks off the court in the third set of her first-round match against Ann Kiyomura at the Avon Championships of Detroit. "Emotionally, I was not up to my game and I could not concentrate on hitting the ball," King says after the 3-6, 6-3, 1-0, retire loss. "I apologize for my behavior. It was not professional."

2008 A crowd of approximately 6,000 Israeli fans mimic the grunts of Maria Sharapova in the final points of the Russian's 6-0, 6-4 Fed Cup win over Tzipi Obziler. Sharapova, playing in her Fed Cup debut at the Ramat Hasharon Tennis Center just outside of Tel Aviv, led 6-0, 5-1 before the partisan crowd try to get under the skin of the freshly-crowned Australian Open champion by imitating her grunts each time she attempts to hit the ball. "I don't mind it," Sharapova says. "It brings out the best in me. I love the atmosphere, the crowd and their craziness. It is what we live for. I got really anxious and excited as I was close to finishing my first Fed Cup match." Sharapova's win gives Russia a 1-1 split with Israel after the first day of play. Earlier, Israel's Shahar Peer rallies to defeat Dinara Safina 0-6, 6-2, 6-2. Russia ends up winning the series 4-1 the next day as Sharapova crushes Peer 6-1, 6-1 and Anna Chakvetadze, a substitute for Safina, beats Obziler 6-4, 6-2 to clinch the victory. After the Russia-Israel series concludes, an International Olympic Committee member Alex Gilady criticizes Peer for her unsportsmanlike behaviour during the series in inciting the crowd to distract the Russian team.

2007 Chilean Nicolas Massu comes back from a 0-6, 2-5 deficit and saves eight match points in defeating Sergio Roitman of Argentina in the quarterfinals of the Movistar Open in Vina del Mar, Chile. Massu benefits when Roitman finally retires with a left thigh injury after Massu wins the second-set tie-break 7-3.

2008 Overcoming two match points and an 18-minute power outage, native son Fernando Gonzalez defeats unseeded Uruguayan Pablo Cuevas

6-7 (4), 7-6 (6), 6-2 in a dramatic semifinal of the Movistar Open in Vina Del Mar, Chile—and then is declared the tournament champion. Following the tense 2 hour, 47-minute match, Gonzalez is awarded the title as Juan Monaco, a winning semifinalist earlier in the day, is declared unfit to play in the final after a serious left ankle sprain suffered in the doubles final. Says Gonzalez, "I'm happy to have won this tournament once again but a little sad for Juan (Monaco) who wasn't able to play the final. He is a great player and even better person." The power outage occurs at the 12th game of the first set, while Gonzalez saves the two match points at 15-40 in the 12th game of the second set, before winning the tie-break (which he trailed at one point 3-5). The title, the ninth career ATP title for Gonzalez, is the Chilean's third in Vina de Mar after also winning in 2002 and 2004. "This is a very special tournament for me," Gonzalez says. "There is only one tournament in Chile every year and each time I look forward to play in front of my home crowd."

1926 Philippe Chatrier, the man largely responsible for tennis returning to the Olympic program in 1988 and the French Championships returning to a prominence as a major championship, is born in Paris. Inducted into the International Tennis Hall of Fame in 1992, Chatrier was a player, journalist and administrator, serving a president of the French Tennis Federation from 1972 to 1992 and as president of the International Tennis Federation from 1977 to 1991. According to tennis historian and writer Bud Collins, Chatrier was "largely responsible for the renaissance of the French Open, placing it on par with the other three majors and overseeing the splendid updating of Stade Roland Garros. He fought valiantly against over-commercialization of the game, and led a carnpaign to restore tennis to the Olympic Games, a goal realized in 1988 after a 64-year interval." To honor his contributions to tennis, the French Tennis Federation named the stadium court at the French Open in his honor.

2004 Roger Federer officially becomes the No. 1 player in the world for the first time in his career, replacing Andy Roddick in the top ranking on the ATP computer.

February 3

1947 President Harry Truman conducts the Davis Cup draw at the White House, joining U.S. President Calvin Coolidge as the only U.S Presidents to conduct the Davis Cup draw. Says Truman during the proceedings, "I hope the time will come when we can settle our international differences in courts, just as we settle our tennis differences on a court."

1989 Sixteen-year-old Michael Chang makes his Davis Cup debut defeating Victor Pecci 6-7 (5), 6-3, 6-4, 6-2 helping the United States to a 2-0 lead over Paraguay in the Davis Cup first round in Ft. Myers, Fla. Chang also becomes the first American to play a Davis Cup tie-break in the first set of his match with Pecci. The tie-break is formally introduced to Davis Cup play (except in the fifth set) beginning in the 1989 season. Chang is also the second youngest player to play Davis Cup for the United States at this tie at the age of sixteen years, 11 months and 12 days. Wilbur Coen, at 16 years, 5 months in 1928, is the youngest American to play Davis Cup.

1985 Nineteen-year-old and No. 19-ranked Stefan Edberg wins his second career singles title, trouncing Yannick Noah 6-1, 6-0 in 54 minutes in the final of the U.S. National Indoor Championships in Memphis. Edberg hits five aces and commits only three unforced errors against the No. 14 ranked Noah, who is slowed by an ankle injury. Says Edberg, "I don't think I ever played so well."

1990 Rick Leach and Jim Pugh make their Davis Cup debuts for the United States and defeat Leonardo Lavalle and Jorge Lozano 6-4, 6-7, 7-5, 6-1 to clinch the 4-0 victory over Mexico in the Davis Cup first round in Carlsbad, Calif. Leach and Pugh become one of the most successful Davis Cup doubles pairings for the United States, posting a perfect 6-0 record in 1990 and 1991.

2000 Zimbabwe President Robert Mugabe presides over the draw ceremony for the USA vs. Zimbabwe Davis Cup first round tie in Harare, Zimbabwe. The African leader, who later earns the reputation as one of the world's most ruthless dictators, calls the first-round match between his tiny nation and the United States, featuring first-year captain John McEnroe and all-time great Andre Agassi, as "the dwarfs against the giants."

February 4

2001 Nineteen-year-old future world No. 1 Roger Federer wins the first ATP title of his career, defeating Julien Boutter of France 6-4, 6-7, 6-4 in Milan, Italy. "What a relief," says Federer after the match. "I'm really happy to have won my first title here in Milan. As a kid you always dream of winning your first title."

2000 John McEnroe sits in the chair as captain of the U.S. Davis Cup team for the first time as the United States and Zimbabwe split the first two matches in their first round tie in Harare, Zimbabwe. Andre Agassi, just five days removed from winning the Australian Open nearly 6,700 miles away in Melbourne, adjusts to the 1,000 foot altitude change and beats Wayne Black 7-5, 6-3, 7-5 in the opening match of the series. Chris Woodruff, the Davis Cup neophyte and a replacement for the injured Pete Sampras and Todd Martin, loses the second match to Byron Black 7-6, 6-3, 6-2.

1979 In his first event of the year, Bjorn Borg breaks the serve of Guillermo Vilas seven out of eight times and wins the WCT tournament title in Richmond, Va., with a 6-3, 6-1 victory over the Argentine in the final.

2001 Lindsay Davenport wins her 31st career singles title when she defeats world No. 1 Martina Hingis of Switzerland, 6-7 (4), 6-4, 6-2, in the final of the Toray Pan Pacific Open in Tokyo. Davenport improves to 13-10 overall against Hingis, including a 10-6 head-to-head advantage in tournament finals.

2006 Former world No. 1 Martina Hingis upsets defending champion and top-seeded Maria Sharapova 6-3, 6-1 to reach the first WTA Tour final of her comeback at the Pan Pacific Open in Tokyo. Hingis goes on to lose the final to Elena Dementieva of Russia 6-2, 6-0, but is pleased with her fast progress in her only her third tournament of her full-time comeback to tennis after a three-and-a-half year hiatus. "I've exceeded my own expectations and am happy to playing good tennis once again," says Hingis, the Pan Pacific singles champion in 1997, 1999, 2000 and 2002. "I've got a couple of things I have to work on and I'll go where this takes me."

February 5

1948 U.S. Secretary of State George C. Marshall, the man who oversaw military victory for the Allies in World War II and whose "Marshall Plan" was the blue-print for a post-war Europe, conducts the Davis Cup draw in Washington, D.C. The Associated Press reports on occasion stating, "While foreign ambassadors and assorted dignitaries watched, Marshall reached in the big Davis Cup, slowly pulled out twenty-nine names, one-by-one."

1985 Ivan Lendl defeats Larry Stefanki 6-2, 6-0 in the first round of the Lipton Championships in Delray Beach, Fla., in a match that ends without an umpire or linesmen. "We have played a few times without the umpire knowing the score, but never without an umpire," says Lendl. After Lendl hits an ace—that was not called—to take a 4-0 lead in the second set, Stefanki is assessed a point penalty for delaying play while speaking with the chair umpire Luigi Brambilla of Italy. While Brambilla and other officials discuss the point penalty, Lendl and Stefanki continue play, prompting the officials and linesmen to leave the court. Lendl and Stefanki then proceed to finish the match without a chair umpire or linesmen. "Lendl said we should play while they are talking it over," says Stefanki. "Tennis is entertainment and the fans loved it. When the umpire said we should start, we were already at deuce and told him that. We kept playing and the umpire left. Lendl and I made our own calls and somebody in the press box kept calling out the score. We were having fun and it was totally in control. The match wasn't close and we just wanted to have some fun."

2007 Xavier Malisse wins his 200th career match win and his third career ATP singles title in a rain-delayed Monday final at the Delray Beach Championships in Florida, defeating James Blake 5-7, 6-4, 6-4. Malisse trails Blake 5-7, 3-3 before the rains came the day before—allowing both players to watch the Indianapolis Colts and Chicago Bears play in the Super Bowl on television. Malisse emerges the next day as a shaper player to win his second title in Delray Beach after winning in 2005. Says Malisse, "If we would have played yesterday, I probably would have lost. The wind slowed down his ball. The wind helped me a little bit today."

February 6

1993 Arthur Ashe, Wimbledon and U.S. Open champion, Davis Cup standout player and captain and the greatest humanitarian and social advocate the sport of tennis ever produced, dies of AIDS-related pneumonia at the age of 49 in New York City. In addition to winning the 1968 U.S. Open, the 1970 Australian Open and Wimbledon in 1975, Ashe spoke out against world injustices including apartheid, poverty and racism and was an advocate for many causes including civil rights, education and curing the AIDS that ultimately claimed his life. He was inflicted with the disease via a blood transfusion during heart by-pass surgery in 1983. He did not disclose his illness publicly until April 8, 1992 when he pre-empted a story that was going to run in *USA Today* disclosing his condition. Writes Robin Finn of the *New York Times* of Ashe in his obituary, "Militant in his convictions but mild in his manner, this slim, bookish and bespectacled athlete never thought himself a rebel and preferred information to insurrection. Since he believed his singular success carried inherent responsibilities, Ashe, during his decade-long professional tennis career and beyond it, dedicated himself to dismantling the barriers of poverty, privilege, racism and social stereotyping. Even the fact of his own mortality became a cause celebre, and Ashe, in the headlines again, conducted his final campaign against the ravages of AIDS."

2000 Chris Woodruff becomes only the second U.S. Davis Cup player to ever win a fifth and decisive match in his Davis Cup debut as he defeats Wayne Black 6-3, 6-7, 6-2, 6-4 to clinch the 3-2 U.S. win over Zimbabwe in the Davis Cup first round in Harare, Zimbabwe. Woodruff, the 1993 NCAA champion from the University of Tennessee and a replacement for the injured Pete Sampras and Todd Martin on the U.S. team, joins 1906 Davis Cup rookie Raymond Little as the only Davis Cup rookies to win a fifth and decisive match. Woodruff's win cap a U.S. comeback from 1-2 down in the best-of-five-match series and prevents tiny Zimbabwe, with a population of 12 million people, from staging one of the biggest Davis Cup upsets over the United States, the all-time winningest Davis Cup nation with a population of over 300 million. Andre Agassi ties the series at 2-2 in the first singles match of the day, overovercoming altitude sickness to defeat Byron Black 6-2, 6-3, 7-6. Agassi throws up into a courtside trash can moments after shaking hands with Black following the match. Agassi and Woodruff's heroics caps the first U.S. Davis Cup comeback from 1-2 down in an opposing nation's country and caps John McEnroe's debut tie as U.S.

captain. The final day of competition is played on the seventh anniversary of the death of Arthur Ashe, the first African-American man to play and captain the U.S. Davis Cup team. Ashe dies in 1993 of complications due to AIDS, a disease that infects one-fifth of the people in Zimbabwe.

1995 Arantxa Sanchez Vicario becomes the No. 1 ranked player in the world on WTA Tour computer for the first time in her career. The reigning French and U.S. Open champion, holds the ranking for a total of 12 weeks during her career.

1983 John McEnroe defeats Ivan Lendl 4-6, 7-6, 6-4, 6-3 to win the U.S. Pro Indoor Championships in Philadelphia, reversing a run of bad results to his Czech rival in which he loses 19 of the previous 20 sets and seven consecutive matches. McEnroe's win also ends Lendl's 66-match indoor winning streak.

February 7

1997 MaliVai Washington performs one of the most courageous Davis Cup performances in the history of the U.S. team, suffering through what ultimately becomes a career-ending knee injury at the tail end of his heroic win over future world No. 1 and future three-time French Open champion Gustavo Kuerten 3-6, 7-6, 7-6, 6-3 to give the United States an early 1-0 lead in the Davis Cup first round in Riberio Preto, Brazil. In the fourth set of his win, Washington shears off a piece of the cartilage in his left knee—an injury that years—and surgeries—later prevents him from successfully continuing his career. Years later, Washington says of his victory over Kuerten, "Beating Gustavo in the opening match was one of my top three or four career highlights. A combination of the occasion, being in Brazil in front of a pretty hostile crowd, and playing the opening match, was very special. Finishing the match with a knee injury made it more painful but more satisfying. Ironically, that was a career highlight but it was also the beginning of the end of my career."

2005 U.S. Davis Cup Patrick McEnroe announces that, after an absence of nearly five years, Andre Agassi will return to the U.S. Davis Cup team for the USA vs. Croatia first round tie in Carson, Calif. Unfortunately for Agassi and the United States, Agassi's return is unsuccessful and short-lived. When he steps back on the Davis Cup court for the United States on March 5, Agassi loses to Ivan Ljubicic 6-3, 7-6 (0), 6-3 as the United States is handed an embarrassing first-round home loss, despite former U.S. Open champion Andy Roddick and the world's No. 1 doubles team, Bob and Mike Bryan, also representing the U.S. on the squad. Agassi does not return to the Davis Cup line-up again and retires after the 2006 U.S. Open. He finishes his career with an incredible 30-6 Davis Cup singles record, leading the United States to Davis Cup titles in 1990, 1992 and 1995.

2008 Amelie Mauresmo needs less than 10 minutes to reach the quarterfinals of the Open Gaz de France in Paris as her opponent, Eleni Daniilidou of Greece, quits the match trailing 0-3 due to the flu. Says the Greek following her retirement from the match, "Unfortunately, last night I got a viral illness and had absolutely no energy to play at 100 percent."

February 8

1930 A chair umpire is so upset at the attitude of Bill Tilden that he walks off the court in the middle of a mixed doubles match at the Carlton Tennis Championships in Cannes, France and the match concludes without an official. A. Wallis Myers, an English writer and player, is the umpire for the match between Tilden and German Cilly Aussem against Louis Worms of Denmark and Phyllis Satterwaite of Britain According to the Associated Press, "the conflict between Tilden and Myers arose when Tilden disputed the Englishman's decision on a service ball. Myers resented Tilden's attitude and left the court. Efforts to enlist another official failed so play continued without an umpire or linesman." Tilden and Aussem win the match 1-6, 6-0, 6-3.

1981 Twenty-three-year-old New Yorker Leslie Allen defeats Hana Mandlikova 6-4, 6-4 in the women's singles final of the Avon Championships of Detroit and becomes the first black woman to win a tour-level event since Althea Gibson wins the U.S. Championships in 1958.

2008 Playing on what he describes as a "terrible" court at the Ferry Dusika Hallenstadion arena in Vienna, Andy Roddick defeats Jurgen Melzer 6-4, 4-6, 6-3, 6-7 (4), 6-3 to pace a 2-0 first day start for the U.S. Davis Cup team over Austria as the United States opens up the defense of its 2007 Davis Cup title. Roddick's teammate James Blake registers what he calls "my best match ever on clay" in defeating Stefan Koubek 5-7, 7-5, 6-2, 6-2 after Roddick dispatches of Melzer. Says Roddick of the soft court that was easily dug up with pot-holes and divots, "The court was terrible, the worst I ever played on in Davis Cup. It was the tough match I expected, but I won and that means we accomplished our goal." Says U.S. Captain Patrick McEnroe of his first day results in the eventual 4-1 victory, "This is probably my best day as captain of the team. Of course, winning the Davis Cup last year was huge, but today I was really impressed by the way the guys battled and showed their physical and mental strength under difficult circumstances."

1987 Tim Mayotte beats John McEnroe for the first time in his career, defeating the former world No. 1 3-6, 6-1, 6-3, 6-1 to win the U.S. Pro Indoor singles title in Philadelphia. Mayotte, winless in five previous meetings with McEnroe, claims the third of 12 singles titles in his career and the first of five singles titles over the 1987 season—his best year as a professional.

February 9

1997 Jim Courier overcomes a hostile Brazilian crowd, dehydration and 110 degree on-court temperatures to defeat upstart Gustavo Kuerten 6-3, 6-2, 5-7, 7-6 (13-11) to clinch the 4-1 United States victory over Brazil in the Davis Cup first round in Ribeirao Preto, Brazil. Says the No. 22 ranked Courier following the 3-hour, 36-minute match, "It was obviously a difficult and close match. I was glad to have it go four sets. But if it went five, I'm sure I would have outlasted him." Kuerten, ranked No. 85 at the time and relative unknown outside of South America, goes on to win the French Open out of nowhere as an unseeded player four months later.

2001 Patrick McEnroe makes his debut as U.S. Davis Cup captain and his top player Jan-Michael Gambill wins his first "live" Davis Cup rubber in defeating Michel Kratochvil 6-3, 7-5, 6-4 as the United States and Switzerland split the opening two matches in the first day of play in the 2001 Davis Cup first round in Basel, Switzerland. Todd Martin is defeated by Swiss No. 1 Roger Federer 6-4, 7-6, 4-6, 6-1 in the opening rubber of the tie.

1991 Brad Gilbert crushes future protégé/pupil Andre Agassi 6-1, 6-2 in just 59 minutes in the semifinals of the Volvo Tennis Championships in San Francisco. Agassi calls the loss to Gilbert his worst since he was straight-setted by Pete Sampras in the finals of the U.S. Open the previous September. Says Agassi, "He steamrolled me. He has never served that well. Even the big servers in the game don't serve that well. I never got rolling. There's not much you can do when he's playing that well. My second serve was a little weak. If he had given me a chance to get in (the match), it might have been different." The Gilbert-Agassi match is the fourth of eight career meetings between the two players, with the series locking at 2-2 after Gilbert's win in San Francisco. The two play four more times during their careers—each winning two more times before Agassi enlists Gilbert to be his coach starting in the spring of 1994. Gilbert ends up losing the San Francisco final the following evening, falling to Darren Cahill of Australia by a 6-2, 3-6, 6-4 margin.

February 10

1893 Six-foot-two "Big" Bill Tilden, regarded as one of the greatest players to ever pick up a tennis racquet, is born in Philadelphia, Pa. Tilden dominates the tennis world in the 1920s winning 20 major titles—10 in singles including three Wimbledon titles and seven U.S. singles titles. Tilden anchors the winning U.S. Davis Cup teams from 1920 to 1926. Writes Bud Collins in *The Bud Collins History of Tennis* of Tilden, "If a player's value is measured by the dominance and influence he exercises over a sport, then William Tatem "Big Bill" Tilden II could be considered the greatest player in the history of tennis."

1992 Jim Courier becomes the No. 1 ranked player in the world for the first time in his career, unseating Stefan Edberg from the top ranking and becoming the first American to hold the position since John McEnroe last holds the ranking on Sept. 8, 1985. Courier holds the ranking for a total of 58 weeks during his career.

2008 Jill Craybas of the United States nearly pulls off one of the greatest final-round comebacks in the history of the WTA Tour at the Pattaya Open in Thailand. The thirty-three-year-old Craybas, the 1996 NCAA singles champion for the University of Florida, fights back from a 1-5 third-set deficit against Poland's Agnieszka Radwanska to win five games in a row, then holds match point at 6-5 in the third set, before losing the final by a 6-2, 1-6, 7-6 (4) margin.

2001 Justin Gimelstob earns a dubious Davis Cup distinction when he and Jan-Michael Gambill are defeated by Switzerland's Roger Federer and Lorenzo Manta 6-4, 6-2, 7-5 as the United States goes down 2-1 to the Swiss after the second day of play in the Davis Cup first round in Basel, Switzerland. The loss, which ultimately becomes his Davis Cup finale, drops Gimelstob's Davis Cup record to 0-3, tying him with Robert Wrenn and Melville Long for the worst-ever record for a U.S. Davis Cup player. Wrenn loses two singles and a doubles match in the 1903 Davis Cup Challenge Round against Britain for his 0-3 record, while Long turns the same trick in the 1909 Davis Cup Challenge Round against Australasia. Gimelstob also loses in doubles with Todd Martin in the 1998 Davis Cup semifinal against Italy and, also in that tie, loses a dead-rubber singles match to Gianluca Pozzi.

February 11

1994 Thirty-seven-year-old Martina Navratilova is so distraught after losing to 18-year-old Maggie Maleeva of Bulgaria 6-4, 6-3 in the quarterfinals of the Virginia Slims of Chicago—a tournament she won a record 12 times—that she fails to participate in a post-match on-court ceremony in her honor in her final year of competitive singles play.

2001 Roger Federer clinches a near single-handed victory for Switzerland over the United States in the first round of Davis Cup, defeating Jan-Michael Gambill 7-5, 6-2, 4-6, 6-2 in the 3-2 win in Federer's hometown of Basel. Federer, who beat Todd Martin in the opening singles and paired with Lorenzo Manta to beat Gambill and Justin Gimelstob in the doubles rubber, becomes one of seven players to win three live matches against a U.S. Davis Cup team, joining Laurie Doherty of Britain, Henri Cochet of France, Frank Sedgman and Neale Fraser of Australia, Nicola Pietrangeli of Italy and Raul Ramirez of Mexico. Says Federer, the future world No. 1, "My total game was good the whole weekend. I can't complain. I was serving well, feeling well from the baseline. ... Usually when I get tired I let go a little bit mentally, but that was absolutely not the case. It was just total relief, total happiness at one time. I was so happy for the team, happy for Switzerland — to beat such a big country." Eighteen-year-old Andy Roddick, another future world No. 1, makes his Davis Cup debut in the dead-rubber fifth-match and becomes the eighth-youngest American to play a Davis Cup match in defeating George Bastl 6-3, 6-4.

1985 Mike Leach, the 1982 NCAA Champion at the University of Michigan whose professional career is characterized as being "mostly a first-round doormat" by Pete Alfano of the *New York Times*, upsets No. 2 ranked Mats Wilander 7-5, 6-2 in the round of 16 at the Lipton International Players Championships in Delray Beach, Fla. Leach credits the gusty winds as being an equalizer in the match, aiding him in his upset victory. Says Leach, "If the earth had opened up in the middle of the court, that would have helped me too."

2001 Venus and Serena Williams as well as Andre Agassi and Pete Sampras appear on the celebrated American television show "The Simpsons."

February 12

1996 Thomas Muster of Austria, the 1995 French Open champion, becomes the No. 1 ranked player in the world, replacing Andre Agassi in the top spot on the ATP computer. Muster holds the ranking for only one week before Pete Sampras takes over the No. 1 spot. Muster then returns to the No. 1 ranking again on March 11 and holds it for another five weeks before surrendering the top spot again, never to rise to the ranking again in his career.

2005 Eighteen-year-old Sania Mirza of India defeats Alyona Bondarenko of Ukraine 6-4, 5-7, 6-3 to win the Hyderbad Open in Hyderabad, India and become the first woman from India to win a title on the WTA Tour.

2008 Gustavo Kuerten plays his final ATP match in his home country of Brazil, losing to Argentina's Carlos Berlocq 7-5, 6-1 in the first round of the Brazil Open in Costa Do Sauipe. The 31-year-old former world No. 1 and three-time French Open champion announces earlier in the year that 2008 would be his final year on tour, after suffering from chronic hip injuries following surgery. Says Kuerten, "It's sad to see your career come to an end. I tried. I played a good first set, but afterward, I just didn't have any strength left in me. I have lived many great moments and this is one of them, but I can no longer play. I'm sorry but I can't."

1989 World No. 1 Ivan Lendl defeats No. 20-ranked Brad Gilbert 6-2, 7-6 to win the Volvo Tennis Championships of Chicago. Says Lendl, "I was trying hard, but I wasn't playing with a game plan. That's why you saw so many strains in my matches this week. I just hit the ball hard, and if it goes in, it goes in, and if it doesn't, it doesn't."

2008 Former world No. 3 and 2004 French Open finalist Guillermo Coria emotionally wins his first ATP match in 19 months, defeating Italian qualifier Francesco Aldi, 6-4, 7-5 in the first round of Brazil Open in Costa do Sauipe. In a career highlighted by nine tournament titles—including the 2004 Monte Carlo Open—Coria calls his win over Aldi as "the happiest moment in my career." Coria drops off the ATP Tour after the 2006 U.S. Open after suffering from a lack confidence as well as problems with his right shoulder.

February 13

2000 Roger Federer plays his first ATP Tour singles final, but loses to countryman Marc Rosset 2-6, 6-3, 7-6 (5) in the final of the Marseille Open in France. The match between to the Swiss players marks the first time in the history of the ATP Tour where two players from Switzerland compete in a singles final.

1984 Thirty-two-old Dick Stockton is nearly knocked unconscious during his first-round match against 16-year-old Aaron Krickstein at the Congoleum Classic in LaQuinta, Calif. After winning the first set 7-5, Stockton runs wide for a ball hit by Krickstein in the third point of the second set. Stockton then trips on the linesperson's box, smashes into a metal railing on the side of the court and falls hard onto the cement court, leaving him groggy and motionless. Stockton is helped to his feet, forfeits the match and is taken to the hospital, where he is diagnosed with bruised ribs. Says Stockton, "I guess I'm too old to try for balls like that."

2008 Eighteen-year-old Donald Young throws his racquet out of the Delray Beach Stadium in frustration of blowing a 5-0 lead in the first set tie-break and six set points in his 7-6 (7), 6-3 first-round loss to fellow American Amer Delic at the Delray Beach International Tennis Championships. The racquet lands in a walkway, just missing unaware strolling spectators. Young, the world No. 1 junior in 2005, is given a code violation and fined for his outburst. Says Young, "Obviously, I was very frustrated. I tried to hold the emotions in. It didn't work."

1985 Upsets continue to highlight the first-ever playing of the Lipton International Players Championships in Delray Beach, Fla., as Scott Davis upsets Stefan Edberg 6-1, 6-4, 7-5, Tomas Smid defeats Yannick Noah 6-3, 6-3, 7-5. and Jan Gunnarsson upsets Vitas Gerulaitis 2-6, 6-3, 6-4, 6-2 in the men's quarterfinals. Tim Mayotte wins the fourth men's quarterfinal match defeating Mike Leach 6-2, 6-3, 6-2.

2007 Gustavo Kuerten ends a two-year winless run on the ATP Tour, defeating Filippo Volandri of Italy 6-3, 6-1 in the first round of the Brazil Open. The match is only Kuerten's fourth since September of 2005 due to hip surgery. Says Kuerten, "I knew it was just a matter of time. I'm improving physically and this win should give me confidence."

February 14

1988 Yaya Doumbia of Senegal, a qualifier ranked No. 453 in the world, becomes the unlikely winner of the ATP singles title in Lyon, France, defeating American Todd Nelson, 6-4, 3-6, 6-3 in the singles final featuring two black players. The previous day, Nelson defeats defending champion Yannick Noah of France, another black player, in the semifinals.

1996 Arriving in Dubai at 5:30 in the morning the day of his evening-scheduled match, Thomas Muster plays—and loses—his first match as the No. 1 player in the world, falling to No. 165-ranked Sandon Stolle of Australia 6-1, 3-6, 7-6 (0) in the first round of the Dubai Open in the United Arab Emirates. Stolle, the son of Hall of Famer Fred Stolle, only gains entry into the tournament as a "lucky loser" when Petr Korda withdraws from the event with a back injury.

2008 Monica Seles, a winner of nine major championships, officially announces her retirement from professional tennis—five years after playing her final singles last match at the 2003 French Open. Seles wins 53 titles during her career, including four Australian singles titles, three French singles title and two U.S. Open singles titles and ranks as the No. 1 player in the world for 178 weeks, staring in March of 1991. The 34-year-old Seles says in a statement released by the WTA Tour, "Tennis has been and will always be a huge part of my life. I have for some time considered a return to professional play, but I have now decided not to pursue that." Seles was the victim of one of the worst tragedies in tennis in April of 1993 when she was stabbed on court by a German fan Gunter Parche in Hamburg, Germany, forcing her off the tour for two-and-a-half years.

1986 Six-foot-eight Milan Srejber of Czechoslovakia, playing in only his second ATP tour level event, upsets reigning Wimbledon champion Boris Becker 7-6 (4), 6-3 in the third round of the Lipton Championships in Boca Raton, Fla.

1982 Johan Kriek defeats John McEnroe 6-3, 3-6, 6-4 to win the U.S. National Indoor Tennis Championships in Memphis, Tenn. Kriek, ranked No. 16 and the fresh off winning the Australian Open earlier in the year, fires 11 aces to earn the $40,500 first-prize paycheck.

February 15

1987 Jimmy Connors sprains a ligament in his right knee and is forced to retire to Stefan Edberg in the final of the U.S. National Indoor Championships in Memphis. Edberg leads 6-3, 2-1 when Connors, 34, falls to the court after hitting an overhead. Says Edberg, "It felt kind of strange when you win the match like this. It's not like winning match point. I served well and played well from the baseline. I am sorry the match had to end like this, but I felt maybe I deserved to win anyway."

1985 Two former Stanford standouts—Tim Mayotte and Scott Davis—advance into the final of the first-ever Lipton International Players Championships in Delray Beach, Fla.—Mayotte defeating Jan Gunnarsson of Sweden 7-6, 6-2, 4-6, 6-1 and Davis upsetting Tomas Smid of Czechoslovakia 7-6, 6-4, 4-6, 6-3.

2007 James Blake is upset in the second round of the SAP Open in San Jose, Calif., falling to No. 103-ranked Ivo Karlovic of Croatia 6-7, 7-6, 6-4. Blake, ranked No. 6 in the world, serves for the match at 5-3 in the second set and blows four match points in the second-set tie-break, before losing. The 6-foot-10-inch Karlovic hammers 29 aces in the upset win. Says Blake of the match, "I had it on my racquet. I was up 5-3, 30-0. No one to blame but myself for that. I made some errors, missed a few serves and that was that. It was my fault."

1981 A battle of different generations, fifteen-year-old Andrea Jaeger beats Virginia Wade, who at 35 years old is old enough to be Jaeger's mother, by a 6-3, 6-1 margin to win the WTA Tour event in Oakland, Calif.

2004 Andy Roddick wins his first tournament title since his 2003 U.S. Open victory, defeating good friend Mardy Fish 7-6 (13), 6-4 in the final of the Sybase Open in San Jose, Calif.,

1987 Zina Garrison defeats Sylvia Hanika of West Germany, 7-5, 4-6, 6-3 to win the Virginia Slims of San Francisco.

February 16

1926 In one of the most hyped and anticipated matches in the history of the sport, Suzanne Lenglen of France beats American Helen Wills 6-3, 8-6 at Cannes, France in the final of the Carleton tournament—the only career meeting between the two tennis legends. The Associated Press calls the encounter, "a wonderful match between the greatest women players of the old and new world...which packed the stands with enthusiastic supporters of the two contestants and brought together huge clamoring crowds outside the gates who were unable to get in." Fans unable to purchase tickets sit on roof tops of neighboring houses to catch a glimpse of the two women's champions. "From the point of view of tennis, the contest was not what had been expected, but after all, the interest lay in the meeting of Suzanne and Helen, long deferred and at one time thought never to come," reports the AP. "For weeks, little else had been talked of."

1959 John McEnroe, known perhaps more for his fiery temper tantrums as much as his deft touch and artistic serve and volley game that corrals seven major singles titles, is born in Wiesbaden, West Germany. McEnroe bursts onto the scene at Wimbledon in 1977 as an 18-year-old qualifier, reaching the semifinals before losing to future rival Jimmy Connors. After one year at Stanford University in 1978—where he wins the NCAA singles title—McEnroe embarks on a professional tennis career that nets him 77 singles titles and 78 doubles titles. He wins his first major singles title at the 1979 U.S. Open, defeating fellow New Yorker Vitas Gerulaitis in the final. He goes on to win the next two Open finals—beating Bjorn Borg both times—and again in 1984 for a fourth time over Ivan Lendl. His battle with Borg in the 1980 Wimbledon final is regarded as one of the greatest matches of all time and the two legends play a 34-point fourth-set tie-break—McEnroe saving five match points to extend the match into a fifth set. McEnroe, however, is denied the Wimbledon title, falling to Borg 1-6, 7-5, 6-3, 6-7 (16), 8-6. A year later, McEnroe finally breaks through to beat Borg in the 1981 Wimbledon final—his first of three singles titles at the All England Club, also winning in 1983 and 1984. McEnroe's best season comes in 1984 when he posts an 82-3 won-loss record, but his French Open loss to Ivan Lendl that year, after leading two sets to love, was one of his career biggest disappoints. McEnroe, a loyal supporter of the U.S. Davis Cup team, helps the U.S. to titles in 1978, 1979, 1981, 1982 and 1992.

1992 Martina Navratilova becomes the all-time singles titles leader in professional tennis, defeating Jana Novotna 7-6 (4), 4-6, 7-5 in the final of the Virginia Slims of Chicago for her 158th career singles crown. Navratilova breaks the tie she previously holds with the retired Chris Evert, but is well ahead of Jimmy Connors, the men's record holder with 109 singles titles. Says Novotna of Navratilova's achievement, "It's a credit to Martina for her comeback and her historic match. I don't think she felt the pressure of the record so much as the pressure I put on her. I was the one who pushed her to the limit."

1968 In the longest doubles match of all-time—6 hours, 20 minutes—Bobby Wilson and Mark Cox of Britain defeat Charlie Pasarell and Ron Holmberg of the United States 26-24, 17-19, 30-28 in the quarterfinals of the U.S. Indoor Championships in Salisbury, Md. The first set lasts 2:05 and the third set lasts 2:35. The match starts at 4:40 in the afternoon and doesn't finish until 11 pm!

1985 Martina Navratilova defeats Chris Evert 6-2, 6-4 to win the first-ever women's singles title at the Lipton International Players Championship in Delray Beach, Fla. "I still have more to do to improve as a player, to show people what I can do," Navratilova says following the match. "There is still a long way to go to be the greatest player in the world. I haven't been playing as well lately. My game is to and I had been giving too much credit to Chris's passing shots."

2003 Playing in his 31st—and ultimately his last—ATP singles final, Marcelo Rios of Chile loses in front of his home crowd to Spain's David Sanchez 1-6, 6-3, 6-3 in the championship match at the BellSouth Open in Vina del Mar, Chile.

1992 MaliVai Washington wins his first ATP singles title, defeating Wayne Ferreira 6-3, 6-2 in Memphis, Tenn. Washington does not lose a set in his five matches en route to the title, including his semifinal win over Jimmy Connors.

February 17

1985 Tim Mayotte wins his first ATP singles title in the first-ever Lipton International Players Championships in Delray Beach, Fla., defeating former Stanford University teammate Scott Davis 4-6, 4-6, 6-3, 6-2, 6-4 in the final. Mayotte, ranked No. 45, benefits from an overruled call that would have given the No. 27-ranked Davis a crucial service break in the third set, but holds serve and comes back to win the $112,500 first prize.

2008 Justine Henin wins her 41st—and final—WTA Tour singles title, defeating Karin Knapp of Italy in the final of the Proximus Diamond Games in Antwerp, Belgium. Three months after the final, the 25-year-old Henin shocks the tennis world by announcing her retirement from the sport, despite ranking No. 1 in the world.

2001 Stanford sophomore Laura Granville sets an NCAA record defeating Vanderbilt's Julie Ditty 6-4, 6-1 in the USTA/ITA National Women's Team Indoor Championships in Madison, Wis., for her 58th consecutive victory. Granville breaks the record she shares with Stanford's Patty Fendick-McCain, who sets the record while at Stanford in 1986-87. Granville's victory at No. 1 singles helps top-ranked Stanford beat No. 13 Vanderbilt 5-1.

2008 The Murray brothers from Scotland—Jaime and Andy—are victorious in events held in different continents. Andy wins his fifth career ATP singles title in Marseille, France, defeating Mario Ancic of Croatia 6-3, 6-4 in the final. In Delray Beach, Fla., Jaime Murray wins his fourth career ATP doubles title, pairing with Max Mirnyi of Belarus to defeat Bob and Mike Bryan 6-4, 3-6, 10-6 (Match Tie-Break) in the final of the Delray Beach International Tennis Championships.

2008 Eighteen-year-old Kei Nishikori of Japan—ranked No. 244—becomes only the second player from Japan to win an ATP singles title, defeating James Blake of the United States 3-6, 6-1, 6-4 in the final of the Delray Beach International Tennis Championships in Delray Beach, Fla. Nishikori, who comes back from facing triple match point a 3-6 in the final-set tie-break in the semifinals the previous day against Sam Querrey, wins eight matches in nine days to win the title, including three matches in the qualifying tournament. Shuzo Matsuoka was the last—and only other—Japanese player to win an ATP singles title, winning in Seoul, Korea in 1992.

February 18

1931 Bill Tilden makes his much hyped and anticipated professional debut defeating Karel Kozeluh of Czechoslovakia 6-4, 6-2, 6-4 in front of 13,000 fans at Madison Square Garden in New York. Tilden and Kozeluh continue on to compete in 32 other matches in a cross-country tour—Tilden winning the tour 27-6. Tilden serves with entrepreneur William O'Brien as the co-promoter of the tour that grosses $238,000.

2007 Former world No. 1 Kim Clijsters plays her final match in Belgium, losing to Amelie Mauresmo 6-4, 7-6 (4) in front of 14,500 fans in the final of the Diamond Games Championships in Antwerp, Belgium. Clijsters, who announced the 2007 season would be her last, breaks down in tears during the awards ceremony as she is showered with praise for her 10-year career. Says the 23-year-old Clijsters, "It was a very emotional day." Mauresmo wins the event for a third year in a row, allowing her to keep the 8.8-pound gold racquet decorated with 1,702 diamonds. The trophy goes to the first three-time winner in any five-year span of the event. Says Mauresmo, "I said all week I didn't think about it, but honestly I thought about it the whole week."

1984 Jimmy Connors needs 3 hours, 15 minutes to defeat Jose Higueras 6-7 (3), 6-0, 7-6 (5) in the semifinals of the Congoleum Classic in LaQuinta, Calif. Higueras serves for the match at 6-5 in the third, but is unable to close out the match. "I thought I had him there," Higueras says after the match. "It was my serve. The wind was on my side, but when you play a guy like Connors, you can't take anything for granted."

2007 Guillermo Canas of Argentina upsets former world No. 1 Juan Carlos Ferrero of Spain 7-6 (4), 6-2 in the Brazil Open in Costa de Sauipe to win his first tournament since returning to professional tennis from a doping ban. Canas is suspended from professional tennis for two years, following a positive test for a banned steroid shortly after the 2005 French Open. The suspension is subsequently reduced to 15 months.

February 19

2006 Forty-seven-year-old John McEnroe, in an unusual return to the ATP circuit, wins his 78th career doubles title, teaming with Sweden's Jonas Bjorkman to win the SAP Open in San Jose, Calif., defeating Paul Goldstein and Jim Thomas 7-6(2), 4-6, 10-7 (Super Tie-break). The tournament is McEnroe's first appearance in an ATP event since he partnered Boris Becker in Rotterdam in 1994 and the title is McEnroe's first since he won at the Paris Indoors with younger brother Patrick in 1992. Says McEnroe after the final, "I felt like I had it in me, but I didn't know quite what was going to happen." McEnroe becomes the oldest player to win an ATP title — singles or doubles—in the last 30 years and Bjorkman becomes the 14th different partner to win an ATP doubles title with McEnroe. In the singles final, eighteen-year-old Andy Murray defeats Lleyton Hewitt 2-6, 6-1, 7-6 (3) in the singles final to win his first ATP singles title.

1984 In a heated match featuring temper tantrums from both players, Jimmy Connors defeats Yannick Noah 6-2, 6-7 (7), 6-3 to win the Congoleum Classic in LaQuinta, Calif. Connors is fined $1,000 following the match for what the *Los Angeles Times* describes simply as "visible obscenities."

1986 Thirty-three-year-old Jimmy Connors defeats Yannick Noah 5-7, 6-4, 7-6, 6-4 in a 3-hour 45 minute quarterfinal match at the Lipton Championships in Boca Raton, Fla. "I feel like I've been put through the wringer," says Connors. "But I wasn't going to roll over at any points and neither was he."

2005 Eighteen-year-old Rafael Nadal wins his second career ATP singles title defeating countryman Alberto Martin 6-0, 6-7 (2), 6-1 in the final of the Brazil Open in Costa Do Suipe, Brazil. Nadal leads 6-0, 4-0 in the match and fights off a furious comeback from Martin to win the match in three sets.

2007 Venus Williams plays her first match after a four-month layoff due to a sprained left wrist and beats Akiko Morigami of Japan 6-1, 2-6, 6-4 in the first round of the Cellular South Cup in Memphis, Tenn. Says the 25-year-old Williams, ranked No. 53. "I definitely was a little rusty, and the first set went so quick, it was fairly easy. In the second set, I started to think and I made a few errors. It seemed like I couldn't stop the errors. It was like a windfall of errors."

February 20

1994 Martina Navratilova wins her 167th and final WTA Tour singles title, defeating Julie Halard of France 7-5, 6-3 in the final of the Paris Open in France. The win gives Navratilova the distinction of winning at least one WTA singles title for an 18th consecutive year.

1982 Yannick Noah defeats Ivan Lendl 3-6, 6-2, 7-5 in the final of the Congoleum Classic in LaQuinta, Calif., ending Lendl's 44-match, eight-tournament winning streak. Noah, the first player to defeat Lendl in a five-month span, calls the win "one of the biggest of my life." Says Lendl, who last lost to Vitas Gerulaitis in round of 16 at the 1981 U.S. Open, "It's just another match and I'm sure I'm going to lose many more in my career." Lendl's streak is the longest in men's tennis since Guillermo Vilas wins 50 straight matches in 1977.

1983 Jimmy Connors captures his record sixth U.S. National Indoor Tennis Championship in Memphis, defeating Gene Mayer 7-5, 6-0 in the singles final. Connors won the tournament previously in 1979, 1978, 1975, 1974 and 1973.

2005 Amelie Mauresmo defeats Venus Williams 4-6, 7-5, 6-4 to win the WTA Tour title in Antwerp, Belgium. Mauresmo trails Williams 3-5 in the second set and 2-4 in the third set before rallying for victory and denying Williams the opportunity to win the $1 million golden tennis racquet encrusted with 1,700 diamonds—the tournament's incentive to any player who manages to win the singles title three times in a five-year period. Williams, the 2002 and 2003 winner of the event, is unable to compete in the event in 2006 due to injury.

1994 Stefan Edberg defeats Goran Ivanisevic 4-6, 6-4, 6-2, 6-2 to win the Eurocard Open in Stuttgart, Germany.

1994 Michael Chang defeats Paul Haarhuis 6-3, 6-2 at the U.S. Pro Indoors in Philadelphia.

February 21

1986 Indignant at chair umpire Jeremy Shales and linesmen during his semifinal match with Ivan Lendl at the Lipton Championships in Boca Raton, Fla., Jimmy Connors walks off the court, defaulting the match to his Czech rival. As Connors sits in his chair trailing 2-5 in the final set, he is assessed three point penalties by Shales for time violations before being defaulted. Lendl wins the match by a 1-6, 6-1, 6-2, 2-6, 5-2, default, decision. "Failure to complete a match is a serious thing," says Marshall Happer, Administrator of the Men's International Professional Tennis Council. "What Connors did is inexcusable." Happer takes action against Connors one month later, issuing a 10-week suspension and a $20,000 fine.

2008 Andy Roddick bullies his way past 18-year-old Kei Nishikori of Japan 6-2, 6-4 in the round of 16 of the SAP Open in San Jose. Roddick says after the match that he wanted to "make my presence felt a little" against the tour rookie, who is playing just days after beating James Blake in the Delray Beach final. A feisty Roddick exchanges words with linespeople, the chair umpire and Nishikori himself throughout the match, highlighted by an alleged obscenity thrown at the young Japanese player after an exchange at the net in the seventh game of the match. Writes Darren Sabedra of the *Oakland Tribune*, "It was a match that will best be remembered for an exchange of shots—and words—at the net late in the first set. Nishikori, 18, ripped a point-blank shot directly at Roddick, but the American somehow got his racket on the ball and eventually won the point. Roddick, ranked No.6 in the world, then tossed in a few verbal bombs at Nishikori for good measure. When someone in the crowd shouted, "What did you say?" during an on-court interview, Roddick replied, "There are kids here."' Roddick says of the exchanges, "There was nothing personal in it. He's probably not that happy with me for doing that. But I don't need any young friends." Asked if he was trying to bully his opponent, like his coach at the time Jimmy Connors was famous for doing during his career, Roddick responds, "I've been a brat for a long time. This isn't something that came along in the last year and a half with Jimmy." Roddick goes on to win the title, defeating Radek Stepanek in the final.

1988 Seventeen-year-old Andre Agassi wins his second ATP title—and his first of six titles during his breakthrough 1988 season—defeating Mikael Pernfors of Sweden 6-4, 6-4, 7-5 in the final of the U.S. Indoors in Memphis, Tenn.

February 22

1983 Bill Scanlon wins the first recorded "golden set" on the ATP Tour, winning all 24 points in the second set of his 6-2, 6-0 win over Marcos Hocevar of Brazil in the first round of the $300,000 WCT Gold Coast Cup in Delray Beach, Fla.

1987 Sixteen-year-old Pete Sampras, who grows into a seven-time Wimbledon champion and 14-time major singles title winner, makes his ATP tournament debut, losing to Sammy Giammalva of Houston 6-4, 6-3 in the first round of the U.S. Pro Indoor Championships in Philadelphia, Pa.

1986 Chris Evert Lloyd defeats 16-year-old Steffi Graf 6-4, 6-2 to win the Lipton Championships in Boca Raton, Fla., her 144th professional tournament victory. "She hit harder ground strokes than any of the girls I have been playing," Evert-Lloyd says of Graf, the future world No. 1 who would win the Grand Slam two years later in 1988. "Her forehand is unbelievable. She was more eager to win, but she was more impatient too." Says Graf. "I had chances, but Chris always knows what to do when it's very close."

1981 In what the *Los Angeles Times* describes as a "match where the tension in the air was so thick, you could cut it with a knife," Jimmy Connors defeats Ivan Lendl 6-3, 7-6 to win the ATP singles title in LaQuinta, Calif. The second set starts off in bizarre fashion as a wide serve by Lendl in the first game strikes a 10-year-old in the nose and Connors rushes to the sidelines to grab ice and a towel to aid the young fan, who is not seriously injured outside of a bloody nose. Lendl rolls to a 4-0 lead in the second set, but Connors surges back to finish off the final in straight sets. Says Connors, "In the second set, I got frustrated because I don't like to play catch up. I want to win the first set and stomp 'em in the second set."

2005 To promote the upcoming Dubai Duty Free Championships, Andre Agassi and world No. 1 Roger Federer conduct a "practice session" on top of the helipad 211 meters above the ground of the Burj Al Arab hotel, the world's most luxurious hotel. The Burj, the most recognizable and famous structure in Dubai, stretches 321 meters above the water on a man-made island in the Persian Gulf. Later in the week—and at ground level—Federer defeats Agassi 6-3, 6-1 in the semifinals of the event.

2007 Wimbledon announces that it will award equal prize money for both men and women for the first time in the history of the event—starting with the 2007 Championships. The All England Club finally succumbs to public pressure and lobbying for years by women's advocates and the WTA Tour. "Tennis is one of the few sports in which women and men compete in the same event at the same time," All England Club Chairman Tim Phillips says at a press conference. "We believe our decision to offer equal prize money provides a boost for the game as a whole and recognizes the enormous contribution that women players make to the game and to Wimbledon. In short, good for tennis, good for women players and good for Wimbledon." Says reigning women's singles champion Amelie Mauresmo, "It is a victory for women's tennis, and a victory for women in general. It was really a matter of principle. It is a question of equality." The U.S. Open is the major championship with the longest history of paying equal prize money—offering equal payouts since 1973. "This is an historic and defining moment for women in the sport of tennis, and a significant step forward for the equality of women in our society," WTA Tour chief executive Larry Scott says in a statement. "We commend the leadership of Wimbledon for its decisive action in recognizing the progress that women's tennis has made."

2006 Lindsay Davenport wins her 700th WTA Tour singles victory in grand fashion, handing Elena Likhovtseva a double-bagel—beating the Russian standout 6-0, 6-0 to reach the quarterfinals of the Dubai Open in the United Arab Emirates.

2004 Joachim Johansson claims his first ATP title with a 7-6(5), 6-3 victory over Germany's Nicolas Kiefer to win the Kroger St. Jude in Memphis. The Swede becomes the fourth different Swedish winner in Memphis, joining Bjorn Borg, Stefan Edberg and Magnus Larsson.

2008 John Isner and Guillermo Garcia-Lopez play for 3 hours, 8 minutes—neither player breaking the others serve—in an epic quarterfinal match at the SAP Open in San Jose that ends in 24-point final-set tie-break. Garcia-Lopez is just slightly better than the 6-foot-10 Isner, winning 7-6 (4), 6-7 (1), 7-6 (11), saving four match points. Says Garcia-Lopez of the no-service-break match, "It doesn't usually happen to me, but he was serving like an animal." Isner fires 22 aces in the match (against Garcia-Lopez's six) Says Isner, "I served well and played well at times, but I could play better on big points."

February 23

1986 World No. 1 Ivan Lendl wins the Lipton Championships in Boca Raton, Fla., defeating world No. 3 Mats Wilander 3-6, 6-1, 7-6, 6-4 in the final. Both players sit through a three-hour rain delay with the score tied at 2-2 in the third-set tie-break. The win is Lendl's 17th straight match victory and his 46th in his last 47 matches.

1994 Steffi Graf blanks 31-year-old Tracy Austin 6-0, 6-0 in 43 minutes in the second round of Evert Cup in Indian Wells, Calif. avenging a loss to Austin 11 years earlier in her pro debut in Filderstadt, Germany. Says Austin, "When I played Steffi the first time, she was a little kid — 13, just starting out—and I was at the top. Now, I'm an old lady at the end of my career and she's at the top."

1996 Jennifer Capriati's second comeback from professional tennis ends as Jana Novotna defeats the 19-year-old 7-6 (6), 2-6, 6-3 in the quarterfinals of the Faber Grand Prix in Essen, Germany. Novotna uses her post-match press conference to criticize the WTA Tour for "hyping" the return of Capriati to professional tennis after her arrest in 1994 for drug possession. "Do you see in any other sport, if someone would have problems like she has or be a drug user that she would be as welcome as she is in women's tennis?" asks Novotna to the press following the match. "I think everyone should be responsible for their actions, no matter how young they are or anything... only see that it makes us feel that women's tennis is so desperate that we are so excited to have somebody with this attitude back. It seems women's tennis is desperate for publicity, and they don't really care if it's good publicity or bad publicity."

1983 Unheralded Mike Bauer, ranked No. 89 in the world, upsets world No. 1 Jimmy Connors 6-3, 6-4 in the second round of the Congoleum Classic in LaQuinta, Calif. "I'm living a dream right now," says Bauer, a former standout at the University of California at Berkeley. "It's going to take a while to sink in...this is the biggest victory of my career...I was serving and all of the sudden realized I had match point against Jimmy Connors."

1974 Seventeen-year-old Bjorn Borg, the future legend of the sport who wins five straight Wimbledon titles and six French Open titles, wins his first pro circuit singles title, defeating Mark Cox of Great Britain 6-7, 7-6, 6-4 in the final of the WCT London Championships at the Royal Albert Hall.

February 24

1985 Twenty-seven-year-old Larry Stefanki, ranked No. 143 in the world, caps off an incredible week of upsets, defeating David Pate 6-1, 6-4, 3-6, 6-3 to win the Pilot Pen Classic in LaQuinta, Calif. Stefanki, the touring pro at the LaQuinta Resort, is given a last minute wild-card entry in the tournament when bigger name players—namely Mats Wilander and Stefan Edberg—decline opportunities to play in the event. Stefanki rides a string of upsets to win the second pro title of his career to go with a 1981 title in Lagos, Nigeria. Writes Mike Penner of the *Los Angeles Times*, "In fact, the Larry Stefanki Story is almost too good, too sensational. This is the stuff of comic books, Steven Spielberg movies and prime-time TV drama." "Unbelievable," says Stefanki of his run. "I've never experienced anything like this. You dream about this." Tournament Director Charlie Pasarell says to the *Times*, "I'm not sure the match would have been any better than this. If we could've written the script, we couldn't have done it any better...I have a tremendous responsibility to this event and to the ticket buyers to bring in some big names. We wanted Wilander and Edberg, but after today's match, I walked over to Larry, shook his hand and said the worst mistake I could've made was getting Wilander and Edberg."

2007 Justine Henin claims her 30th career WTA Tour title—defeating Amelie Mauresmo 6-4, 7-5 in the final of the Dubai Open in the United Arab Emirates. Henin's 2007 title in Dubai is her fourth in the Gulf city to go with her titles in 2003, 2004 and 2006.

2008 Andy Roddick beats Radek Stepanek 6-4, 7-5 to win the SAP Open in San Jose, Calif. Roddick celebrates the win by wiggling his right leg and left arm, mimicking Stepanek, known for performing the belly-on-the-ground dance called "The Worm" on court after big victories. Says Roddick, "Everybody's asking me about the Worm. All I hear is the Worm. I wanted to find something as cheesy if not cheesier to go with, which was tough. I figured one bad leg kick and I'd be on par." Says Stepanek of Roddick's celebration, "I don't know what that was."

1984 John McEnroe and Jimmy Connors join forces on the U.S. Davis Cup team for only the second time in their careers as Connors defeats Florin Segarceanu 6-2, 6-3, 6-4 and McEnroe defeats Ilie Nastase 6-2, 6-4, 6-2 as the United States takes a 2-0 lead over Romania in Bucharest.

February 25

1990 Playing in the same tournament where he made his professional debut two years prior, Pete Sampras wins the first singles title in his illustrious career, defeating Andres Gomez 7-6 (4), 7-5, 6-2 in the final of the U.S. Pro Indoor Championships in Philadelphia. Sampras earns a first-prize check of $135,000 for the first of his 64 ATP singles titles he wins over a 13-year period. Writes Robin Finn of the *New York Times* of Sampras, "There had been no dates, no diploma, no proms and no pranks for 18-year-old Pete Sampras since he turned professional two years back. There had also been no entourage, no hair dye and, until today, no titles for Sampras, an Opie-look-a-like who studied work ethic under the expert tutelage of Ivan Lendl and used it all week here to lay the groundwork for a 7-6, 7-5, 6-2 demotion of Andres Gomez in the Ebel Pro Indoor final." Says Sampras of his motivation for success following the final, "I'm not playing for money. I'm playing for love of the game. And I think I'll keep playing for love of the game for 8 or 10 years." While Sampras was happy with the win in Philadelphia, he says he has his eyes set on bigger prizes, "No one remembers who won Philadelphia or Memphis. Where you make your name is the Grand Slams."

2002 Venus Williams, the two-time reigning U.S. Open and Wimbledon champion, becomes the first black player—man or woman—to rank No. 1 in the world in tennis as she assumes the top ranking on the WTA Tour computer. Williams becomes the 11th player to rank No. 1 on the WTA computer and holds the ranking for 11 weeks during the year.

2001 Identical twins Bob and Mike Bryan win their first ATP doubles title by capturing the Kroger St. Jude championship in Memphis, Tenn., defeating Alex O'Brien and Jonathan Stark 6-3, 7-6 (7-3), in a match-up for former standout players from Stanford University.

1993 Nineteen-year-old Stephanie Rottier of the Netherlands routs 30-year-old two-time U.S. Open champion Tracy Austin 6-1, 6-0 in the third round of the Evert Cup in Indian Wells, Calif., in an abbreviated comeback for the former world No. 1. Says Rottier of Austin's fame, "I heard she won two U.S. Opens. I read it in the paper." The un-ranked Austin, playing in her first tournament since 1989, upsets No. 2 seed and No. 12-ranked Katerina Maleeva 6-2, 2-6, 6-3 in the previous round.

February 26

1989 Sixteen-year-old high school junior Amy Frazier wins the last nine games of the match and defeats Barbara Potter, 4-6, 6-4, 6-0, to win a $100,000 Virginia Slims tournament at Wichita, Kan.—her first WTA Tour singles title.

2007 Roger Federer begins his 161st straight week as the No. 1 player in the ATP rankings, breaking the record of 160 weeks set by Jimmy Connors in 1977. Says Federer, "I have been counting the days....This record is something special to me. Even if I lost it tomorrow it would still take somebody more than three years to beat it."

2008 Four-time Wimbledon champion Venus Williams, the No. 1 seeded defending champion, is stunned by 17-year-old qualifier Petra Kvitova of the Czech Republic 2-6, 6-4, 6-3 in the opening round of the Cellular South Cup in Memphis. Kvitova, ranked No. 143, enters the match having won only one of 13 previous matches on the WTA Tour. "I am very happy," says Kvitova. "It is the biggest (moment) of my life." Says Williams, "She had a good serve and she was left-handed. She mixed it up really well. I'm not happy about the result of the match, but she played well."

1989 John McEnroe comes back from 2-5 deficit in the second set to win his 73rd career singles title, defeating Jakob Hlasek of Switzerland, 6-3, 7-6, to win the ATP title in Lyon, France. "I feel I am getting closer and closer," McEnroe says of returning to his top form that enabled him to win three Wimbledon titles and four U.S. Open titles. "My game is getting stronger and I am very optimistic about this year."

2005 Rafael Nadal claims his second title in two weeks—and his third title overall—when he defeats fellow Spaniard Albert Montanes 6-1, 6-0 in only 52 minutes in the final of the ATP event in Acapulco, Mexico.

1989 Boris Becker defeats two-time defending champion Tim Mayotte 7-6, 6-1, 6-3 to win the U.S. Pro Indoor Championships in Philadelphia, Pa.

1989 Zina Garrison wins her first tournament in two years defeating Larisa Savchenko of the Soviet Union, 6-1, 6-1, to win the $250,000 Virginia Slims of California at Oakland.

February 27

1983 Playing on the same day that Queen Elizabeth of Britain arrives in Palm Springs, Calif., Jose Higueras wins his first hard court tennis title, defeating Eliot Teltscher 6-4, 6-2 to win the men's singles title at the Congoleum Classic in LaQuinta, Calif.

2005 Thirty-three-year old Wayne Arthurs of Australia, playing in his 128th career professional singles tournament, becomes the oldest man to win his first ATP singles title, defeating Mario Ancic 7-5, 6-3 in the final of The Tennis Channel Open in Scottsdale, Ariz. Says Arthurs following his break-through victory, "It feels really good, really satisfying, especially now that I'm older. It's probably more satisfying to win a tournament this late in my career. I'm going to savor every minute of it."

2005 Federer wins his 25th career singles title, defeating Ivan Ljubicic 6-1, 6-7 (6), 6-3 in the final of Dubai Open in the United Arab Emirates. The title is Federer's third in a row in the oil-rich middle eastern city. Says Federer, "To win three times here is fantastic. It's the first time to have achieved that anywhere."

1994 Steffi Graf defeats Amanda Coetzer 6-0, 6-4 in 57 minutes to win the singles title at the Evert Cup in Indian Wells, Calif.

1960 Andres Gomez, best known for his final-round triumph over Andre Agassi at the 1990 French Open, is born in Guayaquil, Ecuador.

February 28

1983 Ivan Lendl becomes the No. 1 ranked player in the world for the first time, taking over the top spot from Jimmy Connors. Lendl ranks No. 1 in the world for a total 270 weeks, a record that would be broken by Pete Sampras, who ranked No. 1 for 286 weeks.

1996 After defeating Jeff Tarango 6-1, 6-1 in the first round of the Kroger St. Jude Championships in Memphis, Tenn., Jim Courier uniquely states that getting to the No. 1 ranking in pro tennis is more fun than being the No. 1 ranked player. "It's like chasing a girl," he says. "The chase is the fun part."

2005 Venus Williams is defeated by Silvia Farina Elia of Italy 7-5, 7-6 (6) in the first round of the Dubai Open in the United Arab Emirates. The loss is the first for Williams in a first round of a tournament in four years—since she loses in the first round of the 2001 French Open to Barbara Schett.

1993 Mary Joe Fernandez saves two match points and wins the singles title at the Evert Cup in Indian Wells, Calif., defeating Amanda Coetzer 3-6, 6-1, 7-5 (6) in a 2-hour, 47-minute singles final. Fernandez fights off two match points serving a 4-5 in the final set, before prevailing 8-6 in the final-set tie-break.

2008 Francesca Schiavone of Italy upsets world No. 1 Justine Henin-Hardenne 7-6 (3), 7-6 (4) in the quarterfinals of the Dubai Open in the United Arab Emirates—ending Henin's 17-match winning streak at the event. Says Henin, "She played really well. She was hitting hard, coming to the net, slicing...really mixing it up. I had my chances but I did not take them, whereas she did. She was definitely a better player and deserved to win." Says Schiavone, "I have beaten (Amelie) Mauresmo when she was world No. 1 in a Fed Cup match, but definitely this win against someone like Justine, who always plays at such a high level, is the biggest win of my career."

February 29

1988 Pete Sampras, a 16-year-old high school junior from Rancho Palos Verdes, Calif., wins his first ATP singles match, defeating No. 37-ranked Ramesh Krishnan of India 6-3, 3-6, 7-6 in the first round of the Newsweek Champions Cup in Indian Wells, Calif. Sampras, an amateur who advances into the tournament via the qualifying rounds, saves five match points in the third set. Sampras goes on to win 761 more ATP tour-level matches in his career, including 14 major singles titles.

2008 Robin Soderling of Sweden slams 16 aces and upsets Andy Roddick 7-6 (6), 6-3, in the quarterfinals of the Regions Morgan Keegan Championships in Memphis, Tenn. In another quarterfinal, 35-year-old Jonas Bjorkman defeats 18-year-old, up-and-coming American Donald Young, playing his first ATP quarterfinal, by a 1-6, 6-2, 7-6 (6) margin. Says Bjorkman after the match, "Well, it's not looking good for (the U.S.) if a 36-year-old can beat the youngsters. No, I'm just kidding. Donald has a great future. He'll just have to learn to play tactically smart. Sometimes he's trying to hit shots that you shouldn't hit." Young was playing in his 21st career ATP match, while Bjorkman was playing in his 759th.

2008 Russians Elena Dementieva and Svetlana Kuznetsova both win three-set semifinals at the Dubai Championships Kuznetsova beats Jelena Jankovic of Serbia 5-7, 6-4, 6-3, while Dementieva defeats Francesa Schiavone of Italy 5-7, 7-5, 6-2. Says Kuznetsova of her victory, "I felt I started playing better and better as the match progressed. I made a slight change of tactics in the second set when I stopped hitting the ball flat and tried to mix it up."

March 1

1998 Venus Williams wins her first WTA Tour singles title, defeating Joanette Kruger of South Africa 6-3, 6-2 in the singles final of the IGA Tennis Classic in Oklahoma City, Okla. After the final, Williams takes a 30-minute break, then returns to the court with younger sister Serena and wins her first career WTA Tour doubles title, defeating Catalina Cristea of Romania and Kristine Kunce of Australia "This is one I will probably always remember," Williams says. "I can say it all started back in Oklahoma City."

2008 Lindsay Davenport wins her 55th career singles title—tying Virginia Wade for seventh place all time on the WTA list—defeating Olga Govortsova 6-2, 6-1 in exactly 60 minutes in the final of the Cellular South Cup in Memphis, Tenn. "Obviously I'm ecstatic to win any tournament," Davenport says. "I've never been one to look at records or anything, but it all seems surreal to me. I love being up there with the greatest players that ever played."

2008 Sergiy Stakhovsky of Ukraine, ranked No. 209, becomes the first "lucky loser" to win an ATP title in 17 years, defeating Ivan Ljubicic of Croatia 7-5, 6-4 to win the singles title in Zagreb, Croatia—his first career ATP singles title. A lucky loser is a player who loses in the final round of the qualifying tournament, but gains entry into the event when a player directly entered into the tournament withdraws. Stakhovsky, who had won only six career ATP-level matches prior to his week in Zagreb, gains entry when Michael Llodra of France withdraws from the event. Before Stakhovsky, the last player to win an ATP title as a lucky loser was Argentina's Christian Miniussi, who wins the title in Sao Paulo in 1991.

1992 Monica Seles drubs Conchita Martinez 6-3, 6-1 in the final of the Evert Cup in Indian Wells, Calif., and celebrates her 23rd career title with a hot air balloon ride over the Coachella Valley of Southern California. Says Martinez of Seles, "She played hard from everywhere on the court. I played the match well, but she's No. 1. She played better."

1998 Playing in the event where he made his pro debut in 1988 and where he won his first career ATP title, Pete Sampras wins his fourth title at the Advanta Championships in Philadelphia, defeating Thomas Enqvist 7-5, 7-6 (3) in the singles final. Says Enqvist of Sampras, "It's a lot of fun to play him, actually. It's an honor. I think he's the best player ever to play the game."

March 2

1988 Sixteen-year-old Pete Sampras, playing only in his second professional event, registers the biggest win of his early career, defeating 28-year-old former U.S. Davis Cup star Eliot Teltscher in the first round of the Newsweek Champions Cup in Indian Wells, Calif. Says the No. 10-seeded Teltscher, "I felt like I lost to a good player. He is a good player. That's the bottom line of it. I didn't play the match of my life out there. I was a little tentative. He serves well and volleys well and he's aggressive. I needed to serve well and keep the ball deep. He was smart. He took my second serve and he came in. Whenever he got a short ball, he hit it and came in. He pressured me throughout the match when I didn't keep the ball deep enough to keep him off the net." Sampras loses his third-round match to Emilio Sanchez of Spain 7-5, 6-2 and 30 months later becomes the youngest U.S. Open men's singles champion at the age of 19.

2003 Ai Sugiyama endures—and enjoys—a four-match, two-title day at the State Farm Women's Tennis Classic in Scottsdale, Ariz., spending 6 hours, 19 minutes on court in winning the singles and doubles titles. Sugiyama starts by playing her rain-postponed singles semifinal match at 10 am, defeating Alexandra Stevenson 6-7 (2), 6-2, 7-6 (7)—saving three match points in the process. Sugiyama then pairs with Kim Clijsters and wins their doubles semifinal over Marion Bartoli and Stephanie Cohen-Aloro 7-5, 6-0. Sugiyama then takes the court with Clijsters for the women's singles final, winning the title with a 3-6, 7-5, 6-4 victory. Next, she and Clijsters play and defeat Lindsay Davenport and Lisa Raymond 6-1, 6-4 to win the doubles title in a match that concludes at 8:10 pm—10 hours after play started in her first match of the day.

1993 Richey Reneberg upsets Stefan Edberg 6-3, 4-6, 6-4 in the second round of the Newsweek Champions Cup in indian Wells, Calif. "This is the first time I've broken through against a highly-ranked guy, a guy in the top five, but there is no question he didn't play his best," says Reneberg.

March 3

1991 Brothers John and Patrick McEnroe play in the singles final of the Volvo Championships in Chicago, with No. 19th-ranked John defeating younger brother and No. 51-ranked Patrick 3-6, 6-2, 6-4 to win his 77th and what would be his final ATP singles title. Says the 32-year-old John following the match, "I have incredibly mixed emotions right now...every emotion you can imagine was there, from worrying how he's doing, to worrying that he might beat you." The final was the third ATP men's singles final involving brothers. Gene Mayer beat Sandy Mayer at Stockholm in 1981 and Emilio Sanchez beat Javier Sanchez at Madrid in 1987.

1980 John McEnroe becomes the No. 1 ranked player in the world for the first time, unseating Bjorn Borg. In all, McEnroe ranks No. 1 for a total of 170 weeks during his career.

2007 Roger Federer wins his 41st straight match, tying Bjorn Borg for the fourth-longest streak in the history of men's tennis, defeating Mikhail Youzhny of Russia 6-4, 6-3 to win the Dubai Open for a fourth time. "It's nice to be playing against the history books," Federer says after the match. "I never thought I would ever do such a thing."

1993 Taking a 23-minute commute via private jet from his home in Las Vegas to Indian Wells, Calif., Andre Agassi is defeated in the second round of the Newsweek Champion Cup by reigning Olympic champion Marc Rosset 3-6, 7-6 (5), 6-4.

1992 Michael Chang comes back from 1-5 down in the third set to defeat Martin Jaite of Argentina 0-6, 7-6 (6), 7-6 (3) in the first round of the Newsweek Champions Cup in Indian Wells, Calif.

2007 Belgium's Justine Henin defeats Russia's Svetlana Kuznetsova 6-4, 6-2 to win the Qatar Open in Doha. Henin's win completes a "Gulf Double"— also winning the title in the Persian Gulf city of Dubai a week earlier. Says Kuznetsova on losing her 14th match in 15 meetings with Henin, "Maybe I have a mental block when I play Justine. She is just too tough mentally and I need to learn this from her."

March 4

1979 Arthur Ashe's quest to win the only important U.S. championship missing from his resume is foiled by Jimmy Connors, who wins the singles final at the U.S. National Indoor Championships in Memphis 6-4, 5-7, 6-3 in what is the 65th and last appearance for Ashe in a professional singles final. Says Ashe to reporters with his second-place trophy in one hand and a beer in his other hand, "Jimmy just played better in times of crises." The title is the fifth for Connors at the world's oldest indoor championship, played for 79 years. Connors, however, skips his post-match press conference as he alleges a virus, but speculation is that he refuses to meet with the media to avoid questions regarding rumors of his marriage to *Playboy* playmate Patty McGuire.

1992 Andre Agassi fends off the challenge of No. 219th-ranked Bernd Karbacher of Germany, playing in his first ATP Tour level tournament, before prevailing 6-1, 1-6, 7-5 in the second round of the Newsweek Champions Cup in Indian Wells, Calif.

1993 World No. 22 Alexander Volkov upsets world No. 2 Pete Sampras 7-5, 6-4 in the round of 16 at the Newsweek Champions Cup in Indian Wells, Calif. Volkov's simple explanation for the victory, in broken English, is, "He was nervous too much, so he lost."

2006 In a battle of the No. 1 and No. 2 players in the world, No. 2 ranked Rafael Nadal defeats world No. 1 Roger Federer 2-6, 6-4, 6-4 in the final of the Dubai Open in the United Arab Emirates. Nadal's win ends Federer's 56-match hard court winning streak. Says Nadal, "I think it is unbelievable to win against the best player in the world—perhaps the best in history of the game."

1927 Bill Tilden fires three aces in the opening game of the match and crushes Frank Hunter 6-1, 6-0, 6-0 in the semifinals of the South Florida Championships at Flamingo Park in Miami Beach, Fla. Manuel Alonso defeats John Hennessey 6-2, 6-0, 6-2 in the other semifinal. Two days later on March 6, Tilden wins the title from the Spaniard, winning the championship match, 6-3, 7-9, 5-7, 6-4, 6-2. Writes the *New York Times*, "Tilden displayed great reserve force and came to the fore with driving strokes in the pinches. Tilden continually came from behind and gradually wore down his rival to win the final two sets and victory."

March 5

1987 Seventeen-year-old world No. 2 Steffi Graf routs top-ranked Martina Navratilova 6-3, 6-2 in the semifinals of the Lipton Championships in Key Biscayne, Fla. Says Navratilova of Graf, "Today, she was the best player in the world and she will be until I play her again." Says Graf of her win, only her second in seven total meetings with Navratilova, "I'm so happy about the match. It's one of the biggest wins I've ever had."

1991 Playing in a dust storm with 30 mile per hour winds, John McEnroe edges Wally Masur 7-6, 2-6, 7-5 in 2 hours, 35 minutes in the first round of the Newsweek Champions Cup in Indian Wells, Calif. Says McEnroe following the match in the challenging conditions, "It was just what I wouldn't have wanted, high winds, and it seemed extra bright to me, but it was a heck of a match, anyway." Says Masur of the third set of the match that features the worst of the conditions, "There was a bit of dust on the court. We both slipped a few times. I made the mistake of not serving and volleying enough in the third, and he continued to serve-and-volley."

1994 After barely winning points against the surging serve of Stefan Edberg, Pete Sampras scrapes out a service break in the final game of the match to overcome the Swede 6-3, 3-6, 6-4 and advance to the final of the Newsweek Champions Cup in Indian Wells, Calif. Writes Jim Murray of Sampras in the *Los Angeles Times*, "Playing Sampras in a three-set match is like fighting a bobcat in a closet. You don't have too much time to figure out strategy. It's tough playing a guy when your best hope is that he will miss. It's like hoping the alligator doesn't see you." In the other semifinal, Petr Korda dispatches of Aaron Krickstein 6-4, 6-4. The following day, Sampras wins the Newsweek title, edging Korda 4-6, 6-3, 3-6, 6-3, 6-2.

2006 James Blake defeats Lleyton Hewitt 7-5, 2-6, 6-3 in the final of The Tennis Channel Open in Las Vegas, Nev. The win is the first in seven tries for Blake against Hewitt. "It's not easy to play against him," says Blake. "I'm just happy to get finally get a win against him. He's one of the best players of all-time."

March 6

1983 John McEnroe is handed his worst Davis Cup defeat of his career, winning only five games in his 6-4, 6-0, 6-1 loss to Guillermo Vilas, which clinches Argentina's 3-2 victory over the United States in the Davis Cup first round in Buenos Aires. Ten years later, in his book *Days of Grace*, U.S. Davis Cup Captain Arthur Ashe tells of the waning stages of McEnroe's one-sided defeat in Argentina writing, "As he was about to trudge back to the baseline, down 1-4 in the third set, facing his and our team's worst defeat in the Cup competition in many years, John turned to me. A smile that mocked us both flirted with a jaunty smirk. 'Well captain,' he said, plucking at his racquet strings, 'do you have any pearly words of wisdom for me?' I smiled, and he went out on the court to be beaten. I thought it was our finest moment together. Sometimes, a defeat can be more beautiful and satisfying than certain victories."

1981 Arthur Ashe makes his debut as captain of the United States Davis Cup team on the opening day of the Davis Cup first round against Mexico in Carlsbad, Calif. John McEnroe defeats Jorge Lozano 6-3, 6-1, 6-3 while Raul Ramirez defeats Roscoe Tanner 3-6, 8-6, 6-3, 8-10, 6-3 as the United States and Mexico split the opening two singles matches.

1975 Thirty-two members of the WTA meet in Boston, Mass., and consider boycotting the U.S. Open tennis championships if it goes ahead with its plan to move the playing surface from grass courts to clay courts. The WTA says they preferred a synthetic surface, Sporteze, over the Har-tru clay court surface and fear that unfavorable publicity from boring, drawn-out matches on the slower clay courts would have a long term effect on women's tennis. Says WTA vice president Chris Evert, "All of the girls, without taking a vote, agreed to play another tournament rather than play on clay at Forest Hills. Women's tennis is more exciting on a faster surface."

1988 Boris Becker needs 3 hours, 4 minutes in 104-degree on-court temperatures to defeat Emilio Sanchez 7-5, 6-4, 2-6, 6-4 in the final of the Newsweek Champions Cup in Indian Wells, Calif.

2006 The USTA, the ATP and the Sony Ericsson WTA Tour announce that electronic line calling technology, along with a player challenge system, will become part of professional tennis in North America, with the 2006 U.S. Open being the first major to introduce instant replay technology and player challenges and the NASDAQ-100 Open being the first WTA Tour and ATP event to utilize the technology and on-court challenges.

2008 Andy Roddick defeats world No. 2 Rafael Nadal 7-6 (5), 6-2 in the quarterfinals of the Dubai Duty Free Open and, following the match in the post-match press conference, announces an end to his 20-month coaching relationship with Hall of Famer Jimmy Connors. "I have the most respect for Jimmy Connors," says Roddick. "I thank him for his time. It was difficult for him to do it part time. He maybe did not exactly get the results he wanted, but at the same time he was retired even before we started. We are amicable, we are friends, and I am thankful for what he has been able to give me and that he took time out of retirement to give me good things." Connors, a winner of 109 tour titles—including five U.S. Open titles, signs on to work with Roddick following Wimbledon in 2006, when Roddick is in a relative slump in his career. "He helped me play up the court and adjust my game," Roddick says. "He's helped my backhand a ton—it's a lot more solid—and fighting spirit. When we got together I was as close to being down and out as I have ever been. I really credit him with getting me back into the top five and into a Grand Slam final."

2001 Hours after Pete Sampras is defeated by Andrew Ilie of Australia 3-6, 7-6 (2), 6-4 in the first round of the Franklin Templeton Classic in Scottsdale, Ariz., Andre Agassi joins his rival on the sidelines, losing in the first round to Francisco Clavet of Spain 6-1, 6-7(2), 7-5, marking the first time since 1989 that both Sampras and Agassi lose in the first round of the same tournament.

1991 Calling it "a huge victory," Jim Grabb, upsets John McEnroe, the brother of his doubles partner Patrick, 7-6 (7), 7-5 in the second round of the Newsweek Champions Cup in Indian Wells, Calif. Says the No. 73-ranked Grabb, "When (Bjorn) Borg and McEnroe used to play, I rooted for McEnroe, and there's a bit of baggage that comes with that."

1993 Saying "the more you win, the more unbeatable you feel," Jim Courier defeats defending champion Michael Chang 6-4, 6-4 in the semifinals of the Newsweek Champions Cup in Indian Wells, Calif. Says Chang of Courier, "His forehand is a weapon, but so is his attitude."

March 7

1960 Ivan Lendl, the man who plays more major singles final than any player in tennis history, is born in Ostrava, Czechoslovakia. Lendl reaches 19 major singles finals—winning eight titles, including three straight U.S. Open titles from 1985 to 1987. Lendl breaks through to win his first major title at the 1984 French Open, coming back from a two-sets-to-love deficit in the final to beat John McEnroe. Lendl also wins in Paris in 1986 and 1987. He wins two Australian titles in 1989 and 1990, but is unsuccessful with his career odyssey of winning Wimbledon, losing in the 1986 and 1987 finals.

2004 Playing in his 223rd career ATP tournament, Vince Spadea finally wins his first ATP singles title, defeating Nicolas Kiefer 7-5, 6-7 (5), 6-3 in the final of the Franklin Templeton Tennis Classic in Scottsdale, Ariz. Says Spadea, "I am very excited and it's a great win for me....A better late than never thing. I didn't think there was that much of a monkey on my back. I didn't think there was that kind of pressure, like I had been to so many finals and it was getting ridiculous. But I was a former top 20 player and you can't find many players that have reached that level without having a title....To win a title, to beat Andy (Roddick) and James (Blake) along the way, and looking comfortable to close it out, and then having to dig as deep as I've ever had to dig and to finish it off is wonderful. I have to look in the Thesaurus for a better word to say."

1987 Seventeen-year-old Steffi Graf needs only 58 minutes to defeat Chris Evert Lloyd 6-1, 6-2 to win the Lipton Championships in Key Biscayne, Fla. Graf's win comes after she beats world's No. 1 Martina Navratilova 6-2, 6-2 in the semifinals. Following the match, Evert Lloyd praises the German teenager, saying she has the game to win all four major tournaments. Says Evert Lloyd, "I don't want to predict who's going to finish No. 1 this year. Whoever it is will have their work cut out for them. But there is no reason why Steffi can't win all the major tournaments. She will be very, very hard to beat this year."

1993 World No. 1 Jim Courier defeats No. 14 Wayne Ferreira 6-3, 6-3, 6-1 in the final of the Newsweek Champions Cup in Indian Wells, Calif., "I got a lot of free points" says Courier who benefits from 51 unforced errors from Ferreira.

March 8

1980 John McEnroe and Jose-Luis Clerc complete one of the longest matches in tennis history—described in wire reports as lasting six-and-a-half hours (no official length of match found)—as Clerc wins a 3-hour, 9-minute, 24-game fourth set in his 6-3, 6-2, 4-6, 13-11 Davis Cup win over the No. 2-ranked McEnroe as Argentina takes a 2-0 lead over the United States in Buenos Aires, Argentina. McEnroe and Clerc's match is postponed the previous evening due to darkness after McEnroe wins the third set. Following his loss, his first career loss in Davis Cup play after 14 previous singles and doubles wins, McEnroe pairs with Peter Fleming to beat Argentina's Carlos Gattiker and Ricardo Cano 6-0, 6-1, 6-4 to cut the U.S. deficit to 2-1.

1981 Needing to sweep the final two matches to avoid a first-round upset by Mexico, Roscoe Tanner and John McEnroe respond without losing a set, defeating Jorge Lozano and Raul Ramirez, respectively, to give the United States a 3-2 win over Mexico in the first round in Carlsbad, Calif. The win is the first for U.S. Captain Arthur Ashe in his first series as U.S. captain.

2008 In the closest match ever between sisters Venus and Serena Williams, Serena saves a match point and defeats big sister Venus 6-3, 3-6, 7-6 (4) in the semifinals of the Bangalore Open in India—the sisters' first visit to India. The meeting is the first between Venus and Serena since 2005 and moves Serena ahead in the rivalry 8-7. Says Serena, "It was definitely hard fought. I need to get refocused in quick time. Neither one of us was playing our best tennis." Says Venus, "She always plays really tough, really challenging. She hit some serves that I really couldn't return."

1987 In a re-match of the U.S. Open men's singles final from the previous September, Miloslav Mecir turns the tables on Ivan Lendl and upsets the world No. 1 7-5, 6-2, 7-5 in the final of the Lipton Championships in Key Biscayne, Fla. Says Mecir of the difference between the two matches, "Today I played much better and had much better confidence... I just wanted to play better than at the Open and I think I was more fit today. I was running well and hitting my passing shots well."

1992 Michael Chang defeats Andrei Chesnokov 6-3, 6-4, 7-5 to win the Newsweek Champions Cup in Indian Wells, Calif. Chesnokov plays the final in noticeable pain, after injuring his back while doing the backstroke in a pool following his third-round upset of world No. 1 Jim Courier. Says

Chang of Chesnokov's injury, "I was trying to get it out of my head that he was hurt. I wanted to close it out as fast as I could. When it got to the third set, I didn't want it to slip away."

2008 Andy Roddick tops a week of excellent tennis beating Feliciano Lopez of Spain 6-7 (8), 6-4, 6-2 to win the Dubai Duty Free Open in the United Arab Emirates, his 25th career ATP singles title. Roddick does not drop his serve throughout the entire tournament, highlighted by victories over world No. 2 Rafael Nadal and world No. 3 Novak Djokovic. Says Roddick, "This is as well as I've played." Roddick, playing in Dubai for the first time, is the first American to win the tournament title.

1995 Two-time champion Jim Courier loses in the second round of the Newsweek Champions Cup in Indian Wells, Calif., falling to No. 34-ranked Carlos Costa of Spain 7-6 (6), 6-3. Says Courier, "Losing is never easy, but I'm at a stage right now where I feel I can handle it."

March 9

2008 In the tallest singles final in the history of professional tennis, six-foot-six Sam Querrey of the United States wins his first ATP singles title, defeating six-foot-seven South African qualifier Kevin Anderson 4-6, 6-3, 6-4 in the final of the Tennis Channel Open in Las Vegas. Says the 20-year-old Querrey, "I started playing better as the match went on. You have to fight your way through and when you have the opportunities, don't make errors. It takes a little time to get into rhythm against a guy who hits it so hard and heavy. He was just bombing it in there."

1980 In the stifling heat of Buenos Aires, John McEnroe is defeated by Guillermo Vilas 6-2, 4-6, 6-3, 2-6, 6-4 in a four-and-a-half hour marathon to clinch Argentina's 4-1 victory over the United States, ending the U.S. hopes for a third straight Davis Cup title. The match comes one day after McEnroe endures five hours on the court in winning his rain-delayed 6-3, 6-2, 4-6, 13-11 loss to Jose-Luis Clerc—McEnroe's first Davis Cup loss—and his 6-0, 6-1, 6-4 win with Peter Fleming over Carlos Gattiker and Ricardo Cano. Says U.S. Captain Tony Trabert of McEnroe, "He's disappointed, of course. The four-setter with Clerc and this one with Vilas were both tremendous matches and long ones, too. You can't play in this kind of heat very long. It's tough staying out there that long and then losing. McEnroe doesn't play as well yet on clay courts as he does on faster surfaces." The series ultimately becomes Trabert's final tie as U.S. Davis Cup captain as he is replaced by Arthur Ashe later in the year.

1971 No. 1 seed Rod Laver wins his opening round match at the Australian Open, defeating Colin Dibley 7-5, 6-3, 6-1. Defending champion Arthur Ashe needs five set to overcome Australian Ray Ruffels 6-4, 6-1, 6-7, 0-6, 7-5.

1986 Jimmy Arias defeats Raul Viver 6-3, 6-1, 6-4 in the fifth and decisive match as the United States defeats Ecuador 3-2 in the Davis Cup first round in Guayaquil, Ecuador. The series is the first for Tom Gorman as U.S. Davis Cup captain.

1991 World No. 5 Guy Forget upsets top-ranked Stefan Edberg 6-4, 6-4 to advance to the final of the Newsweek Champions Cup in Indian Wells, Calif. Jim Courier also advances into the final defeating Michael Stich 6-3, 6-2.

March 10

2008 A sell-out crowd of 19,690 that includes golf legend Tiger Woods pack Madison Square Garden in New York City for the NetJets Showdown exhibition match between Roger Federer and Pete Sampras. Federer, an owner of 12 major singles titles, edges 14-time major singles titlist Sampras in a third-set tie-breaker 6-3, 6-7 (4), 7-6 (6) in the sometimes competitive celebration of tennis. Says Sampras, "It was a great night for tennis." Writes the Associated Press of the match, "There were moments when, if you squinted a bit, you would have sworn that was the Sampras of old, rather than an old Sampras. There were moments when, if you listened to the whip of the racket through the air, you would have been absolutely sure Federer was giving it his all. And then there were moments when, as you watched Sampras throw his racket to the ground in mock disgust or saw Federer raise an index finger to celebrate four aces in a single game, it didn't really matter whether this match counted or not." Says Federer after the match, "I don't think winning or losing was really the issue tonight. I think we both tried to do our best and have a fun night, and that's what it turned out to be."

1991 Twenty-year-old Jim Courier, ranked No. 26 in the world, wins his second career singles title, defeating No. 5 ranked Guy Forget 4-6, 6-3, 4-6, 6-3, 7-6 (4) to win the Newsweek Champions Cup in Indian Wells, Calif. "To win it—and it sounds like a cliché—but it's a big honor for me," says Courier.

2006 The "champions" tennis circuit returns to the United States for the first time since 2001 as the Outback Champions Series begins in Naples, Fla., as Mats Wilander defeats Aaron Krickstein 2-6, 6-2, 10-2 in the opening round robin match of the series. Tour co-founder Jim Courier defeats Mikael Pernfors 6-2, 6-2 and, in the final match of the day, Pat Cash surprises John McEnroe 2-6, 7-6(5), 10-6 in the Champions Tie-break.

1971 No. 1 seed Rod Laver is upset by Mark Cox of Great Britain 6-3, 4-6, 6-3, 7-6 in the third round of the Australian Open in Sydney. No. 3 seed and fellow Australian John Newcombe is also upset, losing to Marty Riessen 7-6, 1-6, 7-6, 7-6.

March 11

2007 Roger Federer's bid to break Guillermo Vilas's ATP record of 46 straight wins in men's tennis ends in his opening round match at the Pacific Life Open in Indian Wells, Calif. Federer, the No. 1 player in the world, is stunned by No. 60 Guillermo Canas of Argentina 7-5, 6-2, ending his match win streak at 41. "He just kept the ball in play and moving me around," Federer says. "He put me away when he had to. He played the perfect match. The right guy won." Canas, recently reinstated into professional tennis after serving a 15-month suspension due to breaking the ATP's banned drug policy, is a "lucky loser" entrant into the event after losing in the qualifying rounds of the tournament. Says Canas, "It's my first Masters Series after I start again and to beat the world No. 1 and to play like this is great for me." Says Federer of the blown match win streak, "Sooner or later it had to happen, so it's OK. It's no problem."

1990 Thirteen-year-old Jennifer Capriati's debut tournament comes to an end as she is defeated by Gabriela Sabatini 6-4, 7-5 in the final of the Virginia Slims of Florida in Boca Raton, Fla. "It's been the greatest week of my life," says Capriati of her first WTA tournament. "It was exciting just to make the finals...I was tired at the end."

1991 Steffi Graf's record reign of 186 weeks as the No. 1 ranked player comes to an end as Monica Seles overtakes Graf as the No. 1 player. Seles goes on to hold the No. 1 ranking for a total of 178 weeks during her career.

1985 Paraguayan riot police storm the court to protect French players after Yannick Noah, star player of the French Davis Cup team, and his captain Jean Paul Loth, charge onto the court and allegedly strike a linesman, Roberto Velazquez, who the French accuse of making distracting noises against their teammate Henri Leconte. With Leconte trailing Victor Pecci 6-3, 1-1 in the fifth and decisive match of the France vs. Paraguay series, Noah and Loth charge the court and confront the linesman. The Associated Press reports that "There was danger of a riot as many of the more than 3,000 fans in the national stadium on the outskirts of the capital surged out of the stands toward the Frenchmen. Policemen with sticks moved in and, according to witnesses, struck at both the French players and the fans, finally restoring order." Noah denies hitting the linesman, stating to the Associated Press, "We had a lot of problems with the umpires and with the crowds during the whole tie...One of the linesmen was making a noise every time Henri was trying to serve—every time. We went to talk to him, and that was it...This guy was too much. If he was some guy from the crowd, we wouldn't bother, but he was a linesman. He's a player. Two years ago, when we played Paraguay (in Davis Cup), he was a player." After officials threaten to postpone the matches, order is restored and Pecci goes on to win the decisive match 6-3, 6-4, 3-6, 7-5. Pandemonium breaks out after Pecci's win as French players, officials and media run for their safety. Says Noah, "At the end of the match, some of the guys (spectators) jumped on the team, and one of the members of the French press was knocked out. We had to send him to a hospital. It was scary. When we left the stadium, we had police following us all over."

1924 Bill Tilden announces that he will not represent the United States in the upcoming Olympic Games in Paris. Tilden's reasoning is that even if he wanted to play for the United States, the U.S. Olympic rule that forbids athletes from writing for newspapers prevents him from competing since he is contracted to write two articles per week. Writes the *New York Times*, "The tennis champion had never definitely announced that he would go abroad this year if picked for the Olympic team. Two months ago, Tilden said he did not think he would go because of the sharp competition expected in the national singles and in the Davis Cup matches. He said he regarded the Davis Cup competition more important than the Olympics and that he felt he could husband his strength for those matches in the event he is to be one of the contestants." The USLTA also had enacted a similar rule for amateur tennis, but it is not scheduled to take effect until Jan. 1, 1925.

1994 The new $20 million Tennis Center at Crandon Park in Key Biscayne, Fla., featuring a 13,800-seat permanent stadium, debuts on the opening day of the Lipton Championships. Karin Kschwendt of Luxembourg defeats Kathy Rinaldi-Stunkel 6-3, 6-4 in the first match played in the new stadium.

2006 In one of the most stunning and disastrous reversals of fortune, Michael Chang, playing in his "champions" circuit debut at the Outback Champions Series event in Naples, Fla., leads Mikael Pernfors 6-0, 5-0 in a round-robin match, only two lose two games in a row and then ruptures his left achilles tendon running for a drop shot. Chang is taken off of the court in a stretcher and loses the match 0-6, 2-5, ret., and is forced to withdraw from the competition. He is not able to play competitive tennis for approximately 18 months.

March 12

1983 In his semifinal match with Vitas Gerulaitis at the Belgian Indoor Championships in Brussels, Peter McNamara of Australia splits his shoe, tries to fit into a shoe that belongs to a ball boy, then uses a pair of shoes rushed from a nearby tennis shop, and defeats his American opponent 6-2, 7-6. McNamara goes on to win the title the next day in the final, handing Ivan Lendl only his second loss in 72 matches on an indoor court by a 6-4, 4-6, 7-6 (4) margin.

1997 Pete Sampras loses his first match of the 1997 season, falling to Bohdan Ulirach of the Czech Republic 7-6 (5), 7-5 in his opening match at the Newsweek Champions Cup in Indian Wells, Calif. Says Sampras who starts the year 17-0, "It was pretty ugly. I just made error after error. ... I was missing a lot of ground strokes, normal shots. I just wasn't very comfortable out there."

1971 Margaret Court needs only 32 minutes to defeat fellow Australian Lesley Hunt 6-0, 6-3 in the semifinals of the Australian Open in Sydney, Australia. Court requires only 10 minutes to win the first set of the match. Thirty-six-year-old Ken Rosewall defeats Tom Okker 6-2, 7-6, 6-4 to advance into the men's singles final.

1989 Ivan Lendl wins his 75th career singles title, defeating Stefan Edberg 6-2, 6-3 in the final of the Eagle Classic in Scottsdale, Ariz.

1995 Pete Sampras and Andre Agassi set up a dream final in the Newsweek Champions Cup by registering semifinal victories over Stefan Edberg and Boris Becker respectively. Sampras defeats Edberg 4-6, 6-3, 6-4, calling Edberg, "one of the classier guys I have ever played" following the match, while Agassi defeats Becker 6-4, 7-6 (4).

1996 Jennifer Capriati, playing her second tournament in her second comeback attempt to professional tennis, loses to fellow American Chanda Rubin 6-3, 6-3 in the round of 16 of the Newsweek Champions Cup in Indian Wells, Calif. Says the 19-year-old Capriati of her form versus Rubin's, "She's been playing and I haven't."

March 13

1998 Serena Williams wins the Evert Cup in Indian Wells, Calif., with a 6-3, 3-6, 7-5 win over Steffi Graf. The 17-year-old Williams comes back from a 2-4 deficit in the third set to win her second title and 11th straight match in the last month. Says Williams, ranked No. 21, following the match, "I definitely think in the next couple of months I'll be in the top 10. The only thing that can keep me away from the top 10 is if I quit playing tournaments for the rest of the year. Other than that, I definitely see myself there soon and farther."

1971 Evonne Goolagong advances into a major final for the first time in her career, defeating Winnie Shaw of Scotland 7-6, 6-1 in the semifinals of the Australian Open in Sydney, Australia. Defending men's singles champion Arthur Ashe defeats Bob Lutz 6-4, 6-4, 7-5 in the men's singles semifinals.

1996 Playing his second match as the world's No. 1 ranked player, Thomas Muster is defeated in his opening round match at the Newsweek Champions Cup in Indian Wells, Calif., losing to Adrian Voinea of Romania 6-3, 7-5. "For me, being No. 1 is maybe the same as Pete (Sampras) winning Wimbledon six times in a row," says Muster of his No. 1 status. "It's a personal thing, a dream come true."

1995 In their 14th career match-up and a re-match of the Australian Open men's singles final six weeks earlier, Pete Sampras defeats Andre Agassi 7-5, 6-3, 7-5 in a sun-down final of the Newsweek Champions Cup in Indian Wells, Calif., avenging his loss in Australia. "If we battle for the next 10 years, it will be great for the game," says Sampras. "It's different when I play Andre. It's like two heavyweights going at it."

1988 Gabriela Sabatini of Argentina ends an 11-match losing streak to Steffi Graf and beats her German rival for the first time to win the Virginia Slims of Florida in Boca Raton, Fla. Sabatini's 2-6, 6-3, 6-1 win over the world No. 1 ends up being one of only three losses for Graf during her eventual "Golden Grand Slam" season. Says the 17-year-old Sabatini, who beat No. 3-ranked Chris Evert in the semifinals, "I guess this has been the best week of my career. This week has given me a lot of confidence for the future. My goal is to be No. 1 someday. That's what I work for."

March 14

1971 Margaret Court and Ken Rosewall win singles titles at the Australian Open at White City in Sydney, Australia. Court defeats first-time major finalist and fellow Australian Evonne Goolagong 2-6, 7-6 (1), 7-5 to win her country's national championship for the 10th time in the last 12 years. Goolagong leads 5-2 in the final set before she is beset with cramping in her legs. Says Court of the final-set deficit, "I thought I'd had it. I don't think I played particularly well, but when Evonne got the cramp, I took advantage." Court's title is her sixth straight major singles title on the heels of her 1970 Grand Slam sweep of all four majors. Rosewall defeats defending champion Arthur Ashe 6-1, 7-5, 6-3, benefiting from 13 Ashe double-faults. Ashe hits four double-faults alone in the sixth game of the match as Rosewall wins the first set in just 19 minutes. Says Rosewall, "I think Arthur lost confidence when his service was not going too well."

1999 One day after defeating Gustavo Kuerten to clinch the world's No. 1 ranking, Carlos Moya is defeated by Mark Philippoussis 5-7, 6-4, 6-4, 4-6, 6-2 in the final of the Newsweek Champions Cup in Indian Wells, Calif. "To be No. 1 and then win the title on top of that would have been the perfect beginning, but today he's better than me so that's it," says Moya after the match.

1966 In a match described by Reuters as "believed to be the longest major tournament match on record," Marty Mulligan of Australia defeats Francois Jauffret of France 9-11, 6-2, 7-5, 2-6, 12-10 in "more than five hours" to win the singles title at Barranquilla, Colombia.

1994 Andre Agassi defeats Boris Becker 6-2, 7-5 in the third round of the Lipton Championships in Key Biscayne, Fla. Down 2-6, 0-2, Becker hands his racquet to ball-girl Stephanie Flaherty who plays a point with Agassi and gains mini-celebrity status at the tournament.

1996 Steffi Graf needs 2 hours, 44 minutes to fight off a bad back and defeats Lindsay Davenport 6-7 (6), 7-6 (3), 6-4 in the semifinals of the State Farm Evert Cup in Indian Wells, Calif. "Every match she plays, there is something wrong with her," says Davenport, "but even when she is so hurt, she always plays real well."

March 15

1987 In one of the strangest Davis Cup matches in the history of the event, No. 285th-ranked Hugo Chapacu of Paraguay defeats American Jimmy Arias 6-4, 6-1, 5-7, 3-6, 9-7 in 5 hours, 5 minutes to square the United States vs. Paraguay Davis Cup first round series at 2-2 in Asuncion, Paraguay. Chapacu is unable to convert a match point at 5-4 in the third set, but comes back from a 1-5 fifth-set deficit and saves three match points to win and force a fifth and decisive match in the series. Writes the Associated Press of the post-match scene, "Jubilant Paraguayans, beating drums and banging tambourines, invaded the center court at the Paraguay Yacht and Golf Club after Chapacu's victory, carrying the 24-year-old off the court on their shoulders. Arias, a 22-year-old from New York, was knocked to the ground in the melee, but later got up, apparently unhurt, and congratulated Chapacu."

1996 Both Pete Sampras and Andre Agassi lose chances of recapturing the No. 1 ranking in the world from Thomas Muster of Austria with quarterfinal losses at the Newsweek Champions Cup. Paul Haarhuis stuns world No. 2 Sampras 7-5, 6-7 (5), 6-1, while Agassi, ranked No. 3, loses to Michael Chang 6-7 (3), 6-2, 6-1. Sampras sums up the lost opportunity to reclaim the world No. 1 ranking by simply saying, "C'est la vie."

1998 Tempermental Marcelo Rios of Chile loses a second-set tie-break in 32 points—the only set he would lose all week—and wins the Newsweek Champions Cup in Indian Wells, Calif., defeating Britain's Greg Rusedski 6-3, 6-7 (15-17), 7-6 (4), 6-4. Says Rios of his reputation as one of the meanest players in tennis, "I'm nice sometimes. In Chile, there's even a lot of kids who want to be like me."

1927 Bill Tilden does not give up a game in winning 24 straight games in his two singles matches to advance to the quarterfinals of the Southeastern Tennis Championships in Ortega, Fla. After beating James Lewin of Kansas City 6-0, 6-0 in his second-round morning match, Tilden also double-bagels William Barrett of Shreveport, La., in his third-round match. Tilden goes on to win the title on March 18, defeating George Lott in the final 6-4, 6-1, 6-3.

March 16

1987 In a match completed at 2:35 am, Victor Pecci of Paraguay defeats Aaron Krickstein 6-2, 8-6, 9-7 to give Paraguay a startling 3-2 upset of the United States in the Davis Cup first round in Asuncion, Paraguay. Pecci's win comes after 285th-ranked Hugo Chapacu upsets Jimmy Arias 6-4, 6-1, 5-7, 3-6, 9-7—saving three match points—in 5 hours, 5 minutes to pull Paraguay even with the United States at 2-2. Pecci's win creates a melee on court as fans envelop the court following match point and carry Pecci—along with teammates Hugo Chapacu and Francisco Gonzalez—around the court. Says U.S. Davis Cup Captain Tom Gorman, "I think the world of tennis must recognize that Paraguay is tough to beat playing in Asuncion. I don't know what we could have done more than we did. Naturally, I have a tremendous feeling of disappointment."

1992 American qualifier Robbie Weiss, a former NCAA singles champion from Pepperdine University ranked No. 289 in the world, registers one of the biggest ranking upsets ever in men's tennis, defeating No. 2-ranked Stefan Edberg 6-3, 3-6, 6-4 in the third round of the Lipton Championships in Key Biscayne, Fla. Says Edberg following the match, "Robbie played a good match. I played a poor match."

1996 Steffi Graf wins her 96th career singles title in her first tournament appearance in 1996, defeating Conchita Martinez 7-6 (5), 7-6 (5) in the final of the State Farm Evert Cup in Indian Wells, Calif.

2007 The French Tennis Federation announces that it will offer equal prize money to men and women starting at the 2007 French Open, becoming the last of the four major tournaments to announce equal prize money offerings for men and women. Says French Tennis Federation President Christian Bimes in a statement, "It has been our objective since 2005. Last year, the first step was to award equal rewards to the winners of the men's and women's singles. In 2007, the parity will be total." Says Amelie Mauresmo of France, the No. 1 ranked woman in the world, "It's very good news for women's tennis and for women in general terms. As a Frenchwoman, I'm happy and proud the French Open organizers took such a decision."

2008 An angry Andy Roddick breaks two racquets and, in a temper fit, hits a ball out of the stadium in his 6-4, 6-4 loss to his ex-coach Dean Goldfine's new pupil Tommy Haas at the Pacific Life Open in Indian Wells, Calif.

March 17

1927 U.S. President Calvin Coolidge conducts the draw for the 1927 Davis Cup competition on the front lawn of the White House in Washington, D.C. Coolidge picks the card with Czechoslovakia on it, which is drawn against Greece in the first round of the European Zone. Writes the *New York Times* of the event, "Surrounded by diplomats from the twenty-five nations entered into the tournament, he drew the card bearing the name of Czechoslovakia from the bowl of the trophy. Joseph C. Grew, Under Secretary of State, then picked Greece, which was paired with the nation of the President's choice. The various diplomats then formed in line and each withdrew the name of one nation from the cup." An ironic event occurs when the representative from Belgium selects his own nation from the cup. Twenty one nations are placed in the European Zone and four in the American Zone. The winner of each zone would meet each other and the winner taking on the United States, the holder of the Davis Cup, in the Challenge Round.

1979 John McEnroe and Peter Fleming make their Davis Cup debut as a doubles team, defeating Ivan Molina and Orlando Agudelo 6-4, 6-0, 6-4 giving the United States a match-clinching 3-0 lead over Colombia in the Davis Cup first round at the Cleveland Skating Club in Cleveland, Ohio. McEnroe and Fleming become arguably the greatest doubles combination the United States has ever fielded in Davis Cup play, ending their patriotic partnership in 1984 with a 14-1 record. They win 14 straight Davis Cup doubles matches—a record among U.S. Davis Cup doubles teams—and represent the U.S. on Davis Cup final-winning teams in 1981 and 1982. Their final Davis Cup doubles match is their only defeat—a 7-5, 5-7, 6-2, 7-5 loss to Stefan Edberg and Anders Jarryd in the title-clinching win for Sweden over the United States in the 1984 Davis Cup final in Goteborg, Sweden.

1992 John McEnroe, whose grandparents on his father's side are born in Ireland, receives no luck of the Irish on St. Patrick's Day in what becomes his final match ever at the Lipton Championships in Key Biscayne, Fla., losing to Richard Krajicek 7-6 (3), 6-4 in the third round.

1996 In a final played with on-court temperatures surpassing 110 degrees, Michael Chang defeats No. 68th-ranked Paul Haarhuis of the Netherlands 7-5, 6-1, 6-1 to win the Newsweek Champions Cup in Indian Wells, Calif. "Today I could actually feel the heat coming through the soles of my shoes," says Chang following the match. "They announced 110 degrees, but I was told it was 130 degrees. They just didn't want to scare anybody."

2001 Booed as she enters the court for her final round match against Kim Clijsters at the Tennis Masters Series–Indian Wells, Serena Williams withstands the harsh fan and media allegations of match-fixing by defeating Clijsters 4-6, 6-4, 6-2. Fans react severely to the Williams family after Venus Williams abruptly withdraws from her semifinal match with Serena the day before. "In the beginning, I was a little shocked," Serena says. "Then I was like, 'Wow, this is getting old. Move on to something new...' I prayed to God just to help me be strong, not even to win, but to be strong, not listen to the crowd." The withdrawal and aftermath comes on the heels of a tabloid story in the *National Enquirer* stating that Williams' father Richard fixed the 2000 Wimbledon semifinal between the two sisters.

2007 Daniela Hantuchova of Slovakia wins her second Pacific Life Open championship in Indian Wells, Calif.—and her second career title—defeating Svetlana Kuznetsova of Russia 6-3, 6-4 in the women's singles final. "I think all the best things in life are worth waiting for, moments like this," says Hantuchova, who wins her first title in Indian Wells five years earlier. "I guess all the hard work and everything I had to go through makes the victory that much sweeter."

March 18

1972 Twenty-nine-year-old Dennis Ralston makes his debut as U.S. Davis Cup captain as the United States takes a 2-0 lead against the Caribbean Commonwealth in their eventual 4-1 victory at the National Arena in Kingston, Jamaica. Erik van Dillen defeats Lancelot Lumsden 6-1, 6-4, 6-2 while Tom Gorman beats Richard Russell 6-4, 6-2, 7-5. Ralston, however, is not the youngest man to captain a U.S. Davis Cup team as he is nine months older than Charles Garland, who first skippers the U.S. Davis Cup team in 1927.

1984 A bomb scare forces the Rotterdam men's singles final between Ivan Lendl and Jimmy Connors to be called off. Lendl sweeps through the first set, 6-0, and breaks service in the first game of the second set when the police, reacting to an anonymous telephone call, order the evacuation of the Ahoy Sports Hall. The caller, claiming to represent an anti-capitalism movement, tells the police that a bomb had been placed close to center court. A search does not yield any suspicious objects, and spectators are then allowed to return to their seats. However, the crowd is then informed that Lendl and Connors would not be resuming their match. Wim Buitendijk, the organizer of the tournament, fails to persuade Lendl to stay and finish the match. He says Connors may have been persuaded to resume the game but "Lendl was not prepared to take any risks."

1992 Jennifer Capriati topples world No. 1 Monica Seles 6-2, 7-5 in the quarterfinals of the Lipton Championships in Key Biscayne, Fla., and avenging her "nightmare" loss to Seles in a third-set tie-break in the semifinals of the 1991 U.S. Open.

2001 In the first all-American Tennis Masters Series—Indian Wells men's final in six years, Andre Agassi defeats two-time champion Pete Sampras 7-6 (7-5), 7-5, 6-1, to capture his first Indian Wells title. Agassi and Sampras also play in the last all-American men's final at Indian Wells in 1995, with Sampras winning, 7-5, 6-3, 7-5.

2006 Maria Sharapova rolls over Elena Dementieva 6-1, 6-2 to win the women's singles title at the Pacific Life Open in Indian Wells, Calif.

March 19

1988 Hana Mandlikova blows five match points, loses her cool and is defeated by No. 289-ranked Sabine Auer of West Germany 4-6, 7-6 (3), 7-5 in the third round of the Lipton Championships. Mandlikova is so upset by an apparent blown call by linesperson Dessie Samuels at 5-5 in the third set that after losing the match, she slams a ball that barely misses Samuels. "I don't regret it," says Mandlikova after the match. "You're struggling out there for three hours. The ball is five yards out and she calls it in. If it wasn't such an important moment, I wouldn't be so upset, but obviously, I couldn't get over it."

1989 Miloslav Mecir becomes the last player to win an ATP tour event with a wooden racquet when he defeats Yannick Noah 3-6, 2-6, 6-1, 6-2, 6-3 in the men's singles final at the Newsweek Champions Cup in Indian Wells, Calif.

1927 Hazel Hotchkiss Wightman wins the singles, doubles and mixed doubles titles—all in one day—at the National Women's Indoor Tennis Championships in her hometown of Brookline, Mass. In the singles final, she defeats Margaret Blake 6-0, 2-6, 6-4 and in the doubles final, she and Marion Zinderstein Jessup defeat Blake and Edith Sigourney 8-6, 1-6, 6-3. In a curiously held mixed doubles tournament, she and G. Peabody Gardner defeat Sarah Palfrey and Malcolm Hill 6-2, 5-7, 6-2.

2005 Kim Clijsters defeats world No. 1 Lindsay Davenport 6-4, 4-6, 6-2 to win the Pacific Life Open in Indian Wells, Calif. The tournament marks only the second tournament since she makes a return to the WTA Tour following surgery on her right wrist that sidelines her for most of 2004.

2006 Roger Federer becomes the first player to win the men's singles title at the Pacific Life Open in Indian Wells, Calif., for a third straight year when he defeats James Blake 7-5, 6-3, 6-0 in the final.

1994 Steffi Graf wins the women's singles title at the Lipton Championships, defeating Natasha Zvereva 4-6, 6-1, 6-2. "I don't expect to win everything, but I know I can do it," Graf says following the victory. "That's what is important, to know that you can."

March 20

1994 In one of the sport's best displays of sportsmanship, Andre Agassi agrees to delay the start of his Lipton Championships singles final against Pete Sampras after Sampras suffers from a stomach ailment, then loses to Sampras 5-7, 6-3, 6-3 in a hard fought final. The rules would have permitted Agassi to claim the match in a walk-over, but Agassi chooses not to be given the match—a decision that costs him $114,000 in prize money. Says Agassi, "If I can't beat the best player in the world, I don't deserve the trophy. And I certainly don't deserve it if I can't beat him when he's sick." Says Sampras of Agassi's gesture, "He showed me a lot of class, and it's something I'll never forget." Sampras wakes up feeling sick and blames a pasta dinner. He receives intravenous fluids for 90 minutes before taking the court on an empty stomach. "I'm as surprised as everyone in this room that I won," Sampras says to the assembled media in the post-match press conference.

1992 Michael Chang defeats Jim Courier 6-2, 6-4 in the semifinals of the Lipton Championships in Key Biscayne, knocking Courier out of the No. 1 ranking after his initial ascent to the mountain-top of men's tennis forty days earlier. "It's certainly nice to be No. 1 and I wish I could be there forever, but the reality is that sometimes you have to relinquish it," says Courier. "It's been a pretty rough ride," he says of his initial reign as world No. 1. "My mind has been on too many things besides tennis, and now I'm trying to get it back."

1967 Fifty-two-year-old Gardnar Mulloy loses in the opening round of the Monte Carlo Open, falling to Canadian Davis Cupper Keith Carpenter 6-4, 4-6, 7-5.

1970 After strong Australian sunshine dries up the soggy grass courts of Sydney's White City courts faster than expected, tournament officials at the Dunlop Tennis Championships hastily seek out Roger Taylor and Arthur Ashe to play their quarterfinal match. Taylor is found at a local landromat doing his laundry, while Arthur Ashe is at a local movie theatre, watching the movie *Paint Your Wagon*. Taylor then beats Ashe 6-3, 8-6, 6-4 to advance in to the semifinals. Taylor loses the next day in the semifinals to Rod Laver.

March 21

1992 Despite a pro-Sabatini crowd that sing *Don't Cry for Me Argentina*, Arantxa Sanchez Vicario defeats Gabriela Sabatini 6-1, 6-4 in the women's singles final at the Lipton Championships in Key Biscayne, Fla. "It was funny because everyone was shouting for Sabatini," says Sanchez Vicario of the fans singing the famed song from the play *Evita*. "I laughed at first and then I concentrated on the game."

2008 Maria Sharapova loses her first match of the 2008 season, losing to fellow Russian Svetlana Kuznetsova 6-3, 5-7, 6-3 in her 19th match of the year in the semifinals of the Pacific Life Open in Indian Wells, Calif. Says Kuznetsova of ending Sharapova's streak, "It feels great. I don't think Maria plays like always she can play. Neither did I. But I think it was very good, interesting third set." Says Sharapova, "I'm human. You know, I'm allowed to make a few mistakes in my life and in my career. That kind of was the story today."

1993 World No. 2 Pete Sampras makes a major move toward his goal of moving up to the No. 1 ranking in the world defeating Mal Washington 6-3, 6-2 to win the Lipton Championships in Key Biscayne, Fla.

2008 Playing the final-set tie-break with a hole in his shoe—and his sock— Mardy Fish outlasts No. 7 ranked David Nalbandian 6-3, 6-7 (5), 7-6 (4) in the quarterfinals of the Pacific Life Open in Indian Wells, Calif. Fish, the 2004 Olympic silver medalist ranked No. 98 in the world, holds two match points in the 10th game of the final set—but squanders them—then has his serve immediately broken, giving Nalbandian the opportunity to serve out the match. Fish then breaks Nalbandian before gutting out the final-set tie break.

2007 In what Charlie Bricker of the *South Florida Sun-Sentinel* calls "one of the more memorable debuts in the 23-year history of this tournament," fourteen-year-old Michelle Larcher de Brito of Portugal defeats U.S. No. 3 Meghan Shaughnessy 3-6, 6-2, 7-6 (3) in the first round of the Sony Ericsson Open in Key Biscayne Fla. "I just went out there and played my best," says de Brito, who at 14 years, two months old is three months older then the event's youngest player to win a match, Jennifer Capriati. "I just try not to worry about who's on the other side of the court. Just try to hit the ball and look for the ball."

March 22

1973 In the first meeting of one of sports most epic rivalries, Chris Evert defeats Martina Navratilova 7-6, 6-3 in the first round of the women's tournament in Akron, Ohio—the first of 80 matches between the two rivals.

2006 American Jamea Jackson becomes a footnote in tennis history after she becomes the first player to challenge a line-call using the new "Hawk Eye" instant replay system in her first-round match with Ashley Harkleroad at the NASDAQ-100 Open in Key Biscayne, Fla. Jackson uses one of her two allowed challenges on the opening point of the second set after seeing a forehand she hits called out. The challenge is referred to another match official, who reviews replays of Jackson's shot and confirms that the ball she hit was out. Says Jackson, "I just wanted to be first." Jackson fights off a match point and beats Harkleroad 7-5, 6-7 (3), 7-5.

2008 Mardy Fish dominates world No. 1 Roger Federer 6-3, 6-2 in 63 minutes in the semifinals of the Pacific Life Open in Indian Wells, Calif. Says the 98th-ranked Fish, "This wasn't, obviously, Roger's best day. But hopefully I had a little something to do with that." Says Federer, "He was just trying to go for everything, and it worked. I didn't even play particularly bad on the break points….Every time he read the right side on the serve, and he kept the ball in play. When he wanted to attack, everything worked. That was just impressive by his side, and I couldn't do much to control it. I didn't even think he served particularly well. It was just impossible to return his first serve, which it normally is anyway. But I couldn't get into his second serves, and that was the disappointing part about today." In the other men's semifinal, Australian Open champion Novak Djokovic defeats defending champion Rafael Nadal 6-3, 6-2. The following day, Djokovic beats Fish for the title 6-2, 5-7, 6-3.

1991 Performing with what Robin Finn of the *New York Times*, describes as "the composure of a fish on a bicycle" Stefan Edberg, the world's No. 1 player, loses in the semifinals of the Lipton Championships to No. 46-ranked David Wheaton 6-3, 6-4. "This is probably my biggest tennis moment for sure," says Wheaton following the match. Jim Courier defeats Richey Reneberg 6-3, 6-4 in the other men's semifinal match.

March 23

1996 Thomas Muster of Austria loses his third match in as many tries as the world's No. 1 player, losing to Nicolas Perreira of Venezuela 7-6, 6-4 in the first round of the Lipton Championships in Key Biscayne, Fla.

1991 Monica Seles overcomes a 0-4, 0-40 second-set deficit to defeat Gabriela Sabatini 6-3, 7-5 to win the Lipton Championships in Key Biscayne, Fla.

1998 World No. 1 Pete Sampras double-faults down match point and is sent packing in the third round of the Lipton Championships, losing to Wayne Ferreira of South Africa 0-6, 7-6 (6), 6-3. "I'm just sitting here just in shock that I lost this match," Sampras says following the loss. "In the first set, he was in another zip code." The loss opens the door for either world No. 2 Petr Korda, world No. 3 Marcelo Rios and world No. 5 Greg Rusedski to seize the No. 1 ranking, which Rios eventually does by winning the event.

1999 One day after clinching his return to the No. 1 world ranking, Pete Sampras is defeated in the quarterfinals of the Lipton Championships in Key Biscayne, Fla., by Richard Krajicek, who defeats Sampras 6-2, 7-6 (6), marking the fourth-straight victory for the Dutchman over the Californian.

1995 Gabriela Sabatini chokes away a 6-1, 5-1 lead against Kimiko Date and loses to the Japanese star 1-6, 7-6 (2), 7-6 (4) in the semifinals of the Lipton Championships in Key Biscayne, Fla. Sabatini hits 18 double-faults in the 3-hour, 5-minute match. Says Date, "I never thought of winning."

2001 Greg Rusedski of Great Britain wins 25 straight points—including the first 20 points of the second set—defeating Nicolas Massu of Chile 6-4, 6-1 in the first round of the Ericsson Open in Key Biscayne, Fla.

1997 Fellow-sixteen year-olds Martina Hingis and Venus Williams compete against each other for the first time in their careers with the No. 2 ranked Hingis defeating the No. 110th ranked Williams 6-4, 6-2 in the third round of the Lipton Championships in Key Biscayne, Fla.

2006 Greg Rusedski of Great Britain opens his first round match at the NASDAQ-100 Open in Key Biscayne, Fla., with five successive double-faults, but recovers to defeat Mikhail Youzhny of Russia 6-3, 6-1.

March 24

1991 No. 18-ranked Jim Courier wins the biggest title of his career to date, defeating David Wheaton 4-6, 6-3, 6-4 in the final of the Lipton Championships in Key Biscayne, Fla. "I feel like I can compete with anybody out there," says Courier following the win, which vaults him into the top 10 for the first time in his career at No. 9.

2000 Jim Courier wins what ultimately becomes his final match on the ATP Tour, defeating 18-year-old David Nalbandian of Argentina 6-3, 3-6, 7-5 in the first round of the Ericsson Open in Key Biscayne, Fla. "This is the golden twilight for a certain period of American tennis, but hopefully the dawning of a new era," says the 29-year-old Courier following the win over Nalbandian, playing his first ATP Tour level match. "What are you going to do? I've been on the tour and this is my 13th year. Pete [Sampras] and [Michael] Chang the same. And Andre [Agassi] has been around even longer. People can't expect us to be around forever. Hopefully we'll be around competitively a few more years, but it's the enjoy-it-while-you-can time of our careers. You start to get limited physically once you get into your 30s." The next day, Courier plays what is his final professional singles match, losing to world No. 7-ranked Thomas Enqvist of Sweden 6-7 (5), 6-3, 6-4.

1927 In a match described by the *New York Times* as "spectacular and bitterly contested," George Lott, the No. 9 ranked American, upsets U.S. No. 1 Bill Tilden 6-3, 0-6, 7-5, 6-3 to win the Halifax Tennis Championships in Ormand Beach, Fla. Writes the *Times*, "Lott stuck stubbornly to his method of going after every return. Long rallies were frequent with Lott winning better than his share. Many of the game went to deuce. The large gallery was on the side of the 20-year-old ninth ranking player."

1990 Sixteen-year-old Monica Seles wins the Lipton Championships in Key Biscayne, Fla.—her second career singles title—defeating Judith Wiesner of Austria 6-1, 6-2 in the final.

1998 Seventeen-year-old Martina Hingis saves two match points and comes back from a 3-5, 15-40 third-set deficit to defeat 16-year-old Serena Williams 6-3, 1-6, 7-6 (4) in the quarterfinals of the Lipton Championships.

March 25

1994 Todd Martin makes his Davis Cup debut at the same time that Tom Gullikson makes his debut as U.S. captain as the United States plays its first round Davis Cup match against India in New Delhi, India. The United States takes a 2-0 lead over the Indians as Martin defeats Leander Paes 6-3, 4-6, 6-1, 7-6, while Jim Courier defeats Zeeshan Ali 6-1, 6-1, 6-2. The U.S. goes on to win the series 5-0 and Martin goes on to become one of the most loyal Davis Cup supporters, never failing to answer the Davis Cup call for the United States. He is the only player to represent the United States every year from 1994 to 2002 and helps the U.S. win the title in 1995.

2001 Eighteen-year-old Andy Roddick, ranked No. 119 in the world, starts the changing of the guard in American tennis as he upsets Pete Sampras 7-6 (2), 6-3 in the third round of the Ericsson Open in Key Biscayne, Fla. Roddick's victory is his first over a player ranked in the top 10. It is the first time Sampras, ranked No. 4, loses to a player outside the Top 100 since losing to No. 205 Karim Alami in the first round of Doha, Qatar in January 1994.

2002 Pete Sampras is defeated by Fernando Gonzalez 7-6 (1), 6-1 in the third round of the Ericsson Open in what eventually becomes his last match at the event.

1990 Nineteen-year-old Andre Agassi defeats Stefan Edberg 6-1, 6-4, 0-6, 6-2 to win the Lipton Championships in Key Biscayne, Fla., for the first time in his career. Agassi goes on to win the tournament a record six times, also winning in 1995, 1996, 2001, 2002 and 2003.

1995 Steffi Graf defeats Kimiko Date 6-1, 6-4 to win the Lipton Championships for a fourth time. The $205,000 first prize puts Graf over the $15 million mark in career earnings.

2006 Defending champion Kim Clijsters loses her opening match at the NASDAQ-100 Open in Key Biscayne, Fla., to No. 54-ranked Jill Craybas of the United States 7-5, 3-6, 7-5. Clijsters double-faults 11 times and commits 78 unforced errors. "It was sort of in my hands," says Clijsters, seeded No. 2. "I was the one making the mistakes. I was just trying to do a little too much."

March 26

1976 Ilie Nastase is defaulted in the quarterfinals of the American Airlines Invitational in Palm Springs, Calif., for stalling, vocal outbursts and continued bad behavior, trailing Roscoe Tanner 6-3, 2-1, 40-0. Nastase spits at a heckling spectator as he leaves the court. Charlie Hare, the tournament referee and a former standout British player from the 1930s, tells the *New York Times* that Nastase crosses the line against Tanner after similar behavior in his previous round match against Dick Stockton. Says Hare, "Let me explain first that I'm an old player. I've been in the Wimbledon finals. I know the game. I am an honorary referee for the tournament and I've had trouble with Nastase all week. I had to go on the court for an hour Wednesday (when Nastase beat Haroon Rahim) and for an hour yesterday (when he beat Stockton). Today, I was forced to sit on the court from the first minute. I've never known any referee, except in Davis Cup, to have this much pressure. (Against Tanner), the first (incident) I had to speak to him, he bowed, giving me his behind. I gave him a warning. In our second altercation, he called me a four-letter word. Nobody can call me that. Then, he actually left the court, sat in a box and put his feet up on the railing. If you leave the scene of the action, under the rules you are defaulted. I had had enough. I had reports on him for three days." Tanner threatens to walk off the court and default the match if Nastase is not kicked out of the tournament. "I had taken out the rule book to show Hare if he hadn't defaulted Nastase for leaving the court, I would have walked away," says Tanner. "For a long time, no referee would stand up to Nastase. They've been afraid, saying the crowd had to be considered. But what about the other guy in the match?" Tanner goes on to reach the final of the event, losing to Jimmy Connors 6-4, 6-4.

1988 Eighteen-year-old Steffi Graf defeats 33-year-old Chris Evert 6-4, 6-4 in 1 hour, 40 minutes to win the Lipton Championships in Key Biscayne, Fla.

1995 Andre Agassi dramatically defeats Pete Sampras 3-6, 6-2, 7-6 (3) in the final of the Ericsson Open in Key Biscayne, Fla., preventing Sampras from winning the title for a third straight year. Writes Robin Finn of the *New York Times* of the match and the Sampras-Agassi rivalry, "They embody a study in contrasts, Pete Sampras the classicist and Andre Agassi the iconoclast, but when their Lipton Championships final came down to a sudden-death third-set tie breaker this afternoon, they were a symphony of squeaking sneakers, smoking racquets and baggy shorts aflutter in the tropical breeze. Nobody else competes better. Rivals with a cause, the two American thoroughbreds are fast discovering that through each other they can goad themselves into reaching their athletic apex and, almost incidentally, revive tennis in the process." The two rivals played the Australian Open final earlier in the year—won by Agassi—and the Indian Wells final— won by Sampras—and fight for the No. 1 ranking throughout the rest of the year. The two also play in the final of the Canadian Championships later in the summer, Agassi winning 3-6, 6-2, 6-3, while Sampras wins the most significant match between the two during the year—and perhaps their careers—in the U.S. Open final 6-4, 6-3, 4-6, 7-5.

1998 Seventeen-year-old Venus Williams upsets world No. 1 and fellow 17-year-old Martina Hingis 6-2, 5-7, 6-2 in the semifinals of the Lipton Championships in Key Biscayne, Fla. "I haven't arrived yet," says Williams following the match, a re-match of the U.S. Open women's singles final from the previous September. "I'm just coming. I'm on my way up." Williams avenges her sister Serena, who loses to Hingis in a three-set thriller in the quarterfinals.

1999 Sisters Venus Williams and Serena Williams each register semifinal victories at the Lipton Championships in Key Biscayne to set up a championship showdown between sisters—the first final-round match-up pitting sister against sister since the 1884 Wimbledon final between Maud and Lillian Watson. In the first semifinal, Serena Williams defeats world No. 1 Martina Hingis 6-4, 7-6 (3), while Venus Williams follows with a 6-2, 6-4 win over Steff Graf. Says Richard Williams, the father of both finalists, "I always knew it would happen. I've been talking about it for years, planning for it, but now that it is here, I don't even know what to think."

1989 Thirty-six-year-old Jimmy Connors leads Kevin Curren two-sets-to-love but fails to close out the hard-serving South African falling by a 4-6, 4-6, 6-3, 6-4, 6-2 margin in the fourth round of the Lipton Championships in Key Biscayne, Fla. Says Connors, "I'm still standing in the 15th round. Nobody's knocking me out."

March 27

1988 Twenty-three-year-old Mats Wilander outlasts 35-year-old Jimmy Connors 6-4, 4-6, 6-4, 6-4 in 3 hours, 39 minutes to win the Lipton Championships in Key Biscayne, Fla.

1999 Richard Krajicek of the Netherlands wins the biggest title of his career besides his 1996 Wimbledon crown, defeating No. 74-ranked Sebastien Grosjean of France 4-6, 6-1, 6-2, 7-5 in the men's singles final at the Lipton Championships. Grosjean becomes the lowest-ranked player to reach the final in Key Biscayne.

1997 With on-court temperatures hovering around 110 degrees, sixteen-year-old Martina Hingis outlasts Jana Novotna 6-3, 2-6, 6-4 in the semifinals of the Lipton Championships. Says Novotna of the hot conditions of the match, "Occasionally I looked in the corner—105 and it's like 'Nice frying, let's pour some olive oil on me.'" Jim Courier, seeded No. 22, defeats No. 4 seed Goran Ivanisevic 6-2, 7-6 (2) in the men's quarterfinals. Says Goran following the match, "I gave him everything—nice presents."

1998 Marcelo Rios allows Tim Henman only five points in the final set in his 6-2, 4-6, 6-0 semifinal victory at the Lipton Championships. Andre Agassi, ranked No. 31 in the world, also advances into the men's singles final, defeating Alex Corretja 6-4, 6-2. Says Agassi of the talk of the race for the world No. 1 ranking between Pete Sampras and Marcelo Rios following his victory, "I don't know why they are all talking about Rios and Sampras, at the end of the year, I'm going to be No. 1." Agassi goes on to finish No. 6, while Sampras finishes No. 1 and Rios No. 2.

2007 For the second time in a month, Roger Federer loses to Guillermo Canas of Argentina, falling by a 7-6 (2), 2-6, 7-6 (5) margin in the fourth round of the Sony Ericsson Open in Key Biscayne, Fla. Canas ends Federer's 41-match win streak in the first round of the Indian Wells two weeks earlier and in Key Biscayne, ends the Swiss maestro's chance at winning his third straight title in the island paradise. Says Federer. "It's one of those matches I never should have lost." Says Canas, "I'm surprised because I beat two times the No. 1 in the world. Really, I don't know what is my secret. I'm just trying to enjoy the moment. For me it's like a dream." Fellow No. 1 seed Maria Sharapova is also eliminated from the event but in a much more convincing fashion, losing 6-1, 6-1 to Serena Williams.

March 28

1999 In the first singles final at an important, big tournament in 115 years played between sisters, Venus Williams defeats younger sister Serena Williams 6-1, 4-6, 6-4 in the women's singles final at the Lipton Championships in Key Biscayne, Fla. The match is highlighted by the charismatic father of both finalists—Richard Williams—who holds various signs during the match with such phrases as "Welcome to the Williams Show" and "It Couldn't Have Happened To A Better Family." The last time the final of a big, important tournament is played between two sisters comes at Wimbledon 1884 when Maud Watson defeats older sister Lillian Watson in the women's final.

1997 No. 30 seeded Sergi Bruguera shocks world No. 1 Pete Sampras 5-7, 7-6 (2), 6-4 in the semifinals of the Lipton Championships. "It's one of the best feelings you can have in tennis, to beat the No. 1 in an important match," says Bruguera. World No. 2 Thomas Muster also advances into the Lipton final, defeating No. 22 Jim Courier 6-3, 6-4.

1998 Seventeen-year-old Venus Williams defeats 16-year-old Anna Kournikova 2-6, 6-4, 6-1 to win the Lipton Championships. Says Kournikova of her loss, "It's good that she didn't really beat me, because I made all the mistakes, right? That gives me some confidence that I could play better. She didn't beat me. I lost."

2002 Serena Williams needs only 50 minutes to defeat older sister Venus Williams 6-2, 6-2 in the semifinals of the Ericsson Open in Key Biscayne, Fla. Jennifer Capriati needs 2 hours, 8 minutes and saves two match points in defeating Monica Seles 4-6, 6-3, 7-6 (3) to also advance into the championship match.

1989 Chris Evert plays a perfect final-set tie-break and escapes the upset bid of Canada's Helen Kelesi, defeating the world No. 11 6-3, 4-6, 7-6 (0) in the quarterfinals of the Lipton Championships. "I played a perfect tie-breaker and I didn't play a perfect match," says Evert. In the early morning hours, world No. 172 Jim Grabb concludes a fourth-round victory over Alberto Mancini, finishing off the Argentine 6-7 (3), 6-4, 7-6 (5), 6-7(4), 6-4 at 1:50 am.

1996 Goran Ivanisevic fires 12 aces in his 6-4, 6-3 quarterfinal victory over Michael Chang at the Lipton Championships, then, in his post-match press conference, vows to set a record for number of aces that will "stand for another 200 years until the robots break it."

2004 Seventeen-year-old Rafael Nadal of Spain registers the biggest win of his young career, upsetting world No. 1 Roger Federer 6-3, 6-3 in the third round of the NASDAQ-100 Open in Key Biscayne, Fla. Says Nadal, the youngest player in the 2004 NASDAQ-100 field, "I played almost perfect tennis." Federer's loss is only his second in 25 matches in the 2004 season. Says Federer of Nadal, his future top rival, "He hit some really incredible shots, and that's what youngsters do. I've heard a lot about him and saw some of his matches, so this is not a big surprise."

2008 Entering the Sony Ericsson Open as the hottest player in men's tennis with victories at the Australian Open and the Pacific Life Open in Indian Wells, Calif., No. 3-ranked Novak Djokovic is cooled off in losing his opening round match to qualifier and No. 122-ranked Kevin Anderson of South Africa 7-6, 3-6, 6-4. Anderson, three weeks removed from reaching his first ATP singles final in Las Vegas, wins 13 points in the a row during a stretch in the third set after Djokovic leads 2-0. Says Anderson, "I kept telling myself, 'I can do this. I've just got to believe in myself.' Even still, just knowing what he's done and what a great player he is, to have beaten him is a tremendous experience for me."

1927 Playing on an injured and banged knee, Bill Tilden gives up only two games in winning his first two matches at the South Atlantic States Tennis Championships in Augusta, Ga. He defeats J.H. Blauvelt 6-0, 6-0 in his morning match and then defeats Frank Capers 6-1, 6-1. Ty Cobb, Jr., the son of the famous baseball player, is defeated by Jack Mooney 6-2, 6-1 in the first round.

March 29

1998 Marcelo Rios of Chile clinches the world No. 1 ranking for the first time when he defeats Andre Agassi 7-5, 6-3, 6-4 in the final of the Lipton Championships in Key Biscayne, Fla. The victory for Rios sets off celebrations in Chile's capital city of Santiago, where thousands for citizens take to the streets in jubilation, waving flags and singing songs celebrating Rios overtaking Pete Sampras as world No. 1. Says Rios of his accomplishment, "First of all, being the best player in the world for Chile is not normal. We have never had a champion be No. 1 in the world in tennis." Writes Lisa Dillman of the *Los Angeles Times*, "Marcelo Rios used his tennis racket like a magic wand, directing none other than Andre Agassi around the court at will Sunday. And, for his final trick, Rios made Pete Sampras' No. 1 ranking disappear."

1992 Andre Agassi defeats Karel Novacek 7-6 (5), 6-0, 6-0 in the fifth and decisive match as the United States defeats Czechoslovakia 3-2 in the Davis Cup quarterfinals in Ft. Myers, Fla. Says Agassi after the match, "There are two things I live by. Number one, you can never drive too far for Taco Bell; and number two, you can never beat somebody too bad, especially in Davis Cup." Earlier, Pete Sampras loses to Petr Korda 6-4, 6-3, 2-6, 6-3 to set up the fifth and decisive match of the series.

1997 Sixteen-year-old Martina Hingis needs only 43 minutes to defeat Monica Seles 6-2, 6-1 in the singles final of the Lipton Championships.

1996 Goran Ivanisevic benefits from a 48-minute rain delay while trailing Pete Sampras 6-1, 1-0 and comes from behind to defeat the world No. 2 1-6, 6-4, 6-4 in the semifinals of the Lipton Championships in Key Biscayne. Says Ivanisevic, "I was thinking I was going to fly home tomorrow and then the rain came and saved me."

1991 Jim Courier makes his Davis Cup debut, losing to Luis Herrera of Mexico 6-4, 2-6, 7-5, 6-4 in opening match of the United States vs. Mexico Davis Cup first round—at 7,250-feet of altitude—in Mexico City, Mexico. Brad Gilbert ties the score at 1-1 for the United States after the first day of play, defeating Leonardo Lavalle 6-3, 6-2, 6-7, 6-3. Says Gilbert of his win that prevents the United States from going down 0-2, "If I didn't win today, we would have been in big trouble."

March 30

1975 Thirty-six-year-old Rod Laver wins his final professional singles title, defeating 20-year-old American Vitas Gerulaitis 6-3, 6-4 in the final of the WCT Championships in Orlando. Laver's title is his 47th in the Open era of tennis, dating to 1968.

1997 Eight years after having to default the final of the Lipton Championships after tearing ligaments in his knee after being hit by a car driven by a drunk driver, Thomas Muster of Austria defeats Spain's Sergi Bruguera 7-6 (6), 6-3, 6-1 to win the Lipton Championships in Key Biscayne, Fla. "It's very emotional for me because of what happened here eight years ago," says Muster of the victory, his 44th and ultimately his final ATP tournament title.

2000 Martina Hingis hands Monica Seles the worst loss of her professional career, defeating the former world No. 1 6-0, 6-0 in 39 minutes in the semifinals of the Ericsson Open in Key Biscayne, Fla. Lindsay Davenport edges Sandrine Testud 6-1, 6-7 (7), 7-6 (7) in a much more competitive women's semifinal match. Seles is hampered by a right ankle sprain that limits her movement and is the major factor in the one-sided match.

2002 Serena Williams fights off seven second-set points and defeats Jennifer Capriati 7-5, 7-6 (4) in the women's singles final at the NASDAQ-100 Open in Key Biscayne, Fla.

1996 Steffi Graf wins her unprecedented fifth title at the Lipton Championships, defeating Chanda Rubin 6-1, 6-3 in 54 minutes in the women's singles final in Key Biscayne, Fla. The title was Graf's 97th of her career in her 124th final. Says Rubin of Graf, "Her game is oppressive, and it forces you to go for too much. I came up quite a bit short today, and that kind of was the story to the match."

2004 Three-time defending champion Andre Agassi sees his 19-match winning streak at the NASDAQ-100 Open end in a 6-2, 7-6 (2) fourth-round loss to Agustin Calleri of Argentina. Agassi holds five set points in the second set, but is unable to convert to even the match at one-set apiece. Says Agassi, who also misses a chance to win his 800th career ATP match victory, "I missed some chances. I needed to step it up and play to his standard, and I didn't do that."

1980 Bjorn Borg dominates Manuel Orantes 6-2, 6-0, 6-1 in the final of the Nice Open in France in a match delayed by 25 minutes when a group of local physical education students storm the court and stage a "sit-in" to protest their department being closed by the French education ministry.

1991 Rick Leach and Jim Pugh need 4 hours, and 24 minutes—marking the longest U.S. Davis Cup doubles match—to defeat Leonardo Lavalle and Jorge Lozano of Mexico 6-4, 4-6, 7-6 (2), 6-7 (3), 6-4 to give the United States a 2-1 lead over Mexico in the Davis Cup first round in Mexico City.

2008 In an exciting day of women's tennis at the Sony Ericsson Open, Lindsay Davenport, playing in Key Biscayne for the first time in five years, upsets world No. 2 Ana Ivanovic 6-4, 6-2, while world No. 3 Svetlana Kuznetsova comes from back a 2-5 third-set deficit—and saves a match point—in defeating Victoria Azarenka of Belarus 1-6, 7-5, 6-0. In the early hours of the day—the night before—Jelena Jankovic rallies from a 1-5 deficit in the third set and saves five match points in the final-set tie-break to register a second-round win over Sofia Arvidsson of Sweden 6-7 (7), 6-2, 7-6 (9) in a match that concludes at 12:30 am. Says Jankovic, "I didn't play well, but I was hanging in there. I really believed in myself. I played one point at a time...I don't like to lose. No matter what the score is, the match is not over until it is over. I'm a big fighter, and it was very important for my confidence to show that I don't give up." Jankovic eventually reaches the final of the tournament, where she is defeated by Serena Williams in a tight three-set final.

1990 Aaron Krickstein defeats Milan Srejber 4-6, 7-6, 7-6, 6-7, 6-3 in the opening match of the United States vs. Czechoslovakia Davis Cup quarterfinal in Prague. Krickstein's victory proves vital in the 4-1 victory over the Czechs.

March 31

2001 In one of the most gripping finals in the history of the WTA Tour, Venus Williams fights off eight match points to win her 16th title of her career at the Ericsson Open in Key Biscayne, Fla., defeating Jennifer Capriati 4-6, 6-1, 7-6 (7-4). Williams clinches the match on her fourth match point to win her 18th consecutive match at the tournament.

2002 Thirty-one-year-old Andre Agassi wins his 700th career match, defeating 20-year-old Roger Federer 6-3, 6-3, 3-6, 6-4 in the final of the NASDAQ-100 Open in Key Biscayne. Says Agassi, "I think as you get older, you have a greater capacity to appreciate everything. Those moments are not promised. Who knows if it will ever happen again? The older I get, the more I keep that in perspective."

2007 Serena Williams stages an incredible comeback and fights off two championship points in the second set to defeat Justine Henin 0-6, 7-5, 6-3 in the final of the Sony Ericsson Open in Key Biscayne, Fla. Says Williams, the reigning Australian Open champion, who nine months earlier languishes at No. 140 in the WTA rankings, "When I get down, a part of me just plays better. I think all champions have that." Says Henin of Williams, "She's a fighter. It's tough to close the matches against her, because she goes for it. She's a champion, and that makes a difference from the other players, for sure."

1995 For only the second time in Davis Cup history, the world's No. 1 and No. 2 ranked players play on the same Davis Cup team as No. 1 Pete Sampras and No. 2 Andre Agassi take the court against Italy in the Davis Cup quarterfinal in Palermo, Italy. Agassi defeats Andrea Gaudenzi 6-4, 6-4, 6-1 and Sampras defeats Renzo Furlan 7-6, 6-3, 6-0 to give the United States a 2-0 lead over the Italians.

1996 Goran Ivanisevic is stricken with a sore neck which forces him to quit trailing Andre Agassi 0-3, 0-40 after only 10 minutes of play in the men's singles final at the Lipton Championships in Key Biscayne, Fla.

1997 Martina Hingis becomes the No. 1 player in the world for the first time in her career, a ranking she holds for 209 weeks during her career.

1973 Billie Jean King ends Margaret Court's 57-match winning streak, defeating the Australian 6-7, 7-6, 6-3 in the semifinals of the WTA Tour event in Indianapolis, Ind.

2008 Mikhail Youzhny of Russia gains more exposure and international attention for a strange outburst of anger in a third-round match at the Sony Ericsson Open in Key Biscayne, Fla., than he does in coming back from two-sets-to love to clinch the Davis Cup title for Russia in 2002. Trailing Nicolas Almagro 4-5 in the third set of their third-round match, the No. 11-ranked Youzhny bangs his head three times with his racquet strings, causing him to bleed down the front of his face. The video becomes a viral video sensation on the internet, registering 500,000 hits on YouTube within 24 hours. Youzhny wins the match 7-6 (4), 3-6, 7-6 (6).

1991 Brad Gilbert defeats Luis Herrera 4-6, 6-3, 7-5, 3-6, 6-3 to clinch the 4-1 victory over Mexico in the Davis Cup first round in Mexico City, Mexico.

April 1

1989 Less than two hours after thrilling 5-7, 3-6, 6-3, 6-3, 6-2 win over Yannick Noah in the semifinals of the Lipton Championships in Key Biscayne, Fla., Thomas Muster's career high goes to a career low as he is hit by a car, tearing ligaments in his left knee and forcing him to default the tournament final to world No. 1 Ivan Lendl. Muster is off the tour for only six months, famously training in a specially-made wheelchair that allows him to hit tennis balls. Oddly, his 44th and final ATP Tour tournament victory comes in 1997 when he returns to the Key Biscayne final and beats Sergi Bruguera for the title.

2000 Martina Hingis defeats Lindsay Davenport 6-3, 6-2 in 58 minutes to win the singles title at the Ericsson Open in Key Biscayne, Fla., ending a five-match losing streak to Davenport and stopping Davenport's 21-match winning streak. Despite the loss, Davenport replaces Hingis as the No. 1 player in the WTA Tour rankings the next day.

2001 Andre Agassi wins the Ericsson Open in Key Biscayne, Fla., for the fourth time in his career, defeating fellow American Jan-Michael Gambill 7-6 (7-4), 6-1, 6-0, in the final. It is Agassi's 48th title of his career.

2006 Svetlana Kuznetsova wins the biggest singles title since winning the 2004 U.S. Open, defeating Maria Sharapova 6-4, 6-3 to win the NASDAQ-100 Open women's singles title in Key Biscayne, Fla.—her sixth career singles title.

2005 Roger Federer defeats Andre Agassi 6-4, 6-3 in the semifinals of the NASDAQ-100 Open in what ultimately becomes Agassi final appearance in the event.

2007 Nineteen-year-old Novak Djokovic of Serbia becomes the youngest men's singles champion in the history of the Sony Ericsson Open, defeating Guillermo Canas of Argentina 6-3, 6-2, 6-4 in the championship match in Key Biscayne, Fla. The title is the first "Masters Series" title for Djokovic, who reached the final at Indian Wells two weeks earlier. Djokovic also wins the title without dropping a set, becoming the first player since Ivan Lendl in 1989 to turn that trick. "Every time you win something or you are the youngest player or you make any record, it certainly feels great," says

Djokovic. "It means that your name is in the history of the sport. I am very proud of that."

2008 One year after Serena Williams saves match points to beat Justine Henin in the Sony Ericsson Open final, Williams dominates her Belgian rival 6-2, 6-0 in the tournament's quarterfinals in 1 hour, 20 minutes. The meeting is the 13ᵗʰ and ultimately final meeting between the two rivals as the No. 1 ranked Henin announces her surprise retirement six weeks later. Williams' decisive win—the most lopsided in their series of matches— pushes her ahead in the rivalry by a 7-6 margin. Entering the match, Henin had won the last three meetings—all quarterfinals matches at major tournaments in 2007 at the French, Wimbledon and the U.S. Open.

1927 Playing on a heavy and damp clay court in front of a crowd of approximately 1,200 fans, Bill Tilden defeats George Lott 11-9, 0-6, 6-2, 6-1 to win the South Atlantic States Tennis Championships in Augusta, Ga. Writes the *New York Times*, "The score does not show the long tussle that Lott and Tilden had, for the first set lasted an hour and had more than fifteen deuces."

April 2

2000 Pete Sampras wins an inspired men's singles final at the Ericsson Open in Key Biscayne, Fla., defeating Brazil's Gustavo Kuerten 6-1, 6-7 (2), 7-6 (5), 7-6 (8) in 3 hours, 18 minutes. Fighting off the hot, humid South Florida conditions, the tenacious groundstrokes of the 1997 French Open champion, and a rare case of nerves at the closing stages of the match, Sampras prevails to win his 62nd—and third to last—title of his career. Says Sampras of the match, "I haven't played a match this tough in many, many months. You can do all the training, all the practicing, but it is always different when you go out and compete. But I can definitely walk out of this tournament feeling real confident about the way things went."

2005 Kim Cljisters defeats Maria Sharapova 6-3, 7-5 to win the women's singles final at the NASDAQ-100 Open in Key Biscayne, Fla. Coupled with her win two weeks earlier in Indian Wells, Calif., Clijsters becomes only the second woman to win the rare "Coast-to-Coast Double" sweep of the two important Indian Wells-Key Biscayne back-to-back tournaments in the spring calendar. Clijsters joins Steffi Graf, who won both Indian Wells and Key Biscayne back-to-back in 1994 and 1996. Her win over Sharapova moves her to No. 17 in the rankings, after missing most of 2004 with a wrist injury. She last ranked No. 1 in the world on Nov. 9, 2003.

2006 Roger Federer wins three tie-breakers in a match for the first time in his career, defeating Ivan Ljubicic 7-6 (5), 7-6 (4), 7-6 (6) to win the NASDAQ-100 Open in Key Biscayne, Fla. The win is Federer's 48 straight match victory in the United States, dating back to August of 2004. Federer also becomes the first player ever to win the "Coast-to-Coast Double"—the American hard court titles in Indian Wells and Key Biscayne—back-to-back in consecutive years.

1999 In the 100th year of Davis Cup play, Roger Federer makes his Davis Cup debut, defeating Davide Sanguinetti 6-4, 6-7 (3), 6-3, 6-4 in the opening day of play in Switzerland's defeat of Italy in Neuchatel, Switzerland. The match is the first for the 17-year-old Federer in a best-of-five-set match. "At first I was nervous but then I calmed down," says Federer. "I didn't do very well in the tie-break and took too many risks. But I think in the end taking a lot of risks combined with the public's support helped me win."

April 3

1920 Playing what Allison Danzig of the *New York Times* calls "a game that no one in the world could have beaten" Bill Tilden wins the U.S. National Indoor Championships at the 7th Regiment Armory in New York City, defeating defending champion Vincent Richards 10-8, 6-3, 6-1 in the final.

2005 Two points from defeat in the third-set tie-break, world No. 1 Roger Federer rallies from two-sets-to-love down to defeat Spain's Rafael Nadal 2-6, 6-7 (4), 7-6 (5), 6-3, 6-1 in 3 hours, 43 minutes to win the NASDAQ-100 Open in Key Biscayne, Fla. Federer trails 4-2 in the third set and 5-3 in the third-set tie-break before rallying to win his 22nd consecutive match and his 18th consecutive final. Says Federer after the match, "I've hardly ever come back in a situation like that. It was a big moment for me. It was uphill. I was trying to force him too much, but I got myself to relax. I thought I'd be all right if I could get him into a fifth set."

2008 With new fiancé and *Sports Illustrated* swimsuit model Brooklyn Decker in attendance, Andy Roddick ends his personal 11-match losing streak to Roger Federer, defeating the world No. 1 7-6 (4), 4-6, 6-3 in a highly-entertaining quarterfinal match at the Sony Ericsson Open in Key Biscayne, Fla. Says Roddick to the crowd following the match, "I came in knowing that nobody has beaten me 12 times in a row. So I had that on my side." Roddick, who last beat Federer in the semifinals of the 2003 Canadian Championships, improves his record to 2-15 against the five-time Wimbledon champion. "I figure I was due," Roddick says. "He hadn't missed a ball in a crucial moment for about six years against me. I figured the law of statistics had to come my way eventually." Earlier in the day, Serena Williams defeats Svetlana Kuznetsova 3-6, 7-5, 6-3 and Jelena Jankovic defeats Vera Zvonareva 6-1, 6-4 in the women's semifinals.

April 4

1999 In one of the most dramatic conclusions ever in a Davis Cup tie, Jim Courier defeats Greg Rusedski 6-4, 6-7 (3), 6-3, 1-6, 8-6 in the fifth and decisive match to clinch a 3-2 win for the United States against Great Britain in the first round of the Centennial year of the competition in Birmingham, England. On day one of the competition two days earlier, Courier gives the United States an early 1-0 lead, defeating Tim Henman 7-6 (2), 2-6, 7-6 (3), 6-7 (10), 7-5. In all, Courier, ranked No. 54 in the ATP Tour rankings, is on court for 7 hours, 58 minutes for his victories over the No. 7-ranked Henman and No. 11-ranked Rusedski. Of Courier's win over Rusedski, Bud Collins of the *Boston Globe* writes, "Seldom, if ever, in the 100 years of the sterling crock's existence has an American guy come through as brawny James Spencer Courier did last night in helping the U.S. seize the 3-2 triumph at the extreme limits of the game—tail end of the fifth set of the fifth match of the best-of-five series."

2004 Andy Roddick wins the NASDAQ-100 Open when his final round opponent, Guillermo Coria of Argentina, retires due to back pain with Roddick leading 6-7 (2), 6-3, 6-1. Coria's ailment is later diagnosed as kidney stones. Says Coria through a translator following the match, "I felt burned out and very sad after all that I had to go through this week. I was hoping that the pain was going to go away, but I knew after a certain point that it was not going to go away. I believe I should have retired after the first set, but nobody wants to retire in a final with all the people that paid the money to come see me play. I knew that I probably couldn't go through."

1998 Andre Agassi defeats Russia's Marat Safin 6-3, 6-3, 6-3 for his 16th consecutive Davis Cup singles victory, tying him with Bill Tilden for the all-time American record. Agassi's win squares the U.S. and Russia at 1-1 after the first day of play in the Davis Cup first round in Stone Mountain, Ga. Agassi remains tied with Tilden as he loses his second match of the series with Russia, losing to Yevgeny Kafelnikov 6-3, 6-0, 7-6 (3). Agassi's streak begins in 1991, following a dead-rubber loss (4-6, 6-4, ret.) to his future coach Darren Cahill in the 1990 Davis Cup Final. Tilden wins his stretch of 16 straight Davis Cup singles matches from 1920 to 1926, ended by Rene Lacoste in the 1926 Davis Cup Challenge Round at the Germantown Cricket Club in Philadelphia.

April 5

1975 In a match highlighted by one of Ilie Nastase's famed on-court incidents, the clown prince from Romania beats Ken Rosewall 3-6, 7-5, 6-2 in the semifinals of the American Airlines Invitational in Tucson, Ariz. Rosewall serves for the match at 6-3, 5-4, but Nastase, frustrated at his play and of his perception of bad line calls, walks off the court with the score at 15-all saying, "I don't want to play anymore." After some delay, Nastase is persuaded to continue the match, where he wins three points in a row to break Rosewall, then runs through and wins a stretch of seven straight games to win the match in three sets. Asked if the stall hurt his chances of winning, Rosewall responds to reporters following the match saying, "Yes, it did break my momentum." Says Nastase, "Maybe I was wrong to do what I did. but I wasn't thinking of upsetting him. He is the most difficult player in the world for me and I still don't know how I beat him." Writes Leonard Koppett in the *New York Times*, "Hours after the match, the switchboard at Margaret Court's Racquet Club Ranch, where it had been played, was still lit up with calls from outraged fans who had watched the contest on television." Nastase goes on to lose the tournament final the following day to John Alexander of Australia by a 7-5, 6-2 margin.

2006 Australia's Nicole Pratt and Bryanne Stewart win the longest tie-break in WTA Tour history, winning a 42-point tie-break that takes 32-minutes to play in their second round 7-6 (7-5), 7-6 (22-20) victory over Rennae Stubbs of Australia and Corina Morariu of the United States at the Bausch and Lomb Championships. Pratt and Stewart have 12 match points in the tie-break and 15 in all during the match, while Stubbs and Morariu hold three set points. The previous WTA record is held by Tara Snyder of the United States and Emmanuelle Gagliardi of Switzerland (Snyder winning a 21-19 first-set tie-break at Madrid in 1999.) The longest tie-break in tennis history is a 50-point tie-break played at Wimbledon in 1985, Michael Mortensen of Denmark and Jan Gunnarson of Sweden winning the decisive fourth-set tie-break 26-24 over Victor Pecci of Paraguay and John Frawley of Australia.

2008 Serena Williams wins her fifth title at the Sony Ericsson Open in Key Biscayne, Fla.—tying the all-time women's record held by Steffi Graf—in a topsy-turvy, entertaining 6-1, 5-7, 6-3 final-round win over Jelena Jankovic of Serbia. Williams needs eight match points to put away the tenacious Serb, who fights through a nasal infection to nearly take the biggest title of her career.

April 6

1997 Andre Agassi comes back from a two-sets-to-love deficit for only the second time in his career and defeats Jan Siemerink 3-6, 3-6, 6-3, 6-3, 6-3 to clinch the 4-1 United States victory over the Netherlands in the Davis Cup quarterfinals in Newport Beach, Calif. Siemerink blows a two-sets-to-love lead for the second straight match, losing two days earlier on the first day of the series to Jim Courier 4-6, 4-6, 6-1, 7-6 (4), 6-3. Janis Carr of the *Orange County Register* calls Agassi's effort "out of a made-for-cable movie" as the struggling Agassi, who enters the Davis Cup series losing his last five matches on a 3-5 record for the year, stages a heroic, come-from-behind victory that saves the day for America's tennis team.

1998 Jim Courier overcomes a 0-6, 1-4 deficit to defeat 18-year-old Marat Safin 0-6, 6-4, 4-6, 6-1, 6-4 in the fifth and decisive match as the United States defeats Russia 3-2 in the Davis Cup first round in Stone Mountain, Ga. Safin, who goes on to become the first Russian man to win a major singles title at the 2000 U.S. Open, easily dictates play from the start, stunning Courier, U.S. Captain Tom Gullikson and all observers. On the changeover after the fifth game of the second set, Gullikson and Courier discuss a strategy change—Gullikson suggesting a change of pace, throwing in with some off-pace slices. A shell-shocked Courier tells Gullikson, "He's blowing the ball right through me. I'm having a hard time changing the pace." Courier's slices and short balls dramatically change the tempo of the match as Courier rallies for the inspired victory. Days after the win, Courier provides perspective on the match, stating, "It is a memory I want to carry with me as long as I can. That was one of the more special matches, having had a couple of days to reflect on it now that I have really played in my career. I want to take as much from that match as I can. I dug myself out of a really deep hole and just kept fighting and kept thinking and really came up with the good shots when I needed them out there."

2001 Marc Rosset of Switzerland fires a men's record 30 double faults against 48 aces in losing a 6-3, 3-6, 7-6 (4), 6-7 (6), 15-13 epic in 5 hours, 47 minutes in the opening match of the France vs. Switzerland Davis Cup quarterfinal in Neuchatel, Switzerland. After France takes a 2-0 lead on the first day of play (Nicolas Escude beating future world No. 1 Roger Federer in four sets), it holds on to win the series 3-2—Escude beating George Bastl 8-6 in the fifth set in the fifth and decisive match. France goes on to win the Davis Cup, beating Australia 3-2 in the final in December.

April 7

2000 Pete Sampras suffers the worst Davis Cup defeat of his career, losing to Jiri Novak of the Czech Republic 7-6, 6-3, 6-2 in the opening day of play in the USA vs. Czech Republic Davis Cup quarterfinal at the Forum in Los Angeles. With Captain John McEnroe sitting with him courtside, Sampras is unable to break serve and fails on all 11 of his break point opportunities. Says Sampras, "I just got out played. I haven't said that too often throughout my career, but today I ran into someone that was pretty much in the zone... It's been a while since I felt I was getting outplayed like that. Right now I'm trying to figure out why and what happened." Andre Agassi defeats Slava Dosedel 6-3, 6-3, 6-3 to even the score at 1-1 after the first day of play.

1980 Seventeen-year-old Tracy Austin assumes the No. 1 ranking on the WTA Tour computer—the fourth player to hold the position following Chris Evert, Evonne Goolagong and Martina Navratilova. Austin holds the ranking for two weeks, before surrendering it back to Navratilova. Ten weeks later, she again assumes the ranking for a 20 week period, before losing the ranking to Chris Evert, never to hold the No. 1 spot again.

1996 MaliVai Washington is defeated by Petr Korda 7-6 (5), 6-3, 6-2 in the fifth and decisive match as the Czech Republic regisers a 3-2 Davis Cup quarterfinal win in Prague over the United States, playing without its top four players—Pete Sampras, Andre Agassi, Michael Chang and Jim Courier. Washington is unable to convert two set points with Korda serving at 4-5 in the first set, which ultimately proves critical in the loss. "When you win that first set, it changes the whole complexion of the match," Washington says after the match. "If I could have won that first set, it would have been a lot different." Earlier in the day, Todd Martin evens the series at 2-2 by routing Daniel Vacek 7-6 (1), 6-3, 6-1 in a flawless display as the American never loses his serve and, during one incredible stretch in the first and second sets, wins 34 consecutive points on his serve, including seven straight love service games. Says Vacek to Martin at the conclusion of the match, "Just how much should I pay you for the lesson?"

1996 In her 10th appearance, Arantxa Sanchez Vicario defeats Barbara Paulus 6-2, 2-6, 6-2 to finally win her first title at the Family Circle Magazine Cup in Hilton Head Island, S.C. Says Sanchez Vicario, "I was coming every year, hoping to do a little better than the year before. Finally, the 10th time has been the one."

April 8

1992 Arthur Ashe holds an emotional press conference in New York to announce that he has contracted AIDS from heart surgery. Ashe, who had known he had the deadly disease for three years, said he decided to disclose the illness publicly only after learning that *USA Today* was preparing an article on his condition. Says the 48-year-old Ashe in his prepared statement, "Beginning with my admittance to New York Hospital for brain surgery in September 1988, some of you heard that I had tested positive for H.I.V., the virus that causes AIDS. That is indeed the case." Ashe says that he believed the virus was transmitted through a blood transfusion after heart surgery in 1983. Ashe states that he did not previously disclose his condition publicly to protect his privacy. Says Ashe, "Just as I'm sure everyone in this room has some personal matter he or she would like to keep private, so did we. There was certainly no compelling medical or physical necessity to go public with my medical condition."

1990 Thirty-three-year-old Martina Navratilova beats 14-year-old eighth-grader Jennifer Capriati 6-2, 6-4 in the final of the Family Circle Cup in Hilton Head Island, S.C. The win is Navratilova's 150th professional singles title, while the Family Circle Cup marks only Capriati's third tournament as a professional. Says Capriati of playing Navratilova for the first time in the final, "It was the greatest feeling of my life. Here I was playing a legend." Says Navratilova, "I think I played a legend-in-the-making."

2005 Russia's Igor Andreev upsets Rafael Nadal 7-5, 6-2 in the quarterfinals of the Valencia Open in Spain. Following this loss to Andreev, Nadal goes on to win his next 81 clay court matches—in winning the 2005 and 2006 French Open titles and setting a new all-time ATP record for consecutive match victories on clay courts. Nadal's streak is broken by Roger Federer, who beats Nadal in the final of Hamburg on May 20, 2007.

2007 Tatiana Golovin of France has an extra special Easter Sunday, winning her first career WTA Tour title, defeating defending champion Nadia Petrova of Russia 6-2, 6-1 in the final of the Bausch & Lomb Championships in Amelia Island. Says Golovin, "I'm a little overwhelmed. This is probably the happiest day of my life in my tennis careeer. I still can't believe it."

April 9

1989 Less than one year after being blanked 6-0, 6-0 by Steffi Graf in the final of the French Championships, Natalia Zvereva of the Soviet Union manages one game in each set against Graf in the final of the Family Circle Cup in Hilton Head, S.C., losing 6-1, 6-1 in 55 minutes. Zvereva uses the platform of one of the biggest events on the WTA Tour—and the national television audience in the United States—to politic the Communist Soviet government to receive a bigger portion of her prize money. She eventually defies the Soviet government and begins claiming her own prize money in the waning years of a Communist Eastern Europe.

2000 Pete Sampras plays a fifth and decisive Davis Cup rubber for the first time in his career and suffers through a strained left calf muscle to defeat Slava Dosedel 6-4, 6-4, 7-6 to clinch a 3-2 U.S. win over the Czech Republic in the Davis Cup quarterfinal at the Forum in Los Angeles. Sampras overcomes a left quad strain suffered in the third game to gut out the match for U.S. Captain John McEnroe and the U.S. team. Says Sampras of his efforts to overcome his injury to win the match, "Adrenaline is the greatest drug of all—that and the crowd support kept me going. I said to John (after suffering the tweek injury), 'I kind of hurt my leg.' I could see in his eyes that he'd strangle me if I said I had to quit. But I never would have. Even if I'd lasted only three sets, Dosedel would have had to beat me. I wasn't walking out." Earlier, Andre Agassi defeats Jiri Novak 6-3, 6-3, 6-1 to square the tie at 2-2.

1988 Andre Agassi completes a darkness-suspended 6-8, 7-5, 6-1, 6-2 victory over Jaime Yzaga in the Davis Cup American zone semifinals in Lima, Peru, Agassi's first-ever Davis Cup match. Agassi's win gives the United States a 2-0 lead over Peru in their eventual 3-0 victory.

1995 Conchita Martinez defeats Gabriela Sabatini 6-1, 6-4 to win the Bausch and Lomb Championships in Amelia Island, Fla., her second consecutive tournament title after winning the Family Circle Cup at Hilton Head Island, S.C. the previous week. Martinez needs only 74 minutes to dismiss Sabatini and win her 22nd career WTA Tour singles title. "It was important to get off to a fast start, especially with the crowd behind her," Martinez says following the match. "I don't mind the fans cheering for her, but it does bother me some when they cheer my mistakes."

April 10

1912 The *Titanic*, touted as the indestructible passenger ship, sinks in the North Atlantic with two of the world's best tennis players on board. Dick Williams and Karl Behr, a future and past U.S. Davis Cup player, respectively, traveling to New York, survive the most famous passenger ship disaster and continue to play top-level tennis. Williams is on the ill-fated ship to travel to the United States to enroll at Harvard University. Williams goes on to win two U.S. singles titles in 1914 and 1916 and helps the United States win five Davis Cup titles from 1921-1926. Behr was a member of the U.S. Davis Cup team in 1907 and actually goes on to face Williams in an intriguing U.S. quarterfinal match in Newport in 1914, won by Williams 6-1, 6-2, 7-5. Behr escapes the *Titanic* by lifeboat, while Williams jumps from the deck of the ship, swimming to a lifeboat and hangs on until rescued. Bud Collins in *The Bud Collins History of Tennis*, tells the fascinating tale of Williams and his survival; "At the insistence of his infirm father, who perished with the ship, Dick dived from the deck at the last possible moment, swam to a half-submerged lifeboat and clung there in near-freezing water for six hours. When rescued by the *Carpathia*, he was advised by a ship's doctor that amputation of the frozen-stiff, apparently useless, legs (common treatment at the time) would save his life. Fortunately, Williams refused, somehow—regardless of intense pain—willing himself to abandon the stretcher and walk the deck. Only months later he was in the quarterfinals of the U.S. Championships, losing in four sets to champion Maurice McLoughlin."

1995 Andre Agassi becomes the No. 1 player in the world for the first time, replacing Pete Sampras, the world's No. 1 for the previous 82 weeks. Agassi becomes the 12th player in the 22-year history of the men's computer rankings to hold the top spot. Agassi positions himself to move up from No. 2 after defeating Sampras in the final of the Lipton Championships on March 26. Says Agassi of his rivalry with Sampras, "The intensity against Pete is above and beyond anything I can feel with anybody at this time," he says after winning the Lipton. "This is a great stage for tennis. It's important for me to be the best that I can. Taking over No. 1 won't have the impact that it is going to have a few years from now when I look back and know that I have maintained it."

1982 Chris Evert loses a match on a clay courts for only the third time in nine years when she is eliminated by 16-year-old Andrea Jaeger 6-1, 1-6,

6-2 in the semifinals of the Family Circle Cup in Hilton Head Island, S.C. Evert had won 199 of 201 matches on clay since 1973—losing only to Tracy Austin in the 1979 Italian Open final and to Hana Mandlikova in the 1981 French Open semifinals. Says Evert of Jaeger and her no pace, moonball style of play, "It's very annoying to play her. I guess I wasn't willing to stay out there all day and moon ball back."

1988 Thirty-one-year-old Martina Navratilova defeats seventeen-year-old Gabriela Sabatini 6-1, 4-6, 6-4 to win the Family Circle Cup in Hilton Head, S.C., for her 20th consecutive match victory and fourth tournament victory in a row. "I don't think I expected to win," says Navratilova, "and she probably thought she would."

April 11

1993 Three days after clinching the No. 1 ranking for the first time in his career, Pete Sampras defeats Brad Gilbert 6-2, 6-2, 6-2 to win the Japan Open in Tokyo and start his reign as the world's best player in style. Says Sampras, "Being No. 1 is a great achievement, but I think the most important thing is to win the big tournaments. My next goal is the French Open." Says Gilbert of Sampras, "He played just like the world's No. 1 player. I couldn't read his serve. He is the top candidate to win Wimbledon and the U.S. Open this season." Sampras assumes the No. 1 ranking officially the following day, replacing Jim Courier.

1983 Martina Navratilova defeats Tracy Austin 5-7, 6-1, 6-0 in the singles final of the Family Circle Cup at Hilton Head Island, S.C. The match ultimately becomes Austin's final appearance in a WTA Tour singles final as back injuries knock off the tour after competing in the pre-Wimbledon tournament at Eastbourne.

1992 Kimiko Date, the most noteworthy player from Japan, wins her first career WTA title at her native Japan Open, defeating Sabine Applemans of Belgium 7-5, 3-6, 6-3 in the women's singles final. Date, who achieves a career-high singles ranking of No. 7 and becomes a semifinalist at the Australian, French and Wimbledon championships, wins the Japan Open three more times in her career, corralling titles in 1993, 1994 and 1996.

1982 Guillermo Vilas defeats Ivan Lendl 6-1, 7-6, 6-3 in the final of the Monte Carlo Open, ending an eight-match losing streak to the Czech great. "It was an important win for me because he had beaten me very badly the last time we played," says the 29-year-old Vilas. "When there's someone whose beaten you a lot, it's important to break that trend."

1982 Martina Navratilova beats 16-year-old Andrea Jaeger 6-4, 6-2 to win the Family Circle Cup at Hilton Head Island, S.C. The win moves Navratilova's record for the year to 32-1 and earns her a first-prize paycheck of $34,000. Says Navratilova after the win, "Who says I can't play on clay?'

1936 John Van Ryn plays his final Davis Cup match and wins his U.S. record 22nd Davis Cup doubles match as he and Wilmer Allison defeat Mexico's Flavio Martinez and Antonio Mestre 6-0, 6-1, 6-2.

April 12

1987 Miloslav Mecir, the world's No. 5 ranked player and seven months removed from his surprise run to the finals of the U.S. Open, wins one of the biggest titles of his career, defeating John McEnroe 6-0, 3-6, 6-2, 6-2 to win the WCT Finals in Dallas. Mecir, from the Slovak part of Czechoslovakia, earns $200,000 for the victory. In the third set, McEnroe threatens to leave the court and default the match after chair umpire Gerry Armstrong does not overrule a call. McEnroe collects his racquets and mutters an obscenity that Armstrong hears and assesses McEnroe a point penalty. After a discussion with referee Keith Johnson, McEnroe returns to complete the match, but continues to badger Armstrong the rest of the match. Says McEnroe to Armstrong, according to the Associated Press, "I'm going to test you the entire match. I'm going to talk to you, but I'm not going to say anything you can make any baloney about. C'mon, big boy, do something about it." Says Mecir of McEnroe and his antics, "It's not nice to play in such an atmosphere. Sometimes it looks like he's going to do it again, then he starts to play."

1998 Kenneth Carlsen becomes the first man from Denmark to win an ATP singles title when he defeats Byron Black of Zimbabwe 6-2, 6-0 in the final of the ATP event in Hong Kong. "It's unbelievable to become the first Dane to win a title on the ATP tour," says Carlsen. "I have been waiting for a title for many years and I am glad I have finally done it."

1999 Andre Agassi wins his first tournament title in Asia—and his first tournament of the 1999 season—when he completes a rain-interrupted 6-7 (4), 6-4, 6-4 victory over Boris Becker in the men's singles final at the Hong Kong Open. Agassi leads Becker 2-0 in the third set, when rain postponed play the previous day.

1981 In a re-match of the U.S. Open women's singles final from 1978, Chris Evert-Lloyd beats Pam Shriver 6-3, 6-2 to the Family Circle Cup for a sixth time. Evert-Lloyd's dominance in the event is reflected in that she has not dropped a set at the Sea Pines Racquet Club in her last 29 matches since she won her first Family Circle title in 1974.

April 13

1986 Sixteen-year-old Steffi Graf wins her first of 107 career WTA singles titles defeating Chris Evert Lloyd 6-4, 7-5 in the final of the Family Circle Magazine Cup in Hilton Head, S.C. With the victory, Graf earns a check for $38,000. Says Evert-Lloyd after the final, "It was nice that Steffi won her first tournament. Unfortunately, it was against me."

1980 Twenty-year-old Ivan Lendl wins his first pro singles title, withstanding cold and blustery conditions to beat Eddie Dibbs 6-1, 6-3 in the singles final of the Houston National Championships in Houston, Texas.

2008 Maria Sharapova wins her first career title on a clay court, defeating 18-year-old Dominika Cibulkova of Slovakia 7-6 (7), 6-3 in the final of the Bausch & Lomb Championships in Amelia Island, Fla. Sharapova commits five double faults and hits 33 unforced errors, but is still able to fend off the young Slovakian. Says Sharapova, "I've been fortunate that I could start the clay season early and that I could get a win and my first title on clay, which is exciting." Says Cibulkova, "I had a lot of chances. I missed so many easy shots. I made quite stupid mistakes today. If you want to beat (a player like Sharapova), you can't make this many mistakes."

1986 Anders Jarryd of Sweden wins the biggest singles title of his career, defeating Boris Becker 6-7, 6-1, 6-1, 6-4 to win the WCT Finals in Dallas. Jarryd, who avenges a semifinal loss to Becker from Wimbledon the previous year, earns $150,000 for the tournament victory. Jarryd leads 5-1 in the first set, but falters to lose in it in a tie-break. Becker struggles with a strained right thigh injury that hampers his movement and his serve. Says Becker, "My injury isn't why I lost. Jarryd played a very good match. I gave it my best."

1997 Lindsay Davenport defeats Mary Pierce 6-2, 6-3 to win the Bausch & Lomb Championships in Amelia Island, Fla.—her third tournament title of the year and her fifth career clay court title.

April 14

1985 Chris Evert Lloyd defeats 14-year-old Gabriela Sabatini 6-4, 6-0 in the final of the Family Circle Cup in Hilton Head, S.C. The title is Evert Lloyd's eighth at the Family Circle Cup and Sabatini's first career WTA Tour singles final. Says Evert Lloyd of the young Argentine, "Everyone loves to see a new face and certainly at 14, she is very advanced. She moves very, very well. For 14, she's got almost everything except probably a really tough first serve."

1992 Thirty-five-year-old Bjorn Borg, 10 years removed from his glory years of tennis, is defeated by Olivier Delaitre of France 7-5, 6-2 in 78 minutes in the first round of the ATP Nice Open in Nice, France. The match is the start of a second comeback to professional tennis for the five-time Wimbledon champion. The previous year, Borg plays an ill-fated comeback match against Jordi Arrese of Spain in the first round of the Monte Carlo Open. "The important thing is to play points and matches in front of people again," says Borg, playing in his third tournament match since 1984.

1996 Pete Sampras wins back the No. 1 ranking, defeating Michael Chang 6-4, 3-6, 6-4 to win the Salem Open in Hong Kong. Sampras again claims the top ranking from Austria's Thomas Muster, who, on the same day, wins the singles title at the Estoril Open in Portugal with a 7-6 (4), 6-4 win over Andrea Gaudenzi of Italy. Says Sampras of the No. 1 ranking, "As I have said before, it is the rankings at the end of the year that count."

2007 Jelena Jankovic wins an epic 3-6, 6-3, 7-6 (5) thriller over Venus Williams in the semifinals of the Family Circle Cup in Charleston, S.C. Leading 6-5 in the final set tie-break, Jankovic hits a winner passed Williams to win the match, but only after the chair umpire confirms the call by inspecting the ball mark that catches part of the sideline. "She kind of like was going to shake my hand and then she was in doubt," Jankovic says of Williams reaction to match point. "So I was really lucky on that one to win. It was great."

2008 Fifteen-year-old Ryan Harrison beats No. 95-ranked Pablo Cuevas of Uruguay 6-4, 6-3 in the first round of the U.S. Clay Court Championships and becomes the 10th player in the Open era to win main draw match on the ATP Tour before his 16th birthday. Harrison wins 17 or 18 points at one stage during the first set.

April 15

2001 Playing in her first WTA Tour doubles final since returning to the tour after a six-year layoff between 1994 and 2000, Martina Navratilova, pairing with Arantxa Sanchez-Vicario, loses to Conchita Martinez of Spain and Patricia Tarabini of Argentina, 6-4, 6-2 in the final of the Bausch and Lomb Championships in Amelia Island, Fla. It was Navratilova's first women's doubles final since the 1994 Bank of the West Classic in Oakland, Calif.

2004 Richard Gasquet, an 18-year-old qualifier ranked No. 101 in the world and playing in his first ATP tournament of the year, upsets world No. 1 Roger Federer 6-7 (1), 6-2, 7-6 (8) in the quarterfinals of the Monte Carlo Open. The Frenchmen fights off three match points in the final-set tie-break to end Federer's 25-match winning streak. The loss is Federer's first since he loses in the semifinals of the Australian Open in January to Marat Safin.

2006 One day shy of her 34th birthday, Conchita Martinez, the 1994 Wimbledon champion, announces her retirement after 18 years on the WTA Tour. "I have been away from the courts for quite some time now due to a serious injury to my Achilles tendon," says the former Spanish No.1. "I have had a lot of time to think and have decided the best thing for me is to retire from singles competition. I am leaving open the slight possibility of playing doubles at some point in the future, depending on the status of my injury following surgery."

2007 Steffi Graf requires three stitches in her mouth after her husband, Andre Agassi, inadvertently hits her in the face with his racquet during a charitable fundraising event with children at the West Side Tennis Club in Houston, Texas. A doctor who paid $70,000 in an auction for a trip to play tennis with Agassi and Graf ends up being the person who stitches up Graf's cut lip.

2006 Justine Henin-Hardenne loses for the first time at the Family Circle Cup, falling to Patty Schnyder 2-6, 6-3, 6-2 in the semifinals. The top-seeded Henin-Hardenne, the tournament's defending champion, wins 14 straight matches at the event before losing to Schnyder.

2007 Ivo Karlovic, the 6-foot-10 Croatian, wins his first career ATP singles title, defeating Mariano Zabaleta of Argentina 6-4, 6-1 to win the U.S. Men's Clay Court Championships in Houston.

April 16

1988 Gabriela Sabatini rallies from a 0-3 third-set deficit to defeat Steffi Graf 6-3, 4-6, 7-5 in the semifinals of the Bausch & Lomb Championships in Amelia Island, Fla. The loss for Graf is one of only three during her eventual "Golden Grand Slam" season. Sabatini previously beats Graf in the final of the Virginia Slims of Florida in March, but later loses to her German rival in the semifinals of the French Open and the finals of both the U.S. Open and the Olympic Games. Graf's only other defeat in 1988 happens in her final match of the year, a semifinal loss to Pam Shriver at the year-end Virginia Slims Championships in New York.

1977 Anti-apartheid protestors spill oil on court to protest the United States competing against South Africa and disrupt the Davis Cup doubles match between Stan Smith and Bob Lutz and Frew McMillan and Byron Bertram in Newport Beach, Calif. U.S. Captain Tony Trabert hits one of the two protestors with a racquet before police apprehend the culprits. After a 45-minute delay to clean the oil, Smith and Lutz defeat McMillan and Bertram 7-5, 6-1, 3-6, 6-3 to give the United States an insurmountable 3-0 lead over the South Africans.

1980 Thirty-six-year-old Arthur Ashe officially announces his retirement from competitive tennis at the age of 36 prior to a lecture at San Francisco University "It is time," he says. "Health is a factor, but that's not the only reason...I feel pretty good. My doctors say I will live to be 100, but they won't put that in writing." His public announcement follows a letter that Ashe sends to friends and business associates, dated April 11, announcing that his days as a playing pro are over and that he is available for other assignments. "Long ago in my Sunday School classes, I learned that 'for everything there is a season," Ashe writes. "After many hours of hard thought and soul-searching, I have decided from today on, to end my non-stop globetrotting odyssey in search of the perfect serve and retire from competitive tennis. In its place, I hope to begin another exciting season of writing, talking, listening, reading and assisting."

1978 Gene Mayer defeats John Newcombe 6-3, 6-4 in the final of the Mexican Open in Guadalajara, Mexico—in what is Newcombe's 53rd and final appearance in an ATP singles final.

April 17

2005 Eighteen-year-old Rafael Nadal wins the first important tournament title of his career, defeating Guillermo Coria of Argentina 6-3, 6-1, 0-6, 7-5 to win the Monte Carlos Open. Nadal, seeded No. 11 in the tournament, wins the most important match of his young career since beating Andy Roddick in Spain's 2004 Davis Cup Final triumph over the United States. Says Nadal, who six weeks later goes on to win his first French Open title, "My first big title. I think I am very happy when I won the Davis Cup, but now is unbelievable."

1979 With the likes of Billie Jean King, Ilie Nastase, Vitas Gerulaitis and Martina Navratilova in attendance, Chris Evert marries fellow tennis professional John Lloyd at the St. Andrew's Roman Catholic Church in Ft. Lauderdale, Fla.

1988 Playing his first tournament since losing in the quarterfinals of the U.S. Open the previous fall, John McEnroe wins his first singles title in 18 months defeating Stefan Edberg 6-2, 6-2 in the final of the Japan Open in Tokyo.

1988 Martina Navratilova crushes Gabriela Sabatini 6-0, 6-2, in just 53 minutes to win the WTA singles title at Amelia Island, Fla. Says the 31-year-old Navratilova, "I played well and she didn't. It's as simple as that." Sabatini has an apparent let down after beating Steffi Graf the previous day, coming back from an 0-3 deficit in the third set. "I was not tired, but maybe I was a little tight. She never let me get into the match."

2008 Jimmy Arias pulls off what is likely the biggest upset in the four-year history of the Outback Champions Series "champions" tennis circuit, defeating former world No. 1 John McEnroe 7-5, 6-2 for the first time in his career at The Residences at the Ritz Carlton, Grand Cayman Legends Championships in Grand Cayman. Arias, who won only one previous match on the Outback Champions Series, dictates play on the red clay surface with his famed whipping forehand and frustrates the 49-year-old McEnroe. The three-time Wimbledon champion is so angered at his play that he is given a point penalty for excessive racquet and ball abuse when trailing 5-2 in the second set. Quips Arias of his win over McEnroe, "I've lost to him 735 times. I don't know the exact count but it's many times that I've lost."

April 18

2004 After missing the entire 2003 season following right rotator cuff surgery, Germany's Tommy Haas captures his first ATP title in three years, defeating reigning U.S. Open champion Andy Roddick 6-3, 6-4 to win the U.S. Men's Clay Court Championships in Houston, Texas. "I am glad to win my first title since coming back," says the 26-year-old Haas. "I didn't expect it to happen this fast." Roddick enters the match having won 18 of 19 matches in Houston, winning titles in 2001 and 2002 and losing in the 2003 final to Andre Agassi.

2004 Venus Williams defeats Conchita Martinez 2-6, 6-2, 6-1 to win the Family Circle Cup in Charleston, S.C.—her first title in 14 months.

1993 In a battle between the world's top ranked players—Pete Sampras and Jim Courier—in the final of the Salem Open in Hong Kong, Sampras further cements his newly acquired No. 1 ranking, beating the man he replaced in the top ranking by a 6-3, 6-7 (1), 7-6 (2) margin.

1993 Qualifier Marc Goellner of Germany, playing in his first ATP singles final, defeats Ivan Lendl, playing in his 143rd ATP final, 1-6, 6-4, 6-2 to win the Nice Open in Nice, France.

1999 Monica Seles, a former Yugoslavian born in the town of Novi Sad, clinches victory for the United States Fed Cup team over Croatia, a former Yugoslavian state, by defeating 1997 French Open champion Iva Majoli 6-0, 6-3 in 43 minutes to give the USA a 3-0 lead in the Fed Cup first round in Raleigh, N.C. The match is originally scheduled to be played in the Croatian capital of Zagreb, but is moved to Raleigh due to NATO-lead bombing of Yugoslavia.

April 19

1992 World No. 1 Jim Courier wins two matches in one day to win the singles title at the Salem Open in Hong Kong. Because of rain the previous day, Courier beats Brad Gilbert 6-4, 6-1 in the morning's semifinal match, and then in the afternoon, he beats Michael Chang 7-5, 6-3 in the championship match. Says Courier, "It is always tough to play Brad because he never beats himself and you have to beat him. You have to come out knowing in the back of your mind that you have to play Michael, who is going to tire you out."

1988 Marian Vajda of Czechoslovakia, a journeyman professional who gains notoriety in 2007 and 2008 as the coach of U.S. Open finalist and Australian Open champion Novak Djokovic, registers a major upset of two-time Wimbledon champion and No. 4-ranked Boris Becker of West Germany, 6-3, 5-7, 6-1 in the second round of the Monte Carlo Open. Says Vajda, ranked No. 42 in the world, "Boris didn't (use) good tactics today. I was more patient in the rallies, so I felt better. I felt I could have played the ball 100 times over the net and not miss." Says Becker, "Marian made my life difficult out there. He played very, very long balls, and I couldn't get in. It's much more difficult for me to get ready on clay. You have to be well prepared. You have to have a few matches under your belt. The longer the rallies were, the worse I played. I had bad groundstrokes out there."

1987 Steffi Graf cruises to win 16 of the first 20 points of the match and defeats Hana Mandlikova 6-3, 6-4 to win the WITA Championships at Amelia Island, Fla., and extends her match winning streak to 22 in a row. "It's difficult to play Steffi because she starts so fast, but I think my serve was the main reason why I lost," Mandlikova says after the match. "I didn't serve well. I double-faulted in the important moments."

1992 Monica Seles needs only 65 minutes to defeat Zina Garrison 6-1, 6-1 to win the Virginia Slims of Houston for her 24th career WTA Tour singles title.

April 20

1982 Reigning French Open champion Bjorn Borg loses in the second round of the qualifying rounds of the Alan King-Caesar's Palace Tennis Classic in Las Vegas, falling to Dick Stockton 7-6, 1-6, 6-2. Borg is forced to play in the qualifying rounds of the tournament for failing to play a minimum of 10 Grand Prix tournaments by a March 31 deadline. Borg, who beat Victor Amaya 6-4, 6-4 in the first round of qualifying, only plays in Las Vegas because of a commitment he made to the tournament before the Grand Prix rule was instituted. Says Stockton of Borg, "I don't think he had his heart in the qualifying. I don't think it was something he really wanted to do." After the loss, Borg declares that he is only going to play exhibition matches the rest of the year and, the following January, announces his complete withdrawal from the men's circuit.

2008 In the 35th anniversary edition of the Family Circle Cup, Serena Williams wins the prestigious women's singles title in Charleston, S.C. for the first time in her career, defeating Vera Zvonareva of Russia 6-4, 3-6, 6-3 in the final. The tournament victory is the first for Williams on clay since the 2002 French Open. Says Zvonareva of Williams, "She always puts pressure on you, so you always have to go for a bigger serve and eventually your serve percentage goes down. I accepted I would have some double-faults today and I knew it was going to happen when I was coming into the match. It's just too bad to have two of them in a row."

2006 Guillermo Coria of Argentina serves an ATP three-set match record of 23 double faults in his 6-7 (5), 6-4, 6-3 round of 16 win over Nicolas Kiefer of Germany at the Monte Carlo Open. In Coria's previous match against Paul Henri Mathieu of France, Coria serves 20 double faults. "Imagine what I will be like when I can serve again," jokes Coria, who hits four consecutive double faults in one game to eclipse Brazilian Jaime Oncins' record of 22 double faults in 1994 at Mexico City.

1986 Sixteen-year-old Steffi Graf wins her second WTA Tour singles title in as many weeks, defeating countrywoman Claudia Kohde-Kilsch 6-4, 5-7, 7-6 (3) in the final of the Sunkist WTA Championships in Amelia Island, Fla. Graf is warned in the third game of the final set for unauthorized coaching from her coach and father Peter Graf, who is accused of signaling strategy to his daughter.

2007 Roger Federer defeats David Ferrer 6-4, 6-0 in the quarterfinals of the Monte Carlo Open to register his 500th career ATP victory and surpass $30 million in career prize money. Says Federer of his milestones, "Those are two incredible numbers."

1983 Trey Waltke, ranked No. 118 in the world, registers one of the biggest upsets of the year in men's tennis, defeating world No. 3 John McEnroe 3-6, 6-3, 6-4 in the first round of the Alan King Tennis Classic in Las Vegas. At 4-4 in the final set, McEnroe is assessed a point penalty when he fires a ball into the stands after losing a point. Waltke goes on to break McEnroe's serve and calmly serves out the match.

1987 A month removed from his devastating loss to No. 285th-ranked Hugo Chapacu of Paraguay in Davis Cup play, Jimmy Arias upsets top-seeded Boris Becker 6-3, 6-3 in the third round of the Monte Carlo Open. The No. 53-ranked Arias, once ranked No. 5 in the world, credits work with sports psychologist Jim Loehr in his post-match press conference with his strong form against the two-time reigning Wimbledon champion. "He (Loehr) showed me films of me when I was 17, 18, 19 years old and they showed I was having fun when I played-laughing and diving around the court. When I saw how I was playing now I looked like I was dead." Arias continues his fine play and reaches the Monte Carlo final, his first final since 1985, but loses to Sweden's Mats Wilander.

April 21

1985 Zina Garrison pulls off a major upset to win her second WTA Tour title, defeating Chris Evert Lloyd 6-4, 6-3 in the final of the Sunkist WTA Championships in Amelia Island, Fla. Prior to the final, Garrison had not even taken a set from Evert-Lloyd. Says Garrison, "I didn't think Chris played as well as I've seen her play, but I'm glad I beat her."

1985 Henrik Sundstrom defeats Hans Gildemeister 6-1, 3-6, 2-6, 7-5, 6-2 in Santiago, Chile to clinch Sweden's 4-1 first round Davis Cup victory over Chile. The Davis Cup series was originally scheduled for March 3, but is postponed after an earthquake strikes the Chilean city.

1992 Playing in the Monte Carlo Open for the first time in his career, Pete Sampras, seeded No. 2, loses to Carl-Uwe Steeb of Germany 6-3, 6-4 in the opening round. Steeb rolls to a 5-0 lead after just 19 minutes and holds on for the win. Says Sampras, "I couldn't get anything going today."

1987 As a result of a lack of crowd control and intimidation of American players during the United States vs. Paraguay Davis Cup first round match, the International Tennis Federation strips Paraguay of its home advantage for the rest of this year's Davis Cup competition.

1996 Pete Sampras and Thomas Muster, the No. 1 and No. 2 players in the world respectively, win titles in different continents and different surfaces on the same day. Sampras defeats Richey Reneberg 6-4, 7-5 on a hard court to win the Japan Open in Tokyo, while Muster defeats Marcelo Rios 6-3, 4-6, 6-4, 6-1 on a clay court to win the Count de Godo Championships in Barcelona.

1985 Playing in front of a crowd of better than 13,000 in Tokyo's Yoyogi Stadium, Ivan Lendl defeats John McEnroe 6-4, 6-2 in just 76 minutes in the final of the Suntory Cup. Says McEnroe of the final, "I didn't play great, but I didn't play terrible. He just overwhelmed me."

April 22

1968 "Open" tennis begins as the British Hard Court Championships—the first tournament open to professionals and amateurs—begins in Bournemouth, England at the West Hants Lawn Tennis Club. British Hard Court Championships. Writes Bud Collins in *The Bud Collins History of Tennis*, "Staged at the coastal resort of Bournemouth, it was the historic first chapter, and it began damply, coolly on a drizzly, raw Monday, April 22. The "open era" lurched into being with a minor young Briton, John Clifton, winning the first point but losing his match, 6-2, 6-3, 4-6, 8-6 against Australian pro Owen Davidson—then the British national coach—on the red shale courts of the West Hants Lawn Tennis Club."

1998 Pete Sampras wins his first—and only—career singles match at the Monte Carlo Open, defeating a familiar foe—Andre Agassi—6-4, 7-5 in the second round of the important French Open prep clay court tournament. The match-up marks the earliest tournament meeting between the two great rivals, who at the end of their careers play 16 of their 34 career matches in tournament finals. Agassi is still trying to return to top form after finishing his 1997 season with a No. 122 ranking, while Sampras is battling Australian Open champion Petr Korda for the world's No. 1 ranking. Says Sampras of the early-round meeting between the two giants of the tennis world. "It was a little bit awkward for Andre and I to play each other in the second round. I'm used to playing him later on in the tournament where I'm playing a little bit better. We were both a little bit nervous out there." Writes Chris Clarey of the *New York Times* of the confrontation, "The former archrivals with the disparate personalities but similar gifts have essentially been out of synchronization since their last major match, the 1995 United States Open final. But on this blustery day at the Monte Carlo Open, their life lines converged again. It might have only been a second-round encounter in an event many Americans consider a glorified French Open warm-up, but it was clear from the opening exchange that it mattered to these Americans a great deal. It was clearer still when Sampras coolly finished off his 6-4, 7-5 victory with an ace and a clenched fist, and a hot and bothered Agassi quickly assembled his belongings and marched off the court." Sampras, appearing in Monte Carlo for the fourth time, emabarrisingly loses 6-1, 6-1 to Fabrice Santoro of France in his second round match and never again returns to the event—his win over Agassi being his lone match victory at the tournament against three first round losses.

2007 Rafael Nadal remains undefeated against Roger Federer on clay courts, defeating the world No. 1 for a fifth straight time on clay 6-4, 6-4 in the final of the Monte Carlo Open. Says Federer, "I lost four times against Rafa. I'd rather have that than lose against four different guys." The title is Nadal's third straight in Monte Carlo and his 67th straight match-victory on clay courts.

2001 Jennifer Capriati defeats Martina Hingis 6-0, 4-6, 6-4 to win the Family Circle Cup in Charleston, S.C., becoming the first American to win the title since Martina Navratilova defeated a 14-year-old Capriati for the 1990 title. Capriati is the first American-born player to win the Family Circle Cup since Chris Evert in 1985.

1984 Chris Evert Lloyd's 85-match clay court winning streak in her home state of Florida is ended abruptly as Martina Navratilova defeats her arch rival 6-2, 6-0 in the final of the WTA event in Amelia Island, Fla. Navratilova only allows Evert Lloyd to get to deuce one time in the last eight games of the match to win her 10th straight match against Evert.

April 23

1991 Playing with a wood-racquet and his trademark headband, 34-year-old Bjorn Borg plays the first match in an ill-fated comeback, losing in 75 minutes to Spain's Jordi Aresse 6-2, 6-3 in the first round of the Monte Carlo Open. The match marks Borg's first appearance in an ATP event since 1984, when he loses in the first round of the event in Stuttgart, West Germany. Says Borg after the match, "I know people have high expectations of me. But I didn't put so much pressure on myself. I enjoyed competing again. I'm ready to continue and, hopefully, I can stay longer in tournaments." Says Aresse, who the following year would again make headlines when he is the surprise silver medalist in men's singles at the 1992 Olympic Games, "At the start, I didn't want to play him. Now, I wouldn't change that moment for anything in life. To see all those people come to see Borg, it was very moving."

1994 Nineteen-year-old Andrei Medvedev of Ukraine wins the biggest title of his professional career, defeating defending champion and reigning French Open champion Sergi Bruguera of Spain 7-5, 6-1, 6-3 in the final of the Monte Carlo Open. Medvedev becomes the youngest player to win the singles title at the prestigious ATP event. Of the 95 points Medvedev wins in the match, 45 are scored with outright winners, illustrating his go for broke style on the day.

1994 Thirty-one-year-old Jeremy Bates of Britain, playing on the ATP Tour for a 15th year, finally wins his first ATP singles title, defeating Joern Renzenbrink of Germany in the final of the Korean Open in Seoul. Bates becomes the first British man since Mark Cox in 1977 to win an ATP singles title.

2000 Cedric Pioline of France wins the biggest title of his career, defeating Dominik Hrbaty of Slovakia 6-4, 7-6 (3) 7-6 (6) in the singles final at the Monte Carlo Open. Says Pioline after winning his fifth career ATP singles final, "I'm like flying, and I don't know when and where I will land."

2000 Mary Pierce dominates Arantxa Sanchez Vicario 6-1, 6-0 to win the Family Circle Cup in Hilton Head, S.C., concluding the tournament's run at Hilton Head Island before moving, after 28 years, to Charleston, S.C. Pierce loses only 12 games during the tournament, besting the record of 15 games lost set by Chris Evert Lloyd in 1985. Says Pierce after pocketing the

$166,000 first prize paycheck, "This has been a great, great week for me. I've just become more and more relaxed and more at peace with everything that I do."

2007 Fourteen months after being diagnosed with skin cancer, Spaniard Felix Mantilla makes an emotional return to the ATP Tour, defeating Farrukh Dustov of Uzbekistan 6-4, 1-6, 6-0 in the first round of the Barcelona Open. The 32-year-old Mantilla, a former top 10 player who defeated Roger Federer in the final of the 2003 Italian Championships, last plays an ATP Tour level match at the 2005 U.S. Open. As he was training for the 2006 season, doctors discovered skin cancer on a black mole on his back. He was told that if not diagnosed at the time, he could have died. Says Mantilla, "I wanted to come back as I did not want to end (my career) that way. To win today is probably as big as winning a tournament for me—people probably don't realize that but it is true." Mantilla goes on to lose to countryman Carlos Moya in the second round.

2008 World No. 1 Roger Federer escapes from a potentially embarrassing opening loss at the Monte Carlo Open, rallying to defeat Spanish qualifier Ruben Ramirez Hidalgo 6-1, 3-6, 7-6 (1). Federer trails 1-5 in the final set and is two points from defeat at 5-4, 30-15. Says Federer, "I felt a bit slow out there. He played so badly in the first set that he almost faked me out. But when he served for the match it became tough on him."

April 24

1983 Martina Navratilova negotiates 35 mile-per-hour wind gusts to defeat Andrea Jaeger 6-1, 7-5 to win the United Airlnes Tournament of Champions singles title in Haines City, Fla., for her 36th consecutive match victory. Navratilova pairs with Pam Shriver in the doubles final, but loses to Billie Jean King and Anne Smith 6-3, 1-6, 7-6 (11-9). Navratilova and Shriver go on to win their next 109 doubles matches—a WTA Tour record—before losing the 1985 Wimbledon final to Kathy Jordan and Liz Smylie on July 6, 1985.

1983 Jose Higueras saves five match points to defeat Tomas Smid of Czechoslovakia 2-6, 7-6, 7-5 in the final of the State Express Tennis Classic in Bournemouth, England.

1955 Tony Trabert wins his ninth consecutive tournament title, defeating U.S. Davis Cup teammate Vic Seixas 6-0, 6-1, 6-4 to win the River Oaks Tennis Championships in Houston.

1983 Jimmy Connors defeats Mark Edmondson, 7-6, 6-1, in a wind-swept men's singles final at the Alan King Tennis Classic in Las Vegas for his 97th singles title in his career.

1988 Martina Navratilova wins her 134th career singles title, defeating Gabriela Sabatini 6-0, 6-2 in the final of the Bausch & Lomb Championships in Amelia Island, Fla.

1989 Stefan Edberg defeats Ivan Lendl 6-3, 2-6, 6-4 in the men's singles final at the Japan Open.

2004 Playing in his fifth consecutive final at the U.S. Men's Clay Court Championships, Andy Roddick wins his third title at the event in Houston, Texas, defeating Frenchman Sebastien Grosjean 6-2, 6-2.

2005 Rafael Nadal defeats fellow Spaniard Juan Carlos Ferrero 6-1, 7-6 (4), 6-3 to win the Open Seat Godo in Barcelona, Spain. The title is Nadal's fifth career title and moves the 18-year-old into the top 10 for the first time in his career.

April 25

1982 Jimmy Connors benefits from Gene Mayer's ankle injury to win the Alan King Tennis Classic in Las Vegas. Mayer severely sprains his ankle trailing 2-5 in the first set and hobbles over in pain after being wrong-footed in a baseline rally at 40-30. Connors hurdles the net and assists Mayer off of the court, before being awarded the title in a retirement.

1999 Jim Courier pairs with Todd Woodbridge of Australia for the first time in his career and wins the doubles title at the U.S. Men's Clay Court Championships, defeating first-time ATP doubles finalists and identical twins Bob and Mike Bryan 7-6 (4), 6-4 in the final. The title ultimately becomes Courier's final ATP championship—his sixth career doubles title and 29th overall career title.

1982 Manuel Orantes needs only 72 minutes to defeat countryman Angel Gimenez 6-2, 6-0 to win the $100,000 British clay-court title in Bournemouth, England. Following the match, Orantes declares he is not going to play Davis Cup for Spain against Britain because of bad treatment he was receiving from the Spanish Tennis Federation. "I don't think I will play for Spain in the Davis Cup against Britain in October because of the way I've been treated by the federation," he says. "There is too much pain in my heart. They treated me like old furniture when I needed help after some arm operations. I played for Spain for 14 years but I had to find out that they did not want me anymore from the newspapers."

1999 Gustavo Kuerten needs only 53 minutes to win the Monte Carlo Open in Monaco after Marcelo Rios retires with a right thigh injury in the singles final with Kuerten leading 6-4, 2-1. The title is Kuerten's second biggest tournament victory at this stage in his career, next to his win at the 1997 French Open that he wins as an unseeded player ranked No. 66 in the world. Says Kuerten of his preparations to perhaps win another title at Roland Garros, "When I won the French Open, I wasn't a big player. After, I had to adapt myself to big tournaments, but now things are clear in my mind. I can save all my energy for the matches. That makes a big difference. I am a more complete player. I can serve and volley, mix my game up and not let the other guy know what I am going to do."

April 26

1981 Chris Evert Lloyd needs only 54 minutes to shockingly defeat Martina Navratilova 6-0, 6-0 in the final of the Murjani Championships in Amelia Island, Fla. The win is Evert Lloyd's 49th straight on clay and her 174th win against one loss on clay since 1973. Says Navratilova to the fans following the match, "When they introduced Chris, they said she was a virtuoso on clay. She showed them they were right. I'm sorry I didn't do much better. I have a check here for $16,000, and I feel like I should give half of it back to you."

1998 Jim Courier defeats Michael Chang 7-5, 3-6, 7-5 in 2 hours, 44 minutes in the final of the U.S. Men's Clay Court Championships in Orlando, Fla. The title is Courier's 23rd and what ultimately turns out to be his final ATP singles title.

1981 Victor Pecci of Paraguay defeats Hungary's Balazs Taroczy 6-4, 6-3 in the singles final of the British Clay Court Championships in Bournemouth, England. The match starts outdoors on a snow-surrounded clay court, but is completed on an indoor carpet. The match is suspended in the ninth game of the first set due to rain and both players decide to resume the match indoors to prevent the possibility of having to stay an extra day to complete the match. Taroczy is in favor of the switch to the indoor venue, saying "He had to change his winning game and besides I have a good indoor record." Says Pecci after winning the $15,000 first prize, "I would like to come back to defend the title next year, because I love playing on clay courts, but if the weather is going to be as bad as it has been this week, I will have to think very seriously about it."

1982 Ivan Lendl defeats John McEnroe 6-2, 3-6, 6-3, 6-3 in the WCT Finals at the Reunion Arena in Dallas, Texas. Lendl, ranked No. 2 in the world. defeats the top-ranked McEnroe for the fourth straight time and claims the first prize of $150,000. Says Lendl, "The more times you can beat a player like John the more you feel like a champion." Says McEnroe, "Ivan is obviously a devastating player. He has shown that this year by dominating the circuit. He played like a dominating player tonight and he deserved to win."

1987 Chris Evert wins her 148th career WTA tournament title, defeating Martina Navratilova 3-6, 6-1, 7-6 (4) in the final of the Virginia Slims of Houston.

April 27

1986 Twelve hours after his wife Cecilia gives birth to a baby daughter in New York, Yannick Noah is defeated by Joakim Nystrom 6-3, 6-2 in the final of the Monte Carlo Open. "I was not into the game," a tired Noah says following the match. "I wasn't thinking about the match because this morning I had a little daughter—and that for me is more important."

2006 The only thing bothering Rafael Nadal during his 6-4, 6-2 second round match with Spanish qualifier Ivan Navarro at the Barcelona Open is a female intruder, who bursts onto the court and handcuffs herself to the net post. Nadal is leading 6-4, 4-0 when the woman enters the court and a brief delay ensues while the protester is cut loose and taken away by security guards.

1985 Martina Navratilova needs only 49 minutes to defeat 15-year-old Katerina Maleeva 6-1, 6-0 win the $50,000 first prize and the WTA singles title in Lake Buena Vista, Fla. Says Navratilova, "I don't think I intimidated her. She's a good player for being that young. She's really burst through the gates."

1997 Michael Chang defeats Grant Stafford of South Africa 4-6, 6-2, 6-1 to win the singles title at the U.S. Men's Clay Court Championships in Orlando, Fla. The title moves Chang into the No. 2 ranking on the ATP computer, the highest ranking he achieves in his career.

2008 Rafael Nadal wins the Monte Carlo Open for a fourth straight time, defeating world No. 1 Roger Federer 7-5, 7-5 in the championship match. Nadal becomes the first player to win four straight in the principality since New Zealand's Tony Wilding from 1911 to 1914. The title is also Nadal's 24th career title and 19th on clay. Federer leads 4-3 by a service break in the first set and 4-0 in the second set, but falters to lose the Monte Carlo final for a third straight year to Nadal. Says Nadal, "Winning four times here is unimaginable."

1997 Marcelo Rios of Chile wins the biggest title of his career, defeating Alex Corretja of Spain 6-4, 6-3, 6-3 in the singles final of the Italian Championships in Rome.

April 28

1996 Kimiko Date of Japan registers the biggest win over her career, upsetting world No. 1 Steffi Graf of Germany, 7-6 (7), 3-6, 12-10 to help Japan upset Germany 3-2 in the first round of the Fed Cup competition in Tokyo. Kyoko Nagatsuka and Ai Sugiyama defeat Graf and Anke Huber 4-6, 6-3, 6-3 in the fifth and decisive match.

1968 Ken Rosewall wins the first ever "Open" tournament, defeating fellow Aussie and fellow professional Rod Laver 3-6, 6-2, 6-0, 6-3 in the final of the British Hard Court Championships in Bournemouth, England. Rosewall pockets the first-prize check of $2,400 in the first tournament open to both pros and amateurs. Rosewall, however, covets the title more than the money stating, "It's worth more than money. It has name value and prestige." Rosewall goes on to win the first major tournament open to amateurs and professionals later in the spring at the French Open, defeating Laver again in the final.

1985 Eighteen-year-old Annabel Croft of Great Britain creates headlines in Britain and causes much excitement of the possibility of a budding British women's tennis star as she wins her first WTA Tour tournament, defeating No. 7 ranked Wendy Turnbull 6-0, 7-6 (5) to win the Virginia Slims of San Diego. Croft, ranked No. 83 at the time, never rises to the expectations caused by this victory and never wins another title before quitting her professional career in 1988.

1996 Thomas Muster successfully defends his title at the Monte Carlo Open, defeating Spain's Albert Costa 6-3, 5-7, 4-6, 6-3, 6-2 in the singles final. Muster becomes only the fourth man to successfully defend his title in Monaco, joining Nicola Pietrangeli, Ilie Nastase and Bjorn Borg. The 3 hour, 8 minute win is Muster's 35th consecutive singles match victory on clay courts.

1932 Ellsworth Vines makes his Davis Cup debut and needs five sets to defeat Jack Wright 8-6, 3-6, 6-4, 4-6, 6-2 as the United States takes a 2-0 lead over Canada in the Davis Cup first round in Chevy Chase, Md.

1999 Tickets for the United States vs. Australia Davis Cup quarterfinal—a centennial celebration of the Davis Cup—at the Longwood Cricket Club in Brookline, Mass., sell out in 81 minutes.

April 29

1970 Andre Agassi, the champion player who transforms himself from a long-haired "Image is Everything" rebel to a bald statesman and ambassador of the game who is one of five men to win all four major singles titles in their careers, is born in Las Vegas, Nevada. Agassi bursts onto the scene as a flamboyant, cocky 18-year-old in 1988, but is unable to win "the big one" until an unlikely triumph at Wimbledon in 1992. His career is full of highs and lows as he wins his second major at the U.S. Open in 1994 as an unseeded player and wins the Australian Open in 1995 en route to ascending to the world No. 1 ranking. After winning Olympic gold in 1996, Agassi plummets to a No. 141 ranking in 1997, but inspires millions around the world by winning the French Open in 1999—completing his career Grand Slam—and returning to the No. 1 ranking in 1999.

2002 Rafael Nadal, at age 15, makes his professional debut at the Mallorcan Open in Spain, and beats Paraguay's Ramon Delgado 6-4, 6-4 in the first round to become the ninth player under the age of 16 to win an ATP match. Says Nadal following the win, "I really wanted to go out there and play well. I knew it was going to be difficult, but I held my game. I thought I played well, keeping the ball deep and maintaining the power."

2001 Eighteen-year-old Andy Roddick wins his first ATP singles title at the Verizon Tennis Challenge in Atlanta, Ga., defeating Belgium's Xavier Malisse 6-2, 6-4 in the final. "I'm glad I got to win it here with my brother John (assistant coach at the University of Georgia) and my parents watching on," says Roddick, who becomes the first American teenager to win an ATP title since 19-year-old Michael Chang wins San Francisco on Feb. 9, 1992. "That makes it that much better. I can look back at the tournament and say I played consistent tennis throughout the week."

2003 The All England Lawn Tennis and Croquet Club announces that players will no longer have to bow or curtsy to the Royal Box at Centre Court during The Championships at Wimbledon. The announcement comes on the same day the All England Club confirms another tradition will continue: men will be paid more than women. Over the years, players have been required to bow or curtsy to members of the royal family when walking onto or leaving Centre Court. But, from now on, they will have to do so only if Queen Elizabeth II or Prince Charles, her eldest son and heir to the throne, are in the box.

April 30

1989 Playing in only her fifth professional tournament, 15-year-old future world No. 1 Monica Seles upsets 34-year-old Chris Evert 3-6, 6-1, 6-4 to win the Virginia Slims of Houston. Says Evert after the match of the future French, U.S. and Australian Open champion, "If you lose to someone who's not a good player, then you should be concerned, but she's a good player. She was able to loosen up and just play and the pressure was on me to win."

1993 Crazed German fan Gunther Parche stabs Monica Seles in the back at a tournament in Hamburg, Germany. Parche, a 38-year-old unemployed machine worker, makes his way courtside during the quarterfinal match between Seles and Maggie Maleeva, comes up behind Seles during a change-over, and stabs her in the back with a five-inch knife. The physical injuries to Seles are minor, but her psychological injuries are more severe as she does not return to competitive tennis for 27 months.

1989 Nineteen-year-old Alberto Mancini of Argentina upsets Boris Becker 7-5, 2-6, 7-6 (4), 7-5 to win the Monte Carlo Open. Ranked No. 31 in the world, Mancini beats No. 1 seed Mats Wilander of Sweden in the semifi-nals, before dismissing the No. 2 seeded Becker in the final. Says Mancini, "This year is beginning very good and giving me a lot of confidence for the rest of the year. To beat Wilander and Becker on center court in Monte Carlo, it's like a dream."

1995 Thomas Muster performs a miracle comeback to defeat Boris Becker 4-6, 5-7, 6-1, 7-6, 6-0 in the final of the Monte Carlo Open, denying Becker of his first clay court tournament victory. Says Muster, "I don't know how I won the match."

2006 Spaniard Rafael Nadal defeats countryman Tommy Robredo 6-4, 6-4, 6-0 to win the Barcelona Open tennis championships for the second con-secutive year. The win over Robredo is the 19-year-old's 47th straight match victory on clay courts, surpassing Bjorn Borg for second place for most con-secutive clay court match victories and landing him just six matches shy of tying the all-time record of Guillermo Vilas of 53 straight matches. Nadal goes on to break the record in the first round of the 2006 French Open.

May 1

1983 John McEnroe wins a fifth-set tie-breaker 7-0 to defeat Ivan Lendl 6-2, 4-6, 6-3, 6-7 (5), 7-6 (0) to win a record third WCT Finals in Dallas. The 4 hour, 35 minute final surpasses the 3 hour, 34 minute 1972 final between Ken Rosewall and Rod Laver, which was previously the longest final in the tournament's history.

1931 Frank Shields, the grandfather of actress Brooke Shields (the former wife of the Andre Agassi) makes his Davis Cup debut as the United States opens up play against Mexico in the Davis Cup first round in Mexico City, Mexico. Shields defeats Ricardo Tapia 6-4, 6-4, 6-2 as the United States takes a 2-0 over Mexico after the first day of play. Famously later in the year, Shields is forced to default the Wimbledon final against teammate Sidney Wood when the U.S. Davis Cup Committee tells Shields to default the final after injuring his ankle in his semifinal match with Jean Borotra of France, so as not to worsen the injury and jeopardize his play for the U.S. series with Great Britain, played one week after Wimbledon. Shields also represents the United States in Davis Cup play in 1932 and 1934.

2007 In a match played in frigid conditions—including snow flurries— Elena Dementieva of Russia defeats Meilen Tu of the United States 6-7 (5), 6-0, 7-5 in 2 hours, 40 minutes the first round of the J&S Cup in Warsaw, Poland. Both players wear pants and long-sleeve shirts during the match— and struggle with their serves as the first set features 10 service breaks. Says Dementieva, "It was extremely difficult conditions. It was freezing out there and also the snow. It was a new experience in my life. It was a very tough match for me."

1937 Don Budge and Gene Mako defeat Fumiteru Nakano and Jiro Yamagishi 6-0, 6-1, 6-4 to give the United States an insurmountable 3-0 lead over Japan in the Davis Cup first round at the Olympic Club in San Francisco, Calif.

1977 Guillermo Vilas clinches victory for Argentina in the Davis Cup Americas Zone Final in Buenos Aires with a 5-7, 6-2, 6-2, 6-2 win over Dick Stockton. Brian Gottfried defeats Ricardo Cano 7-5, 7-5, 6-0 in the dead rubber match to make the final score 3-2 for Argentina.

May 2

1988 Eighteen-year-old Andre Agassi, seeded No. 1, defeats seventh-seeded and fellow American Jimmy Arias to win the singles title at the U.S. Men's Clay Court Championships in Charleston, S.C. Says Agassi, "This means a lot to me because I came in here seeded one and expected to win. I beat the people I was supposed to beat as far as ranking goes, and I've yet to do that. So, from that aspect, it really means a lot."

1993 Thirty-three-year-old Ivan Lendl wins his 93rd—and second to last—ATP singles title, defeating Michael Stich 7-6 (2), 6-3 to win the BMW Open in Munich, Germany. Says Stich following the match, "Lendl was lucky in the first set; I deserved to win it. In the second set, he was clearly better."

2007 In one of the most bizarre exhibitions in the history of the sport, clay-court maestro Rafael Nadal defeats grass court king Roger Federer 7-5, 4-6, 7-6 (10) in Palma de Mallorca, Spain in an exhibition played on a court where one side of the net is a grass surface and the other half is a clay surface. Says Nadal, a native of Mallorca and the two-time reigning French Open champion, of his win over the four-time reigning Wimbledon champion, "It was a long match, with many changes of pace and with little time to adapt. My feet are suffering as a price of having to adapt to the grass." The special court takes 19 days to install and costs $1.63 million to construct.

1988 Coming off a six-week layoff, Pam Shriver defeats Czechoslovakia's Helena Sukova 7-5, 6-1 to win the WTA singles title in Tokyo—her 20th singles title of her career. "It was very important for me because I've never won a singles tournament in Japan and I've taken six weeks off so I wanted to come in and play a very good tournament," says Shriver.

1993 Stefan Edberg plays what he describes as his "best clay court event ever" and defeats Sergi Bruguera 6-3, 6-3, 6-2 to win the City of Madrid Championships in Spain. The win is Edberg's 37th career singles title, but only his third on a clay courts.

1992 Thomas Muster wins the singles title at the Monte Carlo Open for the first time in his career, defeating Aaron Krickstein 6-3, 6-1, 6-3 in the final.

May 3

1968 Twenty-nine-year-old Donald Dell makes his debut as U.S. Davis Cup captain as the United States takes a 2-0 lead over the British West Indies at Byrd Park in Richmond, Va. Arthur Ashe, playing in his hometown, needs only 49 minutes to defeat Lance Lumsden 6-1, 6-1, 6-0. Dell's tenure as U.S. Davis Cup captain last two years, as he steers the U.S. to titles in 1968 and 1969 and a perfect 7-0 record.

1992 Andre Agassi wins his first tournament title of 1992, besting rival Pete Sampras 7-5, 6-4 in the final of the AT&T Challenge in Atlanta, Ga, "I just wish the U.S. Open were played here in Atlanta," says Agassi, who wins the event for a third-straight year, but for the first time since it becomes an official ATP event.

1992 Steffi Graf wins her 63rd career singles title, defeating Arantxa Sanchez Vicario 7-6 (2), 6-2 in the final of the German Open in Hamburg.

2007 Former world No. 1 Kim Clijsters of Belgium is defeated by Julia Vakulenko of Ukraine 7-6 (3), 6-3 in her opening match at the J&S Warsaw Cup in Poland in what ultimately becomes the final match of Clijsters' career. Clijsters, who earlier said that she would only play a limited schedule in 2007 due to her engagement to pro basketball player Brian Lynch, decides to not play the rest of her 2007 schedule and quits professional tennis.

2007 Pete Sampras returns to competitive tournament tennis—emerging on the Outback Champions Series "senior" circuit five years following his dramatic U.S. Open victory—and crushes 1998 Australian Open champion Petr Korda 6-1, 6-2 in his opening round-robin match at the Champions Cup Boston. Says Sampras, "It was great to get back out there and compete. I felt excited walking out there to a nice ovation in front of a large crowd. I've had some trouble with Petr in the past, but felt I was able to play real well on this surface."

1999 Yevgeny Kafelnikov becomes the first Russian to reach the world No. 1 ranking when he replaces Pete Sampras in the top spot on the ATP computer. Kafelnikov holds the top ranking for a total of six weeks.

May 4

1973 Rosie Casals beats Billie Jean King 7-5, 6-4 in the semifinals of the Family Circle Cup in Hilton Head Island, S.C.—her first victory over her doubles partner in over two years and 17 straight matches. The win prevents King, the all-time leading money winner in women's tennis at the time, from playing for the record women's first prize of $30,000 in the championship match of the inaugural event. Casals wins the event the following day, beating Nancy Richey Gunter in the final.

1968 Davis Cup rookies Stan Smith and Bob Lutz pair for the first time as a team in Davis Cup and beat Richard Russell and Lance Lumsden 6-2, 6-3, 6-3 to give the United States an insurmountable 3-0 lead over the British West Indies in a first round at Byrd Park in Richmond, Va.

1980 Twenty-seven-year-old Jimmy Connors defeats John McEnroe 2-6, 7-6, 6-1, 6-2 to win the WCT Finals in front of 16,181 fans at Reunion Arena in Dallas. Connors wins the $100,000 first prize and joins 1971 and 1972 champion Ken Rosewall as a two-time winner of the prestigious event.

2006 In the 20th meeting between Venus Williams and Martina Hingis, Williams come back from a set and 0-3 down to tie the all-time series at 10-10 with her rival in defeating the "Swiss Miss" 4-6, 7-5, 6-4 in the round of 16 of the WTA event in Warsaw, Poland. Says Hingis after the match, "Being up a set, 5-4, 30-0 she's almost like giving it to me, but then she came out fighting and that's what brought her the victory." Says Williams, who suffers from cramps in the third set, "I guess I said that prayer just in time. It was just crazy, it was intense. Even I wouldn't expect that of myself. Definitely just living in the moment."

May 5

2005 Andy Roddick performs one of the greatest gestures of sportsman-ship on a tennis court when he overturns an apparent double-fault—that would have given him the match—and eventually loses to Spain's Fernando Verdasco 6-7 (1), 7-6 (3), 6-4 in the round of 16 of the Italian Open in Rome. Roddick is leading 5-3 in the second set and has triple match point with Verdasco serving. Verdasco's serve appears to land just wide and is called out by the linesperson. Roddick, however, says the ball was in after check-ing the mark on the clay court and concedes the second serve ace to Ver-dasco. "I didn't think it was anything extraordinary," says Roddick. "The umpire would have done the same thing if he came down and looked. I just saved him the trip. Famed American sports journalist Frank Deford says on National Public Radio of the gesture, "In one moment with victory his for the taking—no, not for the taking—is given, is assumed, Andy Roddick went against the way of the world and simply instinctively did what he thought was right. Once upon time we called such foolish innocents sportsmen."

1981 New Yorkers John McEnroe and Vitas Gerulaitis are eliminated from the WCT Tournament of Champions at the West Side Tennis Club in Forest Hills, N.Y. McEnroe is defeated by Brazil's Carlos Kirmayr 5-7, 7-6 (7), 6-2 in a second-round match, while Gerualitis is defeated by fellow American Fritz Buehning 7-5, 7-5. McEnroe holds a match point in the second-set tie-break but is unable to convert, while Gerulaitis loses the last six games of the match after taking a 5-1 lead in the second set. "Inexcus-able," says McEnroe of the loss. "He ran me around like a yo-yo and he deserved to win."

May 6

1999 Trailing 6-2, 1-0, 40-15 in his match against Sebastien Grosjean in the Citrix Championships in Delray Beach, Fla., Cecil Mamiit suffers the indignity of having his cell phone ring during play in the quarterfinal-round match. Mamiit, the 1996 NCAA singles champion from the University of Southern California, is told by chair umpire Tony Nimmons to turn off his phone, which Mamiit obliges before losing the match 6-2, 6-1. Says Mamiit of the call, who was from fellow ATP player David Caldwell, "It affected my concentration." The incident prompts the pubic address announcer at the event to say, "As a courtesy to the fans, will the players keep their cell phones off during the match."

2001 Andy Roddick wins his second career singles title at the U.S. Men's Clay Court Championships in Houston, Texas, defeating Hyung-Taik Lee of Korea, 7-5, 6-3 in the final. Roddick becomes the first American man in 14 years to win his first and second singles titles consecutively, following his tournament victory in Atlanta the previous week. The last American man to win his first and second singles titles consecutively was Andre Agassi. But while Roddick won his first two singles titles in consecutive weeks, Agassi's titles at the 1987 Sul America Open in Itaparica, Brazil, and at the 1988 U.S. National Indoor Championships in Memphis, Tenn., were 12 weeks apart—although consecutive on his playing schedule.

2007 Former World No. 1 Kim Clijsters announces her immediate retirement from tennis, days following her opening round loss in Warsaw, Poland. Cljisters, 23, previously said that 2007 would be her final year on the circuit, so she could properly prepare for marriage and starting a family. However, she announces on her website that she would no longer play in any further events. "It's time to hang up my racquet for good," writes Clijsters on her website."The constantly returning injuries, the laborious crawl out of bed in the morning and the time it takes to warm up tired muscles ... make it all the more difficult to continue"

May 7

1995 Playing in her first career WTA Tour singles final, 14-year-old Martina Hingis is humiliated in the final of the Citizen Cup in Hamburg, losing by a 6-1, 6-0 margin to Spain's Conchita Martinez in 49 minutes. Hingis, a professional for only six months, defeats three higher ranked players en route to the final, including Jana Novotna and Anke Huber, before losing to Martinez.

2008 Rafael Nadal loses for only the second time in his last 104 clay court matches, falling to countryman Juan Carlos Ferrero 7-5, 6-1 in the second round of the Italian Championships. Both Nadal and Ferrero attribute the loss to Nadal's blistering feet after two straight clay court tournaments in Monte Carlo and Barcelona. Says Nadal, "I didn't feel good on court. I couldn't put my legs on the floor with power so every time I played short because I didn't have power in my legs."

2007 Playing in a rain-delayed Monday final, Justine Henin defeats Alona Bondarenko 6-1, 6-3 to win the J&S Cup in Warsaw, Poland for the second time in her career. Says Henin, who also is the 2005 champion in Warsaw, "To wait yesterday was pretty hard, but finally it was a good day today. I'm very happy to win my second title here in Warsaw and the first tournament on clay. That gives me confidence."

1995 Michael Chang defeats world No. 1 Andre Agassi 6-2, 6-7 (6), 6-4 to win the AT&T Challenge in Atlanta, Ga., for a second straight year. Says Agassi of Chang, "Michael is not somebody you can expect to beat unless you are playing your best. He runs for a living."

1995 Wayne Ferreira defeats Michael Stich of Germany for the first time in his career and wins the BMW Open in Munich, defeating the former Wimbledon champion 7-5, 7-6 (6).

May 8

2005 Rafael Nadal and Guillermo Coria play the longest ATP final on record, battling for 5 hours, 14 minutes before the 18-year-old Nadal wins a fifth-set tie-break to win the 6-4, 3-6, 6-3, 4-6, 7-6 (6) marathon in the final of the Italian Open. Coria holds three championship points in the fifth set but is unable to convert. The win for Nadal is his 17th straight match victory and his third title in the last 27 days.

2008 Justine Henin plays what eventually becomes her final professional match as the world No. 1 loses to Dinara Safina 5-7, 6-3, 6-1 in the third round of the German Open in Berlin. Henin, fighting to find motivation to compete at the highest level of professional tennis, shocks the tennis world by announcing her retirement from the sport the following week. Since Henin wins the title at Sydney at the start of the year, she does not win a match against a player ranked in the top 25. Says Henin following the loss to Safina, "It's never easy to lose and to lose that way. During the whole match I didn't have the intensity and the consistency and it was quite tough. There's nothing more I can really say. She's been better. That's it." Says the 17th-ranked Safina, the younger sister of former U.S. Open champion Marat Safin, "Going into the match I had inside the feeling that today I have a chance."

1994 Despite losing the Italian Open final 7-5, 6-4 to Conchita Martinez, the Italian fans at the Foro Italico in Rome give Martina Navratilova a standing ovation in Navratilova's farewell year on tour in 1994. Navratilova, eventually returns to the tour in doubles in 2000, but never claims a singles victory at the Italian Open.

1989 Ivan Lendl defeats Jaime Yzaga of Peru 6-2, 6-1 in a rain-delayed Monday final at the Eagle WCT Tournament of Champions at a cold and windy West Side Tennis Club in Forest Hills, N.Y. The final is watched by only 1,500 fans, who huddle under blankets or wear winter coats in the 40-degree temperatures that keeps the No. 1-ranked Lendl in his sweat pants during the entire duration of the match. The 1989 tournament marks the final year that the West Side Tennis Club, the former long-time home of the U.S. Open, hosts the official ATP event. The new ATP Tour schedule starting in 1990 does not include an event at Forest Hills.

1988 Andre Agassi defeats Slobodan Zivojinovic 7-5, 7-6 (2), 7-5 to win the WCT Tournament of Champions in front of 12,898 fans at the West Side Tennis Club in Forest Hills, N.Y. The title is the most significant to date for the 18-year-old Agassi, who moves to an ATP ranking of No. 15 following the victory. Says Zivojinovic of Agassi, "It's very difficult to say he's good. He looks like he's having a lot of fun, and he's winning. I don't know how long it's [his outlook] going to stay—maybe a year, maybe forever. He doesn't worry about the ball going in or out, winning or losing. He was a hell of a good player today, and with this tournament and maybe one more, he'll be in the top 10."

1988 Gabriela Sabatini of Argentina wins the Italian Open for the first of four times in her career, defeating Canada's Helen Kelesi 6-1, 6-7 (4), 6-1 in the final. Sabatini also claims Italian titles in 1989, 1991 and 1992.

1983 John McEnroe wins his most significant tournament on clay, defeating fellow New Yorker Vitas Gerulaitis 6-3, 7-5 to win the WCT Tournament of Champions at the West Side Tennis Club in Forest Hills, N.Y.

May 9

1915 Four-time Wimbledon champion and the reigning Wimbledon doubles champion Tony Wilding is killed in action in World War I at Neuve Chapelle, France at the Battle of Aubers Ridge on the Western Front. Wilding, from New Zealand, wins four straight Wimbledon singles titles from 1910 to 1913, losing the 1914 title to Aussie Norman Brookes.

2000 At age 29, two-time French and Australian Open champion Jim Courier announces his retirement from tennis after 13 years. "I've been fighting it for seven or eight years," Courier says. "Your enthusiasm ebbs. There was a transition where tennis was my life and somewhere along the way, life became more important than the tennis."

2008 The backhand of Roger Federer completely breaks down as the world No. 1 is stunned in the quarterfinals of the Italian Championships, falling to No. 27-ranked Radek Stepanek of the Czech Republic 7-6 (4), 7-6 (7). Says Federer of the erratic backhand, "You've seen me many times, it happens all the time. It's something I've been trying to get rid of for 10 years but still not today...I don't know if it was just the backhand. I think I missed plenty of opportunities throughout the match. He's difficult to play. He gives you little rhythm and he always changes his game up a lot."

1928 Hall of Famer Richard "Pancho" Gonzales is born in Los Angeles, Calif. Although he wins only two major singles titles—the 1948 and 1949 U.S. Championships, Gonzales is regarded as one of the all-time greatest players in the history of the sport. Gonzales goes after the lure of money and professional tennis after his 1949 U.S. victory. Writes Bud Collins in *The Bud Collins History of Tennis* of Gonzales, "Very much his own man, a loner and an acerbic competitor, Richard Alonzo "Pancho" Gonzales was probably as good as anyone who ever played the game, if not better. Most of his great tennis was played beyond wide public attention, on the nearly secret pro tour amid a small band of gypsies of whom he was the ticket-selling mainstay." When tennis becomes "Open" in 1968, Gonzales makes an immediate impact, beating defending champion Roy Emerson, at age 40, to reach the semifinals of the 1968 French Open. He is the oldest man to win a tour singles title in Des Moines, Iowa in 1972 at the age of 43 years, nine months.

May 10

1935 Don Budge makes his Davis Cup debut and defeats Kho Sin Kie of China 4-6, 6-3, 6-2, 6-2 to help the United States to a 2-0 lead over China after the first day of play of the Davis Cup first round in Mexico City, Mexico. Budge represents the United States for four years (1935-1938), leading the United States to Cup titles in 1937 and 1938 and posts a 25-4 record, including an impressive 19-2 slate in singles.

2006 Inspired by a morning meeting with the Pope, Roger Federer advances into the third round of the Italian Open defeating Potito Starace of Italy 6-3, 7-6 (2). Says Federer of meeting the Holy Father, "It was an emotional day today. In the morning, meeting the Pope was very, very nice and a big honor of course. Got to shake his hand, exchange a few words in German, and that's it. It was very special for me. I'm Catholic after all, so it was very nice. Then, after on, the great match here. It was a perfect day."

1996 Fifteen-year-old Martina Hingis shocks world No. 1 Steffi Graf 2-6, 6-3, 6-2 in the quarterfinals of the Italian Open in Rome, becoming the youngest player to ever beat Graf. Says Hingis, "It was a great chance for me to play, to beat the No. 1 and I took it." Says Graf, appearing in Rome for the first time in nine years, "I didn't have a clue what the hell I was doing out there." Hingis eventually reaches the final of the tournament, losing 6-2, 6-3 to Conchita Martinez.

1987 Steffi Graf wins her 27th consecutive match and her fifth straight WTA Tour title, defeating Gabriela Sabatini 7-5, 4-6, 6-0 in the final of the Italian Open in Rome. Graf, 17, trails 0-4 in the first set, losing 11 straight points at one point, but rallies to fight off four set points to defeat her 16-year-old rival.

1987 Cheered on by flag-waving and cow-bell ringing Ecuadorian fans, Andres Gomez wins the WCT Tournament of Champions at the West Side Tennis Club in Forest Hills, N.Y., defeating Yannick Noah of France 6-4, 7-6 (5), 7-6 (1) in the final. Says Gomez, "I know this is not the U.S. Open, but it's nice. This is the Tournament of Champions, and I'm the champion of this tournament. I'm very happy about that."

May 11

1987 The International Olympic Committee rules in Istanbul, Turkey that tennis professionals are allowed to compete in the Olympic tennis event at the 1988 Olympic Games in Seoul, South Korea, the first Olympic Games where tennis is a full-medal sport after an absence of 64 years. "Officials and players I've talked with agreed that the Olympic tennis tournament would be No. 1 in the world," says Willi Daume, head of the IOC's eligibility commission. "They see the Olympic tennis tournament above Wimbledon and the Davis Cup."

1986 Frenchman and New York resident Yannick Noah wins the WCT Tournament of Champions at the West Side Tennis Club in Forest Hills, N.Y., defeating Guillermo Vilas 7-6 (3), 6-0 in the final. Says Noah, "All wins are big, but this one is very special to me because it's the first one in my new hometown."

1986 Chris Evert Lloyd defeats 17-year-old Kathy Rinaldi 6-4, 2-6, 6-4 to win the Virginia Slims of Houston. "I can't stand to lose to 18-year-olds, I guess that's what keeps me going," Evert says, understating Rinaldi's age by a year. "When you're 18, you recover quicker than at 31. I was a little tired, but I lasted, so that's the important thing."

2003 Felix Mantilla of Spain upends Roger Federer 7-5, 6-2, 7-6 to become an unlikely singles champion at the Italian Open in Rome. The 28-year-old Mantilla, who says that his game does not have "the serve of Pete Sampras, the volley of Pat Rafter, nor the talent of Andre Agassi" capitalizes on 69 unforced errors from Federer to win the biggest title of his career. Says Mantilla following the victory, "I feel like I have found my inner self." Says Federer of the loss, "The whole match was extremely disappointing for me. He (Mantilla) plays patient and it's a little bit boring. Whatever shot you play, good or bad, it comes back the same way. It just became frustrating, and after making such a dreadful start I had the feeling that his victory was meant to be."

2007 Rafael Nadal defeats Novak Djokovic of Serbia 6-2, 6-3 in the quarterfinals of the Italian Open in Rome—his 75th consecutive match victory on clay, matching John McEnroe's streak for most victories on one surface. McEnroe, who is in attendance at the match, won 75 straight matches on indoor-carpet between September 1983 and April 1985.

May 12

1979 Tracy Austin defeats Chris Evert Lloyd in the semifinals of the Italian Open in Rome, ending Evert's 125-match winning streak on clay dating back to Aug. 12, 1973. The match, however, is played in front of a crowd of only 1,500 spectators at Foro Italico.

1984 Ivan Lendl drubs Jimmy Connors 6-0, 6-0—the worst loss for Connors in his professional career—in the semifinals of the WCT Tournament of Champions at Forest Hills "I feel a little bitter—not personally—about Jimmy because he has taken me twice at the U.S. Open," says Lendl of the 52-minute match and his two final-round losses to Connors at the last two U.S. Open finals. Says Connors, "I was in there. I was hitting the ball all right, but he wasn't missing too much." Connors commits 26 unforced errors, wins just 16 points and faces game point only twice.

2002 Fifteen-years after his first visit to the Italian Open, Andre Agassi wins the title for the first time defeating Tommy Haas of Germany 6-3, 6-3, 6-0 in the singles final. Agassi, playing in the Italian Open for the ninth time, plays in one previous singles final, losing in 1989 to Alberto Mancini. Says Agassi, "It's something you don't really admit to yourself because it's pretty much a disappointment when you came so close. But you realize, as you size up all these tournaments outside the Grand Slams, that this has as much, if not probably more history, than all of them."

1987 John McEnroe endures a power-outage at the Foro Italico in Rome and overcomes 17-year-old Franco Davin of Argentina 3-6, 6-2, 6-3 in the opening round of the Italian Open. McEnroe trails by a set and by a service break at 1-0 in the second set when the first of two power failures takes place. After a 30-minute delay, McEnroe wins four straight games before Davin holds serve, then another power outage happens, delaying play for another 55 minutes. After play resumes for a second time, McEnroe takes firm control of the match. Due to the delay, Yannick Noah's match does not take the court until after midnight and he loses to Argentina's Eduardo Bengoechea 7-5, 6-1 in a match that ends at 2:10 am.

2007 Rafael Nadal wins his 76th straight match on clay, breaking John McEnroe's record for most victories on one surface, defeating Nikolay Davydenko of Russia 7-6 (3), 6-7 (8), 6-4 in 3 hours, 38 minutes in the semifinals of the Italian Open in Rome. McEnroe posts a 75-match winning streak on indoor carpet between September 1983 and April 1985. Says Nadal, "It's nice to have these records but the important thing for me is to be in the final right now."

1985 Ivan Lendl routs John McEnroe 6-3, 6-3 to win the singles title at the WCT Tournament of Champions at Forest Hills, Lendl's first win over McEnroe since the French Open final 11 months earlier. Says McEnroe of Lendl, "He seems to be more consistent on clay at this point. This was his best surface and my worst. His game was on today."

May 13

1973 In the prequel to the famous "Battle of the Sexes" match between Bobby Riggs and Billie Jean King, the 55-year-old Riggs crushes No. 1 ranked woman Margaret Court 6-2, 6-1 in 57 minutes in their $10,000 winner-take-all challenge match in Romana, Calif. After the match, that becomes known as the "Mother's Day Massacre," Riggs, the self-described male chauvinist pig, issues the challenge to take on King, saying "I want her. She's the women's libber leader! She can name the place, the court and the time, just as long as the price is right." Riggs, who famously wins the singles, men's doubles and mixed doubles titles at Wimbledon in 1939, calls his win over Court, "the greatest hustle of all time." Writes Neil Amdur of the *New York Times,* "The victory was the latest and perhaps most amazing chapter in the colorful career of one of the games most underrated players and one of the sports most successful hustlers." King eventually accepts Riggs' challenge and in September they play in the famous "Battle of the Sexes" match at the Houston Astrodome.

1958 Mervyn Rose of Australia wins a dramatic final in the Italian Championships, defeating favorite son Nicola Pietrangeli 5-7, 8-6, 6-4, 1-6, 6-2 in 5 hours, 9 minutes. The biggest excitement of the day, however, comes when Kurt Nielsen of Denmark throws his racquet at a linesperson who calls a foot fault on him in the fifth set of the completion of the darkness-delayed men's doubles final. The racquet does not hit the linesperson, but draws boos and jeers from the crowd of approximately 2,500. Nielson and Hungary's Anton Jancso win the title, defeating Luis Ayala of Chile and Don Candy of Australia 8-10, 6-3, 6-2, 1-6, 9-7.

1984 John McEnroe routs Ivan Lendl 6-4, 6-2 to win the WCT Tournament of Champions at the West Side Tennis Club in Forest Hills, N.Y. The title is his seventh of the year and the match victory over Lendl is McEnroe's 32nd of the year without a loss. The victory places McEnroe among the favorites for the French Open later in the month. "I feel better now about my chances going to the French," says McEnroe, who famously loses the French final to Lendl after leading two-sets-to-love. "The French wasn't that important in my mind five or six years ago. I don't think people realize how the French has changed within the last couple of years as far as prestige is concerned."

2001 Juan Carlos Ferrero of Spain upsets world No. 1 and reigning French Open champion Gustavo Kuerten 3-6, 6-1, 2-6, 6-4, 6-2 in 3 hours, 4 minutes to win the Italian Championships in Rome, his first title in a Tennis Masters Series tournament. Says Ferrero, "With Kuerten, it's difficult to win in straight sets. When he started strong, I told myself, 'Don't worry, you have time.'"

2001 France's Amelie Mauresmo defeats Jennifer Capriati 6-4, 2-6, 6-3 to win the German Open in Berlin. Mauresmo also defeats world No. 1 Martina Hingis en route to the title. "Beating who I beat proves I'm playing at a very high level," says Mauresmo. "I started playing well this year and I'm still playing well. It gives me a lot of confidence for the French Open."

2007 Rafael Nadal overcomes dizzy spells and stomach pains but still easily defeats Fernando Gonzalez of Chile 6-2, 6-2 to win the Italian Open, becoming the first player to win three consecutive titles at the event. Says Nadal, "I think I'm in the best moment of my career, playing better than ever, so I'm very happy for that."

May 14

1972 In a match regarded as one of the greatest of all-time, Ken Rosewall wins the final four points in a decisive fifth-set tie-break and defeats Rod Laver 4-6, 6-0, 6-3, 6-7(3), 7-6 (5) in a 3 hour, 34-minute men's singles final at the WCT Finals at the Moody Coliseum in Dallas, Texas. The match, writes Mark Asher of *The Washington Post*, had "more high points than the Himalayas" as both tennis legends battle on national television on Mother's Day for the largest purse in tennis at the time—a $50,000 first prize. Says the 37-year-old Rosewall in the post-match ceremony, "I'm just a bit out of breath and I'm just about out of time." Writes Bud Collins in *The Bud Collins History of Tennis*, "Laver was favored to grab the $50,000 plum that had eluded him the previous November, but Rosewall, an enduring marvel at age 38, again stole it. Laver revived himself from 1-4 in the final set, saved a match point with an ace, and had the match on his racket at 5-4 in the "lingering death" tie-breaker, with two serves to come. He pounded both deep to Rosewall's backhand corner, but the most splendid antique in tennis reached for vintage return winners. Laver failed to return the exhausted Rosewall's last serve and it was over, 4-6, 6-0, 6-3, 6-7 (3-7), 7-6 (7-5)."

2008 Twenty-five-year-old Justine Henin shocks the tennis world by announcing her immediate retirement from the sport, despite holding the No. 1 world ranking. Henin hangs up her racquets with 41 career WTA singles titles, including seven major titles—four at the French Championships, including the last three in a row and the Olympic gold medal at the 2004 Olympics. "It's a page that's turning; I don't feel sadness, it's more relief," Henin says at her retirement press conference. "I know it's a shock for many people, but it's a decision I've thought long and hard about....It's the end of a marvelous adventure, an end of something that I've dreamed about since I was five years old."

2006 In an epic match that officially cements the rivalry between Roger Federer and Rafael Nadal as one of the great rivalries in the sport, Nadal defeats Federer 6-7 (0), 7-6 (5), 6-4, 2-6, 7-6 (5) in 5 hours, 6 minutes in the final of the Italian Open in Rome. Federer leads by 4-1 in the fifth set and holds two match points, before letting the 19-year-old from Mallorca back into the match to successfully defend his Italian title. Says Federer, "I'm on the right track, a step closer with this guy, just got caught at the finish line, but I should have won." The Italian crown is Nadal's 16th career title, equaling Bjorn Borg's teenage record in the early 1970s and his 53rd straight clay court match victory, equaling the record of Guillermo Vilas from 1977.

2000 Magnus Norman of Sweden defeats Brazil's Gustavo Kuerten 6-3, 4-6, 6-4, 6-4 to win the Italian Open singles title in Rome. Norman becomes the first Swede to win the title since Mats Wilander in 1987.

2000 Conchita Martinez of Spain wins her 32nd career singles title defeating Amanda Coetzer of South Africa 6-1, 6-2 in the singles final of the German Open in Berlin.

May 15

1994 Pete Sampras experiences his greatest triumph on clay courts, dominating Boris Becker 6-1, 6-2, 6-2 to win the Italian Open in Rome. "I think he's invincible right now," says Becker after the match. "He's flying right now. He's playing like no one has ever played against me. He's playing like the best of the best." The win is the high-water mark of the clay court career of Sampras, who famously reaches only one semifinal (1996) in 13 appearances at the French Open, the world's premier clay court event. Sampras goes on to reach the French quarterfinals for a third straight later in the spring but loses to Jim Courier.

1977 Jimmy Connors defeats Dick Stockton, 6-7 (5), 6-1, 6-4, 6-3, in 3 hours, 3 minutes to win the WCT Finals in Dallas. "Today I felt I was playing the No. 1 player in the world when he was playing his best tennis," Stockton tells the sellout crowd of 9,352 at Moody Coliseum during the post-match award ceremonies.

1994 Steffi Graf defeats Brenda Schultz of the Netherlands 7-6 (6), 6-4 to win her eighth title at the German Open in Berlin. Graf breaks the booming 120-mph serve of Schultz only once during the match, but it is the only service break needed.

2005 Roger Federer defeats Richard Gasquet of France 6-3, 7-5, 7-6 (4) to win the Tennis Masters Series—Hamburg in Germany. Federer's win avenges his loss to the 18-year-old Gasquet in the quarterfinals of the Monte Carlo Open the previous month—one of only two losses Federer suffers in his last 59 matches.

1989 Ivan Lendl wins his 78th career ATP singles title, defeating Horst Skoff of Austria 6-4, 6-1, 6-3 in a rain-delayed Monday final at the German Open in Hamburg, West Germany.

1994 Luiz Mattar becomes the first Brazilian to win an ATP title in the United States, defeating Jamie Morgan of Australia 6-4, 3-6, 6-3 in the final of America's Red Clay Tennis Championships in Coral Springs, Fla.

May 16

1999 Sixteen-year-old Justine Henin of Belgium, the future world No. 1 playing in her first WTA Tour event, upsets top-seeded Sarah Pitkowksi of France 6-1, 6-2 to win her first career singles title at the Flanders Women's Open in Antwerp, Belgium.

1999 Gustavo Kuerten denies Patrick Rafter the opportunity to seize the No. 1 ranking by defeating the Australian 6-4, 7-5, 7-6 (6) in the final of the Italian Open in Rome. Says Rafter, who would have supplanted Yevgeny Kafelnikov of Russia at the No. 1 ranking with a victory, "It just wasn't happening today. Anything he was doing was too good for me." Rafter eventually assumes the No. 1 ranking later in the year on July 26, but famously only holds the ranking for one week during his career.

1930 The United States wins three points in one day and clinches victory over Canada in the Davis Cup first round at the Philadelphia Country Club in Philadelphia, Pa. John Van Ryn needs two points to finish a rain-delayed 6-2, 6-2, 3-6, 6-2 win over Jack Wright. George Lott then defeats Marcel Rainville 6-2, 6-2, 8-6 to give the United States a 2-0 lead. Wilmer Allison and Van Ryn then clinch victory for the United States with a 6-0, 6-4, 6-2 win over Wright and Willard Crocker.

1993 Jim Courier wins the Italian Open for the second consecutive year, defeating Goran Ivanisevic 6-1, 6-2, 6-2 in the singles final at Rome's Foro Italico. Courier becomes the first player to win consecutive Italian Open titles since Jaroslav Drobny in 1950-51.

2004 Amelie Mauresmo wins one of the biggest titles of her career, defeating Jennifer Capriati 3-6, 6-3, 7-6 (6) in the final of the Italian Open in Rome. Capriati holds a match point at 6-5 in the final-set tie-break on Mauresmo's serve, but hits a forehand long and is not able to convert.

1999 Martina Hingis needs only 42 minutes to defeat Julie Halard-Decugis 6-0, 6-1 to win in the final of the German Open in Berlin, her 23rd career singles title.

1993 Todd Martin wins his first ATP singles title, defeating fellow American David Wheaton 6-3, 6-4 in the final of America's Red Clay Championships in Coral Springs, Fla.

1982 Jose Higueras of Spain wins perhaps the biggest title of his career, defeating Australia's Peter McNamara, 6-4, 7-6, 6-7, 3-6, 7-6 to win the German Open in Hamburg.

1970 Gabriela Sabatini, one of the most graceful and popular women's tennis players and the champion at 1990 U.S. Open champion, is born in Buenos Aires, Argentina. Described by tennis historian Bud Collins as "the most extraordinary Latin American lady since Brazilian Maria Bueno was winning Wimbledon and U.S. titles back in the 1960s," Sabatini wins only one major singles titles was a constant resident of the world's top 10, a Wimbledon finalist in 1991, a U.S. Open finalist in 1988 and an Olympic silver medalist in 1988.

May 17

2008 In a "Battle for the No. 2 Ranking" and a match that Barry Flatman of the *Times of London* describes as "one of the finest matches of this century"— No. 2 ranked Rafael Nadal defeats No. 3 ranked Novak Djokovic 7-5, 2-6, 6-2 to advance into the final of the Hamburg Masters—and keep his No. 2 ranking for a 148th straight week—a record streak at that ranking.

1996 Stefan Edberg receives an emotional farewell from fans at the Italian Open after losing in the quarterfinals of the event in his final appearance at the Foro Italico in his 14th and final year on the professional circuit. After losing 6-4, 6-3 to Richard Krajicek, Edberg bows and waves to all four corners of the stadium and receives a rousing standing ovation from the 10,200 fans in attendance. Says Edberg, "In a foreign country, to have an ovation like that was quite amazing. I expected a nice round of applause, but this was really special....Sometimes I had goose bumps out there. It was great leaving the court. Even if I lost the match, it didn't matter today." Says Krajicek of the atmosphere, "My girlfriend and another friend were supporting me. It was like three against 12,000."

1992 Jim Courier, the reigning French Open champion, adds the Italian Open to his resume and establishing himself as the pre-eminent clay court player in the world, defeating Carlos Costa of Spain 7-6 (3), 6-0, 6-4 in the singles final at the Foro Italico. Says Costa of Courier, "Jim doesn't have ups and downs and you have to be constant playing him. He is stronger physically and more regular than the other players."

1998 For the first time in the tournament's 68-year-history, the men's singles final at the Italian Open is decided by a default as Albert Costa of Spain is unable to play due to a right wrist injury and forfeits to Chile's Marcelo Rios. Costa tumbles onto his wrist, tearing some soft tissue, as he chases a ball on the first point of the final game of his 6-3, 4-6, 6-3 semifinal win over countryman Alberto Berasategui the previous day. Says Costa, "I thought nothing then, but the wrist became swollen and painful during the night. I tried to hit some balls this morning but couldn't do anything."

1929 John Van Ryn wins the first of a record 22 Davis Cup doubles matches for the United States and he and John Hennessey defeat Canada's Arthur Ham and Jack Wright 6-1, 6-1, 1-6, 6-2 giving the United States an insurmountable 3-0 lead over Canada in the Davis Cup first round in Montreal, Canada.

2006 Former French Open champion Gaston Gaudio of Argentina nearly loses his pants, but loses his chance to win the German Open in Hamburg, losing in the second round to unheralded Gilles Simon of France 6-4, 3-6, 6-4. Gaudio rips his shorts when he caught his hand in his pocket running for a ball wide. Says Simon, "[Gaudio] looked at me like 'What is the problem? We could play like this! I was like 'No, you have to change your shorts.'"

2004 Nenad Zimonjic of Serbia, ranked No. 339 in the world, creates world headlines as he defeats Andre Agassi 6-2, 7-6 (6) in the first round of the Raiffeisen Grand Prix in St. Poelten, Austria.

May 18

1909 Fred Perry, the greatest British player in history who leads his nation to supreme heights as a tennis nation, is born in Stockport, England. Perry wins three Wimbledon titles from 1934 to 1936 and, after winning the French singles title in 1935 becomes the first player to ever sweep all four singles titles in their career. In 1934, Perry nearly wins the first Grand Slam, winning three of the four major titles, only to lose in the quarterfinals of the French Championships. Perry famously leads Britain to victory in Davis Cup from 1933 to 1936 before turning professional. He is described by Robin Finn of the *New York Times* in his 1995 obituary as "a player for all surfaces, seasons and continents—adept everywhere it seems, except for the practice court, where he confessed to boredom regardless of the locale."

2008 Jelena Jankovic wins the women's singles title at the Italian Open for the second year in a row, defeating 18-year-old qualifier Alizé Cornet of France 6-2, 6-2 in the final. "I love you. I love Rome," Jankovic says in Italian in the post-match ceremony. "I'm happy to win the title again. I'm just so happy." Despite upsetting No. 3 seed Svetlana Kuznetsova and No. 6 seed Anna Chakvetadze to get to the final, Cornet is only immediately disappointed at losing the final. "I'm very upset," Cornet says. "I couldn't do what I wanted to do on the court. ...Maybe later I will be happy of my tournament, but right now I'm just sad."

1981 Peter McNamara of Australia defeats Jimmy Connors 7-5, 6-1, 4-6, 6-4 to win the rain-delayed Monday final of the German Open in Hamburg, West Germany. McNamara leads two-sets-to-love when the match is postponed until Monday due to rain. "I am always depressed when I leave the court a loser," says Connors after the match.

2008 One year after having his 81-match clay court winning streak snapped on the same court, Rafael Nadal exacts revenge on Roger Federer, beating the world No. 1 7-5, 6-7 (3), 6-3 in the singles final of the Hamburg Masters in Germany. The title was Nadal's first in Hamburg and completed a career sweep of the major clay court titles, joining former world No. 1 players Marcelo Rios and Gustavo Kuerten as only the third man to sweep Monte Carlo, Rome and Hamburg.

May 19

1996 Thomas Muster wins the Italian Open singles title in Rome, defeating Richard Krajicek of the Netherlands 6-2, 6-4, 3-6, 6-3 in the singles final. Muster, the 1990 and 1995 Italian champion, joins Jaroslav Drobny (1950, 1951 and 1953) and Martin Mulligan (1963, 1965 and 1967) as the only men to win the Italian Open three times. Says Krajicek of Muster, "He's not completely unbeatable but almost. What makes him No. 1 or No. 2 is he is winning all the big points, or 99 percent of the big points."

1996 Steffi Graf wins her ninth and final German Open singles title, edging upstart Karina Habsudova of Slovakia 4-6, 6-2, 7-5 in the final in Berlin. The title is also Graf's 98th career singles title.

2002 Roger Federer dominates Marat Safin to win his first Tennis Masters Series title at the German Open in Hamburg, defeating the Russian 6-1, 6-3, 6-4 in the singles final. Says Federer, "I played really well. It has been a wonderful tournament for me, really incredible. I have played well all week and it gives me great confidence going into the French Open." Says Safin, "He played too good, I couldn't do much. I have more experience than him and was probably the favorite but I didn't really play very well, as you can see. I couldn't bring my tennis to the court and he played probably the best game of tennis in his life."

2002 Serena Williams wins her first clay-court title—and her 14th singles title of her career—defeating Justine Henin 7-6 (6), 6-4 in the final of the Italian Open in Rome. Says Williams, "I think I'm a really good clay-court player, but everybody says I can't play on it. This may change some minds."

1991 Emilio Sanchez wins the biggest title of his career, winning the Italian Open in Rome when his opponent, Alberto Mancini of Argentina, retires with a left thigh pull with Sanchez leading 6-3, 6-1, 3-0, 40-0 in the singles final.

1996 Jason Stoltenberg of Australia wins America's Red Clay Championships in Coral Springs, Fla.—his third ATP singles title—edging Chris Woodruff of the United States 7-6 (4), 2-6, 7-5 in a 2-hour, 43-minute singles final. Says Stoltenberg, "I've been playing this game for a long time now, and I feel I know how to play it and work problems out on my own. I battled through my last breath today, and I'm a very happy person."

May 20

1990 Monica Seles ends Steffi Graf's 66-match winning streak, defeating the German 6-4, 6-3 in the singles final of the German Open in Berlin. Says Seles, "I'm much more experienced now and I wasn't afraid of Graf as much as before. This is just one match. I'm just happy that I'm playing well." Says Graf, "I was so far away from playing my best tennis, it was difficult to get into it. If I play like that I can't expect to win."

2007 Roger Federer ends Rafael Nadal's 81-match winning streak on clay, defeating the Spaniard 2-6, 6-2, 6-0 in the final of the Hamburg Masters in Germany. "It was an incredible performance from my side," says the world No. 1. "I had a great day, it's nice to be playing well again. It's my first title on clay in a couple of years." Says Nadal, who had not lost to Federer on clay in five previous matches, "If I have to lose against anyone, then he is the man. I am not sad to lose to the best in the world."

1990 One year after attending the Italian Open on crutches recovering from torn knee ligaments suffering from being hit by a car, Thomas Muster of Austria wins the Italian Open for the first time in his career, defeating Andrei Chesnokov of Russia 6-1, 6-3, 6-1 in the singles final. Says Muster, "When I said then (last year) that I would be back to win this tournament, it was more like a wish. But I worked very hard since then, and it paid off. This is my biggest tournament victory."

2001 No. 40-ranked Albert Portas becomes one of the most unlikely champions of a Tennis Masters Series event when he upsets fellow Spaniard Juan Carlos Ferrero 4-6, 6-2, 0-6, 7-6 (5), 7-5 to win the Tennis Master Series— Hamburg for his first—and only—career ATP singles title. Portas, a qualifier in the tournament, ends Ferrero's 16-match winning streak with the final-round victory. "It was unbelievable, the most incredible experience in my life," Portas says. "It was a beautiful match. Hamburg will be forever in my heart now. It was the best day in my life."

1984 Andres Gomez of Ecuador fends off the challenge of 16-year-old Aaron Krickstein, defeating the American 2-6, 6-1, 6-2, 6-2 in the final of the Italian Open in Rome. Krickstein becomes the youngest men's finalist in the history of the Italian Championships.

May 21

1881 The United States National Lawn Tennis Association—the modern day U.S. Tennis Association—is founded in Room F of the Fifth Avenue Hotel in New York City. The founding of the association is precipitated by the need to bring uniformity to a game that had been imported to this country only six years before. From the time Mary Outerbridge brings a tennis set to U.S. shores from Bermuda until the organizational meeting of what would be known as the United States National Lawn Tennis Association, the rules of the game, including the height of the net, the distance of the service line from the net and, primarily, the size of the ball, varies from region to region. "It was because of the question of the balls, and for the better promotion of the game at large, that I requested the directors of my club to be authorized to try to organize a national association," says Eugenius Outerbridge, Mary's brother and secretary of the Staten Island Cricket and Baseball Club. R.S. Oliver of the Albany Tennis Club is elected as first president of the new USNLTA. In addition, rules are established setting the size of an official tennis ball between 2½ inches and 2-9/16 inches in diameter and between 1-7/8 ounces and 2 ounces in weight.

1989 Alberto Mancini of Argentina continues his romp through the European clay court season, following up his victory at the Monte Carlo Open three weeks earlier by winning the Italian Open in Rome, defeating Andre Agassi 6-3, 4-6, 2-6, 7-6 (2), 6-1 in the singles final. Says Agassi of Mancini's surge in the fifth set after winning the fourth-set tie-break, "There's a funny thing about sports—it's something called momentum. There's not much you can do about it. I had him down but let him go. I don't think it's so much what I did but how well he played."

1994 World No. 2 Michael Stich snaps the 29-match winning streak of Pete Sampras, beating the world No. 1 3-6, 7-6 (3), 6-2 as Germany defeats the United States 3-0 in the World Team Cup in Dusseldorf, Germany.

2006 Former world No. 1 Martina Hingis wins the biggest title following her three-year hiatus from tennis, defeating Russia's Dinara Safina 6-2 7-5 to win the Italian Open in Rome. Says Hingis, "I never thought I'd be here again, but they say never give up hope and keep fighting, and here I am. It's just great to be back on top of the game."

May 22

1977 Vitas Gerulaitis becomes the first American in 17 years to win the men's singles title at the Italian Open, defeating Italy's Antonio Zugarelli 6-2, 7-6, 3-6, 7-6. Gerulaitis becomes the first American man to win the Italian title since Barry MacKay wins the title in 1960. Janet Newberry of the U.S. makes it an American double at Rome, defeating Renata Tomanova of Czechoslovakia 6-3, 7-6.

1995 Thomas Muster wins a rain-delayed Monday final at the Italian Open, defeating Sergi Bruguera 3-6, 7-6 (5), 6-2, 6-3. The title is Muster's 27th title of his career and his 21st consecutive victory in clay court finals dating back to 1990. Says Bruguera, the reigning two-time French Open champion of Muster, who would win the French Open three weeks later. "This year, Muster is the best on clay. He's won all the tournaments. He's had a long undefeated streak. There is no doubt that Muster is the best right now."

1983 Eighteen-year-old Jimmy Arias defeats 30-year-old Jose Higueras 6-2, 6-7 (3), 6-1, 6-4 to win the Italian Open title in Rome, the biggest title of his career. Says Arias, "This is by far the biggest tournament I've ever won."

1930 George Lott wins a Davis Cup match without losing a game for the second time in his career as he defeats Mexico's Ignacio de la Borbolla 6-0, 6-0, 6-0. Lott also turned the trick in 1928 against China's Paul Kong. Lott helps the U.S. take a 2-0 lead over Mexico in the Davis Cup second round at the Chevy Chase Club in Chevy Chase, Md.

May 23

2005 Anastasia Myskina of Russia is defeated in the first round of the French Open, losing to Maria Sanchez Lorenzo of Spain 6-4, 4-6, 6-0 to become the first defending women's champion at Roland Garros to lose in the opening round of the championship. Says Myskina in her post-match press conference, "I was not on top of my game. She (Sanchez Lorenzo) played okay but she didn't do anything special. No matter who I had played today, I would have lost."

1994 In her final year of singles competition, Martina Navratilova loses in the first round of the French Open for the first time in her career, losing to Miriam Oremans of the Netherlands 6-4, 6-4. Navratilova's final swing of her racquet on the day comes against her courtside chair, as the two-time Roland Garros champion shatters her racquet frame before walking off the court. Says Navratilova of her racquet smash, "I've never done it before and I hope I never will again, but at that point, I was too disappointed to care about anything." Navratilova would return to the singles court at the French Open again in a singles cameo in 2004.

1944 John Newcombe, the charismatic Australian three-time Wimbledon champion with the trademark handle-bar moustache, is born in Sydney, Australia. Newcombe wins Wimbledon titles in 1967, 1970 and 1971 and also snatches major singles titles at the Australian Open in 1973 and 1975 and the U.S. Championships in 1967 and 1973. In all, "Newk" wins 25 major titles (including men's and mixed doubles titles), with only fellow Aussie Roy Emerson winning more men's majors with 28.

1981 No. 1 seed Guillermo Vilas of Argentina is upset in the semifinals of the Italian Open in Rome, losing a marathon three-and-half hour straight-set match to Paraguay's Victor Pecci 7-6, 6-4, 7-6. Says Vilas of his reasoning for the upset loss, "I was only thinking of the Sunday final. I thought it would be easy and I wasn't concentrating. That was my biggest mistake. I wasn't thinking of the match." Jose-Luis Clerc, Vilas' Davis Cup teammate, beats Ivan Lendl 3-6, 6-0, 7-5, 6-2 in the other men's semifinal. Pecci is unable to turn an "Argentine double" in the final the next day, losing to Clerc 6-3, 6-4, 6-0.

May 24

2005 Described by Bud Collins in the *Boston Globe* as "a wake masquerading as a tennis match," thirty-five-year-old Andre Agassi hobbles out of the first round of the French Open, losing 12 of the last 13 games in his 7-5, 4-6, 6-7 (6), 6-1, 6-0 loss to qualifier Jarkko Nieminen of Finland. Agassi, playing at the French Open for a 17th time, nearly retires in the match due to severe lower back pain due to a sciatic nerve problem, but tries to compete in the final two sets in the match that eventually becomes his swan song from Roland Garros. Says Agassi after the match, "After the third set, I almost went to the net to shake hands. The pain that was getting worse and worse, running down my back and into my legs. But I wasn't going to walk out. I didn't want to leave that way."

2004 No. 6 seeded Andre Agassi is dimissed in the first round of the French Open by 23-year-old journeyman and qualifier Jerome Haehnel of France by a 6-4, 7-6 (4), 6-3 margin. Haehnel, ranked No. 271 in the world, had never previously played an ATP level match. Says Agassi in the post-match news conference of his poor play, "You know, there's really no explanation for hitting the ball like that. I mean, usually, a few things can go wrong, but striking the ball is not a problem for me. I just was never comfortable with my shot selection, never comfortable with where I was putting the ball. I wish I could give you an excuse."

1999 Carlos Moya flirts with becoming the first defending French men's singles champion to lose in the first round the following year as he comes back from a two-set deficit to beat No. 92-ranked Markus Hipfl of Austria 3-6, 1-6, 6-4, 6-2, 6-4 in the opening round. Says Moya, "The way I was playing, I didn't see any way to escape from this match. But I just kept fighting. I run at all the balls. What can you do when you're losing so badly? You just have to do your best and pray, and that's what I did and it worked."

1899 Suzanne Lenglen, the immensely popular and charismatic French tennis champion, is born in Paris. Lenglen is such a sensation after she wins her first major singles title at Wimbledon in 1919 that three years later, Wimbledon is forced to change locations to a bigger stadium to accommodate the new crowds attending the championships to watch her play. She never loses at Wimbledon in seven visits—the only year she did not win the title, she withdrew due to illness in 1926. She also wins two French titles after the championship becomes international and wins Olympic gold in 1920.

May 25

2004 Frenchmen Fabrice Santoro and Arnaud Clement finish play in the longest-recorded match in tennis history in the first round of the French Open as Santoro edges Clement 6-4, 6-3, 6-7 (5), 3-6, 16-14 in 6 hours, 33 minutes. The match is played over two days and is suspended from the previous day with the two playing for 4:38 the previous day—stopping at 5-5 in the fifth-set—and for 1:55 the second day. Santoro saves two match points during the marathon—one on each day. The first match point comes with Santoro serving at 4-5 in the fifth set on day one and the second comes at 13-14 on the second day. Says Santoro, "I came very close to defeat, it's a miracle. I tried to stay relaxed on the important points and if it looked that way, then I did a good job because I was very tense." Santoro and Clement break the previous record—curiously held by two women in a straight-set best-of-three match—held by Vicki Nelson-Dunbar and Jean Hepner, who play for 6 hours, 31 minutes in the first round of the WTA event in Richmond, Va., in 1984, Nelson-Dunbar winning 6-4, 7-6 (13-11). Says Clement of establishing the new record, "I don't care. What do I get? A medal? There may be an even longer match tomorrow. I don't play tennis to spend as much time possible on court."

1976 Adriano Panatta saves an astonishing 11 match points in defeating Kim Warwick of Australia 3-6, 6-4, 7-6 in the first round of the Italian Championships. The result becomes even more significant when Panatta goes on to win the title, defeating Guillermo Vilas in the final.

1958 In one of the most spectacular comebacks in the history of the French Championships, Robert Haillet of France beats 1950 French champion Budge Patty, 5-7, 7-5, 10-8, 4-6, 7-5 in the fourth round after Patty serves at 5-0, 40-0 in the fifth set and holds four match points.

1999 Ranked No. 111 in the world, 17-year-old Roger Federer plays in his first main draw match at a major tournament at the French Open, losing to two-time reigning U.S. Open champion Patrick Rafter of Australia 5-7, 6-3, 6-0, 6-2. Writes Rene Stauffer in the book *The Roger Federer Story, Quest for Perfection*, "He (Roger) jumped out to win the first set against the world's No. 3-ranked player who then was at the peak of his career. However, the sun came out and the conditions became warmer and faster. The clay courts dried out and balls moved much faster through the court. The Australian's attacking serve-and-volley style seemed to run on automatic and he won in four sets. 'The young man from Switzerland could be one of the people who will shape the next ten years,' the French sports newspaper *L'Equipe* wrote during the tournament. Rafter shared the same opinion. "The boy impressed me very much," he said. "If he works hard and has a good attitude, he could become an excellent player.'"

1993 Three-time French Open champion Ivan Lendl experiences one of the worst losses of his career, losing 3-6, 7-5, 6-0, 7-6 (2) to No. 297th ranked qualifier Stephane Huet of France in the first round of the French Open. The match marks the first ATP level match victory for Huet, against Lendl's 1,027 match victories. It is also Huet's first major tournament match against Lendl's 51st major event.

1993 Brad Gilbert wins his first match at the French Open in six years, registering a two-day 5-7, 4-6, 6-2, 6-1, 10-8 first-round victory over fellow American Bryan Shelton. Gilbert and Shelton share 87 unforced errors in the 3-hour-and-52-minute match. Says Gilbert, the author of the book *Winning Ugly* after the match, "It was a chapter out of my book.... Unequivocally ugly."

1928 George Lott defeats China's Paul Kong 6-0, 6-0, 6-0 in the Davis Cup second round in Kansas City, Mo., to become the first U.S. Davis Cup player to win a match without losing a game. Lott registers another triple-bagel in Davis Cup play in 1930 against Mexico's Ignacio de la Borbolla. Frank Parker is the only other American to win a Davis Cup match without losing a game, turning the trick in 1946 against Felicismo Ampon of the Philippines.

1993 Goran Ivanisevic overcomes throwing up on court in the first set to defeat Franco Davin of Argentina 7-5, 6-3, 6-4 in the first round of the French Open.

2005 No. 2 seed Andy Roddick is eliminated in the second round of the French Open, blowing a two-sets-to-love lead in his 3-6, 4-6, 6-4, 6-3, 8-6 loss to Argentina's Jose Acasuso.

2008 Three-time French Open singles champion and former world No. 1 Gustavo "Guga" Kuerten bids goodbye to tennis, playing the final singles match of his career losing to Paul-Henri Mathieu of France 6-3, 6-4, 6-2 in the first round at Roland Garros.

May 26

1956 Althea Gibson becomes the first black player to win a major singles title, defeating Angela Mortimer of Britain 6-0, 12-10 in 1 hour, 45 minutes, in the final of the French Championships. Gibson's win was her first in her fifth meeting with Mortimer. Writes the Associated Press of Gibson's win, "Miss Gibson was so happy at beating Miss Mortimer for the first time that she leaped over the net to put her arms around her erstwhile jinx." In the men's singles final, Lew Hoad beats Sven Davidson 6-4, 8-6, 6-3.

2004 Top seed Justine Henin-Hardenne is defeated in the second round of the French Open, losing to No. 86-ranked Tathiana Garbin of Italy 7-5, 6-4, marking the earliest loss ever for a top-seeded woman in the 79-year history of women's singles at the event. Henin is not in top form, having not played a tournament for six weeks due to a virus. "I was unable to be positive today, or even to vent my rage or discontentment, all the things you're used to seeing in me," says Henin-Hardenne. "I couldn't express myself. I felt a bit empty somehow." Writes Chris Clarey of the *New York Times*, "It might have been drizzling at Roland Garros, but Garbin was basking in sunlight and the biggest victory of her career, which also happened to be the biggest victory in ages for an Italian woman. Until Wednesday, no Italian had beaten a No. 1-ranked women's player. The closest until now was Linda Ferrando, who just as unheralded as Garbin when she defeated the second-ranked Monica Seles in the third round of the United States Open in 1990."

1978 John McEnroe of Stanford University wins the NCAA singles title as a freshman defeating John Sadri of North Carolina State 7-6, 7-6, 5-7, 7-6 in the final played at the University of Georgia in Athens, Ga.

1928 Wilbur Coen, at the age of 16 years, five months, becomes the youngest American to play Davis Cup as he and Bill Tilden team to defeat Paul Kong and Gordon Lum of China 6-2, 6-1, 6-3 in the Davis Cup second round at the Rockhill Tennis Club in Kansas City, Mo. Coen and Tilden's win gives the United States an insurmountable 3-0 lead over China.

May 27

1992 Jimmy Connors plays his final match at the French Open, enduring 26 aces by Wimbledon champion Michael Stich in a 7-5, 3-6, 6-7(4), 6-1, 6-2 first-round defeat in 3 hours, 52 minutes. "I thought in the first three sets that I played some exciting tennis for me, but unfortunately it didn't last," says the 39-year-old Connors. "I thought I'd let the fourth set go and save my energy for the fifth, but my energy never came back. The years have started to take their toll." Says Stich, who also slaps 68 unforced errors to go with his ace total, "He tried to finish the match, but I think he was just too tired to hang in there."

2002 Pete Sampras loses what eventually becomes his last match at Roland Garros as he is defeated in the first round of the French Open by Italy's Andrea Gaudenzi 3-6, 6-4, 6-2, 7-6 (3). "I don't want to say it's a jinx," says the No. 12 seed Sampras of not winning the French Open, the only major title to elude him. "It's not like I lost four finals here. It's a question of playing well on clay. But, you know, if Paris never happens over my career, life will go on. But I will come back and try again." Says Gaudenzi, ranked No. 69, "What can I say? He's probably the best tennis player who ever breathed [but] you cannot always be at the top and pretending you can win on all surfaces. Definitely his game is not made for clay. It's so much more difficult for him to play good on this surface....It's quite an honor to play him at the end sometimes. And to beat him is a great thing. I know I'm aware I didn't beat him at his best, his best surface, so it doesn't mean a lot."

2003 Michael Chang plays his final match at Roland Garros as the 1989 champion is defeated in the French Open's first round by Fabrice Santoro 7-5, 6-1, 6-1 on Court Central. Chang openly cries into his Roland Garros towel as the crowd gives him a standing ovation following the loss. "I've only cried twice in my career," Chang tells the crowd, "and both times were here on this court."

2004 Juan Carlos Ferrero, who had never lost before the semifinals in four previous appearances at the French Open, matches the earliest loss ever by a men's defending champion at the French Championships, falling in the second round to No. 77-ranked Igor Andreev of Russia, 6-4, 6-2, 6-3. Ferrero, however, is not in top form, slowed by sore ribs and suffering unusually from cramps in his legs midway through the match. Says Ferrero, "I couldn't play my best tennis today. It's pretty difficult to stay in the match with two injuries....It's pretty difficult to defend a title when you're not 100 percent."

1999 Sixteen-year-old qualifier Justine Henin, playing in her first major tournament match, serves for the match against No. 2 seed Lindsay Davenport, but wins only three points in the final three games and loses 6-3, 2-6, 7-5. Davenport praises the No. 121-ranked Henin, a future four-time winner of the French Open, and predicts greatness for her—"The girl is very good."—and laments her sloppy play on clay—"I was just frustrated the way I was playing. I knew I can't be playing like this. On clay, I can't be behind the baseline. I need to be the one attacking." Says Henin of her loss, "I'm very disappointed and very pleased at the same time. I was just one game away from victory. I don't want to do things too quickly, either. It's not good."

1979 Vitas Gerulaitis outlasts Guillermo Vilas 6-7, 7-6, 6-7, 6-4, 6-2 in 4 hours, 53 minutes in the final of the Italian Open in Rome. The final is the longest at the Italian Championships since 1956 when Nicola Pietrangeli defeats Merv Rose in 5 hours, 9 minutes. Says Gerulaitis of the match, "I changed strategy about four times during the match, and played just about every way I know how to."

May 28

1983 World No. 1 and defending champion Martina Navratilova is stunned in the fourth round of the French Open, falling to 17-year-old Kathy Horvath of Hopewell Junction, N.Y. 6-4, 0-6, 6-3. Navratilova enters the match having won her first 36 matches for the year and 126 of 129 since the beginning of 1982. "Obviously I'm not happy about it," says Navratilova of the loss, "but I knew I had to lose sooner or later. It's not a disaster." The loss would be the only one of the year for Navratilova, who finishes the year with an 86-1 record. Writes Bud Collins in *The Bud Collins History of Tennis*, "The ramifications of that upset wouldn't be felt for months. Following the defeat, Navratilova won her next 50 matches and swept the field of Wimbledon, the U.S. Open and Australian Open championships. Not only had Horvath denied her the opportunity of achieving a Grand Slam but spoiled what might have been the first perfect campaign in the Open era."

1962 Rod Laver saves a match point and defeats countryman Marty Mulligan 4-6, 6-3, 2-6, 10-8, 6-2 in the quarterfinals of the French Championships. Laver's dramatic win keeps alive his dreams of achieving a Grand Slam, which he eventually wins by winning the French, Wimbledon and U.S. titles to go with the Australian title that he wins to start the year.

1980 Jimmy Connors trails Jean-Francois Caujolle of France 6-3, 6-2, 5-2 before Caujolle suffers one of the greatest collapses in major tournament history, winning only two of the next 21 games in a 2-6, 2-6, 7-5, 6-1, 6-1 second-round loss to Connors at the French Open. Caujolle holds match point at 30-40 on Connors serve at 2-5 in the third set, but is unable to convert. Writes Barry Lorge of *The Washington Post*, "To paraphrase an old Rodney Dangerfield gag, if you looked up "choke" in the dictionary, you'd find Caujolle's picture."

1976 Harold Solomon walks off the court in disgust, forfeiting his quarterfinal match at the Italian Open in Rome against Adriano Panatta after questioning the call of a linesman and the chair umpire, despite serving for the match leading 5-4 in the third set. Trailing 0-15 in the 10th game of the final set, Solomon questions the call of Panatta's backhand return, which is called good by the linesman and the chair umpire. Says Solomon, who loses the match by a 6-2, 5-7, 4-5, default, scoreline, "I pointed to the mark where the ball landed and told Adriano I'd show him where it hit, but the referee stopped him from coming around the net and told me to continue the match or get off. I was disqualified and for no reason. The referee told me the crowd was going crazy and to play or get off, but he wouldn't let me explain so I said something a little stronger than "good-bye" and left."

1931 After receiving good luck wishes from President Herbert Hoover, the U.S. Davis Cup team opens play against Argentina for the first time in the Davis Cup third round at the Chevy Chase Club in Chevy Chase, Md. Frank Shields and Sidney Wood give the United States a 2-0 lead after the first day of play, defeating Guillermo Robson and Ronaldo Boyd, respectively.

1960 Nicola Pietrangeli of Italy defeats Luis Ayala of Chile 3-6, 6-3, 6-4, 4-6, 6-3 in the final of the French Championships. Darlene Hard defeats Yola Ramirez of Mexico 6-3, 6-4 in the women's final.

2003 Thirty-three-year-old Andre Agassi loses the first two sets and trails in the third, rallies to take the lead, blows one chance to close out the match and finally beats 19-year-old Mario Ancic 5-7, 1-6, 6-4, 6-2, 7-5 in the second round of the French Open. Agassi is twice down a service break in the third set and wins only one more point than Ancic—148 points vs. 147 points—in the 3-hour, 13-minute match. Says Agassi, "Everybody's got a gas tank, and you never know when you are going to have to use it; I had to use mine today,"

2001 Venus Williams exits the French Open on the opening day of play, losing to No. 24 ranked Barbara Schett of Austria 6-4, 6-4 in the first round. Williams, seeded No. 2, is joined on the side-lines by No. 5 seed Amelie Mauresmo, who also loses in the first round, falling to Jana Kandarr of Germany 7-5, 7-5. "I never dreamed it would turn out like this," says Williams. "Normally I do turn it around. Today it just wasn't there. I just had a very rough day."

1984 Seventeen-year-old Manuela Maleeva of Bulgaria defeats Chris Evert Lloyd 6-3, 6-3 in the rain-delayed final of the Italian Open in Perugia, Italy. Maleeva actually finishes three matches during the day, completing the last set of her quarterfinal win over Virginia Ruzici and downing Carling Basset in the semifinals before playing Evert Lloyd in the final. Evert Lloyd also has to play her semifinal during the day, defeating Lisa Bonder before losing to Maleeva.

May 29

1990 For the first time ever in a major tournament, the No. 1 and No. 2 seeds are both eliminated in the first round. Stefan Edberg, the No. 1 seed and reigning Wimbledon champion, is defeated by little-known 19-year-old Spaniard Sergi Bruguera 6-4, 6-2, 6-1, becoming the first No. 1 seed in the 99-year-history of the tournament to lose in the first round. About four hours later, Boris Becker, the No. 2 seed and reigning U.S. Open champion, joins Edberg on the sidelines, losing to little-known Yugoslav Goran Ivanisevic 5-7, 6-4, 7-5, 6-2. "I say, 'Bruguera beat Edberg, why cannot I beat Becker,' you know," Ivanisevic says. "I say, 'Come on, (it) is your chance. He is not playing well, he is not confident.'"

1996 Andre Agassi is defeated in the second round of the French Open by unheralded fellow American Chris Woodruff 4-6, 6-4, 6-7 (7), 6-3, 6-2. Agassi, so dejected by the loss, skips the mandatory post-match press conference and is fined $2,000. Says Woodruff of Agassi to the media following the match, "I'd never met him before, and before we went out on the court he said, 'How ya doing; my name is Andre.' As if I didn't know."Also during the day, Pete Sampras posts one of his most impressive clay court wins, defeating 1993-1994 French Open champion Sergi Bruguera 6-3, 6-4, 6-7 (2-7), 2-6, 6-3 also in the second round. "This match had a lot of everything," Sampras says. "It gives me some confidence that I can play with the Brugueras and whomever, and that's one thing I haven't had before coming into this tournament."

2006 Rafael Nadal wins his 54th consecutive match on a clay court, breaking the Open era record set by Guillermo Vilas, defeating Robin Soderling of Sweden 6-2, 7-5, 6-1 in the first round of the French Open. Nadal is honored for his achievement with an on-court ceremony featuring Christian Bimes, the President of the French Tennis Federation, and Vilas himself, who wins 53 straight matches on clay in 1977. Says Nadal of the record, "Obviously, the record is something just extra. It's something you want. You want to go for it, but the first round in a Grand Slam tournament is always difficult. The first round in any tournament is difficult, but in a Grand Slam, there's a little more pressure." Vilas was not even aware that he held the record for most consecutive clay court victories until weeks before the record was broken. He was, however, well aware of his Open-era records for consecutive victories, regardless of surface (50) and for tournaments won in a year (16)—all accomplished in 1977. Says Vilas, "I'm not sad to lose the minor record, but I'll be mad if he breaks the others." Nadal's streak begins in April of 2005 at the Monte Carlo Open. The streak ends at 81 on May 20, 2007, when Roger Federer beats Nadal in the final of Hamburg, Germany.

2006 For the first time in the history of tennis, a major tournament starts on a Sunday as the French Open starts play a day earlier than the traditional Monday start. Former Wimbledon champion Maria Sharapova saves three match points and comes back from 2-5 down the final set to defeat No. 97-ranked Mashona Washington 6-2, 5-7, 7-5 in the first round in the most exciting match played during the day.

1998 For the first time in the Open era history of major championship play, a qualifier defeats the defending champion at a major event as 18-year-old qualifier Marat Safin from Russia defeats defending champion Gustavo Kuerten 3-6, 7-6 (5), 3-6, 6-1, 6-4 in the second round of the French Open. Safin, ranked No. 114 and playing in his first ever major tournament, defeated Andre Agassi in five sets in the first round. Says Kuerten, "This year I think I had a chance to go far and try to repeat, but there are many dangerous guys in the way, and today he played hard and he played strong and I couldn't finish my work. If the other guy has a great day and you don't have such luck, you can lose to anyone here." Says Safin, who goes on to win the U.S. Open and become the No. 1 player in the world in 2000, "I feel bad for Guga because he's defending champion, but this is tennis life. What can we do? Everybody wants to beat him: a lot of points, money, everything."

2001 Pete Sampras avoids an embarrassing first-round loss at the French Open but hangs on to save three match points and defeat No. 250-ranked qualifier Cedric Kauffmann 6-3, 4-6, 6-2, 3-6, 8-6.

2006 Juan Antonio Marin of Costa Rica loses to Carlos Moya of Spain in the first round of the French Open to drop to a 0-17 career record in Grand Slam tournament play. No man has ever lost as many Grand Slam matches without a victory. Says Marin, "Given my stats, I don't know if I am going to win. ... I'll keep on trying." Marin, the only player from Costa Rica to play in a major tournament, never plays another major tournament match.

2000 Pete Sampras is sent packing in the first round of the French Open, losing 4-6, 7-5, 7-6 (4), 4-6, 8-6 to Australia's Mark Philippoussis.

May 30

1953 Eighteen-year-old Ken Rosewall wins the men's singles title at the French Championships, defeating American Vic Seixas 6-3, 6-4, 1-6, 6-2 in the singles final to become the youngest champion at the event at the time (since eclipsed by 17-year-olds Mats Wilander and Michael Chang). Maureen Connolly wins the women's title, defeating Doris Hart 6-2, 6-4 in the final.

1959 Italy's Nicola Pietrangeli defeats Ian Vermaak of South Africa 3-6, 6-3, 6-4, 6-1 to win the first of his two straight men's singles titles at the French Championships. Christine Truman, the 18-year-old British star, wins the women's singles title, defeating defending champion Suzi Kormoczy of Hungary 6-4, 7-5 in the final.

1969 Rod Laver finishes off the upset bid of Dick Crealy of Australia in the second round of French Open, winning the final two sets of the rain-delayed match to win 3-6, 7-9, 6-2, 6-2, 6-4. Crealy leads two-sets-to-love before the match is suspended the previous day due to rain, with Crealy leading two-sets-to-one. Laver goes on to win the tournament, and with victories later in the summer at Wimbledon and the U.S. Open, his second "Grand Slam."

2007 Venus Williams slams a 128 mph serve—the fastest recorded serve by a woman ever in a major tournament—during her 6-1, 7-6 (8) win over Ashley Harkleroad in the second round of the French Open. Williams hits her serve at 4-1, 30-0 in the second-set, but the serve is not an ace as Harkleroad is able to get her racquet on the ball. Brenda Schultz-McCarthy of the Netherlands is credited with the fastest-recorded serve by a woman—a 130 mph serve in the qualifying tournament at the 2006 WTA Tour event in Cincinnati. Says Williams "When I was younger, I was always trying to serve harder and harder, and now I'm not trying to serve hard." Venus breaks her own major tournament record a year later at Wimbledon, slamming two 129 mph serves, including one in the women's final against her sister Serena.

1999 Andre Agassi wins one of the most important matches of his career, rallying to defeat defending champion Carlos Moya 4-6, 7-5, 7-5, 6-1 in the round of 16 at the French Open. Agassi trails the No. 4-seeded Moya 4-6, 1-4 before rallying to defeat the clay court specialist from Spain en route to winning his only French Open championship. "I was leading pretty easily, 6-4, 4-1 with two breaks," Moya says. "I thought everything was done, you know? That was my problem." No. 5 seed Venus Williams, meanwhile, holds triple match point against Austrian qualifier Barbara Schwartz, leading 6-2, 6-5, 0-40 but is shockingly defeated by a 2-6, 7-6(7), 6-3 margin in the round of 16 of women's singles.

1995 Carsten Arriens of Germany becomes only the second player—after John McEnroe—to be disqualified from a major event in the Open era. After splitting the first two sets with New Zealand's Brett Steven, the 131-ranked Arriens first throws his racquet from the baseline to the net, for which he is warned by the chair umpire Andreas Egli. He then picks the racquet and heaves it towards his chair, but he hits the service linesman on the ankle. Egli then calls for the tournament referee, who agrees that Arriens should be disqualified. McEnroe's abuse of officials and foul language in his 1990 Australian Open match with Mikael Pernfors necessitates his disqualification.

2001 Eighteen-year-old French Open rookie Andy Roddick plays the first five-set match of his career and endures cramps and exhaustion and defeats 1989 French champion Michael Chang 5-7, 6-3, 6-4, 6-7 (5) 7-5 in the second round. Roddick registers 37 aces, marking the most ever for a match at Roland Garros. "The cramps started in my hands, went to my calves, the groin, everywhere. I never played five sets before, probably no more than 2 1/2 hours," says Roddick. "I hit the wall. But I got a burst of energy. I wasn't gonna lay down and die."

1982 Seventeen-year-old Mats Wilander of Sweden upsets Ivan Lendl 4-6, 7-5, 3-6, 6-4, 6-2 in the round of 16 of the French Open. The No. 2 –seeded Lendl, a French Open finalist in 1981, won 92 of his previous 95 matches entering the match, which is the first career five-set match for Wilander. Three matches later, Wilander is crowned the unlikely French Open men's singles champion.

1976 Adriano Panatta defeats Guillermo Vilas 2-6, 7-6, 6-2, 7-6 to win the Italian Open in Rome, becoming the first Italian in 15 years to win his national championship.

May 31

1983 Twenty-five-year-old French journeyman Christophe Roger-Vasselin, ranked No. 130 in the world, registers one of the biggest upsets in the history of the French Open, upsetting No. 1 seed Jimmy Connors 6-4, 6-4, 7-6 in the quarterfinals at Roland Garros. Roger-Vasselin's countryman No. 6-seeded Yannick Noah, accounts for the second big upset on the day, defeating No. 3 seed Ivan Lendl by a 7-6, 6-2, 5-7, 6-0 margin.

1994 Jim Courier defeats Pete Sampras 6-4, 5-7, 6-4, 6-4 in the quarterfinals of the French Open, ending Sampras' hopes of winning a fourth consecutive major tournament title. Sampras falls short in his attempt to join Don Budge and Rod Laver—both of whom won Grand Slams—as the only men to win four straight major titles. Sampras, the 1993 Wimbledon and U.S. Open champion and the 1994 Australian Open champion, sees his major tournament winning streak end at 26 matches. Says Sampras, "I'm kind of down and disappointed. To win four in a row would have been something that would have been written about for years." Says Courier after his first win over Sampras in 18 months, "I was in a lot more rallies and I was able to be the dictator rather than being the person dictated to....It has been a long time since I have won a big match in a big tournament like this against a top player."

1989 Thirty-six-year-old Jimmy Connors plays one of the longest four-set matches in the history of the sport, falling to fellow American Jay Berger 4-6, 6-3, 7-5, 7-5 in 4 hours, 26 minutes in the second round of the French Open. Berger is not surprised that the French crowd is so firmly rooting for the five-time U.S. Open champion. "Hey, if I was in the stands, I would have cheered Jimmy Connors, too," he says. Says Connors after the match, "For me to go out and grind out a match like that. It's fun. To play a kid like that, 14 years younger—I could have played a fifth set. My mouthpiece wasn't knocked out."

1974 Reigning Australian Open champions Jimmy Connors and Evonne Goolagong lose in French appeals court in an attempt to gain entry into the French Open. Both stars are denied entry into the tournament due to their involvement with World Team Tennis. French judge Jean Regnault denies the appeal stating that there was no "emergency" and that both players earned substantial incomes from tennis—with or without playing the French Championships. The decision costs Connors a serious opportunity to become only the third man to win the Grand Slam as he decisively wins Wimbledon and the U.S. Open later in the year. Says Connors of his Parisien court experience, "I'm in the wrong court. I should be on clay."

1998 Alex Corretja completes a 6-1, 5-7, 6-7, 7-5, 9-7 third-round victory over Hernan Gumy of Argentina at the French Open in a match that lasts 5 hours, 31 minutes, the longest match in major tournament history at the time. The match is five minutes longer than Stefan Edberg's semifinal victory against Michael Chang at the 1992 U.S. Open, but it is eclipsed in 2004 when Fabrice Santoro and Arnaud Clement play a two-day 6 hour, 33 minute match in the first round of the French Open.

1996 Pete Sampras outlasts fellow American Todd Martin 3-6, 6-4, 7-5, 4-6, 6-2 in 3 hours, 21 minutes in the third round of the French Open. Sampras serves 19 aces to Martin's 29, believed to be the highest number in one match at the French Open.

2000 Dominique Van Roost of Belgium celebrates her 27th birthday with a 6-7 (5), 6-4, 6-3 win over No. 2 seed Lindsay Davenport in the first round of the French Open.

2001 Pete Sampras is foiled again at the French Open, falling in the second round at the world's premier clay court championship to Spain's Galo Blanco 7-6 (4), 6-3, 6-2. "If I go through my career not winning the French, sure, it's disappointing," Sampras says. "But it's not going to take away from my place in the game, what I've been able to do over the years. I mean, there's still time. There's no reason to think this is it. I mean, I've got plenty of years left."

2003 In a 4-hour, 38-minute epic, defending champion Albert Costa of Spain defeats Nicolas Lapentti of Ecuador 4-6, 4-6, 6-3, 6-4, 6-4 in the third round of the French Open for his third five-set victory in a row at Roland Garros. Lapentti leads two-sets-to-love and 4-1 in the third set before Costa begins his comeback charge. "I'm feeling so proud of myself because I'm not playing my best tennis, but I'm still fighting all the time," Costa says. No. 1 seed Lleyton Hewitt is dismissed in the third round by Spaniard Tommy Robredo by a 4-6, 1-6, 6-3, 6-2, 6-3 margin. "This was the match of my life," Robredo says after his victory "To be two sets down and 0-3 down in the fifth and to have this crowd chanting my name in Paris against a guy like Hewitt, it's close to perfection."

June 1

1993 Mary Joe Fernandez performs one of the greatest comebacks in the history of the sport, rallying against a 6-1, 5-1 deficit and facing five match points before overcoming Gabriela Sabatini 1-6, 7-6(4), 10-8 in the quarterfinals of the French Open. "Never in doubt," Fernandez deadpans in her post-match press conference. With Sabatini serving for the match in the second set, Fernandez says she looked at the match time clock. "I saw that it was only 53 minutes into the match," says Fernandez. "I said, 'This is unbelievable. I've got to make it to the one-hour mark.'" Fernandez ends up winning the match in 3 hours, 34 minutes.

1935 Fred Perry becomes the first player in the history of tennis to win all four major tennis titles during a career when he defeats defending champion Gottfried von Cramm of Germany 6-3, 3-6, 6-1, 6-3 in the final of the French Championships. Perry previously wins the Wimbledon singles title in 1934, the U.S. title in 1933 and 1934 and the Australian title in 1934.

1983 John McEnroe flat out says "I choked" after losing to defending champion Mats Wilander 1-6, 6-2, 6-4, 6-0 in the quarterfinals of the French Open. McEnroe, seeded No. 2, loses the last 11 games of the match and at one point, loses an incredible stretch of 23 straight points.

2004 For the first time in their careers, Venus and Serena Williams are defeated on the same day as both sisters are eliminated in the quarterfinals of the French Open. Serena Williams is defeated by Jennifer Capriati 6-3, 2-6, 6-3, while Venus Williams is defeated by Anastasia Myskina 6-3, 6-4. The conclusion, for the Williams sisters, drawn by Charlie Bricker of the *Ft. Lauderdale Sun-Sentinel* is that "these twin losses probably mark the end of their days of domination of the WTA Tour."

2000 Suffering from a blistered big toe, Andre Agassi loses to Karol Kucera 2-6, 7-5, 6-1, 6-0 in the second round of the French Open, equaling the earliest loss ever by a defending men's champion at Roland Garros. Kucera wins 16 of the last 17 games of the match to take out the No. 1 seeded American. The loss ends Agassi's run of four consecutive Grand Slam tournament finals. Agassi is so distraught by the loss that he leaves the grounds without talking to reporters.

1990 Following a 6-3, 6-2, 6-0 third-round French Open victory over Arnaud Boetsch, Andre Agassi labels French Tennis Federation and International Tennis Federation President Phillipe Chartier as a "bozo" after Chartier and tournament officials issue a statement during Agassi's match criticizing the attire of certain players—presumably Agassi who sports faded black shorts and "hot lava" pink tights. "There is growing concern about this issue," Chatrier says in the statement. "If players go too far in their attire, then something will have to be done." Responds Agassi in his post-match press conference, "Those bozos will look for anyone to talk about. Let them talk. It's some dull guys sitting behind a desk." Continues Agassi, "Tennis players are different. It isn't a team. It's you. I think you should have freedom to express what you feel. Wearing colors is what tennis needs. It adds a little something. Without colors I'd still be me, but I'd be more boring."

June 2

1962 Rod Laver wins the second leg of his eventual "Grand Slam" sweep of all four major singles titles, coming back from two-sets-to-love down to defeat fellow Australian Roy Emerson 3-6, 2-6, 6-3, 9-7, 6-2 in the final of the French Championships. According to UPI wire dispatches of the final, "The last three sets were excellently played, and the fourth and fifth brought the 3,500 fans in Roland Garros Stadium to their feet cheering on a number of occasions." Laver trails 0-3 in the fourth set, but rallies to take the extended fourth set before breaking Emerson twice to ride out the fifth set. The previous day, Laver finishes off a darkness delayed five-set semifinal win over fellow Aussie Neale Fraser 3-6, 6-3, 6-2, 3-6, 7-5, with the match resuming at 2-2 in the fifth set. In the quarterfinals, in another all-Aussie affair, Laver saves a match point in a five-set win over Marty Mulligan. Nineteen-year-old Margaret Smith, who herself would capture a Grand Slam in 1970, wins the French women's singles title, also defeating a fellow Aussie, Lesley Turner, 6-3, 3-6, 7-5 in the final.

1973 Adriano Panatta of Italy ends the upset run of 16-year-old Bjorn Borg of Sweden in the fourth round of the French Open, beating the future six-time champion 7-6, 2-6, 7-5, 7-6. Borg, playing in his first major event, plays the event seven more times in his career and loses one other time—again to Panatta in the quarterfinals in 1976. Borg's string of upset victims in the tournament include No. 9 seed Cliff Richey of the United States in the first round, Pierre Barthes of France in the second round and Dick Stockton of the United States in the third round. Says Stockton of Borg after his 6-7, 7-5, 6-2, 7-6 loss, "He's got a really great future ahead of him. He works really hard and is a dedicated player and he deserved to win."

1994 Steffi Graf is shockingly dominated in the semifinals of the French Open as native hope Mary Pierce of France crushes the world's top-ranked player 6-2, 6-2. Says Graf, "There was very little I could do. She attacked the ball, took it early, played very deep and very hard and my level of game wasn't enough to push her to make some errors." Pierce advances into the final with the loss of only 10 games in six matches, but falls to Arantxa Sanchez Vicario in the championship match.

1976 Adriano Panatta, the No. 5 seed from Italy, saves a match point and survives a first-round scare at the French Open, defeating Czech Pavel Hutka 2-6, 6-2, 6-2, 0-6, 12-10. The match becomes crucial and significant in the annals of the French Championships as Panatta goes on to win the title, becoming the fourth man to win the singles title after trailing by a match point.

1982 Two years removed from a bout of hepatitis that threatens his tennis career, Jose Higueras advances to the semifinals of the French Open with a 6-2, 6-2, 6-2 victory over top-seeded Jimmy Connors. Guillermo Vilas also advances into the semifinals with a 7-6, 6-3, 6-4 win over Yannick Noah of France.

June 3

1967 Roy Emerson wins his 12th—and final—major singles title, beating fellow Aussie Tony Roche 6-1, 6-4, 2-6, 6-2 in the men's final at the French Championships. Not known at the time—in the days before statiscians, record keepers and publicity officials—but Emerson's title furthers his lead as the all-time winner of major men's singles titles—breaking two majors ahead of Bill Tilden, who wins 10 major singles titles from 1920 to 1930. Emerson's victory gives him a second-leg of a possible Grand Slam after winning the Australian Championships, but falters in the fourth round of Wimbledon three weeks later.

1973 Margaret Smith Court wins a record fifth career French singles title, defeating 18-year-old Chris Evert 6-7 (5), 7-6 (6), 6-4 in 2 hours, 17 minutes. Evert leads the match by a set and 5-3—two points from victory—but is unable to close out the match. The win gives Court the second leg of a Grand Slam, but she is foiled at her second run at a calendar year sweep of all major singles titles by Evert in the semifinals of Wimbledon four weeks later. Court, the French champion in 1962, 1964, 1969 and 1970, holds the record for most French women's singles titles until Evert wins her sixth title in 1985 (and a seventh with another title in 1986.)

2001 After fighting back from a two-sets-to-love deficit and saving a match point against unheralded American qualifier Michael Russell, No. 1 seed Gustavo Kuerten shows his appreciation for the French fans of Roland Garros by drawing a heart in the center of the red clay court, collapsing inside of it and showering the fans with blown kisses. "I'm very emotional and everything I got in my life, nothing was for free," says Kuerten, who defeats Russell by a 3-6, 4-6, 7-6 (3), 6-3, 6-1 margin. "I had to fight a lot for everything I got so far. So I like this. I like the battles. I like these challenges that I always get in front of me. Today was special. Maybe one of the greatest feelings in all my life in the tennis court was today." Russell holds a match point serving a 5-3 in the third set and after a 26-stroke rally watches Kuerten stave off elimination with a forehand winner. Kuerten goes on to win the title, defeating Alex Corretja of Spain in the final. Kuerten performs the same heart-drawing antic after winning the title and shaking Corretja's hand.

1995 Jana Novotna performs one of the biggest collapses in major tournament play, leading Chanda Rubin 5-0, 40-0 in the final set in the third round of the French Open and blowing nine match points in losing 7-6 (8), 4-6, 8-6. Says Novotna, who claims she begins cramping in her legs at 5-1 in the third set, "It is always easier to criticize and to say, 'You had this and you had that.' But, of course, you have to also understand that this is tennis. This is happening to everybody, and we are only human beings."

2005 Playing on his nineteen birthday, Rafael Nadal defeats No. 1 seed Roger Federer 6-3, 4-6, 6-4, 6-3 in the semifinals of the French Open. Unseeded Mariano Puerta of Argentina, ranked No. 37, becomes the unlikely finalist, edging No. 12 seed Nikolay Davydenko of Russia 6-3, 5-7, 2-6, 6-4, 6-4 in the other men's singles. Says Nadal, "Federer, for me, is the best player wherever. Not only No. 1 for tennis, but the No. 1 for the person, and for sportsmanship."

1974 Seventeen-year-old Bjorn Borg wins the Italian Open—the biggest tournament victory of his young career at the time—upsetting No. 1 seed Ilie Nastase 6-3, 6-4, 6-2 in the championship match to become the event's youngest champion. "I am very pleased with myself," says Borg after the match. "I think I played well. I hit my forehand very well. Nastase, instead, looked very tired. He can play much better tennis than he did today."

1982 Andrea Jaeger defeats Chris Evert Lloyd 6-3, 6-1 in 68 minutes to advance into the women's singles final of the French Open, handing Evert Lloyd only her fourth defeat on clay in 222 matches since August 1973. Martina Navratilova, the No. 2 seed, also advances to the final overwhelming defending champion Hana Mandlikova 6-0, 6-2, in 41 minutes. "She played me perfectly," says Evert Lloyd, who lost to Jaeger in the semifinals of the Family Circle Cup in Hilton Head, S.C., two months earlier. "She really hit her groundstrokes. And when she was out of position, she'd throw up a lob. She was very patient, and there wasn't much to do except match her patience -which I didn't do today."

1988 Mats Wilander overcomes upstart 18-year-old American Andre Agassi 4-6, 6-2, 7-5, 5-7, 6-0 to reach the French Open men's singles final for the fifth time, while native Frenchman Henri Leconte dispatches of Jonas Svensson of Sweden 7-6, 6-2, 6-3 to reach his first major final. Says Svensson of Leconte, "He closes his eyes and goes for everything. He makes a lot of unbelievable shots. I didn't get to play my game." Says Wilander of Agassi, "He surprised me a lot. I didn't think he was this good. It was the best match I've played so far."

June 4

1955 Tony Trabert wins the men's singles title at the French Championships, defeating Swede Sven Davidson 2-6, 6-1, 6-4, 6-2 in the men's singles final. Trabert becomes the second American to win two straight French men's titles, joining 1948-1949 champion Frank Parker. Angela Mortimer of Great Britain wins the women's singles title, defeating American Dorothy Head Knode 2-6, 7-5, 10-8 in a 2-hour, 15-minute final.

1981 Hana Mandlikova ends Chris Evert's 64-match winning streak on clay, handing the American only her second loss on her favorite surface since August of 1973, a span of 191 matches, in a 7-5, 6-4 victory that propels her into the women's singles final at the French Open. Sylvia Hanika of West Germany registers a 6-4, 1-6, 6-4 win over Andrea Jaeger to also advance into the women's singles final. "It's the best win of my life," says Mandlikova. "Chris is the best clay-court player of all time." Mandlikova goes on to beat Hanika 6-2, 6-4 to win the title.

1982 In one of the greatest displays of sportsmanship seen in the sport, 17-year-old Mats Wilander gives back a winning match point against Jose-Luis Clerc that places him into his first major final, before rightfully earning his place in the French Open final on the next point in his 7-5, 6-2, 1-6, 7-5 semifinal victory. After Clerc's forehand is called long and fans cheer Wilander's advancement into the final, Wilander stands in the backcourt shaking his head and tells chair umpire Jacques Dorfman that the ball was in and that the point should be replayed. Wilander clinches the match rightfully on the next point when Clerc nets a backhand. "I told him I can't win like this," says Wilander of his conversation with Dorfman. "The ball was good. We should play two balls." Says Dorfman to the *New York Times*, "In all my experience, I have never known a gesture of sportsmanship like that on a match point."

1988 In the most lopsided French final in history, Steffi Graf requires only 32 minutes to shut out Natalia Zvereva of the Soviet Union 6-0, 6-0 to win her second French Open women's singles title. No previous French final had resulted in such a lopsided score. The last time a major final featured a 6-0, 6-0 score came in 1911, when Dorothy Lambert Chambers defeated Dora Boothby at Wimbledon. Zvereva wins only 13 points in the match. A one-hour rain delay in the first set proved to be longer than the match itself.

1972 An old man of nearly 36 years of age and self-described "old bag" woman of 28 years old win singles titles at the French Championships in Paris. Andres Gimeno of Spain, age 35 years and 10 months, becomes the oldest man to win the French Open singles title, defeating 22-year-old Patrick Proisy of France 4-6, 6-3, 6-1, 6-1. Billie Jean King, who at age 28 calls herself an "old bag" completes her career Grand Slam, winning her first French singles title, handing 20-year-old Evonne Goolagong her first-ever loss at Roland Garros by a 6-3, 6-3 margin in the final. King, who fights a cold during the match, almost doesn't enter the tournament to better prepare for Wimbledon.

2005 Justine Henin-Hardenne of Belgium, seeded No. 10, wins her second French Open women's singles title in routine fashion, defeating Mary Pierce of France 6-1, 6-1 in the women's singles final. Pierce is a surprise finalist in the tournament, upsetting the No. 9 seed Vera Zvonareva in the third round, No. 8 seed Patty Schnyder in the fourth round, No. 1 seed Lindsay Davenport in the quarterfinals and No. 16 Elena Likhovtseva in the semifinals.

2003 Defending champion Al Costa of Spain comes back from a two-sets-to-love-deficit for the third time in five matches at the French Open, defeating countryman Tommy Robredo 2-6, 3-6, 6-4, 7-5, 6-2 in the quarterfinals. Costa becomes the fifth man in Open era history to win four five-set matches during one tournament (including all events in which five sets are played) and the first to manage this feat at Roland Garros. Costa's third comeback from two-sets-to-love down equals the record for the greatest number of 0-2 comebacks by a player at a single major tournament in the Open era, set by Nicolas Escude at the 1998 Australian Open.

1983 Chris Evert Lloyd wins her fifth French Open and her 15th major singles title with a 6-1, 6-2 win in 65 minutes over Mima Jausovec of Yugoslavia.

June 5

1983 Yannick Noah creates a frenzy of French patriotism at Stade Roland Garros becoming the first Frenchman in 37 years to win the men's singles title at the French Open, defeating Mats Wilander 6-2, 7-5, 7-6 in 2 hours, 24 minutes in a passion-filled final. Noah serves and volleys and chips and charges on the slow red clay court to become the first Frenchman since Marcel Bernard in 1946 to win the French men's singles title. Noah is discovered at age 10 in the African nation of Cameroon, the birthplace of his father, when U.S. Davis Cup star Arthur Ashe informs French Tennis Federation President Philippe Chatrier of Noah's talent after seeing him play—with a tennis racquet carved out of wood. Wilander falls short in his attempt to defend the title he won the previous year as an unknown 17-year-old, unable to hit enough passing shots to fend off the constant net attacks by the dread-locked 23-year-old Noah. Writes Bud Collins in the *Boston Globe*, "Perhaps the French will rename that huge monument at Place de l'Etoile and call it Noah's Arc de Triomphe. The original outlasted a flood, but the current one opened the floodgates of emotion at Stade Roland Garros and washed away not only the Swedish Reign of Terror in the French Open, but also a seemingly impenetrable barrier that has separated French male players from their own title for 37 years."

1999 Twenty-nine-year-old Steffi Graf claims her 22nd—and final—major singles title, upending Martina Hingis 4-6, 7-5, 6-2 in the women's singles final at the French Open. Hingis serves for the title leading 6-4, 5-4, but Graf, inspired by the French crowd chanting "STEF-FEE, STE-FEE" breaks Hingis and wins eight of the next 10 games. "It was my greatest victory," says Graf. "I came here without belief—but the crowd lifted me. At 1-0 in the third I knew the momentum was with me. She got tight. Then at 3-0, I got tight and she almost caught me. It was the craziest match. 'Quit worrying,' I told myself. 'Go for your shots.' I did." The poor behavior of Hingis—and the accompanying boos and whistles from the French crowd—highlights the match as Hingis crosses the net to dispute a line call, takes an extended bathroom break at the end of the second set and serves underhanded on Graf's first championship point. Chair umpire Anne Lasserre issues two warnings to Hingis and penalizes her a point, leaving her one step from a default. Following the loss, Hingis leaves the court, and, in tears, returns to the court in the arms of her mother Melanie Molitor for the trophy presentation.

2003 Serena Williams is defeated by Belgium's Justine Henin-Hardenne 6-2, 4-6, 7-5 in front of a raucously pro-Henin-Hardenne crowd in the semi-finals of the French Open, ending Williams' 33-match major tournament winning streak. The match is highlighted by an incident in the third-set that proves to be contentious and acrimonious between the two rivals for years to come. With Williams serving at 4-2, 30-0 in the final set, Henin-Hardenne raises her hand indicating she is not ready to return serve. Williams serves in the net, then protests, to no avail, to the chair umpire and tournament referee that she should be given a first serve, while Henin-Hardenne says nothing of her gesture. Williams then loses the next four points to lose her service-break advantage and eventually the match. Says Henin-Hardenne, "I wasn't ready to play the point. The chair umpire is there to deal with these kind of situations. I just tried to stay focused on myself and tried to forget all the other things....It's her point of view but that's mine now and I feel comfortable with it....I didn't have any discussion with the chair umpire. He didn't ask me anything. I was just trying to focus on playing the returns. She saw me and she served. It was her decision to serve. I just tried to stay focused on the second serve. One point in the match doesn't change the outcome."

2005 Nineteen-year-old Rafael Nadal of Spain fends off a charge from unseeded Mariano Puerta of Argentina to win his first major singles title at the French Open. Nadal wins the title and his 24th consecutive match with a 6-7 (6), 6-3, 6-1 7-5 decision over the No. 37-ranked Puerta to become the fourth youngest men's singles champion at Roland Garros. Nadal joins 1982 champion Mats Wilander as the only player to win Roland Garros in his debut.

1953 With his bag packed ready for a trip to Cleveland to play in the U.S. Pro Championships, Bill Tilden, regarded by many as the greatest player in the history of the sport, is found dead in his hotel room in Los Angeles at the age of 60. The cause of death for the seven-time U.S. men's singles champion is a heart attack.

1973 In a rare major final played on a Tuesday due to bad weather in Paris, Ilie Nastase beats Nikki Pilic 6-3, 6-3, 6-0 in 90 minutes to win the French Open for the first time. Says Nastase, "It meant much more to me to win Forest Hills last September because I thought I could never win a major grass tournament. Still, this is an important one." Less than one hour after the match, Pilic is notified that he is suspended from competing on the circuit for 25 days for refusing to play for Yugoslavia in Davis Cup, a decision that results in a player boycott of Wimbledon in defense of Pilic. Nastase, however, is one of the few ATP union players who does not honor the boycott.

1982 Martina Navratilova wins the French Open for the first time in her career, defeating Andrea Jaeger 7-6, 6-1 in the final. Following the match, Jaeger accuses Navratilova of illegally receiving coaching signals from her coach, Renee Richards. "It sort of blew my concentration," says Jaeger, the 17-year-old American who was in her first major final. "It's difficult to be playing three people at once. I was trying in the whole first set to deal with it, and I was doing fine. But it was annoying. They've done it in other matches. It's not very good for tennis. She played well and I lost. But it shouldn't happen. I might win, 0-0, or lose, 0-0, but I want to win by myself or lose by myself." Says Navratilova, "This is a shock. All I can say is that I never looked at Renee except for encouragement. Here I have won the final of one of the biggest tournaments in the world. Thank you very much, Andrea. I didn't have to look up at them. Before I played, I went over the match 20 times with Renee. I could have recited in my sleep what I had to do against her. I didn't need to look at Renee."

1988 In a near flawless display of clay court tennis, Mats Wilander wins the French Open for a third time in his career, defeating French native son Henri Leconte 7-5, 6-2, 6-1 in the men's singles final. Wilander misses only two of 74 first serves, commits only nine unforced errors and does not hit a volley during the 1 hour, 52-minute match.

1977 Guillermo Vilas routs Brian Gottfried 6-0, 6-3, 6-0 to win his first major singles title in the most decisive French Open men's singles final in the event's history.

1990 Fourteen-year-old Jennifer Capriati becomes the youngest semifinalist at a major event in tennis history, defeating Mary Joe Fernandez 6-2, 6-4 in the women's quarterfinals at the French Open.

1993 Steffi Graf wins her third French Open women's singles title and her 12th career major singles title, defeating Mary Joe Fernandez 4-6, 6-2, 6-4 in the French Open women's singles final.

June 6

1956 Bjorn Rune Borg, one of the game's all-time greats who wins five straight Wimbledon singles titles from 1976-1980 and 11 career major singles titles, is born in Sodertalje, Sweden. Borg wins his first major title just days after his 18th birthday in 1974 at the French Championships, giving up only two games after dropping the first two sets to Spain's Manuel Orantes. He wins six French titles altogether in eight appearances at Roland Garros (1974-1975, 1978-1981). Adriano Panatta is the only man to beat him there—in the fourth round in 1973 and in the quarterfinals in 1976. In 1975, at age 19, he goes undefeated in Davis Cup singles play, leading Sweden to its inaugural title. One year later, he dominates Ilie Nastase in the 1976 Wimbledon final—the first of five straight championships at the All-England Club. His final Wimbledon title in 1980 is his most famous—a 1-6, 7-5, 6-3, 6-7 (16), 8-6 win over John McEnroe—highlighted by the 18-16 fourth-set tie-break—in a match regarded as one of the greatest of all time.

1989 Seventeen-year-old Michael Chang overcomes a two-sets-to-love deficit, muscle cramps and the world's No. 1 player in upsetting Ivan Lendl 4-6, 4-6, 6-3, 6-3, 6-3 in 4 hours, 39 minutes to advance into the quarterfinals of the French Open. Riddled with cramps in the fifth-set, causing him to stand on changeovers, Chang utilizes an underhand serve in the fifth set and benefits from Lendl's double fault on match point to register one of the biggest upsets in major tournament play.

1999 Andre Agassi becomes only the fifth male player to win all four major championships in a career when he dramatically comes back from a two-sets-to-love deficit to defeat Andrei Medvedev of Ukraine 1-6, 2-6, 6-4, 6-3, 6-4 to win the French Open men's singles title. Agassi joins a select group of men that includes Fred Perry, Don Budge, Rod Laver and Roy Emerson as men to win all four major singles championships. "This is certainly the greatest feeling I've ever had on a tennis court, and I don't think it's even sunk in yet," Agassi says in the post-match ceremony. "It's been a lot of years since I've had this opportunity, and I never dreamed I'd see this day. I just want to say thank you to all the people who never stopped believing in me." Agassi benefits from a rain delay in the second game of the second set to calm him and settle into the match after losing the first set in only 19 minutes. He faces a break point at 4-4 in the third set, but holds serve and breaks Medvedev the next game to win the third set and turn the match around.

1982 Mats Wilander becomes the youngest man to win the French Open when the 17-year-old Swede defeats Guillermo Vilas 1-6, 7-6, 6-0, 6-4 in the men's singles final at Roland Garros. The four-set final is completed in 4 hours, 47 minutes, five minutes longer than the previous record for a French final set in 1929, when Rene Lacoste defeats Jean Borotra. Seven years later in 1989, Michael Chang becomes the youngest French Open men's singles champion, winning the title at the age of 17 years, 3 months—six months younger than Wilander.

1987 Steffi Graf wins her first major singles title when the 17-year-old edges Martina Navratilova 6-4, 4-6, 8-6 in the women's singles final at the French Open to become the youngest French women's champion in history. "I never expected to win a Grand Slam this soon," says Graf, one week shy of her 18th birthday. "I don't think it's hit me yet that I've done it. Martina is still the No. 1 player, but today I took a step, a big step closer. I'm closer now than ever before." Two years later, Graf's "youngest" record is lost when 17-year-old Arantxa Sanchez Vicario, six months younger than Graf, beats her for the title. The next year, in 1990, 16-year-old Monica Seles becomes the youngest French women's titlist.

1992 In the greatest major final between Monica Seles and Steff Graf, Seles wins her third consecutive French singles title, defeating Graf 6-2, 3-6, 10-8 in 2 hours, 43 minutes. Seles becomes the first woman since Hilde Sperling of Germany in 1935-1937 to win three straight French women's singles titles. "I think it was the most emotional match I've played ever, not just in a Grand Slam, but in any tournament," says Seles.

1993 Jim Courier is denied in his attempt to win a third straight French Open singles title as he is defeated by Spain's Sergi Bruguera 6-4, 2-6, 6-2, 3-6, 6-3 in the men's singles final. The 3 hour, 59-minute struggle is played with temperatures hovering near 100 degrees, causing Bruguera to collapse in dehydration in the locker room following the trophy presentations. Says Bruguera of winning his first major title, "I reached my dream that I had since I was five years old, that I had been fighting for since like, I don't know, 15, 17 years."

1998 The emotional run through the French Open ends for Monica Seles, in mourning for three weeks since the passing of her father Karolj, as Arantxa Sanchez Vicario defeats Seles 7-6 (5), 0-6, 6-2 in the French Open women's singles final. The title was the third at Roland Garros for Sanchez-

Vicario and the championship match marks the final major final appearance by both players. "I'm so sorry that I beat you," says Sanchez Vicario in her post-match speech. "I have so much respect for you, and all the players feel so sorry that your father passed away."

1913 Fourteen months after being rescued from the sinking of the *Titanic*, Richard Williams makes his Davis Cup debut defeating Stanley Doust 6-4, 6-4, 1-6, 7-5 to give the United States a 2-0 lead over Australasia (Australia-New Zealand) at the West Side Tennis Club in Forest Hills, Queens, N.Y.

1981 Nineteen-year-old Hana Mandlikova defeats Sylvia Hanika 6-2, 6-4 in the women's singles final at the French Open. Mandlikova streaks to both set victories by winning six straight games after falling down 0-2 in the first set and 0-4 in the second set. "This is the first step to being No. 1, but the competition is very tough," says Mandlikova after the match.

2003 Martin Verkerk of the Netherlands, ranked No. 46, becomes an unlikely finalist at the French Open when he defeats No. 7 seed Guillermo Coria of Argentina 7-6, 6-4, 7-6 in the men's singles semifinals. Juan Carlos Ferrero, in a rematch of the 2002 French Open final, ends the run of defending champion Alberto Costa by a 6-3, 7-6, 6-4 in the other semifinal to reach the French final for a second straight year. Verkerk's run through the French field ends in the final as Ferrero wins the title tilt over the Dutchman 6-1, 6-3, 6-2.

June 7

1981 Bjorn Borg wins his record sixth French singles title and his fourth in a row when he defeats Ivan Lendl 6-1, 4-6, 6-2, 3-6, 6-1 in the men's singles final. The title is also Borg's 11th—and final—title in a major tournament. Says Borg, "It was the toughest final I have ever played here. Ivan and I play similar games, and he was very strong from the back today. His topspin was tiring, and he made the ball bounce awkwardly high."

1986 Thirty-one-year-old Chris Evert Lloyd wins the French Open for a record seventh time, defeating Martina Navratilova 2-6, 6-3, 6-3 in the women's singles final in the 69th meeting between the two rivals. The title is Evert's 18th and final major title and her second straight French final victory over Navratilova. "She seemed to win all the crucial games," Navratilova says after the match. "She won all the turning points. I thought my forehand would be a good enough weapon against her. But I'm not used to running around that much. She was passing well. If I play like I did today, I'll win most of my matches. I would have won last year's final if I played this well."

1987 Ivan Lendl wins his third French Open with a 7-5, 6-2, 3-6, 7-6 (3) victory over Mats Wilander in the men's singles final. The match is played in 4 hours, 17 minutes (not including a 36-minute rain delay) and concludes in a fourth-set tie-break played in a downpour as daylight dims. "This was my toughest Grand Slam win of all," says Lendl. "I had tough matches through the whole tournament, so I had to work for it. I heard coming in I wasn't fit, I wasn't prepared. I had lost confidence. I'm glad I proved everybody wrong. Then I read I wasn't mentally tough, that Mats was mentally tougher than me. I said to myself, 'Where do these guys get these things?'"

1992 Jim Courier repeats as the men's singles champion at the French Open, defeating Czech Petr Korda in the men's singles final by a 7-5, 6-2, 6-1 margin. "Coming in to play again after last year, I wasn't sure how I was going to react mentally," says Courier. "I'm very proud of the way I went out there and played to win, instead of not to lose."

1996 Pete Sampras' furthest penetration into the French Open ends as Russia's Yevgeny Kafelnikov denies Sampras of his elusive French championship, defeating the world's top-ranked player 7-6 (4), 6-0, 6-2 in men's singles semifinals. The 92-degree temperature during the day—equaling a record set in 1873—as well as a grueling road to the semifinals affects Sampras after a tightly-contested first set. "After the first set, I just felt the balloon pop, the tires were flat," says Sampras. "It was the hottest day of the tournament, and it's tough to play out there when you don't have the energy you want, and clay is a surface where you need that energy....The second set I just didn't have anything, and the third, I had a little bit, but I was still running on fumes. It's disappointing because I fought so hard to get here, so many emotional matches throughout the past week." In all, Sampras plays the French Open 13 times and only once reaches the semifinals.

1997 Nineteen-year-old Croatian Iva Majoli registers one of the biggest upsets in the Open era when she hands Martina Hingis the first loss of the year, defeating the world No. 1 6-4, 6-2 in the women's singles final at the French Open. In the process, the No. 9 seeded Majoli becomes the lowest seed to win at Roland Garros in the Open era and becomes the first player from Croatia to win a major title. "I just felt there was more pressure on Martina than on me today, because she's No. 1," Majoli says.

2001 Andre Agassi is defeated by Frenchman Sebastien Grosjean 1-6, 6-1, 6-1, 6-3 in the quarterfinals of the French Open in a match highlighted by the presence of the former U.S. President Bill Clinton, who sits to watch the match after Agassi wins the first set 6-1. With Clinton present, Agassi proceeds to lose 12 of the next 14 games to go down two sets to one. The five-months-out-of-office Clinton then briefly leaves the court, as Agassi goes up a service break in the fourth set 2-1. But when Clinton returns to watch the match, Agassi loses his service break and proceeds to win only one more game in the match. "I was bad for him," Clinton says afterward, referring to Agassi. "I was bad luck. I left, and he won three games. I hated to come back." Quips Grosjean, "We are going to have to invite him back for the semifinal."

1998 Carlos Moya wins his first major title of his career, defeating fellow Spaniard and good friend Alex Corretja 6-3, 7-5, 6-3 in the French Open men's singles final.

2003 Justine Henin-Hardenne becomes the first player from Belgium to win a major singles title, defeating countrywoman Kim Clijsters 6-0, 6-4 in the women's singles final at the French Open.

June 8

1985 Thirty-year-old Chris Evert Lloyd wins her record sixth French Open women's singles title with a dramatic 6-3, 5-7, 7-5 final round victory over arch-rival and two-time defending champion Martina Navratilova. Says Navratilova, "This probably was the best Grand Slam final we've ever played. For sure, it was the closest and most suspenseful." Evert Lloyd describes the match as "certainly one of the most dramatic matches I've ever played in."

1996 Steffi Graf and Arantxa Sanchez Vicario play the longest women's final ever at the French Open, before Graf emerges victorious after 3 hours, 3 minutes with a 6-3, 6-7 (4), 10-8 victory. The title is Graf's 19th major singles title and her fifth at the French Open. Says Sanchez Vicario, "It was very emotional, all the tension and all the nerves. As a matter of fact, we both played our best, but at the end, she pulled away." Says Graf, "These kinds of matches give you such satisfaction and emotions I know I'll never have after my tennis career. I don't think they're going to make me play longer, but they kind of tell me the reason why I'm still there."

1980 Bjorn Borg easily wins his record fifth French Open title, defeating Vitas Gerulaitis 6-4, 6-1, 6-2 in the men's singles final. Borg is given the tournament's championship trophy by 79-year-old Henri Cochet, one of the legendary French "Four Musketeers" and the only other player other than Borg to win the French title four times. Says Borg of what Cochet tells him during the presentation ceremony, "He didn't look too happy. He didn't say anything, really. Just 'Well done.' That's all."

1997 Gustavo Kuerten's incredible run at the French Open ends in victory as the 20-year-old Brazilian becomes the first man from his country to win a major title with a 6-3, 6-4, 6-2 final round win over two-time French champion Sergi Bruguera of Spain. Ranked No. 66, Kuerten is the lowest ranked player to win the French Open men's singles crown. Says Kuerten, "I didn't expect this trophy, that's why I didn't believe that it could happen."

2002 Serena Williams upstages older sister Venus Williams 7-5, 6-3 to win her first French women's singles title. Williams becomes the first African-American woman to win the French Open since Althea Gibson in 1956 and goes on to win the next three major titles at Wimbledon, the U.S. Open and the Australian Open—all at the expense of Venus Williams in the final—to complete a "Serena Slam" of holding all four major women's singles titles at the same time. Writes Australian journalist Linda Pearce in *The Age* of the Williams vs. Williams final, "The crowd appeared not to care, and the same could almost have been said for Venus, but the theory was that Serena wanted this one more."

1986 Ivan Lendl wins the French Open for the second time in two years, defeating unseeded upstart Mikael Pernfors of Sweden 6-3, 6-2, 6-4. Out-matched from the first ball, the former NCAA singles champion from the University of Georgia struggles to stay with the No. 1 player in the world, despite registering upsets over four seeded players en route to the final. "I had to play the best tennis of my life just to win points," Pernfors says. "The guy is just too good. He had too much for me."

1991 Monica Seles wins her second straight French Open women's singles title with a 6-3, 6-4 final round victory over Arantxa Sanchez Vicario. "This is just still incredible to me. I can't believe it's two in a row," the 17-year-old Seles says as she accepts her trophy.

1968 Without their captain Donald Dell, who is attending the funeral of Sen. Robert Kennedy, the United States clinches victory over Ecuador in the Davis Cup second round in Charlotte, N.C. Clark Graebner and Bob Lutz defeat Pancho Guzman and Miguel Olvera 6-3, 6-2, 7-5 to give the United States a 3-0 lead. U.S. team member Charlie Pasarell sits courtside with the Graebner and Lutz in the absence of Dell.

June 9

1990 Sixteen-year-old Monica Seles becomes the youngest player to win the French Open with a 7-6(6), 6-4 final-round victory over Steffi Graf. Graf leads 6-2 in the first-set tie-break, only to lose six points in a row to surrender the first set and ultimately, the match. "I didn't think I would do this well," Seles says. "I thought it was too much to believe I could win."

1984 Martina Navratilova wins her fourth consecutive major tournament when she requires only 63 minutes to defeat Chris Evert Lloyd 6-3, 6-1 in the women's singles final at the French Open. Navratilova is awarded a $1 million bonus from the International Tennis Federation for winning her fourth consecutive Grand Slam tournament title to go with her $98,550 first prize paycheck from the French Tennis Federation.

1985 Mats Wilander institutes aggressive net-rushing tactics on the slow clay court of Stade Roland Garros to win his second French Open men's singles title with a 3-6, 6-4, 6-2, 6-2 final-round victory over Ivan Lendl. "Mats surprised me with how well he hit the volleys at the net," Lendl says. "He came in at the right times and hit good shots." Says Wilander, "I felt like I would be in the match because I would control the points by coming in. I've been working very hard on my volleying and today it paid off."

1976 For the second time in four years, Adriano Panatta beats Bjorn Borg at the French Open as the Italian standout beats the two-time defending champion 6-3, 6-3, 2-6, 7-6 in the quarterfinals. Panatta, who also beats Borg in the fourth round of the 1973 French Open, is the only player to ever beat Borg at the French Championships in the Swede's eight appearances at the tournament.

1979 Chris Evert Lloyd wins her third French Open women's singles title with a 6-2, 6-0 final-round win over Wendy Turnbull. Evert Lloyd needs only 63 minutes to win the championship match and wins 11 straight games after trailing 1-2 in the first set.

1991 Jim Courier wins his first major singles title with a hard-fought 3-6, 6-4, 3-6, 6-1, 6-4 win over fellow American Andre Agassi in the first all-American French Open men's singles final since 1954. The 3 hour, 19 minute wind-swept match marks Agassi's third failure in as many major singles finals after losing the 1990 French final to Andres Gomez and the

1990 U.S. Open final to Pete Sampras. Courier benefits from a rain delay trailing 6-3, 3-1 and is able to confer with his coach Jose Higueras about altering his strategy. "I sat down with Jose and he told me I needed to back up on his serve because I was really getting hurt right away," says Courier. "That really was the turnaround. That was the match. At least, that's what got me into the match. It was the beginning of it for me." Says Agassi, "It turned out that the rain delay worked to his advantage. He changed his strategy, started staying way behind the baseline. I felt like if it hadn't rained I could have kept my momentum, but who knows how long that would have lasted?"

1996 Yevgeny Kafelnikov becomes the first Russian to win a major singles title when he defeats Germany's Michael Stich 7-6(4), 7-5, 7-6 (4) in the men's singles final at the French Open. "It is just a dream," Kafelnikov says. "I never felt I could do it, winning a Grand Slam at age 22.... I never felt I could make it....The first Grand Slam title really means everything. For Russia, it means very much. I know I have many supporters in Russia. I'm going to bring that wonderful trophy back to my country."

2001 Jennifer Capriati captures the women's singles title at the French Open with a gripping 1-6, 6-4 12-10 triumph over Kim Clijsters of Belgium. The 22-game final set marks the longest final set in a women's final ever at Roland Garros. The title gives Capriati her second major title of her career—and of the year—after her break-through win at the Australian Open in January. She becomes the first woman to start the year by winning the first two legs of the Grand Slam since Monica Seles wins the 1992 Australian and French Opens.

2002 Albert Costa defeats fellow Spaniard Juan Carlos Ferrero 6-1, 6-0, 4-6, 6-3 to win the French Open men's singles title. Costa wins the first two sets in just 46 minutes and holds on to win the final in four sets.

2007 Six months removed from her divorce, Justine Henin wins her third straight and fourth overall title at the French Open, defeating 19-year-old Ana Ivanovic of Serbia 6-1, 6-2 in the final. Henin becomes the first woman since Monica Seles from 1990 to 1992 to win three straight women's singles titles at Roland Garros. Says Henin, "It's surreal to win for the third time in a row. I am struggling to take it in."

June 10

1984 Ivan Lendl breaks through to win his first major championship, staging an incredible comeback from a two-sets-to-love deficit to defeat John McEnroe 3-6, 2-6, 6-4, 7-5, 7-5 in the men's singles final at the French Open. The loss is the first of the year for McEnroe, who enters the final with a 42-0 match record on the year. The loss is McEnroe's most devastating of his career, as he is never able to win a French title during his career. Lendl goes on to win seven more major titles. Lendl's post-match speech to the crowd is short and to the point. "I'm very happy that I won my first Grand Slam tournament here in Paris and I will be back next year."

1989 Seventeen-year-old Arantxa Sanchez stuns world No. 1 Steffi Graf 7-6 (6), 3-6, 7-5 to win her first major title at the French Open and stop Graf's run of five straight major singles titles. Graf leads 5-3 in the final set, only to lose the final four games of the match (winning just three points) in her only loss in a major tournament during the year, preventing a sweep of all four majors for a second consecutive year. "I play a great match, and I beat the No. 1 player in the world," says Sanchez, the first Spanish woman to win a major singles title. "I'm so excited, I don't have the words for talking."

1979 Bjorn Borg staves off a spirited comeback run by unseeded Victor Pecci to win the French Open men's singles title for a fourth time, defeating the Paraguayan 6-3, 6-1, 6-7 (6), 6-4 in the final. Borg leads Pecci 6-3, 6-1, 5-2, before Pecci, inspired by the Parisian crowd's chant of "PE-CCI, PE-CCI," rallies to win the third set tie-break, before falling short in the tense fourth set. "I thought I had the match in my hand at 5-2 in the third, but then he started playing better, taking more chances, and I missed a few passing shots. Suddenly it was 5-all," says Borg. "I got to be a little bit scared. I wasn't hitting through my shots and started hitting short, and then he was coming in on every point. He made this the toughest final I have played here." Borg connects on an incredible 100 of 107 first serves during the match—93 percent—and loses only 15 points in his first 13 service games while creating the 5-2 lead in the third set.

2007 For the second straight year, Roger Federer falls one match shy of a French Open title, a fourth consecutive major championship and a career Grand Slam as he falls to Rafael Nadal 6-3, 4-6, 6-3, 6-4 in the men's singles final at Roland Garros. Federer only converts one of 17 break points opportunities on Nadal's serve, allowing Nadal to win his third straight French title. Says Federer, "Spin it any way you want—I'm disappointed to have lost. I couldn't care less how I played the last 10 months or the last 10 years. At the end of the day, I wanted to win that match. I couldn't do it. It's a shame, but life goes on."

2000 Mary Pierce becomes the first French woman to win the singles title at the French Open in 33 years as she registers a 6-2, 7-5 final round victory over Spain's Conchita Martinez. Born in Canada to a French mother and an American father, raised in the United States but a French citizen, Pierce becomes the first "native" woman to hold her nation's national tennis championship since Francoise Durr wins the title in 1967. Says Pierce, "My mother is French, my father American. The reason this tournament means so much to me, more special than my Australian title in 1995, is my Frenchness."

2006 Belgium's Justine Henin-Hardenne defeats Svetlana Kuznetsova of Russia 6-4, 6-4 to win the her second consecutive and third overall French Open singles title. Henin becomes the first player since Steffi Graf in 1995-1996 to win consecutive French Open women's titles. Henin-Hardenne dominates the field over two weeks in Paris, not losing a set in seven matches and not even being pushed to a tie-break. Says Henin-Hardenne, "It's been a lot of sacrifices in my career, a lot of work and now that really pays off."

1990 Ecuadorian Andres Gomez, age 30 and a veteran of 27 major events without a victory, claims his first and only major championship with a 6-3, 2-6, 6-4, 6-4 final round upset of 20-year-old No. 3 seed Andre Agassi at the French Open. "I've been coming here for 12 years and I always dreamed about this moment; it just took too long," says Gomez. "By far this is the best tennis I've ever played. I've gone a step farther in my career."

1995 Steffi Graf wins the French Open for a fourth time with a devastating final-set assault on defending champion Arantxa Sanchez Vicario, relinquishing only six points in a 20-minute final set in her 7-5, 4-6, 6-0 final round victory at Roland Garros.

1993 Twenty-one-year-old Pete Sampras continues to struggle to tune his grass court tennis game as he loses to No. 110-ranked Grant Stafford of South Africa 5-7, 7-5, 6-4 in the first round of the Stella Artois Championships at

Queen's Club in London, England. "I played like an idiot," says Sampras, who wins his first of seven Wimbledon titles four weeks later. "Lethargic, that's the word."

2001 Gustavo Kuerten wins the French Open for a third time with a 6-7 (2), 7-5, 6-2, 6-0 final round victory over Spain's Alex Corretja. After receiving the trophy from former champion Jim Courier, Kuerten speaks to the crowd in French, fulfilling a promise made a year ago after winning his second French title. Kuerten then changes his shirt into a T-shirt with the words "I (love) Roland Garros," with love being represented by a drawing of a heart.

2003 Andre Agassi plays his 1,000th professional tennis match, defeating Australian Peter Luczak to advance to the third round of the Stella Artois Championships at Queen's Club in London, England. "When I first started playing I wouldn't have thought any of my thousand matches would have been on grass," says a smiling Agassi, competing in the Stella Artois Championships for only the second time. "But it's amazing. I have never been a fan of quantity. It's more about quality. For me to be 33 years old and get to No. 1 in the world is a great achievement. I'm proud that I'm still out here, but I don't just want to be out here, I want to do it well."

June 11

1989 Seventeen-year-old Michael Chang becomes the youngest man to win a major title, concluding an improbable run to the men's singles title at the French Open by defeating Stefan Edberg 6-1, 3-6, 4-6, 6-4, 6-2 in the men's singles final at Roland Garros. Chang's victory ends a 34-year drought by American men at the French Championships, becoming the first American man to win the French title since Tony Trabert in 1955. Says Tony Trabert to Bud Collins of the *Boston Globe* after Chang's victory, "What a performance to finish that one off. It was one of the most courageous I've ever seen. Much tougher physically and mentally than mine in '54, straight sets over Art Larsen, and '55, four sets over Sven Davidson. Michael is one of the most remarkable kids to come into this game." Says Chang, "I'm not quite sure how I did it." Says Edberg, "He runs down everything. I had my chances, but I missed too many break points. I got a little tired in the fifth, then it was too late. "

1995 Austrian Thomas Muster breaks through to win a major tournament title for the first time, dominating Michael Chang 7-5, 6-2, 6-4 to win the French Open men's singles title. Muster also becomes the first Austrian to win a major title. Says Muster, "My dreams since I was a kid have come true today."

1978 Bjorn Borg completes one the most devastating runs through a major tournament field as he defeats Guillermo Vilas 6-1, 6-1, 6-3 to win the French Open for a third time in his career. In winning his fifth career major singles title, Borg loses only 32 games in seven matches during his run to the title. Says Vilas, "He played so well, he didn't give me any chances at all. I knew if I was going to play from the baseline all the time, I was going to win more games but not the match. So I tried different tactics, but it did not work. Nothing worked." In the women's singles final, No. 2 seed Virginia Ruzici of Romania defeats top-seeded Mima Jausovec of Yugoslavia 6-2, 6-2.

1938 Don Budge defeats Czech Roderich Menzel 6-3, 6-2, 6-4 in the men's singles final of the French Championships—Budge's second leg of his eventual "Grand Slam." The *New York Times* describes the final as "an unexciting match" and that Budge prevails over a tournament field that "did not include any stars of the first magnitude." Budge wins the first set in 18 minutes, the second in 12 minutes and the third set in 20 minutes.

1975 Eddie Dibbs registers a stunning comeback win against Raul Ramirez in the quarterfinals of the French Open, winning the last six games of the match against the Mexican standout 4-6, 7-6, 6-1, 5-7, 6-4. Dibbs is a point from trailing 0-5 in the fifth-set, but rallies to win the match in 3 hours, 54 minutes. Dibbs also trails 0-4 in the second set, but wins the set in a tie-breaker to prevent himself from going down two-sets-to-love.

2006 Roger Federer's first bid to win a fourth consecutive major tournament title comes to an end as the reigning Wimbledon, U.S. and Australian Open champion falls to Rafael Nadal of Spain 1-6, 6-1, 6-4, 7-6 (4) in the final of the French Open. The No. 2 ranked Nadal wins his second straight French title—his win over Federer his 60th straight match victory on a clay court. Federer falls short of joining Don Budge and Rod Laver as the only men to hold all four major titles at the same time. The loss is Federer's first in a major final in his eighth major tournament final appearances. Says Federer of his lost opportunity, "Obviously, it's a pity, but life goes on, right?"

2000 After letting 10 championship points slip away, Gustavo Kuerten of Brazil finally overcomes Sweden's Magnus Norman 6-2, 6-3, 2-6, 7-6 (6) to win his second French Open men's singles title. Says Kuerten of the assembly line of match points, "Every time I thought I was going to win, and then it was one more, and one more, and one more."

June 12

1983 Billie Jean King, at age of 39 years, 7 months, and 23 days, becomes the oldest woman to win a WTA singles title when she beats 21-year-old fellow American Alycia Moulton 6-0, 7-5 in just 58 minutes to win the Edgbaston Cup in Birmingham, England. Says Moulton of the loss, "I'm quite depressed about the way I played, particularly in the first set. I made a lot of unforced errors and didn't get my serve in. Another thing was that Billie Jean doesn't give you any free points. Even people ranked around 20th do that occasionally."

1988 Boris Becker beats Stefan Edberg 6-1, 3-6, 6-3 to singles title at Queen's Club in London, the premier grass-court tune-up event for Wimbledon. Becker, the Wimbledon champion in 1985 and 1986, wins at Queen's for the third time in four years (1985, 1987, 1988) and sets himself up as the favorite to triumph again at Wimbledon. "Naturally, I must have a good shot for Wimbledon," says Becker. "I could lose. I'm not a machine. But I hope I don't." Edberg, however, avenges his loss to Becker and turns the tables on his German rival in the Wimbledon men's final three weeks later as the Swede wins the first of two titles at the All England Club.

1991 Mark Keil, ranked No. 224 playing in only his second career ATP tour event, stages a staggering upset of future seven-times Wimbledon champion Pete Sampras 6-2, 7-6 in the first round of the Stella Artois Championships at Queen's Club in London. Following his win over the No. 8 ranked player in the world and entering the post-match press conference, he asks reporters, "Is this where I am supposed to sit? I have never done this before." Asked what his previous claim to fame had been prior to beating Sampras, Keil responds, "Nothing."

1983 In a rematch of the previous year's Wimbledon men's singles final, Jimmy Connors again beats John McEnroe 6-3, 6-3 to win the grass court singles title at Queen's Club in London. Says McEnroe of Connors, "He is really playing well. I didn't play badly, but he was one shot better. Right now he must be the favorite for Wimbledon."

2005 Andy Roddick joins John McEnroe and Lleyton Hewitt as the only players to win three-straight singles titles at the Stella Artois Championships at Queen's Club in England, defeating six-foot-10 Croatian Ivo Karlovic 7-6 (7), 7-6 (4) in the final.

June 13

1976 With on-court temperatures reported at 124 degrees, Adriano Panatta of Italy wins the men's singles title at the French Open, defeating Harold Solomon of the United States in the final 6-1, 6-4, 4-6, 7-6 (3). Solomon makes a run in the third and fourth sets and is two points from taking the match to a fifth-set before the Italian snuffs out the rally. Panatta leads 5-2 in the fourth set, before Solomon rallies, winning at one point 12 points in a row. Says Panatta, "I was very nervous with victory in my grasp." Panatta wins the title after escaping from match point down in the first round against Czech Pavel Hutka and after registering a quarterfinal win over Bjorn Borg. In the women's singles final, Sue Barker of Britain beats Renata Tomanova of Czechoslovakia 6-2, 0-6, 6-2.

1989 Defending Wimbledon champion Stefan Edberg of Sweden is a shock first-round upset victim in the first round of the Queen's Club grass court tournament in London, losing to Venezuela's Nicolas Pereira, 7-6 (4), 7-6 (4). Playing two days after losing in a five-set French Open final to Michael Chang, Edberg blames his lack of grass court preparation for the loss. Says Edberg, "You can't expect to play great tennis on grass with 1 1/2 hours practice."

1915 Don Budge, the first man to win the "Grand Slam," is born in Oakland, Calif. After winning at Wimbledon and the U.S. Championships—and leading the United States to the Davis Cup title—Budge delays turning professional after the 1937 season so he can help the U.S. defend the Davis Cup and stake his claim at winning all four major titles in the same calendar year. Budge tells only one person of his ambition to sweep the singles titles at the Australian, French, Wimbledon and U.S. Championships—his doubles partner Gene Mako, whom he beats in the final of the 1938 U.S. Championships to clinch the "Slam." Writes Bud Collins in *The Bud Collins History of Tennis* of Budge, "His serve was battering, his backhand considered perhaps the finest the game has known, his net play emphatic, his overhead drastic. Quick and rhythmic, he was truly a complete player and, what is more, was temperamentally suited for the game. Affable and easygoing, he could not be shaken from the objective of winning with the utmost application of hitting power." Budge wins 14 major titles during this career—including the singles, doubles and mixed—triples!—at Wimbledon in 1937 and 1938 and at the U.S. Championships in 1938. Bill Tilden said of Budge, "I consider him the finest player 365 days a year who ever lived."

June 14

1997 Goran Ivanisevic and Greg Rusedski tie the record for the longest tie-break played in a men's singles match when Ivanisevic wins a 38-point final-set tie-break in his 4-6, 6-4, 7-6 (20-18) semifinal win at the Queen's Club grass court tennis championships in London. Both players hold six match points before Ivanisevic seals the win with his 13th ace of the match. Ivanisevic and Rusedski tie the record previously set by Bjorn Borg and Premjit Lall, who play the first 38-point tie-break at Wimbledon in 1973, and Ivanisevic's record with Daniel Nestor at the 1993 U.S. Open. The record is equaled three more times following Ivanisevic and Rusedski's effort.

1974 Chris Evert overcomes a 1-4 first set deficit to defeat Germany's Helga Masthoff 7-5, 6-4 to reach the finals of the French Open. Says Evert of her first-set turn-around, "I decided I was hitting the ball too soft for her. I wasn't moving her around enough." Olga Morozova of Russia defeats Argentina's Racquel Giscafre 6-3, 6-2 to become the first Soviet player to reach the French Open final.

2007 French tennis player Marc Gicquel is dragged off the court to be treated after being on the receiving end of a 129 mph serve in the groin. Gicquel eventually returns to the court and beats Germany's Benjamin Becker 6-2, 7-6 (5) but spends the night vomiting and suffers with swelling and pain and withdraws from his quarterfinal match with Finland's Jarkko Nieminen the next day.

1963 The United States Davis Cup team is introduced to the Shah of Iran prior to the start of the Davis Cup first round tie against Iran in Tehran, Iran. The tie marks the first time the U.S. Davis Cup team competes in the Middle East. The match is originally scheduled to be held in the United States, but the United States Lawn Tennis Association offers to play the match in Iran, as a good-will gesture to help grow the popularity of tennis in the Arab nation. Gene Scott and Allen Fox give the U.S. a 2-0 lead after the first day of play in their eventual 5-0 victory as Scott defeats Raza Akbari 6-4, 6-1, 6-0 and Fox defeats Taeghi Akbari 6-2, 6-2, 6-2.

1969 Steffi Graf, the only player to win a Grand Slam sweep of all four major championships and win an Olympic gold medal in the same year, is born in Bruhl, West Germany. Graf wins 22 major singles title during her career (second only to Margaret Smith Court's 24 career major singles titles), including every major championship at least four times. The French Open are bookends in her career major tally—winning her first major in Paris as a 17-year-old in 1987 and her 22nd and last as a 30-year-old in 1999. A pair of "Martina's" were her victims in those finals, beating Martina Navratilova 6-4, 4-6, 8-6 in the 1987 final and defeating Martina Hingis 4-6, 7-5, 6-2 in the 1999 final. During her peak years in the late 1980s and early 1990s, she ruthlessly beat opponents routinely under an hour, including her 6-0, 6-0 dismissal of Natalia Zvereva in 32 minutes in the final of the 1988 French Open. She wins four Australian singles title (1988, 1989, 1990, 1994), seven Wimbledon titles (1988, 1989, 1991, 1992, 1993, 1995, 1996), five U.S. Open titles (1988, 1989, 1993, 1995, 1996) and six French titles (1987, 1988, 1993, 1995, 1996, 1999). She wins Olympic gold in 1988 over Gabriela Sabatini and silver in 1992, falling to Jennifer Capriati. She wins 107 career singles titles and ranks No. 1 in the world a record 377 weeks. In 1999, she succumbs to the courtship of fellow player Andre Agassi, whom she marries in 2001.

2003 Andy Roddick launches a 149 mph serve, tying for the fastest serve in tennis history at the time, to defeat Andre Agassi 6-1, 6-7 (5), 7-6 (6) for the first time in his career in the semifinals of the Stella Artois Championships at Queen's Club in London. Roddick fires 27 aces passed Agassi while tying the serve speed record set by Greg Rusedski of Britain. Roddick goes on to break the serve speed record several more times, with this top serve speed registering 155 mph against Vladmir Voltchkov in the 2004 USA vs. Belarus Davis Cup semifinal in Charleston, S.C.

2007 Andy Roddick benefits from the replay "Hawk Eye" system at Queen's Club, edging Alex Bogdanovic of Britain 4-6, 7-6 (5), 6-4. Roddick challenges a call at 5-5 in the second-set tie-break—which would have given his No. 117-ranked British opponent a match point—but the call is overturned and Roddick receives a set point. Roddick converts the set point and goes on to win the third-round match. Says Roddick, "I've been a big supporter of Hawk-Eye and today is the reason why. There's a big difference between being down match point and up set point. Needless to say, I would have been a little perturbed if they'd have got that one wrong."

2007 Marat Safin plays and wins all six points in a resumption of a rain-delayed 3-6, 6-4, 6-4 win over Sebastien Grosjean in the second round of Queen's Club.

June 15

1981 Telling fans to "go jump in a lake" and "shut up you jerks," John McEnroe wins the singles title at Queen's Club for a third straight year, defeating Brian Gottfried 7-6, 7-5 in the final. McEnroe is given an unsportsmanlike conduct warning at the tail end of the match by chair umpire Georgina Clark, whom McEnroe verbally challenges throughout the match. In the post-match press conference, McEnroe suggests it is more difficult for him to play a match with a female chair umpire as "it is harder to get upset with a woman umpire." Says Gottfried of McEnroe's assertion, "An umpire is an umpire, regardless of sex, but Mac may have a problem with women because his language is sometimes a little different."

2003 Andy Roddick wins his first grass court title of his career and his first title in the first tournament with Brad Gilbert as his coach, defeating Sebastien Grosjean 6-3, 6-3 in 59 minutes to win the Stella Artois Championships at Queen's Club in London, England.

1974 With French President Valery Giscard D'Estaing in attendance, Bjorn Borg of Sweden and Manuel Orantes of Spain each win semifinal matches at the French Open in Paris—Borg defeating Harold Solomon of the United States 6-4, 2-6, 6-2, 6-1 and Orantes defeating Francois Jauffert of France 6-2, 6-4, 6-4. Chris Evert and Olga Morozova win the French women's doubles title, defeating Gail Chanfreau of France and Katja Ebbinhaus of West Germany 6-4, 2-6, 6-1.

2008 Rafael Nadal wins his first career grass court title defeating Novak Djokovic 7-6 (5), 7-5 in the final of the Artois Championships at Queen's Club in London. Nadal becomes the first Spaniard to capture a grass-court title since Andres Gimeno wins the title in Eastbourne, England in 1972. Nadal also becomes the first player to win the French Open on clay and turn around a week later and win the title at Queen's Club since Ilie Nastase of Romania captures both titles in 1973. Says Nadal, "This week was amazing for me."

1991 Rick Leach and Jim Pugh defeat Emilio Sanchez and Sergio Casal 7-6, 6-3, 7-6 to give the United States an insurmountable 3-0 lead over Spain in the Davis Cup quarterfinal at the International Tennis Hall of Fame in Newport, R.I.

June 16

1974 Two eighteen-year-olds—Bjorn Borg and Chris Evert—win their first major singles titles with final-round victories at the French Open in Paris. Borg comes back from two-sets-to-love down to defeat Manuel Orantes of Spain 2-6, 6-7, 6-0, 6-1, 6-1 to become the youngest winner of the French Open at the time. Evert encounters much less resistance in defeating her doubles partner Olga Morozova of the Soviet Union 6-1, 6-2 to become the youngest winner in Paris since Christine Truman in 1959. Evert wins a $8,000 first prize, while Borg takes home $24,000.

1985 Three weeks before his break-through victory at Wimbledon as an unseeded 17-year-old, Boris Becker sends a warning shot to the tennis world and wins his first ATP singles title at the Queen's Club championships in London, defeating Johan Kriek 6-2, 6-3 in the final. Says Becker following his first victory, "It has been a dream for me when I was 10 to win a Grand Prix final. This week has been fantastic. I played my best tennis and beat a lot of good players." Says Kriek of Becker and his chances at Wimbledon, "If he plays like that every day at Wimbledon, Becker can win the tournament."

1975 U.S. Open Tournament Director Bill Talbert unveils 11 new clay courts at the West Side Tennis Club in Forest Hills, Queens, N.Y., that will be used in lieu of grass courts for the 1975 U.S. Open. "It will take a complete player to win the Open this year," says Talbert. Asked how he would react to any player criticism of not playing the U.S. Open on the traditional grass courts, Talbert states, "This is the U.S. Open, which I consider the world's major tournament and I believe that every player should consider it a privilege to compete in it regardless of what kind of courts we have. They should be willing to put it on the line for this championship."

1906 The Doherty brothers—Reggie and Laurie—pair to defeat the American doubles team of Holcombe Ward and Raymond Little 3-6, 11-9, 9-7, 6-1 to clinch the Davis Cup title for Britain in the Davis Cup Challenge Round played at Wimbledon's Worple Road courts. The win gives the Brits it fourth straight Davis Cup victory—and its second straight win over the United States in the Challenge Round. It also marks the end of the Davis Cup career of the popular Doherty brothers.

June 17

1980 Venus Ebone Starr Williams, the sensational older Williams sister who, along with younger sister Serena, turn the tennis world on its head by taking their games from the urban streets of Compton, Calif., to Centre Court at Wimbledon, is born in Lynwood, Calif. Williams bursts on the scene as a 17-year-old wunderkind with beaded hair, reaching the final of the 1997 U.S. Open as an unseeded player ranked No. 66. Three years later, she is the champion of Wimbledon, the U.S. Open and singles and doubles gold medalist at the Sydney Olympics. In 2002, Williams becomes the first black player—man or woman—to be ranked No. 1 in the world. She and younger sister Serena play the first all sister major final since 1884 at the 2001 U.S. Open. During a stretch from the French Open in 2002 and the Australian Open in 2003, Venus reaches all four major singles finals, but loses all four finals to sister Serena.

1929 Hall of Fame TV broadcaster, writer and tennis historian Arthur Worth "Bud" Collins is born in Lima, Ohio. Collins is best known for his work with the *Boston Globe* and with NBC Sports during its "Breakfast at Wimbledon" broadcasts from 1979 through 2007. An astute chronicler and tale teller of the history of the game, he is also known for his tennis encyclopedia—that most recent edition called *The Bud Collins History of Tennis*—not to mention his colorful wardrobe, featuring his trademark garish and bright-colored trousers.

1898 In what becomes one of the most peculiar matches in the history of the U.S. Championships, Juliette Atkinson wins her third U.S. women's singles title, coming back from a 3-5 final set deficit and saving five match points to defeat Marion Jones in the five-set women's final 6-3, 5-7, 6-4, 2-6, 7-5 at the Philadelphia Cricket Club. During one of Jones's match points, she loses the point as the ball in play strikes a stray ball on her side of the court. The *New York Times* describes the match's conclusion in the following way; "The final set was the best of all. Five times during this set Miss Jones was only one point from the match and the championship but Miss Atkinson tied her and beat her out each time. In the ninth game of the set, a brilliant rally took place, which was spoiled by the ball in play hitting a ball lying in Miss Jones's court. At that time Miss Jones needed but one point to win, and her supporters groaned as the chance faded away. The score at the time stood five games to three in favor of Miss Jones, but Miss Atkinson won the next four games and the match by fast playing. Both contestants were heartily congratulated for their plucky work."

1939 Don McNeill of Oklahoma City, Okla., upsets fellow American Bobby Riggs, winning a stretch of 13 straight games in a 7-5, 6-0, 6-3 victory in the men's singles final at the French Championships at Roland Garros. Says McNeill, "I never played better in my life." Says Riggs, "Don just beat me." The French Championships suffer a six-year hiatus following the 1939 edition of the event due to World War II and are not played again until 1946.

1911 Hazel Hotchkiss wins her third straight U.S. women's singles title, defeating Florence Sutton 8-10, 6-1, 9-7 at the Philadelphia Cricket Club in Philadelphia, Pa. The *New York Times* describes the match as one "replete with sensational features which kept the large crowd of spectators constantly on edge." Hotchkiss institutes a tactic of lobbing at 7-7 in the third set that helps throw off the upset bid of Sutton, witnessed by approximately 1,000 fans. Hotchkiss also wins the mixed doubles title on this day, pairing with Wallace Johnson to defeat Edna Wildey and Herbert Tilden 6-4, 6-4.

2007 Maria Sharapova's semifinal match with Marion Bartoli at the DFS Classic in Birmingham, England is temporarily delayed twice when two spectators need medical assistance. A woman and a child fall down a staircase in the stadium, knocking the woman unconscious and requiring her to be flown via helicopter to a local hospital. Later, in another part of the stadium, a man faints. Sharapova wins the match with Bartoli 7-5, 6-0 and later in the day, loses the championship match to Jelena Jankovic 4-6, 6-3, 7-5.

June 18

2006 Roger Federer ties Bjorn Borg's record of 41 consecutive grass-court victories with a 6-0, 6-7 (4), 6-2 victory against Tomas Berdych in the final of the Gerry Weber Open in Halle, Germany. It is the fourth consecutive year he wins the tournament. Says Federer, "Winning this tournament gives me enourmous satisfaction. Apart from the Grand Slams, it has been one of the hardest weeks ever."

1976 One hundred and 13 days after Australia and New Zealand began their Davis Cup Eastern Zone Final in Brisbane, the series concludes in Nottingham, England as John Newcombe clinches the 3-1 win for Australia, beating Brian Fairlie 8-6, 5-7, 11-9, 6-3 in three-and-a-half hours. The match is postponed due to rain in February and, due to previously scheduled player commitments, the concluding matches are not scheduled until four months later on the opposite side of the planet.

1955 Ken Rosewall defeats Lew Hoad 6-2, 6-3 to win the London Grass Court Championships at Queen's Club, the tournament immediately preceding Wimbledon. In the women's final, Louise Brough defeats 15-year-old South Africa Jean Forbes 6-3, 6-1 for the title.

2006 Lleyton Hewitt defeats James Blake 6-4, 6-4, to win the Stella Artois Championships at Queen's Club for the fourth time. Hewitt, who wins the event three consecutive times from 2000 to 2002, joins John McEnroe and Boris Becker as the only four-time winners of the event.

2006 One day following her 6-4, 6-4 upset of 2004 Wimbledon champion Maria Sharapova, No. 81-ranked Jamea Jackson of the United States loses a hard-fought final of the DFS Classic in Birmingham, England, falling 7-6 (12), 7-6 (5) to Vera Zvonareva of Russia.

1977 The United States wins the Federation Cup for the sixth time as Billie Jean King defeats Dianne Fromholtz 6-1, 6-2 and Chris Evert defeats Kerry Reid 7-5, 6-3 in the 2-1 U.S. win over Australia in Eastbourne, England.

June 19

1937 Don Budge crushes Britain's No. 1 amateur Bunny Austin 6-1, 6-2 in the final of the Queen's Club Championships in London, placing him firmly as the favorite to win the single title at Wimbledon. Reports the Associated Press of the one-sided affair, "Seldom has a star of Austin's standing absorbed so crushing a defeat in full view of the public."

2003 Dutchman Richard Krajicek, the 1996 Wimbledon champion, announces his retirement from professional tennis at the age of 31. "It's very difficult for me to put into words what I'm feeling right now because it means the definite end of my tennis career, which I started a long time ago when I was three years old," says Krajicek. During his career, Krajicek collects 17 titles, including his Wimbledon title in 1996, and ranks as high as No. 4 in the world in 1999.

1971 Jimmy Connors, a freshman at UCLA, wins the NCAA singles title in South Bend, Indiana, defeating Roscoe Tanner of Stanford 6-3, 4-6, 6-4, 6-4 in the singles final. Connors becomes the first freshman to win the title—a distinction he would share seven years later when his eventual pro rival, John McEnroe, wins the title as a freshman at Stanford in 1978.

1991 Martina Navratilova incredibly loses only two points on her serve and beats Brenda Schultz of the Netherlands, 6-1, 6-2, in only 36 minutes to reach the quarterfinals of the pre-Wimbledon tune-up event in Eastbourne, England.

1993 Martina Navratilova wins the singles title at Eastbourne for a record 11th time, defeating Miriam Oremans of the Netherlands 2-6, 6-2, 6-3. The title is the 164th of Navratilova's singles career.

1983 Johan Kriek wins his ninth of 14 career ATP titles, defeating Tom Gullikson 7-6, 7-5 in 80 minutes in the final of pre-Wimbledon warm-up event in Bristol, England. Kriek earns $17,000.

1993 Twenty-nine-year-old Henri Leconte wins his ninth and final ATP singles title of his career, defeating Andrei Medvedev of Ukraine 6-2, 6-3 in Halle, Germany. Leconte, winning his first tournament in five years, at one point wins 13 consecutive points at the start of the second set against Medvedev, playing only his second career tournament on grass.

June 20

2003 Mohammed Akhtar Hossai of Bangladesh becomes the youngest player to ever compete in Davis Cup when at the age of 13 years, 326 days, he pairs with Abu-Hena Tasawar Collins and loses to Maung-Tu Maw and Min Min of Mynamar 6-4, 6-2 in the Davis Cup Asia/Oceania Zone Group IV round robin match at the National Tennis Centre in Colombo, Sri Lanka. The loss closes out Mynamar's 3-0 win over Bangladesh.

1963 The United States wins the inaugural staging of the Federation Cup, claiming a 2-1 win over Australia at Queen's Club in London. The Federation Cup, the international team competition for women that is the women's equivalent to the Davis Cup, is founded as a part of the celebration of the 50th anniversary of the International Tennis Federation. Billie Jean Moffitt and Darlene Hard clinch the title for the United States in the decisive doubles match in the best-of-three match series, defeating Margaret Smith and Lesley Turner 3-6, 13-11, 6-3.

1987 Helena Sukova overcomes an 0-5 first-set deficit to beat Martina Navratilova 7-6, 6-3—ending Navratilova's 69-match winning streak on English grass courts—in the final of Eastbourne, England. The last time that Navratilova loses on grass in England was in the 1981 Wimbledon semifinals to another Czech, Hana Mandlikova. Says Navratilova, who goes on to win her eighth Wimbledon title two weeks later, "Right now I'm not exactly brimming with confidence. But I'll still go into Wimbledon as the favorite." Earlier in the day, Navratilova beats Pam Shriver, 6-4, 4-6, 6-3 in a rain-delayed semifinal after trailing 0-2, 0-40 in the third set.

1990 Saying "I am like an orange without any juice," 28-year-old Hana Mandlikova announces in Eastbourne, England that she will retire from professional tennis after Wimbledon. Mandlikova, ranked No. 31 in the world, but as high as No. 3 during her career, wins four major singles titles during her career, including the 1985 U.S. Open. Says Mandlikova, "The determination is not there, the motivation is not there and I am too proud to be losing to players I should not lose to. That is why I am walking away." Mandlikova wins the Australian Open in 1980 and 1987 and the French Open in 1981. She reaches the second round in her swan song at Wimbledon the following week, losing her final match to Ann Henrickson 6-3, 6-3.

1991 Mercuial Goran Ivanisevic of Yugoslavia is disciplined on court and close to being defaulted in the quarterfinals of the pre-Wimbledon tune-up event in Manchester, England. The 19-year-old Ivanisevic defeats Arne Thoms of Germany 7-5, 6-3, but receives two warnings for code violations—one for throwing his racquet from the baseline to the umpire's chair and the second for an audible obscenity, costing him a point and a game in the match. One more infraction and Ivanisevic would have been defaulted from the match. Says Ivanisevic, "It was bad because I was swearing in English and if I'd sworn in my own language no one would have understood. It was a mistake." Ivanisevic would go on to win the event—his second career title—defeating Pete Sampras 6-4, 6-4 in the final.

1983 Nigerian tennis has perhaps its greatest day as No. 82 ranked Nduka Odizor saves a match point in the third set and upsets No. 4 seed Guillermo Vilas 3-6, 5-7, 7-6, 7-5, 6-2 on Centre Court at Wimbledon. Odizor, brought to the United States to study as a 15-year-old after living in Lagos, Nigeria, is a standout player at the University of Houston before graduating in 1981. "At first, before I went out on center court, I thought I'd be very nervous," says Odizor. "Amazingly, I was not."

2003 Greg Rusedski has his wallet and cell phone stolen from the locker room as he defeats Hicham Arazi 7-5, 7-5 in the semifinals of Samsung Open in Nottingham, England. Says Rusedski, "Someone's nicked my wallet and phone from the locker room and gone shopping with my credit cards. He got out pounds 600 from a card with my name on it. Who'd be an idiot to let him use it. How many Rusedskis are there in England? There was not too much cash but there were personal items as well which is not very nice. That bothers me. As long as I get them back I'll be a happy man. I was quite happy about the match but you wouldn't expect things to be stolen from the players' locker room here. I hope they catch them. I'll put them in front of my serve and hit them."

June 21

1937 In the first live broadcast of a tennis match, Bunny Austin of Great Britain opens up play on Centre Court at the 1937 Wimbledon Championships and defeats G. L. Rogers of Ireland 3-6, 8-6, 6-1, 6-2. The BBC broadcasts 25 minutes of live play from the match to an estimated television audience of 1,500 Londoners who have the luxury of television at the time. Austin trails a set and 3-5 in the second set before he dons a lucky blue jockey cap and changes his racquet and rallies to win 17 of the next 21 games. The next morning Britain's *Daily Telegraph* describes that viewers could get a clear view of the action and "even the passage of the marks of the lawnmowers were distinctly visible."

1994 In what was regarded as one of the most astonishing upsets in Wimbledon history, Steffi Graf becomes the first defending women's champion at Wimbledon to lose in the opening round of the event, falling to 30-year-old American Lori McNeil 7-5, 7-6. Says Graf, the three-time reigning Wimbledon singles champion, "She was better than me, that was obvious. She served much better and I just didn't have a very good time. On the important points I never really played right. I don't want to think about this for the next few days, but I'm not going to kill myself. Says McNeil, who goes on to reach the semifinals, "It feels great. It is definitely the best win of my career and I'm just happy I'm through to the next round."

1977 Jimmy Connors is loudly booed, jeered and whistled at on Centre Court at Wimbledon during his 6-3, 6-2, 6-4 win over Britain's Richard Lewis in reaction to Connors' snub of the Wimbledon Centenary's "Parade of Champions" featuring all living former singles winners. Says Connors, "I can't let that (the crowd) worry me. I'm out there to play tennis, No. 1. I've had the pleasure of playing in front of both crowds, for me and against me. I would like to have the fans in my corner, no doubt about it, but I still have to go out there and play. I can't let it affect me."

2005 French Open champion and No. 7-ranked Justine Henin-Hardenne is upset by No. 76th ranked Eleni Daniilidou of Greece 7-6 (8), 2-6, 7-5 in the first round of Wimbledon. Henin-Hardenne becomes the first Roland Garros women's champion since Margaret Smith in 1962 to lose her opening match at Wimbledon.

2005 Six-foot-10-inch Ivo Karlovic of Croatia serves 51 aces —the most aces ever recorded in a main draw match in the Open era of tennis—but loses to "lucky loser" Daniele Bracciali of Italy 6-7, 7-6, 3-6, 7-6, 12-10 in the first round of Wimbledon.

1988 John McEnroe returns to Wimbledon for the first time in three years and defeats Horst Skoff in the first round by a 6-1, 7-5, 6-1 margin. McEnroe plays his first match at the All England Club since 1985, when he loses in the quarterfinals to Kevin Curren. Says McEnroe after his win over Skoff, "In 1985, I had been in five straight finals and it was mentally negative for me. In a sense, against Curren I was almost looking for a way to lose. There was a lot of pressure. Now, I'm kind of having to work my way back up. I'll be better in six months than I am now. But on any given day, I can beat anyone. What I want, though, is to be able to look forward to coming here, instead of dreading coming here."

June 22

1922 Centre Court at Wimbledon—featuring 9,989 seats and room for 3,600 standees—is christened as King George V and Queen Mary attend the opening day of The Championships. A pair of British subjects compete in the first match on the famed court—Algernon Kingscote defeating Leslie Godfree 6-1, 6-3, 6-0. Writes Bud Collins in *The Bud Collins History of Tennis*, "Showers delayed the debut of architect Stanley Peach's magnificent dodecagon, Centre Court, by an hour on the opening day. However, with the usual stiffened upper lip of nobility, King George struck a gong thrice at 3:45 p.m. and the Big W was on its frequently wet way into the future, and Centre Court, to its destiny as perhaps the planet's most renowned playpen."

1981 John McEnroe famously calls chair umpire Edward James "the pits of the world" and an "incompetent fool" while exclaiming his famous line "You cannot be serious" in his 7-6 (5), 7-5, 6-3 first-round win over Tom Gullikson on the opening day at Wimbledon. The match is highlighted by McEnroe's verbally entertaining tirades, two point penalties and two smashed racquets. McEnroe's most heated tantrum—featuring the famous phrases—comes with Gullikson serving at 1-1, 15-30. Tournament referee Fred Hoyles is called to the court after James slaps McEnroe with a point penalty. After McEnroe's arguments with Hoyle goes unsatisfied, Gullikson holds serve and McEnroe throws a four-letter expletive to Hoyle on the changeover, prompting another point penalty. Says Gullikson of McEnroe's behavior, "It has no place. Everyone's afraid of these guys. All it would take is one default to put them in line. If it was the 120th player in the world, they would have defaulted him."

1999 In one of the greatest upsets in Wimbledon's 113-year history, top-ranked Martina Hingis loses 6-2, 6-0 in 54 minutes in the opening round to Jelena Dokic, a 16-year-old qualifier ranked No. 129. The match is the first for Hingis since she dramatically loses in the final of the French Open to Steffi Graf, after being booed by the fans at Roland Garros for bad behavior. Says Hingis in the post-match press conference, "It happens to everybody sometimes. I'm not that disappointed." Says Dokic, "It's surprising. You'd expect me to be, but I wasn't. There's no pressure to win. I've been playing well, and I just went for it."

1991 Monica Seles, the No. 1 player in the world seeking the third leg of a possible Grand Slam, mysteriously and controversially withdraws from

Wimbledon in unusual circumstances. Officials of the All England Club receive a fax from Seles' brother Zoltan that she had a "slight accident" that caused her enough injury to withdraw. The mysterious withdrawal and lack of communication between the Seles camp and the media cause for out-of-control speculation and frenzy as to the exact reasoning of her withdrawal. Writes Bill Dwyre in the *Los Angeles Times*, "No top-seeded player has said "thanks, but no thanks" to Wimbledon-especially one who has won the first two legs of the Grand Slam-and that goes back 67 years to when this event started seeding players. The presumption is that, in those 67 years, many a No. 1-seeded player dragged himself or herself onto Centre Court with all sorts of aches and pains-simply because it is Wimbledon." Later in the summer, Seles reveals that her withdrawal is due to shin splits.

1977 In what Barry Lorge of the *Washington Post* describes as "Wild Wednesday" at Wimbledon, two seeded men are upset, five former champions are nearly upset, 14-year-old Tracy Austin makes her Wimbledon debut and Ilie Nastase causes a stir and threatens to kill a reporter from the *New York Times*. No. 5 seed Brian Gottfried is upset by France's Byron Bertam 6-2, 4-6, 6-4, 6-3, while No. 10 seed Adriano Panatta is dismissed by American Alex Mayer 8-9, 6-0, 6-2, 6-4. Six-time Wimbledon champion Billie Jean King is extended by 17-year-old American Anne Smith before prevailing 6-8, 6-0, 6-3, while defending men's singles champion Bjorn Borg comes back from two-sets-to-love to defeat Australian Mark Edmondson 3-6, 7-9, 6-2, 6-4, 6-1. No. 1 seed Jimmy Connors saves two set points in the fourth set before overcoming Marty Riessen 6-4, 8-9, 6-1, 8-6. Nastase stops play for 10 minutes, summoning the referee while down a service break in the fourth set to Andrew Pattison, before breaking back and defeating the South African 7-9, 3-6, 7-5, 8-6, 6-3. Following the match, when Pattison tells Neil Amdur of the *New York Times* that he thought the disruptions were intentional by Nastase, Nastase lunges at Amdur and exclaims "If you write what he says, I kill you." Thirty-seven-year-old Maria Bueno survives a match point before defeating Janet Newberry 1-6, 8-6, 8-6, while Austin defeats Ellie Vessies-Appel 6-3, 6-3. Rod Laver returns to Centre Court at Wimbledon for the first time since 1971 and falls to No. 9 seed Dick Stockton 3-6, 9-7, 6-4, 7-5. Karen Hantze Susman, the Wimbledon champion in 1962, playing at the All England Club for the first time in 13 years, loses to Helle Sparre-Vrragh 6-3, 6-2.

2004 Wayne Ferreira defeats Ivan Ljubicic 5-7, 7-6 (5), 7-5, 6-2 in the first round of Wimbledon, marking his 55th consecutive appearance in a major tournament, setting a new mark previously held by Stefan Edberg. "It's not something that I started out at the beginning of my career, and said, 'Well, this is what I'm going to end off doing,'" says the 33-year-old Ferreira, who starts his streak at the 1991 Australian Open. "It came a couple of years ago, and then I felt like, 'Wow, actually it's not a bad thing.' The last maybe two or three Grand Slams a lot of the players have been congratulating me and saying that they think it's a great thing. A lot of them have thought about how long it would take them to get to this, and they laugh a lot."

1999 Roger Federer makes his main draw debut at Wimbledon and loses in the first round to Jiri Novak of the Czech Republic 6-3, 2-6, 4-6, 6-3, 6-4.

1988 Sixteen-year-old Michael Chang makes his Wimbledon debut and loses in the first round to France's Henri Leconte 2-6, 7-6, 6-2, 6-3. Chang becomes the youngest player to play on Centre Court at Wimbledon since 1927.

June 23

2003 Robby Ginepri of the United States becomes the first player in Wimbledon history to wear a sleeveless shirt in competition in his 6-3, 4-6, 7-6 (2), 6-7 (3), 10-8 first-round loss to Arnaud Clement of France.

1981 Fourteen-year-old American Kathy Rinaldi becomes the youngest player to win a match at Wimbledon at the at the time, saving a match point in defeating Sue Rollinson of South Africa 6-3, 2-6, 9-7 in 2 hours, 36 minutes on Court No. 2 at the All England Club. Rinaldi, a ninth-grader at Martin County High School in Stuart, Fla., enters Wimbledon fresh off reaching the quarterfinals of the French Open. Rollinson serves for the match twice—at 5-4 and 6-5 in the final set and holds at match point in the 12th game of the third set. Rinaldi loses her distinction nine years later when Jennifer Capriati, at the age of 14 years, 90 days—one day younger than Rinaldi—defeats Helen Kelesi 6-3, 6-1 in her first-round match on June 26, 1990.

1976 John Feaver of Britain fires 42 aces, a Wimbledon record at the time, but is not able to put away three-time champion John Newcombe, losing to the Australian legend 6-3, 3-6, 8-9, 6-4, 6-4 in the third round on Court No. 2. Feaver's 42 aces stands as the Wimbledon ace record for a match until 1997, when Goran Ivanisevic fires 46 aces in a 6-3, 2-6, 7-6 (4), 4-6, 14-12 loss to Magnus Norman in the third round. Ivo Karlovic of Croatia breaks Ivanisevic's record in a first round match in 2005, a 6-7(4), 7-6 (8), 3-6, 7-6 (5), 12-10 loss to Daniele Bracciali of Italy.

1992 Jeremy Bates of Britain, a man who Robin Finn of the *New York Times* describes as being "more prone to be written off locally than to pulling off major upsets on the home turf" defeats No. 7 seed Michael Chang 6-4, 6-3, 6-3 in the opening round of Wimbledon. The win marks only the second match victory on the season for the 30-year-old Bates, ranked No. 113. John McEnroe, playing in what ultimately is his final singles sojurn at the All-England Club—and unseeded in the Championships for the first time since his 1977 debut—wins his opening round match with Luiz Mattar 5-7, 6-1, 6-3, 6-3.

1990 Eighteen-year-old Californian Pete Sampras, the future seven-time Wimbledon champion, wins the first grass court tournament title of his career, defeating Gilad Bloom of Israel 7-6 (9), 7-6 (3) in the final of the

Manchester Open in Manchester, England. Says Sampras following the victory, "I was very composed, and he got a little tight on the crucial points." Sampras, however, is not able to translate his grass-court success in Manchester onto the lawns of Wimbledon the following week as he loses in the first round of The Championships to Christo van Rensburg of South Africa 7-6 (4), 7-5, 7-6 (3).

1982 Prior to teeing off for a round of pro-am golf at the Westchester Country Club in support of the PGA Tour's Westchester Golf Classic, Ivan Lendl explains that his decision to skip Wimbledon is based on an allergy to grass. "I sneeze a lot," he says. "I take shots every second day." When pressed about his Wimbledon absence, Lendl says. "I am on a vacation because I need the rest. When you are on vacation you don't write stories. I am not at Wimbledon because I needed the rest. This is when I scheduled my holiday and I didn't want to change it. The grass courts at Wimbledon are also a factor because of my allergy. I'll probably play at Wimbledon next year. "

1987 Stefan Edberg defeats fellow Swede Stefan Eriksson 6-0, 6-0, 6-0 in the first "triple bagel" at Wimbledon since 1947. "It's nice to be able to do whatever you want to do out there," Edberg says, "but I felt sorry for Stefan, too. It was his first match on grass. I thought about giving him a game but you never know when you are going to have another chance to win three love sets again."

1988 John McEnroe suffers a second-round straight-set loss to Wally Masur, losing 7-5, 7-6, 6-3, marking the three-time Wimbledon champion's earliest loss at the All England Club since a first-round loss in 1978. Says McEnroe after the match, "If that's the best I've got to give, I'd quit tomorrow. It's like my body went into some sort of letdown. I wasn't even pushing myself to be my best. It's almost enough to make me sick."

June 24

2003 Lleyton Hewitt becomes only the second defending men's singles champion at Wimbledon to lose in the first round as six-foot-10 Croatian qualifier Ivo Karlovic dismisses Hewitt 1-6, 7-6 (5), 6-3, 6-4 at The Championships. Hewitt joins 1966 Wimbledon champion Manuel Santana, defeated in the first round of Wimbledon in 1967 by Charlie Pasarell, as the only defending champions to be dismissed in the first round.

2004 Forty-seven-year-old nine-time Wimbledon champion Martina Navratilova, in a cameo singles appearance at Wimbledon for the first time since 1994, loses her final singles match at the All England Club on Court No. 3, losing 3-6, 6-3, 6-3 in the second round to 19-year-old Gisela Dulko of Argentina, the same player who ends Navratilova's French Open singles cameo four weeks earlier. Says Dulko, "This is the most special win of my career."

1983 Kathy Jordan upsets Chris Evert Lloyd 6-1, 7-6 (2) in the third round of Wimbledon, marking Evert Lloyd's first-ever loss before the semifinals at a major event. Evert Lloyd's semifinal streak, which dates back to her 1971 U.S. Open debut as a 16-year-old, is stopped at 34 consecutive major semifinals. "I'm disappointed," says Evert Lloyd. "In the past when opponents have been in a winning position against me, they're usually intimidated. Kathy wasn't. When I lose a set, it warms me up and gets me started. But at 3-0 in the tie-breaker, I knew, the way she was playing, I was not going to win."

2004 Chair umpire Ted Watts performs one of the biggest mistakes in Wimbledon history, famously awarding Croatia's Karolina Sprem an extra point in a second-set tie-break in her second-round Centre Court upset win over Venus Williams. Sprem leads Williams 2-1 in a second-set tie-break and wins the next point to lead 3-1, but Watts announces the score as 4-1. The mistake escapes both players and neither player protests the incorrect score. Sprem holds on to win the tie-break 8-6 and wins the match 7-6 (5), 7-6 (6). Says a diplomatic Williams, "I don't think one call makes a match."

2002 Pete Sampras wins what ultimately becomes his final match at Wimbledon, beating Britain's Martin Lee 6-3, 7-6 (1), 6-3 in the first round. Says Sampras of the match, also his final appearance on Centre Court at the

All England Club, "It's nice to play on Centre Court. Stepping out there felt like coming home again....It's like Mecca out there."

2006 In a pre-Wimbledon press conference at the All-England Club, thirty-six-year-old Andre Agassi announces that the 2006 tournament will be his last Wimbledon and he will retire from competitive tennis at the 2006 U.S. Open. Says Agassi, "It's been a long road this year for me, and for a lot of reasons. It's great to be here. This Wimbledon will be my last, and the U.S. Open will be my last tournament."

1996 Andre Agassi, the No. 3 seed and a Wimbledon champion in 1992, is dismissed from the first round of The Championships by No. 281-ranked qualifier Doug Flach 2-6, 7-6 (1), 6-4, 7-6 (6) on the famed "Graveyard" Court, Court No. 2. Says Agassi after the match, "This has nothing to do with Wimbledon. This is just, you know, I came out here and I was one of many guys trying to do well, and I didn't." Michael Chang, the No. 6 seed, joins Agassi on the sideline, also losing on the Graveyard Court, falling to Spain's Albert Costa, 3-6, 7-6 (5), 7-6 (1), 6-4. No. 8 seed Jim Courier is also dismissed in the first round, struggling with a sore leg in his 6-2, 6-4, 2-6, 6-4 loss to former junior doubles partner Jonathan Stark.

1998 Marcelo Rios of Chile takes a swipe at Wimbledon after being unceremoniously dumped in the first round of the world's most prestigious tournament as the No. 2 seed. "I don't take Wimbledon, like playing on grass, like a really important thing," says the dour Chilean, seeded No. 2, after losing to No. 36-ranked Francisco Clavet of Spain 6-3, 3-6, 7-5, 3-6, 6-3. "Tennis, when you see it on grass, it's not tennis. It's not a surface to watch or play tennis on; it's really boring. You just serve, return, go in, that's it." Rios does not return to the All England Club, never playing the event again after competing for three years—1995, 1997 and 1998—with a round of 16 showing in 1997 being his best result.

1977 Twenty-two-year-old world No. 1 Chris Evert defeats 14-year-old Wimbledon rookie Tracy Austin 6-1, 6-1 in 49 minutes in the third round of Wimbledon.

June 25

1969 Forty-one-year-old Pancho Gonzales finishes off his classic, darkness-delayed five-set win over Charlie Pasarell 22-24, 1-6, 16-14, 6-3, 11-9 in 5 hours, 12 minutes—the longest match played at Wimbledon at the time. Gonzales, 20 years removed from when he won his last major at age 21 at Forest Hills, trails Pasarell two-sets-to-love when the match is suspended the night before due to darkness after 2 hours, 20 minutes of play. Gonzales sweeps all three sets on its resumption to move into the second round, but heroically fights off seven match points in the fifth set—at 4-5, 0-40, at 5-6, 0-40 and at 7-8, ad-out. Writes Fred Tupper of the *New York Times* of the match's conclusion, "It was a question of raw courage now. How long could Pancho go on? He was leaning on his racquet between exchanges, flicking globules of sweat off his brow. At 9-9, Pasarell played a bad game. He double-faulted, hit a volley wide, a lob over the baseline and another volley just out. Gonzales served for the match. A serve, a smash to deep court and a backhand volley that creased the sideline put him at match point. In sepulchral silence, Gonzales toed the tape to serve. Then Pasarell lobbed out. Gonzales had taken 11 points in a row. He had clawed his way back and won." In 1989, in a second-round match played over three days, Greg Holmes beats fellow American Todd Witsken 5-7, 6-4, 7-6 (5), 4-6, 14-12 in 5 hours, 28 minutes.

1953 In the what the *New York Times* calls "one of the finest matches seen here since the war," No. 4 seed Jaroslav Drobny defeats 1950 champion Budge Patty 8-6, 16-18, 3-6, 8-6, 12-10 in four-and-a-half hours in the third round of Wimbledon. The match, concluded in fading light on Centre Court, is the longest match played at Wimbledon at the time—eclipsed by the Pancho Gonzales-Charlie Pasarell match in 5:12 in 1969. Patty has six match points in the match—three in the fourth set and three more in the fifth set—but is unable to convert.

1973 The 1973 edition of The Championships at Wimbledon begins, but not with 82 of the top men's players who boycott the event in support of Yugoslav player Nikki Pilic, who is suspended by the International Lawn Tennis Federation for not participating in Davis Cup for his country. The boycott is led by the new men's player union, the Association of Tennis Professionals (ATP) and includes such notable players as defending champion Stan Smith, John Newcombe, Ken Rosewall and Arthur Ashe. Ilie Nastase, Jimmy Connors and Britain's Roger Taylor are among the notable players who refuse to boycott the tournament. Jan Kodes of Czechoslvakia, the No. 2 seed, goes on to win the tournament, defeating Alex Metreveli of the Soviet Union in the men's final.

1979 Wimbledon's famous "Graveyard Court"—Court No. 2—claims two high profile first-round victims as 1975 Wimbledon champion Arthur Ashe, in what ultimately becomes his final match at the All England Club, is defeated by No. 139 ranked Australian Chris Kachel 6-4, 7-6, 6-3, while No. 4 seed Vitas Gerulaitis is defeated by fellow American Pat DuPre 7-6, 6-3, 3-6, 3-6, 6-3.

2001 For the second time in three years, Martina Hingis exits in the first round of Wimbledon as the No. 1 seed. Hingis, 20, loses on Court No. 1 to No. 83-ranked Virginia Ruano Pascual of Spain 6-4, 6-2 in 1 hour, 7 minutes. Two years earlier, in 1999, the top-seeded Hingis is also bounced in the first round by qualifier Jelena Dokic. Says Hingis, the 1997 Wimbledon champion, after her loss to Ruano Pascual, "It seems like I do really well here or I lose in the first round here."

2005 Jill Craybas, the No. 85-ranked player in the world, performs a shocking upset of two-time champion Serena Williams 6-3, 7-6 (3) in the third round of Wimbledon. "Horrible," Williams mutters in a post-match press conference when asked how she was feeling. "I guess I had a lot of rust. I just didn't play well today. I mean, the other days I kind of played through it and got better in the second and third sets. Today, I just didn't do anything right." The match is originally scheduled for Centre Court, but due to weather delays, the match is moved to Court No. 2, the "Graveyard Court" where champions such as Jimmy Connors, John McEnroe and Pete Sampras have all lost. At one point during the match, Williams misses a backhand and exclaims, "What am I doing out here?!"

2002 One year removed from his stunning round of 16 upset of seven-time champion Pete Sampras, No. 7 seed Roger Federer is bounced in the opening round of Wimbledon by 18-year-old Croat Mario Ancic by a 6-3, 7-6 (2), 6-3 margin. Says the No. 154-ranked Ancic, "I came first time to play Centre, Wimbledon, they put me on Centre Court for my first time. I qualified, nothing to lose, I was just confidence. I knew I could play. I believe in myself and just go out there and try to do my best. Just I didn't care who did I play. Doesn't matter...I knew him (Federer) from TV. I knew already how is he playing. I don't know that he knew how I was playing, but that was my advantage. And yeah, I didn't have any tactics, just I was enjoying." Following the loss, Federer goes on to win his next 40 matches at Wimbledon—including five straight titles—before losing in the 2008 final to Rafael Nadal of Spain.

1996 "Hen-mania" begins at Wimbledon as 21-year-old Tim Henman wins his first big match at the All England Club, coming back from a two-sets-to-love deficit—and saving two match points—to upset No. 5 seed and reigning French Open champion Yevgeny Kafelnikov 7-6 (8-6), 6-3, 6-7 (2-7), 4-6, 7-5 in the first round in what Jennifer Frey of the *Washington Post* calls "a cliffhanger that enraptured the winner's countrymen in the Centre Court seats." Henman goes on to reach the quarterfinals, where he is defeated by American Todd Martin 7-6 (5), 7-6 (2), 6-4, but remains a threat to win the title much of the next decade, thrilling British fans in the excitement of the possibility of becoming the first Brit to win the men's singles title at Wimbledon since Fred Perry wins his last of three titles in 1936.

1988 Thirty-five-year old Jimmy Connors fights back after trailing two-sets-to-one to defeat fellow American Derrick Rostagno 7-5, 4-6, 4-6, 6-2, 7-5 in 4 hours, 2 minutes in the third round of Wimbledon. Says Rostagno of Connors, "He comes up with things you haven't seen before. Tennis is an art and he's an artist. It was thrilling, a pleasure to play against." Says Connors, "My game has always been to stay in until I die."

2001 In his third appearance in the main draw at Wimbledon, Roger Federer finally wins his first match in the men's singles competition, defeating Christophe Rochus of Belgium 6-2, 6-3, 6-2 in the first round.

June 26

2002 Seven-time Wimbledon champion Pete Sampras plays what ultimately becomes his final Wimbledon match, losing in the second round—unceremoniously on the Graveyard Court—Court No. 2—to lucky-loser and No. 145-ranked George Bastl of Switzerland 6-3, 6-2, 4-6, 3-6, 6-4. Bastl, who enters the match having won only one main draw grass court match in his career, only gains entry into the tournament when Felix Mantilla of Spain withdraws the day before the tournament begins. Despite the loss, Sampras tells reporters after the match that he would return to the All England Club to play again, but after his U.S. Open triumph later in the summer, he never plays another professional match. "You know, I'm not going to end my time here with that loss," Sampras says after the match. "I want to end it on a high note, and so I plan on being back... As long as I feel like I can continue to win majors and contend, I'll just continue to play." Says Bastl, "It's a nice story isn't it? I gave myself chances because I was practicing on grass for the last three weeks. I had won my last three matches and I knew my game was improving match by match. I felt I would have some sort of a chance."

1951 On a cold and rainy afternoon, Althea Gibson walks on to Centre Court at Wimbledon as the first black player to compete in The Championships. Ten months after becoming the first black player to compete in a major when she plays the U.S. Championships the previous summer, Gibson wins her first match in her debut Wimbledon, defeating Pat Ward of Great Britain 6-0, 2-6, 6-4. Reports the Associated Press of Gibson, "Although the tall Negro girl is unseeded, she convinced the British experts that she has the equipment to rank high in the world within another year or two."

1962 Eighteen-year-old Billie Jean Moffitt beats No. 1 seed Margaret Smith 1-6, 6-3, 7-5 in the opening round of Wimbledon, creating history as the first player to knock off the women's No. 1 seed in the opening round at the All England Club. Smith is the heavy favorite to win the title after winning the Australian, Italian and French Championships entering the tournament. Billie Jean goes on to win six singles titles at the All England Club—and a record 20 titles overall at Wimbledon. Writes Bud Collins in *The Bud Collins History of Tennis*, "Her victory established 'Little Miss Moffitt' as a force to be reckoned with on the Centre Court that already was her favorite stage."

1965 Manuel Santana becomes the first defending champion to lose in the first round of Wimbledon when he is defeated by Charlie Pasarell 10-8, 6-3, 2-6, 8-6. Writes Fred Tupper of the *New York Times* of the Pasarell's upset of the No. 1 seed, "Over 150 spine-tingling minutes this afternoon, the Puerto Rican was the better tennis player, stronger on serve, more secure on volley, and rock steady in the crises." Says Santana, "Charlito was good. He was fast and hit the ball hard."

1978 Bjorn Borg performs a first-round escape on the opening day of Wimbledon as the two-time defending champion staves off elimination by six-foot-seven inch, 220-pound Victor Amaya of Holland, Mich., prevailing in five sets by a 8-9, 6-1, 1-6, 6-3, 6-3 margin. Amaya, who wears size 15 sneakers, leads Borg two sets to one and 3-1 in the fourth set and holds break point in the fifth game to go up two breaks in the fourth set. "He played better than I did on the important points, and that's always the difference in a five-set match," says Amaya. "He came up with great shots like that on crucial points, and that's why he is great."

1998 After no victories in 17 previous matches, including a 6-0, 6-0 loss 10 years earlier in the final of the French Open, Natasha Zvereva wins her first match against Steffi Graf, defeating the German 6-4, 7-5 in the third round of Wimbledon. Graf is hampered by a hamstring injury and is playing in only her fifth event of the year after recovering from knee surgery.

2000 Vince Spadea breaks his ATP record 21-match losing streak by upsetting No. 14 seed Greg Rusedski of Britain 6-3, 6-7, 6-3, 6-7, 9-7 in the first round of Wimbledon. Entering the match, Spadea is winless on the ATP Tour since the previous October in Lyon, France. Says Spadea, "If I had lost this match I was thinking 'Holy goodness! I am going to have to stay in Europe until I win a match.' But here I am, six months on. It was worth the wait." The following day, Rusedski is greeted with the headline in the *Daily Mail* reading, "Rusedski Falls To World's Biggest Loser."

2007 In his last Wimbledon singles match, Justin Gimelstob makes Wimbledon history as the first player to use the "Hawk-Eye" instant replay system at the All England Club. In his 6-1, 7-5, 7-6 (3) first-round loss to Andy Roddick on Court No. 1 on the opening day of play, Gimelstob uses the Hawk-Eye system to challenge one of his serves in the first set. Says Gimelstob of his new status in Wimbledon history, "I'd like to have a few more important records, but I'll take what I can get."

1990 John McEnroe is defeated in the first round of Wimbledon for only the second time in his career as the 31-year-old three-time champion is sent packing by the hands of fellow American Derrick Rostagno by a 7-5, 6-4, 6-4 margin. McEnroe is joined on the sideline by newly-crowned French Open champion and No. 5 seed Andres Gomez, who falls to American Jim Grabb 6-4, 6-2, 6-2. "I'm going home to Ecuador and watch the matches on TV and pretend I never was here," says Gomez. Future seven-time Wimbledon champion Pete Sampras is also sent packing in the first round by South African Christo van Rensburg, who defeats the No. 12 seeded Sampras 7-6, 7-5, 7-6.

1985 French Open champion Mats Wilander of Sweden is dismissed in the first round of Wimbledon as six-foot-six, No. 77-ranked Slobodan Zivojinovic of Yugoslavia defeats the No. 4 seeded Wilander 6-2, 5-7, 7-5, 6-0.

2004 The USTA names the 2004 U.S. Olympic tennis team during the same day that the Olympic flame is run through the All England Club at Wimbledon. Named to the U.S. Olympic tennis team are Andy Roddick, Mardy Fish, Taylor Dent, Vince Spadea, Bob Bryan, Mike Bryan, Venus Williams, Serena Williams, Jennifer Capriati, Chanda Rubin, Lisa Raymond and Martina Navratilova.

June 27

1970 Roger Taylor of Britain ends the 31-match Wimbledon winning streak of Rod Laver, handing the Australian his first loss at the All England Club since 1960 in a 4-6, 6-4, 6-2, 6-1 fourth-round decision. Laver, the Wimbledon champion in 1961 and 1962, did not compete in The Championships from 1963 to 1967 after turning professional. When Wimbledon becomes "open" in 1968, Laver wins the first men's singles title open to amateurs and professionals in 1968, then repeats in 1969, securing the third leg of his eventual Grand Slam. "The day was his," Fred Tupper writes of Taylor in the *New York Times*, "and uproarious applause deservedly celebrated this moment in history. But it must be reported that the little redhead, for so long the champion of the world, lost his touch halfway through the match and double-faulted sadly to finish it." Says Laver following the match, "A few inches make a tremendous gap in the score. I double-faulted the match away. Disappointing. I don't like losing. It is not in my nature."

1985 Anne White turns heads at the All England Club when she sports a white body stocking in her first-round match against Pam Shriver at Wimbledon. White wears an all-body leotard-like outfit to keep her warm during the chilly day in London and splits sets with the No. 5 seeded Shriver before play is suspended due to rain. Wimbledon referee Alan Mills later calls the outfit not appropriate tennis attire and forbids her from wearing it again in the tournament. White returns the next day, without her all-white body suit and dressed in a traditional white tennis skirt and blouse, but loses the third set and the match 6-3, 6-7 (7), 6-3. Says White the following day, "I'm a little aggravated I couldn't wear it today. But it's their tournament and I don't want to do anything to upset them or hurt their feelings. I mean, I don't want people spilling their strawberries and cream because of me."

1992 For the first time in Wimbledon history, a qualifier defeats a No. 1 seeded player as Andrei Olhovskiy of Russia, who wins three matches in the qualifying tournament to gain entry into The Championships, defeats No. 1 seed Jim Courier 6-4, 4-6, 6-4, 6-4 in the third round. Says Courier, the reigning Australian and French Open champion, of losing to the No. 193-ranked Olhovskiy, "Some days you win, some days you lose, and some days it rains, but it didn't rain today. The bottom line is I played as hard as I could and I got outplayed."

2006 Roger Federer wins his record 42nd consecutive win on grass, closing out a 6-3, 6-2, 6-2 demolition of the 20-year-old Frenchman Richard Gasquet in the first round of Wimbledon. The win moves Federer passed Bjorn Borg, who won 41 straight matches from 1976 to 1981. In humble fashion, Federer gives more credit to Borg's streak since all of his matches were won at Wimbledon, "The five Wimbledons and the sixth final is something beyond possibilities for any player," Federer says. "So for me, Borg stays a hero."

1978 One year after being the sensation at Wimbledon by reaching the men's semifinals as an 18-year-old qualifier, John McEnroe is dumped in the first round of The Championships, losing by a 7-5, 1-6, 8-9, 6-4, 6-3 margin to fellow American Erik van Dillen. Arthur Ashe is also defeated in the first round at the All England Club, losing 8-9, 9-8, 6-3, 5-7, 7-5 to six-foot-five Australian Steve Docherty, who played defensive end on the Washington State University football team in 1970. Says Ashe who signs autographs for fans for 20 minutes on court after the loss, "I tried as hard as I could, but the guy just served unbelievably well. The scores attest to the fact that neither of us could do anything but serve and pray. "

1977 Playing "the best match I could possibly play on grass," Chris Evert defeats Billie Jean King, 6-1, 6-2 in 43 minutes in the quarterfinals of Wimbledon. No. 2 seed Martina Navratilova is eliminated by Holland's Betty Stove 9-8, 3-6, 6-1, while two British hopes, Virginia Wade and Sue Barker, also advance to the women's singles semifinals. Wade defeats Rosie Casals 7-5, 6-2, while Barker upends Kerry Melville Reid 6-3, 6-4.

1987 Two-time defending champion and No. 1 seeded Boris Becker is upset in the second round of Wimbledon, falling on Court No. 1 to Australian journeyman Peter Doohan 7-6, 4-6, 6-2, 6-4. Says Becker, "I am disappointed, but it will hurt more tomorrow. I knew the day had to come when I would lose. I am not immortal, but my good feelings about Wimbledon will not go away."

1991 Andre Agassi and Pete Sampras make first-round splashes at Wimbledon—and not just for stepping in water puddles during the rain-marred opening week of The Championships—as both players compete in stand-out matches at the All England Club. Sampras, the future seven-time Wimbledon champion and the No. 8 seed, wins his first-ever Wimbledon match—a 6-1, 6-2, 6-2 win over Brazil's Danilo Marcelino. Sampras, who won the U.S. Open the previous September, advances after losing in the first round of the tournament the previous two years—to Todd Woodbridge in his Wimbledon debut in 1989 and to Christo van Rensburg in 1990. "I just think I'm a little bit stronger physically and mentally than last year," says Sampras after the match. "I think I have grown up a lot since last year, and a lot of things have happened, like winning the U.S. Open and stuff." Agassi's Centre Court match with Grant Connell of Canada creates major fanfare and buzz across Britain—and the tennis community around the world—as the Las Vegan known for his colorful tennis outfits adheres to Wimbledon's "all white" clothing rule and makes his first appearance at the All England Club since losing in the first round in 1987. Agassi and Connell split the first two sets, and stand at 1-1 in the third set before rain postpones play for the day. Agassi returns the next day to finish off the 4-6, 6-1, 6-7(6), 7-5, 6-3 victory, also his first-ever Wimbledon match victory.

1983 Thirty-year-old Jimmy Connors is bombarded with 33 aces by Kevin Curren, who dismisses the No. 1 seed and defending Wimbledon champion 6-3, 6-7, 6-3, 7-6 on Court No. 2 in the round of 16 of The Championships. The loss marks the first time that Connors does reach at least the quarterfinals of Wimbledon since his first visit to the All England Club in 1972.

2008 Jie Zheng of China, a wild card entry ranked No. 133, upsets No. 1 seed Ana Ivanovic of Serbia 6-1, 6-4 in the third round of Wimbledon. Says Ivanovic, a freshly-minted world No. 1 from her French Open victory three weeks earlier, "I didn't play well. But she plays very well on grass and I found it difficult adjusting to the timing of the ball. It was tough, I tried to hit my shots higher and get under the ball to play with speed but I was making too many mis-hits." Zheng, a doubles champion at Wimbledon in 2006, goes on to reach the semifinals of the tournament, losing to Serena Williams.

1988 Ivan Lendl and Mark Woodforde battle for 4 hours, 46 minutes on Centre Court at Wimbledon, before Lendl emerges victorious and advances into the quarterfinals with a 7-5, 6-7, 6-7, 7-5, 10-8 victory.

June 28

1977 Eighteen-year-old John McEnroe becomes the first qualifier to reach the semifinals of Wimbledon when he defeats Phil Dent of Australia 6-4, 8-9, 4-6, 6-3, 6-4 in the men's quarterfinals. Says the No. 270-ranked McEnroe of Jimmy Connors, his semifinal opponent, "I haven't played him. I've never even met him."

1995 Chanda Rubin of the United States defeats Patricia Hy-Boulais of Canada 7-6 (7-4), 6-7 (7-5), 17-15 in a 3-hour, 45-minute second-round match that is the longest women's singles match in Wimbledon history. Played on Court No. 16, the 58-game match is also the longest women's singles match in games in Wimbledon history. Says Rubin after the marathon, "You are never going to forget a match like that. We were friends before this match. Even though somebody had to win, I think we will still be good friends. You definitely won't forget something like this." Says Hy-Boulais, "It's almost a pleasure, knowing that we have both given our best. Like I stretched her or she stretched me. We both took each other one notch higher."

1997 Playing in her first-ever Wimbledon match, future champion Venus Williams, age 17, falls in the first round to No. 91 Magdalena Grzybowska of Poland 4-6, 6-2, 6-4. Says the 59th-ranked Williams after the match, "Everyone does have high hopes and everyone wants to win. I'm not too disappointed. It's my first Wimbledon and there will be many more to come and I think I tried to do my best and I never gave up during the match." The much-hyped and talked about Williams reaches the final of the U.S. Open later in the summer and wins her first major singles title three years later at the All England Club.

1990 Fourteen-year-old Wimbledon debutant Jennifer Capriati, the youngest player to win a match at the All England Club, claws out a 7-5, 6-7, 6-3 win over Robin White to set up a fourth-round confrontation with world No. 1 Steffi Graf. Capriati overcomes missing out on five match points in the second set and wins the final six games of the match. Says Capriati, "I was thinking that it was good that I was able to pull that out. But I was upset, saying, 'Why aren't you closing these matches out?'" Capriati's Wimbledon is ended in the next round in a 6-2, 6-4 loss to Graf.

1979 Eighteen-year-old Californian Linda Siegel wears a backless, braless tennis dress during her 6-1, 6-3 loss to Billie Jean King on Centre Court and has her "peek-a-boo" moments photographed and published in London's tabloid newspapers. Says King of Siegel's dress, "That's great, if she's happy. The audience sure was happy. If you're well-endowed, you might as well show it." Writes Barry Lorge of the *Washington Post*, "A couple of times during her match, the amply-endowed Siegel momentarily fell out of her frock."

1983 Thirty-nine-year-old Billie Jean King reaches the semifinals of Wimbledon for a 14th time with a 7-5, 6-4 quarterfinal victory over Kathy Jordan, while in the men's field, Ivan Lendl reaches his first Wimbledon semifinal, defeating 1979 finalist Roscoe Tanner 7-5, 7-6, 6-3 in the quarterfinals. Lendl returns to the All England Club after skipping the 1982 tournament, citing an allergy to grass. Says Lendl of his win over Tanner, "I would say it was probably my best match on grass courts."

1989 Thirty-six-year-old Jimmy Connors, the oldest player in the Wimbledon field, is defeated in the second round by a 7-6, 5-7, 6-4, 6-2 margin by fellow American Dan Goldie. Says Connors after the match when talk of retirement is brought up in the post-match press conference, "I've put my reputation on the line since I was 18 years old so why should I not do that now? Don't write that I'm retiring and quitting. Just gently write that I'm gonna finish this year and decide after that."

1988 Patrick Kuhnen, ranked No. 90 in the world and No. 9 in Germany, posts the biggest of his career, defeating 35-year-old Jimmy Connors 5-7, 7-6, 7-6, 6-7, 6-3 on Wimbledon's Graveyard No. 2 court in the round of 16. "He's got something no one can take from him, experience," Kuhnen says of Connors. "You have to beat him because he is a fighter and will not make mistakes. He hangs in there."

2007 The Tim Henman era comes to a close at Wimbledon as the four-time semifinalist, four-time quarterfinalist and crowd favorite at the All England Club plays what ultimately becomes his final Wimbledon match, a 7-6 (3), 7-6 (5), 3-6, 2-6, 6-1 second-round loss to Spain's Feliciano Lopez. In his post-match press conference, Henman says he will return to play at Wimbledon, put later in the summer announces that the U.S. Open would be his final tournament and he plays his final two matches—a singles and doubles victory in Davis Cup for Britain—at the All England Club in September.

1902 Trailing Marion Jones 6-2, 1-0 in the challenge round final of the U.S. National Championships (the modern day U.S. Open), Elisabeth Moore faints and is unable to continue play at the Philadelphia Cricket Club. Jones refuses to be given the title and agrees to postpone the match and continue it two days later on a Monday. When Moore still is not feeling well when the match is scheduled to resume, tournament officials award the championship to Jones, her second U.S. national singles title after winning in 1899.

1991 Thirty-year-old former top 10 player Tim Mayotte saves four match points and defeats 19-year-old and No. 9 seeded Michael Chang 6-7 (8-6), 4-6, 6-1, 7-6 (11-9), 6-2 in the first round of Wimbledon. The loss is Chang's first-ever opening round loss in a major tournament, while Mayotte's win comes in his first tournament match since April due to a bad back and bad knees. Says Mayotte, ranked No. 94, of his win, "It was just a good time out there. I came in realizing that, with no preparation and coming off injuries and stuff, I couldn't go out there expecting too much. So I just tried to get into the atmosphere out on the court, and the crowd really got behind it. It was infectious really, and I just started laughing more and more. It was really one of the most fun matches I have played."

1996 Three-time Wimbledon champion and No. 2 seed Boris Becker is forced to retire with a right wrist injury in the first set of his third-round match with No. 223-ranked Neville Godwin of South Africa. In the first point of the first-set tie-breaker, Becker, the reigning Australian Open champion, hits a forehand return of serve off his frame and grabs his wrist in pain. He receives a three-minute injury timeout and has the wrist taped, but realizes he cannot continue, defaulting the match to Godwin by a 6-6, (1-0, retired) scoreline. Says Becker after the match, "My wrist gave way and I heard something pop. I couldn't hold the racquet anymore. I thought I had broken my wrist. I know it's serious. I have had many injuries in my career before, and I know when it's something serious and when something can heal in a few days."

June 29

1984 Jimmy Connors wins his 65th men's singles match at Wimbledon, breaking the men's record set by Arthur W. Gore, defeating Marty Davis 6-4, 6-7 (4), 6-3, 6-4 in the third round. Says Connors, "It's an honor to have won more matches at Wimbledon than any other male, but I play to win tournaments, not matches. Maybe if I'd won three more matches, I'd have won this tournament a lot more. For me, tennis is geared around two tournaments, the U.S. Open and Wimbledon. When I leave here, I go out preparing to win the next year."

1991 Twenty-nine-year-old Nick Brown of Great Britain scores a big upset at Wimbledon, beating 10th-seeded Goran Ivanisevic 4-6, 6-3, 7-6, 6-3 in the second round. Brown, ranked No. 591 and the lowest-ranked player in the men's championship, posts the biggest upset, based on comparative rankings, since the ATP began compiling world rankings in 1973.

1994 Martina Navratilova sets a Wimbledon record, playing her 266th career match as she passes Billie Jean King's record of 265 when she and Manon Bollegraf beat Ingelisa Driehuis and Maja Muric 6-4, 6-2 in the quarterfinals of women's doubles.

1988 In a match featuring the Wimbledon men's singles champions from the previous three years, 1985 and 1986 Wimbledon champion Boris Becker defeats defending champion Pat Cash 6-4, 6-3, 6-4 in the men's quarterfinals. "I watched on television and it hurt when Cash won," Becker says of watching Cash win the 1987 title. "My life changed after that Wimbledon. I realized I am a human being who plays tennis and that I'm beatable, and in the back of my mind, I thought that he was the one to beat to get the title back. But it is not over. This match has given me confidence but not the trophy yet." Mats Wilander's bid for a Grand Slam is ended as the Australian and French and Australian Open champion is defeated by Miloslav Mecir 6-3, 6-1, 6-3 in the quarterfinals. "After the match, I was very disappointed," Wilander says. "I have been thinking of the Grand Slam a little bit. But I am going to get over that in a few days. I don't think you can expect yourself to win the Slam." Ros Fairbank nearly ends Martina Navratilova's six-year grapple-hold on the Wimbledon women's singles championship as she lets 4-2 leads in the second and third set slip away in a 4-6, 6-4, 7-5 loss in the quarterfinals. Says Navratilova, "Several times today I thought I was going to lose the match. I thought, 'What a way to go. On Court 14, to

Ros Fairbank, in the quarterfinals." Says Fairbank, "I thought about ending Martina's streak all the time. Maybe that was my problem."

1977 Thirty-one-year-old Virginia Wade stuns No. 1 seed Chris Evert 6-2, 4-6, 6-1 to become the first British woman to reach the Wimbledon women's singles final since Ann Jones wins the title in 1969. An all-British Wimbledon final, however, is dashed by Holland's Betty Stove, 32, who defeats Britain's Sue Barker 6-4, 2-6, 6-4 in the other women's semifinal. Says Evert, "Virginia played more patiently than I did. I could see in her eyes how much she wanted to win. I just couldn't reach deep down inside myself for what I need to win. I didn't have it."

1946 Frank Parker wins the first 16 games of the match and defeats Rolando Vega 6-0, 6-0, 6-2 to help the United States to a 2-0 lead over Mexico in the Davis Cup second round in Orange, N.J. Parker, a two-time U.S. singles winner, had registered one of the three "triple bagels" in U.S. Davis Cup history in the previous round, defeating Felicisimo Ampon of the Phillippines 6-0, 6-0, 6-0 on June 14.

June 30

1977 Bjorn Borg and Vitas Gerulaitis stage one of the great Wimbledon semifinals in the history of the event, with Borg edging out his good friend and practice partner by a 6-4, 3-6, 6-3, 3-6, 8-6 margin. Playing as the first qualifier and youngest man in a Wimbledon semifinal, 18-year-old John McEnroe is defeated by No. 1 seed Jimmy Connors 6-3, 6-3, 4-6, 6-4 in McEnroe's first major singles semifinal. Says Gerulaitis of the loss, "Maybe a couple of years ago I would have been happy just to play a match like that. But today I really wanted to win and get into the final. I didn't let anything upset me. I had one intention and that was to win the match."

1991 For the first time in the 114-year history of Wimbledon, play is contested on the middle Sunday of The Championships due to excessive rain. The tournament opens all of its seats to fans on a first come, first serve basis that creates a "People's Sunday" as avid tennis fans, who normally do not have access to the prestigious and elite tickets, are allowed to enjoy the tennis—and do so in a carnival type atmosphere of singing, chanting, cheering and standing ovations. Derrick Rostagno and Jimmy Connors play their third round match on Centre Court in front of a raucously appreciative crowd, as Rostagno follows up his second-round win over Pete Sampras by beating Connors 7-6, 6-1, 6-4, in Connors' 101st match at Wimbledon. The most exciting match of the day comes when No. 3 seed Ivan Lendl comes from two sets down to defeat Mal Washington 4-6, 2-6, 6-4, 6-4, 7-5 in the second round.

1979 No. 2 seed John McEnroe falls victim to Wimbledon's infamous Graveyard Court No. 2 and No. 16 seed Tim Gullikson as the 20-year-old is defeated by Gullikson 6-4, 6-2, 6-4 in the round of 16. Says Gullikson of McEnroe, "He's not playing nearly as well as he was. He's not serving as well, and the whole match — just looking across the net at him all the time — he really seemed like he was unsettled. It just seemed like there were a lot of things on his mind. Maybe it's the tremendous pressure that's been put on him. He's been kind of labeled as a bad boy, which he really isn't. He's only 20 years old, and really everybody thought he was going to win Wimbledon this year. That's a lot of pressure on anybody, and you can't play well all the time. There are a lot of good players out there."

1987 In one of the greatest comebacks in the history of the sport, Jimmy Connors trails Mikael Pernfors 6-1, 6-1, 4-1, but incredibly rallies to a 1-6,

1-6, 7-5, 6-4, 6-2 round of 16 victory in 3 hours, 39 minutes. Writes Peter Alfano of the *New York Times*. "Connors added another page in a career that has required several volumes. The complete works of Jimmy Connors will now include what Wimbledon sages are saying was one of the more memorable matches in history, a comeback the equal of any staged here during Wimbledon's 101 years." Says Connors, "I don't think I'm surprised I won. I think I can still play. I didn't have time to be embarrassed today. I was too busy trying to do something to win. If I didn't want to win, I'd just lose, 6-1, 6-1, 6-1, and get off there."

1988 Controversy strikes the 78th meeting between Chris Evert and Martina Navratilova as Evert's cross-court forehand clips the top of the net and apparently lands on the line, only to be called out by the linesman, giving the 6-1, 4-6, 7-5 victory to Navratilova, advancing her into the Wimbledon final. After fighting off a match point in the 10th game of the final set, Evert faces triple-match point serving at 5-6 in the final set. Evert is able to fight off the first two match points, before her controversial missed forehand on the third match point. Says Evert, "But I was sure it was good and I was so happy that I just turned and walked back to the baseline. Then, I turned again and saw Martina with her hand out. I put two and two together and figured the ball was called out....Maybe it was a mixture of me hoping and seeing what I wanted to see. The umpire will rarely overrule on that kind of call. It was bad luck for me considering the match was so close." Says Navratilova, "I cannot say that it was good or that it was out and there was nothing that I could do about it. It's a shame it had to be like that because now, there will always be doubts in people's minds. But we've never had a stranger ending in one of our matches than that."

1983 Thirty-nine-year-old Billie Jean King suffers her worst defeat in 110 Wimbledon singles matches as she is defeated 6-1, 6-1 in 56 minutes by 18-year-old Andrea Jaeger in the women's singles semifinals. "She just cleaned my clock," says King. In the other women's semifinal, Martina Navratilova needs only 36 minutes to defeat Yvonne Vermaak of South Africa by the same 6-1, 6-1 score.

1982 Thirty-eight-year-old Billie Jean King defeats Tracy Austin 3-6, 6-4, 6-2 for the first time in her career to advance to the semifinals of Wimbledon for a 13th time in her career. King's achievement makes her the oldest Wimbledon women's semifinalist since Dorthea Lambert Chambers reaches the last four in 1920 at age 42.

July 1

1977 Virginia Wade of Great Britain wins the women's singles title at the Centenary Wimbledon Championships, defeating Betty Stove of the Netherlands 4-6, 6-3, 6-1 in the women's singles final. Wade, the first British woman to win at Wimbledon since 1969, receives the gold championship plate from Queen Elizabeth II. "I don't think it was by any means the best match there has been this Wimbledon, but the atmosphere was just sensational," says Wade. "I was so excited, the whole thing was like a fairy-tale situation, with everybody cheering for the Queen and cheering for me."

1955 Tony Trabert uses what Fred Tupper of the *New York Times* describes as "crushing display of power worthy of the best players of the bygone eras" to defeat surprise unseeded finalist Kurt Nielsen of Denmark 6-3, 7-5, 6-1 to win the Wimbledon men's singles title. Trabert wins his first—and only— Wimbledon singles title without dropping a set. Says Trabert following his victory, "I've been dreaming of winning this one since I was in knee pants— and I've been working on it for the past five years." Nielsen also reached the Wimbledon final in 1953 as an unseeded player, losing to Trabert's Davis Cup teammate Vic Seixas.

1974 Ismael El Shafei of Egypt crushes 18-year-old Bjorn Borg 6-2, 6-3, 6-1 in the third round of Wimbledon. El Shafei loses only 10 points on his serve against the No. 5 seeded Borg—three on double faults—and becomes the most obscure of the four men to beat Borg at Wimbledon during his career, joining Roger Taylor of Britain (1973), Arthur Ashe (1975) and John McEnroe (1981).

2006 Thirty-six-year-old Andre Agassi plays his final match at Wimbledon in his 14th appearance at the All England Club, losing in the third round to French Open champion Rafael Nadal of Spain 7-6 (5), 6-2, 6-4. Agassi wins his first major title at Wimbledon in 1992, and reaches the final again in 1999. Says Agassi, "It's just nice to come back here on my terms. I'll look back at this as one of my memorable experiences. To say goodbye, for me, this means as much as winning."

1980 Bjorn Borg defeats BalazsTaroczy of Hungary 6-1, 7-5, 6-2 in the round of 16 at Wimbledon, marking his 32nd straight singles match victory at the All England Club, breaking the all-time Wimbledon men's singles record set by Rod Laver. Says Borg, "When I started to play tennis at nine years old, Laver was my idol. To beat this kind of record, especially with Laver involved, when you look at his overall record with two Grand Slams, that's why it means so much to me." Borg goes on to extend his streak to 41 straight Wimbledon victories, before losing the 1981 final—his sixth straight final—to John McEnroe.

1983 Chris Lewis, ranked No. 91 in the world, becomes Wimbledon's most improbable men's singles finalist as he defeats No. 12 seed Kevin Curren 6-7, 6-4, 7-6, 6-7, 8-6 in the men's singles semifinal at the All England Club. Lewis, from New Zealand, trails Curren 0-3 15-30 in the fifth set before rallying to victory with British Prime Minister Margaret Thatcher watching until the bitter end. Lewis becomes the first unseeded man to reach the Wimbledon final since Wilhelm Bungert of West Germany in 1967. John McEnroe reaches the men's singles final for a fourth straight year with a 7-6, 6-4, 6-4 victory over Ivan Lendl in the other semifinal.

1995 Jeff Tarango walks out of a third-round match at Wimbledon, trailing Alexander Mronz of Germany 7-6 (6), 3-1 after a series of disagreements with chair umpire Bruno Rebeuh of France, whom he calls "one of the most corrupt officials in the game." Following his walk-off, Tarango's wife Benedicte slaps Rebeuh in the face and, in his post press conference, Tarango alleges that Rebeuh helps players that he is friends with and is the most corrupt official in the sport. "Well, things were pretty crazy, and I have a lot of basis for what I'm saying," says Tarango following the match, "It's a long, long story. I'm sorry that things happened, but I don't feel that a player has any defense these days in getting some kind of justice when things go wrong against him." Tarango is subsquently fined $63,000 and banned for two major tournaments, including Wimbledon the following year.

1999 Boris Becker's illustrious Wimbledon career comes to an end with a 6-3, 6-2, 6-3 loss to Patrick Rafter in the round of 16 on Centre Court. Becker, a three-time Wimbledon champion and four-time runner-up who wins Wimbledon as a 17-year-old unknown in 1985, returns to Wimbledon for one more sojurn in 1999. He makes his first appearance at Wimbledon since 1997 when, after losing to Pete Sampras in the quarterfinals, he announces that he had played his last match at Wimbledon. Says Becker of his relationship with Wimbledon, "It was a great love affair like nowhere else in the world."

1985 A 50-point tie-break, the longest in the history of professional tennis, is played in the fourth set of a men's doubles match at Wimbledon, between John Frawley of Australia and Victor Pecci of Paraguay against Jan Gunnarsson of Sweden and Michael Mortensen of Denmark. Gunnarson and Mortensen win a 26-24 fourth-set tie-break and the first-round match by a 6-2, 6-4, 3-6, 7-6 (24) margin. The previous longest tiebreak occurred in 1973 at Wimbledon when Bjorn Borg defeats Premjit Lall of India in a first-round match which includes a 20-18 tiebreak.

1966 Manuel Santana becomes the first Spanish champion in the history of Wimbledon, defeating Dennis Ralston of the United States in the final 6-4, 11-9, 6-4. The following year, Santana makes Wimbledon history again, becoming the first defending champion to lose in the first round, losing to Charlie Pasarell of Puerto Rico.

July 2

1988 Nineteen-year-old Steffi Graf ends Martina Navratilova's six-year stranglehold on the women's singles title at Wimbledon, defeating the eight-time champion 5-7, 6-2, 6-1 to win her first Wimbledon singles title and capture the third leg of her eventual Grand Slam. Navratilova fails in her attempt to win her ninth Wimbledon singles title and breaking the record that she shares with Helen Wills. Says Navratilova of the loss, "This is how it should happen. I lost to a better player on the final day. This is the end of a chapter, passing the torch if you want to call it that." Ivan Lendl again fails in his attempt to win the men's singles title at Wimbledon as Boris Becker defeats the No. 1 player in the world 6-4, 6-3, 6-7, 6-4 in a rain-postponed men's singles semifinal. Writes Peter Alfano of the *New York Times*, "As Ahab in this tennis version of Moby Dick, Ivan Lendl will find solace in the belief that he is getting closer to his goal, that eventually, all the hard work and sweat will be rewarded." It is Lendl's eighth appearance at Wimbledon, with his best showings coming in semifinal finishes three times and runner-up appearances twice in 1986 and 1987.

2005 Venus Williams and Lindsay Davenport play the longest women's singles final in Wimbledon history, battling for 2 hours, 45 minutes before Williams saves a match point and prevails by a 4-6, 7-6 (4), 9-7 margin for her third Wimbledon championship. Williams, seeded No. 14, wins her first major singles title since the 2001 U.S. Open. Davenport serves for the match at 6-5 in the second set and holds her match point while up 5-4 in the third set. Says Davenport after the loss, "I don't really feel that I have anything to hang my head for or really be ashamed of. She hit some great first serves at some crucial times. She didn't really give me a look at any second serves on big points. She just took it away from me every time I got up. She was just incredible. Whenever I felt like I was just about to shut the door completely, it was like, 'Oops, let's open that back up.'"

2001 Nineteen-year-old Roger Federer of Switzerland registers a stunning 7-6 (7), 5-7, 6-4, 6-7 (2), 7-5 Centre Court upset of seven-time Wimbledon champion Pete Sampras in the round of 16 at Wimbledon, ending the 31-match wining streak at the All England Club for Sampras as well as his quest for a record-tying fifth straight title. Says Sampras of his four-year run at Wimbledon, "You know something so great isn't going to last forever." Federer, playing on Centre Court for the first time in his career, says that winning the first set after fighting off a set-point against him was a key to the match. "I had the feeling that I really can beat him," he says. "I had that feeling all the way. That's probably why I won."

1977 Bjorn Borg repeats as Wimbledon men's singles champion as he fends off a furious fifth-set challenge from Jimmy Connors in his 3-6, 6-2, 6-1, 5-7, 6-4 final-round victory. Borg leads Connors 4-0 with two break points for a 5-0 lead in the fifth set before Connors wins four straight games before faltering after 3 hours, 14 minutes. Says Borg, "I think I'm even a little happier this year than last because I played Jimmy in the final and I wanted to beat him very badly. He's been beating me a lot of times before, and I lost to him in Forest Hills, in a very close final. I think this is for sure my happiest win."

1932 Ellsworth Vines wins Wimbledon in his first attempt, defeating Britain's Bunny Austin 6-4, 6-2, 6-0 in the men's singles final. Vines fires 30 aces against Austin who only breaks Vines' serve once during the championship match. Writes Bud Collins in *The Bud Collins History of Tennis*, "Competing in his first Wimbledon at 20, Vines was so impressive that some English reporters were calling him the greatest player of all time. He defeated Australian Harry Hopman, 7-5, 6-2, 7-5, in the third round and sailed through Australian Jack Crawford, 6-2, 6-1, 6-3, and Britain's Bunny Austin, 6-4, 6-2, 6-0, in the last two rounds...Ellsworth's match point was a service ace and Austin said: "I saw him swing his racket and I heard the ball hit the back canvas. The umpire called game, set and match, so I knew it was all over, but I never saw the ball."

1937 Don Budge wins the first major singles title of his career, defeating Gottfried von Cramm of Germany 6-3, 6-4, 6-2 to win the men's singles title at Wimbledon. Budge goes on to become the first man to win a Wimbledon "triple" as he also wins the doubles title with Gene Mako and the mixed doubles championship with Alice Marble.

1938 Thirty-two-year-old Helen Wills Moody wins her 19th—and final—major singles title, easily defeating rival Helen Jacobs 6-4, 6-0 in the women's singles final at Wimbledon. Jacobs plays the match despite a severely-strained Achilles tendon, which hampers her as she loses the final eight games of the match. The final is the 11th and final meeting between "the two Helens"—with Wills Moody winning the rivalry by a 10-1 margin. Wills Moody's 19 major singles titles is the all-time record until it is topped in 1970 by Margaret Smith Court, who goes on to win 24 major singles titles.

1954 Thirty-two-year-old Jaroslav Drobny, playing Wimbledon for a 11th time, unexpectedly wins the men's singles title as the No. 11 seed, upsetting Ken Rosewall 13-11, 4-6, 6-2, 9-7 in the championship match. Drobny played three previous finals and six previous semifinals without winning the title. Writes Fred Tupper of the *New York Times*, "The thunderous applause that rang down the crowded center court at Wimbledon must have echoed wherever tennis is played. For "Old Drob" had finally made it. He had been 11 times trying, first in 1938 as a 16-year-old ballboy from Prague."

1983 Martina Navratilova concludes a dominant performance at Wimbledon, defeating Andrea Jaeger 6-0, 6-3 in 54 minutes to win her fourth championship at the All England Club. Navratilova wins seven matches without relinquishing a set en route to the title in less than six hours total time. Says Navratilova, "I've been the favorite the last two years to win every match that I've played. If I don't live up to it, the whole world seems to come tumbling down. It's a disaster, a tragedy, like there's nothing worse that could happen in the world to you but lose a tennis match. After the French, everyone was predicting that I would come apart at the seams. If anything, it inspired me to play better, more aggressively." Entering the final, Navratilova had lost only four matches in 18 months, most recently to unheralded Kathy Horvath in the fourth round of the French Open four weeks earlier in one of the biggest upsets in tennis history.

1904 Rene Lacoste, the most famous of the French "Four Musketeers" who uses his talents and marketability as a tennis player to launch one of the greatest sportswear labels in the world, is born in Paris. Lacoste wins Wimbledon (1925, 1928) and the U.S. Championships (1926, 1927) twice, the French Championships (1925, 1927, 1929) three times and leads the French Davis Cup to its famous 1927 upset of the United States, bringing the world's most famous team tennis trophy to France for the first time. After injuries cut short his career, he starts the famous clothing line bearing his name "Lacoste" featuring a logo of a crocodile—his nickname was the crocodile because he was known to "slither" around the back of the court chasing ball after ball.

July 3

1970 In the longest women's singles final in games in Wimbledon history, Margaret Court defeats Billie Jean King 14-12, 11-9 in 46 games in a two-and-a-half-hour classic women's singles final. Writes Bud Collins in *The Bud Collins History of Tennis* of the match, "Both players were hurt. Court had a painfully strained and swollen ankle tightly strapped as she went on court. She had taken a pain-killing injection beforehand. King was hobbling on a deteriorated kneecap, which required surgery immediately after Wimbledon. Nevertheless, BJK broke service in the first set three times. Each time Court broke back. Their injuries partially dictated the pattern of play, but both players produced magnificent shots under pressure."

1936 A ruptured Achilles tendon suffered by Gottfried von Cramm contributes to the least competitive men's singles final in Wimbledon history as Fred Perry defeats the German 6-1, 6-1, 6-0. Von Cramm suffers his injury in the first set and hopples through the remainder of the match. The championship is Perry's third straight and final singles title at Wimbledon as the 27-year-old jumps from the amateur game into the world of professional tennis. In 1978, when Bjorn Borg becomes the first man to win three straight singles titles since Perry, the Englishman, who by then was a radio commentator, is one of the first to congratulate the Swede.

1954 Nineteen-year-old Maureen Connolly wins her third Wimbledon title, and her ninth—and final—major singles title, defeating Louise Brough 6-2, 7-5 in the final. Two weeks following the win, Connolly suffers a career-ending leg injury when the horse she is riding hits a cement truck. Connolly plays Wimbledon three times—winning the championship all three times. During her career, Connolly plays 11 majors tournaments, winning nine titles.

2005 Roger Federer wins Wimbledon for a third straight year, defeating Andy Roddick, 6-2, 7-6 (2), 6-4 in the championship match. Says Roddick of the match in an entertaining post-match press conference, "I feel like I played decent, the statistics are decent and I got straight-setted. But I am not going to sit around and sulk and cry. I did everything I could. I tried playing different ways. I tried going to his forehand and coming in. He passed me. I tried to go to his backhand and coming in. He passed me. Tried staying back, he figured out a way to pass me, even though I was at the baseline. Hope he gets bored or something." Says Roddick of his personal feelings for

Federer, "I have loads of respect for him as a person. I've told him before, 'I'd love to hate you, but you're really nice'."

2004 Seventeen-year-old Maria Sharapova powers her way to her first major singles title, defeating two-time defending champion Serena Williams 6-1, 6-4 to win the women's singles title at Wimbledon. Sharapova becomes the first Russian to win a Wimbledon singles title as well as the third-youngest women's titlist. Seed No. 13, Sharapova becomes the lowest seeded woman to win the Wimbledon women's singles crown, but loses the distinction in 2007 when Venus Williams, ranked No. 31 and seeded No. 23, claims her fourth title. Says Sharapova after the final, "I knew that the power was within me and that if I put my mind to something, I would do it." Says Williams of the loss, "I think I put too much stress on myself going into it. I really wanted to win more than anything. I was so focused the night before, the day before—I mean, a week before. Maybe I shouldn't be so hard on myself."

1953 Vic Seixas wins the men's singles title at Wimbledon—and his first major singles title—defeating unseeded Dane Kurt Nielsen 9-7, 6-3, 6-4 in the final. Says Nielsen, "I have never seen him play so well. I tightened up. It was like wearing a mental corset." Following the match, Seixas is non-committal on if he would remain on the amateur circuit and defend his title the following year. "I may or may not defend it," he says. "I would like to play in the Davis Cup against Australia, but it is time I joined my father's plumbing business."

1994 Conchita Martinez becomes the first Spanish woman to win the women's title at Wimbledon, defeating 37-year-old Martina Navratilova 6-4, 3-6, 6-3 in Navratilova's 12th and last Wimbledon women's singles final. At the time, Navratilova said the match would be her finale at Wimbledon, but the Czech-born American returns to the All-England Club for nine more tournaments—including another singles sojourn in 2004—before playing her final event at the All England Club in 2006. Writes John Roberts of *The Independent* "It was, the great champion assured us, the last shot she will make at the All England Club, certainly in singles matches, and it may transpire to be the last to be seen from her in any tournament." Says Navratilova of Martinez, "Today she passed me as well as anybody ever has...even Monica Seles."

1983 John McEnroe cruises to his second men's singles title at Wimbledon with a 6-2, 6-2, 6-2 final-round victory over unseeded Chris Lewis of New Zealand. McEnroe loses only nine points in 12 service games during the 1 hour, 25 minute final.

1971 John Newcombe wins his third Wimbledon men's singles title, defeating Stan Smith 6-3, 5-7, 2-6, 6-4, 6-4 in a thrilling final. Writes Bud Collins in *The Bud Collins History of Tennis*, "The final between Newcombe and Smith had fewer breathtaking rallies and was dominated by slam-bang points accentuating the serve-volley power of both, but it also became gripping in the end. Smith seemed in control after a seven-game run that took him to 1-0 in the fourth set, but this was his first major final and he got "a little tired mentally."

1985 Kevin Curren routs two-time defending champion John McEnroe 6-2, 6-2, 6-4 in the quarterfinals of Wimbledon, in the worst loss ever by McEnroe in his Wimbledon career. The loss ends McEnroe's five-year run of reaching at least the Wimbledon final.

July 4

1981 Twenty-two-year-old John McEnroe wins the men's singles title at Wimbledon for the first time in his career, ending five-time defending champion Bjorn Borg's 41-match winning streak at the All England Club with a 4-6, 7-6(1), 7-6 (4), 6-4 final-round victory. "On all the important points," says Borg after the final, "John hit his first serve. And that was crucial, especially in the tiebreakers." McEnroe goes on to win two more Wimbledon titles (1983, 1984), while Borg never again plays in The Championships, virtually retiring from the sport at the end of the 1981 season.

1982 In the longest men's singles final in Wimbledon history at the time, Jimmy Connors edges John McEnroe 3-6, 6-3, 6-7 (2), 7-6 (5), 6-4 in 4 hours, 14 minutes to win his second men's singles title at Wimbledon. Both players finish the match having won 173 points each. Says Connors, who claims his second of two career Wimbledon titles, to go with his 1974 title, "I was going to do anything to not let this chance slip by. I was going to fight to the death." With rain delaying play in the mixed doubles event, Anne Smith and Kevin Curren are forced to play four mixed doubles matches on the final day of the event, winning the title with a 2-6, 6-3, 7-5 final-round decision over Wendy Turnbull and John Lloyd.

1993 Pete Sampras wins the first of his record-tying seven Wimbledon championships, defeating fellow American Jim Courier 7-6 (3), 7-6 (6), 3-6, 6-3 in the men's singles final. Sampras fires 22 aces and puts to rest the controversy of him being ranked No. 1 in the world, despite not having won a major tournament title since the U.S. Open in 1990 and Courier holding the Australian Open title and reaching the final of the French Open. Says Sampras, "There's been a lot of controversy over the computer, how come I'm No. 1 (when) Jim was in the finals of the French and won the Australian. He can't take this title away from me and now I'm No. 1. I don't think there will be any more controversy." Courier's final round showing makes him the 14th man to reach all four major singles finals in his career.

1947 With King George VI and Queen Elizabeth in the Royal Box, Jack Kramer cruises to his first Wimbledon title, defeating fellow American Tom Brown 6-1, 6-3, 6-2 in just 48 minutes. Kramer wins the title losing only 37 games in seven matches and is the first man to win at the All England Club wearing shorts rather than the traditional long flannel pants.

1999 Pete Sampras claims a piece of tennis history winning his sixth Wimbledon crown, defeating fellow American Andre Agassi 6-3, 6-4, 7-5 in the men's singles final. The win was the 12th major singles title for Sampras, tying him with Roy Emerson as holder of the most major men's singles titles. In the women's singles final, Lindsay Davenport wins her first Wimbledon singles title, defeating seven-time champion Steffi Graf 6-4, 7-5. Following the match, Graf announces that she will not return to the All England Club as a player, "I won't be back. I won't be here as a player again," says Graf. "Right now I'm a little sad about everything. I'm not ready to talk about what I'm going to do next." Weeks later, Graf subsequently announces her complete retirement from the game.

1975 Billie Jean King wins the most lopsided Wimbledon women's singles final since 1911, defeating Evonne Goolagong 6-0, 6-1 to win her sixth singles title and 19th overall title at the All England Club. King's 19th title ties her with Elizabeth Ryan for the all-time Wimbledon record. Ryan never wins the singles title at the All England Club but captures 12 doubles and seven mixed crowns between 1914 and 1934. Following the match, King says she is retiring from Wimbledon singles play because of her depilating knee. "I want to quit on top," she says, "and I can't get much higher than this." She, however, eventually returns to singles play in 1977 and reaches the semifinals in 1982 and 1983.

1970 John Newcombe wins his second Wimbledon men's singles title, defeating countryman Ken Rosewall 5-7, 6-3, 6-2, 3-6, 6-1 in the first five-set final in 21 years at the All England Club. Rosewall, denied the Wimbledon title for a third time, reaches the final 14 years after losing to Lew Hoad in the 1956 final.

1987 Thirty-year-old Martina Navratilova wins her eighth Wimbledon women's singles title—tying Helen Wills for the most ever at the All England Club—defeating Steff Graf 7-5, 6-3 in the women's singles final. The win is Navratilova's sixth straight Wimbledon title. Says Navratilova, "I don't know how many of these you have to win to be considered the greatest player of all time. But the closer I get, the more it really doesn't matter. There are great players in different eras and I'm one of the greatest in mine."

1989 In her final Wimbledon, Chris Evert rallies from a deficit of 3-5 in the final set, where she was at one point only two points from defeat, to beat Laura Golarsa of Italy 6-3, 2-6, 7-5 in the women's quarterfinals. The win is ultimately Evert's last at the All England Club after 18 years of competing at The Championships. Writes Robin Finn of the *New York Times*. "Evert has wanted to control the setting and status of her exit, and not until she arrived at Wimbledon for the 18th time had she thought she was ready to begin viewing her tournaments as if she might never see them again. She could bear the thought of leaving the game, but only if she left it with her reputation intact, as a viable Grand Slam challenger and not a hanger-on. To accomplish that, she needed to advance to the semifinals at Wimbledon, a vantage point from which she thinks she can begin to make an honorable exit from tennis." Says Evert in her post-match press conference, "In the third set I thought, this isn't the way I would like to go out of the tournament if it would be my last tournament, which it probably would be."

1988 Twenty-two-year-old Stefan Edberg wins his first Wimbledon men's singles crown, defeating two-time champion Boris Becker 4-6, 7-6, 6-4, 6-2. The final marks the first Wimbledon final to be played over two days as rain postpones play from Sunday with Edberg leading 3-2 in the first set. Says Edberg, "It's hard to believe I really won it. This is something I've worked a long time for. It was my target this year. It's a fantastic feeling that hasn't sunk into my system yet."

1996 Three-time defending champion Pete Sampras is dismissed from the quarterfinals of Wimbledon in a flurry of 29 aces from Richard Krajicek 7-5, 7-6 (3), 6-4. Says Krajicek of his upset victory, "It's a good feeling. I mean, I'm not unbelievably excited yet because I'm still in the tournament, but I have a proud feeling that I'm the first one in four years to beat him at Wimbledon."

July 5

1980 In one of the greatest matches in the history of the sport, Bjorn Borg wins his fifth consecutive Wimbledon singles title defeating John McEnroe 1-6, 7-5, 6-3, 6-7 (16), 8-6 in 3 hours, 53 minutes. McEnroe saves five match points in the titanic 34-point fourth-set tie-break that itself is called "The Battle of 18-16." Writes Neil Amdur of the *New York Times*, "If this marathon was not the greatest major championship final ever played—and tennis historians treasure the past with reverence—it ranked as one of the most exciting." Says Borg, who collects $50,000 first prize for the victory, "For sure, it is the best match I have ever played at Wimbledon."

1975 Thirty-one-year-old Arthur Ashe wins Wimbledon for the first time, becoming the first black man to win the men's singles title at the All England Club, defeating Jimmy Connors 6-1, 6-1, 5-7, 6-4 in a shock upset. The first All-American men's singles final at Wimbledon since 1947 is played under unique and bizarre circumstances as Connors has two lawsuits pending against his opponent—slander and liable—totaling $8 million. Writes Bud Collins in *The Bud Collins History of Tennis*, "Arthur's friends worried that he'd be embarrassed in the title bout as Ken Rosewall had been 12 months earlier. Their concern was unnecessary. Arthur changed speed and spin smartly, fed junk to Connors' forehand, exposing the vulnerability of that wing to paceless shots, and sliced his serves wide to Connors' backhand, exploiting the slightly limited reach of his two-handed shot."

1919 In what is regarded as one of the greatest and most important women's tennis matches in the history of the sport, 20-year-old Suzanne Lenglen defeats Dorothea Douglass Chambers 10-8, 4-6, 9-7 in the women's singles final at Wimbledon. The final is the longest female final at the All England Club (until Margaret Smith Court's 14-12, 11-9 win over Billie Jean King in 1970) and propels Lenglen into international acclaim and the sport of tennis and Wimbledon to greater heights and popularity. Writes the Associated Press of Lenglen, "For one so young, she is said to use remarkable generalship, playing with a dash comparable to that of a masculine expert....Small of stature, she is limber and lithe and frequently recovers a seemingly lost shot."

1968 Rod Laver wins the first "Open" Wimbledon, defeating countryman Tony Roche 6-3, 6-4, 6-2 in a 59-minute men's singles final. It is the third straight title for Laver—who wins Wimbledon titles in 1961 and 1962 before turning professional and being unable to compete at The Championships until 1968 when the event becomes open to professionals and amateurs.

2008 Venus Williams wins her fifth Wimbledon singles title, defeating younger sister Serena Williams 7-5, 6-4 in the women's singles final. The final marks the third Wimbledon final and seventh major final where the two most famous sisters in tennis face off against each other. The sisters also played Wimbledon finals in 2002 and 2003—both won by Serena. Says Venus following the match if she is ever able to block out that she is playing her sister, "At no point am I ever able to forget Serena, because I have the ultimate respect for her game and I have a lot of respect for her serve. If I was playing anyone else I wouldn't have to face what I had to face today, so it's impossible to forget."

1992 Twenty-two-year-old Andre Agassi breaks through and finally wins his first major singles title, withstanding 37 aces from lefty Goran Ivanisevic of Croatia to win the men's singles title at Wimbledon with a 6-7 (10-8), 6-4, 6-4, 1-6, 6-4 final-round decision. It is ironic that Agassi breaks through and makes Wimbledon his first major title as the colorful Las Vegan hated grass court tennis so much that after losing in Wimbledon's first round in 1987 he vowed never to return. He did return in 1991, causing much attention for adhering to Wimbledon's all-white clothing rule despite his objections. Prior to his Wimbledon victory, Agassi loses three major tournament finals—the 1990 French Open final to Andres Gomez, the 1990 U.S. Open final to Pete Sampras and the 1991 French Open to Jim Courier. Says Agassi of his thoughts when Ivanisevic's final volley goes into the net, "I couldn't believe it was over with. Many things were running through my mind. I was Wimbledon champion, Grand Slam (event) winner. Lots of months and years of people doubting me, and I thought of all the people that believed in me and it just was overwhelming. It is quite an irony. You know, I really have had my chances to fulfill a lot of my dreams, and I have not come through in the past. To do it here is more than I could ever ask for."

1987 Pat Cash becomes the first Australian men's singles champion at Wimbledon in 16 years, defeating Ivan Lendl 7-6, 6-2, 7-5 in men's singles final. Seeded No. 11, Cash becomes the first Australian men's champion at Wimbledon since John Newcombe in 1971. Following his victory, the 22-year-old Cash famously climbs into the player's box to hug and share his moment of victory with his friends and family.

1946 In the first post-war staging of Wimbledon—with damage to the club due to bombings still not repaired—Yvon Petra of France wins the men's singles title defeating Geoff Brown of Australia, 6-2, 6-4, 7-9, 5-7, 6-4.

1985 Kevin Curren fires 17 aces in one of the most one-sided and surprising Wimbledon semifinal performances, shell-shocking two-time champion Jimmy Connors 6-2, 6-2, 6-1 to advance in the men's singles final for the first time in his career. Says Connors of Curren's serve, "He just throws it up there and boom, boom. When he's catching the ball on the way up, spanking the ball the way he does, it's tough to counteract."

2003 Serena Williams defeats older sister Venus Williams 4-6, 6-4, 6-2 in 2 hours, 3 minutes to win her second Wimbledon women's singles title. Venus suffers from an aggravated strained abdominal muscle during the final, but plays injured and does not retire from the match for fear of criticism that the match could have been fixed. "First, there's always the 'what if?' in the back of your head," says Venus "And second, it's just hard these days. Serena and I have taken a lot of [flack], so I felt I had to take one for the team. It hasn't been easy. Serena and I, we've been blamed for a lot of things that never even happened. I felt I had to play today. I think everyone's quite familiar with the history. So today was a good effort. And I wanted to play. I had to at least show up and go out on the court. So that definitely was a decision on my own." Says Serena, "In a way it is too bad. I just hope she hasn't injured herself more due to that fact. But I don't know, it's just really taking one for the team. She really took one for the team, and not only in thought. I didn't know it was that serious. I knew it was serious, but ... [she] nearly beat me." The Wimbledon title is Serena's first major title defense and her sixth career major singles title.

July 6

2008 In what is widely described as one of the greatest tennis matches—if not the greatest tennis match—ever played, Rafael Nadal defeats Roger Federer in a Wimbledon final for the ages. Nadal wins his first men's singles title at the All England Club and stops the run of five-straight Wimbledon titles of Federer in a gripping 6-4, 6-4, 6-7 (5), 6-7 (8), 9-7 final in the longest singles final in Wimbledon history at 4 hours, 48 minutes. Nadal, the four-time French Open champion, becomes the first man to win the French title and Wimbledon in the same year since Bjorn Borg in 1980 and prevents Federer from winning his sixth straight Wimbledon men's singles title, an unprecedented feat in the modern era of tennis and only achieved by Willie Renshaw from 1881 to 1887 when reigning champions only had to play the final to defend their championship. In addition to holding a two-sets-to-love lead, Nadal holds two match points in the fourth-set tie-break—at 6-5 and 8-7—the latter being snatched away with a brilliant backhand passing shot from the reigning champion. Federer himself is two points from victory in the fifth set leading 5-4. Three rain delays highlight the match, including a dramatic pause at 2-2, deuce, in the final set. The loss snaps Federer's 40-match win streak at the All England Club and his 65-match grass court winning streak. Praise for the match comes from all observers of the game, including John McEnroe, the three-time Wimbledon champion and TV commentator who labels the encounter, "The greatest match I've ever seen." Jon Wertheim of *Sports Illustrated* describes the match as "a spell-binging men's final that will stand as the benchmark against which all future tennis matches will be measured."

1986 Eighteen-year-old Boris Becker repeats as Wimbledon champion, winning the 100th men's singles title at Wimbledon defeating Ivan Lendl 6-4, 6-3, 7-5 in the final. Becker is given the trophy by 87-year-old Jean Borotra, who was the oldest living men's singles champion. Says Becker, "Winning Wimbledon this year was much more satisfying for me than last year. Then, I was a nobody. This time I really proved that I can play well on grass, proved that I am a legitimate Wimbledon champion." The Centre Court crowd includes British Prime Minister Margaret Thatcher, former men's champions Don Budge and Fred Perry, singer Tina Turner and actress Faye Dunaway.

2003 Roger Federer wins a major tournament for the first time, defeating Mark Philippoussis 7-6 (5), 6-2, 7-6 (3) in the men's singles final at

Wimbledon. The 21-year-old Federer becomes the first Swiss man in 117 editions of The Championships to win the title. Federer hits 21 aces and 50 winners against only nine unforced errors in the 1 hour, 56-minute final. "It's an absolute dream for me coming true," says Federer after the victory.

1962 Rod Laver needs only 53 minutes to dispatch fellow Australian Marty Mulligan 6-2, 6-2, 6-1 to win the men's singles title at Wimbledon and the third leg of his eventual 1962 Grand Slam sweep of all four major singles titles. Writes Fred Tupper of the *New York Times*, "Laver's one-sided triumph confirmed what everybody has known all along: that the 23-year-old Australian is the best player in amateur tennis today and one of the great ones of our time." Says Laver, simply, after the match, "I thought I played very well."

1974 Twenty-one-year-old Jimmy Connors bullies his way to his first Wimbledon men's singles title, defeating 39-year-old Ken Rosewall 6-1, 6-1, 6-4 in the final. Writes Bud Collins in *The Bud Collins History of Tennis*, "Connors' ferocious returns of Rosewall's unintimidating serves kept the old man constantly on the defensive, the young lion always on the attack. Consequently, Connors became the youngest champion since Lew Hoad beat Rosewall at age 22 in the 1956 final. Rosewall, the sentimental choice who had been runner-up in 1954, 56, 70, remains, along with Pancho Gonzalez, Gottfried von Cramm, Fred Stolle and Ivan Lendl, 'the greatest players who never won Wimbledon."

1996 MaliVai Washington rallies from a 1-5 fifth-set deficit to defeat a nerve-rattled Todd Martin 5-7, 6-4, 6-7 (6), 6-3, 10-8 in the men's semifinals of Wimbledon, to become the first black men's singles finalist at Wimbledon since Arthur Ashe in 1975. Richard Krajicek of the Netherlands also advances into the championship match, defeating Jason Stoltenberg of Australia 7-5, 6-2, 6-1. Martin self-admittedly "froze up" when serving for the final on two occasions. Says Martin after the match, "I've played this game a lot and I've never felt a feeling like today. That's why I play, to overcome something like that. I think everybody has experienced some bit of tightness before, and you go through your rituals and routines and make sure those don't change. That didn't happen." Says Washington of his comparisons to Ashe, "I have a lot of support from the black community in the States and around the world. It's great when you when you can win because you're winning for yourself, and you're winning for those who are pulling for you. It's an honor to be the first black since Arthur to be in the final."

1934 Fred Perry of Britain wins Wimbledon for the first of three straight times, playing at times flawless tennis in defeating Jack Crawford of Australia 6-3, 6-0, 7-5 in the final. Perry wins at one stretch 12 games in a row and says after the final, "If I live to be 100, I'll never play so well again." Perry becomes the first Brit to win the men's singles title since Arthur Gore in 1909—the year that Perry is born.

1935 Helen Jacobs loses the Wimbledon women's singles final to Helen Wills Moody in heart-breaking fashion, missing a simple overhead smash on match point leading 5-3 in the final set, only to lose 6-3, 3-6, 7-5. The title is the seventh Wimbledon singles title for Wills, who wins an eighth and final singles title again in 1938. Writes Bud Collins in *The Bud Collins History of Tennis* of Jacobs and her mishap, "Jacobs took a winning 4-2 lead in the third, with one powerful serve knocking the racket from Moody's hand. She then broke Moody's serve to lead 5-2, but Moody broke back to 3-5 in a game where she was facing a match point at 40-30 and Moody flicked a desperation lob with Jacobs at the net. It looked like a simple smash, but a gusty wind caused the ball to sink so swiftly that Jacobs had to drop to her knees to hit it...into the net. That turned the match around. Jacobs went down fighting, serving two aces when trailing 5-6, but losing the match, 6-3, 3-6, 7-5. It was her fourth loss to Moody at Wimbledon, three in a final. Jacobs also lost to Moody in the 1928 U.S. final."

2001 Two points from defeat, Patrick Rafter defeats Andre Agassi 2-6, 6-3, 3-6, 6-2, 8-6 in the semifinals of Wimbledon, in the third consecutive Wimbledon semifinal meeting between the two players. Agassi leads 5-3 in the fifth set—and is two points from victory serving for the match at 5-4, 30-15—but is unable to close out his Australian rival. At 6-6 in the fifth-set, Agassi is unable to convert a break point opportunity, and allegedly utters an obscenity, which a lineswoman reports to the chair umpire Mike Morrissey, resulting a code violation warning. The incident rattles Agassi as he loses the next two games—and the match. Says a classy Rafter, "I think it was that lady that really got him in the end. Just let it go. Only one person heard it...I was just very, very fortunate to get through. Nothing really went his way today even the line judge giving him the code violation. Probably a couple of line calls didn't go his way either. You know, I just feel sort of sad for him but I have to enjoy the moment as well."

1996 Steffi Graf defeats a stubborn Arantxa Sanchez Vicario 6-3, 7-5 to win the women's singles title at Wimbledon. Sanchez Vicario rallies from an 0-4 deficit in the second set to make the final competitive, but is not able to extend Graf into a third set. "It was too little, too late," says Sanchez Vicario.

1985 Martina Navratilova wins her sixth Wimbledon singles title and her fourth in a row, defeating Chris Evert Lloyd 4-6, 6-3, 6-2 in the women's singles final. The win avenges Navratilova's loss to Evert Lloyd from the French Open, where Evert Lloyd returns to the world No. 1 ranking. Says Navratilova, "This was my most satisfying win. I've lost three matches this year and everyone said I was going downhill. Every year, there is more pressure. Every year, there is so much to prove. Six isn't enough." Says Evert Lloyd, "I had chances but Martina rose to the occasion. This match was disappointing to me because I had beaten her in the French and had played so well here. I felt it was 50-50 going into the match even though it was on grass. But I'm not going to pout about it." The victory places Navratilova back at No. 1 in the world rankings. Says Navratilova of her rivalry with Evert Lloyd, "Chris and I are ahead of the field. I don't think I'm going to be around long enough for a future rival to be as great as Chris. Even if I play another three or four years, it will take a while longer for someone else to develop."

1989 Thirty-four-year-old Chris Evert bids adieu to Wimbledon as Steffi Graf defeats the three-time champion 6-2, 6-1 in the women's singles semi-finals in her 109th and final match at the All England Club. Writes Robin Finn of the *New York Times*, "Evert dropped a quick curtsy in front of the royal box, beamed an apologetic grin toward her husband, Andy Mill, the former Olympic skier, gave a sweeping wave of goodbye toward the crowd and vanished down a hallway with the impassive Graf striding at her side. Evert looked, as she had throughout the tournament, unperturbed." Martina Navratilova defeats Catarina Lindqvist of Sweden 7-6, 6-2 in the other women's semifinal.

July 7

1978 Martina Navratilova wins Wimbledon for the first time in her career—the first of her record nine singles titles at the All England Club—rallying to defeat Chris Evert 2-6, 6-4, 7-5 in the women's singles final. Navratilova trails 2-4 in the third set, but rallies and wins 12 of the last 13 points of the match. Says Navratilova, "I thought I could win before the match, but I didn't really believe that I could be the Wimbledon champion. It's only once a year that you get the chance, and this was the first time that I was in the finals. Most people thought that Chris would win, but I came through...I always wondered what it would be like. If I could sleep the night before? How it would feel going on the court? If I could keep walking if I had to serve for the match? What I would do if I ever won? It's very different from what you think."

1985 Seventeen-year-old Boris Becker of West Germany becomes the youngest men's singles champion in Wimbledon history when he defeats Kevin Curren 6-3, 6-7 (4), 7-6 (3), 6-4 in the men's singles final. Becker also becomes the first German to win a singles title at the All England Club and the first unseeded champion. Becker fires 21 aces during the match to Curren's 19. Says Becker "I'm the first German, and I think that will change tennis in Germany. They never had an idol, and now maybe they have one." Says Curren, who defeats both Jimmy Connors and John McEnroe en route to the final, "He never had to play a McEnroe or Connors but what Becker did was a sign of great maturity for someone that young. He's got the qualities of a champion. At 17, I would have been totally intimidated by the whole atmosphere."

1933 Jack Crawford wins the men's singles title at Wimbledon, defeating Ellsworth Vines 4-6, 11-9, 6-2, 2-6, 6-4 in the final to become to the first man in the history of tennis to win three major titles in the same year. Crawford, who earlier in the year wins at the Australian Championships and the French Championships, has his bid to win the first "Grand Slam" in tennis history stopped by Fred Perry in five sets in the final of the U.S. Championships later in the summer.

1934 Forty-two-year-old Elizabeth (Bunny) Ryan pairs with France's Simone Passemard Mathieu to win her 12th Wimbledon women's doubles title and her record 19th Wimbledon title, posting a 6-3, 6-3 win over Dorothy

Andrus and Sylvia Jung Henrotin. Ryan's record stands at the All England Club until 1979 when Billie Jean King wins her 20th Wimbledon title.

1979 Billie Jean King wins her record 20th Wimbledon title, pairing with Martina Navratilova to defeat Wendy Turnbull and Betty Stove 5-7, 6-3, 6-2 in the women's doubles final. King breaks the record that she previously shares with Elizabeth Ryan, who tragically and ironically, dies of a heart attack at age 87 while attending the women's singles final the previous day. Ryan never wins a Wimbledon singles title, but sets the record for titles by winning the women's doubles 12 times and the mixed doubles seven times between 1914 and 1934.

1961 Rod Laver wins Wimbledon for the first time in his career, defeating American Chuck McKinley 6-3, 6-1, 6-4 in the final. Laver goes on to win the title in 1962—then after a six-year hiatus after he turns professional before the advent of the "Open" era in 1968—he wins titles in 1968 and 1969 and reaches the fourth round in 1970 to win 31 straight Wimbledon singles matches.

1979 Borg Borg rallies from a two-sets-to-one deficit to defeat Roscoe Tanner 6-7 (4), 6-1, 3-6, 6-3, 6-4 in 2 hours, 49 minutes to win his fourth straight Wimbledon men's singles title. Borg calls the confrontation, "the toughest match I have played here, absolutely" and admits after the match that when Tanner fights off three match points with Borg leading 5-4, 40-0 in the fifth set, that he had "never been so nervous in my life." Says Borg, "I always felt that I was one step behind Roscoe, even when I was a break ahead of him in the fifth set. I always was a little bit behind because he was serving so well. I had so many problems to break his serve." Says Tanner, "You've got to take chances against Bjorn. You can't go out and just play careful tennis because he's better than anybody else at that type of game. You've got to take some chances on his second serve, mix up your serves and keep him from getting into a groove. If you play just a steady, hard-hitting game, he likes that. You've got to do some things to break up his rhythm, take some gambles, go for your shots all the time. You can't worry if you miss some, because if you start staying back and playing his game, you're going to get beaten for sure."

2007 In a Wimbledon final played between the two lowest-ranked finalists, No. 31 Venus Williams wins her fourth Wimbledon title, defeating No. 20 Marion Bartoli 6-4, 6-1 in the championship match. Williams becomes the lowest ranked woman to win the Wimbledon title. Says Williams, "I was really motivated because no one picked me to win. They didn't even say, 'She can't win.' They weren't even talking about me. I never would doubt myself that way."

1991 In the first all-German men's singles final at Wimbledon—played on what would have been the 82nd birthday of the great German player of the 1930s Gottfried von Cramm—Michael Stich wins his first and only major singles title, upsetting three-time Wimbledon champion Boris Becker 6-4, 7-6 (4), 6-4. Says Stich of his near flawless display of tennis, "I had the feeling I could touch every ball I wanted to that was going into the court." Becker says after the match that he already came to grips with losing well before the final ball is struck. "It hit me already during the match," he says. "I knew that, if he was not going to make big mistakes, I'm not going to win it today because I didn't have enough energy. So I was already, during the match, thinking about why."

1967 John Newcombe wins the final amateur Wimbledon men's singles title—and the first of his three singles titles at the All England Club—defeating unseeded West German Wilhelm Bungert 6-3, 6-1, 6-1 in the final. Bungert's five games are the fewest in a Wimbledon men's final since Marty Mulligan also wins five games against Rod Laver in the 1962 final. The following year at Wimbledon, the tournament is opened to professionals as well as amateur players and prize money begins to be awarded.

1996 Richard Krajicek becomes the first Dutchman to win a major singles title when he is the unlikely men's singles champion at Wimbledon with a 6-3, 6-4, 6-3 victory over MaliVai Washington. "Of course I was unbelievably happy, and then when I did it, I thought, 'Is the match really over?'" says Krajicek after the match. "For a split second, I thought, "Am I making a fool of myself?' but nobody started laughing too much so I thought I won anyway." The beginning of the match is highlighted by a female streaker who runs onto Centre Court just prior to the warm-up.

2002 World No. 1 Lleyton Hewitt of Australia wins his second major singles title, defeating David Nalbandian of Argentina 6-1, 6-3, 6-2 in the men's singles final at Wimbledon. Hewitt becomes the first Australian to win at the All England Club since Pat Cash in 1987 and does it by winning the most-lopsided final since 1984. At age 21, Hewitt is also the youngest men's champion since 1986.

July 8

2007 With Bjorn Borg watching from the Royal Box, Roger Federer wins his fifth-straight Wimbledon men's singles title—equaling the mark set by Borg from 1976-1980—with a dramatic 7-6 (7), 4-6, 7-6 (3), 2-6, 6-2 win over Rafael Nadal. Writes Elizabeth Clarke of the *Washington Post*, "With his idol looking on and his fiercest rival across the net, Roger Federer put an end to a five-set battle of artistry and stamina in Sunday's Wimbledon championship with a thunderous overhead slam. Then he dropped to his knees, fell on his back and wept. The pressure Federer had shouldered with such grace this Wimbledon fortnight erupted in the form of tears the moment his winning shot delivered his fifth consecutive Wimbledon championship, equaling the mark set from 1976 to '80 by the masterful Bjorn Borg, who watched with approval from the Royal Box." Says Federer, "I'm just happy with such a great run, especially at Wimbledon, the most important tournament of my life. I'm loving every moment of it."

1978 Bjorn Borg wins Wimbledon for a third time in a row, easily defeating Jimmy Connors 6-2, 6-2, 6-3 in 1 hour, 49 minutes in the men's singles final. Borg becomes the first man to win three successive Wimbledon singles titles since Englishman Fred Perry in 1934-35-36. Says Borg "I was not scared of his game when he was serving. I felt I could maybe break even every single time." Borg receives $34,200 for winning the title. Perry, a broadcast journalist at the tournament, is one of the first people to offer their congratulations to Borg following the match. Says Perry of Borg to reporters "He's won three French, two Italian and three Wimbledon championships, that is not bad for a beginning, at 22. I didn't win my first Wimbledon until I was 25. This wasn't a great emotional final, in the sense of being close, but it was a demonstration of tennis you'd have to wait a lot of years to see again." Connors famously says of Borg after the match, "I'll chase that son of a bitch to the ends of the earth" in order to beat him.

1996 Martina Hingis becomes the youngest winner of a women's title at Wimbledon when at the age of 15 years and 282 days she pairs with 31-year-old Helena Sukova to defeat Meredith McGrath and Larisa Neiland 5-7, 7-5, 6-1 in a rain-delayed Monday women's doubles final at the All England Club. Hingis is three days younger than Charlotte "Lottie" Dod was in 1887 when she wins the first of her five singles titles. Says Hingis, "For every tennis player, this is a big goal to win Wimbledon, even it it's doubles. But I hope one time it will the singles, too." Hingis, would oblige one year later.

2006 Amelie Mauresmo loses the label of Grand Slam tournament choker as she defeats Justine Henin-Hardenne 2-6, 6-3, 6-4 in the women's singles final at Wimbledon. Mauresmo defeats Henin-Hardenne earlier in the year in the final of the Australian Open for her first major title, but the title is somewhat "tainted" when Henin-Hardenne retires in the championship match, not allowing Mauresmo the opportunity to close out the victory. Says Mauresmo following her victory at Wimbledon, "I don't want anyone to talk about my nerves anymore."

1989 Boris Becker rallies to defeat world No. 1 Ivan Lendl 7-5, 6-7, 2-6, 6-4, 6-3 in the Wimbledon semifinals, again denying Lendl the Wimbledon title that he so desperately seeks after reaching the finals on two occasions and the semifinals on six occasions. Says Lendl, "I don't think I did anything wrong today. I was extremely disappointed and I was pretty upset, too, actually. Last year I really didn't have much of a chance. This year, I thought I played well and I thought I had a good chance."

1984 John McEnroe thrashes Jimmy Connors 6-1, 6-1, 6-2 to win his third—and what ultimately becomes his last—Wimbledon singles title. McEnroe commits only two unforced errors in the 80-minute blow-out, the most lop-sided Wimbledon men's singles final since Don Budge also gives up only four games in beating Bunny Austin in 1938. McEnroe connects on 75 percent of his first serves, fires 11 aces and doesn't allow Connors a break point opportunity. Connors wins only 11 points on McEnroe's serve the entire afternoon. Says McEnroe, "It was one of the greatest matches I've ever played."

1961 Brits Angela Mortimer and Christine Truman play in the first all-British women's final at Wimbledon since 1914 with Mortimer claiming the 4-6, 6-4, 7-5 victory to become the first English champ since Dorothy Round in 1937.

1963 Margaret Smith becomes the first Australian woman to win the singles title at Wimbledon, defeating Billie Jean Moffit 6-3, 6-4 in the final, avenging her loss to Billie Jean in the first round of the tournament the previous year.

2001 Venus Williams successfully defends her women's singles title at Wimbledon, defeating Justine Henin of Belgium 6-1, 3-6, 6-0 in the final. Williams becomes the first repeat women's champion at Wimbledon since Steffi Graf in 1995-96.

July 9

2001 In one of the greatest finals in the history of Wimbledon, Goran Ivanisevic edges Patrick Rafter 6-3, 3-6, 6-3, 2-6, 9-7 in rain-delayed "People's Monday" final. Ivanisevic, previously a three-time runner-up at the All England Club, wins the title with a ranking of No. 125 due to injuries—only gaining entry into the tournament via a wild-card—making him the lowest-ranked player to ever win the Wimbledon title. Rafter, playing in his final Wimbledon, is denied the title he desperately seeks. Writes Christine Brennan of *USA Today*, "Many, many decades from now, on the day that Centre Court finally crumbles, people will talk about this day, this match, this crowd, this man. No one will ever forget what happened Monday at Wimbledon, that Goran Ivanisevic, a wildly popular player who had never won a Grand Slam tournament; a superstitious, outspoken, rather bizarre man who required a special invitation just to get into the tournament this year, finally won the most prestigious title in his sport." Says the 29-year-old Ivanisevic, "This is so great, to touch the trophy. I mean, I don't even care now if I ever win a match in my life again. If I don't want to play, I don't play again. This is it. This is end of the world." The match is also highlighted by the spirited crowd of Croats and Australians who wave flags, sing songs and, in the case of the Australians, wave inflatable kangaroos. With the match being played on Monday, the All England Club make 10,000 tickets available to the average tennis fans. Writes Brennan, "Centre Court, waiting to be filled for this marquee moment, and not by the lords and ladies of Britain who applaud so politely for two straight weeks, but by normal people who scream and yell and actually care passionately about who wins and loses." Adds Rafter, "I don't know if Wimbledon's seen anything like it. I don't know if they will again. It was electric. It's what we play for. It was so much fun." Says Ivanisevic of the atmosphere, "This is just too good. I don't think it's ever going to happen in the history. So many Australian fans, Croatians. I mean, like a football match. I never enjoy more playing tennis than today. The crowd was just too good."

1972 In the first-ever Wimbledon final played on a Sunday—due to a rain delay—Stan Smith and Ilie Nastase compete in an epic men's singles final, with the American edging the Romanian 4-6, 6-3, 6-3, 4-6, 7-5. Writes Bud Collins in *The Bud Collins History of Tennis*, "It was Smith's serve-volley power and forthright resolve against Nastase's incomparable speed, agility and eccentric artistry. The fifth set was electrifying. Smith escaped two break points in the fifth game, which went to seven agonizing deuces, the first with a lunging volley off the wooden frame of his racket. Nastase brushed aside two match points on his serve at 4-5, saved another after having 40-0 at 5-6, then netted an easy, high backhand volley on match point No. 4."

1989 In a hallmark day for German tennis, Boris Becker and Steffi Graf win Wimbledon singles titles as Graf wins a rain-delayed women's singles final, defeating Martina Navratilova 6-2, 6-7, 6-1, while Becker defeats defending champion Stefan Edberg 6-0, 7-6, 6-4 in a rematch of the 1988 Wimbledon men's final. Becker and Graf's sweep mark the first time that Germany takes both titles in the same year and the first time since 1925 that a European nation takes both singles titles at the All England Club. Says Navratilova of her second-straight Wimbledon singles final loss to Graf, "I did everything I could, and I got beat. If I thought there was no chance I would win, or even a 50-50 chance, I wouldn't be playing anymore. I wouldn't be putting myself through this. I absolutely think that I can win." Becker's win is his third major singles title and his third at the All England Club. Says Edberg, "I've lost two Grand Slam finals within a matter of one month, and that hurts. I felt a little bit like I was playing uphill today. Things obviously aren't going much right when you lose a set 6-0."

2006 Roger Federer stops a five-match losing streak to his rival Rafael Nadal to win the men's singles title at Wimbledon, defeating the Spanish world No. 2 6-0, 7-6 (5), 6-7 (2), 6-3 to earn his fourth straight Wimbledon title and eighth career major championship. "I'm very well aware how important this match was for me," says Federer, who lost the last four finals against Nadal, including at the French Open four weeks earlier. "If I lose, it's a hard blow for me. It's important for me to win a final against him for a change, and beat him for a change. Wimbledon I knew was going to be the place for me to do it the easiest way, and it turned out to be tough."

1920 Bill Tilden, one of the greatest U.S. Davis Cup players of all time, makes his Davis Cup debut as he defeats William Laurentz 4-6, 6-2, 6-1, 6-3 to give the United States a 2-0 lead over France in the opening round at Devonshire Park, Eastbourne, England.

July 10

1943 Arthur Ashe, the first black man to win a major tournament title and the sport's leading humanitarian and social advocate, is born in Richmond, Va. Ashe is the first black man to win a major tournament title when, as an amateur, he wins the 1968 U.S. Open, defeating Tom Okker in the final. In 1963, Ashe is the first black to play on the U.S. Davis Cup team and is named captain of the team in 1981. Ashe wins three major titles in his career, also winning the Australian Open in 1970 and in 1975 he wins a magical Wimbledon where he stages a monumental upset of Jimmy Connors in the final. Ashe contracts AIDS via a blood transfusion and becomes a public crusader against the disease, one of the many causes he fights for, including education, health care and an end to apartheid and heart disease.

1981 The USTA National Tennis Center in Flushing Meadows, Queens, N.Y.—the site of the U.S. Open tennis championships—hosts Davis Cup for the first time ever as the United States and Czechoslovakia begin play in the Davis Cup quarterfinal. The U.S. and the Czechs split the first two singles matches as Ivan Lendl tops John McEnroe 6-4, 14-12, 7-5 while Jimmy Connors defeats Tomas Smid 6-3, 6-1, 6-2. A total of 17,445 fans attend the day's matches—setting a Davis Cup record (broken in 1990) for most fans to attend a home U.S. Davis Cup match.

1977 Tim Gullikson defeats fellow American Hank Pfister 6-4, 6-4, 5-7, 6-2 to win his first ATP singles title at the inaugural Hall of Fame Championships played on the grounds of the International Tennis Hall of Fame at the Newport Casino in Newport, R.I.

1999 Highlighted by a 45-minute acceptance speech, John McEnroe is inducted into the International Tennis Hall of Fame in Newport, R.I. McEnroe is introduced by his college friend from Stanford University and Olympic gold medal winning speed skater Eric Heiden. Says Heiden of McEnroe in his introduction speech, "He's probably the most controversial player in modern tennis. He took whining to the next level."

1978 Martina Navratilova becomes the No. 1 player on the WTA computer for the first time in her career. Navratilova holds the ranking for 331 weeks during her career.

July 11

1982 John McEnroe and Mats Wilander play what at the time is the longest recorded match in tennis history—6 hours, 22 minutes—as McEnroe defeats Wilander 9-7, 6-2, 15-17, 3-6, 8-6 in the fifth and decisive match of the 3-2 U.S. win over Sweden in the Davis Cup quarterfinal in St. Louis, Mo. The third set itself lasts 2 hours, 39 minutes as the 17-year-old newly-minted French Open champion and the 23-year-old McEnroe engage in numerous baseline rallies. Says McEnroe, "At one point I thought it was going to go on forever and that's frustrating. It's tough to go out there against a 17-year-old and not know what to do next. That's frustrating. I knew he was capable of playing well. He was psyched up to play." McEnroe and Wilander's time record stands for only two years. In 1984, Vicky Nelson-Dunbar and Jean Hepner play a two-set match in 6:31 in Richmond, Va., while in 2004, the record is broken again as Arnaud Clement and Fabrice Santoro play a first-round French Open match in 6:33. Says U.S. Davis Cup Captain Arthur Ashe after McEnroe's effort against Wilander, "He's entitled to go out and get drunk tonight."

2004 The International Tennis Hall of Fame celebrates its 50th anniversary as its hosts its 2004 induction ceremony of Steffi Graf, Stefan Edberg and Dorothy "Dodo" Cheney. Fifty Hall of Famers grace the grounds for the ceremonies at The Newport Casino, the site of the Hall of Fame and the U.S. Championships (the modern day U.S. Open from 1881 to 1914), including Rod Laver, Margaret Court, Jack Kramer, Chris Evert, John McEnroe, Stan Smith, Roy Emerson, Maria Bueno among others. The induction ceremonies are highlighted by Andre Agassi's induction speech for his wife, Graf, which brings the winner of 22 major singles titles to tears. Says Agassi, "As I attempt to find the words worthy to introduce the person that has changed my life. I realized that the words have yet to be invented that are large enough, colorful enough or true enough to express the heart and soul of this woman I love....You have spent many years of your life competing, but right here, where we stand, in the ears of your children, and right now in my heart, you have no rival. Ladies and gentlemen, I introduce to you the greatest person I've ever known..." Wiping the tears from eyes, Graf says, "Not that this occasion was emotional enough. To hear you are loved so much is amazing. Tennis has been a journey and the best part of this journey is it led to you. I'll be forever grateful for that." John McEnroe gets the biggest chuckle on the day as he introduces Cheney, the 87-year-old winner of hundreds of USTA senior championships who also was the first American woman to win the Australian Championships in 1938. Says McEnroe, "Anyone with a name like 'Dodo' and won as much as she has, has to be mentally tough."

2004 Putting an exclamation point on a week that followed his second Wimbledon title, Roger Federer wins his first pro singles title on Swiss soil at the clay court Swiss Open in Gstaad, defeating Igor Andreev of Russia 6-2, 6-3, 5-7, 6-3 in the final. Writes Rene Stauffer in his book *The Roger Federer Story: Quest for Perfection*, "Federer was the first Swiss champion at Gstaad since Heinz Gunthardt in 1980 and attendance at the Swiss Open during his performance was record-breaking. His relief was as great as his weariness. "Finally," he said. "I can get some sleep."

1981 Stan Smith and Bob Lutz play what turns out to be their final Davis Cup match for the United States as the duo defeat Ivan Lendl and Tomas Smid 9-7, 6-3, 6-2 to give the United States an important 2-1 lead over Czechoslovakia in the Davis Cup quarterfinal at the USTA National Tennis Center in Flushing, N.Y. Smith and Lutz end their Davis Cup careers with a 13-1 record playing for their country.

1993 In only his seventh ATP tournament of his career, 19-year-old Greg Rusedski becomes the first Canadian man to win an ATP event since 1969, defeating Javier Frana of Argentina 7-5, 6-7 (9), 7-6 (5) in the final of the Hall of Fame Championships in Newport, R.I. Says Rusedski, "We're known in Canada for having great hockey players and growing up with a stick and skates. Maybe now people in Canada will start getting excited about tennis. As for me, I'm about the worst hockey player who's ever lived." Rusedski, ranked No. 151 in the world and the last player directly accepted into the Newport draw, remains a Canadian citizen for less than two more years, choosing to represent Britain in May of 1995. Prior to Rusedski's effort on behalf of Canada, Mike Belkin was the last Canadian to win a men's professional event, winning the 1969 Western Open in Cincinnati.

July 12

1981 John McEnroe clinches victory over Czechoslovakia defeating Tomas Smid 6-3, 6-1, 6-4 in the Davis Cup quarterfinal in front of 16,008 fans at the USTA National Tennis Center in Flushing, N.Y. Jimmy Connors completes the 4-1 victory over the Czechs defeating Ivan Lendl 7-5, 6-4. Says Smid of playing McEnroe, the two-time reigning U.S. Open champion fresh off his first Wimbledon title, "John serves well, has a good volley, can guess which way the ball is going and has great touch. What could I do?"

2003 Boris Becker is inducted into the International Tennis Hall of Fame, along with Francoise Durr of France, Texan Nancy Richey and Australian administrator Brian Tobin. Says Ion Tiriac, Becker's manager, in his introduction speech of Becker, "He looked more like a Sumo wrestler than a tennis wrestler. And he wouldn't move his legs. I told him, 'Son, your legs are not moving.' He said, 'I don't need to move my legs. I'm hitting the ball so hard the ball is not coming back. Why do I have to move?' There was never a dull moment with him." Says Becker of his life-time passion, "Tennis has always been my hobby and my passion. To call it my job later in life is something, as boy, I could have never imagined."

2000 U.S. Davis Cup Captain John McEnroe, forced to deal with last-minute injuries to Pete Sampras and Andre Agassi, names himself along with Jan-Michael Gambill, Todd Martin and Chris Woodruff to the U.S. Davis Cup team to face Spain the semifinals in Santander, Spain. Says McEnroe of his playing status in media conference call. "I haven't actually decided to compete at the moment, so this is a stopgap solution. I'd say there's a good chance that I won't play, but there's also a chance that I will, depending on the availability of the other players I'm looking to talk to." A week later, McEnroe pulls himself out of the line-up in favor of Vince Spadea. The United States subsequently is dealt an embarrassing 5-0 loss and McEnroe resigns as U.S. captain four months later.

1998 Leander Paes, the bronze medalist in men's singles for India at the 1996 Olympic Games, wins his first ATP singles title defeating Neville Godwin of South Africa 6-3, 6-2 in the Hall of Fame Championships in Newport, R.I. Paes, ranked No. 120 in the world, plays in his first ATP final in his 52nd singles start.

July 13

1924 Play begins in the tennis competition at the 1924 Olympic Games in Paris as U.S. entries Helen Wills, Vincent Richards, Frank Hunter and Watson Washburn all advance. Suzanne Lenglen, the world's top female player who withdraws from the competition due to illness, makes an appearance at the matches. Reports the Associated Press, "Suzanne Lenglen, the world's champion, watched some of the matches until the sun became too uncomfortably warm for her. She looked thinner than usual. Mlle. Lenglen said she still felt ill and her appearance bore out her statement."

2004 Andre Agassi wins his 800th ATP match as he defeats Alex Bogomolov 6-3, 6-1 in 54 minutes in the first round of the Mercedes Benz Cup in Los Angeles, Calif. Agassi joins Jimmy Connors, Ivan Lendl, Guillermo Vilas, John McEnroe and Stefan Edberg as the only players in the Open era with 800 singles-match victories. For the occasion, tournament organizers make him a cake and present him with champagne following the victory. "Any time you accomplish something only the best have done, it's pretty special," Agassi says. "It takes a lot of time to win that many matches."

1984 In front of 16,279 fans at The Omni in Atlanta—the second largest U.S. home crowd in U.S. Davis Cup history—Jimmy Connors and John McEnroe give the United States a 2-0 lead over Argentina defeating Martin Jaite and Jose-Luis Clerc, respectively, in the Davis Cup quarterfinal in Atlanta.

1980 Vijay Amritraj of India wins the first of his two titles at the Hall of Fame Championships in Newport, R.I., defeating South Africa's Andrew Pattison 6-1, 5-7, 6-3 in the final. The title was 14th of Amritraj's 16 career ATP singles titles. In 1976, Amritraj wins an event in Newport, but it is not recognized as an official ATP tournament.

2008 Thirty-five-year-old Fabrice Santoro, the double-fisted French player nick-named "The Magician" due to his unorthodox playing style and incredible shot-making abilities, beats Prakash Amritraj of India, the son of Indian standout player Vijay Amritraj, 6-3, 7-5 to successfully defend his singles title at the Hall of Fame Championships in Newport, R.I. Amritraj, a wildcard entry into the event and ranked No. 305, falls short in his attempt to win the same singles title that his father won in 1980 and 1984.

July 14

2002 Taylor Dent puts his family into the tennis record books when he defeats fellow American James Blake 6-1, 4-6, 6-4 to win the Hall of Fame Championships in Newport, R.I., making him and his father Phil Dent the only father-son duo to win ATP singles title in the Open era. Phil Dent, a standout Australian who won three titles during his career (Sydney in 1971, 1979, Brisbane in 1979) also was a singles finalist at the 1974 Australian Open. Taylor's mother, Betty Ann Grubb, was also a standout player who was a 1977 U.S. Open doubles finalist. Says the No. 96-ranked Dent, "I'm ecstatic with my first title."

1991 Bryan Shelton, a former All-American from Georgia Tech University ranked No. 147, becomes the first African-American man to win an ATP singles tournament since Arthur Ashe wins in Los Angeles in 1978, defeating Argentina's Javier Frana 3-6, 6-4, 6-4 in the final of the Hall of Fame Championships in Newport, R.I. Says Shelton, "It's exciting and it's an achievement I'm proud of."

1984 Vijay Amritraj of India becomes the first two-time winner of the Hall of Fame Championships in Newport, R.I., defeating Tim Mayotte of nearby Massachusetts 3-6, 6-4, 6-4 in the final. Amritraj also wins the singles title in Newport in 1980.

1985 After 10 years on tour, 33-year-old Tom Gullikson wins his first ATP singles title, defeating John Sadri 6-3, 7-6 (3) in the final of the Hall of Fame Championships in Newport, R.I. "It was good to finally get the monkey off my back," says Gullikson. "At least I can say I won one tournament in my life."

2001 Ivan Lendl and Mervyn Rose are inducted into the International Tennis Hall of Fame in ceremonies at The Newport Casino in Newport, R.I. In his pre-induction press conference, Lendl, a winner of eight major singles titles in his career, is asked of his highlights and proudest achievements and responds, "Quite frankly, I don't think about it. I really don't. When you force me to think about it, I'm very proud. But that's about it." Writes Paul Doyle of the *Hartford Courant*, "Lendl was hardly reflective; his acceptance speech during the induction ceremony lasted about two minutes and there wasn't a tinge of emotion in his voice."

July 15

2006 Thirty-five-year-old Brenda Schultz-McCarthy serves the fastest serve recorded on the WTA Tour, belting a 130 mph serve in her 6-2, 6-4 loss to Julia Cohen in the qualifying rounds of the Western and Southern Group Championships in Cincinnati. "A lot of people were asking me how fast I could serve now that I'm 35 years old," says Schultz-McCarthy, returning to the WTA Tour after an absence of six-years. "This is great, it's very exciting. It was difficult to hear people say I used to have the fastest serve, or that I'm the second-fastest ever; this is definitely something I wanted to do in my comeback." Venus Williams held the previous record, hitting a 127 mph serve in 1998.

2007 Pete Sampras encounters likely his most uncomfortable moments on a tennis court as the 14-time major tournament victor chokes up and cries in an emotional speech as he is inducted into the International Tennis Hall of Fame in Newport, R.I. Sampras is the marquee name in the class of 2007 that also includes Arantxa Sanchez Vicario, Sven Davidson and photographer Russ Adams. Writes Bud Collins in *The Boston Globe*, "As the coolest cat ever to prowl Centre Court, seizing a record seven Wimbledon titles, humble Pete choked on the Casino lawn, overcome by the occasion. His acceptance speech, written for a five-minute distance, seemed more like five sets—"six sets," laughed his father, Sam Sampras. Punctuated by sobs, blank intervals, gulps, and disjointed sentences, it ran 25 nervous minutes. "By far the hardest time I've had on a tennis court," Pete was finally able to smile. Here was Pete Sampras, he of the mesmerizing running forehand, explosive serve-and-volley, and 64 singles titles, stumbling on the doorstep to Fame. "It was tough without a racket.'"

1992 Thirty-six-year-old five-time Wimbledon champion Bjorn Borg is defeated by fellow Swede Thomas Hogstedt 6-4, 7-6 (7-5) in the first round of the Nationsbank Classic in Washington, D.C. The loss is Borg's fourth first-round loss since he begins his comeback in February. "For me, it's nice to see the spectators are happy to see me play," says Borg. "That's a great feeling. These are the kind of matches I need to play. I had quite a few chances today, but I didn't win one important point and that was the difference."

July 16

1942 Margaret Court, the most prolific winner of major championships, is born in Albury, New South Wales. From 1960 to 1975, Court racks up a record 62 major titles (24 singles, 19 doubles, 19 mixed doubles tites) and in 1970, she becomes the second woman to win the Grand Slam, sweeping all four major titles within the calendar year. Court stands alone as the only player to win a Grand Slam in singles and doubles as she and Ken Fletcher win the Grand Slam in mixed doubles in 1963.

1907 Norman Brookes defeats Karl Behr 4-6, 6-4, 6-1, 6-2 clinching a 3-2 win for Australasia (Australia-New Zealand) in the opening round of the 1907 Davis Cup at Wimbledon, England. The loss prevents the United States from reaching the Davis Cup Challenge Round for the first time in its sixth Davis Cup appearance.

2004 Marcelo Rios, the first man from South America to reach the No. 1 ranking in men's singles, announces his retirement from professional tennis due to ongoing back injuries. "It is very sad for me to accept that I must leave tennis. Tennis has been the passion of my life. I am 28 and I have dedicated almost 20 years to tennis. Tennis has been a way of life to me."

2006 Mark Philippoussis, ranked No. 214 in the world, wins his 11th career singles title—and first in three years—defeating Justin Gimelstob 6-3, 7-5 to win the Hall of Fame Tennis Championships in Newport, R.I.

2008 Spain's Carlos Moya requires 2 hours, 45 minutes to beat Viktor Troicki of Serbia 3-6, 7-6 (2), 7-5 to reach the quarterfinals of the Croatian Open in Umag, Croatia. Moya, a five-time champion in the coastal Croatian city, says after the match that losing the match "crossed my mind, but this is Umag. I cannot lose here." The defending champion's statement comes back to bite him in the next round as he falls to Fabio Fognini of Italy 6-4, 6-3.

2007 Nadia Petrova and Elena Vesnina defeat Lisa Raymond and Venus Williams 7-5, 7-6(1) in the fifth and decisive match to give Russia the 3-2 win over the United States in the semifinals of the Fed Cup in Stowe, Vermont.

July 17

1984 Bjorn Borg plays one of his final matches on the ATP Tour, losing to Henri Leconte of France 6-3, 6-1 in only 49 minutes in the first round of the Wiessenhof International tennis championships in Stuttgart, West Germany. Borg, in general retirement since the end of the 1981 season, does not play another tournament match until an ill-fated comeback in 1991. "I didn't expect that he would play so strongly," says Borg of Leconte. "After being at 3-3 in the first set, I thought I still had my chance, but then my lack of match practice began to show...I lacked aggression. It was really tough for me to match him, and he has the stuff to be No. 1 in the world, if he can perform consistently." Leconte also defeated Borg in Borg's previous tournament appearance 15 months earlier in the first round of the Monte Carlo Open.

2007 Anastasia Rodionova of Russia becomes only the second player in the history of the WTA Tour to be disqualified from a match when she is defaulted from her match with Germany's Angelique Kerber in the first round of the Cincinnati Open. Kerber leads Rodionova 4-6, 6-4, 1-0 when the Russian slams a ball at fans cheering for her opponent. Tournament referee Williams Coffey immediately defaults Rodionova for unsportsman-like conduct. The only other player to be disqualified from a match is Irina Spirlea, who is defaulted for abusive language during a match in Palermo, Italy in 1996. Says Rodionova, "I'm shocked. I still don't understand why they defaulted me. I'm really upset. I had no warning. I didn't hit the ball at anybody. I didn't swear at anybody. I didn't throw my racquet."

1994 Jim Courier defeats Jacco Eltingh 6-3, 6-4, 4-6, 6-1 in the fifth and decisive match as the United States defeats the Netherlands 3-2 in the Davis Cup quarterfinal in Rotterdam, the Netherlands. The win is the first of three Davis Cup wins for Courier in fifth and decisive Davis Cup rubbers.

2007 Twenty-seven-year old journeyman pro and former UCLA standout Zack Fleishman registers the biggest win of his career, defeating No. 1 seed and 2007 Australian Open finalist Fernando Gonzalez of Chile 7-6 (5), 6-4 in the first round of the Countrywide Classic on the campus of UCLA in Los Angeles. Says the No. 162nd ranked Fleishman, "I beat a top 10 player, at my school, my former college, my hometown, and the place where I practiced since I was nine years old. I was a ball boy here for years."

July 18

1930 Wilmer Allison saves a record 18 match points in his Davis Cup victory against Giorgio de Stefani of Italy in the Davis Cup Inter-Zone Final at Roland Garros in Paris, France. Allison wins the epic match 4-6, 7-9, 6-4, 8-6, 10-8 after trailing 2-5 in the fourth set and 1-5 in the fifth. Allison and the United States go on to win the series 4-1.

1999 After receiving intravenous fluids prior to the match to combat heat exhaustion, Todd Martin plays one of the most courageous and passionate matches in U.S. Davis Cup history against Patrick Rafter in the Davis Cup Centennial Celebration—a quarterfinal tie between the United States and Australia at the Longwood Cricket Club in Chestnut Hill, Mass. Martin, on the verge of physical collapse the entire match with on-court temperatures hovering around 115 degrees, extends Rafter to five sets before falling 4-6, 5-7, 6-3, 6-2, 6-4 in 3 hours, 14 minutes as Australia clinches a 4-1 victory. The match culminates a strange pre-match drama where U.S. Davis Cup Captain Tom Gullikson attempts to replace Martin with world No. 1 Pete Sampras, who returns to the U.S. team, but only in doubles in respect to Martin and Jim Courier, who win a dramatic 3-2 match with Great Britain in the first round. In Davis Cup rules at the time, Sampras, playing a doubles only role against Australia, is not allowed to replace Martin in singles unless Martin is deemed unfit to play by the ITF referee. In his morning practice, Martin, in the words of U.S. Davis Cup Team Doctor David Altchek, "lost his bearings and had to be helped off the court" due to the late affects of heat exhaustion from Friday's loss to Davis Cup debutant Lleyton Hewitt. Dubious of Martin's ill condition as replacing Martin with the world No. 1 Pete Sampras is an obvious advantage to the United States, the ITF referee and the tie's neutral doctor Richard Paul declare Martin fit for play. Altchek and U.S. Davis Cup team trainer Todd Snyder place ice and cold towels on the back of Martin's neck to help cool his body early in the first set as Martin goes for outright winners against Rafter on almost all shots to keep points short in his condition and in the brutally hot conditions. Says Martin "Basically any ball that I could stand in one place and set up for I tried to hit, if not for a winner, for close to a winner. I had very low expectations of my performance and in that situation, that is not such a bad thing." Martin's go-for-broke style and Rafter's distracted, out-of-sync, tentative and flustered play puts Martin up 4-0 in the first set as he rolls to a two-sets-to-love lead. After Rafter takes the next two sets, Martin leads 3-0 and 4-2 in the fifth set, but Rafter wins the last four games of the match to solidify the Australian win. Writes Michael Madden of the *Boston Globe* of the proceedings, "Martin vs. Rafter moved into the annals of tennis' greatest moments, into the epic list of the most courageous matches of any sport."

1996 Irina Spirlea becomes the first player in the history of the WTA Tour to be ejected from a match when she fires abusive language to the tournament referee in a second-round match with Belgium's Stephanie De Ville at the Palermo Open in Italy. Spirlea, the No. 1 seed in the event, is defaulted from the match at the start of the third set after De Ville wins the second set 7-6 (8) after Spirlea wins the first set 7-5.

2006 Playing her first match in six months due to a chronic knee injury, Serena Williams defeats No. 11-ranked Anastasia Myskina of Russia 6-2, 6-2 in less than an hour in a highly anticipated first round match in Cincinnati. Says Williams, "I felt really relaxed. I haven't felt this way in a long time" Says Myskina of the No. 139-ranked Williams, "She hadn't played in six months, so I didn't know what to expect. Her serve was pretty good. I knew I was going to have to keep winning my serve if I was going to stay in the game."

July 19

1874 On a damp English day, in front of only 200 spectators, Spencer Gore wins the inaugural men's singles title at Wimbledon, defeating William Marshall 6-1, 6-2, 6-4. The first edition of the tournament that becomes known simply as "The Championships" features only a men's singles competition of only 22 entrants, but only 21 show up. Writes Bud Collins in *The Bud Collins History of Tennis*, "The title match was held over until the following Monday. Such delay had been indicated in the prospectus to allow for the Eton-Harrow cricket match at Lords. This was the ultimate sporting event so far as the fashionable London world was concerned, and lawn tennis, itself a fashionable sport, did not dream for many years of coming into conflict with that important fixture. Monday turned out wet, and the final was postponed until Thursday, July 19. That day was also damp, but rather than disappoint 200 spectators, each of whom had paid one shilling (then about 25 cents) to see Wimbledon's baptismal final, Gore and Marshall sportingly agreed to play. Gore came up to the net and volleyed. Whether this was entirely sporting was a matter of some debate, as was his striking the ball before it had crossed the net. He won, 6-1, 6-2, 6-4."

1931 In what *American Lawn Tennis* calls "one of the most thrilling third days ever known in Davis Cup history" Fred Perry and Bunny Austin rally Britain from a 1-2 deficit to defeat the United States 3-2 in the Davis Cup Inter-Zone Final at Stade Roland Garros in Paris, France. Fred Perry defeats Sidney Wood 6-3, 8-10, 6-3, 6-3 to tie the score at two matches apiece, while Bunny Austin wins the fifth and decisive match, overwhelming Frank Shields 8-6, 6-3, 7-5.

1975 The United States Tennis Association announces that for the first time in the tournament's history, night tennis will be played. On eight of the 12 days, night matches would be played during a separate session under the newly installed 150-foot lighting towers, placed on the stadium court at the West Side Tennis Club at a cost of $100,000. Says U.S. Open tournament director Bill Talbert, "The United States Tennis Association wanted play under lights and they've got it."

2006 Former world No. 1 Marat Safin is defeated by No. 512-ranked South African qualifier Wesley Whitehouse 6-1, 6-4 in the first round of the RCA Championships in Indianapolis. Whitehouse enters the match having won only one ATP-level match in his nine-year career. Says Whitehouse, the

1997 Wimbledon junior champion, of Safin, "You never know with him. He can play really well or badly."

2007 Celebrating his 33rd birthday, Vince Spadea advances to the quarterfinals of the Countrywide Classic on the campus of UCLA in Los Angeles, defeating defending finalist Dmitry Tursunov 6-7 (5), 7-5, 6-3. Says Spadea of his career, "I've been around for so long that I might be in the record books for being the longest, weirdest, most pathetic great player ever. Look at how precocious I am at 33."

1946 Ilie Nastase, the clown prince of tennis, is born in Bucharest, Romania. Nastase is perhaps more known for insolent behavior on court than his tremendous tennis talent that brought him victories at the 1972 U.S. Open and the 1973 French Open.

July 20

1937 Don Budge wins one of the most dramatic and politically important Davis Cup matches of all time as he comes back from two-sets-to-love to defeat Gottfried von Cramm 6-8, 5-7, 6-4, 6-2, 8-6 in the fifth and decisive match as the United States defeats Germany 3-2 in the inter-zone final at Wimbledon, England. Von Cramm receives a good luck call prior to the match from Adolf Hitler, who stresses the importance of a German victory over the United States. Says Don Budge many years later of Hitler's call to von Cramm, "I thought why didn't Franklin Roosevelt call me? Didn't he give a damn?"

1924 Americans Vincent Richards and Helen Wills win the gold medal matches in men's and women's singles, respectively, in the tennis competition at the 1924 Olympic Games in Paris. Richards staves off the comeback bid of France's Henri Cochet 6-4, 6-4, 5-7, 4-6, 6-2 to claim gold in men's singles. Wills has little trouble with Didi Vlasto, defeating her French opponent 6-2, 6-2. The Associated Press reports; "A crowd of 8,000 persons, sweltering in the torrid heat, was stirred to a high pitch of enthusiasm by the two Franco-American contests. While the sympathies naturally were with the losers, the spectators, with a few scattered exceptions, gave applause to the youthful contestants impartially and cheered the Americans enthusiastically when the final points were won and lost in each match."

1954 Nineteen-year-old Maureen Connolly suffers a career-ending injury as the horse she is riding, Colonel Merryboy, collides with a cement truck in Mission Valley Polo Grounds near San Diego. Connolly breaks her right leg and suffers torn muscles and tendons in her right calf. Connolly's last tournament comes the day before when she wins the U.S. Clay Court Championships in River Forest, Ill., defeating Doris Hart in the final.

1986 Davis Cup rookie Tim Mayotte, playing in as foreign and uncomfortable environment for him as possible—a clay court in front of a rowdy crowd in Mexico City, Mexico—heroically clinches the 4-1 U.S. victory over Mexico in the Davis Cup quarterfinal, defeating Leonardo Lavalle 7-5, 4-6, 0-6, 6-4, 9-7. The fast-court serve-and-volley specialist saves two match points trailing 3-5, 15-40 in the fifth set, before rallying to victory. Nicknamed "Gentleman Tim" by the British during his 1982 run to the Wimbledon semifinals, Mayotte becomes so irritated with the taunts and jeers of the Mexican crowd early in the third set that he exchanges heated words with fans sitting in the first few rows. Play is interrupted so many times due to the crowd that ITF referee Francis Patrick Loderop penalizes Lavalle a point and threatens to award the match outright to the United States. Mayotte controls his nerves and blocks out the antagonistic fans to help the United States and first-year captain Tom Gorman advance into the semifinals against Australia. Says Mayotte after the match, "I've won some tournaments before, but to come back like that under these conditions and win for a team is the greatest thrill of my tennis life." Writes Bud Collins in *World Tennis* magazine, "When you consider Americans seemingly out of their league on foreign clay, besieged by loud and jeering patriotic crowds, Mayotte's determined victory is in a class with Stan Smith's overcoming Ilie Nastase and Ion Tiriac to win the 1972 Cup in Bucharest. But Smith was an old Cup hand, while this was Mayotte's debut."

July 21

2004 Rainer Schuettler of Germany saves 10 match points in defeating Andreas Seppi of Italy 3-6, 7-6 (15-13), 6-0 in the second round of the Generali Open in Kitzbuhel, Austria.

1951 Tony Trabert, one of America's greatest tennis champions, makes his Davis Cup debut and clinches victory over Japan in doubles with Bill Talbert in doubles, defeating Japan's Fumiteru Nakano and Goro Fujikuru 6-0, 6-2, 10-8 in Louisville, Ky. The doubles win gives the United States an insurmountable 3-0 lead over the Japanese in the Davis Cup first round.

1991 With on court temperatures rising to 106 degrees, Andre Agassi defeats Petr Korda 6-3, 6-4 to win the Sovran Bank Championships in Washington, D.C.

1905 The United States begins play in its first Davis Cup Challenge Round on foreign soil against Britain at Wimbledon. Laurie Doherty of Britain defeats Holcombe Ward 7-9, 4-6, 6-1, 6-2, 6-0 and Sidney Smith of Britain defeats William Larned 6-4, 6-4, 5-7, 6-4. Britain goes on to hand the United States its first-ever shut-out loss in Cup play, posting a 5-0 win. In the doubles match the next day, brothers Reggie and Laurie Doherty defeat Holcombe Ward and Beals Wright 8-10, 6-2, 6-2, 4-6, 8-6 to give Britain the 3-0 lead. The reverse singles matches, Smith defeats William Clothier 4-6, 6-1, 6-4, 6-3 and Laurie Doherty defeats Larned 6-4, 2-6, 6-8, 6-4, 6-2.

1985 Yannick Noah registers his first career win over Jimmy Connors, defeating the five-time U.S. Open champion 6-4, 3-6, 6-2 in the semifinals of the D.C. National Bank Tennis Classic in Washington, D.C. Connors is cited for obscene language several times in the match, including arguing Noah's ace in the match's final point. Says Connors of the line-calling during the match, "The guy was screwing us both from the very beginning, it sets a precedent that the guy can't do the job. They should get somebody who can do the job." Noah wins the title the next day, defeating Martin Jaite of Argentina 6-4, 6-3 in the final.

1985 Mats Wilander dominates fellow Swede Stefan Edberg 6-1, 6-0 in just 59 minutes to win the Swedish Open in Bastad, Sweden.

July 22

1989 In what Boris Becker calls "an exhausting day at the office," the three-time Wimbledon champion from Germany wins the fifth-set of a lateness-suspended match with Andre Agassi, then pairs with Eric Jelen to win a four-set doubles match against Ken Flach and Robet Seguso to give West Germany a 2-1 lead over the United States in the Davis Cup semifinals in Munich. Becker and Agassi's singles match is suspended the previous night after midnight with the score knotted at two sets, Becker trailing two-sets-to-love and Agassi failing to serve out the match at 6-5 in the third set. Becker is the sharper player on the resumption of play and wins the fifth set to close out his 4 hour, 26 minute 6-7 (4), 6-7 (5), 7-6 (4), 6-3, 6-4 win that evens the best-of-five-match series at 1-1. After only 45 minutes of rest, Becker returns to the court in doubles with Jelen and hands Flach and Seguso their first loss as a Davis Cup doubles team in their 12 pairings for the United States in a 3-6, 7-6 (5), 6-4, 7-6 (3) decision. Says Jelen of the Agassi-Becker epic, "That was one of the greatest matches I ever saw." Says Agassi of his loss, "I think, considering the circumstances and the court, I did the best I could do. I don't feel I lost. He beat me. There are times when you pour all your heart and guts into the match. Then you've just got to shake hands with the winner." The following day, Agassi loses to Carl-Uwe Steeb in four sets to give West Germany the semifinal victory. West Germany goes on to beat Sweden 3-2 in the Davis Cup Final.

1979 Guillermo Vilas wins the singles title at the Washington Star International singles when Victor Pecci collapses, overcome by leg cramps, as the two play a second set tie-breaker, with Vilas leading 7-6, 6-6 and 4-3 in the tie-break. Says Vilas, "This is a sad way to win."

1992 World No. 1 Jim Courier loses to No. 157-ranked Diego Perez of Uruguay 7-6 (5), 6-2 in the second round of the Philips Head Cup clay court championships in Kitzbuhel, Austria.

2007 Belgian qualifier Steve Darcis, ranked No. 297 on the ATP computer, defeats Austria's Werner Eschauer 6-1, 7-6 (1) in the final of the Dutch Open in Amersfoort, Netherlands. Darcis, playing in the main draw of only his second ATP event, is the lowest ranked player to win a title since Tommy Haas, who due to injury is ranked No. 349 when he wins the U.S. Men's Clay Court Championships in Houston in 2004. In 1998, Lleyton Hewitt is ranked No. 550 when he wins the title in Adelaide, Australia.

July 23

1992 In their 36th and final meeting as professionals, Ivan Lendl routs rival John McEnroe 6-2, 6-4 in the quarterfinals of the Canadian Open in Toronto. Says Lendl of McEnroe, "If you have him on the ground on his back, you have to step on his throat. You can't put out your hand and say come on over here and hit me. You have to concentrate all the time and not give him any chances." When asked what kind of technique he used on McEnroe's throat, Lendl smiles and replies, "I have spikes in my shoes and I try to twist them as much as I can. That's the killer instinct." Lendl wins the all-time series with McEnroe 21-15, including winning the last six meetings and 10 of the last 11.

1984 Sixteen-year-old Aaron Krickstein becomes the youngest player to win the U.S. Pro Championships, defeating Jose-Luis Clerc 7-6, 3-6, 6-4 in the men's singles final at the Longwood Cricket Club in Brookline, Mass. Clerc leads 3-0 in the final set, before Krickstein rallies for victory.

2000 The United States is shut out for the first time ever in a Davis Cup series other than a Challenge Round or Final as Juan Carlos Ferrero and Juan Balcells complete a 5-0 shutout of the United States in the Davis Cup semifinal in Santander, Spain. In the final day's dead-rubber matches, Ferrero defeats Vince Spadea 4-6, 6-1, 6-4, while Balcells defeats Jan-Michael Gambill 1-6, 7-6, 6-4. The shutout loss marks the end of John McEnroe's short tenure as U.S. Davis Cup captain. In November, McEnroe announces his resignation as U.S. captain after only one year in the position. Pete Sampras and Andre Agassi, the top two U.S. players, beg off the match with Spain with injuries. McEnroe, distraught with the loss, skips out on the post-match press conference, but says to Lisa Dillman of the *Los Angeles Times* in a pool phone interview from his car hours later driving to the Bilboa airport, "I'm totally spent. I'm deflated. It was tough and it was tough for everybody. I feel like I'm going to throw up. I'm not sure if it's emotional or what, but I'm about to heave."

2006 Third-seeded Novak Djokovic of Serbia captures his first ATP title in his first final at the Dutch Open Tennis in Amersfoort. The 19-year-old does not lose a set at the championship and beats No. 4 seed Nicolas Massu of Chile 7-6(5), 6-4 in 2 hours, 41 minutes in the final.

1996 The Olympic tennis competition opens in Atlanta with defending men's singles gold medallist Marc Rosset of Switzerland winning the opening match on stadium court, defeating Hicham Arazi of Morocco 6-2, 6-3.

2006 James Blake defeats fellow American top tenner Andy Roddick 4-6, 6-4, 7-6(5) in the final at the RCA Championships at Indianapolis. Says Blake, "This was extremely exciting for me, to play really my best tennis. It's a little more gratifying to do it when your opponent is playing well. I feel like I've earned the No. 5 ranking. It's crazy what confidence will do. Every break goes against you when you don't have confidence. And every break goes your way when you do have confidence. I have confidence now and they all seem to be going my way."

1991 Michael Chang and Pete Sampras are unceremoniously dumped in the second round of the Canadian Open in Montreal—Chang falls 7-6 (6), 3-6, 6-3 to Italy's Stefano Pescosoliso, while Sampras loses to Japan's Shuzo Matsuoka 2-6, 6-4, 7-6 (10-8)

July 24

1987 John McEnroe and Boris Becker play one of the greatest Davis Cup matches of all time as Becker outlasts McEnroe 4-6, 15-13, 8-10, 6-2, 6-2 in 6 hours, 21 minutes in the Davis Cup Qualifying Round in Hartford, Conn. The match is one minute shy of the 6-hour, 22-minute Davis Cup epic between McEnroe and Mats Wilander in the 1982 Davis Cup quarterfinal, the longest men's singles match in tennis history at the time. The 28-year-old McEnroe, playing in his first competitive match since losing in the first round of the French Open in May, fights to keep the United States out of an 0-2 hole against West Germany on the first day of play as Becker's teammate Eric Jelen opens the series with a 6-8, 6-2, 1-6, 6-3, 6-2 win over Tim Mayotte. Says McEnroe, "I just didn't have much left. I gave it what I had. It was nice to be a part of a great match. I just wish the result had been different." Says the 19-year-old Becker, "It was a war." West Germany goes on to win the series 3-2—relegating the United States to zonal competition for the first time ever for the 1988 Davis Cup campaign—making 28-time Davis Cup champions ineligible to win the 1988 Davis Cup title.

1996 No. 2 seed Goran Ivanisevic of Croatia is upset in the first round of the Olympic tennis competition in Atlanta, as the defending bronze medalist hits 42 unforced errors in a 6-4, 6-2 loss to No. 104-ranked Marcos Ondruska of South Africa. Richey Reneberg, who replaces the injured No. 1-ranked Pete Sampras in the U.S. singles line-up, is defeated by India's Leander Paes in the first round as Reneberg is forced to retire due to a groin pull and a heat illness after 2 hours, 16 minutes in the oppressive Georgia heat, Paes leading 6-7 (2), 7-6 (7), 1-0. Mal Washington of the United States becomes the first African-American man to compete in the Olympics, defeating Slovakia's Jan Kroslak 6-3, 7-6 (3),

1932 Despite suffering from an upset stomach from a pre-match meal of roast pork and cucumbers, Ellsworth Vines defeats Gottfried von Cramm 3-6, 6-3, 9-7, 6-3 to clinch a 3-2 U.S. victory over Germany in the Davis Cup Inter-Zone Final at Stade Roland Garros in Paris, France.

July 25

1970 In a decision called by Neil Amdur of the *New York Times* as "the most revolutionary step in tournament tennis scoring since 'love' became synonymous with losers," the United States Tennis Association announces that a sudden-death nine-point tiebreak will be instituted for all matches at the 1970 U.S. Open tennis championships. Says Bill Talbert, the tournament director for the U.S. Open, "We consider this to be a major step forward for the game of tennis. It provides tennis with a finish line, such as we have in racing, basketball, football and other major sports. No longer will a tennis match drag on for hours. It will be played within a sensible, predictable amount of time, enabling spectators to estimate the length of a match and make their plans accordingly."

1988 Thirty-five-year-old Jimmy Connors wins his first singles title in four years—and the 106th of his career—defeating Andres Gomez 6-1, 6-4 in the final of the D.C. Tennis Classic in Washington. The win is the first for Connors since October of 1984 when he wins the ATP singles title in Tokyo, losing in 11 singles finals before breaking through and winning in Washington, D.C. Says the No. 8-ranked Connors, "I go through a career and win 105 tournaments and it's never enough. Now I guess I'm stuck on 106 until I win 107, right? It doesn't feel as bad not having won a tournament in about 25 minutes than it has in 3 1/2 years. I wanted to win a tournament, no doubt; I just haven't done it. But mostly, I'm just out there to have some fun."

1987 Bjorn Borg is inducted into the International Tennis Hall of Fame in Newport, R.I. in absentia, but is defended for his no-show status by fellow inductee Alex Olmedo. "We all have different problems," says Olmedo. "We're all egomaniacs in a way. Whatever his hang-up was, I don't blame him for not coming. Maybe he was too busy making money or maybe he was afraid to make the flight. Whatever, it doesn't take anything from the presentation...I also think it's a bit of publicity shock for him after all these years. Most of the movie stars I work with sometimes don't like to be in the public eye. I think Borg is in the same category. He's probably publicity shy now." Olmedo is inducted with fellow pros Stan Smith, Dennis Ralston and Billie Jean King.

1996 Andre Agassi defeats Slovakia's Karol Kucera 6-4, 6-4 in the second round of the Olympic tennis competition and, in his post-match press conference, announces that he will compete in the Olympic doubles competition with Mal Washington, replacing the injured Richey Reneberg. Says Agassi, "The team took a hit. You've got to adjust to it. As far as I'm concerned, if it calls for you to give more, you've got to give more. It's as simple as that. Even if it costs me a medal, it is still something that you've got to do."

1982 Martina Navratilova and Chris Evert Lloyd pair to lead the United States to the title at the Federation Cup in Santa Clara, Calif., with a 3-0 win over West Germany. Navratilova defeats Bettina Bunge 6-4, 6-4, while Evert Lloyd defeats Claudia Kohde Kilsch 2-6, 6-1, 6-3. Navratilova, who also wins the Federation Cup for Czechoslovakia in 1975, becomes the first women to win the Cup for two nations.

July 26

1999 Patrick Rafter of Australia begins his one—and only—week as the world's No. 1 ranked player, replacing Andre Agassi in the top spot on the ATP computer. Rafter's curious one-week reign as the No. 1 ranked player is the briefest stint in the top spot of any man or woman. Carlos Moya of Spain ranks No. 1 for only two weeks in March of 1999, while Evonne Goolagong ranks as the No. 1 woman on the WTA Tour for a two-week period in April of 1976 (although not uncovered and announced by the WTA Tour until December of 2007).

1987 The United States is relegated to zonal competition for the first time in Davis Cup history as Boris Becker defeats Tim Mayotte 6-2, 6-3, 5-7, 4-6, 6-2 in the fifth and decisive match as West Germany defeats the United States 3-2 in the Davis Cup qualifying round in Hartford, Conn. The Becker-Mayotte match is called by John Feinstein of the *Washington Post* as, "the match of their lives," as Mayotte, who grew up in Springfield, Mass., 25 miles from the Hartford Civic Center, plays inspired tennis in front of furiously vocal crowd. Says Becker after the epic match, "It was the most difficult match of my life. The circumstances made it hard, the crowd cheering every time I missed a serve made it hard and him playing for two sets like I have never seen him play in his life, it was all very tough. I just had to stay calm—stay calm, be patient and not go mad. If I go mad, I lose the match." Writes Feinstein, "For Mayotte, this was sweet agony. He miraculously came from two sets down to force a fifth set. He was playing in an emotional daze, carried by the fans, by his teammates, by the circumstances."

1969 Nancy Richey is upset in the semifinals of the U.S. Clay Court Championships by Gail Sherriff Chanfreau, 6-3, 6-4—ending her tournament record winning streak at 33 straight matches over seven years. Chanfreau goes on to win the title, beating Linda Tuero, 6-2, 6-2 in the final.

1953 Gardnar Mulloy, at the age of 39 years, 8 months and four days, becomes the oldest man to win a singles match for the U.S. in Davis Cup play as he defeats Ian McDonald of the British West Indies 6-1, 6-3, 6-0 in Kingston, Jamaica.

July 27

1986 Martina Navratilova returns to her native Czechoslovakia and her hometown of Prague in triumph as a member of the U.S. Federation Cup team, clinching the U.S. 3-0 final-round victory over the Czechs with a 7-5, 6-1 victory over Hana Mandlikova. "We all did it for Martina," says Chris Evert Lloyd, whose 7-5, 7-6 victory over Helena Sukova begins the U.S. sweep of Czechoslovakia in the final series. "We dedicate this Federation Cup to her." Says Navratilova of the crowd support she receives all week that results in a tearful closing ceremony for the Wimbledon champion and her U.S. teammates, "I wanted to tell them how special it was for me to be here. It exceeded my wildest expectations."

1946 In the final of the first French Championship since the conclusion of World War II, Frenchmen Marcel Bernard dramatically defeats fellow left-hander Jaroslav Drobny of Czechoslovakia 3-6, 2-6, 6-1, 6-4, 6-3 in the men's singles final. The French have to wait another 37 years before they celebrate another native men's singles champion when Yannick Noah wins the men's singles title in 1983. It will be another 59 years before another all left-handed men's singles final is played at Roland Garros when Rafael Nadal defeats Mariano Puerta in the 2005 final. In the women's singles final, Margaret Osbourne defeats fellow American Pauline Betz 1-6, 8-6, 7-5.

2007 Sam Querrey slams an incredible 10 aces in a row—believed to be a record—in his 7-6(6), 6-7 (4), 7-6 (4) upset win over fellow Ameican James Blake in the quarterfinals of the Indianapolis Tennis Championships. Querrey, a six-foot-six, 19-year-old from Southern California, begins his incredible serving streak with a 113 mph serve out wide at 6-6 in the first-set tie-break. Querrey hits four straight aces in his first two service games of the second set and after a 109 mph ace out wide in the first point of the sixth game of the second set, Querrey's streak ends with a double fault. Querrey, ranked No. 90 in the world, serves a total of 34 aces in the match. Says Blake, "That's the most consistent I've seen him serve. I practice with him quite a bit. I've seen him improve over the last year-and-a-half at an incredible rate. I think it's still going....I don't think I've ever been aced 10 times in a row, until today....The way Sam was locked in, it was tough to deal with. It made me focus on my serve and I needed to hold every time." Says Querrey in his post-match TV interview, "It was just one of those days when I was in the zone serving and it definitely paid off in the end."

1928 Play opens in the 1928 Davis Cup Challenge Round in Paris as Bill Tilden and Rene Lacoste christen Stade Roland Garros, built to honor the French Four Musketeers' victory in the previous year's Davis Cup. Tilden gives the United States an early 1-0 lead by defeating Lacoste 1-6, 6-4, 6-4, 2-6, 6-3. Henri Cochet ties the score at 1-1 as he defeats John Hennessey 5-7, 9-7, 6-3, 6-0.

1988 Roger Smith of the Bahamas, ranked No. 150 in the world, registers a stunning upset of world No. 1 Ivan Lendl, defeating the reigning three-time U.S. Open champion 6-2, 6-3 in the first round of the Volvo International at Stratton Mountain, Vermont. Says Lendl, "He was serving very well and the ball was going very quick, and I couldn't get into the match. It was not a letdown. It was practice for the U.S. Open. This was not the highlight of my year."

1930 Bill Tilden plays his final Davis Cup match, losing to Henri Cochet 4-6, 6-3, 6-1, 7-5 as France completes a 4-1 victory over the United States in the Davis Cup Challenge Round at Stade Roland Garros in Paris. Tilden concludes his Davis Cup career with a 34-7 record and the distinction of leading the U.S. to five Davis Cup titles.

1996 The morning after a bomb kills one person in Centennial Olympic Park in downtown Atlanta, Monica Seles advances into the quarterfinals of the Olympic tennis competition with a 6-3, 6-3 win over Argentina's Gabriela Sabatini. Says Seles, the subject of security at sporting events since her on-court stabbing in 1993, "I'm still going to the track and field (Saturday night) and to other events and go on with my life. That is pretty much all I can do. That is what I did after the stabbing. You just have to go on." Says Sabatini of Seles, "I would think it would be even harder for her because of what happened to her. It's upsetting and it affects you quite a lot because nobody feels secure anywhere." Andre Agassi rallies from a 6-2, 3-0 deficit to defeat Andrea Gaudenzi of Italy 2-6, 6-4, 6-2 to advance into the quarterfinals of the men's singles competition.

1997 Martina Hingis routs Conchita Martinez 6-0, 6-2 to win the Bank of the West Championships at Stanford University in Palo Alto, Calif. The win ups Hingis's won-loss record to 50-1 for the year.

July 28

1996 Jana Novotna rallies from 3-5 deficits in the first and third sets to knock off No. 1 seed Monica Seles 7-5, 3-6, 8-6 in the quarterfinals of the Olympic Games in Atlanta, denying Seles an opportunity to win a medal in her first Olympiad. Says Seles, "I had my chances. Too many chances. Today when it came to the crunch points, she played better." Says the sometimes mentally fragile Novotna, "All the comments some of you have made about me that I'm not strong enough or mentally tough enough at the end, I thought that I didn't prove it today but already in the past. Today I was playing against everybody in a stadium in (Seles') home country and on a occasion like this when you are going for a medal. I think it's pretty gutsy."

1991 Arantxa Sanchez Vicario pairs with Conchita Martinez to defeat Zina Garrison and Gigi Fernandez of the United States 3-6, 6-1, 6-1 in the decisive match of the Fed Cup Final in Nottingham, England, giving Spain its first title in the women's version of the Davis Cup. Earlier, Jennifer Capriati defeats Martinez 4-6, 7-6, 6-1, while Sanchez Vicario defeats Mary Joe Fernandez 6-3, 6-4 to knot the match at 1-1 and setting the stage for the decisive doubles match. Says Gigi Fernandez, "I think basically we choked. That's the biggest choke of my career by far. I think I was way under par today. It happens when you're in the final and you're playing for your country."

1985 Ivan Lendl defeats Andres Gomez 6-1, 6-3 to win the U.S. Clay Court Championships in Indianapolis, but angers fans in his post-match speech by admonishing the crowd for cheering heavily for Boris Becker in his semifinal match the day before. "Thanks for coming even though you didn't like me," he tells the audience in the post-match ceremony. "Maybe next time your Boris will win." Later in the post-match press conference, Lendl tells reporters that he would have rather stayed at home with his pet German shepard than travel to Indianapolis.

1991 Andrei Chesnokov wins the Canadian Open in Montreal, defeating Petr Korda 3-6, 6-4, 6-3 in the final and promises a high-spirited celebration. Says Chesnokov, "I'm going to New York, I'm going to go to Tower Records, have dinner at a very nice Italian restaurant and, of course, I'm going to get drunk."

July 29

1992 The tennis competition at the 1992 Olympics begins as hometown Barcelona natives Arantxa Sanchez Vicario and Emilio Sanchez post first-round victories. Sanchez Vicario defeats Irina Spirlea of Romania 6-1, 6-3 in the first round of women's singles, while her brother Emilio defeats Australia's Todd Woodbridge 6-1, 7-6 (1), 6-2. Boris Becker of Germany wins the most dramatic match of the day, needing nearly five hours to defeat Christian Ruud of Norway 3-6, 7-6 (7-2), 5-7, 7-6 (7-2), 6-3. Defending champion Steffi Graf needs only 35 minutes to defeat Lupita Novelo of Mexico, 6-1, 6-1. Pete Sampras wins his Olympic opener, defeating Australia's Wally Masur 6-1, 7-6 (4), 6-4. Russian Andrei Chesnokov upsets No. 2 seed Stefan Edberg of Sweden 6-0, 6-4, 6-4 in the first round.

1990 Gigi Fernandez and Zina Garrison defeat Natasha Zvereva and Larisa Savchenko of the Soviet Union 6-4, 6-3 to give the United States a 2-1 victory over the USSR, clinching the Federation Cup for the United States in Norcross, Ga. The win is the 14th in 28 years for the United States in Fed Cup play. Earlier Zina Garrison loses 4-6, 6-3, 6-3 to Zvereva, while 14-year-old Jennifer Capriati defeats Leila Meskhi 7-6, 6-2.

1990 Michael Chang defeats Jay Berger 4-6, 6-3, 7-6 (2) in the final of the Canadian Open men's singles final in Toronto. The 24th-ranked Chang's $155,000 winner's check puts him in the million-dollar club for career prize money. "It feels good," says the 18-year-old Chang of his financial achievement. "I think my first priority as far as tennis is concerned is not making money. My priority is to be the best in the world—the best I can be."

1974 Jimmy Connors becomes the No. 1 ranked player in the world for the first time in his career at the age of 21, replacing John Newcombe.

1935 John Van Ryn's 13-match Davis Cup doubles win streak is snapped as the British doubles team of George Hughes and Charles Tuckey defeat Van Ryn and Wilmer Allison 6-2, 1-6, 6-8, 6-3, 6-3 to clinch a 3-0 lead and the Davis Cup title for Britain over the United States at Wimbledon.

2001 Andre Agassi defeats Pete Sampras 6-4, 6-2 in the final of the Mercedes Benz Cup in Los Angeles, Agassi's 17th consecutive match victory on hard courts. Identical twins Bob and Mike Bryan of Camarillo, Calif., win their third ATP doubles title in six weeks, defeating Jan-Michael Gambill and Andy Roddick 7-5, 7-6 (8-6).

2007 Thirty-old-year-old Carlos Moya wins his 20th career ATP title—and his fifth at the Croatian Open in Umag—defeating 33-year-old Andrei Pavel 6-4, 6-2 in the final.

2007 Dmitry Tursunov of Russia wins his second career ATP title, defeating Canada's Frank Dancevic 6-4, 7-5 in the final of the Indianapolis Tennis Championships. Dancevic plays his first career ATP singles final after never previously winning consecutive main draw matches in any ATP event. Ranked No. 109, he is the last player directly accepted into the tournament. He is the first Canadian to advance to an ATP quarterfinal (or better) since Sebastien Lareau reached the Memphis semifinals in 2001. He also is the first Canadian citizen to play in an ATP final since Greg Rusedski captured the Seoul title in 1995. The day before in the semifinals, Dancevic upsets top-seeded Andy Roddick 6-4, 7-6 (1) and admits of the upset win, "To be honest, I have no idea how I pulled it off." Says Dancevic of his upset of Roddick, "Playing against a guy like Andy, you have to keep your level up the whole match. I was focusing on myself and playing point by point. I was pretty mentally sharp."

July 30

1928 France successfully defends its Davis Cup title against the United States as Henri Cochet defeats Bill Tilden 9-7, 8-6, 6-4 clinching the 4-1 victory for France at the newly-dedicated Stade Roland Garros in Paris, which is constructed to host the Davis Cup matches. Writes P.J. Philip of the *New York Times*, "On the central court of the Roland Garros Stadium at Auteuil, that Napoleon of tennis, Big Bill Tilden, met his Waterloo today. In three straight sets, Henri Cochet swept him off the field, holding the Davis Cup for France and writing finis to the world championship career of the most brilliant tennis player of the past decade. It was Waterloo alright." Tilden's career was not entirely finished following the loss. He is kicked off the Davis Cup team prior to this famous series for his "professional" writing from tennis events, which U.S. Lawn Tennis Association officials say violate his amateur status. However, due to the huge demand to see Tilden play against the four French "Musketeers" at the newly-constructed Roland Garros Stadium, the French government and French Tennis Federation pressure the USLTA to re-instate Tilden to the team to appease the ticket-buying public. Tilden is, instead, suspended from the U.S. Championships later in the summer, but continues to play high-level amateur tennis through 1930.

1996 Andre Agassi stages a stunning comeback to advance into the medal round at the 1996 Olympic Games in Atlanta, coming back from a 3-5 third-set deficit to defeat Wayne Ferreira of South Africa 7-5, 4-6, 7-5 in the quarterfinal of men's singles. Ferreira is upset with Agassi's behavior and profane language that results in Agassi receiving a point penalty in the first game of the second set. Says Ferreira, "I honestly believe he should be kicked off the court for the things he was saying. They were pretty rude and actually the worst I've ever heard anybody say. I'm surprised the umpires took it so lightly. If I was sitting in the chair, I probably would have done something different." Retorts Agassi, "It was about the only way he was going to beat me." Also advancing into the medal round in men's singles Leander Paes of India, who defeats Renzo Furlan of Italy 6-1, 7-5, Sergi Bruguera of Spain, who defeats Mal Washington of the United States 7-6 (8), 4-6, 7-5 and Fernando Meligeni of Brazil, who defeats Russia's Andrei Olhovskiy 7-5, 6-3

1932 John Van Ryn and Wilmer Allison dramatically keep the United States alive against France in the Davis Cup Challenge Round as they defeat Henri Cochet and Jacques Brugnon 6-3, 11-13, 7-5, 4-6, 6-4. *American Lawn*

Tennis magazine calls the encounter "one of the best doubles contests in the history of the game." The win by the American duo cuts France's lead over the United States to 2-1 on the second day of play in the Challenge Round played at Stade Roland Garros in Paris, France.

1991 Playing her first official WTA Tour match in nearly two months since the French Open, world No. 1 Monica Seles defeats Pam Shriver 6-2, 6-2 in the first round of the Acura Classic in Carlsbad, Calif. Seles skips Wimbledon and does not explain her absence due to shin splints for several weeks. Seles also skips the Federation Cup but plays in a tennis exhibition in Mahwah, N.J., where she sports a shirt with the words "Rome, Paris, Wimbledon" with the word "Wimbledon" crossed off and "Mahwah" written above it.

1984 Andres Gomez defeats 16-year-old Aaron Krickstein 6-2, 6-2 in the final of the D.C. National Bank Tennis Classic. "It was one of the best matches I have ever played," says the Ecuadorean after the 58-minute victory. "I started a little slowly, but once I picked up my serve, I had no problem."

1992 Top-seeds Jim Courier and Steffi Graf advance into the second round of the Olympic Games in Barcelona, combining to lose a total of three games. Courier defeats Gilad Bloom of Israel 6-2, 6-0, 6-0, winning the final 14 games of the match, while Graf dispatches of Brenda Schutlz of Holland 6-1, 6-0.

July 31

1932 In what Hall of Fame journalist and historian Bud Collins calls "The Great Cup Robbery," France defeats the United States in the Davis Cup Challenge Round for the fifth time in six years as Jean Borotra clinches the Davis Cup for France, erasing a two-sets-to-love deficit, a 3-5 fifth-set deficit and four match points to defeat Wilmer Allison 1-6, 3-6, 6-4, 6-2, 7-5. Allison holds three match points while leading 5-3 in the fifth set—40-15 and then with an advantage—but has his serve broken. In the next game, Allison holds another match point on Borotra's serve. After missing his first serve, Borotra hits a second serve that by all accounts is out—but not called by the linesman. Allison, who did not make a play on the serve, runs to the net to shake hands with Borotra, but stands in disbelief at the non-call. Allison wins only one point in the remainder of the match to lose 7-5 in the fifth set, giving France it's third point of the series, clinching the Cup.

2005 Andre Agassi wins his 60th and what ultimately becomes his final ATP singles title, defeating 22-year-old Gilles Muller of Luxembourg 6-4, 7-5 in 1 hour, 28 minutes to win the Mercedes-Benz Cup in Los Angeles. The title is also the fourth tournament victory at the Los Angeles event for Agassi, who also wins on the campus at UCLA in 1998, 2001 and 2002. "It's been a dream week for me for sure," says the 35-year-old Agassi. "I couldn't have expected to come in here and find my comfort level so early on in the tournament and get better with each match. It's a great sign."

1996 Arantxa Sanchez Vicario and Lindsay Davenport advance into the gold medal match at the Atlanta Olympics with semifinal victories at Stone Mountain Park. Davenport defeats teammate and good friend Mary Joe Fernandez 6-2, 7-6 (6), while Sanchez Vicario defeats Jana Novotna 6-4, 1-6, 6-3. Novotna takes exception to Sanchez Vicario, her WTA Tour doubles partner, and her constant questioning of line calls during the semifinal controntation. Says Novotna, "What is really sad, what is upsetting, is that you are playing against your doubles partner and she's questioning every single call there is, even if there is no reason for it. You wouldn't expect that of a player of her caliber. But it's nothing personal. She doesn't do it only to me, she does it with everybody. That's the way she is, it's her problem." Says Sanchez Vicario, "I didn't question any of the calls. I think that's something that is not right for her to say. I'm very surprised that she says that. Maybe she was disappointed, because every time she has a chance, she has lost against me. But this is tennis and that's the way it is." In men's doubles, Australia's Todd Woodbridge and Mark Woodforde win an epic men's doubles semifinal to advance into the gold medal match, defeating Jacco Eltingh and Paul Haarhuis of the Netherlands, 6-2, 5-7, 18-16, in a semifinal that takes 3 hours, 16 minutes. Woodbridge and Woodforde lead at one point 9-8, 40-love—triple match point—but are unable to put away the Dutch pair. Eltingh and Haarhuis have two match points with Woodforde serving at 11-12, 15-40, but are not able to convert. "It was like, 'What are we going to be doing to ourselves when we lose this match?'" Woodforde says after the match.

1992 Michael Chang is hampered by an upset stomach and loses in the second round of the Olympic Games in Barcelona, losing 6-2, 3-6, 6-3, 6-3 to Brazil's Jaime Oncins. Chang's teammate Pete Sampras, however, advances into the third round with a 6-3, 6-0, 3-6, 6-1 win over Peru's Jaime Yzaga.

2007 Austria's Stefan Koubek saves four match points and comes back from a 6-0, 4-0 deficit to defeat Agustin Callieri of Argentina 0-6, 7-6 (3), 7-5 in the first round of the Orange Prokom Open in Sopot, Poland. Koubek actually overcomes losing 21 straight games over two matches as, entering his match with Callieri, he loses 11 straight games in his 6-4, 6-0 loss to countryman Daniel Koellerer in the first round of Kitzbuhel the previous week. Koubek says he didn't start to think about his losing streak before losing the first set. Says Koubek, "Sitting down on the changeover for those two minutes I said 'Geez, 6-0 and I lost 11 games in Kitzbuhel, which makes it 17.' I said to myself that it was time to win a game because it's not a record you want to hold. When I finally won a game after losing 21 in a row I put my arms up and made fun of myself. In Kitzbuhel it was, uh, no comment, basically. Losing 11 games in a row and then coming here and losing 10 in a row, which makes 21. I didn't feel too comfortable on the court. I didn't know what to do. I was very unhappy with my game. At 6-0, 5-1 down [against Calleri] I didn't really think I could win the match but I thought it was worth trying. It's a great feeling to have won under those circumstances but a comeback like that is nothing you try to reach in your career."

August 1

1921 Jack Kramer, one of the supreme names in tennis who contributes significantly to the game as a player, promoter, administrator and TV broadcaster, is born in Las Vegas, Nev. Kramer is a Davis Cup hero for the United States, helping the U.S. regain the Cup in 1946 and defend it again in 1947, while he also wins Wimbledon in 1947 and the U.S. Championships in 1946 and 1947. He is a major figure in pro tennis starting in 1948 as a player and later as a promoter and administrator who helps start the ATP players union and conceptualize the current "Grand Prix" circuit with a year-end championship.

1982 Nineteen-year-old Tracy Austin wins her 30th—and what ultimately is her last—WTA singles title in San Diego, Calif., defeating 15-year-old Kathy Rinaldi 7-6, 6-3, in the final of the $125,000 Wells Fargo Open.

1992 No. 1 seed and reigning French and Australian Open champion Jim Courier is dismissed in the second round of the Barcelona Olympics, winning only seven games in a 6-4, 6-2, 6-1 loss to eventual gold medalist Marc Rosset of Switzerland. Also joining Courier on the sidelines in the upset-riddled tournament is Boris Becker of Germany, who loses to Fabrice Santoro of France 6-1, 3-6, 6-1, 6-3.

2004 Playing on the second anniversary of the death of his former coach and good friend Peter Carter, Roger Federer defeats Andy Roddick 7-5, 6-3 in the battle of the world's No. 1 and No. 2 players in the final of the Masters Series—Canada in Toronto. Federer dedicates the win to Carter, an Australian who guided Federer during his formative years until he turned professional. Federer also becomes the first player since Björn Borg in 1979 to win three consecutive tournaments on three different surfaces—grass, clay and hard courts.

1996 Andre Agassi overcomes the drop-shoting, chipping and charging Leander Paes of India, defeating the No. 127-ranked player 7-6, (5), 6-3 to advance into the gold medal match at the Olympic Games in Atlanta. Sergi Bruguera of Spain defeats Fernando Meligeni of Brazil 7-6 (9), 6-2 to advance into the gold medal match against Agassi. Says Agassi of the style of play of Paes, "I stopped guessing and I started using a simple philosophy. If I thought it was ridiculous, I was going to plan on him doing it."

August 2

1992 In an astonishing day of disappointment for Pete Sampras, the future 14-time major tournament winner and six-time year-end No. 1 player lets two-sets-to-love leads slip away in losses in singles and doubles on the same day at the Barcelona Olympics. In singles, Sampras blows a two-sets-to-love lead in a 6-7 (7), 1-6, 7-5, 6-0, 6-3 third-round loss to Russian Andrei Cherkasov. Sampras then takes the court in doubles with Jim Courier, losing the two-set lead in their 5-7, 4-6, 6-3, 6-2, 6-2 loss to Spain's Sergio Casal and Emilio Sanchez. Says Sampras, "It was a tough day at the office—a day you just want to get over."

1996 No. 9 seed Lindsay Davenport is the surprise winner of the gold medal in women's singles at the Olympic Games, upsetting No. 2 seed Arantxa Sanchez Vicario of Spain 7-6, 6-2 in the gold medal match at the Atlanta Olympics. Says Davenport, whose father Wink was a member of the 1968 U.S. Olympic volleyball team, "This means everything for me. No matter what else happens in my life, I'll always be a gold medalist." Jana Novotna of the Czech Republic defeats American Mary Joe Fernandez 7-6, 6-4 in the bronze medal match. In men's doubles, Aussies Todd Woodbridge and Mark Woodforde win the Olympic gold medal, defeating Tim Henman and Neil Broad of Great Britain 6-4, 6-4, 6-2.

1971 Twenty-nine-year-old Margaret Court announces that she is pregnant and will not defend her U.S. Open women's singles championship in one month's time. "I hope to return to competitive tennis after my baby is born, but perhaps on a more restricted schedule," says Court. "Ultimately, I plan to continue in some phase of tennis as long as I have something to contribute."

1998 Continuing his dramatic rise from a ranking of No. 141 from the previous fall, Andre Agassi defeats Tim Henman 6-4, 6-4 to win the Mercedes Benz Cup in Los Angeles. The win for Agassi was his fourth title of the year and moves him to a ranking of No. 11. Says Agassi, "It's been a long road. I've climbed 130 spots this year and 11 more to go."

1985 Aaron Krickstein leads unheralded Hansjorg Schwaier two sets to one, but falters to lose to the world No. 39 2-6, 6-1, 2-6, 6-1, 8-6 in 3 hours, 35 minutes giving West Germany a 2-0 lead over the United States in the Davis Cup quarterfinals in Hamburg—spoiling Krickstein's 18th birthday.

August 3

1996 Andre Agassi wins the Olympic gold medal in men's singles, dominating Spain's Sergi Bruguera 6-2, 6-3, 6-1 in only 78 minutes. Agassi becomes the first American to win Olympic gold in men's singles in 72 years—joining Vincent Richards in 1924—although tennis was not on the official Olympic program from 1924 to 1984. Says Agassi of his gold medal, "To me, this is the greatest thing I've accomplished in this sport. I'd keep this over all of them." Agassi, who at the time had won Wimbledon, the U.S. Open and the Australian Open, would go and win the French Open in 1999 to become the only man in tennis history to win all four major singles titles and Olympic gold. Following the victory, Agassi hugs and celebrates with fiancée Brooke Shields, U.S. Coach Tom Gullikson and his father Mike, an Olympic boxer for Iran at the 1948 and 1952 Olympics. Leander Paes of India, ranked No. 127 in the world, wins the bronze medal—India's first medal in 16 years—defeating Fernando Meligeni of Brazil 3-6, 6-2, 6-4 in the bronze medal match. Americans Mary Joe Fernandez and Gigi Fernandez win the gold in women's doubles, defeating the Czech Republic's Helena Sukova and Jana Novotna 7-6 (6), 6-4.

2006 The United States Tennis Association announces that the USTA National Tennis Center—the world's largest public tennis facility and home of the U.S. Open—will be renamed the USTA Billie Jean King National Tennis Center, honoring the tennis legend and trailblazer whose pioneering efforts helped change the sport of tennis and launch the drive for gender equality in sports and in society. Says King in the USTA's official press release, "This obviously is a great honor for me. This outstanding facility is a public park, a place where everyone can come and enjoy our wonderful sport. It is truly humbling that this will link me with Arthur Ashe with whom I celebrated many experiences and shared dreams of the future for this great sport. I know this will continue to be a place where present and future generations of players come out, pick up a racquet, learn a sport and dare to dream big and go for it."

1999 In what ultimately becomes her first WTA Tour appearance, Steffi Graf is forced to retire with a left thigh injury trailing Amy Frazier 6-4, 5-7, 1-2, deuce, in her first round match at the TIG Classic in Carlsbad, Calif. Graf holds a press conference 10 days later, where she officially announces her retirement from professional tennis.

1980 Jose-Luis Clerc of Argentina continues his mastery over John McEnroe on clay with a 6-3, 6-2 victory in the final of the Mutual Benefit Life Open in South Orange, N.J. "Don't take anything away from him," McEnroe says of Clerc. "He's outstanding on clay and played very well today. I didn't. I was stupid because I didn't apply any pressure and move him around." Clerc wins the third of four matches against McEnroe, with all three of his wins coming on clay courts, including a 6-3, 6-2, 4-6, 13-11 decision in Argentina's defeat of the United States in Davis Cup play earlier in the year. The two players conclude their careers splitting the 10 matches they play, McEnroe finally being able to beat Clerc on clay in the World Team Cup in Dusseldorf, Germany in 1984 by a 6-3, 6-3 margin.

1997 Chris Woodruff of Knoxville, Tenn., nick-named "Country" by his fellow American players, wins his first—and biggest—title of his career, defeating reigning French Open champion Gustavo Kuerten of Brazil 7-5, 6-4, 6-3 in the final of the Canadian Open in Montreal.

1981 Fourteen-year-old Kathy Rinaldi plays her first match as a professional player, defeating Cissie Donigan 6-1, 6-3 in the first round of the U.S. Clay Court Championships in Indianapolis. Earlier in the year, Rinaldi, a ninth-grader from Stuart, Fla., reaches the quarterfinals of the French Open playing as an amateur.

1986 Karel Novacek of Czechoslovakia, ranked No. 110 in the world and never previously reaching a quarterfinal of a professional event, defeats No. 2 seed and No. 15-ranked Thierry Tulasne of France 6-1, 7-6 (4) to win the D.C. Tennis Classic in Washington, D.C. The 21-year-old Novacek enters the tournament having lost his last five matches, but upsets five-seeded players during the week, including Guillermo Vilas in the second round and top-seeded Andres Gomez in the semifinals. Novacek goes on to becomes a top 10 player, achieving a career high ranking of No. 8, winning 13 ATP singles titles and reaching the semifinals of the U.S. Open in 1994.

August 4

2007 Six-foot-10 inch upstart American John Isner, less than two months after finishing up his four-year college career at the University of Georgia and playing in only his second career ATP Tour-level event, wins his fifth straight match in a third-set tie-break, defeating Gael Monfils of France 6-7 (4), 7-6 (1), 7-6 (2) in the semifinals of the Legg Mason Tennis Classic in Washington, DC. A last-minute wild card entry into the tournament and ranked No. 416 in the world, Isner beats in succession Tim Henman of Britain 4-6, 6-4, 7-6 (4), Benjamin Becker of Germany 3-6, 7-5, 7-6 (6), fellow American Wayne Odeznik 6-7 (4), 7-6 (3), 7-6 (2) and Tommy Haas of Germany 6-4, 6-7 (6), 7-6 (6) before beating Monfils. Jokes Haas of Isner and his height after his quarterfinal loss, "He served quite well. I think the tour should come up with a system, where if you're over 6-foot-6 you shouldn't be allowed to play.'" Isner's run ends in the final the following day, when Andy Roddick beats the Greensboro, N.C. native 6-4, 7-6 (4) to win his 23rd career title.

1973 The U.S. doubles team of Stan Smith and Erik van Dillen and the Chilean doubles team of Jaime Fillol and Patricio Corneja play the longest set in Davis Cup history as the Chilean team wins the 3-hour, 45-minute second set 39-37 in the Davis Cup quarterfinals in Little Rock, Ark. After Smith finishes a darkness-suspended singles victory over Corneja giving the U.S. a 2-0 lead, Fillol and Corneja lead Smith and van Dillen 9-7, 39-37, 6-8, 1-5 before play is suspended due to darkness.

1991 Pete Sampras wins his first official ATP Tour title since he captures the U.S. Open the previous year, defeating Brad Gilbert 6-2, 6-7, 6-3 to win Volvo Championships of Los Angeles on the campus of UCLA. Afterward, Sampras says he is ready to deal with the pressure of going into the U.S. Open as the defending champion. "I'm not going to worry about being the defending champion," says Sampras. "I'm just going to go out there and play, but I'm sure I will be bombarded." Sampras also beats Gilbert 6-3, 6-4, 6-2 the previous December to win the Grand Slam Cup—and it's $2 million first prize—but the event is not deemed an official ATP event.

1985 Arthur Ashe captains the United States Davis Cup for the last time as 17-year-old Boris Becker, one month removed from winning his first Wimbledon title, defeats 18-year-old Aaron Krickstein 6-2, 6-2, 6-1 to win the fifth and decisive match in West Germany's 3-2 win over the United

States in the Davis Cup quarterfinal in Hamburg. Earlier, Eliot Teltscher wins an inspired 6-4, 2-6, 5-7, 6-4, 6-2 decision over Hansjorg Schwaier in 3 hours, 45 minutes to even the series at 2-2. The previous day, Ken Flach and Robert Seguso rally from a 3-5 fifth-set-deficit to defeat Becker and Andreas Maurer 6-2, 6-8, 6-1, 4-6, 7-5 to stave off elimination and cut West Germany's lead to 2-1. Becker serves to eliminate the United States 3-0 in the doubles match at 5-4 in the fifth set, but is broken by the American duo, who rally to win the final four games of the match. Ashe, after five years as U.S. Davis Cup captain and two Davis Cup titles (1981 and 1982) resigns the post on Oct. 22, 1985.

1996 In his first tournament since he triumphed at Wimbledon three weeks earlier, Richard Krajicek of the Netherlands is defeated in the championship match of the Infiniti Open in Los Angeles, played on the campus of UCLA, losing to Michael Chang 6-4, 6-3. The win marks Chang's first tournament triumph in the Los Angeles event, after losing in the final on three different occasions.

1900 The first-ever British Davis Cup team of Arthur Gore, E.D. Black and H. Roper Barrett arrive by boat in New York Harbor en route to the Longwood Cricket Club in Boston, Mass., for its match with the United States.

August 5

1973 The longest doubles match in Davis Cup history concludes as Stan Smith and Erik van Dillen play only 10 games to complete a darkness-suspended 7-9, 37-39, 8-6, 6-1, 6-3 victory over Jaime Fillol and Patricio Corneja in a match that concludes with a total playing time of 6 hours, 10 minutes. The win gives the United States an insurmountable 3-0 lead over Chile. The match, played in North Little Rock, Ark., is highlighted by calls of the University of Arkansas cheer "Woooo. Pig, Soie" from fans. Says Smith of the Arkansas Razorback cheers, "It was the most tremendous thing I've ever heard." The United States wins the match 4-1.

1986 John McEnroe returns from a six-month sabbatical from tennis—in which he marries actress Tatum O'Neal and becomes a father for the first time—and defeats Yugoslavia's Marko Ostoja 7-5, 6-3 in the first round of the Volvo International at Stratton Mountain, Vermont. McEnroe conducts a 70-minute press conference after the match—his first appearance with the media since he played his last match, a first-round loss to Brad Gilbert in January's Grand Prix Masters. "I felt a little strange," says McEnroe of his first match back against his No. 104th-ranked opponent. "It was hard to get in the flow. It felt good to be out there, but....There's a combination of things here to throw me off. Like the altitude. I have felt myself playing better in practice. Today I wasn't missing the ball by an inch, I was missing it by more. I felt a little flat."

2007 Top-seeded Maria Sharapova wins her first title in 10 months, defeating Patty Schnyder 6-2, 3-6, 6-0 in the final Acura Classic tournament in LaJolla, Calif. Sharapova, who last wins a tournament in Linz, Austria in October of 2006, also wins the Acura title in 2005. "It's always good to win a title," Sharapova says. "But to actually come back the year after and back it up is good." The popular WTA Tour tournament ends its 24-year run in the San Diego area as the tournament promoters sell the event rights back to the WTA Tour.

1990 Stefan Edberg overcomes a twisted ankle to defeat Michael Chang 7-6 (4), 2-6, 7-6 (3) in 2 hours, 37 minutes to win the singles title at Volvo Tennis—Los Angeles on the campus of UCLA. Edberg twists his ankle changing directions in the sixth game of the second set and is forced to abandon his serve and volley tactics. Says Edberg of the injury, "After I twisted it, I had to change my game. I thought about defaulting."

August 6

1902 After a one-year hiatus, the second-ever Davis Cup matches begin at the Crescent Athletic Club in Brooklyn, N.Y., as the United States and Britain split the first two matches. Reggie Doherty of Britain defeats William Larned of the United States 2-6, 3-6, 6-3, 6-4, 6-4 and Malcolm Whitman of the United States defeats Joshua Pim of Britain 6-1, 6-1, 1-6, 6-0. Unlike the first Davis Cup matches in 1900 at Boston's Longwood Cricket Club, admission is free—and 5,000 fans come to watch the spectacle.

1986 Little-known Andre Agassi, a 16-year-old from Las Vegas with a two-toned punk hair cut, defeats No. 5 seed Tim Mayotte 4-6, 6-4, 6-2 in the second round of the Volvo International at Stratton Mountain, Vermont.

1995 Michael Stich and Thomas Enqvist exchange service holds for the first 27 games of the match, before Stich is finally able to secure the service break and go on to defeat Enqvist 6-7 (9), 7-6 (4), 6-2 in the final of the Infiniti Open in Los Angeles, played on the campus of UCLA.

1995 Twenty-year-old Albert Costa of Spain wins his first ATP singles title, defeating reigning French Open champion Thomas Muster 4-6, 6-4, 7-6 (3), 2-6, 6-4 in the final of the Generali Open in Kitzbuhel, Austria. The loss for Muster is his first at the clay court event since 1990.

2006 Playing in the first U.S. final of his 10-year-career, Arnaud Clement of France defeats Andy Murray of Britain 7-6(3), 6-2 to win the Legg Mason Tennis Classic in Washington, D.C.

2006 Maria Sharapova defeats Kim Clijsters 7-5, 7-5 to win the Acura Classic in San Diego to win her first North American summer hard court tournament. The win is Sharapova's first in five meetings with the reigning U.S. Open champion Clijsters. Says Sharapova, "I had lost to her four times in a row, so I thought this might be my lucky day. It's amazing to get the title."

August 7

1903 The Davis Cup is wrestled from American arms for the first time ever as brothers Reggie and Laurie Doherty defeat William Larned and Robert Wrenn, respectively, as Britain completes a 4-1 win over the United States at the Longwood Cricket Club in Boston, Mass. Laurie Doherty clinches the victory with 6-3, 6-8, 6-0, 2-6, 7-5 win over Larned. Reggie Doherty, who pairs with brother Laurie to beat the U.S. sibling pairing of George and Robert Wrenn, beats Robert Wrenn 6-4, 3-6, 6-3, 6-8, 6-4 in the fifth and final match of the series.

1992 Sixteen-year-old Jennifer Capriati is the unlikely gold medal winner in women's singles at the Olympic Games in Barcelona, producing a stunning 3-6, 6-3, 6-4 upset of Steffi Graf of Germany in the gold medal match. Says Capriati, "It was so emotional, I got the chills out there. This is unbelievable. I mean, I can't believe it. The last two weeks, I saw all the other athletes up there on the victory stand and I thought, 'Wow, that would be so cool.'" Capriati, who was a celebrated—and voyeured—as a "about to turn 14-years-old" rookie in March of 1990, fights expectations to win major tournaments and fill the void in women's tennis left by the retirement of Chris Evert three years earlier. After a semifinal upset of local favorite Arantxa Sanchez Vicario and her final round upset of 1988 gold medalist Graf, Capriati begins to show her potential for winning the biggest titles in the sport. Says U.S. Olympic coach Marty Riessen after the match to Mike Penner of the *Los Angeles Times*, "It's her first big win. This is right there with a Grand Slam. How many tournaments has she won? One? Three? Nothing really big. You have to break through and win one like that-and she did it by beating the best players in the tournament-(Spaniard Arantxa) Sanchez in Barcelona (and) Graf, for the very first time. Winning the Olympics, the gold, that's going to change her. The confidence she's going to get from this is going to help her a lot." In men's doubles, Boris Becker and Michael Stich defeat the South African team of Wayne Ferreira and Piet Norval, 7-6, 4-6, 7-6, 6-3 to win the gold medal. Ferreira and Norval's silver medal, however, is South Africa's first Olympic medal since 1960.

2006 Jose Acasuso of Argentina and Germany's Bjorn Phau equal the record for the longest tie-break ever played in men's singles competition when the pair play a 38-point second-set tie-break as Acasuso beats Phau 7-5, 7-6 (18) in the first round of the Masters Series—Canada in Toronto. The 38-point tie-break marks the sixth time a tie-break has extended as long, starting with

Bjorn Borg and Premjit Lall first contesting a 38-point tie-break in Borg's first round win at Wimbledon in 1973. Others include, Goran Ivanisevic defeating Daniel Nestor 6-4, 7-6 (5), 7-6 (20-18) in the first round of the 1993 U.S. Open, Ivanisevic defeating Greg Rusedski, 4-6, 6-4, 7-6 (20-18) in the semifinal of 1997 Queens Club, Roger Federer defeating Marat Safin 6-3, 7-6 (20-18) in the 2004 semifinal of the Tennis Masters Cup in Houston and Andy Roddick defeating Jo-Wilfried Tsonga 6-7 (18-20), 7-6 (7-2), 6-2, 6-3 in the first round of the 2007 Australian Open.

1972 Stan Smith overcomes a slow clay court, dubious line-calling and a partisan Spanish crowd of 7,000 in defeating Juan Gisbert 11-9, 10-8, 6-4 in the fifth and decisive match in the 3-2 victory for the United States over Spain in Barcelona. The win vaults the United States into the Davis Cup final against Romania, an historic Davis Cup final in Bucharest, where Smith again prevails on clay, against suspect line-calling and partisan crowds to lead the United States to victory. Smith calls the 3-hour, 25-minute win over Gisbert "a milestone" and tells Michael Katz of the *New York Times* after the match that he lacked confidence going into the match. "I gave myself only a 50-50 chance of winning," Smith tells Katz. "I was hoping my match wouldn't count." Earlier in the day, with the United States leading the series 2-1, Smith's teammate Harold Solomon is unable to clinch victory for the United States as he loses to Andres Gimeno 6-3, 6-1, 2-6, 6-2 to set up the fifth-and-decisive match.

1978 John McEnroe and Peter Fleming win their first of 50 professional doubles titles together as a team at the end of a chaotic day of tennis at the Grand Prix Championships in South Orange, N.J. McEnroe and Fleming beat Guillermo Vilas and Ion Tiriac 6-3, 6-3 in the doubles final after Vilas plays two other matches during the day. He begins the day at 11 am beating Balazs Taroczy of Hungary 7-6 (3), 6-1 in the singles semifinal. At 3 pm, Vilas and Jose-Luis Clerc take the court for the singles final, but a downpour delays play for nearly an hour before the players return to the court and Vilas wins the singles title 6-1, 6-3. After accepting the trophy and the $12,750 first prize, Vilas says to the *New York Times* while eating an orange and an ice cream sandwich that conditions for playing are challenging to say the least. Says Vilas, "It is difficult to play a tournament like this. One match in the morning; I eat something; I prepare for the finals match; I walk on the court; It rains: I come back here to the locker room; someone comes in again and tells me it is time to play..."

August 8

1900 The first Davis Cup matches are played at the Longwood Cricket Club in Boston, Mass., as Dwight Davis, the donor of the Cup that now bears his name, helps the United States to a 2-0 lead over Britain. Davis, a student at Harvard who purchased the sterling silver bowl as a prize for the international tennis competition among nations, defeats E.D. Black 4-6, 6-2, 6-4, 6-4 in the opening match of the series. Malcolm Whitman, another Harvard student, puts the United States up 2-0 as he defeats Britain's Arthur Gore 6-1, 6-3, 6-2. According to the *New York Times*, "The courts were wet from the heavy rain and afforded the players none too sure of footing." Of Davis, the *New York Times* reports, "Davis played a dashing game running to the net at every opportunity and placing the balls hard and far into the corners" while of Whitman, it states that he was "sending ground strokes first to one corner and then the other, and coming to the net only under the most favorable circumstances."

1992 Marc Rosset is the surprise winner of the gold medal in men's singles at the Barcelona Olympics, defeating another unheralded finalist Jordi Aresse of Spain 7-6 (2), 6-4, 3-6, 4-6, 8-6 in 5 hours, 3 minutes. Rosset serves 33 aces in the match, including a stretch of four in a row when serving at 6-6 in the final set before breaking Aresse's serve to clinch the match. In women's doubles, Gigi Fernandez and Mary Joe Fernandez win the gold medal, defeating Spain's Arantxa Sanchez Vicario and Conchita Martinez, 7-5, 2-6, 6-2.

1902 Ten thousand fans show up to watch the meaningless Davis Cup doubles match between Holcombe Ward and Dwight Davis of the United States and Reggie and Laurie Doherty of Britain at the Crescent Athletic Club in Brooklyn, N.Y. With the United States already assured victory in the match with a 3-1 lead in the best-of-five series, Britain makes for a 3-2 final score as the Doherty brothers defeat Ward and Davis 3-6, 10-8, 6-3, 6-4. The day before, William Larned and Malcolm Whitman clinch victory for the U.S.—Bill Larned defeating Joshua Pim 6-3, 6-2, 6-3, while Mal Whitman defeats Reggie Doherty 6-1, 7-5, 6-4. Curiously, while Davis Cup usually contests the doubles point as the middle match of the best-of-five-match series, the doubles is played last in the 1902 Challenge Round.

1981 Roger Federer, the talented Swiss player regarded by many as the greatest player to play the game, is born in Basel, Switzerland. Federer breaks through and wins his first major title at Wimbledon in 2003, defeating Mark Philippoussis in the final and goes on to win the next four titles at the All England Club, tying Bjorn Borg's modern record of five straight titles. Federer's attempt at a sixth straight title is stopped by his arch rival, Rafael Nadal, in an incredible 6-4, 6-4, 6-7 (5), 6-7 (8), 9-7 final in 2008, regarded by many as the greatest match of all time. Federer is the only man in tennis history to win three majors in a calendar year in three separate years when he sweeps the Australian, Wimbledon and U.S. titles in 2004, 2006 and 2007.

1986 John McEnroe defeats 16-year-old Andre Agassi 6-3, 6-3 in the quarterfinals of the Volvo International in Stratton Mountain, Vermont. Says McEnroe of an Agassi return of serve on the second point of the match, "I've played Becker, Connors and Lendl and no one ever hit a return that hard at me. I never even saw the ball."

August 9

1900 The United States clinches victory in the first-ever Davis Cup matches at the Longwood Cricket Club in Boston, Mass. Holcombe Ward and Dwight Davis defeat E.D. Black and H. Roper Barrett 6-4, 6-4, 6-4 to clinch the 3-0 win over Britain.

1986 John McEnroe and Boris Becker engage in a heated and emotional semifinal at the Volvo International in Stratton Mountain, Vermont with Becker saving three match points and claiming a 3-6, 7-5, 7-6 (10-8) victory. McEnroe, playing in his first tournament of the year after a six-month lay-off, is upset at Becker for returning shots that are already ruled out and asks him during the match: "Who do you think you're dealing with?" and later saying: "Somebody ought to teach you a lesson." Says Becker of McEnroe, "Six and a half months off and he's still the same guy, which is too bad. He always feels that everybody does bad things to him and is trying to cheat him." Says McEnroe of Becker, "I want respect from a younger player. I don't need him to stall on me. I don't feel I should be treated like the 110th player in the world." In the other semifinal at the event, Ivan Lendl defeats Jimmy Connors 6-4, 3-6, 6-2.

1938 Rod Laver, the only player in the history of the sport to win the Grand Slam twice, is born in Rockhampton, Queensland, Australia. "The Rocket" wins 11 major singles titles during his career—including sweeps of all four major titles during the 1962 season as an amateur and in 1969 as a professional. Laver also pockets four men's singles titles at Wimbledon, winning in 1961, 1962, 1968 and 1969. Writes Bud Collins in *The Bud Collins History of Tennis*, "Few champions have been as devastating and dominant as Laver was as amateur and pro during the 1960s. An incessant attacker, he was nevertheless a complete player who glowed in the backcourt and at the net. Layer's 5-foot-8-1/2, 145-pound body seemed to dangle from a massive left arm that belonged to a gorilla, an arm with which he bludgeoned the ball and was able to impart ferocious topspin."

1981 Jose Luis Clerc wins his 25th consecutive match and his fourth straight tournament defeating Ivan Lendl 4-6, 6-4, 6-2 in the final of the U.S. Men's Clay Court Championships in Indianapolis, Ind. Says Clerc, "I'm very tired, but I'm very happy. I prepared for the summer here in America. I think I prepared very good. I play so well in the summer."

August 10

1997 No. 1 ranked Pete Sampras opens his final round match with Thomas Muster at the Thritway ATP Championships in Cincinnati with a 130 mph ace and defeats the Austrian 6-3, 6-4 to win his 49th career ATP singles title. Says Sampras, "I played great all week."

1985 Ivan Lendl defeats Jimmy Connors 6-0, 4-6, 6-4 in the semifinals of the Volvo International at Stratton Mountain, Vermont. John McEnroe also advances to the singles final, defeating Robert Seguso 6-2, 6-3. Says Connors of playing Lendl, "Playing him a best-of-three is like a sprint. If he gets off to a good start he doesn't have time to get nervous and start gagging. The tighter it gets, the tighter he gets." Says Lendl, "The thing about Jimmy is if you beat him, 6-0, in the first set, you still can't count him out. If I had broken him in the first game of the second set, maybe I would have run away with it. But I didn't." McEnroe takes the title the next day, defeating Lendl 7-6 (7-4), 6-2, but Lendl avenges his defeat later in the summer, defeating McEnroe in the final of the U.S. Open to seize the No. 1 ranking away from McEnroe for good.

1980 Jose Luis Clerc ends the string of upsets by Mel Purcell, defeating the American 7-5, 6-3 in the final of the U.S. Clay Court Championships. Purcell, a qualifier who had turned pro only three-weeks before the event, defeats No. 2 seed Harold Solomon and No. 6 seed Wojtek Fibak en route to the final.

1986 Five weeks removed from losing the Wimbledon final to Boris Becker, Ivan Lendl exercises revenge over the 18-year-old German by beating him 6-4, 7-6 in the final of the Volvo International at Stratton Mountain, Vermont. Becker is listless and drained against Lendl after winning an emotionally draining semifinal match with John McEnroe the previous day. "When I got out of bed this morning, I said 'I'm still in the tournament," says Becker. "I thought yesterday (against McEnroe) was the final." Says Lendl of the Wimbledon re-match on the hard courts of Stratton, "Another day. Another match. Another surface. At Wimbledon, on the grass, Becker just cracks the ball. Here, he cracks it and it comes back."

August 11

1923 The new 14,000-seat tennis stadium at the West Side Tennis Club is opened with the inauguration of the Wightman Cup matches. The baptismal match of the USA vs. Great Britain series is played before 5,000 fans who watch Helen Wills of the United States beat Kitty McKane, 6-2, 7-5 to give the U.S. a 1-0 lead in their eventual 7-0 defeat of the Brits. The stadium becomes the host venue for the U.S. Championships/U.S. Open through 1977.

1996 In the shortest recorded final in tennis history, Barbara Paulus of Austria wins her first WTA Tour title defeating Sandra Cecchini of Italy after only three points of play in the final of the event in Maria Lankowitz, Austria. With Paulus leading 30-15 in the first game of the match, Cecchini is forced to retire with a torn tendon in her left foot.

1991 Guy Forget of France defeats Pete Sampras 2-6, 7-6 (4), 6-4 in the final of the ATP Championships in Cincinnati, Ohio. Says Forget of his slow start, "I was a bit tight, and Pete was dominating me. Until the tiebreaker, I could have lost the match. I thought to myself, we can be playing another hour or it can be over in five minutes." Says Sampras, "I started off real well, {but} in the second and third sets I was content just to return his serve and wait for him to make a mistake." The two players play again on a grander scale at the end of the year in Lyon, France at the Davis Cup Final, with Forget again defeating Sampras 7-6 (6), 3-6, 6-3, 6-4 to clinch France's emotional win over the United States to win the Davis Cup.

1996 One year after making a triumphant return to tennis at the Canadian Open in Toronto, Monica Seles wins the Canadian Open for a second straight year, defeating Arantxa Sanchez Vicario 6-1, 7-6 (2) in the final, played in Montreal. In 1995, Seles chooses Canada as the site of her return to the WTA Tour after a two-and-a-half absence following her on-court stabbing by a deranged fan in Hamburg in 1993.

2003 Kim Clijsters of Belgium becomes the No. 1 ranked player in the world for the first time in her career. Clijsters becomes the 13th woman to hold the No. 1 ranking and holds the position for a total of 19 weeks during her career.

August 12

1970 Pete Sampras, the "King of Swing" regarded by many as the greatest tennis player to ever step on a court, is born in Washington, D.C. Sampras re-writes the tennis record book during his storied 14-year career winning a record-breaking 14 men's singles majors beginning with an unexpected win at the 1990 U.S. Open as a 19-year-old—the youngest man to win the U.S. men's singles title. It takes Sampras nearly three years to win his second major—Wimbledon in 1993, defeating friend and fellow American Jim Courier in a Fourth of July four-setter. Sampras goes on to dominate at Wimbledon, winning three straight titles from 1993-1995 and, after a hiccup quarterfinal loss to eventual champion Richard Krajicek in 1996, he wins another four titles consecutively from 1997 to 2000. His win over Patrick Rafter in the 2000 Wimbledon final, his record-tying seventh Wimbledon title, also is his 13th career major singles title, breaking the all-time record he shared with Australia's Roy Emerson. A two-time winner of the Australian Open (1994, 1997), Sampras wins his fifth U.S. Open in 2002, beating Andre Agassi, the same man he beats in the 1990 U.S. Open title tilt. The 2002 Open title becomes Sampras' swan song as 50 weeks later at the 2003 U.S. Open, he officially announces his retirement after a year-long hiatus. Sampras earns the year-end No. 1 ranking for a record six years (1993-1998) and ranks in that position for a record 286 weeks. He nets 64 career singles titles and helps the U.S. to Davis Cup titles in 1992 and 1995.

1990 Stefan Edberg ascends to the No. 1 ranking in grand style, crushing Brad Gilbert 6-1, 6-1 to win the Thriftway ATP Championships in Cincinnati, Ohio. Edberg clinches the No. 1 ranking when he reaches the semifinals of the event to overtake Ivan Lendl in the top spot. "This is one to remember with all the things that have happened this week," says Edberg after beating Gilbert. "I became No. 1 after the quarterfinals, and then I proved it. I've proved it by the way I've played over the last month and a half."

2007 Novak Djokovic of Serbia upsets world No. 1 Roger Federer 7-6 (2), 2-6, 7-6 (2) in an epic final of the Tennis Masters Series—Canada final in Montreal. "It's a dream come true to win such a strong tournament as this and to win against probably the best player ever in the sport," says Djokovic, who would lose to Federer in the U.S. Open final a month later.

August 13

1999 Saying there was "nothing left to accomplish," thirty-year-old Steffi Graf announces her retirement from professional tennis in a press conference in Heidelberg, Germany. "I'm not having fun anymore," says Graf, whose 17-year career includes 22 major singles titles, 107 tournament titles and a record 377 weeks as the No. 1 player in the world. "The weeks following Wimbledon weren't easy for me," she says. "I was pulled back and forth, but when I made my decision, I didn't think about it one minute afterward."

2006 Roger Federer wins his 40th career title, defeating Richard Gasquet of France 2-6, 6-3, 6-2 in the final of the Canadian Open in Toronto. Says Federer of his slow start against the Frenchman, "I just always believe that I can turn any match around. That's what happened today. I know that once I turn it around, once I would take the lead then it would be very difficult for my opponent. That's what I always tell myself. Maybe it's an illusion sometimes, but it definitely works."

1914 As war wages in Europe for a second week, the United States and Australasia (Australia and New Zealand) begin play in the Davis Cup Challenge Round at the West Side Tennis Club in Forest Hills, Queens, N.Y. in front of 12,000 fans—the most to watch Davis Cup tennis at the time. In the opening match of the day, Kiwi Anthony Wilding registers a 7-5, 6-2, 6-3 win over Dick Williams, the man who was pulled from the icy waters of the Atlantic in the *Titanic* disaster two years earlier. "The California Comet" Maurice McLoughlin evens the days play at one match apiece as he defeats Aussie Norman Brookes 17-15, 6-3, 6-3. After Brookes and Wilding defeat Maurice McLoughlin and Thomas Bundy 6-3, 8-6, 9-7 in the doubles the next day, the climatic third day on August 15 features the first recorded example of a rowdy Davis Cup crowd. American fans yell, abuse and throw bottles at Brookes as the Aussie clinches the Davis Cup title for his team with a 6-1, 6-2, 8-10, 6-3 win over Williams. McLoughlin makes the final score 3-2, defeating Wilding 6-2, 6-3, 2-6, 6-2. Wilding would be the most high profile casualty of the war as he is killed in action on May 9, 1915 at Neuve-Chapelle, France.

1990 Stefan Edberg becomes the No. 1 ranked player in the world for the first time in his career, taking over from Ivan Lendl. Edberg holds the ranking for a total of 72 weeks during his career.

August 14

1996 Andre Agassi is disqualified from a professional match for the first and only time in his career when he curses at chair umpire Dana Loconto and hits a ball into the stands during a second-round match against Daniel Nestor at the RCA Championships in Indianapolis. After Agassi wins the first set easily 6-1, he is broken in the fifth game of the second set and slams a ball into the stands. Loconto issues a ball abuse warning to Agassi and Agassi reacts by shouting an expletive at Loconto. ATP supervisor Mark Darby is called to the court, speaks with both Loconto and Agassi, and then instructs Loconto to default Agassi. Fans, angered at the disqualification, throw paper and water bottles on the court.

1983 Martina Navratilova defeats Chris Evert Lloyd 6-1, 6-3 to win the Virginia Slims of Los Angeles in Manhattan Beach, Calif. The victory increases Navratilova's record to 54-1 for the year and is her 10th title in her last 11 tournaments. "A lot of things went my way today," says Navratilova. "I hit a lot of balls on the lines. I made sure I got my first serve in. I kept her guessing on it the entire match. I never let her get grooved. Once she gets grooved, she's tough."

2005 Nineteen-year-old reigning French Open champion Rafael Nadal defeats 35-year-old Andre Agassi 6-3, 4-6, 6-2 in 1 hour, 58 minutes to capture his first ATP hard court title at the Canadian Open in Montreal. Says Nadal, "I knew I could play good on hard courts because I've had some good scores this year, but for me, winning here is very, very nice. I have confidence now. I said before I came here my goal is to win any tournament on hard court this year."

1990 MaliVai Washington, ranked No. 103 in the world, wins the first big match of his career, defeating Ivan Lendl 6-2, 6-3 in the second round of the Volvo International in New Haven, Conn. Lendl, playing his first match since losing to Stefan Edberg in the semifinals of Wimbledon six weeks earlier, arrives only 15 minutes before the start of the match due to traffic on the Merritt Parkway from his home 40 minutes away in Greenwich, Conn.

1994 Michael Chang wins the first 11 points of the match and easily defeats an out-of-sync Stefan Edberg 6-2, 7-5 to win the Thriftway ATP Championship in Cincinnati, Ohio. Says Edberg of his performance, "It was a nightmare. It was just terrible and I almost felt embarrassed."

August 15

1995 Monica Seles returns to the WTA Tour after an absence of 837 days following her on-court stabbing by a German fan in 1993, defeating Kimberly Po 6-0, 6-3 in the first round of the Canadian Open in Toronto. Seles is driven to tears by the affection shown to her by fans, friends and family. "Just playing again—It's all I ever asked for," says Seles. "It's great to be playing. It's so simple. For a long time, everything was so dark. Now, I see the sun."

2004 Rafael Nadal of Spain wins his first career ATP singles title, defeating Jose Acasuso of Argentina 6-3, 6-4 to win the Idea Prokom Open in Sopot, Poland. At 18 years and two months, Nadal becomes the youngest player to win an ATP event since Australia's Lleyton Hewitt wins in Delray Beach, Fla., in 1999 at the same age. Nadal has little time to celebrate as he immediately jumps on a plane to represent Spain at the 2004 Olympics. "I leave to Athens tonight and play doubles tomorrow," says Nadal immediately following his victory. "Of course, I'll be tired after this but its only a doubles match so hopefully it won't affect me too much."

1999 Pete Sampras wins his 60th career title and avenges his final round loss to Patrick Rafter from a year ago, defeating the Australian 7-6 (7), 6-3 in the final of the ATP Championships in Cincinnati. The win marks the 22nd straight match win for Sampras and his fourth title in a row, to go with titles at Queens, Wimbledon and Los Angeles.

2004 The tennis competition at the 2004 Olympic Games in Athens begins as Venus Williams, the defending gold medalist in women's singles, defeats Melinda Czink of Hungary 6-1, 6-2 in the event's opening match. Says Williams, "I had so much fun at the last Olympics and so much success, and then to be here is amazing." American Andy Roddick, seeded No. 2, makes his Olympic debut with a 6-3, 7-6 (4) victory over Flavio Saretta of Brazil, swatting 12 aces and 16 service winners. Says Roddick, "There's definitely something different (about playing in the Olympics.) I was a little more nervous today than I would be normally for a first-round match." At age 47, Martina Navratilova makes her Olympic debut, pairing with Lisa Raymond to defeat Yuliya Beygelzimer and Tetyana Perebiynis of Ukraine 6-0, 6-2 in the first round of the women's doubles competition. Says Navratilova, the oldest competitor to ever play Olympic tennis, of Olympic jitters, "On my first serve of the match, I thought: 'OK, this is your first Olympic toss.'

And it was a good one, and a good serve, and that was all the jitters I had. Navratilova tops Blanche Hillyard of the United States who was 44 at the 1908 London Games and Norman Brookes of Australia who was 46 at the 1924 Paris Games. However, Navratilova is not the oldest U.S. Olympian in Athens as shooter Libby Callaghan is 52, while archer Janet Dykman and equestrian rider Debbie McDonald are 50. Says Navratilova of the Olympics, "I have mixed emotions about how the whole thing is run, because, really, everybody makes money off it but the athletes so I'm not in agreement with this Olympic ideal—amateurism, all this stuff—because that's a bunch of baloney."

1993 Martina Navratilova comes back from 1-5 second set deficit to defeat Arantxa Sanchez Vicario 7-5, 7-6 (4) to win the Virginia Slims of Los Angeles in Manhattan Beach, Calif., for a ninth time in her career. Navratilova plays in the final of the event for the 11th time in the last 13 years. In the semifinals the previous day, Navratilova needs only 51 minutes to defeat Gabriela Sabatini 6-1, 6-1.

1982 Vitas Gerulaitis defeats Ivan Lendl 4-6, 6-1, 6-3 to win the Canadian Open.

1993 Michael Chang edges Stefan Edberg 7-5, 0-6, 6-4 to win a topsy-turvy singles final at the Thriftway ATP Championships in Cincinnati, Ohio. Says Chang, "I decided if I was going to go out losing, I'd rather go out losing by going for my shots and playing the game I want to play." Says Edberg, "Today, I wasn't as sharp as I'd wished to. I wasn't playing badly, I just sort of ran out of steam."

August 16

1994 Andre Agassi, the rebel tennis player who brings the "rock and roll tennis" vernacular into the sport, angrily blasts the ATP officials and organizers of the Volvo International in New Haven for instituting in-stadium music on change-overs during the pre-U.S. Open hard court tune-up event. With music blaring on change-overs, Agassi loses to No. 113-ranked Jan Siemerink of the Netherlands 6-3, 3-6, 6-3 in the feature night match of the first round in front of 10,220 fans. Agassi spends almost his entire post-match press conference ripping the ATP experiment. "It's an embarrassment," Agassi says. "It's a joke. If any other tournament does this, I would quit tennis before I would go out there and be a part of that. And that's no exaggeration. It drove me nuts...It's not just that I was distracted by the music because any athlete has the responsibility to block out things." Continues Agassi, "It's a question of what they are doing to the sport. This is a sport. You come out here and you take pride in what you do. If these people aren't here to watch tennis, they shouldn't come at all." Agassi complains to chair umpire Paolo Pereira about the music early in the match and calls for ATP supervisor Gayle Bradshaw to the court to express his displeasure of the musical distraction. Agassi, however, is told the music would not be turned off. Following the loss, Agassi regroups his game and form very quickly and wins the next event he plays—the U.S. Open.

1921 In her much anticipated debut at the U.S. Championships, Suzanne Lenglen causes one of biggest controversies the tournament has ever experienced, quitting her first match of the tournament with defending champion Molla Bjurstedt Mallory after Mallory leads 6-2 and 0-30 on Lenglen's serve in the first game of the second set. Lenglen claims to be short of breath and stricken with a cough and starts to cry as she tells the chair umpire that she is too ill to continue. Mallory and Lenglen are regarded as the best two players in the draw, but the U.S. Championships are still six years removed from instituting seedings into the composition of the draws. A crowd of approximately 8,000 fans—the largest to ever witness a women's match in the United States—are disappointed not to see the match reach a proper conclusion—some fans even hissing, suspecting that the seemingly invincible Lenglen quits the match as not to acknowledge a proper defeat by the hands of Mallory.

2006 Andy Murray of Scotland hands Roger Federer his earliest tournament defeat in two years, defeating the world No. 1 7-5, 6-4 in the second round of the Western & Southern Financial Group Masters in Cincinnati. The win also ends Federer's 55-match win streak in North America and is Federer's first straight-set loss in 194 matches. "The streaks? I don't care about those now that they're over," says Federer. "It's going to be a relief for everybody, and now we can move on." Federer's last loss on the continent also comes at the Cincinnati-area tournament, when Dominik Hrbaty beat him in the first round in 2004. Says Murray, "I know Federer didn't play his best match, but how many guys beat him when he's playing badly anyway?"

2004 Defending singles and doubles gold medalist Venus Williams loses her first ever Olympic match, pairing with Chanda Rubin women's doubles, losing in the first round 7-5, 1-6, 6-3 to eventual gold medal winners Li Ting and Sun Tian Tian of China. Rubin is a substitute for Venus' sister Serena, who withdraws from the competition with injury and does not travel to Greece.

1998 Reigning U.S. Open champion Patrick Rafter defeats world No. 2 Pete Sampras 1-6, 7-6 (2), 6-4 to win the ATP Championships in Cincinnati. The loss to Rafter prevents Sampras from retaking the No. 1 world ranking from Marcelo Rios of Chile. The win snaps Rafter's eight-match losing streak to Sampras, whose only previous loss to the Australian comes in the quarterfinals of Indianapolis in 1993, their first career meeting.

2007 Carlos Moya wins his first round match with Juan Martin Del Potro at the Western & Southern Financial Group Masters in Cincinnati on a instant replay challenge. After Moya's shot is originally called out, the Hawk-Eye line-calling technology showed the ball just catching the back of the baseline, giving Moya a 7-5, 3-6, 7-5 win.

1930 Hall of Famer and tennis legend Tony Trabert is born in Cincinnati, Ohio. Trabert wins five major singles titles during his career including three of the four major titles in his epic 1955 season where he wins the French, Wimbledon and U.S. titles. Trabert is also an American Davis Cup icon helping the United States to three Davis Cup titles as a player and captain.

August 17

1977 The United States Tennis Association rules that 43-year-old transsexual Renee Richards will be allowed to play in the women's singles championships at the U.S. Open. The USTA statement issued on the day reads, "For the past year, the USTA has been confronted with the difficult problem of balancing consideration for an individual transsexual with considerations of fairness for women tennis players in general, especially the lower-ranked players. On the basis of medical authority, the USTA has had reason to believe that a postoperative transsexual may retain some physical and competitive advantages. It appeared to the USTA that a generally accurate, easily administered and objective test, such as the Olympic type chromosome test, was a desirable screening process in determining sex for the purpose of athletics. The New York State Court ruled in favor of an individual transsexual and places restrictions on the use of the chromosome test. As a result of this proceeding, the USTA will accept Dr. Richards as an entrant into the U.S. Open tennis championships." Richards goes on to draw No. 3 seed and reigning Wimbledon champion Virginia Wade in the first round of the 1977 U.S. Open, losing 6-1, 6-4. She, however, reaches the doubles final partnering with Betty Ann Grubb Stuart (the mother of future U.S. pro Taylor Dent), losing to Martina Navratilova and Betty Stove, 6-1, 7-6.

2004 In a self-described "terrible day," Roger Federer's Olympic dreams come to an end in a matter of hours as he is eliminated from both the singles and doubles competitions at the Athens Olympics. In singles, Federer is dismissed in the second round by unheralded No. 74-ranked Tomas Berdych of the Czech Republic 4-6, 7-5, 7-5. In doubles, an hour after his singles loss, he and partner Yves Allegro, lose to Mahesh Bhupathi and Leander Paes of India 6-2, 7-6 (7). "What can I say? It's a terrible day for me, losing singles and doubles," Federer says. "Obviously, I was aiming for a better result than this, but that's what I got. So I have to live with it."

1987 Steffi Graf ascends to the No. 1 ranking on the WTA computer for the first time in her career—and sits in the spot for a record 186 straight weeks before being bumped by Monica Seles on March 11, 1991. In all, Graf spends a record 377 weeks in the No. 1 ranking.

1970 Jim Courier, the two-time Australian Open and French Open champion and year-end world No. 1 in 1992, is born in Sanford, Fla. A standout

Davis Cupper, Courier helps the United States to two Cup titles in 1992 and 1995. He also reaches the final of the U.S. Open in 1991 and Wimbledon in 1993—earning him the distinction of being one of 15 men to play in all four major singles final during a career.

1952 Guillermo Vilas, the all-time Argentinean tennis legend who wins the French and U.S. Opens in 1977 and the Australian Open in 1978 and 1979, is born in Buenos Aires.

1986 Playing in on-court temperatures close to 115 degrees, Boris Becker defeats Stefan Edberg 6-4, 3-6, 6-3 to win the Canadian Open singles title in Toronto. "It was a tough match because it was very hot," Edberg says. "Boris returns very well on second serves, and I was missing too many first serves today. I was a little bit tired, and Boris put more pressure on me than any of the other guys did."

August 18

1970 Haroon Rahim of Pakistan wins the closest tennis match ever competed, defeating Tom Gorman 6-7 (3-5), 7-6 (5-1), 7-6 (5-4) in the second round of the Pennsylvania Grass in Haverford, Pa. The tournament is one of the first to use the controversial nine-point "sudden death" tie-break—first to win five points. Rahim trails Gorman 1-4 in the final-set tie-break (four consecutive match points) and rallies to win the last four points—and the match. With both players holding match point at 4-4, Gorman nets a return off of Rahim's second serve.

1923 In what the *New York Times* calls "one of the most devastating attacks ever launched at a title-holder," 17 seventeen-year-old Helen Wills of Berkeley, Calif., wins the first of her seven U.S. singles titles, needing only 30 minutes to defeat four-time reigning champion Molla Mallory 6-2, 6-1 in the final, snapping the 22-match winning streak for Mallory at the tournament. Mallory, a seven-time U.S. champion, wins 40 of 41 matches entering her final with Wills, beginning with her first title campaign of 1915.

2004 A black Wednesday for the U.S. Olympic tennis team as U.S. team members Andy Roddick, Venus Williams, Chanda Rubin, Lisa Raymond and the doubles team of Bob and Mike Bryan are all eliminated from the competition. The No. 2 seeded Roddick is upset in the third round by No. 16 Fernando Gonzalez of Chile 6-4, 6-4, while Williams is dismissed by Mary Piece of France by the same score. No. 16 seed Rubin is defeated by No. 2 Amelie Mauresmo of France 6-3, 6-1, while Raymond is defeated by Alicia Molik of Australia 6-4, 6-4. The No. 1 seeded doubles team of Bob and Mike Bryan are upset by Gonzalez and Nicolas Massu of Chile 7-5, 6-4. Says U.S. women's coach Zina Garrison, "Just a pretty rough day for Americans."

2006 Former world No. 1 Martina Hingis, in the full throws of her full-time comeback to the WTA Tour, defeats Svetlana Kuznetsova of Russia 7-6 (4), 6-3 in the quarterfinals of the Rogers Cup in Montreal, Canada. The win clinches a return visit to the top 10 for Hingis, marking the first time she ranks within the elite women of the world since Oct. 13, 2002. Says Hingis of her return to the top 10, "You don't want to squeeze in there by not doing anything on your own so it feels great to make it on my own. It's great I can still handle myself, hold my own out there. This was kind of my secret goal."

August 19

1984 John McEnroe defeats fellow New Yorker Vitas Gerulaitis 6-0, 6-3 after seven failed attempts, to win the Canadian Open. "I am glad to, after eight times coming here I have finally won," says McEnroe. "It was getting to be a mental thing. I didn't think I was ever going to win. I am glad that is off my back."

2007 Roger Federer wins his 50th career singles title, defeating James Blake 6-1, 6-4 in the final of the Western & Southern Financial Group Masters in Cincinnati. Says Federer, "I was mentally much more relaxed today than I was in the first round. I was playing really worried in the first round this week....That was totally different today. I felt I was going to win every point."

1922 Molla Mallory, 38, wins her seventh of eight U.S. singles titles, defeating 16-year-old Helen Wills in the final, 6-3, 6-1 at the West Side Tennis Club at Forest Hills. The 22-year age difference is the greatest disparity in ages for any major final in the history of the sport.

1932 Helen Jacobs wins her first of four straight U.S. singles titles, defeating fellow American Carolin Babcock 6-2, 6-2 in only 31 minutes at Forest Hills. Jacobs finally wins the coveted U.S. title in her seventh attempt, benefiting from the absence of her chief rival, defending champion and seven-time U.S. champ Helen Wills Moody, who decides to stay abroad in Europe after winning the French and Wimbledon titles.

2004 Forty-seven-year-old Martina Navratilova's Olympic medal dreams are dashed as she and Lisa Raymond are eliminated one round shy of the medal round at the 2004 Athens Olympics, falling to Japan's Shinobu Asagoe and Ai Sugiyama 6-4, 4-6, 6-4 in the doubles quarterfinals. Says Navratilova, "This was never a dream of mine when I was growing up. It was a bonus I was able to be here. It's disappointing, of course. We were hoping to get a medal. But the end of a dream? No. I am living my dream." In men's singles play, Mardy Fish of the United States defeats Mikhail Youzhny of Russia 6-3, 6-4 in the men's quarterfinals, while Fish's teammate, Taylor Dent, posts a 6-4, 6-1 win against the Czech Republic's Tomas Berdych, the 18-year-old who knocked off No. 1 Roger Federer.

August 20

2004 Justine Henin-Hardenne of Belgium performs one of the greatest comebacks in Olympic tennis history, coming back from a 1-5 third-set deficit to defeat Russia's Anastasia Myskina 7-5, 5-7, 8-6 in a nearly three-hour match between the past two French Open champions in the women's semifinals. Says Myskina, "I'm really, really upset. If you're up 5-1, you have to finish the match, no matter what." Amelie Mauresmo of France also advances by defeating unseeded Australian Alicia Molik 7-6 (8), 6-3. In men's singles play, Mardy Fish of the United States and Nicolas Massu of Chile advance into the gold medal match with semifinal victories. Fish defeats Fernando Gonzalez of Chile 3-6, 6-3, 6-4 while Massu beats American Taylor Dent 7-6, (5), 6-1. Says the No. 22-ranked Fish, "I didn't expect to be here, so I don't have anything to lose and I'm sure Nicolas would say the same thing. There's less pressure on both of us." In women's doubles, Li Ting and Sun Tian Tian of China defeat Paola Suarez and Patricia Tarabini of Argentina 6-2, 2-6, 9-7, in the women's doubles semifinals guaranteeing China its first Olympic tennis medal.

1995 In her first tournament in two and half years since she was stabbed on court by a deranged fan, Monica Seles wins the Canadian Open singles title in Toronto, defeating Amanda Coetzer of South Africa 6-0, 6-1 in the final. "I just can't believe it," says Seles. "Not playing in such a long time, then playing so well. It's unbelievable....There were so many emotions to get to this point. From that day to this day—what a difference."

1995 Andre Agassi wins his 20th straight match and his fourth straight U.S. summer hard court tournament, defeating Richard Krajicek of the Netherlands 3-6, 7-6(2), 6-3 to win the Volvo International in New Haven, Conn. Agassi saves two match points in the 12th game of the second set en route to his first victory at the Volvo. "There is no way in the world I should have won this match," says Agassi to the 12,065 fans at the Connecticut Tennis Center in the post-match ceremony. "I pulled it out of the hat and was very lucky." Agassi concludes the on-court awards ceremony giving tournament chairman Jim Westhall a buzz cut as the consequence of the challenge Westhall issues to Agassi earlier in the week if he wins the tournament, he would allow the closely shaven Las Vegan to shear his trademark thick hairstyle.

1992 Disgusted with his level of play, John McEnroe, in a fit of anger, pushes over a courtside ESPN TV camera during his 6-7 (6), 7-5, 7-6 (3) third-round win over No. 131-ranked Thierry Guardiola of France at the Volvo International in New Haven, Conn. The camera-pushing incident occurs with the score tied at 5-5 in the first-set tie-break and is met with a chorus of boos from the crowd. McEnroe tells reporters in his post-match press conference that he simply meant to push the camera over, not knock it over after missing a volley. Says McEnroe, "If you can't channel your energies in a more positive way and enjoy it, it's just kind of ridiculous to go out there and put myself in a position where I end up doing something stupid. It's just not necessary. I don't need it and tennis doesn't need it." McEnroe is fined $3,000 for the incident by the ATP Tour.

1931 Helen Wills Moody wins her seventh and final U.S. women's singles title, needing only 35 minutes to defeat Eileen Bennett Whittingstall of England, 6-4, 6-1 in the final.

2006 In a rematch of their U.S. Open singles final of three years earlier, Andy Roddick defeats Juan Carlos Ferrero of Spain 6-3, 6-4 to win the Western & Southern Financial Group Masters in Cincinnati. The tournament win is Roddick's first of the 2006 season and his first since winning in Lyon in October of 2005.

1973 Marty Riessen clinches victory for the United States against Romania in the Davis Cup semifinals in Alamo, Calif., defeating Toma Ovici 6-1, 4-6, 6-1, 7-5 to give the United States a 3-1 lead. Stan Smith defeats Ilie Nastase in the meaningless fifth match 5-7, 6-2, 6-3, 4-6, 6-3 closing out a 4-1 victory for the United States.

August 21

2004 Entering the Olympic Games having won only one match in the past four months due to a viral infection, Justine Henin-Hardenne of Belgium defeats Amelie Mauresmo of France 6-3, 6-3 in 78 minutes to win the gold medal in women's singles at the 2004 Olympic Games in Athens, Greece. Says Henin-Hardenne, "It's difficult for you to imagine the states of depression I went through. I realize how fortunate I am just to be able to be on the court. So I'm really glad to have had the chance to be able to give 100 percent." One day after blowing a 5-1 third-set lead to Henin-Hardenne in the semifinal, No. 3 seed Anastasia Myskina of Russia loses the bronze medal match in women's singles to unseeded Alicia Molik of Australia 6-3, 6-4. Says Myskina, "Emotionally, I was drained. I didn't have any gas left. I couldn't find any motivation." In men's singles, Fernando Gonzalez of Chile outlasts Taylor Dent of the United States 6-4, 2-6, 16-14 in three-and-a-half hours to win the bronze medal. "I can't believe I lost," Dent says. "It was longest match I've played in terms of a set. It was 16-14, is that it? It was a good match. It was a shame I lost, but it was fun to be a part of." The previous night, at 1:05 am local time in Athens, Greece, Mario Ancic and Ivan Ljubicic of Croatia complete a 7-6 (5), 4-6, 16-14 victory over India's Mahesh Bhupathi and Leander Paes in a four-hour bronze medal match in men's doubles. Both teams win 164 points in the match. Says Ljubicic, "Croatia is such a small country, so this is huge. Any medal is huge." Says Paes, "I don't think we've had this much disappointment in a long time."

1984 Thirty-year-old Vijay Amritraj, ranked No. 104 in the world, registers the upset of the year in men's tennis, handing world No. 1 John McEnroe only his second loss of the season in a 6-7, 6-2, 6-3 upset in the first round of the ATP Championships in Cincinnati, Ohio. "I can't take anything away from him," says McEnroe. "He played very well. I was surprised at how well he played, particularly on his serve." McEnroe goes on to finish the year with an 82-3 record, with his only other losses being to Ivan Lendl in the final of the French Open and to Henrik Sundstrom in the Davis Cup Final.

2006 Forty-nine-year-old Martina Navratilova of the United States wins her 177th—and final—WTA doubles title pairing with Nadia Petrova of Russia in registering a 6-1, 6-2 win over Cara Black of Zimbabwe and Anna-Lena Groenefeld of Germany in the final of the Rogers Cup in Montreal, Canada. The event is the second-to-last event in Navratilova's career. Three weeks later, Navratilova concludes her career by winning her 59th career major title—the 2006 U.S. Open mixed doubles title with Bob Bryan. Says Navratilova following her win in Canada, "I have one more to write and then it will be done. It's been great to be able to defend the title and do it in great style." The title with Petrova is Navratilova's fifth Canadian doubles title—each won with a different partner. She also wins in 1981, 1982, 1985 and 2004.

1900 With a packed grandstand and rows of spectators standing four or five people deep around the other three sides of the court at the Newport Casino in Rhode Island, Malcolm Whitman wins the U.S. men's singles title, defeating Bill Larned 6-4, 1-6, 6-2, 6-2 in the championship match. Writes the *New York Times* of the champion, "Whitman's victory was hard-earned and he deserves now the laurel wreath as the greatest of American tennis players. Good judges declare that we have never had such skillful of a champion before."

1961 Bernard "Tut" Bartzen becomes one of the most unlikely U.S. Davis Cup heroes as he caps a comeback by the U.S. Davis Cup team as it defeats Mexico 3-2 at the Cleveland Skating Club in Cleveland, Ohio. Bartzen's 6-3, 6-3, 7-5 victory over Rafael Osuna in the fifth and decisive match clinches victory for the U.S. and gives Bartzen his 16th Davis Cup victory without a defeat in what ultimately becomes his final Davis Cup appearance. Bartzen's 16-0 Davis Cup record for the United States (15-0 in singles, 1-0 in doubles) is tops among all players that have competed for the United States in over 100 years of competition. Setting up Bartzen's clinching victory against Osuna is Chuck McKinley, who evens the score with Mexico at two matches apiece with a 6-4, 7-6, 10-8 win over Mario Llamas.

2006 Eighteen-year-old Ana Ivanovic of Serbia wins the second WTA Tour title of her career, dominating Martina Hingis 6-2, 6-3 in a rain-delayed Monday final at the Rogers Cup in Montreal, Canada. Says Ivanovic of her tournament victory over the 25-year-old Hingis, "This is a big step for me. She's a great player. In juniors, I watched her winning Grand Slam titles and now I played against her and played good tennis. Basically, now I can consider myself one of the top players and that gives me motivation to work even harder to stay at this level."

August 22

2004 In the greatest day in the history of Chilean tennis and Chilean player Nicolas Massu, the South American nation wins its first and second ever Olympic gold medal in a span of 24 hours at the 2004 Olympic Games in Athens, Greece. Chile wins its first ever Olympic gold medal at 2:39 am local time in Athens, when Massu and Fernando Gonzalez save four match points and outlast Rainer Schuettler and Nicolas Kiefer of Germany 6-2, 4-6, 3-6, 7-6 (7), 6-4 in the gold medal match in men's doubles. Just 15 hours later, Massu then returns to the court and defeats Mardy Fish of the United States 6-3, 3-6, 2-6, 6-3, 6-4 in four hours to win the gold medal in men's singles. Massu does not get to bed until 6:30 am the morning of his evening gold medal match, and, in all, plays 24 hours, 43 minutes over 11 matches en route to winning the gold in singles and doubles.

2004 China wins its first ever Olympic gold medal in tennis as Li Ting and Sun Tian Tian beat Conchita Martinez and Virginia Ruano Pascual of Spain 6-3, 6-3 in the gold medal match in women's doubles.

2007 Three months removed from the birth of her son Jagger and 11 months removed from her last WTA Tour match, Lindsay Davenport returns to the court in doubles at the Pilot Pen Championships in New Haven. Davenport and partner Lisa Raymond are defeated by reigning Wimbledon and Australian Open champions Cara Black of Zimbabwe and new U.S. citizen Liezel Huber 6-7 (1), 6-3, and 10-4 in the match tiebreak. Says Davenport, "I feel I'm still very good at my job and having a child doesn't mean you have to abandon all of your career and everything. I feel like while he's this young, and so far so good, I can drag him around the world and try and do what I still love to do."

1982 Ivan Lendl defeats Steve Denton 6-2, 7-6 to win the ATP Championships in Cincinnati, Ohio. "He played a smart match," acknowledges Denton. "He ran me around a lot, but I don't think it hurt me. I felt pretty good. It's just that he played well. He has such good ground strokes. I was just fighting to stay even." The previous day, Denton upsets John McEnroe in the semifinals while Lendl defeats Jimmy Connors 6-1, 6-1—Lendl's first ever win over Connors. "Everything I hit was tentative," says McEnroe of his match with Denton. "There is nothing about my game that is not tentative right now. I have a lot to worry about right now."

August 23

1926 With Helen Wills sidelined after an appendectomy, 42-year-old Molla Mallory wins her record eighth U.S. women's singles title in her record 10th career U.S. singles final and, in the process, becomes the oldest player to win a major singles title. Mallory defeats 24-year-old Elizabeth "Bunny" Ryan 4-6, 6-4, 9-7 in the final after trailing 0-4 in the final set and overcoming a match point.

1985 In a bad remake of the original "Battle of the Sexes," Martina Navratilova and Pam Shriver rout 67-year-old Bobby Riggs and Vitas Gerulaitis 6-2, 6-3, 6-4 in Atlantic City, New Jersey. Says Navratilova. "It was something different. You play tournaments all your life, and this was definitely one of a kind. It can only add to the interest of tennis. People said there would be a lot of pressure on us, but I figured if we can't enjoy this, we can't enjoy anything." Says Riggs, "I knew it was mission impossible going in. They were a little too tough for us and a little too strong. Vitas was not able to cover as much of the court as I thought he could."

1977 Bjorn Borg becomes the No. 1 ranked player in the world for the first time in his career, unseating Jimmy Connors. Borg holds the ranking for only one week, before Connors returns to the No. 1 ranking. Borg does not regain the top ranking for another 84 weeks until April 9, 1979. In all, the Swede holds the No. 1 ranking for a total of 109 weeks during his career.

1973 Ilie Nastase becomes the No. 1 ranked player in the world as the ATP officially unveils its computer rankings. Nastase remains the world No. 1 for 40 weeks before he is overtaken by John Newcombe on June 3, 1974.

1981 John McEnroe defeats unseeded Chris Lewis 6-3, 6-4 to win the ATP Championships in Cincinnati, Ohio. Says McEnroe, "I think the match was closer than the score indicated. I thought I would try to start faster because he really hustles on the court. But I still feel I could be moving a little better."

1981 Tracy Austin defeats Chris Evert Lloyd 6-1, 6-4 to win the Canadian Open singles title in Toronto. Says Evert Lloyd of Austin, "She's playing tough. The one thing that separates her from the other players is that she's fresh and eager to play. You can see her eagerness."

August 24

1925 Helen Wills wins her third consecutive U.S. women's singles title, defeating Britain's Kitty McKane 3-6, 6-0, 6-2 in the final played in front of 7,000 fans at the West Side Tennis Club at Forest Hills. Wills leads 3-1 in the first set, but drops five games in a row to surprisingly lose the first set. The Berkeley, Calif., native, however, needs only 25 minutes to sweep that last two sets. Writes the *New York Times* of the victory, "Miss Wills, at the outset, was rampant. Keenly on edge and keeping right on top of the ball every moment, the champion raised the gallery to a pitch of enthusiasm as she drove the ball to the corners with tremendous sweeping strokes, getting the sharpest angles on them."

1929 With a crowd of 9,000 fans watching on, Helen Wills wins her sixth U.S. women's singles title and her 11th major singles title, defeating Britain's Phoebe Watson 6-4, 6-2 in the final at the West Side Tennis Club at Forest Hills. Wills, who earlier in the year wins at Wimbledon and the French Championships, gives her the distinction of winning three major championships in one season for the second straight year after sweeping all three titles in 1928. Wills devastates the women's field at Forest Hills, losing only eight games in six matches en route to the title. The fact that Watson wins six of those eight games in the final, provides an indication of Wills' dominance. The previous day in the semifinals, the Berkeley, Calif., native destroys Molla Mallory in the women's semifinals, handing the eight-time champion a 6-0, 6-0 loss in just 21 minutes (eight minutes for the first set, and 13 for the second set.)

1997 Carlos Moya defeats Patrick Rafter 6-4, 7-6 to win the singles title at the Hamlet Cup in Commack, N.Y. The final-round loss for Rafter is his fifth without a victory during the 1997 year. The Australian, however, breaks his winless streak in finals for the year two weeks later, defeating Greg Rusedski in the final of the U.S. Open.

1992 Stefan Edberg tops Mal Washington 7-6(4), 6-1 to win the Volvo International in New Haven, Conn., and win his 35th title of his career. The victory provides a solid confidence boost for the Swede, who goes on to win his second straight U.S. Open title three weeks later. "It's necessary for me to win at least once in a while," says Edberg after the match. "I've proved this week that I can play pretty good tennis. I've sort of got the momentum going, and that's what I needed, because I really haven't played that well in the last couple of months. At least I know my game is back in shape." The match is curiously played on a Monday, after the tournament undergoes a major disaster when, after days of heavy rain leading into and during the tournament, the Deco-Turf II court surface becomes soft. A nine-inch tear on the baseline of the Stadium Court, due to the soft nature of the court, makes the court unplayable and tournament officials are forced to rip off the court and re-surface it during the Wednesday session of the tournament, causing for the event to be delayed by a day.

1929 Bill Tilden beats fellow American George Lott 6-4, 7-9, 4-6, 11-9, 6-2 to win the Newport Invitational singles title at The Casino in Newport, R.I. Writes the *New York Times* of the match and atmosphere, "A large gallery surrounded the championship court at the Casino and was held spellbound for more than three hours. It required every wile of the game and every tennis trick that Tilden possessed to beat Lott, and it was a toss up until the fifth and deciding set."

August 25

1997 The United States Tennis Association dedicates Arthur Ashe Stadium with a dramatic on-court ceremony featuring Ashe's widow Jeanne Moutassamy Ashe, Whitney Houston and 38 former champions. Tamarine Tanasugarn wins the first-ever match on Arthur Ashe Stadium defeating Chanda Rubin 6-4, 6-0. Future world No. 1 and two-time U.S. Open champion Venus Williams makes her U.S. Open debut, also on Arthur Ashe Stadium Court, and defeats Larisa Neiland of Latvia in the first round 5-7, 6-0, 6-1.

2003 In an emotional on-court ceremony at Arthur Ashe Stadium on the opening night of the U.S. Open, five-time U.S. Open champion Pete Sampras officially announces his retirement from professional tennis. Just 12 months earlier, Sampras, seeded No. 17, brushes off the critics that say he is washed up and dramatically wins the U.S. Open—ending a tournament title slump of nearly 26 months—beating arch rival Andre Agassi 6-3, 6-4, 5-7, 6-4 in the final. Sampras appears on the court with his wife Bridgette and his 9-month-old son Christian, whom he carries in his arms as he takes one final victory lap around the center court at the U.S. Open. "I'm going to miss playing here," Sampras tells the crowd. "I really loved playing in New York, loved playing in front of you guys. But I know in my heart, it's time to say goodbye."

1927 Althea Gibson, the woman who breaks the color barrier at the U.S. Championships in 1950 and becomes one of the world's most talented and accomplished players, is born in Spring, S.C. Gibson is the first black player to win a major title at the French Championships in 1956 and also becomes the first black player to win at Wimbledon (1957-1958) and at the U.S. Championships (1957-1958).

1950 Play begins at the 50th anniversary edition of the Davis Cup Challenge Round as the United States and Australia open up play at the West Side Tennis Club in Forest Hills, N.Y. Australia takes a 2-0 on the Davis Cup holders as Frank Sedgman defeats Tom Brown 6-0, 8-6, 9-7 and Ken McGregor defeats Ted Schroeder 13-11, 6-3, 6-4. Australia goes on to claim its first Davis Cup title since 1939 the next day as Sedgman and John Bromwich defeat Gardnar Mulloy and Schroeder 4-6, 6-4, 2-6, 6-4, 6-4 giving Australia an insurmountable 3-0 lead.

August 26

1933 Helen Wills Moody's 45-match winning streak at the U.S. Championships ends in controversial circumstances as she quits her match with rival Helen Jacobs while trailing 0-3 in the final set of the women's singles final at the West Side Tennis Club at Forest Hills. Trailing 0-3 in the final set, Moody walks to the chair umpire and informs him that she can no longer continue due to pain in her back. Jacobs pleads with Moody to continue, but the seven-time U.S. champion retreats to the dressing room, giving Jacobs the 8-6, 3-6, 3-0, ret. victory in front of a shocked crowd of 8,000 fans. Moody's loss is the first of any kind, in any circumstance since 1926. Moody issues a statement that reads, "In the third set of my singles match, I felt as though I was going to faint because of pain in my back and hip and complete numbness of my right leg. The match was long and by defaulting I do not wish to detract from the excellence of Miss Jacobs's play. I felt that I have spoiled the finish of the national championship, and wish that I had followed the advice of my doctor and returned to California. I still feel that I did right in withdrawing because I felt that I was on the verge of a collapse on the court." The loss marks the first loss for Moody in the championship since the 1922 U.S. women's final.

1951 Frank Sedgman and Ken McGregor clinch the first Grand Slam in doubles, defeating fellow Aussies Mervyn Rose and Don Candy 10-8, 6-4, 4-6, 7-5 in the doubles final of the U.S. Championships, played at the West Side Tennis Club in Forest Hills, N.Y.

1986 John McEnroe suffers his first—and only—first round loss at the U.S. Open when fellow Long Island native Paul Annacone fires 23 aces and dismisses the four-time champion 1-6, 6-1, 6-3, 6-3 on the opening day of the tournament. McEnroe, the four-time U.S. Open champion, plays only his third event after returning from a six-month sabbatical from the game that featured him being married to actress Tatum O'Neal and the birth of his first child. Says McEnroe of his lack of vigor in his first-round exit, "I have to look at myself in the mirror and ask whether I have the enthusiasm. There's not much sense in pretending it's there." Says Annacone of the victory, "I kind of felt awkward beating him. He's a great champion. He's entertained so many millions of people and done so much for the game. I want to see him come back, but I feel he has got to get some more matches under his belt." While McEnroe is beginning the downward path of his career, Andre Agassi, a standard bearer for the next generation of American tennis, makes his U.S. Open debut as a 16-year-old. The future two-time U.S. Open champion also loses in the opening round, falling to Jeremy Bates of Great Britain, 7-6, 6-3, 4-6, 6-4.

1991 No. 8 seed Andre Agassi commits 61 unforced errors in his 7-5, 7-6, 6-2 first round loss to Aaron Krickstein at the US Open. Says Krickstein simply of Agassi and the upset-win, "He had a lot more to do with what happened than I did." Says Agassi, who lost in the finals of the U.S. Open to Pete Sampras the previous year, "I don't know what is harder, to lose in the first round or to lose in the finals."

2002 The United States Tennis Association pays tribute to the City of New York nearly one year after the Sept. 11 World Trade Center tragedy with a moving on-court "Opening Night" ceremony at Arthur Ashe Stadium. The World Trade Center flag that flew over the Kandahar Airport in Afghanistan is unfurled on-court, then raised over the stadium. New York City Mayor Michael Bloomberg, Tony Bennett, actor Judd Hirsch, Queen Latifah, John McEnroe and Billie Jean King join New York City police and fire fighters during the ceremonies.

1949 Twenty-one-year-old Richard "Pancho" Gonzales makes his Davis Cup debut defeating Frank Sedgman 8-6, 6-4, 9-7 to help the United States to a 2-0 lead over Australia after the first day of the Davis Cup Challenge Round at the West Side Tennis Club in Forest Hills, Queens, N.Y. Born of Mexican parents in Los Angeles, Gonzales wins the singles title at the U.S. National Championships at Forest Hills the year before in 1948 and goes on to defend his title in 1949. Following his triumph at Forest Hills in 1949, Gonzales, short of money, turns professional and never plays Davis Cup again.

1974 Bjorn Borg, who earlier in the year wins the Italian and French Championships, wins the U.S. Pro Championships in Boston, defeating Tom Okker in the final, 7-6 (3), 6-1, 6-1. Borg rallies from being down 2-5 in the first set to easily capture his first title in the United States. Borg comes back from a 1-5 deficit in the fifth set to beat Jan Kodes 7-6 (7-3), 6-0, 1-6, 2-6, 7-6 (7-4) in the semifinals.

August 27

1975 The U.S. Open begins at the West Side Tennis Club at Forest Hills with two major changes in the tournament—clay courts and night tennis. For the first time in history of the tournament, the U.S. Open is not played on grass as the U.S. Tennis Association installs Har-tru clay courts as the surface of the tournament. The first stadium match not contested on grass in the history of the tournament is played between reigning Wimbledon champion Arthur Ashe and fellow American and lucky-loser entrant Victor Amaya, with Ashe registering the 6-3, 7-6 (6) victory. Night tennis makes its debut many hours later as 4,949 fans watch Onny Parun of New Zealand defeat Stan Smith 6-4, 6-2 in the first night match ever played at the U.S. Open.

1985 Mary Joe Fernandez, at the age of 14 years and eight days, becomes the youngest player to win a match at the U.S. Open when she defeats Sara Gomer of Britain 6-1, 6-4 in the first round. Also during the day, defending champion and No. 1 seed John McEnroe survives a five-set, first-round scare by Israel's Shlomo Glickstein, ranked No. 175 in the world, 6-1, 6-7, 2-6, 6-3, 7-6 (9-7). Glickstein is two points from the match with McEnroe serving at 4-5, 15-30 in the fifth set—and again at 6-6 and 7-7 in the final-set tie-break, but is unable to convert. McEnroe closes out the match on his fifth match point of the fifth-set tie-break. Writes Peter Alfano of the *New York Times*, "What should have been nothing more than an afternoon workout became a struggle for survival that lasted until evening and very nearly resulted in what might have been considered the most shocking upset in the history of the United States Open."

1903 Laurie Doherty of Great Britain becomes the first foreign player to win the U.S. Championships, defeating American William Larned 6-0, 6-3, 10-8 in the final in Newport, R.I. The *New York Times* describes the anticipated and excited pre-match atmosphere of the British-American clash, stating, "When the rivals appeared and began their preliminary working out, the interest reached a high pitch and the tension was as severe in the gallery as it was among the players."

1972 Olga Morozova becomes the first Soviet player to win a U.S. tournament when she defeats countrywoman Marina Kroshina 6-2, 6-7, 7-5 to win the Eastern Grass Court Championships at the Orange Lawn Tennis Club in South Orange, N.J. In the men's final, Ilie Nastase needs only 45 minutes to defeat Manuel Orantes 6-4, 6-0.

1909 William Larned wins his fifth U.S. men's singles title, defeating William Clothier 6-1, 6-2, 5-7, 1-6, 6-1 at The Casino in Newport, R.I. Writes the *New York Times* of the match, "Yet with the full limit of five sets being played before the largest gallery that has ever assembled about the court of the Casino, there was relatively but few exciting moments in the competition." Larned goes on to win two more U.S. singles titles to equal the record of seven titles set by Richard Sears and subsequently equaled by Bill Tilden. In addition to being a world champion tennis player, Larned serves militarily for the United States as part of Teddy Roosevelt's "Rough Riders" in the Spanish American War in Cuba in 1898. Roosevelt, in his book *The Rough Riders,* brags of the enlistment of Larned and fellow U.S. Davis Cupper Robert Wrenn along with "an eclectic group of eastern dudes and western deadshots."

1928 Helen Wills, fresh off her public announcement that she is supporting Republican candidate Herbert Hoover for President, needs only 33 minutes to win her fifth U.S. women's singles title, defeating Helen Jacobs 6-2, 6-1 in the final. Wills wins the tournament without the loss of a set and with the loss of only 13 games en route to the title. The win also cements her sweep of the U.S., Wimbledon and French titles for the first of two straight years. Wills also wins Wimbledon and French without losing a set. *New York Times* tennis writer Allison Danzig calls Wills' performance as "the most devastating power ever applied to a tennis ball by a woman." In a press announcement the day before the final, Wills is named by the Hoover campaign as the head of his women's sports committee. A statement from Wills is read at the public announcement where Wills states, "All youth can admire Herbert Hoover because of his sincerity, intelligence and great industry. His achievements in the past have been marked with success because of his ability for organization and his wonderful powers of perseverance." Wills goes on to win two more U.S. titles (1929, 1931), while Hoover goes on to win a landslide victory of Democrat Al Smith in the Presidential election.

1991 Fifteen-year-old Lindsay Davenport, who goes on to become the 1998 women's singles champion, makes her U.S. Open debut, losing in the first round to fellow American Debbie Graham 6-3, 6-2.

August 28

1950 Althea Gibson breaks the color barrier as the first black player to compete in the U.S. Championships when she takes the court in the first round of women's singles at the West Side Tennis Club in Forest Hills, N.Y. Gibson wins her first round match defeating Barbara Knapp of Britain 6-2, 6-2 to set up a second-round match with Wimbledon champion Louise Brough. Writes Allison Danzig of the *New York Times* of Gibson's win over Knapp, "Miss Gibson carried the attack forward continually to score on her volleys with a big crowd gathered around the court."

1914 Dick Williams and Karl Behr, two men who survived the sinking of the *Titanic*, meet in the quarterfinals of the U.S. Championships at the Newport Casino, with Williams emerging victorious by a 6-1, 6-2, 7-5 margin. Williams goes on to win the title, defeating Maurice McLoughlin 6-3, 8-6, 10-8 in the championship match.

1990 With form described by Robin Finn of the *New York Times* as "floundering like a fish out of water on a hot, dry day," Stefan Edberg becomes the first No. 1 seeded player since John Newcombe in 1971 to lose in the first round of the U.S. Open, losing to Alexander Volkov of the Soviet Union 6-3, 7-6, 6-2. Edberg enters the match having won his last 21 matches and his last four tournaments, including Wimbledon. Says Edberg, "This was one of the best summers so far and I really wanted to do well at the Open, but it's too late now."

1984 Fifteen-year-old Steffi Graf, the future five-time U.S. Open champion, makes her U.S. Open debut and loses in the first round to countrywoman Sylvia Hanika 6-4, 6-2.

1989 Eighteen-year-old Pete Sampras, the future five-time U.S. Open champion, wins his first U.S. Open singles match, defeating Agustin Moreno of Mexico 6-3, 5-7, 6-4, 6-1 on Court No. 18 at the USTA National Tennis Center.

1995 After a two-year absence, Monica Seles returns to the U.S. Open and defeats Ruxandra Dragomir 6-3, 6-1 in the first round—28 months after she is stabbed in the back on court in Hamburg, Germany.

1991 In the early hours of the morning (1:35 a.m. to be exact), Jimmy Connors defeats Patrick McEnroe 4-6, 6-7, 6-4, 6-2, 6-4 in one of the most dramatic first round matches ever at the U.S. Open. Connors, ranked No. 174 and five days shy of his 39th birthday, trails McEnroe 4-6, 6-7, 0-3, 0-40 before rallying to victory.

1949 Ted Schroeder clinches the Davis Cup title for the United States, defeating Australia's Frank Sedgman 6-4, 6-3, 6-3 in the Davis Cup Challenge Round at the West Side Tennis Club in Forest Hills, Queens, N.Y. Schroeder's win gives the United States its fourth consecutive Davis Cup title—the third longest stretch the United States has held the Davis Cup. Schroeder, who is a member of all four Davis Cup championship teams, also clinched the Davis Cup title for the U.S. in 1947. Closing out the 4-1 American victory is Richard "Pancho" Gonzales, who in his final Davis Cup match, defeats Bill Sidwell 6-1, 6-3, 6-3.

1955 Vice President Richard Nixon presents the Australian Davis Cup team with the Davis Cup trophy after the Aussies complete a 5-0 shutout of the United States at the West Side Tennis Club in Forest Hills, Queens, N.Y. Nixon is told by Australian Davis Cup Harry Hopman that he might someday be "the youngest president in American history." Nixon next touches the Davis Cup in 1969 when, as the 37th President, he welcomes the victorious 1968 U.S. Davis Cup team that defeats Hopman's Australian team in the 1968 Davis Cup final in Adelaide, Australia.

1959 Barry MacKay defeats 21-year-old Aussie Rod Laver 7-5, 6-4, 6-1 as the United States and Australia split the first two matches on the first day of play in the Davis Cup Challenge Round at the West Side Tennis Club in Forest Hills, Queens, N.Y.

1995 The U.S. Open begins at the USTA National Tennis Center in New York and Shuzo Matsuoka of Japan and Petr Korda of the Czech Republic play a match that is talked about for years. With the score tied at 5-5 in the fifth-set, Matsuoka collapses on the court with cramps in his left leg after 3 hours, 26 minutes of play. For three agonizing minutes, the Japanese player lays on the hard court surface screaming and suffering, but is not allowed to be treated as cramps are considered a loss of condition and helping him would instantly result in a default. USTA Tournament Referee Brian Earley institutes a point penalty after a 60 second delay, then a game penalty after 120 seconds and then defaults Matsuoka after 180 seconds. Says Korda after the match, "He was in tremendous pain because he had a big spasm in both legs. Rules are rules, and it's pretty sad that no one can help him." The incident causes for a rule change where cramping does not constitute a loss of condition and treatment is allowed without a default being instituted.

2006 The U.S. Open becomes the first major tournament to use instant replay and the player challenge system on the opening day of the 2006 U.S. Open. Three hours and fifteen minutes into the tournament, 24-year-old American Mardy Fish makes the first player challenge in major tournament history during his match against Germany's Simon Greul on Louis Armstrong Stadium. With Fish leading 6-4, 6-4, 1-0 and Greul serving at Ad-In, Fish challenges Greul's point-winning shot—that was called in—on the sideline. The call was upheld, leaving the set score at 1-all following the video review which was seen simultaneously by players, officials, fans and television viewers.

2001 Marcelo Rios completes one of the longest days in U.S. Open history, finishing off Markus Hipfl of Austria, 3-6, 7-5, 6-2, 6-0 at 1:25 am on the Grandstand Court. Rain delays cause for many matches to begin later than scheduled, including the Rios-Hipfl match which begins at 10:50 pm.

August 29

1978 The gates open at the new USTA National Tennis Center in Flushing Meadows, N.Y. for the grand opening of the newly-constructed public facility that is the new home of the U.S. Open. "Tonight the U.S. Open belongs to us, the people, the tennis fans," says actor and comedian Alan King, the master of ceremonies for the opening session of the tournament. "Ten months ago when we broke ground I thought they were crazy. But here we are. This is where the legends begin." Bjorn Borg and Bob Hewitt play the first match at the new facility with Borg winning the best-of-three set first round match 6-0, 6-2. "Probably when I get to be 75 years old and look back, I'll say I was the first one to play in the new stadium," says Borg after defeating Hewitt in front of only 6,186 fans during the opening night session of the tournament.

1952 Two years after Althea Gibson breaks the color barrier as the first black player to compete in the U.S. Championships, Dr. Reginald Weir becomes the first black man to accomplish the feat when he takes the court in the first round of men's singles. Weir, however, is defeated in the first round by William Stucki 11-9, 5-7, 8-6, 6-1. One day later, another black man, George Stewart, also loses in the first round of the U.S. Championships to Bernard "Tut" Bartzen 6-3, 9-7, 6-0.

1968 The first professional U.S. "Open" with a tournament field consisting of professional and amateurs begins at the U.S. Championships and Billie Jean King plays the first stadium match at the U.S. Open, defeating Long Island dentist and alternate player Dr. Vija Vuskains 6-1, 6-0. Amateurs Ray Moore and Jim Osborne register upset wins over professionals; Moore defeating No. 10 seed Andres Gimeno 4-6, 6-1, 6-2, 6-1 and Osborne defeating Barry MacKay 8-6, 4-6, 7-5, 6-3.

1951 Described by Allison Danzig of the *New York Times* as "scenes almost unparalleled at Forest Hills," Gardnar Mulloy defeats fellow American Earl Cochell 4-6, 6-2, 6-1, 6-2 in the fourth round in which Cochell hits a ball out of the stadium, tanks a game by returning Mulloy's serve with his racquet switched to his left-hand, and serves underhand to the gross displeasure of the crowd, who shower Cochell with boos and barbs.

1927 Sixteen-year-old Betty Nuthall of Britain advances into the women's singles final of the U.S. Championships at the West Side Tennis Club at

Forest Hills, defeating Charlotte Chapin of the United States 6-1, 4-6, 6-3 in the semifinals. Nuthall, at age 16 years, three months and six days, is the youngest woman to reach the singles final at the U.S. Championships. Helen Wills, a three-time U.S. champion, relents only two games to her rival Helen Jacobs in the other semifinal, winning 6-2, 6-0. The next day, Wills wins the title, defeating Nuthall 6-1, 6-4. Nuthall becomes the first British woman to win the U.S. title in 1930.

1970 Arthur Ashe and Cliff Richey give the United States a 2-0 lead over West Germany in the Davis Cup Challenge Round played at the Harold T. Clark Courts in Cleveland, Ohio. Ashe defeats 1967 Wimbledon finalist Wilhelm Bungert 6-2, 10-8, 6-2, while Richey defeats Christian Kuhnke 6-3, 6-4, 6-2. The United States goes on to clinch the series and its third straight Davis Cup title the following day when Stan Smith and Bob Lutz beat Bungert and Kuhnke 6-3, 7-5, 6-4 in the doubles rubber. The U.S. ultimately wins the series by a 5-0 margin, with Ashe providing the final exclamation point, winning the most dramatic dead-rubber matches in Davis Cup history, overcoming a two-sets-to-love deficit and a match point in the fourth set to defeat Kuhnke 6-8, 10-12, 9-7, 13-11, 6-4.

August 30

1989 Down match point, Boris Becker benefits from a let-cord passing shot just out of the reach of Derrick Rostagno in his 1-6, 6-7(1), 6-3, 7-6 (6), 6-3 come-from-behind second-round U.S. Open victory in 4 hours, 27 minutes. Rostagno leads 6-4 in the fourth-set tie-break and after pushing a forehand long on his first match point, Becker's forehand clips the top of the net and out of Rostagno's reach. Becker then wins the next two points to win the fourth set before running out the fifth-set. Says Becker, who five rounds later claims his first and only U.S. Open singles title, "In a match like that you get many shots in your favor and many against you," Becker says. "When you get a shot like that on match point, it's certainly sweet." Also on the stadium, qualifier Paul Haarhuis, ranked No. 115, stuns No. 4 seeded John McEnroe 6-4, 4-6, 6-3, 7-5 in one of the biggest upsets in U.S. Open history. Says McEnroe following the loss, "I am too disgusted to think straight right now." In the evening session, 18-year-old Pete Sampras upsets defending champion and No. 5 seeded Mats Wilander 5-7, 6-3, 1-6, 6-1, 6-4 to mark his arrival on the top stage of pro tennis. Says Sampras after the match victory, his first over a top 10 player, "At the start I really didn't believe I could beat Mats Wilander. But he gave me a couple of opportunities, and I took advantage. It really all depended on how I was playing. I was going to win it, he wasn't going to lose it."

1979 In one of the most chaotic matches in the history of the U.S. Open, John McEnroe and 33-year-old Ilie Nastase compete in a wild night match featuring, in the words of Neil Amdur of the *New York Times,* "cheers, boos, point penalties, game penalties, police on the court, a switch in chair umpires and even some brilliant shot making." Pandemonium breaks out in the fourth set, starting with Nastase's stall tactics that forces chair umpire Frank Hammond to issue a game penalty to Nastase. As Nastase continues to complain and stall, Hammond then defaults the Romanian exclaiming into his microphone "Game. Set. Match. McEnroe." An 18-minute free-for-all ensues where fans scream, boo and throw objects onto the court—some fans even running onto the court—causing New York City policemen to also enter the court to protect the players and officials. U.S. Open Tournament Referee Mike Blanchard then reinstates Nastase and then replaces Hammond on the chair for the remainder of the match. McEnroe closes out the match at 12:42 am, beating Nastase by a 6-4, 4-6, 6-3, 6-2 margin and goes on to win the tournament five matches later. Earlier in the day, Kathy Horvath is five days past her 14th birthday when she loses a first round match to Diane Fromholtz 7-6, 6-2 to become the youngest person to play a match at the U.S. Open.

1950 Althea Gibson's debut appearance as the first black player to compete at the U.S. Championships comes to a close as she loses all three games played in the continuation of a rain-delayed match with reigning Wimbledon champion Louise Brough. Gibson leads Brough 7-6 in the final set when play resumes after a rain storm from the previous day, but falters to lose the match by a final score of 6-1, 3-6, 9-7.

1986 John McEnroe and Peter Fleming are defaulted from the men's doubles championships at the U.S. Open when they arrive six minutes late for their first round doubles match. The doubles pair get caught in traffic driving from McEnroe's family home in Cove Neck. The normal 30-minute drive takes over an hour. Says Fleming, "I'm shattered right now. It hurts. I thought we were going to win the tournament. You don't get too many chances to win the U.S. Open. We've done it the same way 20 times in the past seven years, and 20 times we've had no problem. It's stupid. What can you say? I mean, you can't say anything. It's stupid, I guess. If I could do it differently, I'd do it 1,000 different ways."

1959 Peruvian born Alex Olmedo, a student at the University of Southern California, defeats Rod Laver 9-7, 4-6, 10-8, 12-10 to even up the Davis Cup Challenge Round at two matches apiece at the West Side Tennis Club in Forest Hills, Queens, N.Y. The fifth and decisive match between Neale Fraser and Barry MacKay is postponed due to rain. The next day, on his 24th birthday, MacKay loses to Fraser 8-6, 3-6, 6-2, 6-4 giving Australia the Davis Cup title by a 3-2 decision.

2005 Life imitates art as No. 4 seed Andy Roddick, featured in an omnipresent American Express marketing campaign in which he loses his "mojo," in fact loses his mojo in an embarrassing straight-set loss to Gilles Muller of Luxembourg in the first round of the U.S. Open. The 7-6 (4), 7-6 (8), 7-6 (1) loss comes on of all days as Roddick's 23rd birthday and marks Muller's first career U.S. Open match. Says the No. 68-ranked Muller of how he defeated Roddick, "I have no idea."

August 31

1881 The first U.S. Championships begin at The Casino in Newport, R.I. as 25 men enter the inaugural competition. Harvard University student Richard Sears goes on to win the four-day tournament defeating William Glyn, a Brit who enters the tournament on a whim while on his Rhode Island holiday, in the final. The first U.S. Championships is a financial success, earning a profit of $4.32.

1977 John McEnroe plays his first U.S. Open match and receives his first U.S. Open code of conduct point penalty in his 6-1, 6-3 win over fellow 18-year-old Eliot Teltscher in a first-round night match at the West Side Tennis Club at Forest Hills. Chair umpire Patti Ingersol of Chicago issues the conduct violation after McEnroe stalls and argues over several calls in the second set. Following the point penalty, McEnroe serves the next point underhand and Teltscher, in a show of solidarity to McEnroe over the point penalty, lets the ball bounce twice, surrendering the point to McEnroe. Says McEnroe of his point penalty, "I was just mumbling under my breath and she assumed I said something. No one knows what I said. I was just saying I can't believe the match was going like this and she said "Love-15." I guess she was just trying to show her authority, but I think she went overboard."

1999 Patrick Rafter becomes the first defending U.S. Open champion to lose in the first round as he is defeated by Cedric Pioline 4-6, 4-6, 6-3, 7-5, 1-0, ret. Rafter is forced to quit the match due to a shoulder injury. Earlier in the day, No. 1 seed Pete Sampras, in full pursuit of his record-breaking 13th major singles title, withdraws from the event with a herniated disc in his back suffered in a pre-event warm-up session on site at the USTA National Tennis Center.

1990 Unheralded and No. 82-ranked Linda Ferrando of Italy upsets No. 3 seed and 16-year-old Monica Seles 1-6, 6-1, 7-6 (3) in the third round of the U.S. Open. Says Seles, "I've never seen her play before so I didn't know what to expect from her. After the first set, I knew she was going to be a bigger problem to finish off."

1969 Two 41-year-olds, Torben Ulrich and Pancho Gonzales, thrill the crowd at the West Side Tennis Club with an exciting, five-set match in the third round of the U.S. Open, won by Gonzales, 3-6, 6-4, 4-6, 8-6, 6-2.

1979 Sixteen-year-old Tracy Austin defeats 14-year-old Andrea Jaeger 6-2, 6-2 in the second round of the 1981 U.S. Open. Six years later, both players would be out of the game. Earlier in the day, John Lloyd defeats Paul McNamee 5-7, 6-7, 7-5, 7-6, 7-6 in the longest match by games at the U.S. Open since the introduction of the tie-break. The two players contest 63 of a maximum 65 games, before Lloyd is victorious in 3 hours, 56 minutes on Court No. 17.

2002 The first-ever all-women's night session at the U.S. Open is played in Arthur Ashe Stadium as Martina Hingis defeats Amanda Coetzer 6-3, 6-4, Jennifer Capriati tops Meghann Shaughnessy 6-2, 6-2 and the doubles team of Hingis and Anna Kournikova defeat Laura Granville and Jennifer Hopkins 6-1, 6-2.

1923 The new 13,500-seat stadium court at the West Side Tennis Club at Forest Hills, Queens, N.Y. hosts Davis Cup matches for the first time as the United States and Australasia (Australia and New Zealand) split the first two singles matches in the Davis Cup Challenge Round. James Anderson of Australasia defeats Bill Johnston 4-6, 6-2, 2-6, 7-5, 6-2 and Bill Tilden of the United States defeats John Hawkes 6-4, 6-2, 6-1.

September 1

1914 Richard Norris "Dick" Williams, a survivor of the sinking of the *Titanic*, upsets Maurice McLoughlin 6-3, 8-6, 10-8 to win the U.S. men's singles title in the final staging of the U.S. Championships at The Casino in Newport, R.I. The men's tournament moves to the West Side Tennis Club at Forest Hills, N.Y., where it is predominantly played until 1977. The *New York Times* calls the result "one of the great surprises of the age."

1971 Wimbledon champion John Newcombe of Australia becomes the first top-seeded man to lose in the first round of the U.S. Open when he is defeated by Czech Jan Kodes 2-6, 7-6, 7-6, 6-3. Kodes, the reigning French Open champion, is strangely unseeded in the tournament and goes on to reach the final, losing to Stan Smith.

1975 Nineteen-year-old Bjorn Borg ends the Rod Laver era at the U.S. Open, defeating the 37-year-old two-time U.S. titlist 6-1, 6-4, 2-6, 6-2 in the round of 16 in Laver's final U.S. Open match. Laver, who completes both of his Grand Slams at the U.S. Championships in 1962 and 1969, blames the loss on his inability to effectively handle the heavy and high-bouncing top-spin ground strokes of his much younger opponent on the clay court. Asked if he is disappointed with the loss, Laver says to the *New York Times*, "Yes, but not that disappointed. I've had my shakes over the years. It's time for the younger players to take over."

1977 Renee Richards, the 43-year-old transsexual who fights for more than a year for the right to play in the women's singles field of a major tennis championship, is beaten in the first round of the U.S. Open by Wimbledon champion Virginia Wade, 6-1, 6-4. Barry Lorge of the *Washington Post* describes the match as a media event as "a swarm of photographers, broadcasters and reporters were on hand to record the details of what was purposed to be a grand gesture for human rights by some, and a freak show by others." Later that evening, 5-foot tall, 90-pound Tracy Austin, at the age of 14 years, eight months, 20 days, becomes the youngest player to play in the U.S. Open, defeating Heidi Eisterlehner of West Germany 3-6, 6-3, 6-1 in the first round. Austin's mark is broken in 1979 by 14-year-old Kathy Horvath.

1987 Fifteen-year-old Michael Chang defeats Paul McNamee of Australia 6-3, 6-7, 6-4, 6-4 to become the youngest man to win a match at the U.S.

Open in the Open era. Chang, at the age of 15 years, six months and 30 days is almost two months older than the all-time youngest player to win a match at the championship—Vincent Richards—who was 15 years, five months and eight days at the start of the 1918 U.S. Championships. Other highlights of the day are Ivan Lendl's 6-0, 6-0, 6-0 whitewash of Barry Moir of South Africa and, in the evening session, Boris Becker needing more than four hours to come back from two-sets-to-love to beat Tim "Dr. Dirt" Wilkison 4-6, 4-6, 7-5, 6-4, 6-2. Says Becker, "It was one of my biggest matches. He's a fighter and the crowd was getting into it."

1993 Goran Ivanisevic and Daniel Nestor play the longest tie-break in the history of the U.S. Open (38 points)—and equal the longest tie-break in men's singles ever played as Ivanisevic prevails 6-4, 7-6 (7-5), 7-6 (20-18) in a first-round encounter. The tie-breaker ties the all-time record in men's singles set by Bjorn Borg and Premjit Lall at Wimbledon in 1973—Borg prevailing 6-3, 6-4, 9-8 (20-18). The longest tie-break played—50 points—is played at Wimbledon in 1985 —Michael Mortensen and Jan Gunnarson defeating John Frawley and Victor Pecci 6-4, 6-4, 3-6, 7-6 (26-24) in the first round of men's doubles.

1994 Thirty-four-year-old Ivan Lendl plays what ultimately becomes his final professional tennis match as he is forced to retire with back pain trailing Bernd Karbacher of Germany 6-4, 7-6, 1-0 in the second round of the U.S. Open. Lendl announces his retirement from competitive tennis due to his back problems on Dec. 20, 1994.

1939 As Adolf Hitler launches blitzkrieg against Poland at the start of World War II, the United States and Australia conduct the draw ceremony for the Davis Cup Challenge Round at the Merion Cricket Club in Philadelphia, Pa. The war prevents Davis Cup from being contested from 1940 to 1945, but the trophy sits in the safe of a bank in Melbourne, Australia as the Aussies go on to stage an incredible comeback win over the United States at Merion, coming back from an 0-2 deficit to beat out the Americans 3-2. John Bromwich wins the anti-climatic fifth and decisive match, beating Frank Parker 6-0, 6-3, 6-1 on September 4.

September 2

1991 In one of the most celebrated and famous matches in the history of the U.S. Open, Jimmy Connors turns 39-years-old and comes back from a two-sets-to-one and a 2-5 fifth-set deficit to defeat 27-year-old Aaron Krickstein 3-6, 7-6 (8), 1-6, 6-3, 7-6 (4) in a rousing fourth round match in the late afternoon of Labor Day Monday, "This is what I live for, to win a match 7-6 in the fifth," says Connors, who pulls a similar escape in the first round against Patrick McEnroe, trailing two-sets-to-love and 3-0 in the third set. "For me to pull out another stunt like this, how can you not laugh about it? What the hell is going on here?" Connors struts, fist-pumps and grinds around the court in the 4-hour, 42-minute encounter, telling TV viewers before the fifth-set tie-break, "This is what they paid for. This is what they want." Writes Tommy Bonk in the *Los Angeles Times*, "Connors came from a break down in the fifth set, got it back even as Krickstein served for the match at 5-3, climbed into the deciding tiebreaker with a windmill overhead on which his feet cleared the court by a good two inches and knocked a backhand volley into the open court to end it on the first match point. Along the way, Connors carried on in what has become his time-honored tradition, alternating somewhere between reform school and charm school."

1970 The tie-break makes its debut in major tournament tennis on the opening day of the 1970 U.S. Open. A total of 26 tie-breaks (the VASSS, nine-point sudden death tie-break) are played on the first day of the tournament with Bob McKinley and Ray Ruffels both winning matches in fifth-set tie-breaks. Jimmy Connors plays his first match at the U.S. Open on his 18th birthday, losing to Mark Cox 6-2, 6-4, 6-2.

1971 Chris Evert and Jimmy Connors win their first U.S. Open singles matches. Playing in her first U.S. Open, the 16-year-old Evert wins the first of her record 101 U.S. Open match victories, defeating Edda Buding 6-1, 6-0 in 42 minutes. Playing on his 19th birthday, Connors comes back from a two-set deficit to defeat Alex Olmedo 2-6, 5-7, 6-4, 7-5, 7-5.

1993 Karel Novacek upsets two-time defending champion Stefan Edberg 7-6, 6-4, 4-6, 6-4 in the second round of the U.S. Open, ending the Swede's 15-match U.S. Open winning streak.

1969 John Newcombe defeats Marty Riessen 4-6, 6-3, 6-4, 25-23 in the fourth round of the U.S. Open in 4 hours, 10 minutes. The 48 games played in the fourth set in the most number of games played in a set in U.S. Open history.

1924 Bill Tilden wins his fifth straight U.S. men's singles title with a 6-1, 9-7, 6-2 victory over chief rival and U.S. Davis Cup teammate Bill Johnston in the final at the West Side Tennis Club at Forest Hills.

1977 Using the eventually outlawed "spaghetti strings," 22-year-old Mike Fishbach upsets No. 16 seed Stan Smith 6-0, 6-2 in a best-of-three-set second round match at the U.S. Open. Fishbach, described as "an amply beared, amusing, apple juice-slugging refugee from the satellite circuit" by the *Washington Post*, uses a racquet that he has strung with two interwoven layers of gut reinforced with fish test line, adhesive tape and twine that helps him generate extraordinary amounts of spin. The stringing method is eventually outlawed by the governing bodies of tennis.

1921 Bill Tilden is two points from defeat, but comes back from two-sets-to-love down to beat Japan's Zenzo Shimizu 5-7, 4-6, 7-5, 6-2, 6-1 to give the United States a 2-0 lead over Japan in the Davis Cup Challenge Round at the West Side Tennis Club in Forest Hills, Queens, N.Y. The 5-foot-six Shimidzu leads Tilden 5-3, 30-15 in the third set, but Tilden, suffering from a boil on his foot during the 100-degree afternoon, rallies to win four straight games to win the third set. Between the third and fourth sets, Tilden has his boil lanced by a doctor and goes on to lose only three more games in the five-set victory. The U.S. goes on to sweep Japan 5-0 to retain the Davis Cup.

1952 Jimmy Connors, the five-time U.S. Open champion and the only man to win the U.S. Open on three surfaces, is born in East St. Louis, Ill. Connors wins his first U.S. Open in 1974 on grass and his second on clay in 1976. His last three titles—1978, 1982 and 1983—are won on hard courts. He wins a record 109 singles titles that also include two Wimbledon titles in 1974 and 1982 and the Australian Open in 1974. Writes Bud Collins in *The Bud Collins History of Tennis* of Connors, "Fiery of temperament and shot-making, this lefty with a two-fisted backhand pounded foes for more than two professional decades in rip-roaring baseline style, a rag doll throwing himself into his groundies with utter gusto. Often controversial, he fought verbally with opponents, officials and the crowd."

September 3

2006 Thirty-six-year-old Andre Agassi bids adieu to competitive tennis, losing his career finale 7-5, 6-7 (4), 6-4, 7-5 to No. 112th-ranked qualifier Benjamin Becker of Germany in the third round of the U.S. Open. Agassi, the 1994 and 1999 champion, competing in his 21st U.S. Open, is forced to have cortisone shots to relieve the pain in his back and is visibly hurting in the latter stages of the match. Writes Bud Collins in the *Boston Globe* of the match's conclusion, "Those 21 wondrous years were wrapped up in the cascade of hurrahs, lengthy applause, and a ton of handclapping. As ever, Agassi bowed in all directions and flung kisses as waterfalls of tears trickled everywhere, his along with so many among his flock. He sat down to compose himself, then returned to the blue court to brush away the crowd's blue mood with a valedictory delivered from the heart amid sobs" Says Agassi to the crowd and the global television audience, "The scoreboard said I lost today, but what the scoreboard doesn't say is what it is I have found. And over the last 21 years, I have found loyalty. You have pulled for me on the court and also in life. I've found inspiration. You have willed me to succeed sometimes even in my lowest moments. And I've found generosity. You have given me your shoulders to stand on to reach for my dreams, dreams I could never have reached without you. Over the last 21 years, I have found you and I will take you and the memory of you with me for the rest of my life. Thank you."

1989 Thirty-year-old Chris Evert defeats 15-year-old Monica Seles 6-0, 6-2 for her 101st and last U.S. Open singles victory. Evert commits only 17 unforced errors—compared to 34 from Seles—to advance into the U.S. Open quarterfinals for a 19th time in 19 U.S. Opens. Says Evert of her near flawless performance, "I don't know where it came from." Writes Sally Jenkins of the *Washington Post*, "In many ways this was a match of remembrance. Evert had played it countless times before, against all the Tracy Austins and Andrea Jaegers she has outlasted over her 19-year era. Seles was a pogo stick of a girl with harmful, two-fisted strokes like those of a younger Evert. Ranked No. 12 in the world, she defeated the slowing, tiring fourth-seeded Evert in straight sets in April's Virginia Slims of Houston, and was widely expected to do so again today. Instead Evert accomplished her 101st Open victory, a record for men and women."

1975 Eighteen-year-old Martina Navratilova, competing in her third U.S. Open, defeats 33-year-old Margaret Court, competing in her 11th and final

U.S. Open, 6-2, 6-4 in the women's quarterfinals. Navratilova goes on to win 18 major singles titles, while Court concludes her career with 24 major singles titles.

1945 Sgt. Frank Parker, after enduring a 9,000 mile flight from Guam to defend his U.S. title, defeats Bill Talbert 14-12, 6-1, 6-2 in the final of the first post-war U.S. Championships. Talbert endures what must have felt like a 9,000 mile flight on the day, playing three finals, despite being a diabetic. After losing to Parker, Talbert and partner Gardnar Mulloy complete their doubles final—suspended the previous night with the score at 10-10 in the third set—defeating Jack Tuero and Bob Falkenburg 12-10, 9-10, 12-10, 6-2. Then, he and Margaret Osborne win a semifinal match over Louise Brough and Frank Shields and finally, in a match that starts at 6:45 pm, they win the mixed title, defeating Doris Hart and Bob Falkenburg 6-4, 6-4.

2001 Four-time U.S. Open champion Pete Sampras defeats two-time U.S. Open champion Patrick Rafter 6-3, 6-2, 6-7 (5), 6-4 in a highly-anticipated round of 16 encounter at the U.S. Open in what is Rafter's final U.S. Open match. Approximately 18 hours earlier, No. 1 seed Gustavo Kuerten finishes off a two-sets-to-love comeback at 12:17 am defeating Max Mirnyi 6-7 (5), 5-7, 7-6 (4), 7-6 (3), 6-2 to become only the third No. 1 seeded man to come back from two-sets down in the Open era at the U.S. Championships. Kuerten serves 33 aces and hits 104 winners and celebrates his victory with many flag-waving, singing Brazilian fans.

1968 Cliff Drysdale of South Africa, the U.S. singles finalist in 1965 described by the *New York Times* as "more a stylist than a tiger except when he is lashing his vicious two-fisted backhand from any spot on the court," defeats Wimbledon champion Rod Laver 4-6, 6-4, 3-6, 6-1, 6-1 in the fourth round of the U.S. Open. Says Laver after the disappointing loss, "Confidence plays a big part of this game. I lost confidence in my serve and he had the confidence to stay back and rely on his ground strokes."

1977 Ken Rosewall, two months shy of his 43rd birthday, is defeated by 24-year-old Jose Higueras 6-4, 6-4 in a best-of-three-set third round match that marks Rosewall's final U.S. Open singles match.

1990 Twenty-one-year-old Steffi Graf needs only 53 minutes to end 14-year-old Jennifer Capriati's first U.S. Open with a 6-1, 6-2 fourth round dismissal.

September 4

1977 James Reilly, a 33-year-old resident of New York City, is shot in the left thigh as a spectator at the John McEnroe—Eddie Dibbs third-round night match at the U.S. Open at the West Side Tennis Club in Forest Hills. The shooting, from a .38 caliber gun, occurs at the start of the match near Portal 8 in the north section of the stadium and delays play for about six minutes as Reilly is taken from the stands to the first aid station and then to nearby St. John's Hospital. Most of the 6, 943 fans in attendance are not aware that a shooting had occurred. Police conclude it was likely a shot that came from outside the stadium. McEnroe wins the best-of-three set match 6-2, 4-6, 6-4.

1992 In his record 115th what ultimately is his final U.S. Open singles match, five-time U.S. Open champion Jimmy Connors is defeated by three-time champion Ivan Lendl 3-6, 6-3, 6-2, 6-0 in a 2-hour, 37-minute second-round night match. Connors, who famously wins two U.S. Open titles in 1982 and 1983 defeating Lendl in the final, is unable to foment the shot-making skills and the frenzied atmosphere of the previous year's tournament, when as a 39-year-old, he reaches the "Final Four" of the tournament. In a final attempt to get under the skin of Lendl after the 35th and final meeting between the two legends, Connors tells reporters after the match that Lendl's skills have diminished, "He was just bunting the ball back. He doesn't play anything like he used to." Counters Lendl, a winner of 22 of the 35 matches with Connors, "If it works, why not?" Writes Harvey Araton of the *New York Times* of the match, "What began with Jimmy Connors trying to drag Ivan Lendl all the way back to 1983 ended with Lendl making it painfully clear to Connors the consequences of it being 1992."

1959 Sixteen-year-old Arthur Ashe makes his debut at the U.S. Championships and loses to 21-year-old Rod Laver 6-2, 7-5, 6-2 in the first round. Allison Danzig of the *New York Times* says Ashe "served well and hit with a good pace and length off the ground, particularly on his forehand." Danzig however notes that Ashe was "not so effective in his volleying."

1983 Confessing that "I was a little nervous in the first two sets," 16-year-old amateur Aaron Krickstein comes back from two sets down and from 2-4 down in the fifth set to upset 29-year-old and No. 15 seeded Vitas Gerulaitis 3-6, 3-6, 6-4, 6-3, 6-4 in the third round of the U.S. Open. "I'm not intimidated by the older players," says Krickstein after the match. "When the chips are down, I usually play my best." The two-sets-to-love comeback win becomes a trademark of Krickstein's during his career as he turns the trick 10 times in his career. In all, he plays 28 five-set matches in his career and wins 20 of them. His 1983 tournament ends in the round of 16, when he is dismissed by Yannick Noah.

1993 Mats Wilander finally defeats Mikael Pernfors 7-6 (7-3), 3-6, 1-6, 7-6 (8-6), 6-4 in a 4 hour, 1 minute match that concludes at 2:26 am—the latest ever conclusion of a U.S. Open match. In the post-match press conference, when asked if he had ever played this late in the evening, Wilander deadpans, "Played what?"

1999 In a battle of teenagers, 17-year-old Serena Williams, the eventual champion, defeats 16-year-old Kim Clijsters 4-6, 6-2, 7-5 in a dramatic third-round U.S. Open match on Louis Armstrong Stadium. Williams comes back from a 3-5 third-set deficit and wins 16 of the last 17 points of the match.

2003 The U.S. Open's first "four-day" match is completed as Francesca Schiavone of Italy completes a 6-7 (5), 7-5, 6-2 victory over Ai Sugiyama of Japan in the round of 16. The match begins four days earlier on Monday, Sept. 1 on Louis Armstrong Stadium and finally concludes on Court No. 10 after the two players go on and off the courts seven times during four days of rain at the USTA National Tennis Center.

2007 Saying her opponent "made a lot of lucky shots," Serena Williams is defeated by Justine Henin 7-6 (3), 6-1 in the quarterfinals of the U.S. Open. The match marks Henin's third quarterfinal win over Williams in a major tournament in 2007, also beating the 2007 Australian Open champion in the quarterfinals of the French Open and Wimbledon.

1981 Unranked 17-year-old amateur Andrea Leand upsets No. 2 seed, and 16-year-old Andrea Jaeger 1-6, 7-5, 6-3 in the second round of the U.S. Open. Jaeger leads the match 6-1, 5-2 before letting the match slip away. Says Leand of her deficit, "I decided to play each point as if it were the most important point of the match." Says Jaeger, "She played well and I let her in the match when I had it won."

September 5

1989 The storied U.S. Open career of Chris Evert comes to an end as the six-time champion is defeated by Zina Garrison 7-6 (1), 6-2 in Evert's final U.S. Open match in the women's quarterfinals. Says Evert, "I'm not disappointed that it's my last match at the Open, I'm disappointed isolating the match and thinking how I played it, and, well, that's one of the reasons I'm retiring." Evert, a six-time U.S. Open champion, makes her debut at the U.S. Open in 1971 as a 16-year amateur, reaching the semifinals en route to winning a record 101 of 113 tournament matches. Says Garrison, "When I went over and sat down, I thought about what had just happened, that this is the last time we'll see Chris here. She's been so much to the game. She's such a lady. To be the villain to have to take her out of this tournament, it's good for me, but it wasn't good for me. It might not be the way I want people to remember me, but at least I will be remembered." Writes Robin Finn in the *New York Times* of Evert's emotional and dramatic final moments on a U.S. Open court, "Evert calmly packed up her racquets on the Stadium Court for the last time, gave a smile and a rotating wave of farewell to her fans and put a steadying arm around the shoulders of Garrison, who couldn't suppress a few confused tears."

1996 Defending champion and No. 1 seeded Pete Sampras, fighting off fatigue and becoming ill on court, outlasts Alex Corretja 7-6 (5), 5-7, 5-7, 6-4, 7-6 (7) in the quarterfinals in one of the most dramatic matches ever at the U.S. Open. Sampras vomits on the court after the second point of the final-set tie-break and fights off a match point at 6-7 in the tiebreaker with a stab volley. At 7-7, Sampras, struggling with his strength, serves a second-serve ace to take an 8-7 lead. Sampras appears barely able to play another point—and doesn't need to—as Corretja double-faults the match away on the next point. Says Corretja following the match, "It was probably the best match of my career—the best one and the worst one."

1949 In one of the greatest U.S. championship finals in the history of the sport, 21-year-old Pancho Gonzales needs 67 games—the most ever in a U.S. final—to defeat Ted Schroeder 16-18, 2-6, 6-1, 6-2, 6-4 for his second straight U.S. title. Allison Danzig of the *New York Times* writes of Gonzales and his two-sets-to-love comeback that "no holder of the crown has shown more perseverance in enduring and surmounting the barbs of adversity than did the 21-year-old, six-footer from Los Angeles." Fifteen days later, Gonzales turns professional and does not appear again at the U.S. Championships at

Forest Hills until 1968, when the tournament is finally open to professional players.

1932 Bunny Austin, the British Davis Cup standout and losing Wimbledon finalist to Ellsworth Vines earlier in the summer, introduces tennis shorts to the sport in his four-set win over Berkeley Bell of the United States in the first round of the U.S. Championships at Forest Hills. Writes John Kieran of the *New York Times*, "Austin came dressed for the occasion. He was practically in running costume."

1951 Sixteen-year-old Maureen Connolly wins the U.S. women's singles title for the first of three times with a 6-3, 1-6, 6-4 victory over Shirley Fry, played in front of a surprisingly small crowd of 2,500 at the West Side Tennis Club at Forest Hills. Connolly becomes the youngest player to win U.S. singles title—a record broken in 1979 by Tracy Austin, who is three months younger the Connolly. Writes Allison Danzig of *The New York Times*, "The final was so nerve-wrecking in the concluding stages, with the outcome hanging in the balance to the last stroke, that Eleanor Tennant, Miss Connolly's coach, was near collapse at the end. She had to be administered to in a box in the marquee as her pretty little protégé let out a scream of joy and ran forward to great her beaten opponent."

1979 Roscoe Tanner fires 11 aces, breaks the net with his bullet serve and upsets top-seeded Bjorn Borg 6-2, 4-6, 6-2, 7-6 (2) in 2 hours, 26 minutes in a much-hyped night match in the quarterfinals of the U.S. Open. Tanner's win avenges his five-set loss to Borg in the Wimbledon final two months earlier. Tanner's blistering serve breaks the net cord in a crucial part of the match—with Tanner serving for the match at 5-3 in the fourth set and the score knotted at deuce, Tanner just serving an ace to save a break point. Tanner and Borg leave the court while a maintenance crew fixes the net, causing a six-and-a-half minute delay. Borg saves two match points before breaking Tanner's serve to even the set score at 5-5. Each player holds serve again before Tanner runs away with the fourth-set tie-breaker 7-2. Says Borg of the upset loss, "I made too many errors and Roscoe put the pressure on my all the time that I had to break his serve. Tonight, I couldn't do that."

1978 Jimmy Connors rallies from a 3-5 fifth-set deficit and defeats Adriano Panatta 3-6, 6-4, 6-1, 1-6, 7-5 in 3 hours, 36 minutes in the fourth round of the U.S. Open. Panatta serves for the match at 5-4 in the fifth set and is two points from victory at 30-30. Connors hits one of the most incredible shots in the history of the Open at 5-6, deuce in the final set—an around the post backhand passing shot. Writes Barry Lorge of the *Washington Post*. "Panatta saved four match points as he served at 5-6 in the tingling final set, but Connors got to match point for the fifth time on an astounding shot—a running backhand down the line off a ball 10 feet out of court and practically behind him. Panatta's forehand cross-court volley would have been a sure winner against virtually any other player. Connors played the shot one-handed, unable to get his right hand on the racket for his usual two-fisted grip on the backhand, and drilled the ball around the net post. It landed inches inside the sideline as Panatta watched forlornly." Says Connors, "When I took off after that ball, I knew I could get to it, but I didn't know what I'd be able to do with it. First, I just wanted to get it back, to make him play another shot. But he wasn't in great position, so I went for it. It nearly took the net judge's head off." Says Panatta, "In Italy, we have a saying: "He did not want to die." I think that is the biggest positive point for Jimmy. He fights on every point, so you can't relax, not even one single point."

September 6

1943 An unusual ending to a major final occurs in the men's singles final at the U.S. Championships as Joe Hunt, a lieutenant in the U.S. Navy, defeats Jack Kramer of the U.S. Coast Guard 6-3, 6-8, 10-8, 6-0 at Forest Hills. As Hunt serves at match point in the fourth set, Kramer's forehand return of serve lands long as Hunt buckles to the court with cramps. Writes Allison Danzig in the *New York Times*, "As Kramer knocked the last ball out of the court, Hunt, turned at the baseline to run to the net to greet his opponent, fell to the ground in pain, seized with a cramp in his left leg, which had been bothering him through the last set. Kramer walked over to his fallen rival and, with Hunt holding on to his leg, they shook hands on the turf as camera men rushed to "snap" the unusual scene." Says Kramer of the match in *The Bud Collins History of Tennis*, "I hit a forehand long on match point. If I'd kept that ball in court I think I would have been the champ by default." Hunt does not defend his title in 1944, due to his military obligations, and is killed in a plane crash on a training mission in 1945 off Daytona Beach, Fla.

1975 Four years after her debut at the U.S. Open as a 16-year-old, Chris Evert wins her first Open title, defeating Evonne Goolagong 5-7, 6-4, 6-2 in the women's singles final. "All through the match, I never thought I'd win," says Evert. "I was pretty down the whole way." The final marks the first year the tournament is played on clay and Evert goes on to dominate the Open on the surface, not losing a singles match during the event's three-year-run on clay from 1975 to 1977. After Jimmy Connors beats Bjorn Borg 7-5, 7-5, 7-5 in the first men's semifinals, Manuel Orantes performs one of the greatest comebacks in tennis history, saving five match points in defeating Guillermo Vilas 4-6, 1-6, 6-2, 7-5, 6-4 in 3 hours, 44 minutes after trailing two-sets-to-love and 0-5 in the fourth set.

1977 Top-seed Bjorn Borg dramatically quits his round of 16 match with Dick Stockton at the U.S. Open—a sore right shoulder not allowing him to continue as Stockton advances into the quarterfinals by a 3-6, 6-4, 1-0, ret. margin. Says Stockton, "I'll take the victory any way I can get it, but I would liked to have seen the match continue. I think I would have won it anyway." Also in the round of 16, Manuel Orantes ends the debut U.S. Open of John McEnroe, defeating the 18-year-old New Yorker 6-2, 6-3.

1986 Martina Navratilova and Steffi Graf complete one of the greatest U.S. Open women's semifinal matches ever as Navratilova comes back from three match points down to claim a 1-6, 7-6 (7-3), 7-6 (10-8) semifinal victory over the 17-year-old West German. Navratilova, who displays fist-shaking and finger-waving emotion, leads 4-1 in the first set before the match is delayed a day due to rain and completes the inspired victory in a total match-playing time of 2 hours, 19 minutes. Writes Roy Johnson of the *New York Times*, "It took more than 24 hours to complete, with emotions that ranged from exultation to disappointment. In between, two players tested and stretched one another and provided a sellout crowd at the National Tennis Center with the most dramatic match of the tournament."

1998 Patty Schnyder defeats Steffi Graf 6-3, 6-4 in the round of 16 in what ultimately becomes Graf's final match at the U.S. Open. Graf announces her retirement 11 months later on August 13, 1999.

2001 At 12:14 am, Pete Sampras and Andre Agassi complete one of the greatest tennis matches of all time as Sampras finishes off a 6-7 (7), 7-6 (2), 7-6 (2), 7-6 (5) victory in the quarterfinals of the U.S. Open. Neither player has his serve broken in the 3-hour, 32-minute match. As the clock strikes midnight, the fourth set-tie break is played and both players receive a standing ovation from the 23,033 fans in attendance.

2003 Andy Roddick saves a match point and advances into the final of the U.S. Open—his first major final—defeating David Nalbandian of Argentina 6-7 (4), 3-6, 7-6 (7), 6-1, 6-3. Roddick, who fires 38 aces in the match, saves his match point at 5-6 in the third set tie-breaker with a service winner. Says Roddick, "The turning point was clearly the third set tie-break. At that point I was nearly down and out. I had no pressure at that point so just went for it."

1991 Seventeen-year-old Monica Seles and 15-year-old Jennifer Capriati slug it out in the dramatic women's semifinal at the U.S. Open with Seles hanging on to advance into the U.S. Open final for the first time with a nail-biting 6-2, 3-6, 7-6 (4) victory. Capriati serves for the match on two occasions—at 5-4 and 6-5 in the final set—but is unable to convert. Says Capriati, "I guess it just wasn't meant to be." Says Seles, "We both didn't want to give up unitl the last ball....There was a lot of pressure on me because she was running every ball down." In the first women's semifinal, 34-year-old Martina Navratilova knocks off top-ranked Steffi Graf 7-6 (2), 6-7 (6), 6-4.

2003 Twenty-two hours after walking off the court after a dramatic semi-final win over Jennifer Capriati, Justine Henin-Hardenne becomes the first Belgian to win a U.S. title, defeating countrywoman Kim Clijsters 7-5, 6-1 in all-Belgian women's singles final. In the wee-hours of the morning the night before, Henin-Hardenne finally defeats Capriati 4-6, 7-5, 7-6 (4) in the women's semifinal in a match that concludes at 12:27 a.m. The Capriati-Henin-Hardenne match lasts 3 hours, 3 minutes with Capriati serving for the match in both in the second and third sets. She is two points from winning the match 11 times, but is unable to break through. Curiously, both Capriati and Henin-Hardenne win 127 points in the match.

2000 At 1:22 am, Todd Martin completes an incredible two-sets-to-love comeback to defeat former world No. 1 Carlos Moya of Spain 6-7 (3), 6-7 (7), 6-1, 7-6 (6), 6-2 in the fourth round of the U.S. Open. Martin saves a match point at 6-5 in the fourth-set tie-break to win the 4-hour, 17-minute struggle. Following the match, Martin laps center court and exchanges high-fives with the die-hard fans that stay to the bitter end of the match.

September 7

1980 Two months after their epic Wimbledon final, John McEnroe and Bjorn Borg stage one of the greatest U.S. Open finals as the 21-year-old McEnroe fends off a Borg comeback to win his second consecutive Open title and avenge his Wimbledon loss by a 7-6 (4), 6-1, 6-7 (5), 5-7, 6-4 margin. Borg, attempting to win the third leg of a possible Grand Slam, is denied by the tempestuous native New Yorker. Writes Neil Amdur of the *New York Times*, "The match may have lacked Wimbledon's fourth-set tie-breaker intensity and fifth-set drama in the minds of the players. But it had the same number of total games, 55, two tense tie-breakers and was especially noteworthy for McEnroe's amazing stamina."

1953 Eighteen-year-old Maureen Connolly win her third straight U.S. women's singles title and becomes the first woman to complete a Grand Slam when she defeats Doris Hart 6-2, 6-4 in the women's singles final. Connolly needs only 43 minutes to win the final and finishes 10 days of tennis at Forest Hills without losing a set. In the men's singles final, Tony Trabert wins his first U.S. men's singles title, defeating Vic Seixas 6-3, 6-2, 6-3 in exactly one hour in the final.

1991 Seventeen-year-old Monica Seles defeats 34-year-old Martina Navratilova to win her first U.S. Open women's singles title and complete the season winning all three major tournaments she enters. Seles wins the Australian and French titles, but withdraws from Wimbledon with shinsplits. Says Seles of her Wimbledon absence, "Not playing Wimbledon, it will always be there, a little emptiness, but I have to put that behind me. It would've have been fair to my legs. I would've been able to play the U.S. Open. I really feel that way." Following the 1 hour, 9-minute women's final, Jim Courier ends the dramatic U.S. Open run of 39-year-old Jimmy Connors in the men's semifinals—Courier beating the five-time Open champ 6-3, 6-3, 6-2.

1942 Described by Allison Danzig of the *New York Times* as "one of the most enthralling matches the tournament ever has provided," Ted Schroeder, five days shy of reporting for duty in the U.S. Naval Reserve, outlasts Frank Parker 8-6, 7-5, 3-6, 4-6, 6-2 to win his first and only U.S. singles title.

1975 Less than 18 hours removed from escaping five match points and an 0-5 fourth-set deficit in the semifinals against Guillermo Vilas, Manuel

Orantes stages one of the biggest upsets in U.S. Open history and shocks No. 1 seed and defending champion Jimmy Connors 6-4, 6-3, 6-3 to win the men's singles title. Orantes, seeded No. 3, becomes the first Spaniard to win the title since Manuel Santana wins the title on grass courts in 1965. The 1975 U.S. Open marked the first year that the U.S. Open is not played on grass, but a Har-Tru clay surface. Writes Parton Keese of the *New York Times*, "Off-speed ground strokes and passing shots from both sides were two of the tactics that blunted the bullish tactics of the defending champion. But Orantes' most devastating weapon was the forehand topspin lob, a shot that typified the tone of a tournament that had switched from grass to the clay-like Har-Tru surface."

2002 For the second consecutive year, sisters Venus and Serena Williams meet in a prime time U.S. Open women's singles final. However, unlike 2001, younger sister Serena turns the tables on her older sister, defeating the two-time defending champion 6-4, 6-3 to win her second U.S. Open women's singles title.

2007 One round after defeating Serena Williams in quarterfinals, Justine Henin defeats older sister Venus Williams 7-6 (2), 6-4 in the semifinals of the U.S. Open. After her final-round victory over Svetlana Kuznetsova of Russia the following evening, Henin becomes the first player to beat both Williams sisters en route to a major tournament title. Says Henin after her win over Venus, "I really believed I could do it, and that's maybe why I did. I don't think a lot of people thought I could beat her here in this tournament. I was really proud. It's not easy to play Serena and Venus, you know."

1992 Andre Agassi defeats Carlos Costa of Spain 6-4, 6-3, 6-2 in the round of 16 of the U.S. Open. Sitting in Agassi's box is actress and singer Barbra Streisand, who describes Agassi's game and mental capabilities on court as that of a "Zen Master." Says Streisand, "He's very much in the moment."

1993 Wally Masur of Australia stages one of the most improbable comebacks in U.S. Open history, coming back from a two-set deficit and fighting back from an 0-5 hole in the fifth set to beat countryman Jaime Morgan 3-6, 4-6, 6-3, 6-4, 7-5 in the fourth round of the U.S. Open. In addition to winning the last seven games of the match, the 30-year-old Masur wins 18 of the last 19 points in the match. "I cannot believe that I won that match," Masur says. "I mean it was just ridiculous. It was incredible." Says the 22-year-old

Morgan of the 3 hour, 25 minute match played on the Grandstand Court at the USTA National Tennis Center, "I got up and I gagged, I guess."

1997 The first two U.S. Open singles titles are played on the new Arthur Ashe Stadium Court as 16-year-old Martina Hingis and 17-year-old Venus Williams play the youngest major tournament final in the Open era and Hingis wins her first U.S. Open title by 6-0, 6-4 margin. Patrick Rafter of Australia outduels Greg Rusedski of Britain 6-3, 6-2, 4-6, 7-5 to win his first of two U.S. Open men's singles crowns.

1999 Todd Martin stages one of the greatest comebacks in U.S. Open history, defeating Greg Rusedski of Britain 5-7, 0-6, 7-6 (3), 6-4, 6-4 in the round of 16. Rusedski serves for the match at 5-4 in the third set and leads 4-1 in the fifth-set, but is unable to convert. Among chants of "Let's Go Todd" from the evening crowd at Arthur Ashe Stadium, Martin wins 20 of the final 21 points of the match that concludes at 12:50 am.

1969 Margaret Court defeats Nancy Richey 6-2, 6-2 in the women's singles final at the U.S. Open and is presented the championship trophy by U.S. Vice President Spiro Agnew.

1941 Bobby Riggs wins his second of two U.S. singles titles, defeating Frank Kovacs 5-7, 6-1, 6-3, 6-3. Sarah Palfrey Cooke wins her first U.S. singles title, defeating Pauline Betz 7-5, 6-2 in the final.

1985 Hana Mandlikova wins her only U.S. Open singles crown defeating Martina Navratilova in the final 7-6 (3), 1-6, 7-6 (2). The 23-year-old Czech becomes the first non-American woman to win the U.S. singles title since Margaret Court of Australia in 1970. Mandlikova, who beat Chris Evert in the semifinals, bursts out to a 5-0 lead in the first set and hangs on to win the first set in a tie-breaker. Mandlikova, seeded No. 3, wins the last six points of the decisive, third-set tie-breaker. Says Mandlikova, "I just think that finally everything fell into place and I showed I can play."

1986 An all-Czech day at the U.S. Open as all four singles finalist are Czechoslovakian-born. Ivan Lendl, a Czech living in Greenwich, Conn., defeats Miloslav Mecir for the men's title, while Martina Navratilova, a Czech-born naturalized U.S. citizen, defeats Helena Sukova for the women's crown.

September 8

1969 Rod Laver becomes the only player in tennis history to complete a second Grand Slam defeating Tony Roche 7-9, 6-1, 6-3, 6-2 in a rain-delayed Monday final at the U.S. Open. Laver equals the same sweep of all four major titles that he did as an amateur player in 1962. However, his 1969 Grand Slam is won in the "Open" era open to all players—amateurs and professionals. The Australian also claims a first prize paycheck of $16,000— the largest cash first prize in tennis history at the time—to lift his earnings for the year to a record $106,000. Says Laver after the match of his unprecedented Grand Slam accomplishments, "Tennis-wise, winning this Slam was a lot tougher because all of the good players. Pressure-wise, I don't think it was any tougher. There's always pressure when you are playing for something over nine months." The final is delayed by 1 hour, 35 minutes due to soggy conditions on the grass court that drives tournament officials to rent a helicopter to hover just over the stadium court to help dry the court in preparation for play. Laver makes an important strategic decision late in the first set, switching his footwear to spikes to help his footing on the slippery grass. Laver plays in the U.S. Open final with his wife, Mary, at the couple's home in Newport Beach, Calif., three days late in delivering their first child.

2002 Pete Sampras puts a final exclamation point on his storied and historic tennis career, beating arch rival Andre Agassi 6-3, 6-4, 5-7, 6-4 to win his fifth U.S. Open singles title and his 14th career major singles title in what ultimately becomes the final match of his career. Seeded No. 17 and without a tournament title since Wimbledon in 2000, Sampras silences his critics that offer that he is washed up and, at age 31, becomes the U.S. Open's oldest men's singles champion since 35-year-old Ken Rosewall wins the title in 1970. "To beat a rival like Andre, in a storybook ending, it might be nice to stop," Sampras says in his post-match press conference. "But I still love to compete. I'll see in a couple of months where my heart is and my mind. My head is spinning." Fifty weeks later—without striking another competitive shot following his match-clinching last backhand volley winner against Agassi—Sampras officially announces his full retirement from the sport on the opening night of the 2003 U.S. Open.

2001 In an historic evening for women's tennis, Venus Williams wins her second U.S. Open singles title, defeating younger sister Serena Williams 6-2, 6-4 in the first-ever all-sister U.S. singles final in the first-ever prime time major singles final. The 69-minute final marks only the second time in the history of tennis that two sisters compete in the final of the major singles final—the only other occasion coming 117 years earlier in the Wimbledon final in 1884, when Maud Watson beats her younger sister Lillian for the title. The Associated Press calls the match "a very public spanking...that was far more historic than dramatic." Says Venus in the post-match trophy ceremony of the final, "There have been some good things and bad things. I always like to win. But I'm the big sister. I want to make sure she has everything, even if I don't have anything. It's hard. I love her too much. That's what counts." Diana Ross opens the magical evening at the USTA National Tennis Center by singing "God Bless America."

1957 Althea Gibson, raised on the streets of nearby Harlem, becomes the first black player to win a title at the U.S. Championships as she defeats Louise Brough 6-3, 6-2 in the women's singles final at the West Side Tennis Club in Forest Hills, N.Y. One year removed from winning her first French singles title and two months removed from winning the singles title at Wimbledon for the first time, Gibson is presented with the championship trophy by U.S. Vice President Richard Nixon. Writes Allison Danzig of the *New York Times*, "The girl who was playing paddle tennis on the streets of Harlem some fifteen years ago found herself, at the age of 30, at the pinnacle of tennisdom as she completed a year of almost uninterrupted conquest." In the men's singles final, Mal Anderson becomes the first unseeded player to win the U.S. men's singles title, defeating Ashley Cooper 10-8, 7-5, 6-4 in the final.

1996 Pete Sampras and Steffi Graf win the men's and women's singles titles respectively in the last U.S. Open championship matches played in Louis Armstrong Stadium. Sampras defeats Michael Chang 6-1, 6-4, 7-6 (3), while Graf defeats Monica Seles 7-5, 6-4. Arthur Ashe Stadium becomes the U.S. Open's new center court beginning with the 1997 tournament. The title is especially poignant for Sampras, who wins the title on what would have been the 45th birthday of his mentor, coach and friend Tim Gullikson, who passes away earlier in the year on May 3 due to brain cancer.

1973 Margaret Court wins her final 24th—and final—major singles title, defeating Evonne Goolagong 7-6, 5-7, 6-2 in the U.S. Open women's singles final. The 31-year-old Court claims her fifth U.S. singles crown and her third major of the year to go with triumphs in Australia and France.

1984 The U.S. Open hosts perhaps the single greatest day in tennis history as each of the four matches played on stadium court extends to the maximum number of sets— Stan Smith defeating John Newcombe in the men's 35s semifinal, Ivan Lendl defeating Pat Cash 3-6, 6-3, 6-4, 6-7 (5), 7-6 (4) in the men's semifinal, Martina Navratilova defeating Chris Evert 4-6, 6-4, 6-4 for the women's title and John McEnroe defeating Jimmy Connors 6-4, 4-6, 7-5, 4-6, 6-3 in the men's semifinal. Play begins at 11:07 a.m. and ends at 11:16 p.m.

1985 After three failed attempts in U.S. Open men's finals, Ivan Lendl finally breaks though and wins the national championship of his adopted homeland, beating John McEnroe in the men's singles final 7-6 (1), 6-3, 6-4. Says Lendl, "To me, this is the biggest tournament in the world. It's the championships of the country where I enjoy living very much. I'm just so happy that I'm not even going to try and describe it." The following day, Lendl takes over the No. 1 ranking from McEnroe, who never again attains the top ranking in men's tennis.

1991 Playing nearly flawless tennis, Stefan Edberg dismantles Jim Courier, 6-2, 6-4, 6-0 in devastating fashion to win his first U.S. Open singles title and his fifth major singles title. Says Edberg of his near perfect display of tennis, "It's pretty hard to believe. It's almost like a dream. I felt like I could do anything out there." Says Courier of his lop-sided loss, "I've been pummeled before, but this is the worst beating I have taken this year. He was making my shots look like I don't know what."

1946 Jack Kramer finally claims his first U.S. singles title, defeating Tom Brown 9-7, 6-3, 6-0 in the men's singles final in front of 14,000 fans at the West Side Tennis Club at Forest Hills. Allison Danzig of the *New York Times* writes that Kramer is "indisputably the master of the court, so sound and faithful to the tenets of orthodoxy and keeping on such grinding pressure with his lethal service, return of service and volleys that the lacerating drives of Brown were reduced to impotency in the final set."

1990 Gabriela Sabatini captures her first—and only—major singles title of her career, upsetting top-seeded Steffi Graf 6-2, 7-6 (4) to win the U.S. Open women's singles title. Says the soft-spoken Sabatini after the match, "It's hard for me to talk right now. I just can't believe that I won this tournament. There are no words to describe this emotion."

September 9

1968 Arthur Ashe, an amateur and lieutenant in the U.S. Army, wins the U.S. Open to become the first black man to win a major singles title, defeating Tom Okker in the final 14-12, 5-7, 6-3, 3-6, 6-3. The tournament is the first of the "Open" era—open to professionals and amateurs and Ashe, an amateur, is not eligible to collect the $14,000 first prize and is given a $20 per day per diem for 14 days, while Okker is awarded the first prize paycheck. Dave Anderson of the *New York Times* calls Ashe's win, "the most notable achievement made in the sport by a Negro male athlete." Ashe fires 26 aces in the 2-hour, 40-minute final.

1956 Ken Rosewall prevents fellow 21-year-old Aussie Lew Hoad from becoming the second man to complete a Grand Slam, beating Hoad 4-6, 6-2, 6-3, 6-3 to win his first U.S. singles crown. Hoad, aiming to equal Don Budge's feat of 1938 of sweeping all four major titles in the calendar year, is denied by his Davis Cup teammate, doubles partner and good friend. Allison Danzig of the *New York Times* describes the confrontation as a "madcap, lightning fast duel" that despite a strong wind, features dazzling displays of shot-making. Writes Danzig, "The breakneck pace of the rallies, the exploits of both men in scrambling over the turf to bring off electrifying winners, their almost unbelievable control when off balance and the repetition with which they made the chalk fly on the lines with their lobs, made for the most entertaining kind of tennis. In time, the gallery was so surfeited with brilliance that the extraordinary shot became commonplace, particularly by Rosewall."

1990 At the age of 19 years and 28 days, Pete Sampras becomes the youngest U.S. Open men's singles champion with a 6-4, 6-3, 6-2 victory over Andre Agassi. Says Agassi of the match, "It was a good old-fashioned street mugging." Says Sampras after winning the first of his record 14 major singles titles, "I'm just a normal 19-year-old with an unusual job, doing unusual things."

1979 John McEnroe defeats Vitas Gerulaitis 7-5, 6-3, 6-3 in an All-New Yorker U.S. Open men's singles final. Tracy Austin, at the age of 16 years, 8 months and 28 days, becomes the youngest U.S. Open women's singles champion, ending Chris Evert's 31-match win streak at the U.S. Open with a 6-4, 6-3 victory.

2000 Venus Williams wins her first U.S. Open singles title, defeating Lindsay Davenport 6-4, 7-5 in the women's singles final. Combined with younger sister Serena's U.S. Open title from 1999, the Williams sisters become the first set of sisters to win U.S. Open singles titles. Earlier in the day, President Bill Clinton becomes the first sitting U.S. President to attend the U.S. Open and watches Marat Safin defeat Todd Martin 6-3, 7-6, 7-6 and Pete Sampras defeat Lleyton Hewitt 7-6, 6-4, 7-6 in the men's singles semifinals.

1984 Less than 15 hours after winning a knock-out, drag out five-set semi-final over Jimmy Connors that ends at 11:13 pm the previous evening, John McEnroe wins the U.S. Open for a fourth time, defeating Ivan Lendl in the final 6-3, 6-4, 6-1. "I feel unbelievable and terrible at the same time," says McEnroe following the final of his physical and mental state.

1974 Twenty-two-year-old Jimmy Connors needs only 78 minutes to defeat 39-year-old Ken Rosewall 6-1, 6-0, 6-1 in the most one-sided final in the history of the U.S. Championships. Billie Jean King wins her final U.S. Open singles title, defeating Evonne Goolagong in the final 3-6, 6-3, 7-5.

1978 Chris Evert wins her fourth consecutive U.S. Open title with a 7-5, 6-4 victory at the new USTA National Tennis Center over 16-year-old amateur Pam Shriver.

1995 Steffi Graf wins her fourth U.S. Open women's singles crown, fending off Monica Seles 7-6, 0-6, 6-3 in the women's singles final. Seles plays in her first U.S. Open since she wins the second straight title in 1992 before dropping off the circuit for over two years after being stabbed in the back by a crazed fan in Hamburg, Germany in April of 1993.

2001 Lleyton Hewitt wins his first major singles title, defeating four-time champion Pete Sampras 7-6, 6-1, 6-1 in the men's singles final of the U.S. Open.

2007 Roger Federer saves seven set points and defeats Novak Djokovic of Serbia 7-6 (4), 7-6 (2), 6-4 to win his fourth consecutive U.S. Open singles title and 12th major singles title. Djokovic, who defeats Federer earlier in the summer in the final of Montreal, holds five-set points in the first set and two-set points in the second set, but is unable to convert.

September 10

1962 Rod Laver becomes the first man since Don Budge in 1938 to win the Grand Slam as he defeats fellow Aussie Roy Emerson 6-2, 6-4, 5-7, 6-4 in the final of the U.S. Championships, avenging his loss to Emerson in the previous year's final. Budge is at the West Side Tennis Club at Forest Hills to congratulate Laver and is called to the podium during the award ceremony to comment on Laver's achievement. Says Budge, "If anyone ever deserved winning the Grand Slam, Rod Laver certainly deserved it. I was lucky in not having to compete against such a player as Rod, and Roy's has been impeccable. A lot of our boys and players from other countries could learn something from them." Laver also beats Emerson in the final of the Australian and French Championships. Margaret Smith wins the women's singles title, beating Darlene Hard 9-7, 6-4, to become the first Australian woman to win the U.S. women's title. Hard hits 16 double faults in the final.

1988 Steffi Graf becomes the third women to complete the Grand Slam, defeating Gabriela Sabatini 6-3, 3-6, 6-1 to win the U.S. Open and clinch the sweep of all four major titles for the year. Graf joins Maureen Connolly (1953) and Maureen Connolly (1970) as the only women to win the Slam. Don Budge (1938) and Rod Laver (1962 and 1969) are the only other players to achieve the feat. Says a relieved Graf following the match, "I'm very happy all the talk about the Grand Slam is over. That's a nice relief. Now I've done it and there's no more pressure on me. There's nothing else you can tell me that I have to do."

1933 Fred Perry ends Jack Crawford's bid for the first Grand Slam of tennis and wins his first U.S. men's singles title with a 6-3, 11-13, 4-6, 6-0, 6-1 victory over the Australian. Crawford plays the U.S. Championships against his will as the Lawn Tennis Association of Australia forces him to compete—based on a $1,500 "appearance fee" the association receives from the U.S. Lawn Tennis Association to guarantee Crawford's participation. Crawford prefers to return home to Australia after five months on the road where he wins 13 straight tournaments, but is in ill-health and suffers from insomnia, asthma and exhaustion. Crawford's wins in Australia, France and Wimbledon have the tennis world buzzing at the prospects of an unprecedented sweep of all of majors. *New York Times* columnist John Kieran writes: "If Crawford wins, it would be something like scoring a grand slam on the courts." Crawford nearly pulls off the feat, leading Perry two-sets-to-one in the final, but following the intermission between the third and fourth sets, the Australian is only able to win one more game.

1978 Jimmy Connors becomes the first player to win the U.S. Open on three different surfaces as he defeats Bjorn Borg, 6-4, 6-2, 6-2 in the men's final played on the Deco Turf II hard courts at the new USTA National Tennis Center. Connors previously wins the 1974 U.S. Open on grass and the 1976 U.S. Open on clay courts. The win snaps Borg's 39-match winning streak and avenges Connors' loss to Borg in the Wimbledon final. Connors also becomes the first man since Bill Tilden in the 1920s to reach the singles final five consecutive years, and becomes the first man since Fred Perry in 1933-34, 36 to win three U.S. singles titles.

1995 Pete Sampras wins his third U.S. Open men's singles title, defeating No. 1 seed and defending champion Andre Agassi 6-4, 6-3, 4-6, 7-5 in the final, snapping Agassi's 26-match winning streak. The match is highlighted by an incredible baseline exchange between the two tennis giants on set point for Sampras in the first set. Writes Robin Finn of the *New York Times* of the famed point, later to be recreated in Nike television commercials, "Sampras and Agassi hurtled 19 crosscourt lasers at one another and drew each other ever more dangerously off to the sidelines, until a sharply angled backhand from Sampras turned out to be too swift for Agassi to chase. He took two steps toward it, then waved his racquet as if to say goodbye to the set." Sampras calls the point that won him the first set, "probably one of the best points I've ever been a part of."

1983 Playing in her 10th U.S. Open, Martina Navratilova finally wins her first U.S. Open women's singles championship, defeating Chris Evert Lloyd 6-1, 6-3 in a 63-minute singles final. Navratilova's determination to win the national championship of her adopted homeland results in a dominating performance as the Czech-born left-hander jumps to a 5-0 lead in the first set in 15 minutes and wins the first set in 22 minutes. Writes Bud Collins in the *Boston Globe* of Navratilova, "A skirted zephyr, whose strength, mental resolve and relentless attacking nature are so grandly blended, Martina is currently playing tennis at a level most likely the highest a woman has ever reached."

1927 Needing only one victory in the final two singles matches to retain the Davis Cup against France in the Davis Cup Challenge Round at the Germantown Cricket Club in Philadelphia, the United States is shocked and loses both matches and loses its seven-year stranglehold on the Davis Cup. Rene Lacoste defeats Bill Tilden 6-3, 4-6, 6-3, 6-2, while Henri Cochet clinches victory in the fifth and decisive match defeating Bill Johnston 6-4, 4-6, 6-2, 6-4, giving France the 3-2 victory.

2006 With golfing great Tiger Woods sitting in his box, Roger Federer wins the U.S. Open for a third consecutive year, defeating Andy Roddick 6-2, 4-6, 7-5, 6-1 in the final.

1932 Henri Cochet finishes off a five-set 6-1, 10-12, 4-6, 6-3, 7-5 win over Wilmer Allison in the semifinals of the U.S. Championships—then is given only a two-hour rest period by tournament officials before he is forced to play the championship match with Ellsworth Vines, who beats the Frenchmen 6-4, 6-4, 6-4 for his second straight U.S. title.

2000 Marat Safin becomes the first Russian to win the U.S. Open as he defeats four-time champion Pete Sampras 6-4, 6-3, 6-3. At age 20 years, 7 months and 14 days, Safin is the third-youngest men's singles winner in the Open era behind Sampras and John McEnroe.

1967 John Newcombe and Billie Jean King become the last winners of U.S. Championships in the "amateur" era—Newcombe defeating Clark Graebner 6-4, 6-4, 8-6 and King beating Ann Jones 11-9, 6-4. King and Graebner are the first players to compete in U.S. finals with steel racquets.

1972 Ilie Nastase trails two-sets-to-one and faces break point at 1-3 in the fourth set, but comes back to defeat Arthur Ashe 3-6, 6-3, 6-7, 6-4, 6-3 in the stunning men's singles final at the U.S. Open.

1989 Boris Becker becomes the first German man to win the U.S. Open, defeating Ivan Lendl in the final 7-6 (2), 1-6, 6-3, 7-6 (4). Lendl appears in his eighth straight U.S. Open final, which ties him with Bill Tilden for the all-time record.

1994 Arantxa Sanchez Vicario becomes the first Spanish woman to win the U.S. Open as she defeats Steffi Graf 1-6, 7-6 (3), 6-4 in the women's singles final.

September 11

1955 Tony Trabert defeats Ken Rosewall 9-7, 6-3, 6-3 to win the U.S. Championships at Forest Hills—his third major championship of the season. Allison Danzig of the *New York Times* calls Trabert's accomplishments in the major championships "the finest record in amateur tennis since Don Budge's grand slam of 1938 in the world's major championships." Trabert's lone blemish during the major championship campaign during the year comes in a semifinal loss to Rosewall at the Australian in January. Trabert, also the 1952 U.S. champion, wins the title without the loss of the set, turning the same trick he turned in winning Wimbledon in July.

1994 Andre Agassi becomes the first unseeded player since Fred Stolle in 1966 to win the U.S. title as he defeats No. 4 seed Michael Stich of Germany 6-1, 7-6, 7-5 in the men's singles final. Agassi's victory comes 28 years to the day that Stolle wins his title as an unseeded player when he defeats John Newcombe in the 1966 final 4-6, 12-10, 6-3, 6-4. Agassi also becomes the second man—joining Vic Seixas in 1954—to beat five seeded players in the U.S. Championships, beating No. 12 Wayne Ferreira, No. 6 Michael Chang, No. 13 Thomas Muster, No. 9 Todd Martin and No. 4 Stich.

1937 Don Budge defeats Germany's Gottfried von Cramm 6-1, 7-9, 6-1, 3-6, 6-1 to win his first U.S. men's singles title and establish what Allison Danzig of the *New York Times* describes as "the greatest record of conquest compiled by an American tennis player since the heyday since William Tilden." The match is played nearly two months since the two players compete in an epic Davis Cup match at Wimbledon where Budge comes back from a two-sets-to-love deficit to beat von Cramm in five sets in the fifth and decisive match-clincher for the United States over Germany, the round before the U.S wins the Cup from Britain. Two weeks prior to that match, Budge beats von Cramm to win the singles title at Wimbledon. The victory is redemption of sorts for Budge, who falters when holding two match points against Fred Perry in the 1936 final, only to lose 10-8 in the fifth set.

2005 Andre Agassi calls Roger Federer to best player he has ever faced in losing to Federer 6-3, 2-6, 7-6 (1), 6-1 in the finals of the U.S. Open. "Pete (Sampras) was great, no question," Agassi says. "But there was a place to get to with Pete. It could be on your terms. There's no such place with Roger. I think he's the best I've played against." Says Federer of Agassi's comments, "It's fantastic to be compared to all the players he's played throughout his career. We're talking about the best—some are the best in the world of all time. And it's still going and I still have chances to improve." The title is Federer's sixth major tournament victory and second in Flushing Meadows.

1977 Guillermo Vilas and Jimmy Connors compete in the final U.S. Open match played at the West Side Tennis Club at Forest Hills with Vilas pulling a 2-6, 6-3, 7-6 (4), 6-0 upset of Connors in the men's singles final. After hosting the U.S. Championships since 1915, the U.S. Open moves from the private club in Forest Hills to the other side of the Queens borough of New York City to the new USTA National Tennis Center, a public tennis facility, in Flushing Meadows.

1983 Thirty-one-year-old Jimmy Connors wins his second consecutive and fifth overall singles title at the U.S. Open, defeating Ivan Lendl in the final 6-3, 6-7 (2), 7-5, 6-0. Lendl holds a set point serving for the third set—and a two-set-to-one lead—at 5-4 in the third set, but double faults and falters and loses the last 10 games of the match. Says Lendl, "After I double-faulted, I never recovered."

1988 Mats Wilander out-lasts three-time defending champion Ivan Lendl 6-4, 4-6, 6-3, 5-7, 6-4 in 4 hours, 55 minutes—the longest men's final in U.S. Open history. Wilander's victory gives him a third major tournament victory for the year—to go with his wins in Australia and France—and earns him the No. 1 world ranking for the first time in his career. Says Lendl of losing his three-year grip on the U.S. Open title and the No. 1 ranking, "It's a lousy feeling."

1999 Seventeen-year-old Serena Williams becomes the first black woman since Althea Gibson in 1958 to win a major singles title, defeating Martina Hingis 6-3, 7-6 (4) in the U.S. Open women's singles final. Says Williams of her post-match victory reaction, "It was pretty exciting I'm thinking, 'Should I scream? Should I yell? Should I cry? What should I do?' I guess I ended up doing them all."

2004 Svetlana Kuznetsova becomes the first Russian woman to win the U.S. Open when she defeats countrywoman Elena Dementieva 6-3, 7-5 in the women's singles final. The women's final is played on the fourth anniversary of the Sept. 11 attacks on the United States and both Russian finalists pay tribute in pre-match and post-match activities. Kuznetsova enters stadium court for the final wearing an FDNY hat for the Fire Department of New York, while Elena Dementieva wears a NYPD hat to honor the New York Police Department. In post-match speeches, both players pay tribute the heroes and victims of Sept. 11 as well as the Russian school massacre 11 days earlier in Beslan, Russia.

1982 Chris Evert Lloyd wins her sixth and final U.S. Open singles crown defeating Hana Mandlikova 6-3, 6-1 in 1 hour, 4 minutes in the women's singles final. "I may have my place in history now," says Evert of her sixth U.S. title.

1966 Brazil's Maria Bueno wins her fourth U.S. singles title—and her last of seven major singles crowns—defeating Nancy Richey 6-3, 6-1 in just 50 minutes at the West Side Tennis Club in Forest Hills.

1993 Steffi Graf wins her third U.S. Open singles title with a 6-3, 6-3 victory over Helena Sukova.

1926 With the United States leading France 4-0 at the Germantown Cricket Club in Philadelphia, Pa., "French Musketeer" Rene Lacoste defeats Bill Tilden 4-6, 6-4, 8-6, 8-6 ending Tilden's unbeaten run in Davis Cup singles matches at 16.

September 12

1981 A tie-breaker determines the winner of a major singles title for the first time as 18-year-old Tracy Austin wins her second U.S. Open singles title edging first-time finalist and newly-minted American citizen Martina Navratilova in the final 1-6, 7-6 (4), 7-6 (1). "This means more to me than the last one," says Austin. "At 16, it all came so fast. It was kind of like the stepping stone. I had come onto the women's tour and gradually had gotten better and better. I was too young to realize how important it was."

1936 Fred Perry becomes the first foreigner to win three U.S. men's singles titles as he dramatically defeats Don Budge 2-6, 6-2, 8-6, 1-6, 10-8 in the men's singles final. Budge holds two match points serving for the match at 5-3 in the fifth set, but falters. Writes Bud Collins in *The Bud Collins History of Tennis*, "Point and counter-point they went as Budge, in his first major final, neared the championship again and again, two points away at 7-6 and 8-7, only to be blocked. Every point was a war, but Perry coolly won the last three games, the only man other than Bill Tilden to carry off three titles from Forest Hills. It was Fred's eighth major singles, good for second place all-time then behind Tilden's 10. Budge would play six more major finals, winning them all."

1965 Spain's Manuel Santana becomes the first man from his nation to win the U.S. men's singles title, defeating Cliff Drysdale of South Africa 6-2, 7-9, 7-5, 6-1. In the women's singles final, Margaret Smith beats Billie Jean Moffitt 7-5, 8-6 after trailing 3-5 in both sets. Robert F. Kennedy, the New York Senator and younger brother of President John F. Kennedy, presents both winners and runners-ups with their trophies in post-match ceremonies. The Santana-Drysdale match is postponed 40 minutes by rain at which time Santana buys wool socks from the pro shop of the club to wear over his sneakers for better traction on the muddy grass court. Drysdale becomes the first player to hit with a two-handed backhand to play in a U.S. singles final.

1992 Stefan Edberg and Michael Chang play what is the longest match on record in the history of the U.S. Championships as the No. 2 seeded Edberg needs 5 hours, 26 minutes to defeat the No. 4 seeded Chang 6-7 (3), 7-5, 7-6 (3), 5-7, 6-4 in the men's semifinals. Monica Seles wins her second straight U.S. Open singles title, defeating Arantxa Sanchez Vicario of Spain

6-3, 6-3 in the final. Pete Sampras advances into his second U.S. Open final, defeating fellow American Jim Courier 6-1, 3-6, 6-2, 6-2.

1982 Thirty-year-old Jimmy Connors returns to the winner's circle at the U.S. Open for the first time since 1978, defeating 22-year-old Ivan Lendl in the men's singles final 6-3, 6-2, 4-6, 6-4. Connors claims his fourth Open singles title to go with his championship runs in 1974, 1976 and 1978 and, coupled with his Wimbledon title won two months earlier, earns him the returned status as top dog in men's tennis. Writes Neil Amdur of the *New York Times* of Connors following his victory, "His relentlessly aggressive, uninhibited, all-court style, is more than a trademark: It is a mold of competitive excellence, carved in a tradition of baseball's Pete Rose and basketball's John Havlicek."

1999 Andre Agassi wins his second U.S. Open singles title, coming back from two-sets-to-one down to defeat Todd Martin 6-4, 6-7 (5), 6-7 (2), 6-3, 6-2. Agassi never loses his serve in the 3-hour, 23-minute long match—the first five-set U.S. Open final in 11 years. Coupled with his win at the French Open earlier in the year—and his final-round showing at Wimbledon— Agassi stakes his claim as the top player in men's tennis—just over 18 months after he was seemingly out of the game with a ranking of No. 141 at the tail end of the 1997 season. Says Agassi after the match of the highs and lows of his career, "Part of me is convinced that if it wasn't for those valleys, these peaks wouldn't be this high. It's kind of how my spirit has always worked. To say I regret [the valleys] would be inaccurate."

1993 Pete Sampras defeats Cedric Pioline 6-4, 6-4, 6-3 to win his second U.S. Open singles title in a match described by Tommy Bonk of the *Los Angeles Times* that "failed as far as drama goes, but nevertheless went a long way toward cementing Sampras' reputation as the best player in tennis in 1993." The championship is the third at a major championship for Sampras after also winning at Wimbledon earlier in the year and his initial U.S. Open win in 1990. Says Sampras, "I mean, it has been a great year. The Wimbledon victory was really big for me and now I have won the two biggest tournaments in the world."

1998 Lindsay Davenport wins her first major singles title, defeating Martina Hingis 6-3, 7-5 in the final of the U.S. Open. Davenport also becomes the first American-born woman to win the U.S. Open since Chris Evert wins her last of six U.S. Open singles titles in 1982.

2004 A 23-year-old Roger Federer wins the U.S. Open for the first time, overwhelming Lleyton Hewitt 6-0, 7-6 (3), 6-0 in 1 hour, 51 minutes in the men's singles final. The U.S. Open title adds to his Australian and Wimbledon titles also won in 2004 making Federer the first player since Mats Wilander in 1988 to win three Grand Slam tournament titles in the same year.

1936 Alice Marble, sidelined for much the previous two years with anemia and pleurisy, ends the four-year reign of Helen Jacobs as U.S. champ, ending her 28-match Forest Hills match winning streak by a 4-6, 6-3, 6-2 margin in the final of the U.S. Championships. Marble wins 10 of 11 games from 0-2 down in the second set.

September 13

1970 Margaret Court becomes the second woman after Maureen Connolly in 1953 to achieve the Grand Slam, finishing her sweep of the four major titles by defeating Rosie Casals 6-2, 2-6, 6-1 in the U.S. Open women's singles final. Says Court, "I felt the pressure quite a bit at times. I played very tentative but I sort of made myself concentrate. I'm tired. I guess I haven't realized that it's all over." The Grand Slam is not the only prize Court achieves at Forest Hills as she also pairs with Marty Riessen to win the mixed doubles title and teams with Judy Tegart Dalton to win the women's doubles title to claim a rare "triple." In the men's singles final, 35-year-old Ken Rosewall, who at 5-foot-7 is two inches shorter than Court, wins the men's singles title defeating Tony Roche 2-6, 6-4, 7-6 (5-2), 6-3. Rosewall, whose previous U.S. title in 1956 is won as an amateur, is awarded $20,000 and a new Ford Pinto car for his tournament victory. The third-set tie-break is the first to be played in a major singles final.

1981 Bjorn Borg leaves the U.S. Open—never to return to major championship tennis—losing to John McEnroe 4-6, 6-2, 6-4, 6-3 in the men's singles final. McEnroe earns his third straight U.S. Open singles crown with the victory, while Borg is left to ponder his fourth defeat in an Open final. Due to two death threats phoned into the USTA National Tennis Center telephone switchboard, Borg immediately leaves the court following the loss, surrounded by plain-clothed policemen, skipping the trophy ceremony and post-match press conference. Borg drops out of the sport at the start of the 1982 season and never plays another major tournament in his career. McEnroe becomes the first player to win three straight U.S. men's singles titles since Bill Tilden wins six straight titles from 1920 to 1925.

1964 Maria Bueno needs only 25 minutes to win the most one-sided U.S. women's final as the Brazilian standout dominates Carole Caldwell of the United States 6-1, 6-0. Roy Emerson of Australia needs only 41 more minutes than Bueno to win his best-of-five set final with countryman Fred Stolle, winning his second U.S. men's singles crown by a 6-4, 6-1, 6-4 margin in the final.

1992 Defending champion Stefan Edberg defeats 1990 U.S. Open champion Pete Sampras 3-6, 6-4, 7-6 (5), 6-2 in the first U.S. men's singles final since 1947 to feature the last two singles champions.

1998 Patrick Rafter defends his U.S. Open men's singles title, defeating fellow Australian Mark Philippoussis 6-3, 3-6, 6-2, 6-0. The singles final is the first all-Australian men's singles final at the U.S. Open since Ken Rosewall defeats Tony Roche in the 1970 men's singles final.

1930 John Doeg of the United States beats 19-year-old Frank Shields, the grandfather of actress Brooke Shields, 10-8, 1-6, 6-4, 16-14 in the final of the U.S. Championships. Shields, seeded 11th, holds a set point at 13-14 in the fourth set that is cancelled by an ace.

September 14

1929 Thirty-six-year-old Bill Tilden wins his seventh—and final—U.S. men's singles crown, defeating fellow "oldie" 35-year-old Francis Hunter 3-6, 6-3, 4-6, 6-2, 6-4 in the championship tilt. Tilden's seventh title ties him with Richard Sears and Bill Larned for the record of most U.S. men's singles titles. At age 36, Tilden becomes the oldest U.S. singles champion since Larned wins his last two titles in 1910 and 1911 at ages 37 and 38. Writes Allison Danzig of the *New York Times*, "The match went to five sets, with Tilden trailing 2 to 1, but there was never any question as to the ultimate reckoning and the final two chapters found the once invincible monarch of the courts electrifying the gallery as of yore with a withering onslaught of drives and service aces that brooked no opposition." Bud Collins, in his book *The Bud Collins History of Tennis*, calls the 1929 U.S. men's final "The Geezer's Gala" as the combined age of both finalists—71 years—ranks second only to the 1908 Wimbledon final played between Arthur Gore, 40 and Herbert Roper Barrett, 34.

1947 Jack Kramer drops the first two sets to Frank Parker, but rallies in dramatic fashion to nudge out a 4-6, 2-6, 6-1, 6-0, 6-3 victory to win the U.S. Championships. The title is Kramer's swan song in major tournament tennis as he subsequently turns professional.

1987 Ivan Lendl requires 4:47 to defeat Mats Wilander 6-7 (7), 6-0, 7-6 (4), 6-4 to win his third straight U.S. Open men's singles final in a rain-delayed Monday final. The match is the longest men's singles final in time in the history of the event (only to be surpassed by seven minutes the next year by the same two players). Says Lendl after the epic final, "Mats forced me to be a little more aggressive than I wanted to be. But that is what I had to do. Mats always makes me work. But I didn't expect to last that long with Mats." Writes Peter Alfano of the *New York Times*, "The men's final had already been delayed a day by rain, and then Mats Wilander and Ivan Lendl—tennis players working without a net—sat on the baseline in no particular hurry to leave. For four hours, 47 minutes they engaged in a match of attrition, like marathoners whose biggest concern was finishing the race."

September 15

1971 Stan Smith fends off the challenge of Jan Kodes to win the U.S. Open, his first major singles title, by a 3-6, 6-3, 6-2, 7-6 (5-3) margin. After winning the singles title, Smith returns to the court to compete in the doubles final, which ends in peculiar circumstances as a sudden-death tie-breaker is played in lieu of a decisive fifth set by mutual consent of all four players. Smith, pairing with Erik van Dillen, splits the first two sets of the doubles final with John Newcombe and Roger Taylor, and, with darkness closing in, all four players elect to play a sudden-death tie-breaker in lieu of a fifth set to prevent a resumption of the match the following morning. Newcombe and Taylor win the nine-point tie-breaker 5-3 to claim the men's doubles title by a 6-7, 6-3, 7-6 (5-4), 4-6, (5-3) abbreviated score. Billie Jean King wins the women's singles title, defeating Rosie Casals 6-4, 7-6 (2).

1963 Arthur Ashe makes his Davis Cup debut, defeating Orlando Bracamonte 6-1, 6-1, 6-0 as the United States completes a 5-0 shutout of Venezuela in the Davis Cup third round at the Cherry Hills Country Club in Denver, Colo. Ashe goes on to become one of the greatest figures in U.S. Davis Cup history, helping the United States win the Davis Cup five times as a player and two times as a captain. Ashe competes in 18 ties as a player and compiles a 28-6 Davis Cup record (27-5 in singles). He serves as U.S. captain from 1981 to 1985 and guides John McEnroe and the U.S. team to Davis Cup titles in 1981 and 1982.

1986 In the first professional final played between two black players, Lori McNeil defeats childhood friend Zina Garrison 2-6, 7-5, 6-2 at the Virginia Slims of Tampa, marking McNeil's first singles title on the WTA Tour. Says McNeil of the significance of the final, "I didn't think it was any big deal. It was emotional, because Zina and I are friends, actually we operate like sisters. We're both competitive, and it was too bad Zina had to lose. But I'm also happy I won.'"

2002 Gustavo Kuerten saves a match point and wins the Brazil Open, the national tournament of his home country, defeating Guillermo Coria of Argentina 6-7 (4), 7-5, 7-6 (2). The title ends a 13-month title drought for the former world No. 1 as he wins his 17th career singles title. Says Kuerten, "I'm sure that if they had written a soap opera about this final, they couldn't have come up with anything more dramatic."

September 16

1922 Rivals and Davis Cup teammates "Big" Bill Tilden and "Little" Bill Johnston, each two-time U.S. champions, play in the final of the U.S. Championships at the Germantown Cricket Club with Tilden rallying from a two-set deficit to defeat Johnston 4-6, 3-6, 6-2, 6-3, 6-4. As a three-time winner, Tilden wins—and gets to retire—the silver championship bowl that goes to the U.S. champion.

1978 A 19-year-old John McEnroe makes his Davis Cup debut, clinching the United States victory over Chile in the Davis Cup quarterfinals in Santiago, Chile. McEnroe and Brian Gottfried give the United States an insurmountable 3-0 lead over the Chileans with a 3-6, 6-3, 8-6, 6-3 win over Jaime Fillol and Belus Prajoux. McEnroe goes on to become the greatest American Davis Cup player in history. An owner of 22 U.S. Davis Cup records, McEnroe leads the United States to five Davis Cup titles and posts an incredible 59-10 Davis Cup record (18-2 in doubles).

2007 In her first singles tournament in her post-pregnancy comeback, Lindsay Davenport wins the singles title at the Bali Open in Indonesia, defeating Daniela Hantuchova 6-4, 3-6, 6-2 in the singles final. The 31-year-old former world No. 1 plays just three months after giving birth to her first child, son Jagger. Says Davenport, "I'm a little bit in shock....It's just overwhelming and exciting. I swear this is probably the first tournament I've played in four years where I didn't have anything wrong with my lower extremities." Her last singles appearance on the tour comes one year earlier in Beijing. Her last singles title was nearly two years earlier in Zurich in 2005.

2001 Monica Seles of Sarasota, Fla., wins her 49th career singles title at the Brazil Open in Bahia, Brazil. Seles defeats Jelena Dokic 6-3, 6-3, in the final. While the title was Seles' first since she won the IGA U.S. Indoor Championships in February, it was her third final in her last five events.

2007 Russia wins its third Fed Cup title when Svetlana Kuznetsova defeats Francesca Schiavone 4-6, 7-6 (7), 7-5 in Moscow, giving her nation an insurmountable 3-0 lead over defending champion Italy. Schiavone serves for the match at 5-4 in the second set, but is unable to convert. "(Schiavone) made me play some very inconvenient tennis," says Kuznetsova.

September 17

1960 In the most delayed conclusion to a major tournament in tennis history, Neale Fraser of Australia and Darlene Hard of the United States win the singles titles at the U.S. Championships at Forest Hills—one week after winning semifinal matches to advance into the championship match. The tournament is delayed a full seven days as Hurricane Donna slams New York and soggies up the grass courts at the West Side Tennis Club. Fraser finally defends his 1959 title, defeating fellow Aussie Rod Laver 6-4, 6-4, 10-8, becoming the first repeat men's winner at Forest Hills since fellow Aussie Frank Sedgman in 1951 and 1952. Hard finally breaks through and wins her first U.S. singles title, upsetting defending champion Maria Bueno of Brazil 6-3, 10-12, 6-4. Fraser and Hard both win semifinal matches on September 10—Fraser beating Dennis Ralston and Hard beating Donna Floyd—before the rains come. The Fraser-Laver final is a rubber match for the two Aussies, who split their two previous meetings in major finals on the year—Laver winning the Australian title in January for his first major singles title and Fraser turning the tide on "The Rocket" at Wimbledon. Fraser also ends Laver's 29-match winning streak secured on the Eastern grass court circuit following his loss to Fraser at Wimbledon. Hard finally breaks through and wins her first U.S. title after five previous attempts to win the title. Says Hard, "I never thought I would do it. That girl (Bueno) never gives up. She hits winners when she least expects it."

1927 In a match that Allison Danzig of the *New York Times* calls "a match the like of which will not be seen again soon," defending champion Rene Lacoste defeats 1920–1925 champion Bill Tilden 11-9, 6-3, 11-9 in the men's singles final of the U.S. Championships. Writes Danzig, "On one side of the net stood [Tilden] the perfect tactician and most ruthless stroker the game probably has ever seen, master of every shot and skilled in the necromancy of spin. On the other side was the player who has reduced defense to a mathematical science; who has done more than that, who has developed his defense to the state where it becomes an offense, subconscious in its workings but nonetheless effective in the pressure it brings to bear as the ball is sent back deeper and deeper and into more and more remote territory." Lacoste's career is cut short due to ill health, but becomes one of the sports greatest entrepreneur's—best known for conceiving the famed polo shirts bearing the crocodile emblem. He never again competes at Forest Hills.

1939 Bobby Riggs, the charismatic American player best known as Billie Jean King's opponent in the 1973 "Battle of the Sexes" match, wins his first of two U.S. singles titles at the age of 21, defeating fellow American Welby van Horn 6-4, 6-2, 6-4 at Forest Hills. Riggs also wins the title in 1941, but due to the spreading war around the world, the field is considerably weaker due to a major lack of foreign participation.

2006 Marcos Baghdatis of Cyprus wins his first ATP title and becomes the first player from his country to win a professional tour title, winning the last eight games of the match in his 6-4, 6-0 win over Mario Ancic of Croatia in the final of the China Open in Beijing. Baghdatis, a finalist at the Australian Open and a semifinalist at Wimbledon earlier in the year, is only the third player of the 133 players to rank in the top 10 of the ATP rankings (since 1973) to break into the top 10 without having won an ATP title (joining Cedric Pioline and Mikael Pernfors.)

September 18

1926 Rene Lacoste performs a French breakthrough at Forest Hills, beating Davis Cup teammate Jean Borotra 6-4, 6-0, 6-4 to win U.S. singles title—the first Frenchman to win the national championship of the United States. Lacoste, in fact, is only the second non-American player to win the U.S. men's singles title, following Laurie Doherty, who wins the U.S. singles title in 1903 in Newport, R.I. The all-French final is the first U.S. singles final since 1917 that does not feature Bill Tilden, who is upset in the quarterfinals of the tournament by Lacoste and Borotra's teammate Henri Cochet. Lacoste's title ends the six-year reign of Tilden as U.S. champion. Writes Allison Danzig of the *New York Times* of Lacoste, "The victory of the youthful Lacoste marks the fulfillment of a prophecy made three years ago, when he first came to the United States as a member of the French Davis Cup team. The schoolboy wonder of France, as he was called then, has borne out the prediction made in many quarters and by Tilden himself, that he was the man of destiny in tennis, for whom fortune held her most treasured jewel in store."

2000 Marat Safin follows up his historic and surprising win at the U.S. Open by winning the singles title at the Tashkent Open in Tashkent, Uzbekistan, defeating Davide Sanguinetti 6-3, 6-4 in the final. Tennis is a global game and Safin proves to be a jet-setter as he flies to Uzbekistan the evening after winning the U.S. Open in New York, and, after his win over Sanguinetti, immediately boards a plane for Sydney, Australia for the Olympic Games. Safin's globetrotting catches up to him in Sydney where, as the No. 1 seed, he is defeated in the first round of the competition by France's Fabrice Santoro 1-6, 6-1, 6-4.

1977 Australia advances to the Davis Cup final with a 3-1 win over Argentina in Buenos Aires as Phil Dent wins the clinching singles victory, defeating Ricardo Cano 6-4, 6-4, 6-3. Earlier in the day, Dent pairs with John Alexander to finish off a darkness-suspended doubles win—that puts Australia up 2-1—defeating Cano and newly-crowned U.S. Open champion Guillermo Vilas. Dent and Alexander win the only four games played in the resumption of play, winning 6-2, 4-6, 9-7, 4-6, 6-2—play being suspended at 2-2 in the fifth set the previous night. Italy clinches victory over France in the other semifinal the previous day in the doubles rubber, but extends its margin of victory when Adriano Panatta beats Francois Jauffret 6-4, 6-2 in Italy's 4-1 win in Rome.

September 19

2000 The tennis competition begins at the 2000 Olympic Games in Sydney, Australia as Venus Williams and Monica Seles—half of the U.S. women's tennis "Dream Team"—need less than one hour each to advance into the second round of women's singles. Seles requires only 50 minutes to defeat Katalin Marosi-Aracama of Hungary 6-0, 6-1 in the day's first match on Centre Court. Playing in the final match of the day on Centre Court, Williams requires only 53 minutes to defeat Henrieta Nagyova of the Slovak Republic 6-2, 6-2. Says Williams, "I'm looking to get the gold. Everyone is. I feel it's a long way to the gold medal and lot of opponents who will want the gold."

1925 Despite an injured shoulder, which prevents him from holding barely half his service games in a long, five-set match, "Big" Bill Tilden defeats "Little" Bill Johnston, 4-6, 11-9, 6-3, 4-6, 6-3 in the U.S. men's singles final at Forest Hills. Says Johnston immediately after the match, "I can't beat him; I can't beat the son of a bitch, I can't beat him." The title marks the last of Tilden's six straight U.S. titles and the last time he and Johnston play for the title.

1970 A 5-foot-3, 98-pound, 15-year-old named Chris Evert shocks Margaret Court 7-6, 7-6 in the semifinals of the Carolinas International Tennis Classic in Charlotte, N.C. Court is only two weeks removed from becoming the second woman in tennis history to achieve a Grand Slam sweep of all four major titles in winning the U.S. Open. Evert loses to Nancy Richey in the final the next day by a 6-4, 6-1 margin.

1997 Michael Chang defeats Patrick Rafter 6-4, 1-6, 6-3, 6-4 to help the United States take a 2-0 lead on the opening day in the Davis Cup semifinal in Washington, D.C. and avenges his devastating loss to Rafter in the semifinals of the U.S. Open two weeks earlier. Pete Sampras puts the U.S. up 2-0 on opening day with a 6-1, 6-2, 7-6 (7-5) win over Mark Philippoussis. Says Aussie Captain John Newcombe of being down 0-2 on the first day, "We're down, we're in trouble, but the fat lady hasn't called for a limo yet."

1969 Arthur Ashe and Stan Smith give the United States a 2-0 lead over Romania in the Davis Cup Challenge Round played at the Harold T. Clark Courts in Cleveland, Ohio. Ashe defeats Ilie Nastase 6-2, 15-13, 7-5, while Smith defeats Ion Tiriac 6-8, 6-3, 5-7, 6-4, 6-4

September 20

1973 In perhaps the most socially significant event in the history of tennis and the history of sports, 29-year-old Billie Jean King defeats 55-year-old Bobby Riggs 6-4, 6-3, 6-3 in 2 hours, 4 minutes to win the "Battle of the Sexes" played at the Houston Astrodome in Houston, Texas. The match is played in a circus-like atmosphere in front of a world record crowd of 30,492 fans and millions in front of televisions around the world. "She was too good," says Riggs, the 1939 Wimbledon champion, following the match. "She played too well. She was playing well within herself and I couldn't get the most out of my game. It was over too quickly." Writes Neil Amdur of the *New York Times*, "King struck a proud blow for herself and women around the world."

1988 The sport of tennis returns to official status as an Olympic sport for the first time since 1924 as the tennis competition opens at the Seoul Games. Wimbledon champion Stefan Edberg, the winner of the gold medal in men's singles at the 1984 demonstration in Los Angeles, plays the first match on stadium court, defeating Austria's Horst Skoff 7-6, 6-2, 6-3. Says Edberg of tennis being part of the Olympics, "I don't really know whether we should be here in tennis, but it is worth giving it a chance. It needs some time. In the 1920s, there weren't that many countries competing in the Olympics. Now, here, all the top players aren't competing so that hurts it a little bit. Plus, we have all the Grand Slam events we play in, and those are the most important right now to us. But this is only played every four years, so there's nothing wrong with trying it."

1977 Ilie Nastase is upset in the first round of the Grand Prix tournament in Paris by Frenchman Georges Goven, who uses a double-strung "spaghetti" racquet to post the 6-4, 2-6, 6-4 victory. The spaghetti-strung racquet provides added speed and lift to shots. "That's the first time I've played against someone using one of those things," says Nastase of the spaghetti-strung racquet.

1969 Stan Smith and Bob Lutz give the United States an insurmountable 3-0 lead over Romania, clinching the Davis Cup title, defeating Ilie Nastase and Ion Tiriac 8-6, 6-1, 11-9 in Cleveland, Ohio.

September 21

1997 World No. 1 Pete Sampras defeats reigning U.S. Open champion and No. 3-ranked Patrick Rafter 6-7 (8), 6-1, 6-1, 6-4 to clinch the 4-1 victory for the United States over Australia in the Davis Cup semifinal in Washington, D.C. Says Sampras of the satisfying win over the man who took the U.S. Open title he held since 1995, "I couldn't play any better. I did everything that I could do very well. I served and returned well. If I can play at that level and with that intensity, I feel like I am going to be pretty tough to beat." Sampras never faces a break point on the afternoon and gives up only 18 points on his serve over four sets. Says Rafter, "Pete served too well today. I played Pete a lot of times before and I've always had at least one chance to break him. But today I couldn't read his serve and just didn't pick the ball up. He was too good for me on the day." After Sampras and Michael Chang win opening day singles matches over Mark Philippoussis and Rafter, respectively, Australia cuts the U.S. lead to 2-1 in the doubles contest, defeating Sampras and Todd Martin 3-6, 7-6 (5), 6-2, 6-4. Sampras is so angry at the doubles loss that he refuses to attend the post-match press conference, causing the International Tennis Federation to fine the U.S. team $1,000. "I really didn't have anything to say. I really didn't," Sampras says after his win over Rafter of skipping his media session after the doubles loss the previous day. "I was getting a rubdown, and the key thing was to recover, because I played back-to-back matches. It was more important to get ready for an early match, an 11 o'clock match. It is early for me."

2000 Venus Williams defeats Tamarine Tanasugarn of Thailand 6-2, 6-3 in the second round of the 2000 Sydney Olympic Games and then pairs with younger sister Serena in the pair's Olympic doubles debut, defeating Canada's Vanessa Webb and Sonya Jeyaseelan 6-3, 6-1 in the first round. In between matches, Venus meets with Janette Howard, the wife of Australian Prime Minister John Howard, and trades pins with The Right Honorable Hage Geingob, the Prime Minister of the African nation of Namibia.

2003 Agustin Calleri of Argentina, substituting for teammate Mariano Zabaleta, connects on an incredible 109 winners in just three sets in beating reigning French Open champion Juan Carlos Ferrero 6-4, 7-5, 6-1 to level Argentina even with Spain in the Davis Cup semifinal in Malaga, Spain. Carlos Moya beats Gaston Gaudio in the fifth and decisive rubber of the tie 6-1, 6-4, 6-2 to elevate Spain to the final.

September 22

2000 The U.S. men's Olympic tennis team concludes a dismal showing at the 2000 Sydney Olympic Games as its last remaining entries in singles and doubles are eliminated. Jeff Tarango, the last remaining American man left in singles play, is defeated in the second round by Argentina's Mariano Zabaleta 6-2, 6-3, while in doubles play, the lone American doubles team, Alex O'Brien and Jared Palmer, are eliminated in the second round after a first round bye by Mark Knowles and Mark Merklein of the Bahamas by a 6-2, 6-4 margin. The U.S. team concludes play at the Games with a 1-5 record. U.S. team members Todd Martin, Michael Chang and Vince Spadea all lose first round singles matches the previous day. In women's singles, with first daughter Chelsea Clinton and billionaire Bill Gates in attendance, Venus Williams advances to the quarterfinals defeating Jana Kandarr of Germany 6-2, 6-2 in 52 minutes.

1997 Roger Federer, less than two months after turning 16 years old, debuts on the ATP computer with a world ranking of No. 803. Nearly six and half years later, the man from Basel, Switzerland moves into the No. 1 ranking on the computer, and keeps the top spot for more consecutive weeks than any man in the history of the sport.

1998 U.S. Vice President Al Gore visits with U.S. Davis Cup Captain Tom Gullikson and team members Todd Martin, Jan-Michael Gambill and Justin Gimelstob in Milwaukee, Wisc., prior to the Davis Cup semifinal between the United States and Italy. Gullikson asks Gore if he and President Clinton would host the U.S. team should they defeat Italy and then win the Davis Cup final at which Gore emphatically responds "Absolutely." Unfortunately, in a dismal showing, the U.S. is upset by the lightly regarded Italians 4-1 in one of the most disappointing results for a U.S. team in the history of the competition.

1985 Paul Annacone edges Stefan Edberg 7-6 (3), 6-7 (8), 7-6 (4) to win Volvo Tennis—Los Angeles men's singles title at UCLA. Annacone lets five match points slip away in the second set tie-break before winning the 2-hour, 6-minute final by a 7-4 final set tie-break.

1991 Andre Agassi defeats Carl-Uwe Steeb 6-2, 6-2, 6-3 in the fifth and decisive match as the United States defeats Germany 3-2 in the Davis Cup semifinal in Kansas City, Mo.

September 23

1938 After a delay of six days due to a hurricane hitting the New York area, play is resumed at the U.S. Championships at the West Side Tennis Club at Forest Hills as Don Budge keeps his dream of being the first player to win a Grand Slam alive by beating 1931 Wimbledon champion Sidney Wood 6-3, 6-3, 6-3 in the men's semifinals. Advancing to play Budge in the final is his unseeded doubles partner, Gene Mako, who defeats Australia's John Bromwich 6-3, 7-5, 6-4 in the other men's semifinal. In the women's singles semifinals, Alice Marble beats Sarah Palfrey Fabyan 5-7, 7-5, 7-5, saving two match points at 2-5, 15-40 in the second set, while Nancye Wynne defeats Dorothy Bundy 5-7, 6-4, 8-6.

1969 Ray Moore snaps the 31-match winning streak of Rod Laver, beating the Australian legend in his second "Grand Slam" season in the second round of the Pacific Southwest Open 7-5, 3-6, 6-2. Laver's last loss came at the Bristol Open grass court tournament, a Wimbleon warm-up event, on June 11. Says Moore, "This is my most gratifying victory because he is the best player in the world."

2000 Venus and Serena Williams fend off the upset bid of Russia's Elena Likhovtseva and Anastasia Myskina to advance into the quarterfinals of the women's doubles competition at the 2000 Sydney Olympic Games. The sisters fight off a shaky first set to defeat the Russian duo 4-6, 6-2, 6-3 to score their 30th doubles victory in their last 31 matches. Says Venus Williams, "We played pretty satisfactory. We are looking to improve our level, though. Everyone is coming out with their best tennis. These girls came out today playing some of their best tennis."

1989 Down 6-1, 5-2 Aaron Krickstein fights off seven match points and defeats Brad Gilbert 1-6, 7-6 (0), 6-2 in the semifinals of the Volvo Tennis-Los Angeles played on the campus of UCLA. The following day in the final against Michael Chang, Krickstein finds himself in a 6-2, 4-1 hole, but performs another incredible comeback and defeats Chang 2-6, 6-4, 6-2 to win his sixth career title. Says Krickstein of his art of the comeback, "I've watched a lot of sports all my life and I know it's never over. I'm the kind of player who it takes one or two points to get it going."

September 24

1938 Don Budge achieves the first "Grand Slam" of tennis when he defeats doubles partner and Davis Cup teammate Gene Mako 6-3, 6-8, 6-2, 6-1 in the final of the U.S. Championships at Forest Hills. At the beginning of the year, Budge made a sweep of all four major titles his secret goal for the year and one by one claims all four tournament goals—the Australian Championships in January, the French Championships in June, Wimbledon in July and finally, the U.S. Championships. Writes Allison Danzig of the *New York Times* of the final, "The book was closed yesterday on the greatest record of success ever compiled by a lawn tennis player in one season of national and international championships competition." Mako, who also wins the U.S. doubles title with Budge, is the only player to win a set from Budge in the tournament. Their final is played in great spirits and with a high quality of play, despite the fact that many of the crowd of 12,000 is certain that Budge, the overwhelming favorite, would easily win the match. Writes Danzig, "The play was animated with friendly manifestations across the net whose contagion was communicated to the gallery, particularly in the third set when the crowd was roaring with mirth as the doubles champions trapped each other repeatedly with drop shots. But there was no holding back on either side and there was no trace of amiability in the scorching forehand drives with which Mako caught Budge in faulty position inside the baseline or the murderous backhand and volcanic service which Budge turned loose." In the women's final, Alice Marble defeats Australia's Nancye Wynne 6-0, 6-3.

1988 Thirty-three-year-old Chris Evert defeats Sandra Cecchini of Italy 6-2, 6-2 in her debut match at the Seoul Olympic Games. Says Evert of being part of the Olympics, the first time tennis is part of the program since 1924, "I wanted to be a part of this the first time. I've been trying to think about it, to decide whether I really feel included in this Olympics. So many of the other athletes here—well, for four years, their goal is the Olympics. They have other meets, but all their training is essentially for the Olympics. It's different with us. We have Wimbledon and the U.S. and French Opens, and we have to get pumped up for those. We just finished the U.S. Open a week or so ago, and that makes me look around at the other athletes in other sports—they are so hungry for this—and wonder just how many of the tennis players here are really that hungry."

1984 Vicky Nelson defeats fellow American Jean Hepner 6-4, 7-6 (11) in the first round of the Virginia Slims of Richmond in 6 hours, 31 minutes—the longest women's tennis match ever. The tie-break alone takes 1 hour, 47 minutes, with one point in the tie-break lasting 29 minutes in which the ball crosses the net 643 times.

2007 Dmitry Tursunov, a Russian raised and living in the United States, and Andy Roddick, the fiery and loyal American, play in one of the most dramatic Davis Cup matches in the history of the event, exchanging ferocious groundstrokes for 4 hours and 49 minutes before Tursunov clinches team victory for Russia over the United States with a 6-3, 6-4, 5-7, 3-6, 17-15 win on a clay court in Olympic Stadium in Moscow. The match equals the Davis Cup World Group record for longest fifth set, set in 1985 between Michael Westphal and Tomas Smid. Roddick, ranked No. 6 in the world, actually serves for the match at 6-5 in the fifth set, but is unable to convert and the No. 22-ranked Tursunov is able to hang on and break Roddick's serve to win the match in the 32nd game of the final set. Says Roddick of the final throws of the match, "I don't know which is worse at that stage—the physical or the mental stress. Both equally, I suppose, because everything is made worse by the tension of the occasion." Says U.S. Davis Cup Captain Patrick McEnroe, "It was a classic Davis Cup match and I am only sorry so many people back home won't appreciate just what it takes for both guys to play at that level for nearly five hours. Andy laid everything on the line and you can't ask for more."

2000 Venus Williams and Arantxa Sanchez Vicario collide in an epic Olympic quarterfinal at the 2000 Sydney Games, with Williams winning her 30th straight singles defeating the 1996 Olympic silver medalist 3-6, 6-2, 6-4 in 2 hours, 2 minutes. Says U.S. Coach Billie Jean King of the Williams vs. Sanchez Vicario match, "It was great for Olympic tennis. That's by far the best match so far at the Olympics." Monica Seles needs only 61 minutes to easily defeat Belgium's Dominique Van Roost 6-0, 6-2 to advance into the Olympic medal round for the first time to face Williams.

1990 Michael Chang wins the final two-sets of his dramatic 3-6, 6-7, 6-4, 6-4, 6-3 win over Horst Skoff in the fifth and decisive match of the 3-2 win over Austria in the Davis Cup semifinals. Chang joins Don Budge as the only two American players to come back from two-sets-to-love deficit in the decisive match of a Davis Cup tie.

September 25

1988 Chris Evert is surprisingly eliminated in the second round of the Olympic tennis competition, as Raffaella Reggi of Italy, ranked No. 19 in the world, posts the 2-6, 6-4, 6-1 upset victory over the No. 2 seeded Evert. "At this point in my career, I'm afraid I'm going to have a few more bad days than I used to," the 34-year-old Evert says. "I had a bad one today, and I certainly would have preferred that it not happen like this here. I really don't have any excuses. I just played badly. It's kind of too bad for me that the Olympics came so late in my career. I'm proud and happy with what I've done in my career, and I've had worse losses than today. It's just that an Olympic medal would have been some nice icing on the cake."

2000 No. 2 seed Venus Williams advances to the gold medal match in women's singles at the 2000 Olympic Games in Sydney with a 6-1, 4-6, 6-3 win over teammate Monica Seles. Elena Dementieva of Russia, seeded No. 10, also reaches the gold medal match with a 2-6, 6-4, 6-4 win over Australia's Jelena Dokic. Says Williams of where an Olympic gold medal would rate against winning a major singles title, "This is a once-in-a-lifetime thing. The next time I come here, I'll be 24, if I can get to the Olympics again. Obviously, there's not too much time to win a medal in your lifetime and it's probably bigger than a Grand Slam." In the men's quarterfinals, fifth-seeded Yevgeny Kafelnikov of Russia defeats No. 2 Gustavo Kuerten of Brazil 6-4, 7-5, while unseeded Arnaud Di Pasquale of France defeats No. 8 Juan Carlos Ferrero of Spain 6-2, 6-1. Tommy Haas of Germany edges Max Mirnyi of Belarus 4-6, 7-5, 6-3, while Roger Federer of Switzerland eliminates Karim Alami of Morocco 7-6 (2), 6-1.

1978 Arthur Ashe wins his 33rd and final professional singles title, defeating Brian Gottfried 6-2, 6-4 in the final of the Los Angeles Open at Pauley Pavilion on the campus of UCLA. Says Ashe, the 1965 NCAA singles champion for UCLA, "There are certain places I always seem to play better. Los Angeles is one of them. It's like a second home to me."

1992 Forty-year-old Jimmy Connors defeats 35-year-old Martina Navratilova 7-5, 6-2 in a pro-type "Battle of the Sexes" match in Las Vegas in front of a sellout crowd of 13,832 outdoors at Caesars Palace. Connors wins $500,000 in the match in which he is only allowed to hit one serve, against Navratilova hitting the traditional two serves. Navratilova is also allowed to hit the ball in an extra half of the doubles alley. "I didn't take advantage of the alleys," says Navratilova. "I served poorly today. I was more nervous today than any match I've ever been in." Say Connors, "I thoroughly enjoyed playing Martina. I didn't know what to expect going out there playing her." The match is witnessed by both Riggs and King, who engage in their "Battle of the Sexes" in 1973, won by King 6-4, 6-4, 6-3.

1993 Patrick McEnroe makes his Davis Cup debut for the United States, pairing with Richey Reneberg to clinch the 5-0 victory over The Bahamas with a 6-7, 7-5, 6-4, 6-2 win over Roger Smith and Mark Knowles in Charlotte, N.C. Patrick's Davis Cup representation ensures that he and older brother John McEnroe become the second brother combination to represent the United States in Davis Cup play, joining Robert and George Wrenn, who compete on the 1903 Davis Cup team. The previous day, MaliVai Washington also makes his Davis Cup debut and joins Arthur Ashe as only the second African-American man to represent the United States in Davis Cup as he defeats Knowles 6-7, 6-4, 4-6, ret. (leg cramps). Andre Agassi opens the series for the United States beating Smith 6-2, 6-2, 6-3.

1977 Transsexual Renee Richards wins her first—and only—professional women's singles title, defeating fellow American Caroline Stoll 7-5, 6-1 in the final of the Pensacola Open in Florida.

September 26

2000 Monica Seles clinches the bronze medal in women's singles at the Olympic Games in Sydney, defeating Australia's Jelena Dokic 6-1, 6-4 in the bronze medal play-off match. After losing to teammate Venus Williams in a hard-fought three-set women's semifinal match, Seles says a call from former Olympic teammate Mary Joe Fernandez motivates her in the bronze medal match after the disappointment of not reaching the gold medal match. Says Seles, "I'm happy that I won a medal. I've never had a medal in my life and I had to fight hard for it...I wasn't wanting to play at all today. I was really down. Mary Joe called and got me going and I said okay, I'm really going to come back today and fight for this." In 1996, Seles is denied a medal opportunity, losing in the quarterfinals to eventual champion Jana Novotna of the Czech Republic—a loss that Seles calls "one of my tougher losses in my career."

1988 Brad Gilbert and Tim Mayotte clinch Olympic medals for the United States at the Seoul Olympic Games with quarterfinal victories in men's singles. Gilbert defeats Martin Jaite of Argentina 5-7, 6-1, 7-6, 6-3, while Mayotte defeats Germany's Carl Uwe Steeb 7-6, 7-5, 6-3. Says U.S. Olympic coach Tom Gorman, "This is probably the most pressure any player will ever feel for a quarterfinal match. It was a whole different thing with both of them (Gilbert and Mayotte) in the locker room before the matches today. They knew this was for a medal (guaranteed bronze), and they were feeling it. This is one of the bigger deals in either of their tennis lives." Says Gilbert, "It's different. It dawns on you that, unlike other tournaments, if you lose in the quarters, you go home empty-handed. No medal, no money, no nothing."

1981 Bill Scanlon upsets a tempermental John McEnroe 3-6, 7-6, 6-2 in the quarterfinals of the Transamerica Open in San Francisco in a match that features two "delay" warnings issued to McEnroe. The first comes when the chair umpire forgets to change to new balls after the 11th game of the second set and McEnroe gathers all of the balls and throws them in the middle of the court. The second delay warning comes in the first game of the third set, when McEnroe recognizes linesmen Bill Ruehl and asks him, "Why are you on my match? I thought I told you I didn't want to see you again."

September 27

2000 Venus Williams wins the gold medal in women's singles at the Olympic Games in Sydney with a 6-2, 6-4 victory over Elena Dementieva of Russia in the gold medal match. Williams becomes the third different American to win Olympic gold in women's singles in the last three Olympiads, joining 1996 champion Lindsay Davenport and 1992 champion Jennifer Capriati. Says Williams, "Obviously, the Wimbledons and the Grand Slams, you have so many opportunities to win those, but this gold medal is just every four years. Who knows in 2004, I won't be chosen or you never know what is going to happen, so this is the one moment in time for me, for my country, for my family, for the team."

2000 Unheralded Arnaud DiPasquale of France, ranked No. 62 in world, defeats 19-year-old Roger Federer of Switzerland 7-6 (5), 6-7 (7), 6-3 to win the bronze medal playoff at the Olympic Games in Sydney. The medal is the first for France since tennis returns to the Olympic fold in 1988.

1981 Bjorn Borg wins his 61st and final professional singles title, defeating Tomas Smid 6-4, 6-3 to win the Martini Open in Geneva, Switzerland. Playing just two weeks after losing the U.S. Open men's singles final to John McEnroe, Borg plays only one more tournament for the remainder of the 1981 season, before dropping off the professional circuit for good early in the 1982 season.

1988 Zina Garrison defeats teammate and doubles partner Pam Shriver 6-3, 6-2 in the quarterfinals of the Olympic tennis competition in Seoul, Korea, clinching at least a bronze medal. Garrison advances to play No. 1 seed Steffi Graf, who defeats Larisa Savchenko of the Soviet Union 6-4, 4-6, 6-3.

September 28

2000 In the most decisive gold medal match in Olympic tennis history, Sisters Venus and Serena Williams win the Olympic gold medal in women's doubles at the Sydney Olympic Games with a 49-minute 6-1, 6-1 victory over Miriam Oremans and Kristie Boogert of the Netherlands. Venus Williams becomes only the second woman to win Olympic gold medals in singles and doubles, joining 1924 Olympic singles and doubles champion Helen Wills. The win completes a sweep of the gold medals for the United States women for a third straight Olympiad. In 1996, Lindsay Davenport capture singles gold, while Mary Joe and Gigi Fernandez wins doubles gold. In 1992, Jennifer Capriati wins singles gold, while Mary Joe and Gigi Fernandez captures doubles gold. The dynasty of dominance by the USA women's tennis team since 1992 is the most dominant performance by any country in any Olympic sport that has more than one discipline with the exception of the U.S. women's diving team, which swept all gold medal opportunities from 1924 to 1952 and the U.S. men's diving team, which swept all gold medal opportunities from 1928 to 1952. Says Serena Williams of the gold medal, "We have won a Slam in singles, in doubles and mixed doubles, but this takes the cake. Every year I can win a Slam. But this, it's every four years. You never know what is going to happen. You have one moment in time and Venus and I were able to capitalize on it." Says Venus Williams of the doubles gold medal, "For me this is almost bigger than singles. To have a victory like this with Serena, my sister, my best friend, doesn't happen often. It's very rare. So just to be able to stand up together and have success together on this level has been really, really good. We really worked hard for it and we beat a lot of tough teams along the way. Everyone gave a hundred and ten percent and, honestly, nobody plays like this in a Grand Slam. We had to beat everyone when they are playing better than their best because they are representing their countries."

2000 After winning 61 ATP doubles titles, including 11 Grand Slam titles, one Davis Cup title and an Olympic gold medal, "The Woodies"—Mark Woodforde and Todd Woodbridge of Australia—play their final match as a team, losing to Canada's Daniel Nestor and Sebastien Lareau 5-7, 6-3, 6-4, 7-6 (2) in the gold medal match at the Olympic Games in Sydney. Says Woodbridge, "I'm not disappointed about losing because I know we played as hard as we possibly could. I was just emotional because it was over, and I'd blocked it out basically the whole year. I guess some things you don't expect to end, and when they do come to an end, it's just sad." Says

Woodforde, "It's a big, big moment for the both of us and there's a lot of great memories now to live a dream on."

2000 Yevgeny Kafelnilkov of Russia defeats Tommy Haas of Germany 7-6 (7-4), 3-6, 6-2, 4-6, 6-3 in the gold medal match in men's singles at the Sydney Olympic Games. Says Kafelnikov of serving out the match at 5-3 in the fifth set, "I talked to myself, you know. You came all the way here to play the final match in the Olympics and if you lose that match, you are going to regret it for the rest of your life. That's what kept me motivated today. And I give everything what I had....I was just hoping to participate in the Olympics, to have the record that I was in the Olympics. To win the gold medal is beyond my expectation. I am really proud of myself. I am really proud of my country."

1988 Tim Mayotte and Miloslav Mecir advance to the gold medal match at the 1988 Olympic tennis competition in Seoul, Korea with semifinal victories. Mecir upsets No. 1 seed Stefan Edberg 3-6, 6-0, 1-6, 6-4, 6-2 in the men's singles semifinals, while Mayotte defeats teammate Brad Gilbert 6-4, 6-4, 6-3.

1982 Jose Higueras and Ivan Lendl finish their Volvo International final in North Conway, N.H. that was started on July 26 and postponed due to rain. Lendl leads the match 6-3, 3-2, 15-30 two months earlier, but needs only seven-and-a-half minutes to win the final three games of the match and take championship match 6-3, 3-2. Lendl flies to New Hampshire from Los Angeles, while Higueras travels to the match all the way from Spain.

September 29

1988 Steffi Graf and Gabriela Sabatini advance into the gold medal match at the 1988 Olympic Games in Seoul, Korea with semifinal victories. Graf defeats Zina Garrison 6-2, 6-0, while Sabatini defeats Manuela Maleeva 6-1, 6-2. Says Graf of the possibility of winning a "Golden Grand Slam,""I won a Grand Slam, and now I am trying to do the best I can do to win a gold. One has nothing to do with the other."

1984 John McEnroe and Peter Fleming pair to clinch victory for the United States over Australia in the Davis Cup semifinal, defeating Mark Edmondson and Paul McNamee 6-4, 6-2, 6-3 for a 3-0 lead over the Aussies in Portland, Ore. The win is McEnroe and Fleming's 14th win—against no losses—in Davis Cup play since the duo begin playing for their country together in 1979. The win, however, is their last as a Davis Cup doubles team as their next match—against Stefan Edberg and Anders Jarryd of Sweden in the Davis Cup Final in December—results in their first Davis Cup loss in the their swan song as a U.S. Davis Cup doubles team. Jarryd and Edberg, meanwhile, clinch Sweden's semifinal win over Czechoslovakia in Bastad, Sweden, coming back from two-sets-to-love down to beat Tomas Smid and Pavel Slozil 2-6, 5-7, 6-1, 10-8, 6-2, giving Sweden the unbeatable 3-0 margin.

1985 Nineteen-year-old Stefan Edberg uses his kick-serve to near perfection in defeating Johan Kriek 6-4, 6-2 in the singles final of the Transamerica Open at the Cow Palace in San Francisco. Edberg wins his first ATP title on U.S. soil by losing his serve once during the week. Says Kriek after the match, "It's not that I played badly, it's just that I didn't get a chance to play. If you don't return well, he's got you out of the court. Last week, his (Edberg's) serve was even more overpowering. If a guy serves full throttle and gets 80% of his first serve in...."

1985 Chris Evert Lloyd defeats Pam Shriver 6-4, 7-5, in the final of a Virginia Slims tournament at New Orleans, Lloyd's 16th straight victory over Shriver dating back seven years.

1985 Thierry Tulasne of France comes back from losing the first set, 0-6, to surprise top-seeded Mats Wilander 0-6, 6-2, 3-6, 6-4, 6-0 and wins the Conde de Godo tournament in Barcelona, Spain.

September 30

1988 Miloslav Mecir defeats Tim Mayotte 3-6, 6-2, 6-4, 6-2 in the gold medal match at the Olympic Games in Seoul, Korea becoming the first man to win Olympic gold since tennis returns as a full-medal Olympic sport after a 64-year hiatus. The No.-10 ranked Mecir, from the Slovak portion of Czechoslovakia, throws his racquet into the air and runs to the net after Mayotte nets a backhand volley on match point. "It's a very good feeling," Mecir says of winning gold. "It's difficult to say how this rates, however. I've played in so many tournaments. It is nice, though, to hear people cheering not only because I'm a good player, but because I am playing for them also." Says Mayotte, "It's strange because here, the emphasis is on medals instead of 100 percent on winning. So there is consolation in getting to the medal group. The ceremony was fantastic, it's such a different way of doing things." In women's doubles, Pam Shriver and Zina Garrison win the gold medal, edging Helena Sukova and Jana Novotna of Czechoslovakia 4-6, 6-2, 10-8 in the gold medal match. "If I never do anything else in my life, this will be the highlight," says Shriver. "It's been a long time since I've gotten a charge like this from anything. This is just so different. Zina and I didn't even know each other that well before we came here. And then we got here, were roommates, did everything together—including having her beat my brains out in singles the other day—and then we win this. It's going to be hard to top for a while." Says Garrison, "It was really strange to be on the victory stand and hear your national anthem. It's just got to be the most special moment in your life."

2007 Richard Gasquet of France defeats Olivier Rochus of Belgium 6-3, 6-4 in the final of the Kingfisher Airlines Open in Mumbai, India to win his first career hard-court title and achieve a rare feat of winning titles on all four surfaces—grass, clay, indoor synthetic and hard. Says the 21-year-old Gasquet, "I'm very happy to have won a title on hard court. I had won on grass, clay and indoor (synthetic), so it shows I can play on every court, which is very important for me....It's my first title of the year and my first title in India, so I will have great memories of this tournament for sure. The conditions were tough here with the humidity—it's not the same in France—and maybe I got a little tired. I didn't lose a set all week, which was very good."

1998 Seventeen-year-old Roger Federer defeats Guillaume Raoux of France 6-2, 6-2 in the first round in Toulouse, for his first ATP singles match victory.

Rene Stauffer, in his book *The Roger Federer Story, Quest for Perfection*, summarizes Federer's achievement, "Yet, before the chase for the year-end No. 1 junior ranking reached its decisive phase, the unexpected happened. Federer achieved his first great breakthrough on the ATP Tour. With a ranking of No. 878, he traveled to Toulouse, France at the end of September and, to his own surprise, advanced through the qualifying rounds to progress into the main draw of the tournament. In only his second ATP tournament, the 17-year-old registered an upset victory over No. 45-ranked Guillaume Raoux of France—his first ATP match victory—allowing the Frenchman just four games. In the next round, Federer proved this win was not a fluke by defeating former Australian Davis Cup star Richard Fromberg 6-1, 7-6 (5). In the quarterfinals—his sixth match of the tournament including matches in the qualifying rounds—Federer lost to Jan Siemerink 7-6 (5), 6-2, with a throbbing thigh injury hampering him during the match. The Dutchman was ranked No. 20 and went on to win the tournament two days later, but Federer was also handsomely rewarded. He received a prize money check for $10,800 and passed 482 players in the world rankings in one tournament—moving to No. 396."

1983 John McEnroe defeats Ireland's Sean Sorensen 6-3, 6-2, 6-2 to tie two U.S. Davis Cup records in the Davis Cup qualifying round against Ireland in Dublin, Ireland. McEnroe's win over Sorenson ties him with his Davis Cup Captain Arthur Ashe for the most singles victories by an American Davis Cupper with 27. The win also ties McEnroe with Vic Seixas for the most total wins (singles and doubles) with 38.

October 1

1988 Steffi Graf clinches the "Golden Slam" as the 19-year-old West German defeats Gabriela Sabatini 6-3, 6-3 in the gold medal match in women's singles at the Seoul Olympic Games in Korea. Earlier in the year, Graf becomes the third woman to sweep all four Grand Slam tournament titles in the same year, joining Margaret Court and Maureen Connolly. Says Graf, "I'm very excited. It's something not many people after me will achieve. It's amazing." Writes Bill Dwyre of the *Los Angeles Times* of Graf, "Most people, writers included, have long ago run out of superlatives for her." In men's doubles, in an epic gold medal men's doubles match, Americans Ken Flach and Robert Seguso hang on to defeat Emilio Sanchez and Sergio Casal of Spain 6-3, 6-4, 6-7 (5), 6-7 (1), 9-7. Flach and Seguso lead two sets to love and 5-3 in the third-set tie-break, with Flach serving, before Casal and Sanchez rally to take the match into a fifth set. Flach serves for the match twice in the fifth set, but falters before Seguso serves out the match at 8-7 in the fifth set.

1983 John McEnroe sets an American Davis Cup record for most total wins (singles and doubles) as he teams with Peter Fleming to defeat Matt Doyle and Sean Sorensen 6-2, 6-3, 6-4 in the Davis Cup qualifying round against Ireland in Dublin, Ireland. McEnroe's doubles victory is his 39th career Davis Cup victory, breaking the previous U.S. record of 38, set by Vic Seixas. McEnroe and Fleming's victory gives the United States a 2-1 lead over Ireland.

2006 The third time is a charm for Italy's Filippo Volandri, who after two consecutive defeats in the final of the Sicilian Championships in Palermo, finally wins the title—his second career ATP title—defeating Ecuador's Nicolas Lapentti 5-7, 6-1, 6-3 in the final. Volandri loses to Igor Andreev of Russia in the 2005 final and to Czech Tomas Berdych in the 2004 final. Says Volandri, "I wanted this win so much. This was my third final in a row here and maybe one of the last occasions to win this tournament."

2006 James Blake needs only 58 minutes to dispatch Ivan Ljubicic 6-3, 6-1 to win the Thailand Open in Bangkok. Says Blake, "It was one of those days where everything was going my way, and everything was going against him. It happens to everyone at some point, where everything you hit seems to go in. It's great to do it against a champion like Ivan and to beat him for the first time."

October 2

1977 Guillermo Vilas has his record 50-match win streak snapped when, trailing two-sets-to-love to Ilie Nastase in the final of the Aix-en-Provence final in France, he walks of the court and defaults to protest Nastase using an illegal "spaghetti" racquet. Vilas trails 1-6, 5-7 when he suddenly walks off the court in protest of the racquet, which is labeled illegal by the International Tennis Federation. The ban, however, does not go into effect until the next day. Says Vilas, "I am completely disconcerted and discouraged by the trajectory of those balls. You can understand that Nastase, plus the racquet, that's just too much." The loss also ends the 53-match clay court win streak for Vilas. The Argentine, however, goes on to win his next 29 straight matches, losing next in January to Bjorn Borg in the semifinals of the Masters.

1988 Sixteen-year-old Michael Chang wins his first career ATP singles title, defeating Johan Kriek—14 years his senior—by a 6-2, 6-3 margin in the final of the Transamerica Open in San Francisco, Calif. At the age of 16 years and eight months, Chang is the second youngest player to win an ATP event behind Aaron Krickstein who was five months younger when he won his first ATP title in Tel Aviv, Israel in 1983. Says Kriek, "He's another phenomenon. I tried my absolute best."

1988 Mats Wilander wins his only tournament as the world's No. 1 player, beating fellow Swede Kent Carlsson, 6-1, 3-6, 6-4, to win the Sicilian Open in Palermo, Sicily. The event is Wilander's first event since he beats Ivan Lendl to win the U.S. Open to become the new world No. 1.

1983 John McEnroe defeats Ireland's Matt Doyle 9-7, 6-3, 6-3 for his 28th career Davis Cup singles victory, breaking the record of his Davis Cup captain, Arthur Ashe. McEnroe's win clinches the eventual 4-1 American victory over Ireland in the Davis Cup qualifying round in Dublin, Ireland.

2005 In the first-ever ATP tournament played in Vietnam, Jonas Bjorkman of Sweden defeats Czech Radek Stepanek 6-3, 7-6 (4) in the final of the Vietnam Open in Ho Chi Minh City. The title is Bjorkman's sixth ATP singles title.

October 3

1982 The United States completes a 5-0 shutout of Australia in the Davis Cup semifinal in Perth, Australia as Gene Mayer defeats Mark Edmondson 6-3, 6-3 and John McEnroe defeats John Alexander 6-4, 6-3. The most difficulty the U.S. team has with Australia is getting there, as McEnroe and teammate Peter Fleming encounter a frightening flight experience and travel delays that place them on the ground in Perth approximately 40 hours before the start of play. Leaving San Francisco Monday night after playing in the final for the Transamerica Open, McEnroe and Fleming's flight stops in Honolulu to refuel. As reported in the *New York Times*, the flight from Honolulu to Australia aborts its first takeoff, but blows a tire when the plane finally does take off, but the problem is not discovered for two hours. The plane is forced to return to Honolulu and the pilots warn McEnroe, Fleming and other passengers that they should prepare for a crash landing. The plane safely lands back in Honolulu without incident, but McEnroe and Fleming are forced to wait 10 hours before a plane can be flown from Los Angeles to take them to Australia. They arrive in Perth at 9:30 pm Wednesday night, the night before the official draw ceremony for the series, which starts on Friday.

1981 John McEnroe and Peter Fleming put the United States into the Davis Cup final for a third time in four years as they defeat Phil Dent and Peter McNamara 8-6, 6-4, 8-6 to give the U.S. an insurmountable 3-0 lead over Australia in the Davis Cup semifinals in Portland, Ore.

1986 Paul McNamee wins 12 of the last 13 games to defeat Brad Gilbert 2-6, 6-3, 3-6, 6-0, 6-1 to give Australia a 1-0 lead over the United States in the Davis Cup semifinal in Brisbane, Australia. The second singles match of the day—Tim Mayotte against Pat Cash—is postponed due to rain with Mayotte leading 6-4, 1-2.

2004 Roger Federer defeats Andy Roddick 6-4, 6-0 in the final of the Thailand Open in Bangkok for his 10th title of the year, making Federer the first player to win 10 titles in a season since Thomas Muster wins 12 in 1995. Federer also wins his 12th straight final, joining Bjorn Borg and John McEnroe as the only players to achieve that feat in the past 25 years.

October 4

1994 Future world No. 1 Martina Hingis of Switzerland, two weeks past her 14th birthday, makes her professional debut with a 6-4, 6-3 victory over Patty Fendick in the first round of the Zurich Indoors. The Hingis debut comes after a celebrated junior career where she becomes the youngest player to win a major junior title at age 12 at the 1993 French Open and earning the world No. 1 junior ranking the next year with wins at the junior French and Wimbledon. Says Hingis of her debut match, "The first time is always difficult. But I didn't have anything to lose, and I enjoyed it toward the end especially." Hingis goes on to lose to Mary Pierce of France 6-4, 6-0 in the next round.

2007 Austrian Stefan Koubek is disqualified from his second-round match with Sebastien Grosjean at the Metz Open in France when he uses inappropriate language in an argument with tournament referee Thomas Karlberg. With Koubek leading 5-7, 7-6, 4-2, the Australian left-hander argues with Karlberg over the ruling to replay a point due to a linesperson being unsighted and missing a call. Says Karlberg, "On the first point of the seventh game, on Grosjean's serve, a Koubek forehand close to the baseline gave a 0-15 advantage to Koubek, but the umpire realized Grosjean was in the way of the line judge, who was therefore unable to judge the point. In this case, the rule is to replay the point. Koubek disagreed and asked for the supervisor's intervention. He did not want to accept the rules and used strong language. I told him the match was over and asked the umpire to announce it."

1986 Pat Cash wins 16 of 20 games played and defeats Tim Mayotte 4-6, 6-1, 6-2, 6-2 in the completion of a rain-postponed match to give Australia a 2-0 lead over the United States in the Davis Cup semifinals in Brisbane, Australia. Mayotte begins play leading Cash 6-4, 1-2. Cash then pairs with John Fitzgerald in the doubles match, and nearly puts away the Americans by an insurmountable 3-0 margin, but darkness postpones their match with the ad-hoc U.S. doubles team of Ken Flach and Paul Annacone, with the Aussies leading 10-8, 6-1, 5-7. Annacone, in his Davis Cup debut and what ultimately becomes his only Davis Cup playing experience, substitutes for an injured Robert Seguso.

October 5

1967 The British Lawn Tennis Association votes to allow professional tennis players to compete at Wimbledon starting with the 1968 Championships. The decision, which is ratified and approved at the associations annual meeting on December 16, is one of the most important single decisions in the development of the sport as it ushers in the "Open" era where the tournament circuit moves from becoming amateur-only events into professional events. Says Judge Carl Aavold, the President of the British Lawn Tennis Association to the *New York Times*, "We have hopes of not going it alone, but we have had no assurances from anyone. It is a grave and serious step that could have serious consequences." Wimbledon's ground-breaking decision eventually opens the floodgates for all four major tournaments to become "open" starting with the 1968 French Championships.

1986 Ken Flach and Paul Annacone keep American hopes alive against Australia in the Davis Cup semifinal as they complete a come-from-behind, darkness-delayed victory over Pat Cash and John Fitzgerald by a 8-10, 1-6, 7-5, 13-11, 7-5 margin. Entering the day's play trailing two sets to one, Flach and Annacone prevent a 3-0 shutout by the Australians by rallying to win the final two sets in dramatic fashion.

2006 Benjamin Becker of Germany and Jiri Novak of the Czech Republic conclude their round of 16 match at the Japan Open in Tokyo at 3:24 am local time, Becker emerging victorious by a 6-3, 3-6, 7-6(4) margin. Becker saves a match point while serving at 5-6 in the third set in the latest recorded finish to a singles match in ATP history at the time. Months later, the record is broken by Andreas Seppi of Italy and Bobby Reynolds of the United States, who conclude a match at 3:34 am at the 2007 Australian Open. Another year later, Lleyton Hewitt and Marcos Baghdatis play until 4:34 am at the 2008 Australian Open, setting the new standard.

1918 French aviator Roland Garros, whose name graces the stadium at the French Championships in Paris, is shot down and killed near Vouziers, Ardennes in the waning days of hostilities of World War I. In 1928, when the French Tennis Federation created its tennis stadium to stage the USA vs. France Davis Cup Challenge Round, the French government stipulates that the stadium must honor a military hero, thus the aviator's connection to the nation's biggest tennis tournament.

October 6

1977 Ground is broken for the new USTA National Tennis Center and the new Louis Armstrong Stadium in Flushing Meadows, N.Y. In a ceremony shortened to five minutes due to a rain squall, USTA President Slew Hester, Mrs. Louis Armstrong, New York City Parks Commissioner Joe Davidson and Queens Borough President Donald Manes break ground with shovels to signify the construction of the new stadium and facility that hosts the U.S. Open the following summer.

1978 Bjorn Borg, in his only Davis Cup confrontation against the United States, defeats Arthur Ashe 6-4, 7-5, 6-3 to give the Sweden a 1-0 lead over the United States in the Davis Cup semifinal in Goteborg, Sweden. Vitas Gerulaitis ties the score for the United States at 1-1, defeating Kjell Johansson 6-2, 6-1, 6-4.

1986 In a Monday finish to the Davis Cup semifinals in Perth, Australia, Pat Cash defeats Brad Gilbert 3-6, 6-2, 6-3, 6-4 to give Australia a 3-1 victory over the United States. Cash enters the match having played a total of 120 games in three days of play—including 40 games of doubles the day before. Gilbert wins the first set in 38 minutes, before Cash finds his groove to roll through the next three sets to send Australia into the Davis Cup Final. Bad blood erupts between Cash and Gilbert as Cash accuses him of "quick-serving" him and Gilbert chirping to chair umpire Guy Nash that Cash is stalling and not playing to the server's pace. Says Gilbert of Cash's alleged stall tactics, "The umpire should have done something about it because he did it 30 times. If I'm ready to serve, he shouldn't be able to walk away. It's unfair. Play should be continuous." Says U.S. Davis Cup captain Tom Gorman. "It is the first time I have heard a receiving guy saying: 'Wait, I'm not ready' between first and second serves. I always thought that when a guy is at the line looking at the server, he is ready. They have 30 seconds to start the point, but if he wanted to take extra time he should take a step back, like our players do." Counters Cash, "Three weeks ago, he (Gilbert) quick-served me in Los Angeles and he did it to me 20 times again today. I have a right to slow him down. If I didn't, he'd have 100 more points. The guy just rolls up and serves. He doesn't even look across the court to see if you're there."

1905 Helen Wills, one of the greatest women to ever play the sport, is born in Centreville, Calif. Wills wins 31 major titles, including 19 singles titles.

October 7

1999 Less than one month after being named captain of the U.S. Davis Cup team and John McEnroe creates his first international incident as the United States is drawn to play an away match against the African nation of Zimbabwe in the first round the 2000 Davis Cup. Speaking to reporters at a U.S. Tennis Association organized event at the ESPN Zone in New York City, McEnroe says of the away match against Zimbabwe, "I am sure that word is seeping out that our worse case scenario has just taken place. We need like 27 shots or something to go down there." After meeting with reporters, McEnroe takes questions from fans at the theme restaurant and is asked what surface he expects the match to be on. Responds McEnroe, "That is their choice. They are going to try to pick a surface that they feel they have the best chance of beating us on which will probably be cow dung ..." The following day, "Page Six" the famous gossip column in the *New York Post* reports the Zimbabwean government's outrage over McEnroe's comments. "This is disparaging," Immanuel Gumbo, attache at the Zimbabwe mission to the UN tells Page Six. "When we beat Australia last year we didn't play on a cow dung court. We admire Mr. McEnroe for his gifts but you have to wonder what must go on inside his head."

2001 Monica Seles wins her 50th career singles title by capturing the AIG Japan Open in Tokyo, defeating Tamarine Tanasugarn of Thailand, 6-3, 6-2. Seles wins a total of 53 singles titles in her career with the 2001 AIG Open being her sixth and final title she wins in Japan.

2007 Justine Henin's third appearance in the final of Porsche Grand Prix final in Stuttgart is a charm and the world No. 1 wins her first title in the German city with a 2-6, 6-2, 6-1 victory over Tatiana Golovin of France. The title is Henin's 37th career title, and eighth of the 2007 season. Henin previously loses finals in Stuttgart in 2001 and 2003. Says Henin, "I finally got this title."

2007 Tommy Robredo, the Spanish player who is named after the rock-opera *Tommy* written and recorded by the British rock group The Who, wins his first title not on a clay court, defeating Andy Murray of Britain 0-6, 6-2, 6-3 in the final of the Metz Open in France. Robredo loses the first set in just 23 minutes, but rallies to win his sixth career title in 1 hour, 52 minutes. Says Robredo, "It's my first title on a hard court, that is great. My goal here was at least to reach the final."

October 8

1874 The earliest found recorded play of lawn tennis in the United States takes place in the then remote Camp Apache, Arizona Territory, north of Tucson. In Mary Summerhates book, *Vanished Arizona*, she reports tennis being played by an Army officer's wife, Ella Wilkins Bailey. The date is confirmed by her husband's records.

1989 Unseeded Jim Courier upsets No. 1 seed Stefan Edberg of Sweden, 7-6 (8-6), 2-6, 3-6, 6-0, 7-5, to win his first ATP Tour singles title at the Swiss Indoor Championships in Basel, Switzerland. Says Courier, "This was by far my best tennis. It's an incredible feeling. I took advantage of the fact that Stefan could have played better." Courier goes on to lose the U.S. Open men's singles final to Edberg in 1991, but turns the tide and beats Edberg in the 1992 and 1993 Australian Open finals.

1971 Stan Smith defeats Ilie Nastase 7-5, 6-3, 6-1 to give the United States a 1-0 lead over Romania in the Davis Cup Challenge Round at the Julian J. Clark Stadium in Charlotte, N.C. Darkness postpones the second singles match with Ion Tiriac and Frank Froehling tied at 6-6 in the fifth set. Froehling, ranked No. 18 in the United States in singles and a surprise selection for singles by U.S. Captain Ed Turville, trails two sets to love, but rallies to force a fifth set.

1978 Arthur Ashe plays what ends up to be his final Davis Cup match, defeating Kjell Johansson 6-2, 6-0, 7-5 to clinch a 3-2 U.S. victory over Sweden in the Davis Cup semifinal in Goteborg, Sweden.

2006 Roger Federer wins his 42nd career title—but his first in Japan—defeating former nemesis Tim Henman 6-3, 6-3 in the final of the Japan Open in Tokyo in the Swiss maestro's maiden trip to Japan. The win is Federer's sixth straight over Henman to take the lead in their head-to-head series 7-6. The final-round showing is the 28th and last final-round appearance for Henman, who wins 11 of the 28 championship matches during his ATP career. Says Henman of his match with Federer, "I'm not the first guy to lose in a final to Roger and I won't be the last. I would have loved to have won today but he was simply too good."

October 9

1989 Chris Evert plays her final match as a professional, defeating Conchita Martinez 6-3, 6-2 to help the United States to a 3-0 victory over Spain in the final of the Federation Cup in Tokyo, Japan. "If this is it, I think I'm going out on the highest note possible," Evert says. "I came here thinking this is my last tournament scheduled for this year, and maybe forever, and what better note could there be to end it on, playing on a great team for my country." Says Evert's teammate and legendary rival Martina Navratilova, "I think all of us really wanted to win it for Chris, but she won it for herself, too. She won all her matches so she played a huge part in it. It was great to be on the team with her."

1938 Harry Hopman, the non-playing captain of the Australian Davis Cup team, defeats Don Budge 6-2, 5-7, 6-1 in the quarterfinals of the Pacific Coast tennis championships in Berkeley, Calif., snapping Budge's 92-match, 14-tournament winning streak. Hopman, who holds three match points at 5-3 in the second set, goes on to win the title defeating Jack Tidball in the final.

1971 Frank Froehling wins two games and completes a darkness-suspended 3-6, 1-6, 6-3, 6-1, 8-6 win over Ion Tiriac to give the United States a 2-0 lead over Romania in the Davis Cup Challenge Round in Charlotte, N.C. Tiriac and Ilie Nastase team to defeat Stan Smith and Erik van Dillen 7-5, 6-4, 8-6 in the scheduled doubles match to cut the U.S. lead to 2-1.

1926 French tennis sensation Suzanne Lenglen makes her pro debut in front of 13,000 fans at Madison Square Garden in New York. Lenglen, a winner of six Wimbledon singles titles, debuts against Mary Browne, who she dominates during the tour, winning all 38 matches.

2005 Lindsay Davenport wins her 50th career WTA singles title, defeating Amelie Mauresmo 6-2, 6-4 in the final of the Porsche Grand Prix in Filderstadt, Germany.

October 10

1971 Stan Smith defeats Romania's Ion Tiriac 8-6, 6-3, 6-0 in 1 hour, 35 minutes to clinch the Davis Cup title for the United States in the Davis Cup Challenge Round in front of 5,500 fans at the Julien J. Clark Stadium in Charlotte, N.C. Due to heavy rains the night before and early in the morning of the match, organizers rent a helicopter to hover in the stadium to help dry the clay court. The soggy court is also doused with gasoline and lit on fire to try and improve its playing condition.

1985 Forty-six days after their final-round match at the Hamlet Challenge in Jericho, N.Y. is rained out, Ivan Lendl and Jimmy Connors return to the Long Island community and play their singles final—Lendl emerging victorious by a 6-1, 6-3 margin. Lendl, who beat Connors 6-2, 6-3, 7-5 in the U.S. Open semifinals the previous month, needs a little more than an hour to win the title. Says Connors after the match, "I was trying to get it done with and go home to see my family."

1989 Play begins at the Virginia Slims of Moscow, the first professional tennis tournament to be held in the Soviet Union, as 18-year-old Natasha Zvereva of Minsk wins the opening match of the tournament, defeating fellow Soviet Aida Khalatyan 6-3, 6-0. Says Zvereva, "I can't remember being as nervous for a first round match."

2007 Maria Sharapova is upset in the second round of the Kremlin Cup in Moscow, losing to Victoria Azarenka of Belarus 7-6 (9), 6-2. Sharapova leads 5-3, 40-0 but loses 10 straight points and eventually loses the first set after holding three more set points. Says Sharapova, "Maybe I was too self-assured at 5-3. But it all went downhill after." Says Azarenka, "I tried to stay concentrated and believed I could win the match."

1976 Chris Evert withstands the hard-hitting tactics of Diane Fromholtz to win the singles title at the Talley tennis tournament in Phoenix, Ariz., defeating her Australian opponent 6-1, 7-5 in the final. After losing the first set in just 20 minutes, Fromholtz dramatically changes tactics in the second set, deciding to hit every ball as hard as she can and rush to the net. Fromholtz jumps to a 3-0 lead in the second set, before Evert resorts to "moonball" tactics to disrupt the rhythm of Fromholtz and close out the second set—and the match.

October 11

1940 German bombs first hit Wimbledon's Centre Court at the All England Club during the Battle of Britain of World War II. Bombs cause significant damage to a section of the stadium, blowing a hole in the Centre Court roof and destroying 1,200 seats. The Championships are not held due to the war from 1940 to 1945 and the club is used as a civil defense center as well as farmyard with pigs, hens, geese and rabbits.

1971 Despite the U.S. clinching the Davis Cup title over Romania the previous day on Stan Smith's victory over Ion Tiriac, Ilie Nastase and Frank Froehling return to the Julien J. Clark Stadium in Charlotte, N.C. to finish their rain-suspended, meaningless "dead rubber" match. After Smith's 8-6, 6-3, 6-0 win over Tiriac on Sunday gives the U.S. an insurmountable 3-1 lead, Nastase leads Froehling 6-3, 2-0 before rain suspends play. Davis Cup referee Harry Hopman, the former long-time Australian Davis Cup captain, rules that the match be continued the next day, despite it having no bearing on the final result. Davis Cup organizers admit fans free of charge to the Monday conclusion and 300 fans oblige, watching Nastase cut the U.S. winning margin to 3-2 with a 6-3, 6-1, 4-6, 6-4 win.

1999 In a match delayed one day because of a typhoon hitting the coast of China, Magnus Norman wins his fifth title of the 1999 season, defeating Marcelo Rios in the final of the Heineken Open in Shanghai, China.

1992 Spurred by a rowdy pro-Croatian crowd who chant "GOR-AN" and wave Croatian flags between games, Goran Ivanisevic defeats Stefan Edberg 6-4, 6-2, 6-4, to win the Australian Indoor Championships in Sydney. Following his victory, Ivanisevic shakes Edberg's hand and runs into the packed upper deck, tosses his shirt to the Croatian fans and hugs supporters.

1998 Britain's Tim Henman defeats Andre Agassi 6-4, 6-3, 3-6, 6-4 in the final of the Swiss Indoors in Basel. "I played some of the best tennis of my career, the kind I only dreamed about," says Henman after the match. "The level was just so high and I was very consistent."

1992 Steffi Graf loses the first set in 24 minutes, but rallies to defeat 35-year-old Martina Navratilova, 2-6, 7-5, 7-5, in the final of the European Indoors tournament in Zurich, Switzerland.

October 12

2001 One hundred and one years after three Harvard students make up the first U.S. Davis Cup team, former Harvard student James Blake makes his Davis Cup debut against India in the Davis Cup Qualifying Round at the Joel Coliseum in Winston-Salem, N.C. Blake defeats India's Leander Paes, playing in his 79th Davis Cup match, 7-5, 6-3, 6-3 to give the U.S. a 2-0 lead. Blake also becomes the first Harvard student to play Davis Cup for the U.S. since *Titanic* survivor Richard Norris Williams in 1926 and becomes only the third African-American man to play Davis Cup for the U.S.—joining Mal Washington and Arthur Ashe. Earlier in the day, Andy Roddick defeats India's Harsh Mankad 6-3, 6-4, 6-1 to give the U.S. a 1-0 lead.

1994 Boisterous American Jeff Tarango performs one of the most unusual on-court activities ever in pro tennis, dropping his shorts after having his serve broken in the first game of the third set in his loss to Michael Chang in the second round of the Seiko Championships in Tokyo. Following his serve being broken, Tarango, in the words of Britain's *Daily Record*, "pulled his shorts down, raised his arms and waddled to his seat courtside with his shorts around his ankles and his underpants in full view." Says Tarango, "I felt that I let the match slip away a little bit, and I wanted to make light of it. I had exposed my weakness to Michael." Tarango, who would famously walk off the court in a third round match at Wimbledon in 1995, retires from his match with Chang with a left forearm injury, trailing 1-4 in the third set. Tarango is given a code violation for unsportsmanlike conduct and is fined $3,000. Says Chang, who goes on to lose to Goran Ivanisevic in the final of the event, "I know the ATP has been trying to create a little bit more interest in the game but I don't know if that is what they had in mind."

1998 Lindsay Davenport ascends to the No. 1 ranking in women's professional tennis for the first time in her career, taking the No. 1 WTA ranking from Martina Hingis, whom she beat in the U.S. Open final the previous month. Davenport holds the No. 1 ranking for 98 weeks in her career.

2003 Roger Federer wins his 10th career ATP singles title and successfully defends a title for the first time in his career when he defeats Carlos Moya of Spain 6-3, 6-3, 6-3 to win the CA Trophy in Vienna, Austria. Says Federer of successfully defending a title for the first time, "I'm over the moon about that."

October 13

1972 Amid high security and terrorist threat tension, the United States and Romania open play in the Davis Cup Final in Bucharest, Romania, as Stan Smith defeats Ilie Nastase 11-9, 6-2, 6-3 while Ion Tiriac defeats Tom Gorman 4-6, 2-6, 6-4, 6-3, 6-2. The spirit of the Davis Cup Final permeates all corners of Bucharest as posters of Nastase and Tiriac are found everywhere—even bakeries sell giant cakes in the shape of the Davis Cup. Security is high during the series as false rumors are spread that the same assassins who struck during the 1972 Munich Olympics would strike the U.S. team during the final. Smith plays what Bernard Kirsch of the *New York Times* calls "unexciting tennis" to beat Nastase in 2 hours, 14 minutes. Says Smith of Nastase, "He knows I'm always bearing down. He's knows I'm not going to get discouraged and he knows he's got to play well all the time." Gorman is bothered by not only fatigue, but questionable line calls from Romanian linespeople, who are accused of favoritism to the home team. Argentinean chair umpire Enrique Morea overrules six line calls in the match, causing for "do overs."

1985 With singles victories by Hana Mandlikova and Helena Sukova, Czechoslovakia captures its third consecutive Federation Cup title defeating the United States in the final in Nagoya, Japan. Mandlikova defeats Kathy Jordan, 7-5, 6-1, in the rain-delayed second singles match on the hard courts of the Nagoya Green Tennis Club to clinch the victory.

2007 Wimbledon champion Venus Williams is upset by Flavia Pannetta of Italy 6-4, 7-6 (8) in the semifinals of the Bangkok Open in Thailand. "She had nothing to lose against me," says Williams of the No. 49-ranked Pennetta. "She did a great job of staying in the match and staying in the point." Says the 25-year-old Pennetta, who goes on to win the title, "I think it is one of the most beautiful wins of my career, for sure."

1985 Top-seeded Yannick Noah of France wins the Toulouse Open, defeating Tomas Smid of Czechoslovakia, 6-4, 6-4. Noah finishes the match hitting a "tweener" shot between his legs, a shot he first makes famous two years earlier at the U.S. Open.

1985 Top-seeded American Paul Annacone scores a 6-3, 6-3 victory over Kelly Evernden of New Zealand in the final of the $100,000 GWA Mazda Classic in Brisbane, Australia.

October 14

2007 Elena Dementieva, the 2000 Olympic silver medalist and 2004 U.S. and French Open finalist, rallies to defeat Serena Williams 5-7, 6-1, 6-1 to win her hometown tournament—the Kremlin Cup in Moscow—and register her first win over the younger Williams sister in their fifth career meeting. Says Dementieva of her eighth career title, "It's an incredible feeling when you win at home. I knew that if I did not beat Serena today, it would never happen again."

1982 John McEnroe struggles with indecisive calls from linespeople in his 6-4, 6-4 win over Australian Peter McNamara in the quarterfinals of the Australian Indoor Championships in Sydney. Leading 3-2 in the second set and serving at 15-30, McEnroe becomes angry with the sideline umpire who calls his serve out. McEnroe kneels to the ground, grabs the ball and screams at the umpire. McEnroe's behavior solicits a strong fan reaction as patrons yell at him to continue play and to stop being a brat. Says McEnroe, "I let some go by in the first set, but some of those calls were 10 seconds late. What am I supposed to do?" McEnroe, subsequently, has his serve broken for the first time in the tournament, but goes on to break McNamara back to close out the straight-set win. McEnroe goes on to win the title, defeating Davis Cup teammate Gene Mayer 6-4, 6-1, 6-4 in the final.

1972 Stan Smith and Erik van Dillen give the United States a 2-1 lead over Romania in the Davis Cup final in Bucharest, Romania, dominating Ilie Nastase and Ion Tiriac 6-2, 6-0, 6-3 in just 68 minutes. After the score is tied at 2-2 in the first set, the Americans reel off 11 straight games to run away with the match. Smith and van Dillen's run of games solicits the biggest cheers of the afternoon from the small contingent of American fans, which prompts an English-speaking Romanian spectator to yell "Quiet! It's not a baseball game." Says Nastase after the match, "We didn't expect them to play so well."

2001 Nineteen-year-old Andy Roddick defeats India's Leander Paes 4-6, 6-3, 6-2, 7-5 clinching victory for the U.S. Davis Cup team in the Davis Cup Qualifying Round in Winston-Salem, N.C. James Blake closes out the 4-1 U.S. victory with a 6-3, 6-0 win over Harsh Mankad.

October 15

1972 In one of the greatest Davis Cup matches in history, Stan Smith overcomes "the worst officiating I ever had" and a partisan Romanian crowd to defeat Ion Tiriac 4-6, 6-2, 6-4, 2-6, 6-0 in 2 hours, 50 minutes to clinch the Davis Cup title for the United States over Romania in Bucharest. Smith's victory gives him the distinction of clinching the Davis Cup victory for the fifth straight year (he would also clinch a sixth Cup-victory for the U.S. in the 1979 title in doubles with Bob Lutz). Smith struggles mightily against Tiriac, who calls himself, "the best player in the world who can't play tennis" as well as the Romanian linespeople, who are suspect in their fairness. "I started to believe they weren't going to let me win... no matter how well I played," Smith says following his victory. Writes Bud Collins in *The Bud Collins History of Tennis*, "Despite numerous pro-Tiriac officiating calls, Smith, knowing he had to hit winners inside the lines, was too good for Ion." The fifth set is one of the finest sets of tennis ever played by Smith or seen in Davis Cup play as the reigning Wimbledon champion plays near perfect tennis to roll through the decisive set in just 20 minutes to clinch the 24th Davis Cup title for the United States. Writes Bernard Kirsch of the *New York Times*, "When Smith hit a passing shot for Cup point, he threw his racquet high in the air, went to the net, shook hands with Tiriac and said: 'I really lost a lot of respect for you.'"

2001 More than 11 years after her celebrated and hyped professional debut as a 14-year-old, Jennifer Capriati finally moves to the No. 1 ranking in women's tennis for the first time. Capriati, the reigning Australian and French Open singles champion and the only woman to reach the semifinals of all four Grand Slam tournaments during the year, ends Martina Hingis's 73-week hold of the top ranking. "When I look back on my career, I am very proud of the two Grand Slams I won this year and, obviously, getting to No. 1," says Capriati. "I am also proud to be able to come back from everything that has happened in my life and just to enjoy tennis and play this well. This shows everybody that it's never too late to realize your talent, or your dream. If you think positive and believe in yourself, good things are going to come."

1983 Aaron Krickstein becomes the youngest player to win an ATP singles title when, at the age of 16 years, two months, defeats Christophe Zipf of West Germany 7-6, 6-3 to win the Israeli Open in Tel Aviv.

October 16

1983 John McEnroe curses at the let-cord judge, is fined $1,500—resulting a 21-day suspension—and beats France's Henri Leconte 6-1, 6-4, 7-5 in the final of the Australian Indoor championships in Sydney. Serving at 2-3 in the second set, McEnroe swears at let-cord judge Barry Hill and asks him, "How many more imaginary let-cords are you going to call?" McEnroe's cursing results in a $1,500 fine which pushes him over the $7,500 yearly limit imposed by the Men's International Professional Tennis Council, necessitating an automatic 21-day suspension. After the match, McEnroe acknowledges abusing Hill and says the $1,500 fine is excessive and counters, "If I'd known that was going to happen, I would have really let him have it."

1988 Jimmy Connors wins his first tournament in France—and the 107th of his career—defeating Andrei Chesnokov 6-2, 6-0 in the final of the Toulouse Open in Toulouse, France. The title is the third-to-last title for Connors, who repeats as the champion of Toulouse again in 1989 and wins his 109th and final singles title in Tel Aviv, Israel in 1989.

1988 In the 79th and second-to-last career meeting between Martina Navratilova and Chris Evert, Navratilova needs only 75 minutes to defeat Evert 6-2, 6-3 to win the singles title in Filderstadt, Germany. Navratilova wins the title for a fifth time in her career and extends her lead over Evert in their career head-to-head to 42-37.

2005 James Blake wins his first ATP singles title outside of the United States and his third overall defeating Paradorn Srichaphan of Thailand 6-1, 7-6 (6) in the final of the Stockholm Open in Sweden.

1983 Vitas Gerulaitis wins the men's singles final at the Swiss Indoor Championships in Basel when Wojtek Fibak of Poland rushes off the court with a stomach ailment with Gerulaitis leading 4-6, 6-1, 7-5, 5-5. Says Fibak after the match of his stomach cramps, "I couldn't stand it anymore."

1833 Major Walter Clompton Wingfield, the English military man who conceives the idea of the modern form of tennis—and patents the game in 1874—is born in Wales.

October 17

1975 Jimmy Connors makes his Davis Cup debut, defeating Humphrey Hose of Venezuela 6-4, 6-1, 6-3 in the first round of the 1976 Davis Cup (which was actually played in the end of the 1975 year) in Tucson, Ariz. Connors says of the experience playing Davis Cup, "It's great to be playing for 210 million Americans instead of just Jimmy Connors." Connors has an indifferent attitude toward Davis Cup and only participates in seven ties for the United States over his career.

1982 Jimmy Connors is successful in his wish to have chair umpire Peter Duncan removed from service during his semifinal match with Gene Mayer in the Australian Indoor Championships in Sydney, but is unsuccessful in his attempt to reach the event's final, falling to Mayer 6-3, 2-6, 6-3. After a series of incidents with Duncan in the second set of the match, Connors tells tournament referee Bill Gilmour that "one of us has to go" before Gilmour convinces Connors to continue playing the match. However, as the Associated Press reports, "the situation almost got out of hand after the first point of the fourth game of the second set, when Duncan first ruled a Mayer shot in, then out, then in again." Gilmour then returns to the court and calls for a let to be played, but Connors refuses to play unless Duncan is replaced. Two games later, Duncan is replaced in the chair by Max Ward.

2004 Jerome Haehnel, a qualifier ranked No. 185 in the world, is an unlikely winner of his first ATP title, defeating countryman Richard Gasquet 7-6 (11-9), 6-4 in the Open de Moselle in Metz, France. The match marks the first career ATP final for both Haehnel and Gasquet.

2004 Russia's Nikolay Davydenko fights off three match points to defeat Greg Rusedski of Britain 3-6, 6-3, 7-5 to win the Kremlin Cup singles title in Moscow. In the women's singles final, reigning French Open champion Anastasia Myskina defeats fellow Russian Elena Dementieva, 7-5, 6-0 in a re-match of their final at Roland Garros.

October 18

1956 Martina Navratilova, the woman whose unparalleled tennis career extends four decades from 1973 to 2006, is born in Prague, Czechoslovakia. The left-hander re-writes the record books in tennis, especially at Wimbledon where she wins an unprecedented nine women's singles titles (1978, 1979, 1982, 1983, 1984, 1985, 1986, 1987, 1990) and ties Billie Jean King's record of 20 overall titles when she wins the mixed doubles title with Leander Paes in 2003. At the U.S. Open, she wins four singles titles (1983, 1984, 1986 and 1987) and after losing in the women's singles semifinals to Chris Evert in 1975, defects to the United States. In 2006, she finally bids adieu to competitive tennis, six weeks shy of her 50th birthday, winning the U.S. mixed doubles title with Bob Bryan for her 59th career major.

2004 The Madrid Masters tennis tournament in Spain debuts its controversial model ball girls on the opening day of play, also highlighted by victories by Spaniards Albert Costa and Alex Corretja. The models debut during Costa's 6-2, 5-7, 7-5 win over Iraki Labadze of Georgia and are greeted by cheers and whistles at the Madrid Rockodrome indoor court. Says Costa, "They did it very well. I didn't notice any difference. It's entertaining, and I like the idea that the tournament should do this." Corretja defeats fellow Spaniard David Ferrer 7-5, 6-1.

1987 Martina Navratilova celebrates her 31st birthday by defeating Chris Evert 7-5, 6-1 to win the WTA Tour title in Filderstadt, West Germany. Navratilova is given the choice of collecting $36,000 or a Porsche sports car and chooses the car.

1992 Martina Navratilova turns 36 years old in style, defeating Gabriela Sabatini 7-6, 6-3 to win the Porsche Grand Prix in Filderstadt, Germany, her 161st career singles title. Says Sabatini of Navratilova, "It is really astonishing what she can still do. It would have been unfair of me to beat her today. After all, it is her birthday."

1993 Ivan Lendl wins his 92nd—and final—pro singles title, defeating Todd Martin 6-4, 6-4 in the final of the Seiko Super men's tennis championships in Tokyo. The title is Lendl's fifth at the Tokyo indoor event.

October 19

1978 Fifteen-year-old ninth-grader Tracy Austin announces in a press conference that she is turning professional. Says Austin of turning pro, "Instead of getting just roses, I will be getting prize money."

1980 Chris Evert Lloyd wins the 100th tournament of her career, defeating 15-year-old Andrea Jaeger 6-4, 6-1 to win the Linda Carter Tennis Championships in Deerfield Beach, Fla.

2003 Justine Henin-Hardenne defeats Jelena Dokic 6-0, 6-4 to win the Swisscom Challenge in Zurich, Switzerland, clinching the world No. 1 ranking, which she assumes the next day, overtaking countrywoman Kim Clijsters. "All my life I have dreamed about winning Grand Slams and being No. 1 in the world," says Henin-Hardenne. "This is a very special day for me and one I will remember forever. It's taking a while to sink in now, and I think it will take a few days to truly realize what has happened here."

1975 Former Wimbledon and U.S. Open champion Stan Smith wins his first tournament in 15 months, defeating doubles partner Bob Lutz 7-6, 6-2 in the Australian Indoor Championships in Sydney. Smith dedicates the victory to his wife of 12 months, Margie. "I think Margie thought she was a jinx," says Smith of his title drought. "I haven't won a tournament since we've been married."

2006 A strong opponent of the Hawk-Eye replay challenge system, Roger Federer wins his round of 16 match at the Madrid Masters against Robin Soderling by using a challenge that overrules an original call on match point. In the final point of his 7-6 (5), 7-6 (8) victory over the Swede, Federer challenges the linesman's call on Soderling's cross-court forehand winner, which the Hawk-Eye replay reveals to be out. Says Federer of the final replay, "I thought it was really funny, especially waiting like this for the match point. This has never happened before and I thought it was kind of silly."

1980 Ivan Lendl wins his fourth career singles title with a dramatic 6-3, 6-2, 5-7, 0-6, 6-4 upset of world No. 1 Bjorn Borg in the Swiss Indoor Tennis Championships in Basel, Switzerland.

1980 Jimmy Connors defeats Eliot Teltscher 6-2, 6-4 to win the Canton Open in Canton, China, the first professional sports event ever held in China.

October 20

1985 A religious fanatic walks on the court, serves drinks to Ivan Lendl and Henri Leconte and preaches a sermon in the middle of the final round match of the Australian Indoor Championships in Sydney. In the ninth game of the third set, the man, wearing a caterer's uniform, walks onto the court with a tray with two glasses of orange juice and religious pamphlets that he presents to both Lendl and Leconte. Reports the Associated Press of the incident, "To the astonishment of the players, officials and crowd, he put the tray down in the center of the court and proclaimed loudly, 'I would like to bring these gentlemen two drinks.' He then began babbling about the evil of credit cards and the devil before being escorted away by embarrassed officials. The tournament was sponsored by a credit finance company." Says Lendl of the incident, "I was really, really mad at that. Not for the security reason, but because they were too gentle with him. They should have been rougher with him." Lendl wins the match from Leconte by a 6-4, 6-4, 7-6 margin.

2006 Czech Tomas Berdych illicts jeers from an angry Spanish crowd after putting his finger to his lips in a silencing motion after defeating Spanish favorite son Rafael Nadal 6-3, 7-6 (6) in the quarterfinals of the Madrid Masters. Nadal calls Berdych a "bad person" because of the gesture. Berdych responds that is done in response to the Spanish crowd cheering his mistakes. "I can understand they want him to win the match and the tournament, but this is not a Davis Cup where you can expect this—not in this tournament," Berdych says. Counters Nadal, "When I played him in the Czech Republic, the crowd was the same and I didn't say anything. If you play against a local player, that's normal. That's good for tennis because the public supports you."

1974 Evonne Goolagong defeats Chris Evert 6-3, 6-4 to win the Virginia Slims of Los Angeles and the first prize paycheck of $32,000, at the time, the largest payout ever in women's tennis.

2003 Justine Henin-Hardenne of Belgium officially becomes No. 1 in the world for the first time in her career. Henin-Hardenne holds the ranking for a total of 117 weeks during her career. Her last week in the No. 1 ranking comes on June 2, 2008, when she announces her shocking retirement from the sport and has the WTA Tour immediately pull her name off of the rankings.

October 21

1989 Jimmy Connors wins his 109th and final professional singles title, defeating No. 181-ranked Gilad Bloom of Israel 2-6, 6-2, 6-1 in the final of the ATP tour event in Tel Aviv, Israel. The 109 professional singles titles for Connors is the most of any male player in the history of the sport and dates back to 1972 when he wins his first title at London's Queen's Club tournament. Ivan Lendl eventually wins 94 pro singles title in his career that ends in 1994 for second place on the all-time list, followed by John McEnroe with 77 singles titles. The only players to win more titles than Connors are Martina Navratilova with 167 singles titles and Chris Evert with 154 singles titles.

2007 David Nalbandian pulls of a rare "trifecta" in men's tennis defeating No. 1 Roger Federer, 1-6, 6-3, 6-3 in the final of the Madrid Masters in Spain, giving the Argentine the distinction of beating the No. 1, No. 2 and No. 3 ranked players in the same tournament. Nalbandian, ranked No. 25, beats No. 2 Rafael Nadal in the quarterfinals and No. 3 Novak Djokovic before dismissing Federer in the final. "It's very important at this moment, a great way to finish the season and to go into the next one," says the 25th-ranked Argentine, once ranked as high as No. 3 in the world. "To beat such great players as I did this week makes it important." Nalbandian becomes only the third player in 13 years to perform the sweep of the top three players in the same event—Novak Djokovic turning the trick earlier in the year at the Canadian Championships—and Boris Becker pulling off the feat in Stockholm in 1994.

2007 World No. 1 Justine Henin wins her ninth tournament of the season, defeating 19-year-old Tatiana Golovin of France 6-4, 6-4 at the Zurich Open. Henin trails 4-1 in the first set but rallies to win five games in a row to win the first set. "That really changed the match," Henin says of the five-game stretch. "She put me under pressure but slowly and surely I came back."

2001 Lindsay Davenport wins singles and doubles titles at the Swisscom Challenge in Zurich, Switzerland, defeating Jelena Dokic of Yugoslavia 6-3, 6-1 in the singles final and pairing with Lisa Raymond to defeat Sandrine Testud of France and Roberta Vinci of Italy 6-3, 2-6, 6-2.

October 22

2001 Andre Agassi and Steffi Graf, two of the greatest champions tennis has ever produced, are married in a small, private ceremony in Las Vegas, Nevada. The two all-time greats date for more than two years since both win the singles titles at the 1999 French Open. "We are so blessed to be married and starting this chapter of our lives," Agassi and Graf says in a joint statement after the ceremony. "The privacy and intimacy of our ceremony was beautiful and reflective of all we value." Agassi and Graf are the only two players in the history of the sport to win all four major singles titles—and an Olympic gold medal—in their careers.

1985 Arthur Ashe resigns as captain of the U.S. Davis Cup team after a tenure of five years. Ashe resigns "in the best interests of me personally and of the team," according to a statement released by Ashe's agency, ProServ. The United States wins the Davis Cup during Ashe's first two years as captain in 1981 and 1982, but the U.S. loses in the first round in 1983 and the second round in 1985. Ashe's overall record as U.S. Davis Cup captain concludes at 13-3.

1982 Vitas Gerulaitis defeats Gene Mayer 7-5, 6-2 in the semifinals of the Mazda Super Challenge in Melbourne, Australia and then blasts the officiating as the worst he has seen in his career. Says Gerulaitis, "From Egypt to Zambia, it has never been as bad as this. This is the worst place I have ever played."

1995 Wayne Ferreira of South Africa ends the three-year reign of Pete Sampras as champion of the Lyon Open in France, defeating Sampras 7-6 (2), 5-7, 6-3 in the final. Says Ferreira, "I played one of the best matches I could play. I tired a little at the end but I wasn't going to get tight." Ferreira has surprising success with Sampras during his career, winning six of 13 matches against the seven-time Wimbledon champion.

1995 Mary Joe Fernandez celebrates her 24th birthday by defeating South Africa's Amanda Coetzer 6-4, 7-5 to win the Brighton Indoors in England. The title is the fifth of seven career WTA Tour singles titles for Fernandez.

October 23

2005 Rafael Nadal of Spain outlasts Ivan Ljubicic 3-6, 2-6, 6-3, 6-4, 7-6 (3) to win the Tennis Masters Series Madrid. The win is the first time that Nadal comes back from two-sets-to-love down and ends Ljubicic's 16-match win streak.

2005 Lindsay Davenport defeats Patty Schnyder 7-6(5), 6-3 to win the Zurich Open for the fourth time in her career. Says Davenport, "Patty's a great player. The first set was very up and down. She really fought hard. I served for it, got broken, she had three set points in a row up 6-5, but I just told myself to go for it, step inside the court and be more aggressive. In the second set we had a couple of breaks there but from 3-1 down, I felt I got a better rhythm going and played quite well by the end of the match."

2007 World No. 1 Roger Federer loses a rare set in a first-round match as he defeats No. 56-ranked Michael Berer of Germany 6-1, 3-6, 6-3 at his hometown tournament, the Swiss Indoors in Basel. Says Federer, "I'm now having to explain why I lost a set. It's almost laughable. It happens."

2007 Charismatic American Justin Gimelstob plays the final match of his career, losing to Mikhail Youzhny of Russia 6-2, 6-4 in 1 hour, 7 minutes in the first round of the St. Petersburg Open in Russia. Gimelstob, who wins the French and Australian Open mixed doubles titles with Venus Williams, reaches a career-high ranking of No. 63 in April 1999 and reaches one career ATP singles final, losing to Mark Philippoussis in Newport in 2006. Says Gimelstob post-match, "Today it was hard to concentrate in the match. I faced a great player and I knew this could be my last match. During my entire career I tried to do the best I could every day; always gave my best. Very few people get to be good at what they do, enjoy it and still make a living of it. I think I'm blessed to be one of those people....I think what I will miss the most are the guys in the tour. I made great friends throughout my 12-year career. These last couple months of my career were very enjoyable. I want to thank everyone who supported me during my career and apologize to the umpires for the problems I might have created."

October 24

1999 Future world No. 1 player Amelie Mauresmo of France wins her first career WTA Tour title, defeating another future world No. 1 Kim Clijsters 6-3, 6-3 to win the Eurotel Slovak Indoor in Bratislava, Slovakia. Mauresmo advances to the final of the event a day earlier when her opponent, Kveta Hrdlickova of the Czech Republic, withdraws after being stung by a wasp on her right hand. Hrdlickova is strung after her quarterfinal win while signing an autograph, but by Saturday's semifinal match, she is unable to hold her racquet due to the swelling from the sting.

1982 Martina Navratilova ends the four-year reign of Tracy Austin at the Porsche Championships in Stuttgart, Germany, defeating Austin 6-3, 6-3 in the final of the event. Given the choice between the $22,000 first prize check and a new Porsche, Navratilova doesn't flinch and chooses the car.

1989 Steffi Graf gives up only 15 points—including only one in the first five games—in defeating Italy's Laura Garrone 6-0, 6-0 in 34 minutes in the first round of the WTA Tour event in Brighton, England.

1999 Nicolas Lapentti of Ecuador becomes the unlikely winner of the Lyon Open in France, defeating Lleyton Hewitt 6-3, 6-2 in the final. Until Lyon, Lapentti had never previously won a match on indoor carpet and had won only two matches indoors in his career before Lyon.

2004 Marat Safin of Russia has little difficulty in beating David Nalbandian 6-2, 6-4, 6-3 to win the Madrid Masters in Spain. Says Safin, "The match was quite a lot easier than I'd expected. I don't think I can go on playing like this forever—it's too good."

1993 Cedric Pioline nearly avenges his final-round loss to Pete Sampras from September's U.S. Open, but narrowly falls 7-6 (5), 1-6, 7-5 in the final of the Lyon Open in Lyon, France. Sampras, playing in his first event since he beats Pioline 6-4, 6-4, 6-3 in the U.S. Open final, claims his third straight tournament title in Lyon, the site of his disastrous Davis Cup debut in the 1991 Davis Cup Final. Sampras also beats Pioline 6-4, 6-2 in the final of the event in 1992. Pioline and Sampras will again play in a major tournament final at Wimbledon in 1997, with Sampras again winning by a 6-4, 6-2, 6-4 margin.

October 25

1981 Vitas Gerulaitis is defaulted in the final of the Miracle Indoor Tennis Championships in Melbourne, Australia when, playing against Australia's Peter McNamara, he refuses to play on after a disputed line call at 5-5 in the third and final set. Gerulaitis leads 6-4, 1-6, 4-0 and serves for the match at 5-4 in the third set, before McNamara breaks Gerulaitis' serve to even the final set at 5-5 with a down the line passing shot that is called good—despite a late call being issued. Gerulaitis argues with chair umpire David Bierwirth and demands to tournament referee Jim Entink and Grand Prix supervisor Keith Johnson that Bierwirth and all the linesmen be removed or else he will not continue to play the match. After Entink and Johnson refuse the request, Gerulaitis sits on his courtside chair and is assessed a time warning, two point penalties, followed by a game penalty, followed by the match default. Gerulaitis then collects his racquets, shakes hands with McNamara and leaves the court. Gerulaitis is later fined $1,990.

2007 Olivier Rochus of Belgium overcomes 43 aces from American Mardy Fish—and saves five match points—and defeats the 2004 Olympic silver medalist 6-7 (5-7), 7-6 (8-6), 7-6 (17-15) to advance into the quarterfinals the Lyon Grand Prix quarterfinals.

2005 Andy Roddick wins his 300th career ATP match victory, defeating Thierry Ascione of France 7-5, 6-3 in the first round of the Lyon Grand Prix.

1992 Steffi Graf beats Jana Novotna 4-6, 6-4, 7-6 (7-3) in 2 hours, 32 minutes to win the singles title at the Brighton (England) Indoor championships for the sixth time in seven years. Novotna leads by a set and 3-1 and is two points from victory in the 10th game of the third set, but is unable to put away the world No. 2.

October 26

2003 Todd Woodbridge wins his 78th career ATP doubles title—tying Tom Okker for the all-time record for most doubles titles—pairing with Jonas Bjorkman of Sweden to win the Stockholm Open, defeating Wayne Arthurs and Paul Hanley of Australia 6-3, 6-4 in the final. "What I feel great about today is that the record is mine and Tom's," says Woodbridge. "It was my first final with a shot at tying the record and now I have it and can look at breaking it." In the men's singles final, American Mardy Fish wins the first ATP singles title of his career, defeating Robin Soderling of Sweden 7-5, 3-6, 7-6(4).

2006 Mary Pierce of France, the 1995 Australian Open champion and the 2000 French Open, endures a career-altering injury, falling and tearing her cruciate ligament in her left knee in a second-round match against Vera Zvonareva in Linz, Austria. Pierce is leading 6-4, 6-6—after having three match points the previous game—before she suffers the injury in the tie-break.

2007 Croatia's Ivo Karlovic saves five match points and defeats Czech Tomas Berdych 6-7(5), 7-6(2), 7-6(13) in a 2-hour, 37-minute quarterfinal match without a service break at the Swiss Indoor Championships in Basel. Berdych holds match points at 6-4, 7-6, 9-8 and 11-10 in the third set tie-break, but is unable to convert. Karlovic seals victory on his fifth match point and fires 38 aces in the match.

1982 Chris Evert Lloyd defeats Virginia Wade for an 18th straight time, defeating the British great 6-1, 6-1 in only 58 minutes in the first round of the WTA event in Brighton, England.

1985 Ivan Lendl out-slugs Boris Becker 6-3, 7-6 (1) in the semifinals of the Seiko Super Tennis in Tokyo, Japan. Mats Wilander advances to the final to face Lendl by default when Jimmy Connors is unable to compete and defaults due to a back injury. Lendl goes on to win the title the next day, needing only 54 minutes to beat Wilander 6-0, 6-4. Says Lendl of his status as the No. 1 tennis player in the world, "You can't ever say that anyone is far superior in the game of tennis. I'm doing my job, which I enjoy. If I do it well, I'm No. 1."

October 27

1996 In an epic five-set final played in a pro-German atmosphere, Boris Becker defeats world No. 1 Pete Sampras 3-6, 6-3, 3-6, 6-3, 6-4 in the final of the Stuttgart Open, ending a 21-match win streak for Sampras. "He was just too good today—a great comeback," says Sampras. "There's only one king in Germany and his name is Boris. Becker is the best indoor player I've ever played." Says Becker, "I am a bit perplexed. I never expected to be able to beat him, but you try everything against Pete in a final like this. My muscles started to hurt in the fifth but I gritted my teeth and hung on."

1991 Defending champion Boris Becker ends a nine-month title drought and defeats world No. 1 Stefan Edberg 3-6, 6-4, 1-6, 6-2, 6-2 in the final of the Stockholm Open in Sweden. In winning his first tournament title since the Australian Open in January, Becker snaps Edberg's 21-match winning streak in front of the pro-Edberg Swedish crowd of 14,000. Becker wins the title in an impressive series of victories, beating Pete Sampras in the quarterfinals, Jim Courier in the semifinals and Edberg in the final. Says Becker of his win over Edberg and his run to the title, "Every win against Stefan is important. It feels good to have beaten the No. 7, No. 3 and No. 1 players in a row here."

1991 World No. 2 Steffi Graf wins the last nine of 10 games to defeat Zina Garrison 5-7, 6-4, 6-1 in 2 hours, 12 minutes in the final of Midland Bank Championships in Brighton, England. The title is Graf's seventh title of the year and fifth career title at the Brighton event. Says Graf after the match, "Zina played a great match, so this was very satisfying for me," Graf nearly loses the match in straight sets as Garrison breaks the Wimbledon champion to take a 4-3 lead in the second set, but is unable to hold on and close out the match. Says Garrison, "She moved me around a lot, and after that (seventh game) I think I played defensively. If it had been a quicker game, I think I would have had a lot more energy."

October 28

1990 Fourteen-year-old Jennifer Capriati wins the first of her 14 career singles titles, defeating Zina Garrison 5-7, 6-4, 6-2, in the finals of the Puerto Rico Open in San Juan, Puerto Rico. Capriati, however, is not the youngest player to win a professional women's event as Tracy Austin, at the age of 14 years, 28 days wins the title in Portland, Oregon in 1977. Capriati's age at the time of her tournament victory is 14 years, seven months.

2007 Roger Federer beats Jarkko Nieminen 6-3, 6-4 to win his hometown tournament—the Swiss Indoor Championships in Basel—for a second consecutive year. The win officially clinches the year-end world No. 1 ranking for a fourth consecutive year. Federer joins Pete Sampras, Jimmy Connors, John McEnroe and Ivan Lendl as the only men to finish the year ranked No. 1 for at least four years since the rankings begin in 1973. Says Federer, "It's nice to win again and go into the next year as No. 1 again."

2001 Lindsay Davenport wins her third consecutive tournament in as many weeks, winning the Generali Ladies Open in Linz, Austria, defeating Jelena Dokic of Yugoslavia 6-1, 6-4 in the final for her 12th consecutive singles victory. The last woman to win three consecutive titles in a three-week period was, in fact, Davenport. In 1998, she wins the Bank of the West Classic in Stanford, Calif., the Toshiba Tennis Classic in San Diego, Calif., and the Acura Classic in Los Angeles consecutively.

1911 The U.S. Davis Cup team of Beals Wright, William Larned and Maurice McLoughlin arrive by boat in Christchurch, New Zealand for the Davis Cup Challenge Round against Australasia (combined Australian-New Zealand team). The trip "Down Under" is the second such trip for a U.S. Davis Cup team after a two-man team of McLoughlin and Melville Long make the trip in 1909. Unfortunately for the U.S. team, like the 1909 trip, the United States is shut out 5-0 in the Challenge Round.

1990 World No. 2 Boris Becker cruises to a 6-4, 6-0, 6-3 win over No. 1 ranked Stefan Edberg in the final of the Stockholm Open in Sweden.

2007 Andy Murray beats Fernando Verdasco 6-2, 6-3 to win his third career ATP title in the St. Petersburg Open in Russia. Says Murray, "I played a pretty solid match, not too many mistakes. I came to the net at the right time and put a lot of pressure on his serve."

October 29

1995 Fourteen-year-old future world No. 1 Serena Williams makes an auspicious, humbling professional debut, losing in the first round of qualifying of the Bell Challenge in Quebec City, Canada to 18-year-old Anne Miller 6-1, 6-1. The match is played at Club Advantage, a private tennis club in Quebec with little fanfare. Writes Robin Finn of the *New York Times,* "Instead of a stadium showcase, she competed on a regulation practice court at a tennis club in suburban Vanier, side by side with another qualifying match. There were no spotlights, no introductions, not even any fans. Her court was set a level below a smoky lounge that held a bar, a big-screen television, an ice cream cart and 50 or so onlookers with varying stages of interest in her fate." Says Williams to Finn, "I felt bad out there because I lost. I didn't play like I meant to play. I played kind of like an amateur." Says Miller, "I guess I played a celebrity....She has as much power as anybody around, but maybe she needs to play some junior events the way Anna Kournikova has to learn how to become match-tough. There really is no substitute for the real thing. I felt like a complete veteran compared to her."

2006 World No. 1 Roger Federer hosts a victory pizza party for ball kids at the Swiss Indoors in his hometown of Basel, Switzerland as he finally wins his hometown tournament with a 6-3, 6-2, 7-6 (3) final-round win over Fernando Gonzalez of Chile. "It's a dream to finally win my home tournament," says Federer, "This is an exciting moment and one of the nicest titles (out of 44) of my career." In the on-court trophy ceremony, Federer, a former ball boy at the tournament, tells ballkids, "Don't go away, there's pizza coming for you later, that's something I remember from here."

1983 Twenty-one-year-old Scott Davis of Santa Monica, Calif., six months into his professional career after leaving Stanford University, upsets Jimmy Connors 6-3, 6-4 in the semifinals of the Seiko Super Tennis in Tokyo, Japan. "It was one of those days," says Connors. "He played very well." Davis loses the final the next day, falling to Ivan Lendl 3-6, 6-3, 6-4.

1927 Frank Sedgman, the first great champion of the "Aussie Invasion" of the 1950s and 1960s, is born in Mount Albert, Victoria. Sedgman stands in the No. 3 position all-time winning 22 career major titles—despite only competing from 1949 to 1953.

October 30

2003 Andy Roddick clinches the No. 1 ranking for the first time in his career when he defeats Tommy Robredo of Spain 6-3, 6-4 to reach the quarterfinals of the Tennis Masters Series in Paris. Roddick's win—coupled with Juan Carlos Ferrero's 7-5, 7-5 loss to Jiri Novak of the Czech Republic—ensures that Roddick will move to the No. 1 ranking. "I like to be greedy, and I want to stay there for a long time," Roddick says. "When I was 12 years old, I was still trying to figure out how to tie my shoelaces. Being No. 1 was a long way off. It's not something I thought would happen."

1994 Boris Becker wins the Stockholm Open for a fourth time in his career, defeating Goran Ivanisevic 4-6, 6-4, 6-3, 7-6 (7-4) in the final. The victory over the No. 2-ranked Ivanisevic gives the No. 6-ranked Becker the distinction of winning the tournament by beating the world's No. 1, 2 and 3 ranked players. In the quarterfinals, Becker beats his fellow German Michael Stich, the world No. 3, while the semifinals, Becker beats world No. 1 Pete Sampras. Says Becker, "It must be something in the air in Stockholm that makes me play great here. I can't remember playing as good tennis three days in a row against the best players in the world."

1988 Amos Mansdorf of Israel, ranked No. 33 in the world, defeats No. 23 ranked Brad Gilbert 6-3, 6-2, 6-3 to win the singles title at the Paris Open Championships—at the time, the richest indoor tennis tournament in the world, offering $1.1 million in prize money. Mansdorf wins $262,000 by winning the tournament—four times his previous best pay day.

2005 Twenty-three year-old Nadia Petrova of Russia finally gets the monkey off her back, winning her first WTA Tour singles title, defeating Patty Schnyder 4-6, 6-3, 6-1 in the Generali Ladies Open in Linz, Austria. Petrova, a stalwart in the top 20 of the WTA rankings, wins the title in her fifth career WTA singles final appearance. "This is a great step forward for me," says Petrova. "It gives me a lot of confidence for next year and allows me to aim for more finals and more titles. It was very important that this happened finally. I've now achieved everything I wanted to this year—to play very consistently, to have good results in the Grand Slams, and now to win a title. I'm very happy."

October 31

1994 Fourteen-year-old future world No. 1 Venus Williams makes her celebrated professional debut, defeating No. 59th-ranked Shaun Stafford 6-3, 6-4 in the first round of the Bank of the West Classic in Oakland, Calif. Robin Finn of the *New York Times* describes Williams as "the most unorthodox tennis prodigy her sport has ever seen" stating that she is "a 14-year-old African-American girl with a ghetto in her past, a total absence of junior competition in her present and a plan to spend no more than a decade pursuing Grand Slam titles and six-digit purses so she can put a college degree in her future." Says Stafford, "She moves extra well for her height, she's got a great serve and it'll get better. It's exciting for tennis to have her here. When I came on the tour at 19, I was intimidated, but here she is at 14, ready to play the pros. It's unique."

2007 In a Halloween match between "The Magician" and "Zorro" in the second round of the BNP Paribas Paris Masters, Fabrice Santoro, nicknamed "The Magician" due to his unusual double-fisted playing style, defeats world No. 3 Novak Djokovic, who enters the court wearing a black Zorro eye mask, by a 7-6, 6-3 margin in the second round.

1980 Bill Scanlon registers one of the biggest wins of his career, defeating Bjorn Borg 7-5, 3-6, 7-5 in the quarterfinals of the Seiko Championships in Tokyo. "I was surprised by myself," says Scanlon. "It's my biggest victory."

1981 Vince Van Patten, son of Hollywood actor Dick Van Patten and ranked No. 83 in the world, defeats John McEnroe 6-3, 7-5 in the semifinals of the Seiko Super Tennis in Tokyo, marking the biggest victory of his career. The next day, Van Patten beats Australia's Mark Edmondon 6-2, 3-6, 6-3 to win the tournament title, his first and only ATP singles title of his career.

1986 John McEnroe is defeated, fined and suspended in the quarterfinals of the Paris Open. McEnroe is upset by Spain's Sergio Casal 6-3, 7-6 and is fined $3,000 for outbursts against chair umpire Jeremy Shales, forcing a 42-day suspension from tournament play. At one moment in the match, McEnroe says to Shales, "You are the worst umpire I have ever seen in my life. You'll never work another one of my matches again."

1982 Martina Navratilova plays near flawless tennis, defeating Chris Evert Lloyd 6-1, 6-4 in the final of the Daihatsu Challenge in Brighton, England.

November 1

1911 Sidney Wood, the only player to win a Wimbledon final without striking a ball, is born in Bridgeport, Conn. In 1931, Wood is scheduled to play Frank Shields in the Wimbledon men's singles final, but Shields, who injures his ankle in his semifinal win over No. 1 seed Jean Borotra, is pressured by the U.S. Davis Cup committee to default the final in order to rest up and prevent further injury in preparation for the U.S. Davis Cup team's match with Britain the following week. Says Wood of the incident to Bud Collins in *The Bud Collins History of Tennis*, "Frank wanted to play, and so did I. It was insulting to the fans and the tournament. I didn't want to win that way. But the U.S. Davis Cup committee ordered Frank to withdraw so he'd be ready for Davis Cup the next weekend against Britain, which we lost. It shows you the control the USTA had over us amateurs." Wood, at age 19, was the youngest man to win Wimbledon at the time, a record that a 17-year-old Boris Becker eclipsed in 1985.

2007 David Nalbandian beats Roger Federer for the second time in two weeks, beating the world No. 1 6-4, 7-6 (3) in the third round of the Paris Masters. The Argentine, a thorn in the side of Federer through the years, evens his series record with the Swiss maestro at 8-8. Says Federer of Nalbandian, "It's not easy being aggressive against him when you're 3 meters (10 feet) behind the baseline. He's got a phenomenal backhand and can dictate play from both sides."

1990 Playing his second tournament since his surprise win at the U.S. Open, 19-year-old Pete Sampras is upset by No. 134-ranked qualifier Guillaume Raoux of France 6-3, 3-6, 6-3 in the second round of the Paris Open. Says Sampras, "This is a real downer. He was going for broke on every shot. He was playing in front of his home crowd and he had nothing to lose. He was going for it on every serve. Sometimes he double-faulted by 20 feet."

1987 Eliot Teltscher comes back from a two-sets-to-love deficit to beat Australia's John Fitzgerald 6-7, 3-6, 6-1, 6-2, 7-5 to win the Hong Kong Open. The title is the American's 10th and final ATP singles title. Says Teltscher, "It's great to end the year with a victory. A 2-0 lead (in sets) is good but is not incredible. It could be very deceiving. I have seen so many players lose after leading 2-0 before." Says Fitzgerald, "I lost my legs in the third set and allowed Eliot to get a roll on."

November 2

1986 Boris Becker wins the Paris Open indoor championships—his third tournament title in three weeks on his third different continent—defeating Spain's Sergio Casal 6-4, 6-3, 7-6 in the final. Becker wins titles in the previous two weeks in Tokyo, Japan and Melbourne, Australia, before winning the title in Paris. Says Becker, "Under such circumstances, to fly all those many hours, the different continents, the different cities, and different surfaces, let's say, I didn't think I could do it."

1994 The first professional tennis tournament for 14-year-old Venus Williams comes to a close with a 2-6, 6-3, 6-0 second-round loss to reigning U.S. and French Open champion Arantxa Sanchez Vicario of Spain. According to Robin Finn of the *New York Times*, Williams "displayed plenty of precocious pyrotechnics in the opening set, where her athleticism reduced the world's second-ranked player to merely another player." Says Williams, "I think my game was solid; I just need to improve it. If I told myself, 'You played great, Venus; she's No. 2 in the world and you're just a 14-year-old kid,' then I wouldn't be attaining my goals." Says Sanchez Vicario, "In the first set I was watching more the way she hit the ball instead of thinking about my shots. She did very well. She's a big girl, and she can serve and volley or stay back. Sometimes she hit the ball so well there was nothing you could do."

2000 Just five days before the Presidential election, it is revealed publicly for the first time that Republican Nominee George W. Bush was arrested for drunken driving in Maine in 1976, with Aussie tennis legend John Newcombe in the car with the future president. "I was drinking beers, yeah, with John Newcombe," Bush says in a briefing with the press. "I'm not proud of that. I made some mistakes. I occasionally drank too much, and I did that night. I learned my lesson. I told the guy (the arresting officer) I had been drinking, what do I need to do? He said, 'Here's the fine.' I paid the fine." Thirteen days later, Newcombe emerges from going "underground" and makes his first statements on the situation. Says Newcombe to the Australian Associated Press, "When (the news of the Bush's arrest) came out, I just did the first thing that came into my mind—I went underground mate. I didn't put my head up." Newcombe describes Bush as a "good bloke" who would make a "pretty good president" and says the drunk-driving incident was minor in terms of how far Bush was over the limit. "That's something I've laughed about with George for the last 24 years," Newcombe says. "That's something that just happened that night. We were just a couple of young blokes going out and having a good time. We didn't do anything wrong, basically....We probably shouldn't have been driving at that stage but it wasn't that anyone was badly inebriated."

1980 Jimmy Connors defeats Tom Gullikson 6-1, 6-2 to win the singles title in Tokyo, Japan and the $48,000 first prize. Says Gullikson of how he will make get over his poor play in the final, "The $24,000 (runner-up prize) will make up for it."

1963 The United States opens up play against India on courts made of cow dung in the Davis Cup Inter-Zone Final in Bombay, India. Chuck McKinley defeats Premjit Lall 6-4, 6-3, 6-0, while Dennis Ralston defeats Ramanathan Krishnan 6-4, 6-1, 13-11 to give the U.S. a 2-0 lead after the first day, in the eventual 5-0 victory.

1933 Ken Rosewall, the smooth-stroking Australian who plays his first major final in 1953 and his last in 1974, is born in Sydney. Nick-named "Muscles" (because of his lack of them), Rosewall wins a total of eight major singles titles—and 18 total major titles—during a career that stretches until 1980, when Rosewall is 45 years old. Wimbledon is the famous missing trophy from his trophy case, losing four finals (1954, 1956, 1970, 1974), but he tallies four Australian titles (1953, 1955, 1971, 1972), two French titles (1953, 1968) and two U.S. titles (1956, 1970).

November 3

1975 The WTA Tour computer rankings debut and Chris Evert is the first player to achieve the No. 1 ranking. Evert holds the top ranking for 262 weeks during her career, including the first 26 weeks of the computer rankings.

2003 Andy Roddick takes over as No. 1 player in the world for the first time in his career, replacing Juan Carlos Ferrero in the top ranking position. Roddick, the 22nd player to hold the ranking, holds the top spot for a total of 13 weeks before surrendering it to Roger Federer on Feb. 2, 2004.

2001 Lindsay Davenport defeats Kim Clijsters 1-6, 6-3, 7-6 (3) to reach the final of the year-end Sanex WTA Tour Championships in Munich, Germany and clinches the year-end No. 1 ranking. Davenport finishes the year No. 1 despite not reaching a major final during the year. Writes Christopher Clarey of the *New York Times*, "Since computer rankings began in 1975, no player has finished No. 1 with such a suspect resume."

1985 Ivan Lendl defeats John McEnroe 1-6, 7-5, 6-2, 6-2 to win the European Champions Championship in Antwerp, Belgium, in the first meeting between the two players since Lendl beats McEnroe to win the U.S. Open two months earlier. Lendl wins $220,000 by winning the title and, by virtue of winning the event for a third time in five years, wins a diamond-studded 13.2 pound gold tennis racquet valued at $700,000.

2006 Kim Clijsters loses only 12 points in a 36-minute 6-1, 6-0 rout of No. 119th-ranked Sandra Kloesel in the quarterfinals of the WTA Tour event in Hasselt, Belgium. Clijsters, ranked No. 6 in the world, is playing in her first event after a 10-week layoff due to an injured wrist. Says Clijsters, "I was seeing the ball and moving a lot better. I was doing those things for a few games here and there in previous matches this week but today, I played well throughout the whole two sets." Clijsters goes on to win the tournament, defeating Kaia Kanepi of Estonia in the final, 6-3, 3-6, 6-4.

1937 Roy Emerson, the most prolific winner of men's majors, is born in Black Butt, Australia. Emerson wins a record 28 major championships—including 12 in singles that stands as a record for 33 years before Pete Sampras breaks the record by winning his 13th of 14 majors at Wimbledon in 2000.

November 4

1984 John McEnroe conducts one of his worst on-court tirades of his career, slamming a ball into the stands, calling the chair umpire a jerk and slamming a soda can with his racquet during a change-over in a 1-6, 7-6, 6-2 semifinal win over Anders Jarryd at the Stockholm Open in Sweden. Says McEnroe, who is fined $2,100, "I'm mentally tired at the moment. That's one of the reasons I lost my temper." Says Jarryd, "It is very difficult to play against someone who behaves like McEnroe." In the second game of the match, McEnroe hits a fan with a ball, giving him his first penalty of the match. Following the infraction, he goes on to lose the next 15 points of the match. Leading 4-2 in the second set, McEnroe exclaims to the chair umpire "Answer my question, jerk!" causing for a point penalty for verbal abuse. After losing his serve for 4-3 moments later, McEnroe then slams a soda can with his racquet on the changeover, resulting in a game penalty.

2001 Serena Williams wins the year-end Sanex Championships in Munich, Germany in bizarre circumstances as Lindsay Davenport is forced to default the final due to her re-injured right knee that she suffers at the end of her semifinal win over Kim Cjlisters the previous day.

1989 Boris Becker overcomes a second-set charge from John McEnroe—and his famed on-court antics—to defeat the three-time Wimbledon champion 7-6, 4-6, 6-3 in the semifinals of the Paris Open. Say Becker of McEnroe's outbursts, "He's been doing that for 10 years, but that's John McEnroe."

2007 David Nalbandian hands world No. 2 Rafael Nadal his first career defeat in the city of Paris, defeating the three-time French Open champion 6-4, 6-0 in the final of the BNP Paribas Paris Masters. The loss is Nadal's first in 26 career matches in the French capital. "All week I was playing great, and I don't know why the result was so easy," says Nalbandian who in the third round of the event defeats world No. 1 Roger Federer. "After I broke him, I felt that I was playing better than him. I play more relaxed, start hitting winners almost from everywhere. That gave me confidence."

2007 Lindsay Davenport, continuing a comeback to the WTA Tour after becoming a mother earlier in the year, defeats Julia Vakulenko of Ukraine 6-4, 6-1 in the final of the Bell Challenge in Quebec City. The title is Davenport's 53rd singles title on tour—tying her for eighth place all-time with Monica Seles.

November 5

2006 Marion Bartoli of France needs only 41 minutes to register a white-wash 6-0, 6-0 victory over Russia's Olga Poutchkova in the final of the Bell Challenge in Quebec City, Canada in the first double-bagel WTA Tour final in 13 years. Says Bartoli, "I didn't have expectations coming into this match, so maybe that helped. Also, maybe she was tired from yesterday. She's a little younger and less experienced, too. Whenever she'd start taking control of the points I'd hit it just as hard back, and I think that discouraged her a little bit."

1980 Bjorn Borg is fined for the first time in his professional tennis career when he is docked $500 for not attending a post-match press conference following his 6-4, 6-3 victory over Tomas Smid in the first round of the Stockholm Open in Sweden. Borg, in an attempt to avoid the Swedish press asking him of his initial decision to play an exhibition match in South Africa despite its apartheid policies, skips three more post-match press conferences and is fined a total of $2,000. He meets with the press after winning the title, defeating John McEnroe in the final.

2006 Nikolay Davydenko of Russia crushes Slovakia's Dominik Hrbaty 6-1, 6-2, 6-2 in 1 hour, 38 minutes to win the BNP Paribas Masters in Paris and the biggest title of his career. The victory vaults Davydenko to the No. 3 world ranking, behind Roger Federer and Rafael Nadal, who both withdraw from the event with injures. Says Davydenko, "This is amazing. Winning a Masters Series for the first time is important and being number three in the world behind players such as Roger Federer and Rafael Nadal is quite an achievement."

1989 Boris Becker dominates Stefan Edberg 6-4, 6-3, 6-3 in the final of the Paris Open.

2000 In the third consecutive all-American singles final of the Bell Challenge in Quebec City, Canada, Chanda Rubin defeats Jennifer Capriati, 6-4, 6-2, avenging her 4-6, 6-1, 6-2 loss to Capriati in the 1999 final. Rubin also reaches the 1998 Bell Challenge final, but loses to fellow-American Tara Snyder, 4-6, 6-4, 7-6. The title is Rubin's first of the year, but the third of her career.

November 6

1994 Playing in her second-to-last event in her final year of singles play, 38-year-old Martina Navratilova competes in her last WTA singles final, losing 1-6, 7-6 (5), 7-6 (3) to Spain's Arantxa Sanchez Vicario of Spain in the final of the Bank of the West Championship in Oakland, Calif. Says Navratilova, "It's nice to be able to play great tennis. I just wish I could finish it off. When I play tennis like this, I know I didn't retire too late. "

1994 Andre Agassi wins his first title in Paris, defeating Marc Rosset of Switzerland 6-3, 6-3, 4-6, 7-5 in the final of the Paris Open. Says Agassi, "I have been to the final of the French Open at Roland Garros twice but never won. Now, I know what it is like to win in Paris." Five years later, in 1999, Agassi finally adds the French Open to his career resume.

2007 Ana Ivanovic turns 20 years old and celebrates with a 6-1, 4-6, 7-5 opening round-robin win over world No. 2 Svetlana Kuznetsova at the year-end Sony Ericsson Championships in Madrid, Spain. Says Ivanovic of the 2-hour, 18-minute victory, "I knew I had to start well because she is such a strong player and I tried not to give her too many chances and it worked well for me. At the end, I tried not to think about the score any more, but I'm really happy I was able to stay calm and break her."

2005 Unseeded 20-year-old Thomas Berdych of the Czech Republic defeats Ivan Ljubicic of Croatia 6-3, 6-4, 3-6, 4-6, 6-4 to win the BNP Paribas Masters in Paris—his first Tennis Masters Series title and his second career ATP singles title.

1985 Trailing 5-4 in the second set-tie break to Ramesh Krishnan, John McEnroe smashes his racquet in anger, then wins the last three points of the match to defeat the Indian 6-4, 7-6 in the first round of the Stockholm Open in Sweden. Says McEnroe, "I was not into the match today."

November 7

1993 With the Parisien crown occasionally booing his boring play of 27 aces and 32 service winners, Goran Ivanisevic defeats Andrei Medvedev 6-3, 6-2, 7-6 (2) to win the Paris Open. Says Ivanisevic of the booing French crowd, "'I don't care. They want five sets but I don't want to play five sets."

1999 Reigning French and U.S. Open champion Andre Agassi defeats Russia's Marat Safin 7-6 (1), 6-2, 4-6, 6-4 in 2 hours, 32 minutes to win the Paris Open in France. The title marks Agassi's second victory in the prestigious indoor tournament after also winning the title in 1994. Says Agassi, "I thought we were both outstanding. He kept it together very well today and made me earn it from start to finish. Against Safin, every point is important because a couple of swings of his racquet and he breaks your serve." Says Safin of the match, "The problem was I started to play his game, running all the time. I prefer to play short points. I was also very nervous...I got very tired at running along the baseline."

1983 With the King of Sweden Karl Gustav XVI in attendance, Mats Wilander honors his nation's royalty by defeating Tomas Smid 6-1, 7-5 in the final of the Stockholm Open.

1993 Martina Navratilova improves her record to 33-1 against Zina Garrison, beating her former Fed Cup teammate for the final time in their careers 6-2, 7-6 (1) in the final of the Bank of the West Classic in Oakland, Calif. Says Navratilova of the win over Garrison, "Once I got into the tiebreaker I was confident. Everything was working. I was faultless. I served well and backed it up with a decent volley." Garrison's lone career singles win over Navratilova comes in the quarterfinals of the 1988 U.S. Open, Garrison upsetting the two-time defending champion Navratilova in dramatic fashion 6-4, 6-7 (3), 7-5.

1989 Alexander Volkov of the Soviet Union saves a match point and upsets Jimmy Connors, 3-6, 6-4, 7-6 (8-6) in the first round of the Wembley Championships in London. Connors holds a match point at 6-5 in the final set tie-break, but is unable to put away Volkov, who breaks a seven-match losing streak with the win.

November 8

2007 Justine Henin avenges her semifinal loss to Marion Bartoli at Wimbledon in torrid fashion, ripping the Frenchwoman 6-0, 6-0 in 57 minutes in round-robin play at the year-end Sony Ericsson Championships in Madrid. The loss is the most lopsided result in the 35-year history of the year-end women's championships and extends Henin's winning streak to 23 straight victories since her semifinal loss to Bartoli at Wimbledon in July. Says Henin, "I wanted to take revenge. Wimbledon is far away now. She was better than me that day and that was it. Now a few months later I'm fresh and in Wimbledon I was pretty tired. I had a pretty good reaction after that defeat though and it helped me. It was not really about the score, it was the way I played. You could see I had a lot of determination out there tonight. I really played unbelievable tennis. I was aggressive. I went to the net pretty much and everything was working pretty well tonight and that gives a lot of confidence." Bartoli is a substitute player in the event, being called up as a late replacement for an injured Serena Williams. "I think she played an amazing match, she didn't miss anything," says Bartoli. "When she plays good it is hard to beat her but when she plays awesome she's almost unbeatable."

1992 Brothers John and Patrick McEnroe pair together to win the doubles title at the Paris Open in France, defeating Patrick Galbraith and Danie Visser 6-4, 6-2 in the final. The title is the second for the brother tandem having also won the title in 1984 in Richmond, Va. In the singles final, Boris Becker defeats defending champion Guy Forget 7-6 (3), 6-3, 3-6, 6-3—both players firing 21 aces.

1998 Calling it "definitely the best victory of my career," Greg Rusedski defeats world No. 1 Pete Sampras 6-4, 7-6, 6-3 to win the Paris Open, a win called perhaps the most historic tournament victory by a British citizen in over 30 years. Says Sampras, "He basically outplayed me for the most part. He has been hot all week and my hat is off to him. He is tough when he is on and he was definitely on today."

2003 Andy Roddick, two months removed from winning his first major title at the U.S. Open, hosts the popular American Saturday evening comedy television show "Saturday Night Live," joining Chris Evert as only the second tennis player to host the popular U.S. entertainment program.

November 9

1993 Bjorn Borg ends his comeback to the ATP Tour—10 years after dropping completely off the tour—losing to Alexander Volkov in the first round of the Kremlin Cup in Moscow. Borg, 37, blows a match point losing to the Russian star 4-6, 6-3, 7-6 (7), then announces that he will not play any more ATP tournaments. He begins his ill-fated comeback in 1991 and goes 0-12 in ATP matches, including his loss to Volkov, his closest match of the comeback. Says Borg of his match with Volkov, "I'm just glad I played a good match on the tour."

1980 Bjorn Borg and John McEnroe register semifinal victories at the Stockholm Open in Sweden to set up their third meeting of the 1980 season—after splitting major finals earlier in the year. Borg defeats Gene Mayer 6-2, 7-5, while McEnroe defeats Bob Lutz 6-3, 6-3 to set up their final round match at the world's oldest indoor tennis tournament. Borg wins the final the next day 6-3, 6-4.

1997 Marcelo Rios suffers a humiliating day as he is easily defeated by Julian Alonso 6-2, 6-1 in the final of his hometown tournament in Santiago, Chile, and with the loss, fails to qualify for the year-end ATP Tour World Championships in Hannover, Germany.

1975 Adriano Panatta of Italy wins his fourth of nine career titles, upsetting world No. 1 Jimmy Connors 4-6, 6-3, 7-5 in the final of the Stockholm Open.

1997 Yevgeny Kafelnikov of Russia wins the first of five straight singles titles at the Kremlin Cup in Moscow, defeating Petr Korda 7-6, 6-4 in the final. The title is Kafelnikov's 14th of 26 career ATP titles.

1997 Lindsay Davenport wins the first set in 26 minutes and comes back from a 1-4 deficit in the second set to defeat Nathalie Tauziat, 6-0, 7-5, to win the Ameritech Cup in Chicago.

1997 Jonas Bjorkman trails Jan Siemerink 3-6, 2-4, before rallying to win the Stockholm Open in his native Sweden for the first time in his career, defeating his Dutch opponent by a 3-6, 7-6 (2), 6-2, 6-4 margin.

November 10

2003 Kim Clijsters defeats Amelie Mauresmo 6-2, 6-0 in 52 minutes to win the year-end WTA Championships at the Staples Center in Los Angeles for a second consecutive year. Clijsters collects the first prize pay check of $1,000,030—the extra $30 in honor of the WTA Tour's 30th anniversary. Says Clijsters, "I think I saw the ball like a football. I was seeing it really well. And that is a nice feeling to have, knowing you can do whatever you want with the ball."

1997 In the world singles rankings released by the ATP, Andre Agassi sits at a ranking of No. 141—his lowest ranking since August 4, 1986. On the verge of retirement, Agassi re-dedicates himself to the game and returns to the No. 1 world ranking on July 5, 1999—four weeks after winning the 1999 French Open and completing a career sweep of all four major championships.

1973 In the first meeting between Bjorn Borg and Jimmy Connors, the 17-year-old Borg defeats 21-year-old Connors 6-4, 3-6, 7-6 in the semifinals of the Stockholm Open. The two rivals play 31 more times on the ATP Tour—never before a tournament semifinal—Borg winning the head-to-head series 14-8. The two play eight times in major championships—Borg winning five of the eight—with Connors winning the 1976 and 1978 U.S. Open finals and Borg winning the 1977 and 1978 Wimbledon finals. Tom Gorman ends the string of upsets of Borg in the final, winning the title by a 6-3, 4-6, 7-5 margin.

1974 Thirty-one-year old Arthur Ashe needs only 55 minutes to defeat Tom Okker 6-2, 6-2 in the final of the Stockholm Open in Sweden.

1981 Angry fans demand their money back from the Wembley tennis tournament in London when John McEnroe's match with Britain's John Feaver is postponed, due to a mix-up in the tournament's scheduling. McEnroe requests and is granted a Wednesday start by tournament director Len Owen, but his match mistakenly is placed on the Tuesday schedule of play.

1970 Graham Stilwell of Great Britain defeats No. 1 seeded Rod Laver 6-3, 6-3 in the first round of the Paris Open in France.

1986 Martina Navratilova defeats Hana Mandlikova 6-2, 6-2 in 57 minutes in the final of the Virginia Slims of New England in Worcester, Mass.

November 11

2002 Nineteen-year-old Kim Clijsters wins the year-end WTA Tour Championships at the Staples Center in Los Angeles, defeating Serena Williams 7-5, 6-3 in the Monday night championship match. The loss to Clijsters ends Williams' 18-match winning streak and is only her fifth loss of the season.

2006 Justine Henin-Hardenne clinches the year-end No. 1 ranking for the 2006 season after beating Maria Sharapova 6-2, 7-5 (5) in the semifinals of the year-end WTA Championships in Madrid, Spain. Henin-Hardenne's win also avenges her loss to the Russian in the U.S. Open final earlier in the year.

2007 Justine Henin and Maria Sharapova battle for 3 hours, 24 minutes in the longest three-set final in the history of the women's year-end championships with Henin claiming the Sony Ericsson Championships crown with a 6-7, 7-5, 6-3 victory. The title is Henin's 10th on the season and earns her $1 million to make her the first woman to eclipse $5 million in season-single prize money. "What a way to finish the season," says Henin, who closes the season with 25-straight wins, including her second U.S. Open victory. "I just enjoy my tennis so much and I just wish I can keep playing like that for more years...I played with my heart. I had to find the resources, mentally and physically, but I think it's a match everyone will remember."

1997 With a ranking of No. 141, former world No. 1 Andre Agassi resorts to playing on the Challenger Circuit—the minor leagues of professional tennis—and defeats Michael Tebbutt of Australia 6-2, 6-4 in the first round of the Luxor Challenger in his hometown of Las Vegas, Nev. Agassi's 1997 season features opening round losses in eight of his 12 events, while missing three of the four major tournaments. Says the 27-year-old Agassi, "I feel like this is a step for me, and it's part of my preparation in hopes of really getting myself back to where I know I can be. My shots haven't gone anywhere. ...I think since the summer of the Olympics, Cincinnati and the U.S. Open (in 1996) was the last stretch of really great tennis I've played. Since then, my foot speed lacked a little bit, which I'm starting to get back...once the footwork comes back and I'm in position, I've still got great shots....It feels good for me to come out here and grind it out with the boys. If I can get a day better every day, that's all I can ask for."

November 12

1978 In the first-ever meeting between John McEnroe and Bjorn Borg, the 19-year-old McEnroe defeats the 22-year-old Borg 6-3, 6-3 in the semifinals of the Stockholm Open in Sweden. The loss marks the first-ever professional loss for Borg to a younger player. The McEnroe-Borg rivalry becomes one of the greatest in the sport as the two titans square off 14 times in all—each player winning seven times. The two play in four memorable major finals, McEnroe winning three of the four at the 1980 and 1981 U.S. Opens and at Wimbledon in 1981. Their epic final at Wimbledon in 1980 is regarded as one of the greatest matches of all-time, Borg winning his fifth consecutive title in a 1-6, 7-5, 6-3, 6-7 (16), 8-6 epic. McEnroe wins the Stockholm singles title the next day, defeating fellow American Tim Gullikson 6-2, 6-2 in the final.

2006 Despite missing the entire fall WTA Tour schedule with a right knee injury, Justine Henin-Hardenne reigns supreme at the year-end Sony Ericsson WTA Tour Championships, defeating Amelie Mauresmo 6-4, 6-3 in the final. "No excuses—she just played better than me today," Mauresmo says. "She took the opportunities when she had them, and I felt I didn't serve so well, and wasn't so effective on the forehand side when I was going to the net. But that's just the way it is."

2003 Andre Agassi defeats Juan Carlos Ferrero of Spain 2-6, 6-3, 6-4 in round-robin play at the Tennis Masters Cup in Houston, Texas in a victory that eliminates Ferrero from advancing into the semifinals of the event, and clinching the year-end No. 1 ranking for fellow American Andy Roddick. Says Agassi, "Andy had No. 1 in his hands the whole week, so regardless if I beat Ferrero or not, it was going to be up to him to solidify it. So, you know, glad I could help. I aim to please."

2007 For the first time in four years, world No. 1 Roger Federer loses consecutive matches as the Swiss maestro is a shock loser to hard-hitting Fernando Gonzalez of Chile in the opening round-robin match of the year-end Tennis Masters Cup in Shanghai, China. Gonzalez's 4-6, 7-6 (1), 7-5 win comes after Federer loses to David Nalbandian in the semifinals of the BNP Paribas Masters in Paris earlier in the month. The win was Gonzalez's first over Federer in 11 meetings and Federer's first-ever loss in a round-robin match in 15 previous round-robin matches at the event.

November 13

1988 Martina Navratilova defeats Chris Evert 6-2, 6-2 in the final of the Virginia Slims of Chicago in the 80th and final professional match between the two tennis legends. In a rivalry that begins in 1973, Navratilova defeats Evert 43 times to Evert's 37 victories over her Czech-born left-handed rival. Sixty-one of their matches are contested in finals, including fourteen major tournament finals. Says Navratilova to the crowd following the final in Chicago, "The older we get, the more you guys appreciate us. I think Chris and I are like wine. We get better with age."

1977 At the age of 43 years, 11 days, Ken Rosewall wins the singles title at the Hong Kong Open, defeating 31-year-old Tom Gorman 6-3, 5-7, 6-4, 6-4 in the final. Rosewall is nine months younger than 43-year-old Pancho Gonzales, who wins the title in Des Moines, Iowa in 1972 to become the oldest man to win an ATP title. The title is Rosewall's 32nd and last singles championship of the Open era.

2005 Amelie Mauresmo wins the biggest title of her career—and begins to silence the talk of being able to big titles—defeating Mary Pierce 5-7, 7-6 (7-3), 6-4 to win the year-end WTA Tour Championships at the Staples Center in Los Angeles. Serving the match at 5-4 in the final set, Mauresmo shows her nerves when she double faults to fall into a 0-40 hole, but benefits from five straight errors from Pierce to hold serve and win the title. Says Mauresmo, who goes on to win her first major title two-and-half months later at the Australian Open, "I really think that's a huge step for me...I don't know where it's going to take me, but it is a step. You know that it's an important moment. It's just a great reward for me to be able to hold the trophy...It's the biggest win, so it has to be ranked as the best emotional moment for me. I'm just proud of what I did. I kept fighting."

2007 World No. 2 Rafael Nadal is upset by countryman and Tennis Masters Cup rookie David Ferrer 4-6, 6-4, 6-3 in a ground-stroking slugfest in round-robin play at the year-end championships in Shanghai, China. Says Nadal, "David is playing with unbelievable confidence and moving unbelievable—just crazy. No excuse. This is the toughest tournament of the year. Anything can happen. I didn't play a bad match. I played well. He played better."

November 14

1994 Martina Navratilova is defeated by Gabriela Sabatini 6-4, 6-2 in the first round of the year-end Virginia Slims Championships at Madison Square Garden in Navratilova's swan song to professional tennis. Well, almost her swan song to tennis as Navratilova emerges from retirement six years later to play full-time doubles on the WTA Tour. Navratilova has a banner retired at Madison Square Garden during the on-court post-match festivities. Says Navratilova, "I got blown off the court tonight by someone who was playing in another zone. If I have to lose my last match to anyone, I'd want to lose it to Gabriela Sabatini because she's a very, very nice human being besides being a hell of a tennis player.'

1973 Margaret Court lobs verbal volleys at both Billie Jean King and Bobby Riggs almost two months following the King-Riggs "Battle of the Sexes" match at the Houston Astrodome and five months following Court's embarrassing loss to Riggs in the Mother's Day match. "I believe Billie Jean is dodging me and I'm trying to escape Bobby," says Court. "Billie Jean is frightened to lose since she won that bally-hoo match against Bobby Riggs...and I'm not interested in taking on Riggs again. The taxman would be the only winner."

1993 Conchita Martinez defeats Steffi Graf 6-3, 6-3 in the final of the WTA Tour event in Philadelphia, ending Graf's 44-match winning streak.

1976 Vitas Gerulaitis defeats Jorge Andrew 6-3, 1-6, 6-3, 7-5 to finish off a 4-1 U.S. win over Venezuela in the first round of the 1977 Davis Cup campaign (begun in 1976) in Caracas, Venezuela.

1877 Norman Brookes, one of the early greats of Australian tennis and the man whose name graces the men's singles trophy at the Australian Open, is born in Melbourne. In 1907, Brookes becomes the first man from overseas to win the singles title at Wimbledon, and also wins the title in 1914. He wins only one Australian title—in 1911—but helps Australasia (Australia and New Zealand) win the Davis Cup in 1907, 1908, 1909 and 1914. In 1926, he becomes the first president of the Lawn Tennis Association of Australia. The name of the Australian Open men's singles trophy is officially called "The Norman Brookes Challenge Cup."

November 15

2004 Serena Williams leads seventeen-year-old reigning Wimbledon champion Maria Sharapova 4-0 in the third set in the singles final of the year-end WTA Tour Championships at the Staples Center in Los Angeles, but becomes hampered with a pulled stomach muscle, and loses six straight games to lose the final by a 4-6, 6-2, 6-4 margin. Sharapova wins $1 million for claiming the championship, while Williams picks up the runner-up paycheck of $500,000. Says Williams of her runner-up prize, "It's definitely not a million but with the right investments it will be."

2006 Andy Roddick lets three match points fall by the wayside—and a golden opportunity to beat the near-unbeatable world No. 1 Roger Federer—in a 4-6, 7-6(8), 6-4 loss in round-robin play at the year-end Tennis Masters Cup in Shanghai, China. Says Federer of Roddick, "He served out of a tree. It was incredible. He was serving a lot of aces. Pretty much for two sets I was trying to stay in and I was a bit lucky in the end because the second-set tiebreak, he should have gotten it. He served for it at 6-4 and he was disappointed, I think, but for me it was a hell of a win...I think he played the perfect match for two sets. Maybe he lacked one serve in the end, so it was unfortunate for him."

1981 Jimmy Connors registers a stunning, 3-6, 2-6, 6-3, 6-4, 6-2 final-round victory over John McEnroe in 3 hours, 37 minutes at Wembley, England, to win a $175,000 Grand Prix tennis tournament in a match that is highlighted by numerous acts of unsportsmanlike conduct. Connors is fined $400 by tournament officials for shouting an obscenity on the court, while McEnroe is fined a total of $700, including $350 for racquet abuse and abuse of the umpire's chair and $350 for ball abuse. McEnroe is involved in numerous verbal exchanges with chair umpire John Parry and tournament referee Colin Hess. Parry twice announces the score of the match incorrectly and enrages both McEnroe and Connors during the last three sets by continually overruling line judges' calls. Says McEnroe, "It's not fun to play tennis anymore. There are so many rules; I don't think anyone knows them all. Tennis is a great sport and if it's to survive you can't suppress everyone's personality."

November 16

2001 Twenty-year-old Lleyton Hewitt clinches the No. 1 year-end ranking, becoming the youngest player to accomplish the feat in the history of the ATP rankings since 1973. Hewitt clinches the ranking when he defeats fellow Aussie Patrick Rafter 7-5, 6-2 in his final round-robin match at the Tennis Masters Cup in Sydney, Australia. Hewitt's victory, coupled with the loss of Gustavo Kuerten to Yevgeny Kafelnikov, ensures the top year-end ranking for the Adelaide, Australia native. Says Hewitt, the first Australian to finish the year ranked No. 1, "It's an unbelievable feeling. To become No. 1 at 20 years of age, and to do it in Australia, you couldn't have written a better dream." Hewitt, at 20 years, 8 months, is younger than the previous year-end No. 1 Jimmy Connors, at 22 years, 3 months, in 1974.

1997 Pete Sampras wins the year-end ATP Tour Championships for a fourth time, defeating Russia's Yevgeny Kafelnikov 6-3, 6-2, 6-2 in Hannover, Germany. Sampras becomes the first player to win the season-ending championships for a second consecutive year since Ivan Lendl in 1986 and 1987.

2003 Roger Federer routs Andre Agassi 6-3, 6-0, 6-4 to win the year-end ATP Masters Cup for the first time in his career. Playing at the West Side Tennis Club in Houston, Texas, Federer fires 11 aces in the 88-minute match that is delayed two-and-a-half hours due to rain. "It was one of the best matches for me this season," Federer says. "I'm very happy how the whole year went, especially this tournament. I worked hard this year. You always have ups and downs but I feel this season has been complete."

1997 Returning to the minor league Challenger circuit to try and resurrect his game, Andre Agassi is surprisingly defeated by No. 202-ranked Christian Vinck of Germany 6-2, 7-5 in final of the Luxor Challenger in Las Vegas, Nev. "I have my goals long-term, and this week was assisting me to getting there," says the former No. 1 ranked Agassi, whose ranking drops to No. 141 after a dismal stretch of play over 18 months. "I can't start questioning the big picture because of this. It's ridiculous. That's what the press' job is. For me, it's just to go one at a time."

November 17

1991 Pete Sampras rallies to defeat Jim Courier 3-6, 7-6 (5), 6-3, 6-4 in 3 hours, 10 minutes to win the year-end ATP Tour Championships in Frankfurt, Germany. Says Courier of Sampras, "When he is hot, he is hot, he can knock you off the floor. He goes for shots most of us wouldn't even think of hitting. It was his day today."

1991 Monica Seles defeats Jennifer Capriati 7-5, 6-1 to win the Virginia Slims of Philadelphia. Says Seles, "Whenever Jennifer and I play, it's great tennis. We both hit the ball as hard as we could, and I had to play well to win."

2002 World No. 1 Lleyton Hewitt battles Juan Carlos Ferrero for four hours and five sets, but successfully defends his title at the year-end ATP Masters Cup in Shanghai, China, defeating the Spaniard 7-5, 7-5, 2-6, 2-6, 6-4. The event is the biggest sporting event ever to be staged in China at the time, with 9,000 fans in attendance and global television audience of millions.

1963 Dennis Ralston of the United States wins the singles title at the New South Wales Open in Sydney, Australia, defeating Mike Sangster of Great Britain 6-8, 6-3, 6-4, 6-4 in the final and breaking an 11-year stranglehold of Australian dominance at the Australian event. It marks the first time since 1952—when American Vic Seixas wins the title—that a non-Australian wins the title.

2006 Marcelo Rios, the No. 1 ranked player on the ATP Champions Tour, has his undefeated 25-match Senior Tour winning streak for 2006 end in a 6-3, 7-6(3) loss to Dutchman Paul Haarhuis in round robin play at the Merrill Lynch Tour of Champions stop in Frankfurt. Says Haarhuis, "I'm proud of my achievement today. The player that no one could beat has finally been beaten. It's what all the players wanted—to beat Rios, and I think it makes life more interesting on the tour. The other players will now know that he is beatable and think that they can do it as well, and maybe Rios will feel a little less confident knowing that he can be beaten." Says Rios, "I don't think anyone likes to lose—it's not a good feeling."

November 18

1990 In the first five-set women's tennis match since 1901, sixteen-year-old Monica Seles defeats 20-year-old Gabriela Sabatini 6-4, 5-7, 3-6, 6-4, 6-2 in 3 hours, 47 minutes in the singles final of the Virginia Slims Championships at Madison Square Garden. "It was an unbelievable match; we both played great," says Seles, who becomes the youngest player to win the year-end women's championships. "I think women's tennis is at its best right now." The last recorded five-set match among women comes in 1901, at the U.S. Nationals, when Bessie Moore defeats Myrtle McAteer at the Philadelphia Cricket Club.

1990 Twenty-year-old Andre Agassi defeats defending champion and world No. 1 Stefan Edberg 5-7, 7-6, 7-5, 6-2 in 3 hours, 15 minutes to win the year-end ATP Tour Championships, played in Frankfurt, Germany. Says Agassi, "It's unbelievable to accomplish this at my age. It's very special. I am proud. There is no question that this is the high point of my career." The tournament is played for the first time in Germany after a 13-year stint at Madison Square Garden in New York City.

2007 Roger Federer wins the year-end Tennis Masters Cup for a fourth time, defeating surprise finalist David Ferrer of Spain 6-2, 6-3, 6-2 in Shanghai, China. The title is Federer's 53rd of his career and his eighth on the season, which for the third time, sees him win three of the four major tournaments (Australian Open, Wimbledon and the U.S. Open.) Says Federer. "It was a nice victory, especially proving it, to myself and the world, that I can do it over and over again. This is the year-end tournament that only the best can make it to...I practiced hard to get (to) this level. So when it all comes together in a final like today against Ferrer—it's fantastic."

2001 Twenty-year-old Lleyton Hewitt dominates Sebastien Grosjean 6-3, 6-3, 6-4 to win the year-end ATP Masters Cup in Sydney. Grosjean actually hits significantly more winners than Hewitt in the championship match—31 to Hewitt's 12—but also registers 47 unforced errors.

November 19

1988 Describing her post-match feeling as "disgusting," Steffi Graf ends her Grand Slam season of 1988 on a low note in a 6-3, 7-6 (5) upset loss to world No. 5 Pam Shriver in the semifinals of the year-end Virginia Slims Championships at Madison Square Garden in New York. Says Graf after the last match of her year where she sweeps all four major titles—Wimbledon, the Australian, French and U.S. Opens, "What I've achieved this year, no one can take away from me. I just wish it had a better ending." Says Shriver of her upset win, one of the biggest of her career, "Moments like this one, I treasure them. They don't come every day." Shriver is one of only two players to beat Graf during her famed year—joining Gabriela Sabatini who beats Graf in Boca Raton and Amelia Island.

2000 In the 22nd and final staging of the year-end WTA Tour Championships at Madison Square Garden, Martina Hingis beats Monica Seles 6-7 (5), 6-4, 6-4 in a 2-hour, 21-minute final, preventing Seles from winning the title for a fourth time. After being held at Madison Square Garden since 1979, the event moves to Munich, Germany starting in 2001. Hingis uses her victory platform of the "World's Most Famous Arena" to ask for more respect as the world's No. 1 player, despite Venus Williams winning at Wimbledon, the U.S. Open and the Olympics. Says Hingis, "This is like the fifth Grand Slam. I think I deserve now the respect of being No. 1."

2006 Roger Federer concludes one of the most dominating seasons in tennis history, defeating James Blake 6-0, 6-3, 6-4 in the final of the Tennis Masters Cup in Shanghai, China. Federer finishes the year with 12 titles in 16 final-round appearances in 17 total tournaments played, three major championships (Australian Open, Wimbledon and the U.S. Open) and becomes the first player to exceed $7 million in prize money in a season with a $8.34 million during the 2006 campaign. Only two players manage to beat Federer during the year—Rafael Nadal and Andy Murray. Says Blake of the undisputed world No. 1, "Obviously, we're all chasing Roger. It's no secret. He's playing head and shoulders above the rest of us." Says Federer of his epic year, "To finish it off by winning the Masters Cup, the world championship so to speak, it's the perfect ending to an incredible season. There's not much more I could have done." Federer is one match from winning the Grand Slam—losing in the final of the French Championships to Nadal. He finishes the year with a 92-5 record—winning his last 29 matches.

1995 Steffi Graf edges countrywoman Anke Huber 6-1, 2-6, 6-1, 4-6, 6-3 in 2 hours, 47 minutes in only the second five-set women's match in 94 years to win the year-end WTA Tour Championships at Madison Square Garden in New York. Says Graf, "It's an incredible end to an unbelievable year,"

1995 Boris Becker defeats Michael Chang 7-6 (3), 6-0, 7-6 (5) in the year-end ATP Tour Finals in Frankfurt, Germany. Says Becker, "This was the best crowd I've ever had in Germany."

1989 Steffi Graf, overcoming a sore left ankle, holds off Martina Navratilova in four sets 6-4, 7-5, 2-6, 6-2 to win the year-end Virginia Slims Championships at Madison Square Garden in New York. Says Graf after the match, "My feet are gone, I'm gone, I'm just happy everything is over. I was worried, but because I always had the feeling, 'I can do it, I can do it,' I just played and played. But I think I could have played a fifth set. I don't know what the result would be."

2005 World No. 1 Roger Federer blanks Gaston Gaudio of Argentina 6-0, 6-0 in the semifinals of the year-end Tennis Masters Cup in Shanghai, China—the first ever white-wash in the 35-year history of the year-end men's championships.

1999 The United States Tennis Association announces John McEnroe's resignation as U.S. Davis Cup captain after only one season at the helm. McEnroe outwardly lobbies for the job since he plays his final match for the United States in the 1992 Davis Cup final and is finally awarded the position at the 1999 U.S. Open by USTA President Judy Levering. McEnroe's frustration at instilling the same passion that he feels for the competition to top players Pete Sampras and Andre Agassi ultimately leads to his decision to step down as captain.

2000 One day before officially being crowned as the No. 1 player in the world, Marat Safin gets bloody in winning the title at the Paris Open in France, defeating Mark Philippoussis 3-6, 7-6 (7), 6-4, 3-6, 7-6 (8). Trailing 4-3 in the third set, Safin dives headfirst for a backhand return and hits himself with his racquet above his eye. Two doctors tend to Safin, who after an eight-minute interval off court for treatment, returns to the court with a butterfly bandage taped to his eyebrow.

November 20

2005 David Nalbandian of Argentina stuns world No. 1 Roger Federer 6-7 (4), 6-7 (11-13), 6-2, 6-1, 7-6 (3) in 4 hours, 33 minutes to win the year-end Tennis Masters Cup in Shanghai, China. Nalbandian's win snaps the 35-match win streak for Federer and ends his string of 24 straight victories in singles finals. Says Nalbandian to Federer in the post-match ceremony, "After knowing you a long time, don't worry, you'll win a lot more trophies. Let me keep this one." Federer finishes his 2005 season with an 81-4 record.

2004 World No. 1 Roger Federer wins a 38-point tie-break—the longest tiebreak in the history of the Tennis Masters Cup—as he defeats Marat Safin 6-3, 7-6 (20-18) in the semifinals of the event in Houston, Texas. The tiebreak is the longest in men's tennis history, equaling the mark last set at the 1993 U.S. Open, when Goran Ivanisevic and Daniel Nestor also play a 38-point tie-break in the third set.

1994 World No. 1 Pete Sampras defeats Boris Becker 4-6, 6-3, 7-5, 6-4 to win the year-end ATP Tour Championships in Frankfurt, Germany. Sampras loses to Becker in the opening round-robin match and only advances into the semifinals when Becker defeats Stefan Edberg in round-robin play two days earlier. "I want to thank you, Boris, for letting me be here," says Sampras to Becker at the awards ceremony, also promising to buy Becker "an apartment, anything you want."

1988 One day after ending the Grand Slam season of Steffi Graf, Pam Shriver is defeated by Gabriela Sabatini 7-5, 6-2, 6-2 in the final of the year-end Virginia Slims Championships in Madison Square Garden.

1994 Gabriela Sabatini ends her two-and-a-half title drought and defeats Lindsay Davenport 6-3, 6-2, 6-4 to win the year-end Virginia Slims Championships at Madison Square Garden in New York. In winning her first tournament in her last 44 attempts, Sabatini says, "It's been a long time. I've had a lot of frustration, a lot of tough matches that I lost." Her last title prior to winning in New York is the Italian Open in May of 1992.

2000 Marat Safin ascends to the No. 1 ranking in men's tennis, replacing Pete Sampras in the top spot on the ATP computer.

November 21

2004 Roger Federer wins an Open era record 13th final in a row, defeating Lleyton Hewitt 6-3, 6-2 in the final of the year-end ATP Tennis Masters Cup in Houston, Texas. The victory caps a fantastic season for the Swiss world No. 1, who also wins the Australian Open for the first time, Wimbledon for a second time and the U.S. Open for a first time. The title in Houston is his 11th for the year. "It's just an unbelievable end to a fantastic season for me," Federer says.

1992 A crowd of 18, 257 fans descend on Madison Square Garden in New York to watch the singles semifinals and the doubles final of the Virginia Slims Championships, marking the largest crowd to watch a WTA tournament match (non-Grand Slam). Monica Seles defeats Gabriela Sabatini 7-6 (6), 6-1, while Martina Navratilova defeats Lori McNeil 7-6 (5), 6-4 in the women's singles semifinals. In the women's doubles final, Arantxa Sanchez Vicario and Helena Sukova defeat Jana Novotna and Larisa Neiland 7-6 (4), 6-1.

1999 Lindsay Davenport routs world No. 1 Martina Hingis 6-4, 6-2 in the final of the year-end Chase Championships at Madison Square Garden. Davenport knocks Hingis, according to Bud Collins of the *Boston Globe*, "flatter than the world before Columbus." Says Hingis, "She didn't give me a chance." Says Davenport, "It was the best match I've played, especially when you consider the opposition."

1993 Michael Stich wins his biggest title since claiming the men's singles title at Wimbledon in 1991, slamming 27 aces in defeating Pete Sampras 7-6 (3), 2-6, 7-6 (7), 6-2 in 2 hours, 57 minutes to win the year-end ATP Tour World Championship in Frankfurt, Germany. The win over the world No. 1 places Stich to the No. 2 world ranking. Says Stich, "It's a great finish to a great year."

1993 Steff Graf outlasts Arantxa Sanchez Vicario 6-1, 6-4, 3-6, 6-1 in the final of the year-end Virginia Slims Championships in New York. The title ends another fantastic year for Graf, who wins three of the four major tournaments (French, Wimbledon and U.S .Open) and earns $2.8 million in prize money.

November 22

1992 Boris Becker celebrates his 25th birthday in style, defeating world No. 1 Jim Courier 6-4, 6-3, 7-5 to win the year-end ATP Tour World Championship in front of a decidedly pro-Becker German crowd in Frankfurt, Germany. "I am playing maybe better than I have in my whole career," says Becker, whose best major performance during the 1992 season is a quarter-final showing at Wimbledon. "To come back that quickly, I didn't expect...I had to suffer a lot this summer. Not playing the French and then not being able to do great at Wimbledon and the U.S. Open...and I felt like I still had it in me, and I wanted to bring it out."

1992 Monica Seles wins the year-end Virginia Slims Championships for a third consecutive year, defeating Martina Navratilova 7-5, 6-3, 6-1 in the final. Says Navratilova of the match, "Today is probably as well as I've ever played and I still got beaten—and beaten in straight sets, as well. At her best, Monica is as good as anybody ever was. It's amazing to me how she can hit the ball that hard and still hit the lines. Nobody hits the corners and the lines more than she does—except Jimmy Connors, and I don't have to play him all that often."

1987 Steffi Graf defeats Gabriela Sabatini 4-6, 6-4, 6-0, 6-4 to win the year-end Virginia Slims Championships at Madison Square Garden. Graf's victory completes an incredible season for the 18-year-old in which she posts a 75-2 record with her only two losses coming to Martina Navratilova in the finals of Wimbledon and the U.S. Open. "It's been quite a year," Graf says simply.

1967 Boris Becker, the Wimbledon wunderkind who was the youngest men's singles champion at age 17 in 1985, is born in Liemen, Germany. Becker wins three Wimbledon finals in his career—also in 1986 and 1989—and is the runner-up on four other occasions (1988, 1990, 1991, 1995). He also wins the U.S. Open in 1989, the Australian Open in 1991 and 1996 and an Olympic gold in men's doubles with Michael Stich in 1992.

1943 Billie Jean King, one of the most iconic figures in tennis and in women's sports and women's equality around the world, is born in Long Beach, Calif. While King wins 39 major titles—including a record 20 Wimbledon titles—she is perhaps best known for her win over Bobby Riggs in the 1973 "Battle of the Sexes" that is a catalyst for women's rights around the world.

November 23

1963 Heart-sick over the news of U.S. President John F. Kennedy's death, 21-year-old Dennis Ralston reluctantly plays the final of the South Australian Tennis Championships in Adelaide, Australia, and loses to Australian John Newcombe 6-1, 6-3, 15-17, 6-1. Ralston is urged to take the court by U.S. Ambassador to Australia William Battle, a close friend of Kennedy's who assures Ralston that the President would have wanted him to take the court and play the final. "Our entire team was distressed over the news of the President's assassination," says Robert Kelleher, the captain of the U.S. Davis Cup team. "Denny didn't know whether he should play or not."

1997 World No. 2 Jana Novotna wins the year-end Chase Championships at Madison Square Garden, defeating Mary Pierce 7-6 (4), 6-2, 6-3 in the best-of-five-set women's singles final. The title is the biggest of Novotna's career at the time—four years removed from her Wimbledon final collapse against Steffi Graf. Says Novotna of her triumph in New York, "I have come a very long way, there's no question about it. I made it three times to the finals of the Grand Slams, and I was twice close to winning, and, after winning this tournament, I have proved to myself that I am a great champion. Even if I don't win a tournament from now on, even if I don't win another match, I just proved to myself that I am the player I expected to be." Novotna breaks through seven months later and wins her first—and only—major singles title at Wimbledon.

1986 One month beyond her 30th birthday, Martina Navratilova wins the year-end Virginia Slims Championships for a fourth straight year and for a seventh time overall, defeating Steffi Graf 7-6, 6-3, 6-2 in the best-of-five-set final in front of 16,175 fans at Madison Square Garden. Says Navratilova of her age, "People have such a hang-up about 30. To me 40 is young. It's just a number. I've never been scared by numbers." Navratilova ends her 1986 season with a 86-3 won-loss record, winning 53 straight matches to end the year. She plays her last competitive match at age 49, winning the 2006 U.S. Open mixed doubles title.

1934 Lew Hoad, the man who falls one match shy of winning the Grand Slam in 1956, is born in Sydney, Australia. Hoad wins 13 major titles, including four in singles, including back-to-back Wimbledon titles in 1956 and 1957.

November 24

1996 Pete Sampras and Boris Becker play what many say is one of the greatest matches of all-time, with Sampras fending off Becker and a raucous pro-German crowd 3-6, 7-6 (5), 7-6 (4), 6-7 (11), 6-4 to win the year-end ATP Tour World Championship in Hannover, Germany. Sampras says the match is perhaps the most dramatic of his career. "This is one of the best matches I have ever been part of," says Sampras. "This is what the game is all about. It's not the money, it's not all that, it's the great matches."

1996 Steffi Graf needs five sets to defeat 16-year-old Martina Hingis 6-3, 4-6, 6-0, 4-6, 6-0 to capture the year-end Chase Championships at Madison Square Garden in New York. Graf wins despite twisting her knee in the seventh game of the fourth set. Hingis, herself, considers quitting the match after pulling her left thigh muscle in the fourth set.

1991 Seventeen-year-old Monica Seles wins the year-end Virginia Slims Championships, defeating Martina Navratilova 6-4, 3-6, 7-5, 6-0 in a rematch of the U.S. Open women's singles final. The win ends one of the most lucrative years in the history of women's tennis as Seles wins three major singles titles—the Australian Open, the French Open and the U.S. Open—as well as 10 tournament titles. She reaches the final of all 16 tournament she enters and earns $2.457 million in prize money, a record at the time.

1999 Andre Agassi defeats top rival Pete Sampras 6-2, 6-2 in round robin play at the year-end ATP Tour World Championships in Hannover, Germany. Playing only his third match after recovering from hip and back injuries, Sampras gives much of the credit to Agassi for his victory, "I was a touch rusty, but it had a lot to do with Andre," Sampras says. "It's not an excuse, he clearly outplayed me." Says Agassi, "On my best day, I couldn't beat Pete 2 and 2 if he's playing what he's capable of. I could have everything go well for me and I am not going to beat him 2 and 2."

1969 Neale Fraser, the retired Australian tennis standout and current insurance salesman, is named captain of the Australian Davis Cup team. The 36-year-old Fraser replaces Australia's legendary Harry Hopman, who steers the Australian Davis Cup team for 22 years—and 16 titles—since 1939. Fraser goes on to captain the Aussie Davis Cuppers for one more year than Hopman—a record 23 years—and guides Australia to four titles.

November 25

1999 Andre Agassi defeats Gustavo Kuerten 6-4, 7-5 to advance into the semifinals of the ATP Tour World Championships. Following the victory, Agassi is officially awarded the ATP Tour trophy for finishing the year as the No. 1 player. "It symbolizes a lot for me professionally and personally," Agassi says after receiving the glass trophy which depicts an athlete holding up his index finger in a No. 1 sign. "It's a big accomplishment for me."

1981 First-year U.S. Davis Cup Captain Arthur Ashe announces that John McEnroe, Roscoe Tanner, Eliot Teltscher and Peter Fleming will represent the United States against Argentina in the Davis Cup Final starting December 11 in Cincinnati, Ohio. Absent from his team announcement is Jimmy Connors, who Ashe worked tirelessly to return to the Davis Cup fold after an absence of five years earlier in the year. Says Ashe to the *New York Times,* "I'm quite disappointed. We are all disappointed. Even John's disappointed. We will win without Jimmy, but it will make it a tiny bit more difficult." Says Connors by phone to the *New York Times* from his home in Miami, "I never have any time for my family, to be alone without any demands. Everyone wants me to do something here or there. The final just happens to be at a bad time of the year. It doesn't seem like there is ever a letup in tennis." The U.S. encounters more difficultly than Ashe or anyone would anticipate in the final, with the U.S. claiming a 3-1 win over Argentina with McEnroe and Fleming winning an 11-9-in-the-fifth-set doubles match over Guillermo Vilas and Jose-Luis Clerc and McEnroe beating Clerc in a five-set match-clinching epic.

1982 In extreme heat and wind conditions at the New South Wales Open in Sydney, Australia, Leslie Allen of the United States defeats Hana Mandlikova of Czechoslovakia 6-7, 7-6, 6-3 to reach the quarterfinals of the event and win her third straight match against her Czech opponent. Reports the Associated Press of the weather conditions of the match, "Temperatures reached 115 degrees and winds gusted to more than 50 miles per hour, sometimes creating a haze from brushfires than ringed the city."

November 26

1982 John McEnroe comes back from two-sets-to-one down to beat Yannick Noah 12-10, 1-6, 3-6, 6-2, 6-3 in 4 hours, 21 minutes in the opening match of the United States-France Davis Cup Final on indoor clay at the Palais des Sports in Grenoble, France. Gene Mayer, McEnroe's teammate and a fellow New Yorker, gives the United States the 2-0 lead beating Henri Leconte 6-2, 6-2, 7-9, 6-4.

1998 Pete Sampras clinches the year-end No. 1 ATP Tour world ranking for a sixth straight year, breaking the record he shares with Jimmy Connors, who finishes five straight years as the No. 1 player from 1974-1978. Sampras clinches the No. 1 ranking when his challenger, world No. 2 Marcelo Rios of Chile, withdraws with a back injury from round robin play at the ATP Tour World Championships in Hannover, Germany and Sampras finishes with a perfect 3-0 record with a 6-2, 6-1 win over Karol Kucera of Slovakia. Says Sampras, "It's an ultimate achievement. It will probably never be broken. I'm trying to stay humble through all this, but the record speaks for itself. It's a little overwhelming."

1972 Arthur Ashe beats Bob Lutz 6-2, 3-6, 6-3, 3-6, 7-6 (2) in 2 hours, 25 minutes to win the year-end WCT Championships in Rome, Italy and the first prize paycheck of $25,000. Bernard Kirsch of the *New York Times* writes that with the win, Ashe "helped re-establish a reputation that he said he had prematurely built." Says Ashe to the *New York Times* after the victory, "In 1968, all I really did was reach the semis at Wimbledon and win at Forest Hills. I established my reputation on those two tournaments. It's what you've done in the long run (that counts)."

1999 World No. 5 Pete Sampras defeats Nicolas Lapentti 7-6 (2) 7-6 (5) to clinch a place in the semifinals of the ATP Tour World Championships in Hannover, Germany for a ninth straight year.

November 27

1973 Arthur Ashe becomes the first black player to win a title in the apartheid nation of South Africa, winning the doubles title at the South African Open with Tom Okker, defeating Lew Hoad and Bob Maud 6-2, 4-6, 6-2, 6-4 in the final. After initially being denied a visa based on his anti-apartheid views, Ashe is permitted to play in the event by the South African government. Ashe requests to tournament officials that the bleacher seating not be segregated during the tournament, but his wishes are not granted. Says Ashe to local reporters, "You can't integrate the place in one full sweep. It is important to recognize the progress that has been made." Ashe loses the singles final the day before to Jimmy Connors 6-4, 7-6 (3), 6-3. Chris Evert wins the women's singles title, defeating Evonne Goolagong 6-3, 6-3.

1982 John McEnroe clinches his fourth career Davis Cup title for the United States as he and Peter Fleming defeat Yannick Noah and Henri Leconte 6-3, 6-4, 9-7 to give the U.S. an insurmountable 3-0 lead over France in the Davis Cup final in Grenoble, France. McEnroe is also on victorious U.S. teams in 1978, 1979 and 1981—winning the clinching singles point in the fourth rubber in 1978 against Britain and in 1981 against Argentina. Says McEnroe of his title-winning performances, "Each one is different and each one's nice in its own way. This was one of the best, if not the best, because we beat their team in front of a large crowd and played well, and I played on my worst surface and won the matches. Argentina, when we beat them last year in Cincinnati, was probably the most exciting final I was involved in. This and Argentina were definitely the two biggest."

1999 Andre Agassi and Pete Sampras each win semifinal matches to set up a dream final at the ATP Tour World Championships in Hannover, Germany. World No. 1 Agassi defeats world No. 2 Yevgeny Kafelnikov 6-4, 7-6 (7-5) for his 600th career match victory and Sampras defeats Nicolas Kiefer 6-3, 6-3. Says Agassi, "It's not good for me just to get to the final. I want to be the best. I'm inspired by what I accomplished this year. And I always look forward to playing Pete." Says Sampras, "It is going to be two heavyweights going at it. This is a fitting way to end the decade."

November 28

1999 Pete Sampras wins the year-end ATP Tour Championships for a fifth time, defeating world No. 1 Andre Agassi 6-1, 7-5, 6-4 in the championship match in Hannover, Germany. Agassi had defeated Sampras 6-2, 6-2 in round-robin play earlier in the tournament. Writes British journalist Stephen Bierley, "It was perhaps fitting, given that this was the last major singles tournament of the millennium, that the best player of modern times won it so emphatically."

1998 One day after clinching the year-end No. 1 ranking for a record sixth consecutive year, Pete Sampras is un-gloriously dumped in the semifinals of the ATP Tour World Championships by Alex Corretja of Spain, who defeats the world No. 1 4-6, 6-3, 7-6 (3) after saving three match points. Fellow Spaniard Carlos Moya also advances into the championship match, defeating Tim Henman of Great Britain 6-4, 3-6, 7-5. Says Sampras, who hits 50 unforced errors in the loss. "It's a tough way to end it. I had mixed emotions, coming so close to winning, being in the final. But the achievement of doing it six years in a row, and the fans giving me a nice ovation, it was a very good feeling. But it wasn't the way I wanted to end the year."

1997 Pete Sampras suffers one of the most unfortunate injuries in Davis Cup history as he tears a left calf muscle and is forced to retire in the third set, trailing Magnus Larsson 3-6, 7-6, 2-1, giving Sweden a surprising 2-0 lead over the United States after the first day of play in the Davis Cup Final in Goteborg, Sweden. Jonas Bjorkman opens the series with a 7-5, 1-6, 6-3, 6-3 win over Michael Chang to put the Swedes up 1-0. The United States goes on to suffer one of its most disappointing losses in Davis Cup history as it is blanked 5-0 in the series, despite having the world's No. 1 (Sampras) and No. 3 (Chang) players as well as Jonathan Stark, fresh off of winning the year-end ATP doubles championship, and Todd Martin. Stark and Martin are defeated by Bjorkman and Nicklas Kulti 6-4, 6-4, 6-4 the following day, clinching victory for Sweden with a 3-0 lead. Sampras, so upset at his condition and the entire Davis Cup scenario and schedule, does not return to the U.S. team for nearly two years. Says Sampras the day after his match with Larsson, "The schedule for Davis Cup is horrendous. To play after the Lipton (in April) and to play in late November, it's too much. Sure it would be great to get every top American to play every tie but I don't see that happening. It's a big commitment. It's too much tennis."

November 29

1991 Pete Sampras makes an inauspicious Davis Cup debut, losing to Henri Leconte 6-4, 7-5, 6-4 in the Davis Cup Final in Lyon, France. The 28-year-old Leconte, the former top 10 player ranked No. 159 in the world and recovering from back surgery that threatened his career, plays perhaps the most inspirational tennis match of his career. Says Leconte, "It's the greatest day of my life, the win of my career. I've proved I'm still around." Says French captain Yannick Noah "He played like I dreamed he would." Says Sampras, ranked No. 6 in the world of his baptismal Davis Cup appearance, "It's certainly a different experience." Andre Agassi's earlier 6-7, 6-2, 6-1, 6-2 victory over Guy Forget makes the score 1-1 after the first day of play.

1985 John McEnroe rips the Australian Open and the grass court at the Kooyong Tennis Club calling it "without a doubt the worst grass court" in his second-round 6-4, 6-3, 3-6, 6-3 victory over Danie Visser of South Africa. Says McEnroe, "The court is simply not good enough to play a Grand Slam tournament on."

1998 Alex Corretja rallies from a two-sets-to-love deficit to win the biggest title of his career, defeating fellow Spaniard Carlos Moya 3-6, 3-6, 7-5, 6-3, 7-5 in four hours to win the year-end ATP Tour World Championship in Hannover, Germany. Corretja, who lost to Moya in the French Open final earlier in the year, says he used Ivan Lendl's two-set-to-love comeback win over John McEnroe in the 1984 French Open final as inspiration for his comeback. Says Corretja, "At that time Lendl was my idol. Today I was thinking, 'Come on, try to do like your idol' ... try to find some energy from somewhere and try to think about your tennis and try to push him to see if he is going to be able to finish in straight sets. Even when I was two sets down, I was still thinking that I could win this match. That's why I think I won." Says Moya, "Two sets up, maybe I relaxed a bit. I thought the match was not over. It's never over when you play against Alex. But I had a really big advantage. I had many chances to beat him, but they went and he started to play better. It's a big disappointment."

1980 Eighteen-year-old Hana Mandlikova of Czechoslovakia advances to the final of the Australian Open, defeating unseeded Mima Jausovec of Yugoslavia 6-4, 6-1. Wendy Turnbull of Australia upsets No. 1 seed Martina Navratilova 6-4, 7-5 in the other women's semifinal.

November 30

1973 Rod Laver and John Newcombe each win five-set struggles to give Australia a commanding 2-0 lead over the United States, the five-time defending Davis Cup champions, in the Davis Cup Final in Cleveland, Ohio. Twenty-nine-year-old Newcombe beats 26-year-old Stan Smith 6-1, 3-6, 6-3, 3-6, 6-4 in the opening rubber, while 35-year-old Laver defeats 27-year-old Tom Gorman 8-10, 8-6, 6-8, 6-3, 6-1. The loss is Smith's first-ever defeat in five previous Davis Cup Final appearances and only his second singles loss in 17 previous Davis Cup singles matches in all. Says Smith, "I played tougher matches under tougher conditions, but it's the best I've seen Newk play." Newcombe, the reigning U.S. Open champion, calls the win, "the toughest five-set match I have won in the last five years." Laver, playing in his second Davis Cup series in his return to the competition for the first time since 1962, needs 3 hours, 22 minutes to outlast Gorman.

1990 Andre Agassi wins a dramatic five-set match over Richard Fromberg, while Michael Chang is steady in a straight-set dismissal of Darren Cahill as the United States takes a 2-0 lead over Australia in the Davis Cup Final at the Florida Suncoast Dome in St. Petersburg, Fla. Agassi, the world No. 4 and a French Open finalist earlier in the year, struggles on the indoor red clay court against Fromberg, playing in his first career Davis Cup match, but barrels through to win 4-6, 6-2, 4-6, 6-2, 6-4. Chang, the 1989 French Open champion, has little difficultly with Cahill, a serve and volleyer, winning 6-2, 7-6 (4), 6-0.

2003 Mark Philippoussis wins the most heroic match of his career as he clinches Australia's 28th Davis Cup title, defeating Juan Carlos Ferrero 7-5, 6-3, 1-6, 2-6, 6-0 to give Australia the 3-1 victory over Spain on a grass court at the Rod Laver Arena in Melbourne. Philippoussis, playing in his hometown, fights through a torn pectoral muscle that inflicts him with sharp pain with every serve and groundstroke he hits. Spurred on by a screaming crowd of 14,000 supporters, Philippoussis, the losing finalist to Roger Federer earlier in the year at Wimbledon, plays the match as if his life were on the line. "The crowd was incredible," says Philippoussis after the match. "This is what Davis Cup is all about. There is no way I could have got through without them. It gets you up and numbs the pain because they are so loud." Eleanor Preston writes in *The Guardian* that Philippoussis "veered between triumph and disaster before fighting back nerves, fatigue and pain."

December 1

1995 In one of the most dramatic moments of his career, Pete Sampras collapses in cramps on match point as he outlasts Andrei Chesnokov 3-6, 6-4, 6-3, 6-7 (5), 6-4 to give the United States a 1-0 lead over Russia in the Davis Cup Final in Moscow, Russia. Struggling with cramps in both hamstrings in the latter stages of the fifth set, the top-ranked Sampras guts out a 25-stroke rally on the final point of the match to dramatically fend off the pesky No. 91-ranked Chesnokov in 3 hours, 38 minutes. Writes Lee Hockstader of the *Washington Post*, "Pete Sampras didn't walk off the court after his grueling five-set victory against Russia's Andrei Chesnokov. He didn't limp off the court. He didn't even manage to crawl off the court. He was dragged from it—his cramped legs limp beneath him—by two U.S. Davis Cup teammates seconds after a heart-stopping, hair-raising, 25-stroke match point that left the Russian crowd in an uproar and Sampras flat on his back in pain. You might say he was lucky to get out alive." Says U.S. Davis Cup Captain Tom Gullikson of Sampras and overcoming his cramping in the fifth set, "Pete has that low-key approach—and I think that helps him, because in tight spots a lot of people show their competitiveness more and get fired up. But then their muscles get so tight they can't swing at the ball. One of Pete's real strengths is that he hits out in the big moments." Yevgeny Kafelnikov defeats Jim Courier 7-6 (1), 7-5, 6-3 to even the score at 1-1 after the first day of play.

1991 France wins the Davis Cup for the first time in 59 years—since the last of six titles by the famed Four Musketeers in 1932—as Guy Forget upsets Davis Cup rookie Pete Sampras 7-6 (6), 3-6, 6-3, 6-4 to clinch France's 3-1 triumph over the United States in the Davis Cup Final in Lyon, France. The win causes an uproarious celebration as the crowd sings the French national anthem, *The Marseilles*, dance and applaud, while Forget, teammate Henri Leconte and French captain Yannick Noah run around the court with the French Flag. Noah then leads his team and support staff in a conga-line around the court. Says Forget of the glory of winning the Davis Cup, "I don't think the Americans realize how much the Davis Cup means to the French team and the public. We have World Cup soccer, the Tour de France and the Davis Cup. In America, they have 10 different things more important than the Davis Cup." Sampras, playing in his first Davis Cup series, also loses on the opening day of the best-of-five-match series to Henri Leconte. Says the world No. 6 of the loss, "It's very disappointing. I feel like I've let down my team...so life goes on, really."

1996 France wins the Davis Cup title for an eighth time in the wildest final day in Davis Cup history as the final two singles matches last a total of 9 hours, 12 minutes in Malmo, Sweden. With France leading 2-1 entering the third and final day of the best-of-five-match series, Cedric Pioline of France nearly clinches victory in the fourth rubber, leading No. 9-ranked Thomas Enqvist of Sweden two-sets to love and 5-2 in the final set, only to lose 3-6, 6-7 (8), 6-4, 6-4, 9-7 in 4 hours, 25 minutes. Arnaud Boetsch of France, ranked No. 31, then wins the closest Cup-deciding match in the event's history, beating No. 64-ranked Nicklas Kulti, 7-6 (2), 2-6, 4-6, 7-6 (5), 10-8. Boetsch saves triple-Cup point, down at 6-7, 0-40 in the fifth set, but wins the epic in 4 hours, 47 minutes.

2007 The United States ends its longest title drought in Davis Cup history, winning its first title in 12 years as identical twins Bob and Mike Bryan defeat Nikolay Davydenko and Igor Andreev 7-6 (4), 6-4, 6-2 giving the United States a clinching 3-0 lead over Russia in the Davis Cup Final in Portland, Ore. "No words can explain how we feel right now, except Wooooooooo!" Mike Bryan says to the crowd following the victory, the record 32nd title for the United States. The Bryans victory comes a day after their teammates Andy Roddick and James Blake put the United States up 2-0 on the first day of play. Roddick, the No. 6 player in the world, defeats Dmitry Tursunov 6-4, 6-4, 6-2 in the opening match and No. 13-ranked Blake beats Mikhail Youzhny 6-3, 7-6 (4), 6-7 (3), 7-6 (3). Says U.S. Davis Cup Captain Patrick McEnroe after the Bryans clinching victory, "It's been a long road; I couldn't be happier for those guys, because they've been through it all together."

1990 In front of a crowd of 18,156 fans at the Florida Suncoast Dome—the most to watch a Davis Cup match in the United States—Rick Leach and Jim Pugh clinch the 29th Davis Cup title for the United States as they defeat Australia's Pat Cash and John Fitzgerald 6-4, 6-2, 3-6, 7-6 (2) in 3 hours, 6 minutes in the Davis Cup Final in St. Petersburg, Fla. The title is the first for the United States in eight years when John McEnroe leads the U.S. to victory over France in the 1982 final in Grenoble, France.

1973 Rod Laver and John Newcombe defeat Stan Smith and Erik van Dillen 6-1, 6-2, 6-4 giving Australia a match-clinching 3-0 lead over the United States in the Davis Cup Final in Cleveland, Ohio. The win ends the five-year reign of the United States as Davis Cup champions and earns Australia its 23rd Davis Cup title. Laver and Newcombe's win takes only 66 minutes and is the worst doubles loss ever inflicted upon a U.S. Davis Cup team.

Newcombe and Laver never face a break point, serve nine love games and lose only one point on serve in the third set. Says Laver, "I think it's the best I've played in doubles."

1985 Nduka Odizor of Nigeria aces John McEnroe in embarrassing fashion—hitting an underhand drop-shot serve—up 40-love in the sixth game of the second set—but loses to the three-time Wimbledon champion 4-6, 6-2, 6-4, 6-2 in the third round of the Australian Open on the grass courts of the Kooyong Tennis Club in Melbourne.

1997 Playing his second consecutive "minor league" Challenger Series event, Andre Agassi defeats Sargis Sargsian 6-2, 6-1 to win the HealthSouth USTA Challenger in Burbank, Calif. Says Agassi, "No question, I definitely put my game in a place where every day I was getting better." The former world No. 1 enters the event with a No. 122 world ranking, after being ranked No. 141 two weeks earlier when competing at the Las Vegas Challenger. "Every match feels important to me now, every single one," says Agassi. "But I must say it feels better to win a tournament than just another match....It's just a great way to get started. I took a couple years sabbatical, but there's no reason to believe I can't train hard and come back. I'm excited to be challenged by the game." Agassi eventually returns to the No. 1 ranking in 1999.

1984 Chris Evert Lloyd wins her 1,000th career pro tennis match, defeating Pascale Paradis of France 6-1, 6-7 (5), 6-2 in the round of 16 at the Australian Open in Melbourne. Says the 29-year-old Evert Lloyd, "It's pretty interesting, I feel like I've played that many on some days, and other days it feels like I haven't been around that long."

December 2

2001 Nicolas Escude, ranked No. 27 in the world, clinches victory for France in the Davis Cup Final, defeating No. 64th-ranked Wayne Arthurs 7-6(3), 6-7 (5), 6-3, 6-3 in the fifth and decisive match in France's 3-2 victory over Australia at Rod Laver Arena in Melbourne. Arthurs is a last minute substitute for Patrick Rafter, who is replaced due to tendonitis in his right arm. Says Escude, 'This might take a while to sink in. To win twice here is unbelievable, to win the Cup even better. Earlier Sunday, Lleyton Hewitt sends the final to the fifth match with a 6-3, 6-2, 6-3 win over Sebastien Grosjean. France leads the series 2-1 entering the final day of play as Cedric Pioline and Fabrice Santoro pair to defeat Rafter and Hewitt 2-6, 6-3, 7-6 (5), 6-1.

1995 One day after collapsing in cramps after defeating Andrei Chesnokov in five sets, Pete Sampras teams with Todd Martin to give the United States an important 2-1 over Russia in the Davis Cup Final in Moscow. Sampras and Martin defeat Yevgeny Kafelnikov and Andrei Olhovskiy 7-5, 6-4, 6-3 in a match that proves pivotal in the United States claiming its 31st Davis Cup title.

1973 Rod Laver and John Newcombe complete a 5-0 shut out of the United States in the Davis Cup Final in Cleveland, Ohio as Newcombe defeats Tom Gorman 6-2, 6-1, 6-3 and Laver defeats Stan Smith 6-3, 6-4, 3-6, 6-2. With the victory, captain Neale Fraser's team goes down in Davis Cup history as one of the greatest of all time. The four team members—Newcombe, Laver, Ken Rosewall and Mal Anderson—combine for a total of 25 major singles titles on their resumes

1989 Stefan Edberg and Boris Becker register semifinal victories at the year-end Nabisco Masters Championships at Madison Square Garden in New York. Becker defeats John McEnroe 6-4, 6-4, while Edberg defeats world No. 1 Ivan Lendl 7-6 (5), 7-5. Becker finishes off his win over McEnroe with a backhand crosscourt passing shot that he says was probably the hardest backhand he had ever hit in his life. Says Becker, "I think if John had been there in the middle, there would have been a hole in his body."

1973 Monica Seles, the youngest woman to win the French Open at age 16 and a winner of nine major singles titles, is born in Novi Sad, Yugoslavia.

December 3

1995 Pete Sampras concludes one of the finest performances of his career, dominating Russia's Yevgeny Kafelnikov 6-2, 6-4, 7-6 (4) on a clay court—his worst surface—to almost single-handedly win the 31st Davis Cup title for the United States against Russia in Moscow. Sampras, the world No. 1 and the reigning Wimbledon and U.S. Open champion, accounts for all three points in the 3-2 U.S. victory, dramatically recovering from being dragged off the court in cramps following his 3-6, 6-4, 6-3, 6-7 (5), 6-4 win over Andrei Chesnokov in the opening match of the series. The day after his epic first day heroics, Sampras returns to the court and, with Todd Martin, dominates Kafelnikov and Andrei Olhovskiy in a straight-sets doubles victory, before beating Kafelnikov to give the U.S. the match-clinching 3-1 lead. "I've never seen better clay court tennis," U.S. captain Tom Gullikson says of the performance of Sampras. "The combination of power and patience and precision serving. It was flawless tennis....The great players have a sense of history. When the great players go down in the history books, not only will they be remembered by Grand Slam singles titles but how many times did they help their country win the Davis Cup."

1989 After a 13-year stint at New York's Madison Square Garden, the year-end Nabisco Masters stages its final match at the world's most famous arena as Stefan Edberg defeats Boris Becker 4-6, 7-6, 6-3, 6-1 to win the year-end championship in men's tennis. The Masters, which is first held at Madison Square Garden in 1977, is moved to Frankfurt, Germany starting in 1990. Edberg enters the match having lost major singles finals to Michael Chang at the French Open and to Becker at Wimbledon and holding a 1-6 career record against Becker. Says Edberg, "I've been waiting for this one. It is something I really needed. I'm going to start believing in myself, and that's something I needed to do because I know I've got the game and the talent to challenge for the No. 1 spot."

2000 Gustavo Kuerten defeats Andre Agassi 6-4, 6-4, 6-4 to win the year-end ATP Tour Tennis Masters Cup in Lisbon, Portugal and clinch the No. 1 ranking in the world. Kuerten, from Brazil, becomes the first South American to finish the year as the No. 1 ranked man. Says Kuerten, "It's been a great week, the last tournament, the last match. I had to give everything." Kuerten enters the tournament trailing U.S. Open champion Marat Safin by 75 points in the rankings and has to win the season-ending event to finish with the No. 1 ranking.

December 4

1977 Australia wins the Davis Cup for the 24th time as John Alexander defeats Adriano Panatta 6-4, 4-6, 2-6, 8-6, 11-9 in 3 hours, 54 minutes to clinch the 3-1 victory for the Australians in Sydney, Australia. Neale Fraser, the Australian team captain, describes the match "one of the greatest of all time," while Italian captain Nicola Pietrangeli labels it "one of the greatest I have ever seen." Panatta serves for the match at 6-5 in the fourth set and comes within three points of winning the match.

1985 Slobodon Zivojinovic of Yugoslavia defeats No. 2-seeded John McEnroe 2-6, 6-3, 1-6, 6-4, 6-0 in the quarterfinals of the Australian Open—ending McEnroe's season without a major singles title for the first time since 1978 and preventing him from overtaking Ivan Lendl as the world's No. 1 player. Zivojinovic, affectionally known as "Bobo," gains the crowd support of the Australian fans when in the fourth set, while McEnroe waits for tournament referee Peter Bellenger to come to court in a dispute, he sits in a courtside box and eats a sandwich. Says Zivojinovic of McEnroe, "You know how McEnroe is. Every match he tries to do the same things. I just sat down." In the fifth game of the final set, the Associated Press reports that McEnroe says to Zivojinovic "You are going to pay for this. I mean it." The two also play an epic third round match at the U.S. Open in 1987, McEnroe being fined $17,500 for his foul language and eventually suspended two months after his 6-4, 5-7, 6-7, 6-4, 6-3 win. Two days before his quarterfinal loss in Melbourne, McEnroe stages an incredible comeback over Henri Leconte, coming back from two sets to one and 1-5 in the fourth-set tiebreaker but rallies for a 5-7, 7-6, 3-6, 7-6, 6-1 win, winning six straight points in the fourth-set tie-breaker.

1992 With the sound of Swiss cowbells reverberating throughout the Tarrant County Convention Center in Ft. Worth, Texas, play opens up in the first Davis Cup Final on American soil in 11 years as the United States and Switzerland split the opening day singles matches. Wimbledon champion Andre Agassi puts the United States up 1-0, crushing Jakob Hlasek 6-1, 6-2, 6-2 in the opening match of the series, while Olympic champion Marc Rosset upsets world No. 1 and Australian and French Open champion Jim Courier 6-3, 6-7, 3-6, 6-4, 6-4 in 4 hours, 23 minutes to even the series at 1-1.

December 5

1988 A backhand let-cord winner after a 37-ball rally is all that separates Boris Becker from Ivan Lendl in an epic final at the Nabisco Masters in front of 17,792 fans at Madison Square Garden in New York. In arguably, one of the greatest matches in the sport, Becker defeats the world No. 1 5-7, 7-6, 3-6, 6-2, 7-6 (5) in 4 hours, 42 minutes, with Becker clinching victory when his backhand crawls over the top of the net to conclude the fifth-set tiebreak. Says Lendl of the let-cord winner to lose the match, "What can you do? It's just heartbreaking, but there's nothing you can do about it." Says Becker, "At the end, I was just playing. I didn't even know the score. This tournament has a lot to do with prestige and pride. Beating Ivan in the final gives me even more satisfaction. I am playing the very best tennis of my life."

1982 Calling it "the missing link in my career," Chris Evert Lloyd wins the Australian Open for the first time in her career, defeating Martina Navratilova 6-3, 2-6, 6-3 in the women's singles final. "I've wanted this tournament badly," says Evert Lloyd. "I'm not thinking about retiring, but if I hadn't won, in 10 years time, I would have looked back and thought that something is lacking."

1992 John McEnroe plays what ends up to be his final Davis Cup match as he and Pete Sampras defeat Jakob Hlasek and Marc Rosset 6-7 (5), 6-7 (7), 7-5, 6-1, 6-2 in 4 hours, 18 minutes to give the United States an important 2-1 lead over Switzerland in the Davis Cup Final in Ft. Worth, Texas. The match is highlighted by the fiery tenacity of McEnroe, whose fist-pumps—and volleying and return of serve prowess—leads the U.S. comeback. After McEnroe's forehand return of serve to Rosset's feet gives the U.S. the third set, the four-time U.S. Open champion has an adrenaline-induced "win one for the Gipper" tirades in the U.S. locker room during the then traditional Davis Cup match-break between the third and fourth sets. Says Sampras of McEnroe's locker room antics, "Mac was just ranting and raving. He was getting pumped up. `Let's kick some....' It was on that level." Says Hlasek of his team's fourth and fifth set fade away, "I think we ran out of steam."

December 6

1992 Jim Courier, the No. 1 player in the world, clinches the 30th Davis Cup title for the United States defeating Jakob Hlasek 6-3, 3-6, 6-3, 6-4 to give the United States a 3-1 victory over Switzerland in the Davis Cup Final in Ft. Worth, Texas. Says Courier following the title-clinching win, "There is certainly nothing like winning for a team. It's not something we get to do too often as tennis players. Hopefully we'll win this thing for the next eight or nine years." Adds U.S. Davis Cup Captain Tom Gorman of his team's performance, "They felt very proud to be in the final and they were going to make sure they did themselves proud. They had their entire country behind them." Following his victory Courier is carried off the court by his teammates John McEnroe, Pete Sampras, Andre Agassi and team support staff. All four players then take victory laps around the court waving the American flag.

1984 Helena Sukova snaps Martina Navratilova's 74-match winning streak in the semifinals of the Australian Open, defeating Navratilova 1-6, 6-3, 7-5 and ending her dream of completing a Grand Slam. Says Navratilova, "It hurts, but I will get over it. If I had won, I would have done it all. If I lost, I would have to start from scratch. Both are hard to cope with." Navratilova, the winner of the previous six major singles titles, was aiming to become only the third woman to win a calendar year Grand Slam, joining American Maureen Connolly, who accomplished the feat in 1953, and Margaret Court, who completed the feat in 1970. The surprising win for the 19-year-old Sukova, the daughter of 1962 Wimbledon finalist Vera Sukova, moves her into her first major singles final. In the other women's semifinal, Chris Evert Lloyd runs her head-to-head record to 19-1 over Wendy Turnbull, defeating the Australian 6-3, 6-3. Says Evert, "Wendy kept coming and applying pressure. I think she played a smart game, but I was pleased with the way I hit out. The lob is one of my best shots and I went out there feeling it would be a very effective shot against Wendy, who is short."

1957 Gardnar Mulloy becomes the oldest American to win a Davis Cup match at the age of 44 years and 14 days when he and Vic Seixas defeat Felicissimo Ampon and Raymudo Deyro 6-1, 6-3, 6-2 to give the U.S. a match-clinching 3-0 lead over the Philippines in the Davis Cup Inter-Zone First Round at Memorial Drive in Adelaide, Australia.

December 7

1985 Martina Navratilova defeats Chris Evert Lloyd 6-2, 4-6, 6-2 to win the Australian Open in Melbourne for her 17th victory over Evert Lloyd in the last 19 matches and her third career Australian singles title. "That was tough on the nerves," says the 29-year-old Navratilova after the match. "It seems Chris and I always play great matches. Even though I lost the second set, I felt in control. I knew this was it. I knew it was for the No. 1 ranking. I was going to go after it, and I did." Navratilova previously wins in Australia in 1981 and 1983. Says Evert, the defending champion, "After the second set, there was a lot of pressure on both of us, and she handled it better." In men's singles, Mats Wilander advances into the final, finishing up a 7-5, 6-1, 6-3 rain-delayed victory over unseeded Slobodan Zivojinovic of Yugoslavia. The other men's singles semifinal between Ivan Lendl and Stefan Edberg is suspended due to rain after only 10 minutes of play, Edberg leading 2-1.

1987 Ivan Lendl defeats Mats Wilander 6-2, 6-2, 6-3 to win the year-end Nabisco Masters Championship for a fifth time. Says Lendl, "Today may have been the best I hit the ball and moved. I think I still can get better, though. I can work on new shots and my physical strength and conditioning." Wilander implements a more aggressive strategy against Lendl, coming to net more often and using his one-handed chip backhand in an attempt to close the gap between he and Lendl. Earlier in the week, Wilander says that his goal is to become the No. 1 player in the world. Says Wilander, "I tried to come in on his backhand, but that didn't work. After a while, you don't know what to do. A couple of times I was thinking, 'He's just too good for me.'" Says Lendl of his goals and how he can he can improve his game, "There are millions of ways I could improve. There are new shots, new ways to hit the shots, ways to become more flexible, stronger....There are still so many things I want to do. Everyone in tennis would like to win a Grand Slam...I paid my dues on and off the court and now I'm enjoying the fruits of it."

1980 December 7 becomes a day of infamy for Pam Shriver as the American blows seven match points in losing to Wendy Turnbull of Australia 3-6, 6-4, 7-6 (6) in the final of the New South Wales Open in Sydney. Turnbull trails 6-2 in the final-set tie-break against the 18-year-old Shriver.

December 8

1978 Play begins at the Davis Cup Final between the United States and Great Britain at the Mission Hills Country Club in Rancho Mirage, Calif., as 19-year-old John McEnroe, playing his first Davis Cup singles match, has little trouble with John Lloyd in a 6-1, 6-2, 6-2 win in the opening match of the series. The day's drama, however, occurs in the second match as McEnroe's teammate Brian Gottfried lets a two-sets-to-love lead and a match point disappear in dramatic turn of events against Buster Mottram. Gottfried leads Mottram 6-4, 6-2, 7-6 (the tie-breaker is still 11 years away from being played in Davis Cup), and holds a match point with Mottram serving at 30-40. Gottfried decides to attempt to lob over the net-rushing Mottram, but the Brit puts away the ball away with an overhead. Mottram then squeaks out the third set 10-8 and takes advantage of the momentum turn and wins the final two sets 6-4, 6-3 to win the match in 4 hours, 49 minutes and square the series at 1-1. Writes Neil Amdur of the *New York Times*, "As the sun dipped behind the San Jacinto Mountains in the mid-afternoon and the desert temperature dropped from 59 degrees to 37, the drama on the court seemed more like a change in the seasons. By the time Gottfried lost his serve on the second match point at 5:54 p.m. local time, only about 500 spectators remained from the crowd of 3,553 that had watched 19-year-old McEnroe complete an impressive Davis Cup singles debut in 1 hour 40 minutes."

1984 Chris Evert Lloyd defeats Helena Sukova 6-7, 6-1, 6-3 to win the Australian Open women's singles title. Evert Lloyd's title is her 16th major singles title, her second Australian title and continues her streak of winning at least one major title every year since 1973. Says the 19-year-old Sukova, playing in her first major singles final, "Chrissie just started to pass me so much better. She just hit so many passing shots down the line or just a couple of inches away from the line."

1985 Stefan Edberg upsets No. 1 seed Ivan Lendl 6-7, 7-5, 6-1, 4-6, 9-7 in the semifinals of the Australian Open in Melbourne, advancing the 19-year-old Swede into his first major final. Following the loss, Lendl rips the Australian Open for its lack-luster status, continuing the trend of tournament criticism all week due mainly to the rough conditions of the grass courts at the Kooyong Tennis Club. "I don't call this a major championship," says Lendl. "I put it in the second class." The match is resumed after rain interrupts play the previous day with Edberg leading 2-1.

December 9

1985 Nineteen-year-old Stefan Edberg wins a major singles title for the first time in his career, defeating fellow Swede Mats Wilander 6-4, 6-3, 6-3, preventing Wilander from winning a third-straight Australian title. Says Wilander on the rain-delayed Monday final, "If there's somebody I don't mind very much losing to, its Stefan. He's a very good friend." Wilander and Edberg are so chummy in preparation before the final that they share beers the night before their match and even practice with each other the morning of the final. Says Ederg following the match, "I have never been so happy. This is a wonderful day for me and for Sweden. I am very glad to be able to win for my mother and father."

1984 Mats Wilander wins the Australian Open men's singles title for the second year in a row, defeating Kevin Curren of South Africa 6-7 (5), 6-4, 7-6 (3), 6-2 in 2 hours, 52 minutes in the singles final. The title is the 20-year-old Wilander's third major title to go with this 1982 French title and his 1983 Australian title.

1960 Butch Buchholz defeats Orlando Sirola 6-8, 7-5, 11-9, 6-2 to give the United States a 1-0 lead over Italy in the Davis Cup Inter-Zone Final in Perth, Australia. The second singles match between Barry MacKay and Nicola Pietrangeli is suspended due to darkness with Pietrangeli leading 6-8, 6-3, 10-8, 5-5. MacKay saves five match points in the 10th game of the fourth set before tying the score at 5-5, just before play is suspended for the day.

1983 Mats Wilander upsets John McEnroe 4-6, 6-3, 6-4, 6-3 in 2 hours, 45 minutes in the semifinals of the Australian Open. Wilander, known as a clay court specialist, receives a standing ovation from the crowd at the Kooyong Tennis Club for his grass-court victory over the reigning Wimbledon champion.

1978 Stan Smith and Bob Lutz have little difficulty with David Lloyd and Mark Cox, defeating the British pair 6-2, 6-2, 6-3 in just 74 minutes to give the United States a 2-1 lead over Britain in the Davis Cup Final in Rancho Mirage, Calif. The win is the 10th straight—and most one-sided—Davis Cup doubles victory for the reigning U.S. Open champions. Says Smith, "I think it is one of the best matches we have played in Davis Cup."

December 10

1978 John McEnroe, playing only his second career Davis Cup singles match, completes the most devastating run through a Davis Cup final in the history of the competition, dominating Buster Mottram 6-2, 6-2, 6-1 to clinch the 25th Davis Cup title for the United States in Rancho Mirage, Calif. Combined with his 6-1, 6-1, 6-2 defeat of John Lloyd on the opening day of play, McEnroe gives up at total of 10 games in his two singles matches, besting the previous record for fewest games allowed in the Davis Cup final of 12 set by Bill Tilden in 1924 and Bjorn Borg in 1975. Says McEnroe, "It's probably the best I've played in an important match." Says Paul Hutchins, the British Davis Cup captain, of McEnroe, "On form, he's probably the No. 1 player in the world at the moment. This was the Davis Cup and it was just like a normal tournament for him." Brian Gottfried beats John Lloyd in the meaningless fifth match to make the final score 4-1 for the United States. For his efforts, McEnroe not only goes into the Davis Cup history books, but also earns him the cover of *Sports Illustrated* for the first time.

1960 Barry MacKay completes a darkness-suspended 8-6, 3-6, 8-10, 8-6, 13-11 win over Nicola Pietrangeli, giving the United States a 2-0 lead over Italy in the Davis Cup Inter-Zone Final in Perth, Australia. MacKay trails 5-3 in the fifth-set and fights off another three match points in the fifth set (he faced five match points in the fourth set the day before) before winning 13-11 in the fifth set.

1983 Martina Navratilova defeats Kathy Jordan 6-2, 7-6 (5) in 78 minutes to win the Australian Open women's singles title in Melbourne. Navratilova concludes her year losing only one match in 86 matches—that to Kathy Horvath in the round of 16 in the French Open. Navratilova also wins $75,000 with the title, raising her 1983 tournament winnings to $1,443,030.

1995 Goran Ivanisevic fires 28 aces on a lightning fast indoor court at the Olympiahalle in Munich, Germany to defeat Todd Martin 7-6, 6-3, 6-4 to win the Grand Slam Cup and the first prize of $1.6 million. Says Ivanisevic, "Today I achieved what I've always wanted to. I played my best tennis in a final. I was not scared to hit any shot at any time and I served unbelievably."

December 11

1983 Mats Wilander wins the Australian Open for the first time in his career, defeating Ivan Lendl 6-1, 6-4, 6-4 in the first-ever Australian Open final contested between Europeans. Wilander becomes the first European to win the men's title since France's Jean Borotra in 1928. The loss is Lendl's fourth in a major final without a victory—losing the 1981 French final to Bjorn Borg and the 1982 and 1983 U.S. Open finals to Jimmy Connors. Says Lendl, "I knew it was going to depend on how I served and volleyed, and most of the time, when I tried to come to the net, I just wasn't able to."

1960 Chuck McKinley hurls his racquet into the stands following a 3-6, 10-8, 6-4, 13-11 doubles loss with Butch Buchholz to Orlando Sirola and Nicola Pietrangeli of Italy in the Davis Cup Inter-Zone Final in Perth, Australia. The racquet nearly hits a group of Italian fans, who in turn, throw insults at the American. McKinley is later suspended by the U.S. Lawn Tennis Association. The doubles win for the Italians cuts the American lead to 2-1 after the second day of play.

1994 Magnus Larsson of Sweden virtually equals his career prize money by winning $1.5 million in upsetting world No. 1 Pete Sampras 7-6 (6), 4-6, 7-6 (5), 6-4 in the final of the Grand Slam Cup in Munich, Germany. Says Larsson, who earned $1.69 million dollars in career prize money entering the tournament, "This is the best Christmas present I could get." Larsson, a semifinalist at the French Open earlier in the year, is fresh off helping Sweden win the Davis Cup title against Russia in Moscow. Says Sampras, "I felt a bit tired, but you've got to give Magnus credit. He played too good, he served too big, and he's coming off the Davis Cup victory. "

1981 John McEnroe defeats Guillermo Vilas 6-3, 6-3, 6-2 while Jose-Luis Clerc defeats Roscoe Tanner 7-5, 6-3, 8-6 as the United States and Argentina split the first two matches in the Davis Cup Final at the Riverfront Coliseum in Cincinnati, Ohio. Clerc, ranked No. 5 in the world but a weaker player on fast indoor surfaces like the carpet laid in the Riverfront Coliseum, surprises the No. 11-ranked Tanner with the ease in which he wins points and calls his effort "a lovely match." Says Clerc, "I play with too much nerves in Davis Cup before today, but this one or two or three best matches I ever play. I'm really surprised I win in three sets. I think maybe four, five—but three?" Counters the hard-serving Tanner, "I think that's the worst I've served in 10 years. I probably never got in the match."

December 12

1981 In a match described by Bud Collins of the *Boston Globe* as "a shiver-and-sweat epic that included pandemonium, chaos, family squabbles, flag waving, traded insults...an earthquake of sorts, not to mention a Davis Cup tennis match that defied all predictions and possibilities in achieving an extremely high level of frenzy," John McEnroe and Peter Fleming defeat singles specialists Guillermo Vilas and Jose-Luis Clerc 6-3, 4-6, 6-4, 4-6, 11-9 to give the United States a 2-1 lead over Argentina in the Davis Cup Final at the Riverfront Coliseum in Cincinnati, Ohio. The four players nearly come to blows in the hotly contested match in which Vilas actually serves for victory at 7-6 in the 91-minute fifth and final set. Writes Collins "Several times the North Americans and Argentineans swore at each other. Each side blamed the other for starting it. (U.S. Captain Arthur) Ashe came onto the court a couple of times to tone down his men..."

1993 Petr Korda concludes two of the most remarkable days of tennis of his career, defeating world No. 2 Michael Stich 2-6, 6-4, 7-6, 2-6, 11-9 in 3 hours, 48 minutes to win the Grand Slam Cup in Munich, Germany and a first prize of $1.6 million. Korda's epic win comes one day after he saves five match points in defeating world No. 1 Pete Sampras 13-11 in the fifth-set in 4 hours, 32 minutes in the semifinals.

1976 Manuel Orantes of Spain performs a stunning comeback to defeat Poland's Wojtek Fibak 5-7, 6-2, 0-6, 7-6, 6-1 in the final of the year-end Grand Prix Masters Championships in Houston, Texas. The match turns when Fibak is just two games from the match, having just broken Orantes' serve for a 4-1 lead in the fourth set. Fibak then hears courtside TV reporter Vic Braden interviewing celebrities in the crowd, piped into the public address system at the Summit and broadcast to 61 nations, including Fibak's native Poland. Says Fibak, "Instead of thinking about the Masters, about the last tournament, instead of putting all of my thoughts on the match, I was thinking about the TV to Poland. I was caring how it looked and what was to be said, especially when they had those interviews."

1960 The U.S. blows a 2-0 lead for only the second time in Davis Cup play as Italy's Nicola Pietrangeli and Orlando Sirola sweep the final matches in the Inter-Zone Final in Perth, Australia - Pietrangeli defeating Butch Buchholz 6-1, 6-2, 6-8, 3-6, 6-4 and Sirola beating Barry MacKay 9-7, 6-3, 8-6.

December 13

1981 Wimbledon and U.S. Open champion John McEnroe clinches the Davis Cup title for the United States, defeating Jose-Luis Clerc 7-5, 5-7, 6-3, 3-6, 6-3 in 4 hours, 8 minutes to clinch the 3-1 win over Argentina at Cincinnati's Riverfront Coliseum. Writes Neil Amdur of the *New York Times* of the post-match scene, "It was unlike anything ever seen at a Davis Cup match in the United States. John McEnroe, clinching the final in five tense sets, hurdles the net, shook hands with Jose-Luis Clerc, his Argentine opponent, and joyously jumped into the arms of Arthur Ashe, the team captain, and Bill Norris, the trainer. Meanwhile, 13,327 spectators at Riverfront Coliseum stood and cheered, and chanted "U.S.A.! U.S.A!" And at a far end of the arena, a white bedsheet inscribed with "McEnroe We Love You" fluttered aloft."

1982 For the first—and likely only time—in the history of tennis, a player wins two major singles titles in the same calendar year, at the same tournament and against the same opponent as Johan Kriek repeats as Australian Open champion, defeating No. 2 seed Steve Denton 6-3, 6-3, 6-2. The two players also play in the 1981 Australian Open final that is played on January 3, 1982, Kriek winning 6-2, 7-6 (1), 6-7 (1), 6-4. A newly naturalized American citizen, Kriek saves a match point in beating Australia's Paul McNamee in the semifinals by a 7-6, 7-6, 4-6, 3-6, 7-5 margin.

2000 In a press conference staged at Brasserie 8½ on West 57th street in his hometown of New York City, Patrick McEnroe is named the 38th U.S. Davis Cup captain, replacing older brother John McEnroe, who resigned after only 14 months in the position.

1975 In a match that lasts a mere 40 minutes, Raul Ramirez defeats Harold Solomon 6-1, 6-1 in round robin play at the year-end Masters Championships in Melbourne, Australia.

1992 Michael Stich of Germany concludes an otherwise disappointing season winning the $2 million first prize at the Grand Slam Cup in Munich, Germany, defeating Michael Chang 6-2, 6-3, 6-2 in the final. Says Stich after winning in Munich, "I would be much happier winning Wimbledon and getting $10,000 than winning here and getting two million."

December 14

1979 The United States and Italy open up play in the Davis Cup Final in San Francisco, Calif., as Vitas Gerulaitis and John McEnroe give the United States a 2-0 lead with respective singles victories over Corrado Barrazutti and Adriano Panatta. McEnroe is labeled "a new phenomenon" by Panatta after the Italian is crushed by a 6-2, 6-3, 6-4 margin. Says Panatta of McEnroe, "I think he will be No. 1 for a long time to come." Barrazutti becomes the first player to ever retire in a Davis Cup Final when he injures his right ankle and quits the match with Gerulaitis leading 6-3, 3-2.

1988 Carl-Uwe Steeb of West Germany saves a match point and upsets world No. 1 Mats Wilander of Sweden in the opening match of the Davis Cup Final in Goteborg, Sweden. Boris Becker makes it a 2-0 lead for West Germany, trouncing Stefan Edberg 6-3, 6-1, 6-4. One day later, Becker and Eric Jelen defeat Edberg and Anders Jarryd 3-6, 2-6, 7-5, 6-3, 6-2 to clinch the Davis Cup for West Germany.

1957 Vic Seixas defeats Jacques Brichant 10-8, 6-0, 6-1 in the fifth and decisive match as the United States advances to the Davis Cup Challenge Round with a 3-2 win over Belgium in Brisbane, Australia.

1974 With on-court temperatures hovering around 125 degrees, Guillermo Vilas outlasts Raul Ramirez 4-6, 6-3, 6-2, 7-5 to advance to the singles final of the Grand Prix Masters in Melbourne, Australia. Ilie Nastase also advances into the singles final defeating John Newcombe 6-3, 7-6, 6-2. Fifty spectators out of a crowd of 8,000 at the Kooyong Tennis Club receive medical treatment due to the intense heat during the Vilas-Ramirez match.

1946 Stan Smith, the winner of the U.S. Open in 1971 and Wimbledon in 1972 and a legendary figure on the U.S. Davis Cup team, is born in Pasadena, Calif. Smith clinches a six Davis Cup titles for the United States—a record achievement. He and Bob Lutz make up of one of the most accomplished doubles tandems ever in the game, winning four U.S. Open titles and one Australian title. Smith wins 35 ATP singles titles in his career, and 54 doubles titles, including 36 with Lutz.

December 15

1979 Stan Smith plays a hand in clinching a Davis Cup title for the United States for a record sixth time as he and Bob Lutz clinch the 26th Cup win for the U.S., defeating Adriano Panatta and Paolo Bertolucci 6-4, 12-10, 6-2 giving the U.S. a match-clinching 3-0 lead over Italy in San Francisco, Calif.

1974 Guillermo Vilas defeats Ilie Nastase 7-6, 6-2, 3-6, 3-6, 6-4 to win the year-end Grand Prix Masters in Melbourne, Australia. Says Vilas of his victory on grass courts, "Two months ago, I thought grass was for cows, now I think that some of it should be kept for tennis."

1990 Brad Gilbert and David Wheaton nearly come to blows on court during their semifinal match at the Grand Slam Cup in Munich, Germany before Gilbert wins by a 6-3, 3-6, 7-6 (7), 2-6, 6-4 margin. With at least $550,000 on the line in their semifinal confrontation (losing semifinalists earning $450,000, the event's runner-up earning $1 million and the tournament winner winning $2 million) both players exchange heated words and push each other before being separated by tournament officials. Wheaton is angered at Gilbert after Gilbert loudly protests a call at 6-6 in the third-set tiebreak that is overruled in Gilbert's favor by chair umpire Stephen Winyard. Wheaton protests the overrule and asks tour supervisor Ken Farrar to the court, but the overrule stands. Says Wheaton of the overrule, "It was a million dollar mistake. You don't overrule a line call on the far side at 6-6 in the tie-break unless you are absolutely sure." Says Wheaton of the confrontation, "Brad said something about my brother that I didn't like. I told him to withdraw his remarks. If he had thrown the first punch, I would have been pretty happy. He started crying and whining like a child and got his way."

1985 Henri Leconte becomes the first Frenchman to win the men's singles title at the New South Wales Open in the 100th year of the event when he defeats Kelly Evernden of New Zealand 6-7(6), 6-2, 6-3 at White City in Sydney, Australia. Following his victory, Leconte rushes to the airport to catch a flight, but furiously returns to the tennis club at White City when he learns that had mistakenly been given Evernden's runner-up prize money check. Leconte misses his flight, but buys drinks for Evernden at the club bar.

December 16

1984 In an ignominious low for the United States Davis Cup team, future Hall of Famers and the world's No. 1 and No. 2 ranked players, John McEnroe and Jimmy Connors, are embarrassingly straight-setted by Henrik Sundstrom and Mats Wilander, respectively, as Sweden takes a surprising 2-0 lead over the United States in the Davis Cup Final in Goteborg, Sweden. Wilander easily defeats Connors 6-1, 6-3, 6-3, while Sundstrom hands McEnroe only his third loss in the calendar year in a 13-11, 6-4, 6-3 upset. Connors is criticized for his rude and boorish behavior highlighted by many obscenity-laced tirades against chair umpire George Grime. Alan Mills, the event's referee, considers tossing Connors from the series due to his behavior, but his decision to simply fine Connors $2,000 the next day is made a moot point when Sweden closes out the victory over the United States the next day in the doubles rubber. The behavior of McEnroe and Connors causes for the U.S. Tennis Association to implement a code of conduct for its players following the eventual 4-1 loss. Connors never plays Davis Cup again and McEnroe refuses to sign the USTA's contract and does not play Davis Cup again until 1987.

1990 Pete Sampras wins $2 million—the largest payout in tennis history at the time—by defeating Brad Gilbert 6-3, 6-4, 6-2 in the final of the inaugural Grand Slam Cup in Munich, Germany, a year-end tournament that features the 16 players who perform the best in all four major tournaments during the year. Sampras compares his win over Gilbert to his win over Andre Agassi in the final of the U.S. Open earlier in the year saying "I just felt similar to when I beat Agassi at the U.S. Open—that anything I hit turned to gold." Says Gilbert, whose runner-up showing earned him $1 million, "I have bought a lot of bad stock and I would like to buy some stock in him (Sampras) because his stock is rising."

December 17

1984 John McEnroe and Peter Fleming lose their only Davis Cup doubles match and it costs the United States the 1984 Davis Cup title. Stefan Edberg and Anders Jarryd defeat McEnroe and Fleming 7-5, 5-7, 6-2, 7-5 giving Sweden a match-clinching 3-0 lead over the heavily-favored Americans in the Davis Cup Final in Goteborg, Sweden. "We played badly, so we lost," says McEnroe simply. "But they (Sweden) have a great team on any surface and they are the best on clay." McEnroe and Fleming never again pair up for the United States in Davis Cup play, finishing their Davis Cup careers with a 14-1 record.

1989 Boris Becker finishes off the worst thrashing of top players in the history of the Davis Cup final, crushing Mats Wilander, the previous year's No. 1 ranked player, 6-2, 6-0, 6-2 to clinch West Germanys 3-2 victory over Sweden in the Davis Cup Final in Stuttgart. "This is the best someone's ever played against me," Wilander says following his defeat. "Nobody can beat Becker on a day like this. Not on this surface." Says Becker, "I never dreamed I'd play so well in the final. Today I played the best match of my life. It's almost impossible for me to play better." Two days earlier, Becker dominates French and Wimbledon runner-up, Masters champion and world No. 3 Stefan Edberg 6-2, 6-2, 6-4. Becker loses only 12 games in both singles victories and pairs with Eric Jelen the previous day in the doubles, beating Jan Gunnarson and Anders Jarryd 7-6 (6), 6-4, 3-6, 6-7 (4), 6-4. Says Becker's Davis Cup captain Nikki Pilic of the weekend performance, "Being objective, I never saw anyone play that kind of tennis for three days in such an important match."

1978 Chris Evert defeats Martina Navratilova 7-5, 6-2 to win the WTA Tour title in Tokyo, Japan. Navratilova is rattled when a shot that Evert hits apparently lands out with Navratilova leading 5-4 in the first set. Says Navratilova after the match, "I'm frustrated about the bad linesman's call. That bad call cost me the set and probably the match. I don't mind if I lost on my stupidity but with the bad line call, I felt I was being robbed of $50,000."

December 18

1977 Roscoe Tanner fires 29 aces and defeats fellow American Brian Teacher 6-3, 3-6, 6-3, 6-7, 6-3 to win the New South Wales Open in Sydney, Australia. Says Tanner, who completes one service game by hitting four straight aces, "That was the fastest I have ever served." Says Teacher of the Tanner serve, "It's not that much fun standing there watching the balls whiz by." The match is nearly postponed after the fourth set due to darkness caused by smoke from nearby brushfires. In the women's final, Evonne Goolagong defeats Sue Barker 6-2, 6-3 to win the New South Wales Open title for a fourth time.

1995 Two-time Australian, U.S. and Wimbledon champion Stefan Edberg announces that 1996 will be his last year as a professional. "I thought it was best to announce my decision now," says Edberg. "Everyone keeps asking when I'm quitting. It will be in a year's time, whether I'm ranked second or 100 in the world."

1982 Chris Evert Lloyd embarrasses Tracy Austin 6-0, 6-0 in the semifinals of the Toyota Championships in East Rutherford, N.J., marking the first time that Austin is defeated without winning a game in her career. Says Austin, "I guess there is a first time for everything." Austin, the defending champion in the event, wins only 14 points in the 46-minute match.

1976 Stan Smith and Bob Lutz defeat Raul Ramirez and Emilio Montana 6-2, 6-3, 6-4 to give the United States a third and clinching point against Mexico in the first round of the 1977 Davis Cup competition—curiously played within the 1976 calendar year—in Tucson, Arizona. The win for the United States avenges losses to Mexico in the previous two Davis Cup campaigns.

1984 Sweden completes a 4-1 victory over the United States in the Davis Cup Final in Goteborg, Sweden as Henrik Sundstrom defeats Jimmy Arias, who substitutes for Jimmy Connors who flies back to the United States for the birth of his second child. John McEnroe registers the only point for the United States defeating Mats Wilander 6-3, 5-7, 6-3.

1971 Arantxa Sanchez Vicario, the three time French Open women's champion who in 1994 also wins the U.S. Open and becomes the No. 1 player in the world, is born in Barcelona.

December 19

1987 Mats Wilander pairs with Joakim Nystrom to clinch the Davis Cup for Sweden, defeating brothers Anand and Vijay Amritraj 6-2, 3-6, 6-1, 6-2 to give Sweden a match-clinching 3-0 lead over India in Goteborg, Sweden. The win gives Sweden its fourth Davis Cup title to go with victories in 1975, 1984 and 1985 and ends the incredible run of India, led by the Amritraj brothers and Ramesh Krishnan. India advances into the final with victories over Argentina, Israel and Australia. However, all three victories are contested on grass courts—against Argentina and Israel in New Delhi and against Australia in Sydney. The final against Sweden, however, is played on indoor red clay. The previous day, Wilander and Anders Jarryd give Sweden the 2-0 lead—Wilander defeating Krishnan 6-4, 6-1, 6-3 and Jarryd beating Vijay Amritraj 6-3, 6-3, 6-1. Krishnan's appearance in the final gives he and his father Ramanathan Krishnan, the unique distinction of fathers and sons to play in Davis Cup finals. Ramanathan leads India to the 1966 Davis Cup Challenge Round against Australia, before losing 4-1.

1982 Martina Navratilova puts to rest any conversation that anyone other than herself is the No. 1 player in the world for the 1982 season, defeating world No. 2 Chris Evert Lloyd 4-6, 6-1, 6-2 in the final of the Toyota Championships in East Rutherford, N.J. Says Navratilova, "I didn't want there to be any question about who was No. 1. Now there should be no question."

1975 Jimmy Connors wins a dramatic five-set match over Marcelo Lara 6-2, 6-1, 3-6, 4-6, 7-5 as the United States and Mexico split the first two singles matches in the 1976 Davis Cup second round (begun in 1975) in Mexico City, Mexico.

1952 Tony Trabert and Vic Seixas defeat Gianni Cucelli and Marcello Del Bello 6-4, 6-3, 6-2 to give the United States its match-clinching third point in its 5-0 win over Italy in the Davis Cup Inter-Zone Final in Sydney, Australia. The Italians are so dismissive of their chances of defeating the United States and advancing to the Davis Cup Challenge Round that the team books airline reservations back to Italy before the match is even contested.

1953 Tony Trabert defeats Jacques Brichant 6-4, 6-3, 6-1 in 58 minutes to give the United States a match-clinching third point in its 4-1 victory over Belgium in the Davis Cup Inter-Zone final in Brisbane, Australia.

December 20

1994 Thirty-four-year-old Ivan Lendl, the Czech player who plays in a record 19 major singles finals, announces his retirement from tennis after a 15-year career due to continued back problems. Lendl wins eight major titles, including three straight U.S. Open titles from 1985 to 1987. He also wins the French Open in 1984, 1986 and 1987, two Australian titles in 1989 and 1990 and ranks No. 1 in the world for 270 weeks. Says Lendl in a media conference call where he announces his decision, "This is a very difficult and sad time for me. This is not the way I would have chosen to retire and I'm sure I will miss the game I love. I enjoyed playing the game, had a lot of great times, and I will miss it."

1998 Roger Federer ends his career as a junior tennis player by winning the prestigious singles title at the Orange Bowl in Key Biscayne, Fla., defeating Guillermo Coria of Argentina, 7-5, 6-3 in the final. The win over Coria moves Federer to the No. 1 ranking in the ITF world junior rankings for the first time. Writes Rene Stauffer in *The Roger Federer Story, Quest for Perfection*, "Federer had to endure one more week of uncertainty until his year-end No. 1 ranking was official. It wasn't until an upstart American junior named Andy Roddick defeated (Julien) Jeanpierre in the semifinals of the last junior tournament of the year—the Yucatan Cup in Mexico—that Federer clinched the year-end No. 1 ranking."

1981 Tracy Austin withstands the loss of eight straight games to defeat Martina Navratilova 2-6, 6-4, 6-2 in the final of the Toyota Championships in East Rutherford, N.J. "Martina always seems to start out pretty fast," says Austin. "I just tried to hang in there and play one point at a time."

1974 John Newcombe expresses relief at losing 6-4, 6-4 to Phil Dent in the quarterfinals of the New South Wales Open in Sydney. Says Newcombe, "I'm glad I'm out in a way. I need some mental stimulation. I feel like a draft horse being flogged to win a six-furlong race."

December 21

1954 Chris Evert, the enduring American champion who helps vault the popularity of tennis around the United States and the world in the 1970s and 1980s, is born in Ft. Lauderdale, Fla. Evert wins 18 major singles titles (tied for fourth place all time with Martina Navratilova behind Margaret Court's 24, Steffi Graf's 22 and Helen Wills Moody's 19) including a record seven titles at the French Open (1974, 1975, 1979, 1980, 1983, 1985,1986). She wins at least one major final between 1974 and 1986, also winning six U.S. Open titles (1975-1978, 1980, 1982), three Wimbledon titles (1974, 1976, 1981) and two Australian titles (1982, 1984). She wins 154 career singles titles, second all-time to Martina Navratilova's 167 and ranks as the No. 1 player in the world for 260 weeks.

1975 Nineteen-year-old Bjorn Borg clinches the first-ever Davis Cup title for Sweden, defeating Jan Kodes of Czechoslovakia 6-4, 6-2, 6-2. The victory for Borg, his 19th straight in Davis Cup play, gives Sweden a 3-1 lead in their eventual 3-2 win over the Czechs in Stockholm, Sweden. "This was my finest victory ever," says Borg, who goes on to win the men's singles title at Wimbledon for the next five years. "I've always dreamt of winning the Davis Cup since I played my first match in the tournament three years ago."

1972 Chris Evert turns 18 years old and turns professional after playing the circuit as an amateur for 18 months. Says Evert to the Associated Press, "I'll miss the senior prom, but it will be worth it. I think I am ready to play tennis for money....I'm eager not only to become a pro, but to get out of school."

1980 Tracy Austin needs only 65 minutes to defeat Peanut Louie 6-2, 6-0 to win the Colgate Championships of Tucson, Ariz.

1975 Brian Gottfried fends off Marcelo Lara 3-6, 6-2, 3-6, 8-6, 6-1—saving two match points in 3 hours, 26 minutes—to pull the United States even with Mexico at 2-2 in the 1976 Davis Cup second round (curiously played in 1975 calendar year) in Mexico City, Mexico. In the fifth and decisive match, Jimmy Connors trails Raul Ramirez 2-6, 6-3, 6-3, 2-3 before darkness suspends play.

December 22

1975 Jimmy Connors loses four of five games played as Raul Ramirez completes a darkness-suspended 2-6, 6-3, 6-3, 6-4 victory to give Mexico a 3-2 victory over the United States in the 1976 Davis Cup second round (played in 1975) in Mexico City, Mexico. Ramirez leads Connors 2-6, 6-3, 6-3, 2-3 as play is resumed from the evening before. For the second straight year, Ramirez almost single-handedly beats the U.S. Davis Cup team as his win over Connors, coupled with his first-day singles win over Brian Gottfried and his doubles victory with Marcela Lara over Dick Stockton and Erik van Dillen, puts away the United States. In the 1975 Davis Cup, Ramirez accounts for all three points in the upset of the United States in Tucson, Ariz. Says Ramirez, "The most important thing in tennis is to play for my country. Those other tournaments—they are only for money." Some observers pin-point this Davis Cup loss as a turning point for Connors as he avoids Davis Cup play for most of the rest of his career, re-appearing for one series in 1981 against Czechoslovakia and for all four matches in 1984 as the U.S. loses to Sweden in the Davis Cup Final.

1977 Defending champion Roscoe Tanner is defeated in the opening round of the Australian Open, losing to New Zealand's Chris Lewis 3-6, 6-3, 6-2, 1-6, 6-4 to become the first defending Aussie champion to lose in the first round. Tanner, coming off a tournament victory at the New South Wales Open in Sydney the previous week, claims fatigue as the reason for his early defeat. He angrily brushes off reports that he is more interested in returning home for the holidays than defending his Australian singles title. "I think that is an insult," says Tanner of the charges. "If I wanted to lose, I would have defaulted and said I had a headache."

1985 Stefan Edberg clinches the Davis Cup for Sweden defeating West Germany's Michael Westphal 3-6, 7-5, 6-4, 6-3 in the fifth and decisive match in Munich, Germany. "I was a bit nervous when I went out there," says the No. 5-ranked Edberg of walking out to play the No. 51-ranked Westphal in the decisive match. "I was not playing well, but I was battling and it paid off." Boris Becker ties the series at two matches apiece, defeating Sweden's Mats Wilander 6-3, 2-6, 6-3, 6-3 in the fourth rubber of the series earlier in the day.

December 23

1973 Australian Evonne Goolagong defeats Chris Evert 6-4, 6-3 that begins a three-match Australian sweep of the United States giving Australia a 6-3 win over the U.S. in Sydney in the Bonne Bell Cup, an annual competition featuring the United States against Australia. Kerry Melville of Australia defeats Julie Heldman of the U.S. 2-6, 6-1, 6-4 to give Australia the insurmountable 5-3 lead, while Goolagong and Janet Young close out proceedings, defeating Pam Teeguarden and Janet Newberry 6-2, 6-3. The win for Australia gives them a sweep of the Davis Cup, Fed Cup and Bonne Bell Cup competitions for the year.

1984 Peter Doohan of Australia defeats Huub van Boeckel of the Netherlands 1-6, 6-1, 6-4 to win the singles title at the South Australian Championships in Adelaide, Australia.

2003 Zina Garrison, the 1990 Wimbledon finalist, 1988 Olympic gold medalist in women's doubles and an eight-year veteran of the U.S. Fed Cup team, is named the captain of the U.S. Fed Cup team, replacing Billie Jean King.

December 24

1978 Unseeded Tim Wilkison wins his first career ATP Tour singles title, outlasting No. 14 seed Kim Warwick of Australia 6-3, 6-3, 6-7, 3-6, 6-2 in the final of the New South Wales Open at White City, Sydney, Australia. Wilkison wins five more ATP singles titles during his career and earns cult-like status for his blue-collar, workman-like attitude and earns the nickname "Dr. Dirt" for his propensity to dive for shots. His best career result comes in reaching the quarterfinals of the 1986 U.S. Open, highlighted by a five-set win over Yannick Noah, before losing to Stefan Edberg. In the women's final, Dianne Fromholtz defeats fellow Australian Wendy Turnbull 6-2, 7-5.

December 25

1910 Bryan "Bitsy" Grant, a Hall of Famer and standout on the U.S. Davis Cup team in the 1930s, is born in Atlanta, Ga. Standing at only 5-foot-4, Grant is the smallest American player to become a world class player, helping the U.S. to Davis Cup title in 1937.

1942 Francoise Durr, the odd-stroking Frenchwoman who wins 12 major titles in singles and doubles, most notably at the French singles title in 1967, is born in Algiers, Algeria. Nick-named the "Psychedelic Strokeswomen" by Hall of Fame journalist Bud Collins, Durr is a strange striker of the ball with wristy ground strokes and peculiar grips.

1943 Bill Bowrey, the man who wins the last major singles title in the "amateur year" at the 1968 Australian Championships, is born in Sydney. Bowrey defeats Juan Gisbert of Spain in the men's singles final of the 1968 Australian Championships, shortly before the dawning of the "Open" era in which professionals and amateurs compete side-by-side and against each other in major tournaments and on the tour.

1966 Javier Frana, 1992 Olympic bronze medalist in doubles, is born in Rafaela, Argentina.

December 26

1947 Jack Kramer makes his pro debut at Madison Square Garden against Bobby Riggs as a blizzard hits New York. With taxis, buses and commuter trains and private cars stalled and subways limping, 15,114 fans came to the arena on Eighth Avenue and 50th Street. Riggs spoils the debut of Kramer, winning 6-2, 10-8, 4-6, 6-4. Writes Lincoln Werden of the *New York Times*, "The former amateur king pin piled up error after error throughout and indications that he lacked complete poise and control brought an occasional reassuring cry from the fans 'Come On Jackie.'"

1972 Top-seeded Ken Rosewall loses his opening round match at the Australian Open, falling to Karl Meiler of West Germany 6-2, 6-3, 6-2. Says Rosewall following the match, "I've never heard of Meiler. I'm not even sure about his first name."

1980 In front of a noisy and boisterous crowd described as "lacking common decency," Sandy Mayer defeats fellow American Fritz Buehning 6-1, 3-6, 7-5, 4-6, 6-3 in the opening round of the Australian Open. Following the match, Buehning says he is irritated with the crowd that he calls "disrespectful" and "horrendous." Says Buehning, "They were bad. They screamed out and talked whenever they wanted to. They had no common decency the way they kept talking and drinking between games and I don't think the umpire controlled them well." Mayer calls the fans, "the noisiest crowd I have played before."

1946 The United States and Australia begin play in the first post-war Davis Cup final at Kooyong Tennis Club in Melbourne, Australia. Ted Schroeder and Jack Kramer register wins over John Bromwich and Dinny Pails, respectively, to give the United States a 2-0 lead after the first day of play.

1957 Barry MacKay and Vic Seixas both lose five-set matches as the United States goes down 2-0 to Australia in the Davis Cup Challenge Round at the Kooyong Tennis Club in Melbourne, Australia. Mal Anderson, the reigning champion at the U.S. Nationals, defeats MacKay 6-3, 7-5, 3-6, 7-9, 6-3, while Wimbledon champion Ashley Cooper defeats Seixas 3-6, 7-5, 6-1, 1-6, 6-3. Australia goes on to clinch the victory—and the Davis Cup title—the next day as Anderson and Mervyn Rose beat Barry MacKay and Seixas 6-4, 6-4, 8-6 to give Australia the match-clinching 3-0 lead.

December 27

1954 A crowd of 25,578—the largest audience to watch a tennis match at the time—gathers at the White City courts in Sydney, Australia as the United States and Australia open up play in the Davis Cup Challenge Round. The United States takes a commanding 2-0 lead as Tony Trabert defeats Lew Hoad 6-4, 2-6, 12-10, 6-3 and Vic Seixas defeats Ken Rosewall 8-6, 6-8, 6-4, 6-3. The following day, Seixas and Trabert pair in the doubles to defeat Hoad and Rosewall 6-2, 4-6, 6-2, 10-8 to clinch the Cup for the U.S. The crowds to watch the USA-Australia series remains a world record until 1973 when 30, 492 fans pack the Astrodome in Houston, Texas to watch the "Battle of the Sexes" match between Billie Jean King and Bobby Riggs. In 2004, when daily crowds of 27,200 watch the USA-Spain Davis Cup final in Seville, Spain, the 1954 USA-Australia Davis Cup series loses its status as the largest crowds to watch an officially sanctioned match.

2007 Evonne Goolagong joins the list of women players to be ranked No. 1 in the world on the WTA computer—albeit it 31 years after the fact. The WTA Tour announces that the Australian should have been ranked No. 1 in the world for a two-week period from April 26 to May 9 in 1976, but due to missing paper records, the results were not calculated. "Evonne was always one of the most beloved and gracious of champions," WTA Tour Chief Executive Larry Scott says in a press release issued by the WTA Tour. "We felt once it came to light that she did in fact assume the No. 1 ranking for a period in 1976, it was important to recognize the achievement, just like with all the other 15 women who have achieved that pinnacle in women's tennis."

1976 John McEnroe wins the boys' 18 singles title at the Orange Bowl junior championships in Miami, defeating Eliot Teltscher 7-5, 6-1 in the final.

1980 Brad Drewett of Australia upsets No. 4 seed Vitas Gerulaitis 2-6, 6-4, 1-6, 6-4, 6-4 in the first round of the Australian Open. Gerulaitis is fined $500 when he does not attend a post-match news conference.

December 28

1946 The United States completes a 5-0 shutout of Australia at the Kooyong Tennis Club in Melbourne, Australia as Jack Kramer and Gardnar Mulloy register wins over John Bromwich and Dinny Pails, respectively. As the U.S. is officially presented with the Davis Cup as the first post-war victor of the competition, U.S. team member Ted Schroeder salutes friend and former U.S. Davis Cupper Joe Hunt, who is killed in during a training flight off the coast of Florida in World War II. "Joe the dog-faced boy, where ever you are, I wish you were here today," says Schroeder. "We owe a lot to you."

1986 Pat Cash defeats Mikael Pernfors 2-6, 4-6, 6-3, 6-4, 6-3 in 3 hours, 27 minutes in the fourth rubber to clinch a 3-2 victory for Australia over Sweden in the Davis Cup final at Kooyong Tennis Club in Melbourne, Australia. "This is a fantastic feeling," Cash says of clinching Australia's 26th Davis Cup championship. "In a way, this is my greatest moment in tennis." Australian Davis Cup Captain Neale Fraser describes Cash's performance as the greatest he had seen by an Australian in Davis Cup play. "That's the best comeback I've ever made," says Cash. "(Pernfors) just played amazing tennis in the first two sets. I gutted out the match better than I've ever done before."

1963 Chuck McKinley clinches the Davis Cup title for the United States, defeating 19-year-old John Newcombe 10-12, 6-2, 9-7, 6-2 in the fifth and decisive match of the Davis Cup Challenge Round at the Memorial Drive Courts in Adelaide, Australia. The win concludes a whirl-wind championship year for the U.S. team, starting with an opening round match against Iran in Tehran. Twenty-six physicians are consulted during the year by the U.S. team because of a wide array of injuries to the players. Dennis Ralston nearly loses an eye in a freak accident in England, while McKinley suffers from dysentery in Bombay, India during the U.S. victory over the Indians in the Inter-Zone Final. Frank Froehling has an abscess removed from his back just before the final with Australia and is not able to play for the United States in the Challenge Round.

1983 Pat Cash clinches the Davis Cup for Australia with a 6-4, 6-1, 6-1 win over Sweden's Joakim Nystrom giving Australia the match-clinching 3-1 lead at the Kooyong Tennis Club in Melbourne. The eighteen-year-old Cash becomes the youngest player to play singles for Australia in a Davis

Cup final. Australia wins the trophy for the 25th time and for the first time since 1977.

1951 In front of 15,300 fans, Frank Sedgman defeats Vic Seixas 6-4, 6-2, 6-2 in the fifth and decisive match to give Australia a 3-2 win over United States and the Davis Cup title for 1951 at White City, Sydney, Australia.

1971 Forty-four-year-old Frank Sedgman upsets No. 5 seed Owen Davidson 6-3, 1-6, 6-1, 7-5 to reach the round of 16 at the Australian Open. Joining Sedgman in the fourth round is 37-year-old Neale Fraser, who defeats Geoff Masters 7-5, 7-5, 6-2. Both old-timers are defeated in the next round, Sedgman losing to fellow Aussie John Cooper 3-6, 6-3, 6-1, 6-3 while Fraser falls to Mal Anderson 6-2, 6-3, 6-1.

1957 Vic Seixas plays his final Davis Cup match as he defeats Mal Anderson 6-3, 4-6, 6-3, 0-6, 13-11 in a dead-rubber singles match in the Davis Cup Challenge Round against Australia in Melbourne, Australia. Trailing 3-0 entering the final day, wins by Seixas and Barry MacKay give the United States a respectable 3-2 loss to the Australians. Seixas is regarded as one of the greatest Davis Cuppers the United States ever produces, representing the United States in 23 series, posting a 38-17 won-loss record.

December 29

1958 Peruvian-born University of Southern California student Alejandro "Alex" Olmedo, the reigning U.S. intercollegiate champion, opens play in the Davis Cup Challenge Round in Brisbane, defeating Australia's Mal Anderson 8-6, 2-6, 9-7, 8-6 as the U.S. and Australia split the opening day singles matches. Olmedo, known affectionately as "The Chief" because of his Peruvian background, is a controversial selection to the U.S. team by captain Perry Jones as Olmedo is not a U.S. citizen but is eligible to play Davis Cup for the United States because of a rule allowing a nation to name a player who has been a resident for three years and who had not represented any other country. Olmedo's play is the difference in the series as he and Ham Richardson win the crucial doubles match—putting the United States up 2-1 after day two—defeating Cooper and Neale Fraser 10-12, 3-6, 16-14, 6-3, 7-5. On the third day, Olmedo clinches the Cup for the U.S., defeating Cooper, the reigning Wimbledon, U.S. and Australian champion, 6-3, 4-6, 6-4, 8-6.

1952 The United States and Australia open up play in the Davis Cup Challenge Round as Australia takes a 2-0 first-day lead as Frank Sedgman defeats Vic Seixas 6-3, 6-4, 6-3 and Ken McGregor beats Tony Trabert 11-9, 6-4, 6-1 at the Memorial Drive Courts in Adelaide, Australia. Sedgman and McGregor clinch the Cup for Australia the next day with a 6-3, 6-4, 1-6, 6-3 win over Seixas and Trabert, giving Australia its third-straight Cup final victory over the United States. Seixas prevents an American shut-out on the final day of play, winning the fifth match of the series 6-3, 8-6, 6-8, 6-3 over McGregor.

1980 Unseeded American Pat DuPre overcomes a match point in the final set tie-breaker to complete a rain-delayed 7-5, 6-3, 3-6, 2-6, 7-6 (6) upset of No. 2 seed Ivan Lendl of Czechoslovakia in the second round of the Australian Open. Lendl holds a match point at 6-5 in the final set tie-breaker but loses the next two points and then meekly serves a double fault to give DuPre the victory.

December 30

1953 Lew Hoad of Australia and Tony Trabert of the United States contest one of the greatest Davis Cup matches in the history of the event as Hoad beats Trabert 13-11, 6-3, 2-6, 3-6, 7-5 to even the United States vs. Australia Davis Cup Challenge Round at 2—2 at the Kooyong Tennis Club in Melbourne. Playing in front of 17,500 fans and in a steady drizzle that causes for slick conditions on the grass court, Trabert, choosing to wear spikes, is unable to complete his two-sets-to-love comeback against the spikeless, 19-year-old Hoad and clinch the Cup for the United States. Serving at 5-6 in the fifth set, Trabert loses his serve at love to lose the match. The fifth and decisive match between Vic Seixas and Ken Rosewall is postponed until the next day, due to the soggy conditions, with the 19-year-old Rosewall eventually winning the Cup for Australia with a 6-2, 2-6, 6-3, 6-4 decision.

1977 John Lloyd becomes the first British man to reach a major singles final since Fred Perry in 1936, defeating Bob Giltinan of Australia 6-4, 6-2, 6-0 in the semifinals of the Australian Open. Vitas Gerulaitis advances into his first major final with a 6-1, 6-2, 6-4 win over John Alexander of Australia in the other men's semifinal.

1974 Jimmy Connors, heckled and jeered by a spectator who is escorted out of the stadium by police, defeats Kim Warwick of Australia 6-3, 6-2, 6-2 in the quarterfinals of the Australian Open. Says Connors of the heckler, "I don't mind them making comments, but this guy obviously had drunk gallons of beer before coming to the match."

1972 John Newcombe defeats Patrick Proisy of France 7-6, 6-4, 6-2 to reach the final of the Australian Open, joining New Zealand's Onny Parun, who defeats West Germany's Karl Meiler in the other semifinal match 2-6, 6-3, 7-5, 6-1.

1981 American Hank Pfister upsets top-seeded Guillermo Vilas of Argentina, 6-3, 6-4, 6-4 to reach the quarterfinals of the Australian Open. The day is highlighted by an umpire's walkout as a veteran official Tom Gray of Adelaide leaves the court during a doubles match, saying that Chris Lewis of New Zealand had ridiculed him over a call. It marks the first time in the 70 years of the championships, or in any other Australian tournament, that a linesman quits after a dispute.

December 31

1977 Vitas Gerulaitis wins his first—and only—major singles title, overcoming a severe case of cramping in defeating John Lloyd of Great Britain 6-3, 7-6, 5-7, 3-6, 6-2 in the final of the Australian Open. "Today was my lucky day and the good Lord looked down on me," says Gerulaitis. "The pain was dreadful and I remember looking up toward the sky in the fourth set and saying to myself I couldn't win without some sort of help. My muscles were popping out because of the cramp, which spread right through my body, but I wasn't about to give up in such an important final."

1972 Margaret Court routs fellow Australian Kerry Melville 6-1, 6-0 in the semifinals of the Australian Open to advance into her first major final since becoming a mother. "It would be a thrill to win the title after having a baby," says the 30-year-old Court. "It would show that tennis mums can play and play well." Court goes on to win the title, defeating fellow Aussie Evonne Goolagong 6-4, 7-5 in the final.

1974 John Newcombe wins a titanic struggle with fellow Aussie Tony Roche, saving two match points in the eight game of the final set in defeating his countryman and good friend 6-4, 4-6, 6-4, 2-6, 11-9 in the men's semifinals of the Australian Open. Newcombe goes on to win the title, upsetting defending champion Jimmy Connors in the final.

1930 Bill Tilden's amateur tennis career comes to an end as the seven-time U.S. men's singles champion announces that he is turning professional. During his amateur career, Tilden also wins three Wimbledon titles and helps the United States to seven straight Davis Cup titles from 1920 to 1926.

1920 Bill Tilden clinches the first of six straight Davis Cup titles for the United States as he and Bill Johnston defeat Norman Brookes and Gerald Patterson of Australasia 4-6, 6-4, 6-0, 6-4 at the Domain Cricket Ground in Auckland, New Zealand.

Also From New Chapter Press

The Bud Collins History of Tennis—By Bud Collins

Compiled by the most famous tennis journalist and historian in the world, this book is the ultimate compilation of historical tennis information, including year-by-year recaps of every tennis season, biographical sketches of every major tennis personality, as well as stats, records, and championship rolls for all the major events. The author's personal relationships with major tennis stars offer insights into the world of professional tennis found nowhere else.

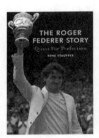

The Roger Federer Story, Quest For Perfection— By Rene Stauffer

Regarded by many as the greatest tennis player in the history of the sport, this authoritative biography is based on many exclusive interviews with Federer and his family as well as the author's experience covering the international tennis circuit for many years. Completely comprehensive, it provides an informed account of the Swiss tennis star from his early days as a temperamental player on the junior circuit, through his early professional career, to his winning major tennis tournaments, including the U.S. Open and Wimbledon. Readers will appreciate the anecdotes about his early years, revel in the insider's view of the professional tennis circuit, and be inspired by this champion's rise to the top of his game.

Boycott: Stolen Dreams of the 1980 Moscow Olympic Games—By Tom and Jerry Caraccioli

With a thorough exploration of the political climate of the time and the Soviet Union's invasion of Afghanistan, this book describes the repercussions of Jimmy Carter's American boycott of the 1980 Olympic Games in Moscow. Despite missing the games they had trained relentlessly to compete in, many U.S. athletes went on to achieve remarkable successes in sports and overcame the bitter disappointment of a once-in-a-lifetime opportunity dashed by geopolitics.

www.newchapterpressmedia.com